D1511576

The Consultant's Guide to SAP® SRM

SAP PRESS

SAP PRESS is a joint initiative of SAP and Galileo Press. The know-how offered by SAP specialists combined with the expertise of the publishing house Galileo Press offers the reader expert books in the field. SAP PRESS features first-hand information and expert advice, and provides useful skills for professional decision-making.

SAP PRESS offers a variety of books on technical and business related topics for the SAP user. For further information, please visit our website: *www.sap-press.com.*

Martin Murray
SAP Warehouse Management: Functionality and Technical Configuration
2007, 504 pp.
978-1-59229-133-5

Sachin Sethi
Enhancing Supplier Relationship Management Using SAP SRM
2007, 696 pp.
978-1-59229-068-0

D. Rajen Iyer
Effective SAP SD
2006, 365 pp.
978-1-59229-101-4

Martin Murray
Understanding the SAP Logistics Information System
2006, 336 pp.
978-1-59229-108-3

Padma Prasad Munirathinam, Ramakrishna Potluri

The Consultant's Guide to SAP® SRM

Galileo Press

Bonn • Boston

ISBN 978-1-59229-154-0

1st edition 2008

Acquisitions Editor Jawahara Saidullah
Developmental Editor Jutta VanStean
Copy Editor Mike Beady
Cover Design Silke Braun
Layout Design Vera Brauner
Production Iris Warkus
Typesetting III-satz, Husby
Printed and bound in Germany

© 2008 by Galileo Press
SAP PRESS is an imprint of Galileo Press,
Boston, MA, USA
Bonn, Germany

All rights reserved. Neither this publication nor any part of it
may be copied or reproduced in any form or by any means
or translated into another language, without the prior con-
sent of Galileo Press, Rheinwerkallee 4, 53227 Bonn, Germany.

Galileo Press makes no warranties or representations with
respect to the content hereof and specifically disclaims any
implied warranties of merchantability or fitness for any particular purpose. Galileo Press assumes no responsibility for
any errors that may appear in this publication.

All of the screenshots and graphics reproduced in this book
are subject to copyright © SAP AG, Dietmar-Hopp-Allee 16,
69190 Walldorf, Germany.

SAP, the SAP logo, mySAP, mySAP.com, mySAP Business
Suite, SAP NetWeaver, SAP R/3, SAP R/2, SAP B2B, SAPtro-
nic, SAPscript, SAP BW, SAP CRM, SAP EarlyWatch, SAP
ArchiveLink, SAP GUI, SAP Business Workflow, SAP Busi-
ness Engineer, SAP Business Navigator, SAP Business Frame-
work, SAP Business Information Warehouse, SAP inter-
enterprise solutions, SAP APO, AcceleratedSAP, InterSAP,
SAPoffice, SAPfind, SAPfile, SAPtime, SAPmail, SAP-access,
SAP-EDI, R/3 Retail, Accelerated HR, Accelerated HiTech,
Accelerated Consumer Products, ABAP, ABAP/4, ALE/WEB,
BAPI, Business Framework, BW Explorer, Enjoy-SAP,
mySAP.com e-business platform, mySAP Enterprise Portals,
RIVA, SAPPHIRE, TeamSAP, Webflow and SAP PRESS are
registered or unregistered trademarks of SAP AG, Walldorf,
Germany.

All other products mentioned in this book are registered or
unregistered trademarks of their respective companies.

Contents at a Glance

Contents

4   SAP SRM Deployment Scenarios 103

5   Operational Procurement 119

Dedications

Ramakrishna dedicates this book to his parents, Mrs. and Mr. Sreeramulu, his wife Vijitha, and his son Prajwal, for their unconditional love and support.

Prasad dedicates this book to his parents, Mrs. and Mr. Munirathinam, his wife Praveena, and his sisters Vijayalakshmi and Devika, for the positive energy he has received from them throughout his life.

Acknowledgments

Knowledge is gained from every walk of life, and for us, a major source of knowledge has come from our customers' implementations on which we have worked during our 12-year consulting career. This book would not have been possible for us to write without the knowledge gained from these implementations. Hence, we want to thank all of our customers — to whom we are greatly indebted — for having given us the opportunity to learn the processes, procedures, and practices in purchasing.

We thank our SAP management team, in particular SRM Management, who have supported and encouraged us in writing this book. Special thanks go to our managers, Peter Welter, Norbert Koppenhagen, Diego Devalle, and Jerome Levadoux. Recognizing talent and encouraging their people to go that extra mile is key for success, and we thank John Zepecki and Armin Schwarz for doing exactly that. We also thank them for the confidence they have shown in our knowledge. We are also grateful to Clas Neumann, President, SAP Labs India, for inspiring us with his vision to have many "Thought Leaders" from SAP Labs India.

Knowledge gained without sharing does not grow and we have learned even more by sharing our knowledge with our colleagues. We wish to thank the entire SAP SRM Regional Implementation Group team, and our consulting and other field colleagues, both from SAP and partners, who have worked with us on many challenging projects and participated in countless brainstorming sessions to design solutions for customer requirements. We would also like to thank our SAP SRM development colleagues whose enthusiasm and energy encouraged us to put in that extra effort to write this book.

We would like to sincerely thank our colleagues who spent their valuable time reviewing this book and gave their invaluable suggestions. The list of people is long, and unfortunately we are not able to mention everyone who has contributed. However, even if your name does not appear here, know that we are grateful for your help. We would like to thank the following people: Masayuki Sekihara, Yeu Sheng Teo, and Syamala Parimi from the SRM Regional Implementation group; Divyesh Jain, Vanishree Malagi, Chander Viswanathan, Mradul Kumar, Katta Nageshwara Rao, Pritesh Jain, and Wolfgang Hofher from the development team; Ota Noboru, Vishal Gupta, and Deepak Singh from the consulting team; Alexa MacDonald from the knowledge management team; David Marchand, Florian Seebauer, and Daniela Schweizer from the solution management team; and Emily Rakowski from the marketing team.

Our heartfelt gratitude to those who stood by us during our challenging times: Andy Waroma, Usman Sheikh, Alexander Obe, Stanley Young, Mohan Das, Potluri Seshagiri Rao, and Suresh Ramanathan.

Special thanks to our editors Jawahara Saidullah and Jutta VanStean. We deeply appreciate their patience, guidance, and constant support. We also want to thank all of the other people from Galileo Press/SAP PRESS who were involved in publishing this book.

Foreword John Zepecki

In the past decade, businesses have increasingly globalized their operations and developed new business models. These drivers have led many organizations to develop a much stronger reliance on suppliers to fulfill the requirements of their customers and deliver services and products to market. Markets and products continue to change frequently. Flexibility and agility continue to increase in importance — not just for success, but for survival.

Increased complexity has come along as organizations address these new challenges. One important consequence is a supply base that is more important and a new type of supplier relationship. At the same time, businesses continually look toward cost reduction to stay competitive or become more profitable. These macro factors have driven procurement to become an increasingly important element of business strategy — both providing means to deliver products and services while effectively managing costs, driving both the top line and reducing the bottom line.

SAP is the leader in enterprise applications across the globe. Many organizations have standardized on SAP for all business functions. A challenge for many companies is, "Where to start?" or "How to start?" a transformation of their procurement function. The challenges vary from organization to organization, but understanding the capabilities and value derived from various modules of a Supplier Relationship Management (SRM) application suite and the approaches to leverage these capabilities can be daunting. There are many paths to success or value, but the appropriate size, scale, and scope has to fit each organization.

This book provides an overview of the SRM application suite, practical case examples, and how to effectively leverage SAP's SRM capabilities to dramatically change and expand the impact of the procurement function. Many groups will benefit from reading this book — either to leverage SAP's SRM system to effectively make a procurement transformation happen, or to understand more about procurement and how SAP SRM can make procurement more strategic.

The authors of this book have a deep knowledge of both the procurement topic and SAP's SRM product offerings. Through years of active work on projects with customers, Ramki and Prasad have seen how SAP's SRM can drive change in organizations and have expert knowledge in the various paths to success.

I have had the good fortunate to have Ramki and Prasad work on my team and provide their insights to help SAP build a better SRM suite. I am happy that

Ramki and Prasad have taken the time and extensive effort to provide their insights and expertise to the broader community. I hope that you will find their insights on procurement and details on how to proceed with the SAP SRM application valuable.

Best regards,

John Zepecki

SVP and GM
SAP

Foreword Armin Schwarz

Few corporate functions have undergone such dramatic changes in recent years as procurement. Procurement today is taking significant steps into new areas. While in the past the major tasks in procurement had been to follow and administer manual processes, most purchasing organizations today make significant contributions at strategic levels to an organization's long-term overall success.

SAP, as the leading provider of business solutions, is supporting and enabling these developments with its world-class procurement solutions. According to the increasing importance of procurement in organizations, SAP offers a complete portfolio of procurement applications. The bandwidth and the flexibility of the solutions are enormous: almost 20,000 customers are using SAP procurement solutions across 25 plus industries. Companies ranging in size from multimillion dollar organizations with global operations to small and midsize enterprises with only a couple of hundred employees are relying on SAP in procurement.

One significant cornerstone in this offering is SAP SRM. It is built to work as both a standalone product, or closely integrated to complement other procurement offerings — specifically SAP ERP Materials Management. SAP SRM offers everything that is needed to support purchasing organizations to be successful today. While focal points are contract management, sourcing, and e-procurement, SAP SRM especially improves the creation of transparency about supplier activities and helps companies to stay compliant.

With the same path and speed at which business is changing, IT applications have to follow. Business transformation, for example, via mergers and acquisitions, new organizational models, outsourcing or new supply markets need to be easily reflected and managed in the procurement solution. Business configuration and low total-cost-of-ownership are therefore equally important as innovative and supportive business processes. As SAP is continuously striving forward to allow for even faster change cycles, we are delighted to see that this publication is an essential reference book for SAP SRM implementation teams and business users alike. This book is a comprehensive guide for SAP users who are looking to implement functions within SAP SRM and it also gives great insights into the important integration aspects of the SAP SRM solution.

The authors have been personally involved with implementing the products described in this book. The knowledge shared here comes from actual field experience working with corporations. Their practical and real-world approach to implementing SAP SRM will be invaluable to readers who are implementing for the first time, or adopting their solution to the ever-changing business world.

Armin Schwarz

SVP — Head of SAP SRM Development

Foreword Clas Neumann

Today, you cannot imagine Global IT without India. SAP has realized the potential of this country very early, by implementing its first ERP packages in 1990/1991. In 1995, SAP realized it had to increase its footprint and opened its first fully owned subsidary, followed in 1998 by the founding of SAP Labs India. During those years, we have learned a great deal from the emerging global companies operating out of India — how they overcome their challenges and how they use IT in ways even we never thought about.

Reliance, Tata, Mittal Steel, Infosys, and Wipro are very well-known companies around the globe and they have all been running their businesses on SAP software for more than 10 years. Their knowledge is world class in all respects, may it be in entering foreign markets, trading, or sourcing. Our consultants in India have the unique opportunity to work with these emerging giants from the Indian subcontinent as well as with our multinational clients from around the globe.

At the same time, we have built up SAP Labs India to more than 4,000 software engineers — which represents nearly 1/3 of SAP's global R&D. We did this by carefully building up knowledge in core product and business areas and blending it with the knowledge of our global customer base. SAP never used India as a pool for cheap engineering, but as a resource hub of tremendous potential and capabilities. We have pioneered processes to engineer software in completely new ways across borders and continents and went far beyond the usual way of working in service organizations from India or in distributed parts of projects, where mostly the lower end of the value chain lands in Bangalore. In return, that means that our engineers and managers do not only have world-class education and experience, but also in-depth technical knowledge about the solutions and products they own.

Prasad and Ramki have written a book, which comes at the right time. The combination of people focus, business process knowledge, and technical capabilities that this book outlines to be mandatory for successful implementations is unique indeed. This goes, of course, far beyond the usual technical descriptions of functions and features in implementation guides. Ramki and Prasad, having built their careers in our field organization and at SAP Labs India respectively, are very well positioned to share their knowledge on SAP SRM implementations — a rare combination — that the reader will soon discover.

The reader will participate with the authors in the unique learning one can only have working out of Asia Pacific and at the same time, the reader can be ensured that this knowledge is state of the art in terms of technology, processes and concept applied. This book is a book for the successful, global SAP SRM consultant, written by two colleagues from our global organization.

Clas Neumann

President – SAP Labs India

Preface

Purchasing has traditionally been perceived as a back-office clerical function, but today many organizations realize that it can play a strategic role in facing the competitive pressures from globalization and innovation. *The Consultant's Guide to SAP Supplier Relationship Management (SRM)* is the result of our endeavor to help fellow consultants deliver successful SAP SRM implementations. In this book, we discuss the changing needs of purchasing professionals, whose roles have evolved over the last few years from being operational purchasers to being strategic business partners. We will also share with you the knowledge and experience gained from numerous customer projects we have worked on, which enabled us to address real implementation issues faced by consultants and customers.

We strongly believe that consultants implementing SAP SRM should analyze the dynamics of procurement processes within the organization before suggesting a solution, to derive maximum value for the customer from SAP SRM. In other words, rather than looking at the SRM project as a mere software implementation project, it should be considered as a procurement process optimization project. A software implementation is successful only when a customer uses it and realizes value from it. Value can be derived by addressing the critical business challenges faced by the customer. The business challenges vary from customer to customer; for some customers cost savings is critical, for others compliance is a key challenge, and for yet others, maintaining relationships with their business partners is of importance. Consultants should understand the critical business issues faced by their customers and provide best-practice insights while implementing software solutions.

In this book, we have consolidated our experiences from numerous SAP SRM and SAP ERP implementations with information derived from publicly available help manuals and documents to give you a comprehensive reference guide on SAP SRM. The book explains the implementation of SAP SRM scenarios in both SAP SRM 5.0 and SAP SRM 2007. We also consciously decided to focus on core SAP SRM scenarios in this book, although SAP offers a suite of SAP SRM applications today (including SAP SRM, SAP E-Sourcing, SAP xCLM, and SAP xSA). The book also contains practical tips on enhancing the standard SAP SRM scenarios to implement complex customer business processes by leveraging SAP NetWeaver and other SAP Business Suite applications.

Although this book is primarily targeted toward consultants, we strongly recommend it for anyone involved in SAP SRM implementations: consultants implementing SAP SRM projects, customer IT teams planning to implement SAP SRM, business users and procurement professionals involved in SAP SRM projects, solution architects, and project managers involved in providing SAP SRM solutions to customers.

How This Book is Organized

This book covers the following topics in 17 chapters:

- In Chapter 1, we explain general SRM concepts and factors affecting purchasing. We will discuss how product segmentation and the industry in which a company operates determine the procurement process in an organization. We will also discuss several procurement models, explaining the organizational structures for procurement and supply management groups in a company. Awareness of the factors affecting purchasing and procurement models is crucial to defining the purchasing process in a customer project.
- In Chapter 2, we will provide a brief overview of the functionalities offered by SAP SRM.
- Chapter 3 contains an introduction to the definition of organization and master data in SAP SRM. Related settings are explained for a fictitious organization with a global presence.
- Chapters 4 to 14 will explain different scenarios and processes in SAP SRM and the configuration of these scenarios. Each scenario is explained with the help of a case study to illustrate how customers use SAP SRM. We have selected case studies from different industries to explain different scenarios. Each case study is followed by a detailed description of the scenario with a process flow. Configuration is explained with screenshots to make it simple and precise, based on the SAP SRM process implemented.

  Also, integration points needed with SAP ERP and other SAP application processes are explained in these chapters because processes, such as design collaboration, supply chain management, and so on, are essential ingredients of the purchasing process in some industries. Even though this book focuses mainly on SAP SRM, we have incorporated the necessary configuration for these other applications to make this a comprehensive reference book. Furthermore, SAP NetWeaver platform configurations associated with SAP SRM scenarios are also included in these chapters. Even though the NetWeaver configuration is very technical in nature, due consideration has been taken while explaining it, making it easy for functional consultants and customer teams to understand the issues surrounding technical configuration.

- ▶ In Chapter 15, we will discuss in detail how SAP SRM leverages SAP NetWeaver capabilities.
- ▶ In Chapter 16, we will discuss Frequently Asked Questions and provide Troubleshooting Tips and Tricks to help consultants address commonly encountered implementation problems.
- ▶ This book also includes bonus material, in Chapter 17, as follows: Enhancements in SAP SRM, with the help of customer scenarios, will provide real-life examples of how SAP SRM functionality can be improved to handle critical business issues.

Note
We have used the terms SAP ERP and SAP R/3 interchangeably in this book. Unless a specific version is mentioned, wherever we mention SAP ERP or SAP R/3 individually, we are referring to both.

We hope that this book will help consulting and customer project teams understand the concepts and configuration of SAP SRM, and enable consultants to examine issues from their customers' perspective. This will help enable them to provide solutions to critical business issues, and deliver successful SAP SRM implementations.

Purchasing has experienced a sea of change in recent years and is poised to undergo further transformation in the coming decade. Purchasing is becoming more strategic and procurement strategies are becoming vital in extending a company's competitive advantage.

— *"The New Face of Purchasing" by Economist Intelligence Unit, 2005*

1 Supplier Relationship Management

When we did an Internet search for a definition of Supplier Relationship Management (SRM), we got about two million hits. While some definitions revolved around suppliers and relations with suppliers, others veered toward comprehensive procurement and supply management. SAP SRM is a comprehensive approach to managing all procurement and supplier interactions in an organization. This includes spend analysis, procurement, sourcing, managing supplier relations, and involving suppliers in regular procurement requirements and in innovation. In this chapter, we will discuss the evolution of procurement, factors affecting procurement, procurement models, and how software applications like SAP SRM are transforming procurement.

1.1 The Evolution of Procurement

During the past 20 years or so, purchasing has undergone a kind of revolution that has redefined the way business processes are conducted and relationships are managed with suppliers driving innovation and value in these processes. New business models, like outsourcing and low-cost-country-sourcing (LCCS), have emerged from this revolution. Purchasing has evolved from a back-office intra-enterprise function to a strategic function driving innovation in collaboration with external business partners. There are many drivers that contributed to this revolution, including advances in Information Technology (IT) and Enterprise Resource Planning (ERP) applications, competitive pressures due to globalization, and an increased pace of innovation.

1.1.1 Advances in IT Driving Procurement Transformation

The evolution of procurement followed the trends in information technology and enterprise software applications. What started as an ERP initiative to integrate intra-enterprise processes has evolved into integrating processes with external business partners, such as suppliers, and redefining the boundaries in which processes are defined. These cross-enterprise processes require organizations to maintain deeper relationships with external business partners, mainly suppliers and customers. We will discuss this in detail in this section.

Figure 1.11 illustrates the process view of the purchasing evolution. Stages **3** to **5** in the figure are more strategic in nature. The figure also identifies the required procurement software capabilities for each stage of the purchasing evolution.

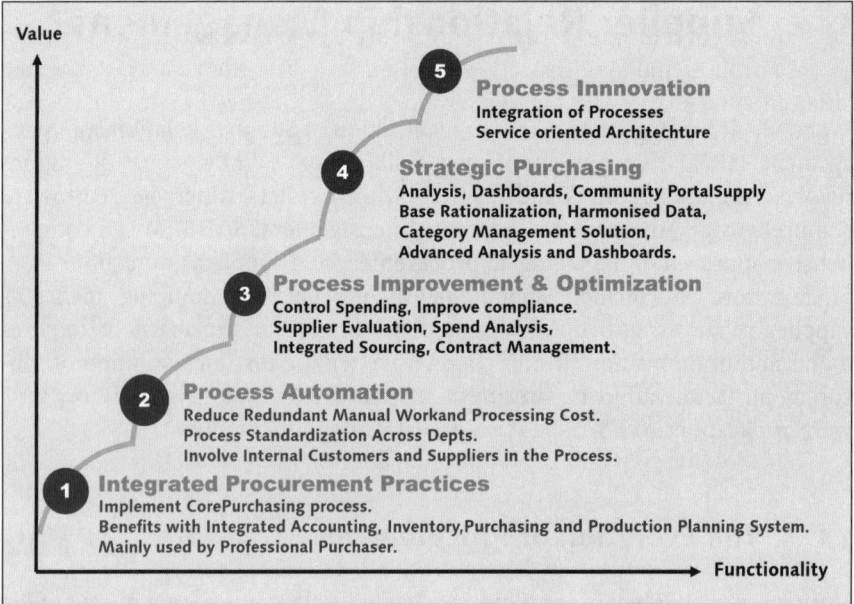

Figure 1.1 Purchasing Evolution: Process View

Integrated Procurement Processes with ERP Applications

Until the late 1980s, organizational processes were organized by functions, that is, purchasing, sales, production, stores, etc. In the 1990s, the need of organizations was to get these loosely integrated functions across different departments into integrated, well-defined processes. This resulted in great demand for ERP applications like SAP ERP, which enabled organizations to gain considerable benefits from integration. With integrated logistics and financial processes, purchasing departments were able to identify the procurement demands from various departments more precisely, reconcile the demands with available stock, identify the source of supply, and define streamlined order-to-pay processes. The Materials Management (MM) component in ERP applications enabled purchasers to automate their processes and eliminated the manual coordination with other departments in the organization, like production and account payables. This greatly enhanced the capabilities of purchasing departments by considerably reducing internal procurement lead times and process costs. Further, the automation and resulting time savings enabled purchasers to look more closely at the products and services the organization is procuring, as you'll see next.

Product Categorization

ERP applications facilitated purchasers to analyze the spend and procurement processes. It became evident to buyers that each product has its own characteristics and needs a different way of purchasing. Purchasers also learned to categorize products and services to be procured based on the characteristics that differentiate each category, having recognized that they need to streamline procurement processes around these categories. They also started focusing their efforts on defining and streamlining their processes around top spend categories, which are critical for the organization to reap maximum value. Examples include the following:

▶ An automotive company will be interested in defining procurement processes around direct materials, for example, components and sub-contracting of components. Because automotive companies buy most of their components from suppliers, they pioneered the concept of strong, long-term relationships with suppliers.

▶ Companies in asset-intensive industries, like oil and gas, utilities, etc., will be interested in defining their processes around assets and spare parts to maintain their critical assets. Well-defined contracts and agreements with original equipment manufacturers are the key focus here.

We will further discuss product categorization in Section 1.2

Employee Self-Service

During the late 1990s, purchasers sensed another opportunity to realize value, by deploying employee self-service systems for low spend categories. By then, enough measures had been taken to streamline and control the process for major spend categories, but the procurement of low spend categories or less-critical categories (which had less visibility in the organization) was not managed by the procurement department.

That is, to save on ERP license and training costs, many organizations did not extend ERP implementations to cover the process for low spend category procurement, and requirements for products and services in such categories originated from all employees, resulting in maverick buying. To address this issue, many companies implemented employee self-service systems.

As an example, a maintenance engineer typically requires spare parts for equipment maintenance and office supplies to perform his regular tasks. Procurement of spare parts is taken care of by the integrated maintenance and procurement process in ERP without the direct involvement of the maintenance engineer in creating purchase requests and ordering. However, the engineer needs to create purchase requests for office supplies requirements, as do employees in other departments such as production, quality control, and so on. Employees, however, were either reluctant to use the ERP system as they felt it was tedious to use and not worth the effort for low-cost items, or the ERP system was not available for procurement of these items. As a result, manual, paper-based processes were used for such categories, and in many cases, paper requisitions were routed to the purchasing department, also increasing the manual work load of purchasers. In time, purchasers realized that the volume of these transactions was so high that they consumed most of their available time.

Internet-based self-service applications like catalogs, search technologies, and mail-based workflow engines provided an economical solution to this issue. Applications using these technologies require little or no training and are extremely easy to learn and use. Business-to-Business (B2B) procurement applications facilitate purchasers to publish products with negotiated prices as catalogs. Employees can search the products they need from these catalogs and order in two or three steps. Integrated approval workflow ensures that the process can still be controlled by purchasers, and if needed, allows purchasers to get involved in the process. The process helps organizations reduce maverick buying and automate manual, paper-based processes while reducing the burden of the purchasing department. Organizations globally have started implementing these self-service procurement systems to control the spend from low-value spend categories.

Engaging Suppliers

Actively involving internal users in the procurement process has enabled purchasing departments to realize benefits through cost savings and compliance. In the early 2000s, the attention of purchasing departments turned toward involving bidders and suppliers in the procurement process. Processes like bidding or sourcing, and order follow-up require active involvement of suppliers.

In a sourcing process, suppliers have to come to buyers' locations to understand requirements, or obtain information about the request for quotation (RFQ) through mail or fax. This process is time-consuming and inefficient. Purchasers now rely on Internet-based sourcing applications to make the process more efficient. The new systems allow purchasers to publish RFQs online, where suppliers can see and respond to them. This greatly reduces the cycle time and the costs involved as compared to the manual process. It also reduces purchasers' workload, as there is no need to input the responses from suppliers into the system. Also, because the data is stored in the system, it allows for a systematic analysis of the data submitted and evaluate suppliers' quotes. Additionally, reverse auction capabilities of some sourcing applications allow purchasers to tap the competition for certain products and ensure cost savings.

In order to follow-up, the main issue is getting confirmation from suppliers for goods ordered and the visibility of goods in transit. Many purchasers spend considerable time and effort in 'chasing' suppliers. In the past, purchasers and suppliers had to work with unreliable and inefficient communication modes like mail, fax, and phone calls. Now, procurement applications with order collaboration capabilities facilitate effective communication between purchasers and suppliers. In typical order collaboration, suppliers can access purchase orders online, confirm the orders and provide advance shipping information to buyers in real time. This helps organizations to reliably plan their supply chain activities.

Advanced SAP SRM Applications for Strategic Purchasing

Automation of procurement transactions involving both internal and external business partners have resulted in reducing the process cost and cycle time, and improving compliance. Automation also relieved purchasers' burden of dealing with routine transactions, freeing up their time for more strategic activities. This started the next wave of the purchasing evolution — *strategic purchasing*. Strategic purchasing initiatives include the following:

▶ It has become evident that the automation of transactional processes can bring value from efficiency and process cost perspective. But to extend this value, it is important to measure the efficiency of the procurement supply chain. This includes measuring the internal and external process efficiencies, continuous development and evaluation of suppliers, global contract management, etc. Purchasers started harnessing the data in their systems by integrating procurement analysis and spend analysis applications directly in the process. These analyses can be used to improve transactional and process efficiency or to improve the performance measures to streamline the process. For example, analysis related to bid evaluation is mainly used to determine the winning bid in a bidding process. Similarly, supplier evaluation is a compilation of supplier performance from past transaction history and qualitative inputs from buyers and is used in sourcing and the supplier development process. Contract monitoring enables purchasers to proactively analyze the contract usage and take actions on expiring contracts.

▶ Globalization helped purchasers to source products from across the globe. This also increased the risk as the interpretation of terms of contracts is different in different countries. Therefore, contract management has become an essential strategic tool in the era of globalization. Multinational companies (MNC) with operations in many countries have realized that by entering into central global contracts with suppliers they can achieve greater cost savings on globally aggregated demand for common products. However, these MNCs realized that their systems do not contain the same set of data in all countries. For example, a product like personal computers may have different product codes in different countries. Demand aggregation and central global contracts require the data to be harmonized with uniform data across systems in different countries. Many companies are currently engaged in various initiatives to harmonize data and harness the power of demand aggregation and central contracts.

Companies that have already benefitted from the strategic purchasing initiatives we just described have started looking for new initiatives to harness the innovation. As a result, category management, procurement outsourcing, and so on, are slowly becoming buzzwords.

Software Evolution

Software applications evolve with procurement practices and often even drive new innovations in procurement. One example of how SAP SRM has evolved and kept pace with customer requirements can be seen in Figure 1.2. SAP SRM started as a B2B procurement application in the late 1990s that enabled catalog-based self-service procurement. Enterprise Buyer Professional (EBP) replaced B2B procurement with enhanced capabilities to help all activities of buyers. SAP SRM replaced EBP with many enhanced capabilities and enabled organizations to integrate their processes with suppliers' processes.

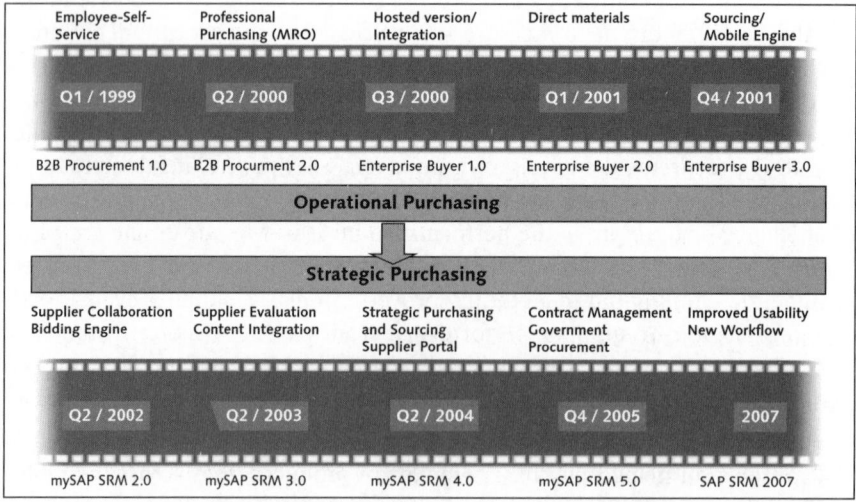

Figure 1.2 Purchasing Process: Software Evolution

1.1.2 Globalization and Innovation Driving Procurement

Bottom-line results are the focus of every company competing in today's tough economy. To improve the bottom line, there are two choices — grow revenues or decrease costs:

▶ In a sluggish economy, revenue growth is challenging at best. Fortunately, the cost-reduction side of the equation is vastly more promising.

▶ By reducing the costs associated with the purchase of goods and services, companies can boost profitability without having to generate more sales. That is the kind of bottom-line result that makes shareholders happy and keeps companies ahead of the competition.

Marketplace trends, such as globalization, increasing specialization, and outsourcing, are fueling the pressure to reduce costs while increasing adaptability, speed, and innovation. Organizations are responding to this pressure by centralizing their purchasing operations, outsourcing to low-cost regions, and implementing transformation initiatives. They are moving beyond outmoded order faxing and "squeeze" tactics when dealing with suppliers.

Modern purchasing is driven by strategic agendas and guided by policies that are clearly segmented across spend categories and across the supplier portfolio. Competitive companies are now managing demand actively. Their purchasing teams are working across organizational boundaries and geographic regions. And there is an infrastructure in place to manage compliance.

Today, companies are nurturing collaborative relationships with strategic suppliers, a tactic that leads to margin improvement and fosters innovation. Such transformations have made purchasing a key influence on corporate strategy. Of course, most organizations have not yet completed this transformation. Improvement initiatives may be in place, but often they have not been coordinated, focused, or prioritized to maximize their potential benefits.

Typically, the initiatives are focused on spend reduction alone. While this may bring short-term cost savings, it does not help organizations transform sourcing practices to gain a competitive advantage and create new market opportunities. Change programs must be based on cultural and organizational development. Building strategic relationships with suppliers requires a new approach and skill set. The underlying infrastructure of business processes, business data, and technology also plays a role, because it enables the workforce that manages supply and suppliers to work together. The business infrastructure is the foundation that allows an empowered workforce to accelerate business innovation in purchasing. And nobody is suggesting that companies should cozy up to their suppliers just to be friendly. Behind the new face of purchasing are core economic issues and hard realities driving real business change — the kind of change companies desperately need to resolve the conflicting pressures they face.

As we've seen, on the one hand, companies are pressured to reduce costs and mitigate risk while on the other hand, they are pressured to innovate, adapt, and speed up processes. And the old ways of managing the supply base, which might be good for random cost savings, do not deliver the kind of sustainable business value companies can bank on.

Companies are revising their perspective on supply management. Rather than, for example, seeking the lowest price for a transaction, they are seeking the best price possible for sustained savings and high levels of quality and service. Further, rather than keeping suppliers at arms' length, they are partnering with suppliers to mitigate supply risk and get products to market faster than ever before. This change in perspective is triggering new initiatives in purchasing that require a broad supply management perspective:

- For example, many companies are attempting to manage the supply base as a corporate asset by extending internal processes outward to trustworthy partners and enhancing the value of supplier relationships.

- Others are trying to strike favorable agreements through global leverage, reducing overall spend by enforcing agreements throughout the enterprise and controlling access to approved vendors and materials.

These emerging trends represent a significant shift away from tactical purchasing techniques toward a more strategic approach that can deliver long-term measurable value by reducing supply risk, improving margins, and tapping supplier innovation.

Let us now look into factors that are important for defining the purchasing in an organization.

1.2   Factors Affecting Purchasing

Many factors drive the way procurement function operates in an organization. It is important to understand these factors to redesign or optimize a procurement process in an organization. We will discuss three important factors — product segmentation, industry in which a company operates, and procurement models — in this section.

1.2.1   Product Segmentation

A product may refer to a material or a service, and products can be divided based on the process in which they are used in the organization. They can be further divided based on the criticality of the product, nature of the product, and on its complexity. The procurement processes for materials and services are also different. We will discuss several product segmentations in this subsection, including direct and indirect materials, stock and nonstock materials, critical and non-critical products, spares, services, and high cost and complex products.

Direct and Indirect Materials

Direct materials refer to materials used directly in production or service delivery. They include raw materials, parts, and subcontracted items required to manufacture an organization's product. *Indirect materials* refer to materials that are not directly used in production but are required for organizational activities. For example, while steel sheets and tires are direct materials for an automobile manufacturer, stationery items and printer cartridges are indirect materials.

Some characteristics of direct materials include the following:

▶ They typically form part of a finished product of the organization.
▶ They are part of production plans, and typically procurement requirements are generated automatically as a result of material requirements planning (MRP).
▶ They are stocked in warehouses and issued for consumption as required.
▶ They typically have a part number or product master code.
▶ Their cost is included in the product cost of finished products.
▶ They form the bulk of procurement spend in an organization.

Some characteristics of indirect materials include the following:

▶ They may or may not have a part number or product master code.
▶ They are not typically stocked. However, equipment spare parts, which may not be direct materials, are typically stocked in many organizations.
▶ They are typically delivered to the consuming department on receipt and thus consumed immediately.
▶ Their cost is typically part of overhead costs of the organization.

> **Note**
>
> Although the number of procurement transactions for indirect materials can be very high, the value is typically very low.

While most e-procurement software offerings help organizations manage indirect materials, applications like SAP SRM help organizations manage both direct and indirect materials. Further, although the automation of indirect materials processes brings savings to organizations, companies can achieve greater value by effectively managing direct material procurement.

Stock and Nonstock Materials

Stock and nonstock materials are another segmentation that plays a significant role in purchasing. *Stock materials* are materials that are bought in bulk, kept in stock, and consumed whenever required. A material number or product master code exists in the buyer's system for such materials. They can be direct materials like raw materials, components, etc., or indirect materials like spares, etc. *Nonstock materials* are used less frequently, may not have material numbers, and are ordered as needed. Services provided by external companies that are requested as and when needed may be handled as nonstock material purchases.

Some characteristics that affect stocking decisions and purchasing include the following:

▸ **Raw materials and components**
  The procurement and stock planning for raw materials and components depend on the production model used in the organization. For example, in a make-to-stock scenario, sufficient stock based on the production plans of the finished product should be maintained. In a make-to-order scenario, raw materials and components are ordered based on the requirements of the finished product. Just-in-time (JIT) scenarios require that raw materials and components are received from suppliers as and when required for the finished product production and therefore strong relationships with suppliers as well as supplier collaboration are crucial.

▸ **Dangerous materials**
  If a material is classified as dangerous, it is important that minimum and maximum stock levels are closely monitored. Purchasing contracts and instructions to suppliers should be in accordance with the respective country's laws regarding dangerous goods.

▸ **Critical materials**
  With materials critical for production it is necessary to keep a fair amount of stock. Also, it is important to have multiple sources of supply to avoid supply risk.

Critical and Noncritical Products

How critical a product is can be defined based on different characteristics like availability, safety, etc. Criticality of a product also depends on the industry and affects the purchasing process. Some examples include the following:

▸ From a production point of view, a product can be considered critical if it affects the final output. In this case, the purchasing department should ensure that critical items are always available to production on time. Stock planning, order follow-up, and reducing procurement lead time are important here.

▸ From a safety point of view, a material can be classified as critical if the consequence of a material failure will be catastrophic, possibly resulting in severe injury or loss of life, or if the material failure can result in excessive repair or replacement cost. Again, safety consideration may be taken into account in different ways. For example, for the pharmaceutical industry, the end product can be affected if the molecules don't pass the critical product standards, resulting in loss of life. In the process industry, spare parts used in critical equipment (e.g., coils for furnaces) should pass stringent quality norms to prevent accidents. Quality and supplier reliability are the most important factors here.

Spares

In any organization, spares are needed for maintaining equipment. These spares can be stock or nonstock spares, and critical or noncritical spares, depending on the industry and availability. Spares may be procured from the original equipment manufacturer (OEM) or distributors of OEM products, or from any other manufacturer producing similar items. Some spares may have to be procured only from OEMs as they are proprietary in nature. Based on the use of the spares they can be divided into several categories:

▸ **Capital (insurance) spares**
Parts or assemblies that are purchased along with the original equipment. Usually one-of-a-kind assemblies such as rotor assemblies, reduction gear sets, special forgings, etc. These are normally capitalized in the balance sheet.

▸ **Warehouse spares**
Complete assemblies that are purchased along with the original equipment and are stocked. Stock levels are maintained for these types of spares and they are reordered whenever stocks dip below the reorder point.

▸ **Construction spares**
Parts and assemblies normally used or consumed during installation of equipment, cleaning, flushing, and inspection. These spares might be needed only once during installation or reinstallation. These are one-off purchases.

▸ **Commissioning spares**
Parts and assemblies that are required from the time of mechanical completion to the point at which equipment is ready for start-up. Commissioning spares include items required for testing, calibration, etc. These are also one-off purchases.

▸ **First Year spares**
Parts required to safeguard the operation of equipment during the running-in and start-up periods and during the first complete year of plant operation.

Most of the time they are purchased once the installation is complete and ready to run.

▸ **Normal operation spares**
Parts required for the regular maintenance of equipment, including slow-wearing parts and consumables like oil, grease, etc. Such spare parts are kept in stock and are maintained regularly.

Services

At most companies, business services — from outsourced travel booking, to temporary and contract labor, to IT support and consulting services — account for the bulk of purchasing dollars spent. Yet the majority of services have not been subject to the discipline of well-defined procurement procedures because of the complex nature of services, and the multiple activities and parties involved in procuring and managing services. In fact, services such as contracting, consulting, printing, and travel and entertainment make up a bigger percentage of indirect spend than office supplies.

Enterprises utilizing contract labor procurement technologies have been able to cut costs through better negotiation for rate reductions, shortened recruiting cycles, improved candidate selection, and rationalized and reduced supply bases. Companies deploying automation in all service procurement areas report improved spend visibility, better supplier intelligence, and enhanced decision-making capabilities. Service procurement offers a huge and largely untapped opportunity for cost savings and process improvements at most organizations. Unlike materials, it is often difficult to precisely define service requirements. Many times, the actual services required are known only during the delivery of service. However, traditional applications were not designed to support the complexities and dynamics of service procurement. In fact, service procurement processes are ripe to respond to the information collection, compliance, and collaboration capabilities of online procurement automation. So the purchasing process defined for service procurement should be capable and dynamic enough to consider the previously mentioned facts.

High Cost and Complex Products

High cost and complex products is another segmentation that may affect the procurement process. In the case of high cost and complex products, like assets, defense items, etc., you must ensure that transparency and compliance to the predefined procedures are followed during evaluation of suppliers and products. In such cases, procurement processes should be well-documented and all contract actions should be in accordance with applicable laws and predefined procedures. It is important to ensure that records are maintained in sufficient detail so as to provide a significant history of the procurement action. These records must include, but are not necessarily limited to; rationale for the method of procurement, the selection of agreement type, awardees selection or rejections, and the basis for the agreement type.

Some products or services can be very complex to define. Depending on the characteristics of the product or service, the complexity of the purchasing process also varies. For example, in the case of procuring a gas turbine, the bill of materials and specifications may be large. In the case of service procurement for maintenance of the same equipment, the steps and processes involved may be complex. In the case of enterprise software implementation or consulting services procurement, defining the problem to be resolved or consulting deliverables may be very complex. Purchasers should ensure well-drafted contracts are in place to cover all of the risks associated with high cost and complex products purchases.

Let us now look at the other important factor, the industry in which a company operates, which drives the purchasing processes.

1.2.2 Industry in which the Organization Operates

A critical factor that may affect the procurement processes in an organization is a category's industry-specific characteristics. The following points should be taken into consideration while procuring complex categories:

▶ Some categories are specific to the industry. For example, steering gear assembly is a specific direct material in the automobile industry.

▶ Some categories are common across different industries and will be treated the same way in all of the industries during the procurement process. This is mainly applicable to indirect materials used for operational purposes. For example, stationery or IT purchases are considered to be part of office supplies or office equipment and are treated more or less the same way in all industries.

▶ Some categories are common across different industries, but during the procurement process, the methodology varies. For example, cable buying may be considered a direct material in the utilities industry, where cable is used for the transmission and distribution of electricity and is purchased on a regular basis. Proper planning is required for cable buying in this case. Cables may be bought in the manufacturing industry also, but mainly for maintenance activity within the plant or facilities. In this case, cable buying is not a regularly occurring activity, but rather cable is bought only when there is a breakdown, or when preventive maintenance is needed.

▶ Some categories, depending on the industry in which they are used, need special attention, as they have direct impact on production capabilities. This mainly applies to consumables that are used in process industries. For example, in the case of lubricants, a main raw material that is considered input for the production process is crude oil. During the processing of crude oil, catalysts and additives are needed to make lubricants. Once the lubricant is ready, packaging materials are required. These categories should be taken into consideration in the production planning and given the importance of direct materials, even though they are not raw material for production.

Note
While implementing purchasing process in an organization, it is very important to understand the dynamics of the various categories being used.

Let us now look at the typical procurement organization models that influence the procurement processes.

1.2.3 Procurement Models

Traditionally, enterprises have had two primary options for organizing procurement operations — centralized and decentralized. Let us look at each in more detail.

Centralized Procurement Model

Organizations that use centralized procurement leverage corporate spending and drive sourcing, process, and technology decisions as well as execution from a central command and control group. Although they offer greater spending leverage and operational efficiencies, centralized structures result in higher incidences of unapproved spending, process circumvention at the business unit level, and uneven performance.

Centralized procurement models provide economies of scale that improve spending power, enhance operational efficiencies and knowledge sharing, and help enforce process and policy standardization.

While good in theory, these models have not always performed well in practice. This has been particularly true for large, geographically dispersed organizations, especially those that have grown through mergers and acquisitions. In these environments, site and plant managers often resist centralization, because they feel that centrally mandated supply decisions and policies slow operations and do not satisfy local supply and quality needs. As a result, centralized procurement groups often report high incidences of maverick spending, process and policy circumvention, and uneven supply measurement and performance.

Decentralized Procurement Model

Organizations that use decentralized procurement provide business units and sites with autonomy and control over supply, process, and technology decisions, as well as sourcing and procurement execution. This improves satisfaction at the site and business unit level. It also speeds process and issue resolution by avoiding much of the bureaucracy and red tape that comes with centralized procurement models.

Decentralized procurement, however, doesn't leverage corporate spending, and is costly to operate. It does not share systems, expertise, and resources across sites, and leads to enterprise-wide inconsistent supply cost and performance.

With market pressures, such as globalization, outsourcing, and compliance, pushing procurement to the frontlines of corporate strategy, an increasing number of enterprises are transitioning to a new procurement model to position themselves for supply management success: the center-led procurement model. We will look at this model next.

Center-Led Procurement Model

The center-led procurement model is a hybrid model that blends spend leverage, process standardization, and knowledge- and resource-sharing attributes of centralization with the local empowerment and execution characteristics of the decentralized model. These factors make it clear that fully centralized or decentralized organizational models are ill-suited to support and sustain procurement's new strategic role and address the higher expectations and new (and global) market pressures.

The center-led procurement model relies on cross-functional and divisional teams, flexible process and policy standards that can be customized at the local level, coordinated metrics and incentives, and an integrated procurement information systems infrastructure that automates and aligns source-to-settle processes across the enterprise.

1.3　Summary

Over the next five years, as the advantages of managing supplier relationships become more widely accepted, new practices for supply management will emerge. Transaction processing, for example, will become increasingly automated or eliminated wherever possible. Supply chains will embrace process collaboration, leading to significant advantages for suppliers with the technical abilities to get on board early. At the same time, outsourcing will spur further innovation as competitive companies work harder and dedicate increasing resources to identifying and nurturing important relationships.

Ultimately, these changes point to one simple fact: building solid relationships with the supply base bodes well for the long-term health of business. The challenge is to form partnerships and grow relationships in a way that ensures favorable pricing and guarantees efficient procurement, delivery, and production. These partnerships help to place the purchasing organization in a stronger position to influence supplier behavior. When it comes to enforcing adherence to technical standards or inducing response to performance incentives, companies that build solid relationships with their supply base consistently outperform companies that do not.

In this chapter, you learned how procurement evolved from a back-office function to a strategic supply management function. In Chapter 2, we will discuss how SAP SRM helps organizations transform their procurement processes and effectively manage their relationships with suppliers.

SAP is making significant investments in SAP SRM, resulting in differentiating applications that will enable our customers to continue to innovate and meet their procurement needs in an increasingly competitive marketplace.

— *John Zepecki, SVP, SRM Strategy and Development*

2 An Overview of SAP Supplier Relationship Management (SAP SRM)

According to SAP's product literature, "SAP Supplier Relationship Management (SAP SRM) provides organizations with the tools to drive superior results through an end-to-end procurement process." Having been in the market since 1999, SAP SRM has matured into a comprehensive purchasing solution that enables procurement organizations to provide strategic value through sustainable cost savings, regulatory compliance, and quick time-to-value. SAP SRM covers the full supply cycle from strategy to execution, enabling the procurement organization to optimize supplier selection, increase collaboration, and compress cycle times. SAP SRM also offers consolidated content and analytics functions that enable making and executing decisions aligned with corporate strategy. The SAP SRM solution provides capabilities in the following areas:

- Sourcing
- Operational Procurement
- Supplier Enablement
- Contract Management
- Category Management
- Catalog Management
- Analytics

In this chapter, we will provide an overview of each of these key capabilities, with more detailed information provided on each capability in later chapters in this book. In addition, we will provide a brief overview of the different SAP SRM deployment scenarios available to purchasing departments in this chapter.

Before we start looking at SAP SRM's key capabilities in more detail, note that they are delivered through the following application components of SAP SRM:

- ▸ Enterprise Buyer Professional (EBP)
- ▸ Bidding Engine (BE) and Live Auction Cockpit (LAC)
- ▸ Supplier Self-Services (SUS)
- ▸ SRM-MDM Catalog
- ▸ Category Management
- ▸ SRM Analytics with SAP NetWeaver Business Intelligence (SAP NetWeaver BI).

> **Note**
>
> EBP, BE, and SUS are delivered with the software component *SRM Server*.

Let us now start our discussion of the key SAP SRM capabilities by providing you with a brief overview of the concept of sourcing.

2.1 Sourcing

Many organizations focus their initial IT-based strategic sourcing initiatives on gaining some quick savings for the business. Online negotiations help companies to achieve quick savings, increased participation in bidding events, and transparency. SAP SRM offers various reverse auction and bidding techniques, delivered through the BE component of SAP SRM. Further, the sophisticated analytical functions of SAP SRM expedite the decision-making process and enable evaluation based on a broad range of criteria. SAP SRM supports informed sourcing decisions that are aligned with a company's sourcing strategy.

SAP SRM creates a common view of purchasing data, develops well-segmented supply strategies, and brings analytical insight into both supplier performance and the internal purchasing process. Through these capabilities, the solution supports sourcing professionals in analyzing spend patters and streamlining sourcing processes. In addition, it provides support for managing an integrated supplier negotiation and award process that includes the following:

- ▸ Preparing a bidding event
- ▸ Executing electronic requests for quotes and reverse auctions
- ▸ Evaluating bids
- ▸ Awarding suppliers
- ▸ Creating and managing contracts.

Next, in Sections 2.1.1 and 2.1.2 respectively, we will discuss the bidding process and the live auction process.

2.1.1   The Bidding Process

SAP SRM helps companies achieve quick savings using online bidding events. Using *Requests for Quotations* (RFQs), companies invite qualified suppliers to submit proposals to provide materials or services according to the specified requirements. The *Bidding with collaboration* scenario enables companies to innovate in collaboration with suppliers. RFQs are created from a requirement without an assigned source of supply, or from existing expiring contracts. SRM also supports the *Request for Information* (RFI) and *Request for Proposal* (RFP) functionalities. Further, the *dynamic attributes* functionality allows companies to also incorporate qualitative parameters in the selection process. *Expressive bidding* enables suppliers to offer alternatives or substitutes to the requested products. SAP SRM also provides the tools to quickly convert received bids into *purchase orders* (POs) or *contracts*. SAP SRM supports sophisticated analysis that helps you make quick decisions by assigning scores to both price and qualitative factors, such as the quality of materials and services, delivery times, past experience with a supplier, dependability, and the ability to scale up. SAP SRM provides tools that let you perform complex, multi-parametric analyses so that buyers can easily generate bidding statistics and perform side-by-side comparisons of individual bids and vendors.

2.1.2   Live Auction Process

The process for creating bids for auctions starts in a similar manner as bid invitations using RFQs. Unlike with RFQs, in which bids are hidden from other bidders, reverse auctions allow bidders to bid against each other. This technique can drive bottom-line results significantly because it puts suppliers in direct competition with each other. Invited suppliers receive an email that includes a link to an auction in the SAP bidding engine. Bidders can then enter the live auction cockpit that lets them participate in the real-time bidding process. Once in the cockpit, bidders can monitor bidding activity, receive chat messages from and send chat messages to the purchaser, and place bids. The live auction cockpit offers real-time information, so new bids immediately update the information in the cockpit, including charts and current prices. Purchasers can control the information that is shown to bidders using a variety of auction types, such as rank-only bidding or blind bidding.

> **Note**
>
> We will discuss sourcing in more detail in Chapter 10.

Now, let us take a closer look at the next SAP SRM key capability, operational procurement.

2.2   Operational Procurement

SAP SRM operational procurement enables companies to optimize and automate the procurement process for direct and indirect materials and services by providing the specific functionalities necessary to cater to these items' requirements. Optimizing procurement helps companies reduce cycle times and costs by automating and streamlining the purchasing process. The operational procurement capabilities of SAP SRM are delivered through the Enterprise Buyer Professional (EBP) component of SAP SRM.

SAP SRM has its heritage in the procurement of indirect materials through catalog-based requisitioning over the Internet. Direct materials require planning and inventory capabilities. SAP SRM plan-driven procurement enables companies to integrate the procurement optimization capabilities of SAP SRM with the planning and inventory management capabilities of SAP ERP.

Operational procurement facilitates the following three scenarios, which we'll look at next:

- Self-service procurement
- Service procurement
- Plan-driven procurement

2.2.1   Self-Service Procurement

The procurement functions of SAP SRM complements the ERP-based procure-to-pay process with integrated catalog-based requisitioning often referred to as *self-service procurement*. Easy-to-use browser-based screens enable every employee in an enterprise to search for products, requisition products, and then place purchase orders. The process also ensures that employee transactions comply with corporate purchasing policies and internal controls. Empowering employees to carry out routine procurement reduces overhead and allows purchasing professionals to focus on managing strategic relationships.

Purchasing departments are often burdened with administrative tasks involved in the procurement of routine maintenance, repair, and operations (MRO) items and services, such as office supplies, machine parts, janitorial goods, repairs, and professional, travel, and educational services. Centralizing the purchasing process requires the purchasing department to spend much of their time in organizing and processing requisitions and in answering queries about standard materials. Paper-based processes are slow, bureaucratic, and costly. Further, transaction costs are often extremely high compared with the value of the goods and services purchased and frequent errors and maverick buying lead to inefficiency in the process. Manual procedures impede transparency, preventing corporate decision makers from understanding the impact of purchasing choices and making it difficult to consolidate purchasing power across the enterprise.

Self-service procurement addresses these issues by empowering employees to create and manage their own requisitions. This relieves the purchasing department of a huge administrative burden and makes the procurement process faster, more cost-effective, more user friendly, and more responsive. Creating requisitions and purchase orders with SAP SRM is simple and efficient. Shopping carts can be created in SAP SRM using catalog, product master, templates, free texts, etc. SAP SRM automatically generates requisitions and routes them through the approval process. On approval, a purchase order is created and dispatched to suppliers using different communication mediums without the delay or expense of additional user intervention.

In addition, providing catalogs of the most frequently ordered services and materials ensures that users can easily manage their own purchase orders in line with company rules. Purchases can be restricted to approved vendors and business rules are established to enforce limits on the ordering process. SAP SRM uses a robust workflow to route documents for approval in accordance with existing business processes, ensuring complete transparency. Employees can check the status of their orders at any time and confirm receipt from their desktops. With SAP SRM integrated with a backend financial system, confirmations of receipt also trigger the appropriate accounting activities.

Self-service procurement with SAP SRM also supports *limit shopping carts* for unplanned purchases, which have a value limit and a validity period. Items or services can be added during confirmations and invoices up to this limit. This approach guarantees cost monitoring. A *procurement card* issued to employees or physically or logically deposited at a particular supplier, can simplify the procurement process for MRO items.

> **Note**
>
> Self-service procurement is explained in detail in Chapter 5, and procurements cards are explained in detail in Chapter 7.

2.2.2 Service Procurement

Companies in all industries rely on supplemental workforces — from temporary workers to consultants — for full-time staff requirements. Temporary and consulting services can add greatly to enterprise agility and competitive advantage. These services can also help the bottom line by making costs more predictable and by reducing in-house management efforts for peripheral business activities. Service procurement solutions help to manage resources and monitor costs over a whole range of services. The process of service procurement is often more complex and less standardized than materials procurement. Furthermore, service requirements are often undefined in quantity, duration, and price at the point of purchase until the supplier confirms the actual services rendered. SAP SRM helps to close the gap between the strategic needs of service purchasers and the operational needs of requesters. Service procurement supports fully automated procurement processes for services and includes a response function so suppliers can indicate the availability of a service agent.

> **Note**
>
> Service procurement is explained in detail in Chapter 11.

2.2.3 Plan-Driven Procurement

Plan-driven procurement enables you to link the streamlined procurement processes in SAP SRM with backend SAP or non-SAP planning and operations systems. With SAP SRM, it is possible to purchase goods and services to fulfill requirements generated by SAP or non-SAP applications for plant maintenance, project management, and production planning. Companies can also centralize the procurement for requirements generated in many planning and operational systems.

Plan-driven procurement takes requirements from an SAP or non-SAP planning and operations system in the form of purchase requisitions and carries out automatic procurement for the requirements. With SAP SRM, professional purchasers have a variety of sourcing tools at their disposal to find reliable sources of supply quickly and easily.

> **Note**
>
> Plan-driven procurement is explained in detail in Chapter 6.

Next, let's take a look at the SAP SRM capability of supplier enablement.

2.3 Supplier Enablement

SAP SRM supplier enablement lets suppliers connect to an organization's procurement systems to process orders using a web-based front end. Suppliers just need Internet-enabled computers; there is no need for any special software or integration effort. Supplier enablement is delivered through the Supplier Self-Services (SUS) component of SAP SRM.

Supplier enablement within SAP SRM provides suppliers with a streamlined order management system. Outbound purchase orders are sent from the purchasing system — which can be either SRM EBP or Enterprise Resource Planning (ERP) — to SUS, where suppliers can view, change, respond, print, and download them. All subsequent communications relating to a purchase order, such as acknowledgements, confirmations, and invoices are exchanged electronically

SAP NetWeaver Exchange Infrastructure (SAP NetWeaver XI) is used to achieve the integration between the purchasing system and SUS. Depending on the security policies of the purchasing organization, multiple deployment options are supported:

▶ The purchasing system and SUS are on different servers, separated by a firewall, if necessary. This mode is supported for ERP materials management integration with SUS.

▶ The purchasing system and SUS are both part of the SAP SRM web application server (WAS) instance, but on different clients. This is supported only with the EBP purchasing component.

▶ The purchasing system and SUS are both part of the SAP SRM WAS instance and on the same client. This is supported only with the EBP purchasing component.

The process of using SRM SUS with the EBP system is as follows:

1. A supplier logs on to SRM SUS, processes the order, and creates an order response, which is forwarded to the e-procurement system. If the supplier cannot meet all of the order terms specified by the original purchase order and changes them, the purchaser may not agree to the changes and may decide to change them once again. In this case, the supplier receives a changed purchase order and must send a new response. This cycle is concluded when both parties agree on the terms of the purchase order. When the goods ordered have been shipped or the service has been performed, the supplier prepares one or more confirmation sheets.

2. For orders that simply state the services type and total cost without including a breakdown of activities and materials, as in limit purchase orders for unplanned services or materials, confirmation sheets can be prepared by selecting and including the appropriate items from the catalog. This is possible because of the Open Catalog Interface (OCI) connection to the product and service catalog. The confirmation is sent to the EBP system, where purchasing organization can approve or reject it. Generally, the procurement system initiates a workflow to obtain the necessary approvals.

3. After approval, the e-procurement system sends a confirmation response to the supplier, which updates the status of the confirmation sheet. In the final step, the supplier creates an invoice, which the purchasing organization must verify and approve or decline. This cycle may be repeated until the buyer and seller agree on the content of the invoice. For legal reasons, a purchasing organization can't modify an invoice received from the supplier. Invoices are

created within SUS and suppliers do not need a financial accounting system to do this. On approval, an invoice response is sent to the supplier, and the invoice status is updated.

> **Note**
>
> SUS integration with the EBP system is explained in detail in Chapter 14. Similar order processing is also supported in SUS with ERP materials management systems. SUS integration with the Materials Management (MM) system is explained in detail in Chapter 13.

2.4 Contract Management

Most solutions for contract management usually focus on either preparing and negotiating contracts before they are signed, or fulfilling and monitoring them after they are signed. The SAP SRM solution addresses both of these issues, providing control over the complete contract management life cycle. SAP SRM supports centralized contract management and decentralized fulfillment, enabling purchasing organizations to develop global contracts that help increase compliance throughout the enterprise. Stored electronically for easy access, all business units and subsidiaries can tap into these contracts to secure the most favorable terms and conditions. At the same time, this approach provides the necessary flexibility for storing business unit or subsidiary-specific exceptions, modifications, and conditions, as requirements demand.

Better management of contracts throughout their life cycle results in more efficiently negotiated terms, cross-enterprise contract visibility, higher compliance, and reduced administrative costs. SAP SRM workflows allow an efficient method of handling contracts during the preparation and negotiation phase by monitoring and tracking all changes to ensure consistency. In addition to the functionalities provided in SAP SRM, SAP also has a solution called SAP xApp Contract Life Cycle Management (xCLM) to help organizations manage contracts. xCLM is built on the SAP E-Sourcing platform and facilitates collaborative contract creation and authoring, contract performance management, and compliance monitoring.

> **Note**
>
> More details on xCLM can be found on SAP's website at *http://service. sap.com/xapps*.

Next, we will discuss briefly the three phases of contract management, namely, contract development, contract execution, and contract monitoring.

2.4.1 Contract Development

SAP SRM lets you reuse organizational knowledge so you don't have to start from scratch when creating new contracts, reducing contract creation lead time. Users can search for contracts based on different attributes, use free-text searches for attachments and long text fields, and copy information from existing contracts or predefined templates into new contracts. This saves time and ensures both compliance with external regulations and adherence to internal business rules and best practices. It also provides an authorization concept, a rule-based approval workflow, and a contract release strategy for security.

2.4.2 Contract Execution

SAP SRM streamlines the centralized contract creation process by distributing contracts from a central contract repository to one or more backend execution systems. After distribution and release, values are transferred back to SAP SRM. SAP SRM supports real-time rebate calculations and the ability to quickly and easily maintain product catalogs. Contract items can also be distributed to an SRM MDM catalog so that all employees use only contracted items in their requisitions. This process automates contract compliance and eliminates maverick buying. Further, approval workflows and version control functions ensure that the proper version of a contract is released, enhancing purchasing departments' ability to enforce contract compliance and promoting contract reuse.

Based on the materials or services required, SAP SRM identifies the optimal contract to fill the need while taking into consideration factors such as price, delivery time, and plant location. SAP SRM can also account for different types of discounts, such as value discounts, quantity-based step ladder discounts, group discounts, or rebates based on released values. These functions combine to provide automated contract compliance, helping organizations extract the most value out of negotiated agreements.

2.4.3 Contract Monitoring

SAP SRM continuously updates all active contracts, providing you with up-to-the-minute information on contract status and usage. It also helps you track vendor performance and oversee internal contract compliance. Decision makers receive alerts when contracts are about to expire and when suppliers should be contacted for renewal or renegotiation. The alert notification can be triggered by the contract's expiration date or by exceeding the contract's target release value. If supplier performance has degraded, or if marketplace changes warrant new terms and conditions, authorized purchasing professionals can recommend contract renegotiation. This helps you maintain a base of contracts that are always optimized to meet your enterprise's overall business objectives.

> **Note**
>
> Contract management is discussed in detail in Chapter 12.

2.5 Category Management

Purchasing departments are increasingly centralizing management and are shifting their focus from the tactical tasks of procurement to the more strategic tasks of sourcing. Companies are looking for tools to help them manage new strategic procurement and sourcing initiatives like Low Cost Country Sourcing (LCCS), global sourcing, commodity management, outsourcing, etc. Most companies rely heavily on office tools like Microsoft Word, Microsoft Excel, etc., which forms the unstructured knowledgebase of any company, but do not provide control and efficiency to manage these sourcing initiatives.

Category management addresses this key requirement of organizations and helps procurement departments establish, execute, and monitor strategic goals and initiatives. Category segmentation, gaining spend visibility per category, and initiating and executing a sourcing project based on careful analysis is the lifeblood of the modern purchasing organization. Lack of category-specific visibility has always hindered category managers in making accurate decisions. Category management provides central access to all relevant aspects of spend categories that are mission critical for strategic buyers.

The objective of category management is to establish a procurement standard to be applied to sourcing strategy development and execution. It is a structured approach using consistent methodology, standard software tools, and data analysis to support sourcing decision making. Using category management, procurement departments can establish category-specific methodology for procurement and sourcing process. They can collaboratively execute the process while sharing unstructured, as well as structured, knowledge. Category management is enabled through the SAP E-Sourcing project management capabilities.

2.6 Catalog Management

SAP SRM enables faster, more convenient access to product information than traditional methods such as printed catalogs, supplier sales persons, or phone or fax inquiries through online catalogs. SAP SRM supports internal catalogs, catalogs on the web, and external punch-out catalogs provided by suppliers via OCI. Providing catalogs of the most frequently ordered services, materials, and contracts ensures that employees can easily manage their procurement in line with company rules. SAP SRM supports the following catalog integration models:

▶ **Buyer managed and maintained**
With this catalog type, the main source of information is the purchasing system of the buyer. Buyers upload material master, services master, contracts, or source of supply information from ERP and SAP SRM into the catalog.

▶ **Supplier managed, buyer maintained**
With this catalog type, suppliers provide product and price information in the form of spreadsheets or XML files. Buyers first upload the necessary data into an internal catalog and then make this catalog available for users to search in their shopping carts. If needed, an approval process can be included before publishing the content.

▶ **Supplier managed and maintained**
With this catalog type, catalogs are managed by suppliers in their own system. Supplier catalogs are integrated with SAP SRM using OCI, and should comply with the OCI 4.0 standard.

SAP's own catalog product SAP SRM-MDM Catalog helps content managers with all of the necessary tools to manage catalogs. It is based on SAP NetWeaver Master Data Management (SAP NetWeaver MDM) technology, delivered with preconfigured content adapted to support SAP SRM procurement processes. The SRM-MDM catalog consists of the following main components:

▶ **Repository**: Built-in data model and repository for SAP SRM processes on the MDM server.

▶ **Import manager**: Feature that enables uploading and extracting catalog content.

▶ **Data manager**: Feature that takes care of enriching and approving catalog content.

▶ **User interface for catalog search**: Search interface that is based on WebDynpro for Java technology.

> **Note**
>
> Catalog and content management is discussed in more detail in Chapter 9.

2.7   Analytics

SAP SRM analytics helps customers develop a sound supply management strategy and put it into practice with sourcing and contract management. SAP SRM helps you analyze suppliers and evaluate their performance for better supply management. It also helps you make decisions and take actions that can improve the quality of your supplier base.

It is estimated that sourcing accounts for up to 75% of the total opportunity for procurement savings within an enterprise. To capitalize on this opportunity, buyers should carefully weigh cost-reduction goals against issues of quality, risk, and innovation. SAP SRM helps you strike this balance by using a systematic approach for formulating and optimizing a global sourcing strategy. By consolidating and anticipating supply needs, analyzing historical buying patterns, and tracking current market trends, SAP SRM can help you evaluate suppliers' capacity to deliver high-quality goods that match the specific needs of your organization.

Note
SRM analytics functionalities in global spend analysis, supplier evaluation, and transaction analysis are described in Sections 2.7.1, 2.7.2, and 2.7.3 respectively.

Let's take a brief look at the concepts of spend analysis, purchasing control, supplier evaluation, and transactional analysis next.

2.7.1   Spend Analysis

High-quality spend analysis is the cornerstone of strategic sourcing initiatives. By highlighting spend volume, supplier redundancies, and demand aggregation opportunities, SAP SRM helps organizations control procurement costs. The true challenges of spend analysis are fragmented content and master data — including multiple material classifications, and duplicate vendors and materials — as well as spend data that is inaccessible because of disconnected purchasing execution systems. SAP SRM uses SAP NetWeaver BI for data extraction and analysis. Prepackaged data extractors, reports, and roles in SAP NetWeaver BI minimize deployment efforts.

SAP NetWeaver BI allows slicing and dicing of data, using multiple dimensions, such as product category, region, purchasing organization, and time. Reports include aggregated views of purchasing documents and functionality for drilling down to the line-item level for analysis, providing information at every level of granularity.

2.7.2   Purchasing Control

It is important to know whether your sourcing goals are being achieved and to what degree. How successful was your strategic sourcing initiative? Is contract leakage diminishing the efficiency of your corporate sourcing efforts? With purchasing control functions, SAP SRM helps purchasers answer these and other critical questions. It also helps you assess the value of the purchasing organization in the context of the larger enterprise. SAP SRM provides an array of tools to measure internal performance against defined objectives. For example, you can compare actual prices against historical pricing data or combine internal price developments with external market trends to benchmark performance. SAP SRM also lets you compare purchases made according to existing contracts against those made without contracts. Ready-made reports that reveal important information, such as volume developments by purchasing organization, shifts in allocation to preferred vendors, or vendor improvement measurements, can be easily generated with SRM analytics.

2.7.3 Supplier Evaluation

With supplier information spread across many heterogeneous systems and locations, supplier evaluation can be a daunting task. Typically, purchasing professionals use a collection of tools to assist them in evaluating suppliers. SAP SRM consolidates these tools for optimal use. Information can be pulled in quickly from sourcing cycles on an ongoing basis to provide sourcing teams with instant access to relevant information. To make performance measurable, SAP SRM business content offers two ways to capture performance data:

► Quantitative data from purchasing documents such as purchase orders, goods receipts, and invoices, are collected and interpreted for performance measurement.

► Qualitative data in the form of web surveys is collected from SRM users. Soft facts about suppliers are collected during a specific procurement process step, for example, information about packaging quality of the goods received during entry of goods receipt.

It is possible to define hierarchical key performance indicators (KPI) such as service, price, quality, etc. Subcriteria can be defined for each KPI. For example, goods receipt quality, packaging quality, and process quality may be defined as subcriteria for the quality KPI. Depending on organizational priorities, weights are assigned to each KPI and subcriteria.

Both quantitative procurement data and qualitative web survey information is interpreted in SAP NetWeaver BI, which leads to consolidated supplier evaluation scores based on the weightings. With SAP SRM, suppliers can also access their evaluation data, giving them the opportunity to proactively improve their processes.

2.7.4 Transactional Analysis

Transactional analysis helps buyers monitor their business processes and improve the efficiency of these processes. In this section, we discuss transactional analysis related to contract monitoring, bidding analytics, and operational purchasing analysis, as follows:

▶ **Contract monitoring**

Contracts and global outline agreements and their relations can be monitored in SRM Analytics. This lets you regularly monitor contract usage and patterns of maverick buying. For expiring contracts, you can define alerts, in which case purchasers will receive information as soon as the contract expiry date is approaching or contract utilization reaches a pre-defined limit. An RFQ can be created from the expiring contract to find new suppliers or negotiate better prices.

▶ **Bidding engine analytics**

Bidding engine analytics supports all process steps from RFQ creation to winner determination. They can be classified into historical event analysis and historical participants analysis:

  ▶ *Historical event analysis* helps maximize effectiveness by learning from past bidding experience. Some of the analyses include analysis of bid invitations, analysis of bid invitation items, and analysis of attributes of a bid invitation.

  ▶ *Historical participants analysis* displays detailed historical information about individual bids, per bidder. The analysis displays bidders' behavior, such as the number of bids by bidder and the number of bids won, etc., in multiple dimensions.

▶ **Operational purchasing analysis**

Operational purchasing analysis helps analyze purchasing data for purchasing processes. This includes reports that let cost center managers monitor purchases in their departments, monitor budget utilization, analyze maverick buying etc. They enable users at different levels to monitor the purchasing process, thus allowing better control of purchases.

2.8 Deployment Scenarios

SAP SRM supports different deployment scenarios to enable flexible integration with the backend enterprise resource planning (ERP) system. Which scenario is used depends on which system the purchasing department decides to work with and where follow-on documents are created. The deployment scenarios include the following:

▶ **Classic**

The *classic* scenario relies strongly on the backend system. In this scenario, requisitions are created in SAP SRM and purchase orders are created in the ERP system. Confirmations and invoices can be entered in either the ERP system or SAP SRM.

- **Extended Classic**

  In the *extended classic* scenario, both requisitions and purchase orders are created in SAP SRM. A copy of the SAP SRM purchase order is created in the ERP system. Confirmations and invoices can be entered in either the ERP system or SAP SRM.

- **Standalone**

  In the *standalone* scenario, all of the procurement transactions are handled in SAP SRM. Only the accounting information is sent to the ERP system.

- **Decoupled**

  In the *decoupled* scenario, customers can implement any combination of the other three scenarios, based on the product category.

> **Note**
>
> Deployment scenarios are explained in more detail in Chapter 4.

2.9   Summary

In this chapter, we introduced the various functionalities of SAP SRM. SAP SRM helps organizations effectively manage their supply management processes. By improving supply-related efficiency and enhancing the value of supplier relationships, SAP SRM delivers significant business benefits. Procurement and sourcing are integral to supplier relationship management. Providing the insight and discipline that is needed for well-tuned sourcing and procurement processes requires closing the loop between them. Next, in Chapter 3, we will discuss the basic settings required to implement SAP SRM.

Mapping a company's organizational structure to organizational elements in SAP applications and defining master data are the first steps in the design of a good SAP implementation. In this chapter, we will discuss the basic settings required for these steps in SAP SRM implementations.

3 SAP SRM Basic Settings

Organizational structure, master data, and technical settings to connect to backend systems form part of the basic settings in SAP Supplier Relationship Management (SAP SRM) implementations. SAP SRM, being a procurement application integrated with SAP ERP and other SAP applications, can receive basic master data through replication from SAP ERP, eliminating the need to re-create master data in SAP SRM.

However, organizations can also create the master data in SAP SRM. Further, SAP SRM can be integrated with non-SAP applications and master data can be replicated from non-SAP applications as well. The basic master data comprises material master, service master, and vendor master. The organizational structure can be either replicated from the SAP ERP Human Capital Management (SAP ERP HCM) application or directly created in SAP SRM.

In this chapter we will cover the following:

- The case study in Section 3.1 describes the requirements for an SAP SRM implementation in a fictitious global organization.
- In Section 3.2, we will discuss the system landscape requirements for SAP SRM.
- In Section 3.3, we will provide an overview of master data in SAP SRM.
- In Section 3.4, we will explain the basic technical settings and the configuration required to replicate product master data.
- In Section 3.5, we will discuss the organizational structure in SAP SRM and the configuration required for setting up an organizational plan in SAP SRM.
- In Section 3.6, we will explain vendor master replication and the associated configuration settings.
- Finally, in Section 3.7, we will explain a few common, basic technical settings required for all SAP SRM scenarios.

It is important for consultants to understand the basic settings for SAP SRM so let's us get started by introducing you to Besttec Industries, our fictional corporation in need of an SAP SRM solution.

3.1 Case Study: Procurement Automation at Besttec Industries

Besttec Industries is a world leader in transformers and switchgears with presence on three continents and in 12 countries. Besttec Industries was one of the leading manufacturers of electrical transmission equipment in Europe. Superior product quality and excellence in customer service have helped Besttec Industries obtain its leadership position. When it was ready to go global, Besttec Industries initially exported its products to other countries through local agents and franchisees, but established its own facilities in other countries later, to meet the growing demand. Besttec Industries implemented SAP R/3 to enable the corporate headquarters to cope with the rapid growth and rolled out ERP in all locations over the next 2 years.

The purchasing managers have been with the organization from the early stages on, and a few of them were also involved in the SAP R/3 implementation as the core team from the business side. This team was instrumental in designing the processes in SAP R/3 to reap the benefits of integrating procurement processes with production, sales, inventory, and financials. They defined the master data, transactional processes, interface points with other departments, and analytical processes. This helped the purchasing department to synchronize their activities with the production, sales, and financial accounting departments. Better planning and integration helped Besttec Industries to achieve inventory reduction, streamlined processes, and a reduction in cycle times.

The ERP transformation started with headquarters going live first, followed by its subsidiaries around the globe. It took two years to roll out ERP-based, streamlined processes around the globe. Besttec Industries used a global template to rollout the common processes across locations. Global templates were adjusted to suit local requirements and regulations. Each subsidiary is defined as a separate company in the SAP system, with its own organizational data. The ERP implementation has also enabled Besttec Industries to define a global strategy for each major process in the organization. For example, Besttec Industries set up a central purchasing department for the entire organization as part of the global strategy for the procure-to-pay process.

Project Automation: Needs and Driving Factors

ERP enabled Besttec Industries' rapid growth without the corresponding increase in procurement staff. However, the volume of procurement transactions increased phenomenally over the years and the procurement department started looking at ways to further automate the procurement process. A team was formed to look into the procurement automation problem. The team analyzed the company's transactions and found that most of them do not need procurement department involvement because they can be either automated or simplified by enabling the requesting employees to perform their own purchasing. The team decided that this can be achieved by providing an easy-to-use self-service procurement application to all employees. Employees should be able to use this application with little or no training. The application should enable users to enter only a minimum of data, with most of the required data getting defaulted in from the user master, so that very little time would be required to complete a transaction. The application should also automate most of the procurement process.

It was also determined to be important that the automated self-service procurement process complement the core purchasing process implemented in SAP R/3, and to leverage the strengths of SAP R/3. Further, the process should be integrated with the SAP R/3 financials, budgeting, and inventory systems. Redundancy must be reduced in the automation solution, and perfect synchronization of data must be achieved between SAP R/3 processes and self-service procurement processes.

During the team discussions, three possibilities for self-service procurement were discussed:

▸ **Extending the ERP functionality to all requesting employees**
ERP Materials Management (MM) transactions are defined for the needs of professional purchasers and may be too complex for regular employees to use. Also, transactions require too much data to be entered manually.

▸ **Enhance existing ERP functionality by developing a Web-based wrapper around the MM transactions, using methods provided by Business Application Programming Interfaces (BAPI)**
By defaulting most of the organizational data in the wrapper, it is possible to improve the usability of the transaction. But the development associated with the wrapper is very complex and is less flexible.

▸ **Use packaged software**
The third option is to use packaged software for self-service procurement that can be integrated with SAP R/3 processes. This software should take care of the usability and development complexity issues associated with the other two approaches. At the same time, self-service procurement should be separate from mission-critical SAP R/3 purchasing processes to allow higher flexibility. This is advantageous, for example, if there is a need to upgrade the self-service procurement solution as downtime for SAP R/3 processes would be near zero.

After several discussions between the purchasing department and its internal customers, it was decided that the third option is the best way to go forward. The team decided to implement SAP SRM, because it meets all of the stated requirements and provides built-in integration with SAP R/3.

> **Note**
>
> SAP SRM processes in operational procurement are explained in Chapters 5, 6, and 7.

> **Summary of the case study company and its situation**
>
> **Organization**: Besttec Industries
>
> **Current situation**: ERP has been implemented in the organization. The purchasing department has had prior exposure to the advantages of integrated planning, procurement, inventory, and financials processes.
>
> **Problem**: High load of operational procurement transactions.
>
> **Need**: Solution to automate procurement transactions and to facilitate distribution of work through controlled automation.
>
> **Solution**: Enabling requesting employees to execute their own procurement for identified categories of purchases.

We will now discuss the following important elements of Besttec Industries' SAP SRM implementation:

- System landscape
- Master data
- Organizational plan

3.2 System Landscape

The system landscape refers to the hardware composition along with the necessary software components installed for an SAP SRM implementation. Before finalizing the system landscape for Besttec Industries, it is important to understand the software components required to implement the functionalities of SAP SRM.

> **Recommendation**
>
> You should refer to the SAP SRM master guide provided in the SAP Service Marketplace at *http://service.sap.com/instguides* before finalizing the system landscape in your implementation.

To start, we will give you an overview of the SAP SRM 2007 components.

3.2.1 SAP SRM 2007 Components Overview

Figure 3.1 illustrates the software components for SAP SRM 2007. These components are explained briefly in the following list:

▶ **SAP SRM Server 6.0**: This is the main SAP SRM software component. It is an ABAP-based application with a Web Dynpro user interface (in SAP SRM 5.0 and lower versions, the user interface is based on Internet Transaction Server (ITS)) and consists of the following application components:

▶ **Enterprise Buyer Professional (EBP)**: Software component for implementing operational procurement.

▶ **Bidding Engine**: Software component for implementing the bidding and reverse auction processes. In case of the auction process, the business logic is contained in the bidding engine, where users submit bids using a Java-based *Live Auction Cockpit* (LAC) Web Presentation Server (WPS) as the frontend.

▶ **Supplier Self-Services (SUS)**: Software component for implementing the supplier order collaboration process.

▶ **Supplier Self-Registration (ROS)**: Software component for implementing supplier self-registration process.

▶ **cProjects**: Software components that are shipped together with SAP SRM Server 6.0. However, the user interface for cProjects is a Java-based component, which should be installed separately, if required. The Java-based cProjects user interface can be installed on the Enterprise Portal. Note that in SAP SRM 5.0 and lower versions, cProjects was shipped separately as the SAP PLM cProjects Suite. cProjects software consists of two application components — cProjects and cFolders. cProjects is used for online collaborative project management and cFolders is used for design collaboration.

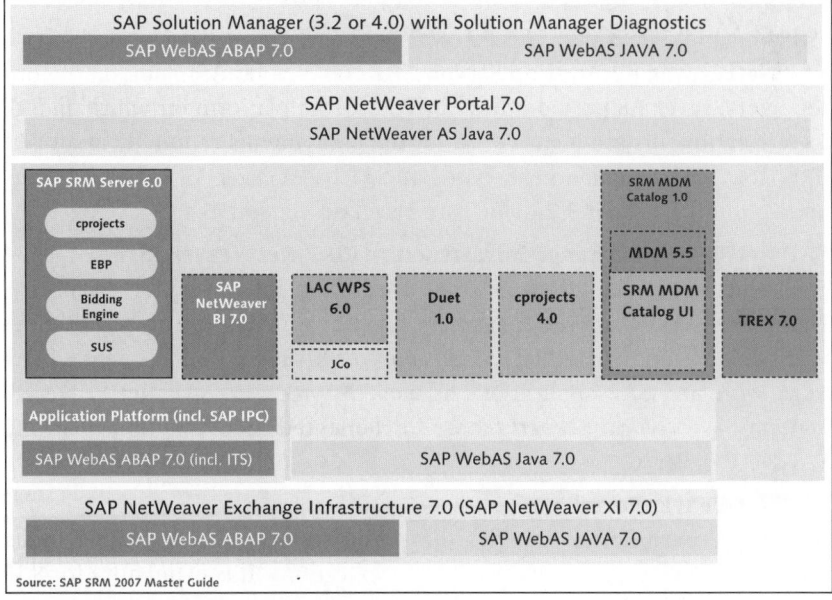

Figure 3.1 SAP SRM 2007 Components Overview

▶ **SRM-MDM Catalog 2.0**
SRM-MDM Catalog is used for managing catalog content in SAP SRM. SRM Server transactions access and import catalog information through Open Catalog Interface (OCI). SRM-MDM Catalog replaces SAP Catalog Content Management (CCM), which was used to manage catalogs in earlier versions of SAP SRM, that is, in SAP SRM 4.0 and SAP SRM 5.0. SRM-MDM Catalog can also be used with earlier versions of SAP SRM, and its user interface is based on Webdynpro Java. SRM-MDM Catalog is built on SAP NetWeaver MDM. Refer to Figure 3.3 for more details on the SRM-MDM Catalog architecture.

▶ **SRM Live Auction Cockpit (SRM LAC) 6.0**
Deployed on the SAP J2EE engine, SRM LAC is used as a frontend client for the reverse auction process. LAC provides the user interface for real-time online bid submission for suppliers, and the user interface for auction administration for purchasers. LAC can be installed on the Enterprise Portal.

▶ **SAP NetWeaver Business Intelligence (SAP NetWeaver BI) 7.0**
SAP NetWeaver BI is used for analytics in SAP SRM processes. SAP SRM content is imported into SAP NetWeaver BI to enable the analysis.

▶ **SAP NetWeaver Text Retrieval and Information Extraction (SAP NetWeaver TREX) 7.0**
SAP NetWeaver TREX is used for advanced search functionality in SAP SRM contracts. It is also used when you want to use the metadata search functionality or use the SAP NetWeaver BI accelerator in SRM Analytics, and for catalog searches in SAP CCM. However, the SRM-MDM Catalog does not require SAP NetWeaver TREX for catalog searches.

▶ **SAP NetWeaver Application Server (SAP NetWeaver AS) 7.0**
SAP NetWeaver AS provides the ABAP and Java platform on which all SAP SRM components are installed. All of the components required for an SAP SRM 2007 implementation are based on SAP NetWeaver AS 7.0, except Duet and Solution Manager 3.2, which are based on version 6.4.

▶ **SAP NetWeaver Exchange Infrastructure (SAP NetWeaver XI) 7.0**
SAP NetWeaver XI provides the integration platform for SUS. SAP NetWeaver XI is also used for certain functionalities in integrating catalogs with SAP ERP and SAP SRM. SAP NetWeaver XI is required to integrate SAP SRM with non-SAP applications as well. Appropriate SAP NetWeaver XI content based on the scenario to be implemented should be imported into SAP NetWeaver XI.

▶ **SAP NetWeaver Portal 7.0**
SAP NetWeaver Portal provides the portal framework for unified login, security, and single sign on for all SAP applications. It is mandatory for SAP

SRM 2007 and optional for SAP SRM 5.0 and lower versions. The appropriate business package for SAP SRM should be imported into portal.

▶ **Duet 1.5**
Duet provides the integration of SAP SRM with Microsoft Office applications. Duet installation requires SAP NetWeaver AS Java 6.4. Duet is optionally used for the following functionalities:

  ▶ Workflow approvals

  ▶ SRM Analytics with Duet

▶ **SAP NetWeaver Adobe Document Server (SAP NetWeaver ADS) 7.0**
SAP NetWeaver ADS is a NetWeaver component used to integrate Adobe forms with SAP SRM. SAP ADS is used to define skill profiles in service procurement and exception mail attachments in the invoice management system. All SAP SRM document outputs are also provided in Adobe format in SAP SRM 2007. This Java-based component can be installed on the SAP NetWeaver Portal.

▶ **Solution Manager 3.2 or higher**
Solution Manager contains the configuration guide and other useful documentation required for SAP SRM implementations. Solution Manager can also be used to manage and maintain SAP implementations. Solution Manager Diagnostics is a Java-based component that facilitates monitoring of Java-based software components.

▶ **SAP R/3 Plug-In 2004 or higher**
This component is required to integrate SAP SRM with the backend SAP ERP application. SAP R/3 Plug-in contains programs that communicate through Remote Function Calls (RFCs). SAP R/3 Plug-in is not required when the backend system is SAP ERP 6.0 or higher.

Note
The listed components and versions may vary depending on the SAP SRM version. For example, the user interface in SAP SRM 5.0 and earlier versions is based on ITS.

Depending on the scenario you need to implement, the system landscape and components involved will vary. Figure 3.2 illustrates the components required in various SAP SRM scenarios according to the SAP SRM 2007 master guide. In Figure 3.2, scenarios are shown as columns and application components as rows. SAP NetWeaver components required for each application component are also given.

	SRM standard scenarios								NetWeaver components						
Legend: O = optional, M = mandatory	Self Service Procurement	Plan Driven Procurement	Service Procurement	Catalog Content Mgmt.	Analytics	Category Management	Contract Management	Strategic Sourcing	WebAS ABAP 7.0	SAP ITS 7.0	WebAS Java 7.0	MDM 5.5	BI 7.0	EP 7.0	PI 7.0
Solution Manager (3.2 or higher)	M	M	M	M	M	M	M	M	M		O				
SAP SRM Server 6.0	M	M	M	M	M	M	M	M	M						
Live Auction Cockpit (LACWPS) 6.0								M			M				
SRM-MDM Catalog 1.0 or 2.0	M	O	O	M			O	O			M	M			
SAP Netweaver TREX 7.0	O	M				O	O	O							
SAP NetWeaver BI_CONT 7.0.3	O	O	O		M	M	O	O	M				M		
Business Package for SRM Server 6.0	M	M	M	M	M	M	M	M						M	
Business Packages for Category Mgmt.	O	O	O	O	O	M	O	O						M	
XI Content for SAP SRM Server 6.0	O	M	M	O			O	O							M
XI Content for SAP NetWeaver BI Content 7.0.3	O	O	O	O											M
XI Content for SRM MDM Catalog 1.0	O	O	O	O			O	O							M
SAP NW Adobe Document Server 7.0	O	O	M				O	O			M				
Duet 1.0 and SAP Document Builder							M				M				
cProjects 4.0		O		O		O		O			M				

Source: SAP SRM 2007 Master Guide

Figure 3.2 SAP SRM 2007 Scenario-Component Matrix

3.2.2 Sample SAP SRM System Landscape

In an SAP environment, it is possible to have multiple instances of SAP NetWeaver AS in one physical server, and multiple clients in one SAP NetWeaver AS server. Application components are defined in individual clients, and it is possible that multiple application components are defined in one client. For example, EBP and cFolders are two different application components that can be implemented in the same client. Similarly, application components of SAP SRM can be implemented in different clients within the same WAS instance. For example, EBP and SUS are normally deployed in different clients.

Figure 3.3 illustrates a sample system landscape depicting the installation of various software components on a set of servers. It is assumed that all SAP SRM components, except Duet, are required for the customer. The sample landscape consists of six servers and a PC-based MDM client. Please note that the software components SAP NetWeaver XI, SAP NetWeaver BI, SAP NetWeaver TREX, MDM Server, and Solution Manager need not be exclusively installed for the SAP SRM application. These components can also be used for other SAP and non-SAP applications. Unicode installations for SAP SRM are highly recommeded. Please also note that SUS and ROS are implemented in the same client and EBP is implemented in a different client in the sample landscape. It is recommended to implement EBP and SUS in different clients.

The sizing of the servers is based on sizing guidelines provided in the SAP service marketplace (*http://service.sap.com/sizing*). SAP Web dispatcher is recommended as the application gateway to log on securely from outside the firewall. Alternatively, a reverse proxy can be implemented as the application gateway outside the firewall.

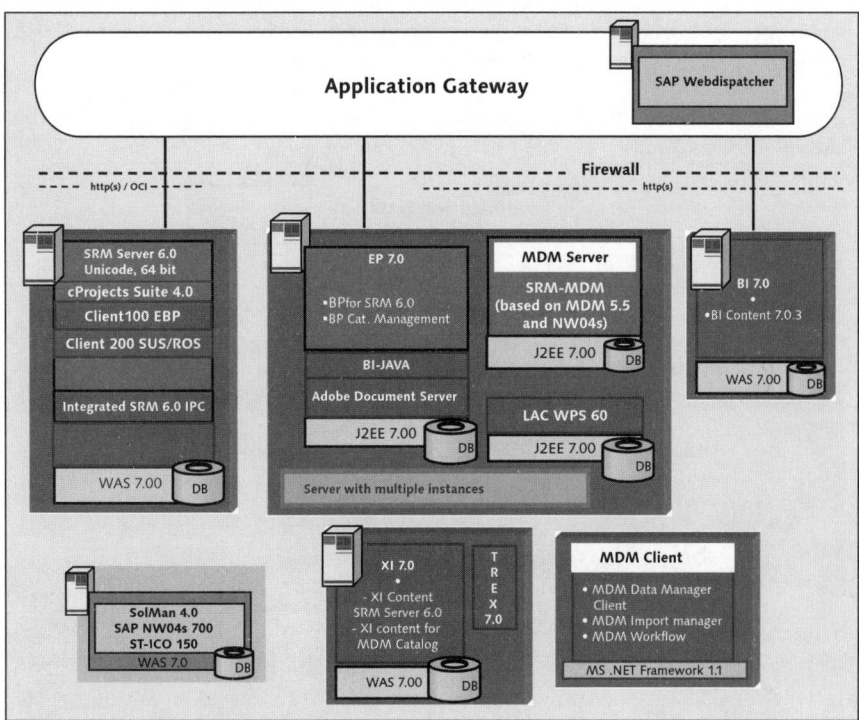

Figure 3.3 Sample SAP SRM 2007 System Landscape

3.2.3 System Landscape for Besttec Industries

Getting back to our sample company, Besttec Industries, recall that their goals are to achieve automation, empower employees, and ensure seamless process and data integration with SAP ERP processes. Therefore, a self-service procurement scenario will be implemented at Besttec Industries, using the following components:

- ▸ SRM Server 6.0
- ▸ SRM-MDM Catalog 2.0
- ▸ SAP NetWeaver XI 7.0
- ▸ SAP NetWeaver BI 7.0
- ▸ SAP NetWeaver Portal 7.0
- ▸ Plug-In for the SAP R/3 System.

A sample system landscape for the self-service procurement at Besttec Industries is shown in Figure 3.4.

Note

System landscapes vary depending on customer requirements and server sizing requirements. For example, SAP NetWeaver XI is not required if you do not need to transfer contract items and the product master from SAP SRM to an SRM-MDM Catalog.

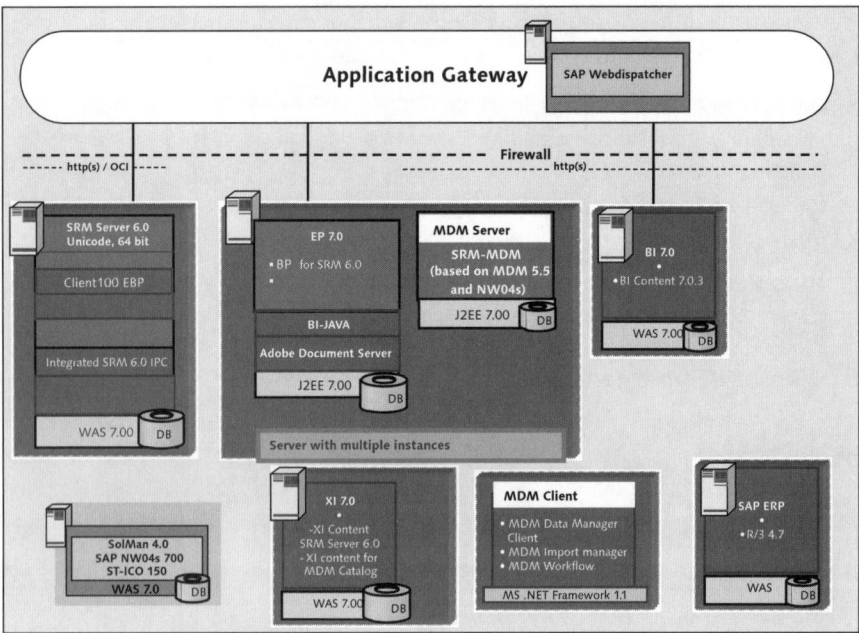

Figure 3.4 System Landscape for Self-Service Procurement at Besttec Industries

After finalization of the system landscape, the next big task for the Besttec Industries implementation team is the master data definition in SAP SRM and synchronization with the SAP R/3 system.

3.3 Master Data in SAP SRM

The two key masters required for procurement are *product master* and *supplier master*. Product master refers to both materials and services. SAP SRM lets you create the product and supplier masters directly in SAP SRM, or they can be replicated from the backend system.

The master data in SAP SRM is only a subset of the master data maintained in ERP systems. For example, while the material master in SAP ERP contains data that pertains to planning, accounting, sales, production, and purchasing, the material master in SAP SRM contains only purchasing data. Many organizations have established master data maintenance procedures while implementing ERP. These organizations should keep maintaining the master data in the backend system and replicate it to SAP SRM to avoid duplication and inconsistency.

Classifications of Master Data Replicated from SAP ERP to SAP SRM

Master data that needs to be replicated from SAP ERP to SAP SRM can be classified into data from global settings, basic customizing data, and master data:

▸ **Data from global settings**
This data is generic in nature and should be the same in ERP and SAP SRM. Units of measure (UOM), currencies, and exchange rates form part of global settings data.

▸ **Basic customizing data**
This includes data that needs to be attached to master data during transactional processes. For example, purchasing organization and purchasing group, plant, company code, document type, number range, etc., fall under this category of data. They can be replicated from SAP ERP to SAP SRM or can be defined directly in SAP SRM.

▸ **Master data**
This includes product master (material and services), supplier master, and product category (material group in SAP ERP).

It is very important to keep data synchronized between the SAP ERP and SAP SRM systems. If there are differences, mapping between the two should be maintained through appropriate Business Add-In (BAdI) implementations.

The Besttec Industries team considered all of the aspects of master data maintenance and decided to replicate the data from SAP ERP. Before doing so, however, a few basic technical and other configuration settings required for master data synchronization need to be configured in SAP SRM, as we will discuss next.

3.4   Basic Technical Settings and Maintaining Product Master Data

In this section, we will take a look at the configuration settings required to connect to backend systems, as well as how to replicate product master data from the backend SAP ERP system. In addition, we will discuss how to maintain product master data in SAP SRM. Let's get started.

3.4.1 Basic Technical Settings

The basic technical settings we describe in this subsection are common for all SAP SRM processes, and include the following:

- Regenerate role profiles
- Define logical systems
- Assign logical system to the client
- Define SAP SRM logical system in the backend system
- Define the RFC user
- Define RFC destination in SAP SRM
- Define RFC destination in the backend system
- Define backend systems
- Check UOM
- Align currencies and exchange rates
- Maintain time zone settings
- Maintain TWPURLSVR settings
- Publish ITS services

Define Roles

All SAP SRM-relevant authorization profiles should be regenerated before starting the configuration. This ensures that the profiles belonging to these roles are assigned all of the required authorizations.

Use the menu path **SPRO · SAP Implementation Guide · Supplier Relationship Management · SRM Server · Cross Application Basic Settings · Roles · Define Roles** or Transaction code PFCG to access the Define Roles functionality.

To define roles, perform these steps:

1. Select **Utilities · Mass generation**.
2. Select all roles.
3. Enter "SAP_EC_BBP*" in the Role field.
4. Click on the execute icon.

> **Tip**
>
> You should refer to the configuration documentation provided at the Define Roles menu path given in this section, if you want to learn how to define your own customer-specific roles.

Define Logical Systems

You need to define a logical system name for all of the systems connected to, as well as for, SAP SRM, using the menu path **SPRO • SAP Implementation Guide • Supplier Relationship Management • SRM Server • Technical Basic Settings • ALE Settings • Distribution • Basic Settings • Logical Systems • Define Logical System**.

Typical systems connected to SAP SRM include ERP, cFolders, cProjects, SUS, SAP APO, SAP NetWeaver BI, etc. Remember that logical systems are tied to a client and each client in the server will have a different logical system name. Common nomenclature used to define a logical system name is the following:

```
<SID>CLNT<client number>
```

With this nomenclature, SID refers to the system ID, and a numerical value refers to the client. For example, in the logical system name SRDCLNT100, SRD represents the system ID, and 100 refers to the client.

Assign Logical System to the Client

You need to assign the SAP SRM logical system name to the client using Transaction code SCC4.

Define SAP SRM Logical System in a Backend System

You also need to define the logical system name for SAP SRM in each backend system using the menu path **ALE Settings • Basic Settings • Logical Systems • Define Logical System** after executing Transaction code SALE.

Define RFC User

Using Transaction code SU01, you need to define RFC users. RFC users are used to communicate between the systems using RFC calls.

You should create a system user in the SAP SRM system and in each of the backend systems. For security reasons, when you create a system user (for example, RFCUSER), assign authorization profiles according to SAP Note 642202, instead of assigning the SAP_ALL profile. Create an additional dialog user (for example, RFC_Dia) in the backend ERP system with authorizations according to SAP Note 656633.

Tip

Use capital letters for RFC passwords. In older versions of SAP systems that are based on Basis technology, passwords are not case sensitive. They are entered on a screen, converted to capital letters, and stored in these systems. However, in SAP systems based on SAP NetWeaver AS, passwords are case sensitive. This can sometimes cause confusion and you might face logon failure problems despite entering the correct password in RFC destination settings. Using capital letters for all passwords circumvents this issue.

Define RFC Destination in SAP SRM

SAP SRM communicates with a backend system using RFC calls. Therefore, you have to define RFC destinations for these systems, and assign an RFC user with appropriate authorizations, using Transaction code SM59.

Perform the following steps:

1. Define an RFC destination for all backend systems connected to the SAP SRM system. The RFC connection type for the SAP R/3 system is 3.

2. Use the Logon & Security tab to maintain the backend system client, the RFC user defined in the backend system, and the password.

3. Using the Test connection and Remote logon buttons, test the connection and remote logon in each RFC destination. If the remote logon is successful, you should be logged on to the system to which you tried to connect.

4. Define a second RFC destination for the backend SAP ERP system to enable search help in account assignment. To enable backend search help in SAP SRM, the RFC user should be a dialog user according to SAP Note 656633.

5. Assign the RFC dialog user to the second RFC destination you created for SAP ERP.

6. Connections you can define are as follows:

▶ For connection to ADS, define an HTTP connection to the external server with connection type G. "/AdobeDocumentServices/Config?style=rpc" should be entered in the Path prefix field.

▶ For connecting to LAC, define an RFC destination called SRM_LIVE_AUCTION with connection type G (HTTP connection to external server).

▶ For connecting to SAP NetWeaver XI, define an RFC destination with connection type H (HTTP connection to ABAP system). "/sap/xi/engine?type= entry" should be entered in the Path prefix field.

  ▶ For connecting to SAP NetWeaver XI, two additional RFC destinations, LCRSAPRFC and SAPSLDAPI, are defined with connection type T (TCP/IP connection). For LCRSAPRFC, enter the Registered server program ID as "LCRSAPRFC_XI1" where XI1 is the system ID of the SAP NetWeaver XI server. Similarly, enter "SAPSLDAPI_WS2" as the Registered server program ID for SAPSLDAPI. Maintain gateway host and gateway service for both the connections.

▶ For connecting to TREX, define an RFC destination with connection type T.

> **Note**
>
> In the Define Backend Systems setting in SAP SRM, which we will talk about in a little while, remember to specify the RFC destination with the dialog user in the RFC (Dialog) field for the SAP ERP system entry.

Define RFC Destination in a Backend System

Use Transaction code SM59 to define an RFC destination for the SAP SRM system in each of the backend systems connected to SAP SRM. You should define the RFC destination for the SAP SRM system using the same name in all backend systems.

Define Backend Systems

You need to maintain backend system definitions to link the backend systems with SAP SRM. This enables linking between logical systems and RFC destinations. In addition, these settings allow maintaining backend system applications and versions (e.g., SAP R/3 4.6C) based on which metadata BAPI calls to backend SAP R/3 systems are triggered. For example, while BAPI_PO_CREATE is used for replicating purchase orders from SAP SRM to R/3 31H, a new BAPI, BAPI_PO_CREATE1, is used for SAP R/3 46C.

To define backend systems, use menu path **SPRO • SAP Implementation Guide • Supplier Relationship Management • SRM Server • Technical Basic Settings • Define Backend Systems**.

Figure 3.5 and Figure 3.6 illustrate sample settings.

Change View "Definition of Backend Systems in B2B": Ov

Logical s	Description	RFC Destination	Sys. type	RFC	Local	FI valid
	SRM_Live_Auction	SRM_LIVE_AUCTION	SRM_AUC	☐	☐	0 real-time
ERPCLNT800	ECC/ERP system	ERPCLNT800	ERP_1.0	☑	☐	0 real-time
SRDCFL100	Cfolder in SRE 100	SRDCFL100	CFOLDERS	☑	☐	0 real-time
SRDCLNT100	EBP System	SRDCLNT100	LOCAL	☐	☑	0 real-time
SRDCLNT200	SUS system	SRDCLNT200	SUS_1.0	☑	☐	0 real-time
TREX	TREX_06	TREX_06	TREX	☑	☐	0 real-time

Figure 3.5 Define Backend Systems Sample Settings — 1

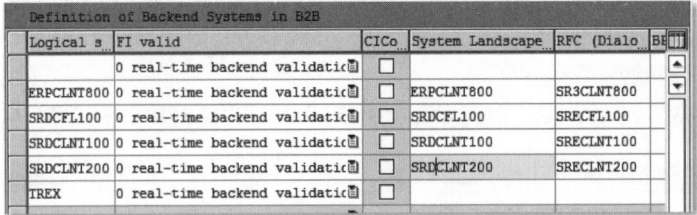

Figure 3.6 Define Backend Systems Sample Settings — 2

To define backend systems, perform these steps:

1. Enter the logical system, description, and RFC destination of the backend system. Maintain an entry for the SAP SRM system, also. If two or more applications are defined in the same system client, then maintain a dummy logical system to create multiple entries. For example, in the sample settings shown in Figure 3.5, SAP SRM and cFolders are in the same system and client (SRD and 100). Therefore, a dummy logical system **SRDCFL100** is maintained in these settings. RFC destinations **SRDCLNT100** and **SRDCFL100** both point to the same system.

2. Select the appropriate checkboxes in the **RFC** column to specify the system type for the backend systems.

3. Select the checkbox in the **Local** column to specify the system type for the SAP SRM system.

4. Select an appropriate entry in the **FI valid** column. The entry decides the validation method of account assignment entries in SAP SRM purchasing documents.

5. Select the appropriate checkboxes in the **CIConnect** column shown in Figure 3.6 if you use the SAP content integrator (CI) to map product codes.

6. Remember to provide the System Landscape Directory (SLD) ID for all systems whose product ID should be mapped using CI. You specify the name of the associated system in XI SLD in the **System Landscape Directory ID** column.

7. In the **RFC (Dialog)** column, enter the RFC destination with the dialog user. This is required, especially for SAP ERP backend systems, when you want to use backend search help.

Check Units of Measurement

Now, ensure that the UOM settings in SAP SRM are identical to the settings in SAP ERP. To do so, use the menu path **SPRO • SAP Implementation Guide • SAP Web Application Server • General Settings • Check Units of Measurement** or Transaction code CUNI.

SAP delivers a standard set of UOMs in all SAP applications. Only additions or changes to these need to be maintained in SAP SRM to synchronize data between both systems.

To check UOMs, follow these steps:

1. Click on the ISO codes button.
2. Select **Utilities • Adjustment**.
3. Enter the RFC destination for SAP ERP and click Enter. The ISO codes will be synchronized between the SAP ERP and SAP SRM systems.
4. Click on the Units of measurement button and maintain the UOM according to the changes made in the SAP ERP system.

Align Currencies and Exchange Rates

You also need to ensure that the currency settings and exchange rates are synchronized with the settings in SAP ERP. Run the programs BBP_GET_CURRENCY and BBP_GET_EXRATE whenever currencies and exchange rates are updated in the backend system.

Maintain Time Zone Settings

To maintain time zone settings, follow the path **SPRO • SAP Implementation Guide • SAP Web Application Server • General Settings • Time Zones • Maintain System Settings** or use Transaction code STZAC. Then perform these steps:

1. Maintain the system time zone and default time zone for users.
2. Select the indicator Time Zones Active.

Maintain TWPURLSVR Table Settings

This setting is relevant for SAP SRM 5.0 and lower versions. URLs for various SAP SRM transactions (e.g., BBPSC01) are generated based on the settings in table TWPURLSVR. Use Transaction code SM30 and then click on the New Entries button to maintain the settings in this table for each logical system, as follows:

▶ **Logical system**: Specify the logical system of the EBP client
▶ **Web server**: Specify the domain and port information of the ITS server (e.g., "ebp.sap.com:1080")
▶ **Web protocol**: Specify the Web protocol used (http or https)
▶ **GUI start server**: Specify the domain and port information of ITS server (e.g., "ebp.sap.com:1080")

- ▸ **GUI start protocol**: Specify the Web protocol used (http or https)
- ▸ **KW Web server**: Specify the domain and port information of the ITS server (e.g., "ebp.sap.com:1080")
- ▸ **KW protocol**: Specify the Web protocol used (http or https)

Publish ITS Services

This setting is relevant for SAP SRM 5.0 and lower versions. The ITS services should be published on the ITS server. Follow these steps to publish ITS services:

1. Execute program W3_PUBLISH_SERVICES using Transaction code SA38.
2. In the screen that appears next, click on the execute icon.
3. All ITS services are listed in the "WAB:Publish Services" screen that appears. Click on the Workbench settings button.
4. Select the Publish tab. Select the Integrated ITS radio button and click on the enter icon. In SAP SRM 4.0 and lower versions, select the appropriate external ITS server.
5. Click on the select all icon to select all of the services and click on the Publish button. All ITS services will be published on the given ITS server.

> **Note**
>
> You can publish individual ITS services using Transaction code SE80.

3.4.2 Settings for Product Master Data Replication

This section contains the settings required in both SAP SRM and SAP ERP systems to replicate product master data from SAP ERP to SAP SRM.

Define Output Format and Storage Form of Product ID

You use the "Define Output Format and Storage Form of Product IDs" setting to maintain the output format and storage format for the product master. To do so, follow the path **SPRO • SAP Implementation Guide • Supplier Relationship Management • SRM Server • Master Data • Products • Define Output Format and Storage Form of Product IDs** or Transaction code COMCPRFORMAT.

Settings for lexicographical or nonlexicographical storage of the product master are important. You should maintain the same format in this setting as that used in the backend SAP ERP settings for the material master. The SAP ERP settings for the output format of the material master can be found in Transaction code OMSL.

Setting the Middleware Parameters in SAP SRM

In this section, you define receiving and sending systems for the master data as sites. The site for the receiving system is delivered in the SAP standard as site CRM. Therefore, only the sending systems, that is, backend SAP ERP systems, need to be configured. To define the sending system, use the menu path **Tools • Middleware:Basis • Administration • Administration Console** or Transaction code SMOEAC. Follow these steps:

1. Select the Object Type Site.
2. Click on the create object icon or press the F6 key.
3. Enter a name for the backend SAP ERP system in the Name field (for example, "ERP- 800"), and a description (for example, "ERP Dev client 800") in the Description field.
4. Select SAP R/3 from the dropdown list in the Type field.
5. Click on the Site Attributes button.
6. Enter the RFC destination for the SAP ERP system in the RFC- Destination field and click on the enter icon.

If you connect multiple backend ERP systems to SAP SRM, repeat these steps to create additional sites for each backend system.

Configure Settings in SAP R/3 or SAP ERP for SAP SRM Master Data

These settings should be configured in the backend SAP ERP or SAP R/3 system. You'll need to create table entries in the CRMCONSUM, CRMSUBTAB, CRMR-FCPAR, CRMPAROLTP, and TBE11 tables, as described in this section, using Transaction code SM30 (or SE16 in older versions of SAP SRM). You should read SAP Notes 430980 and 720819 before configuring these settings. Proceed as follows:

1. Maintain the table entries in the table CRMCONSUM as shown in Table 3.1. Note that the **Remarks** column is included to describe each setting and is not part of the table. If you have only one SAP SRM system connected to SAP ERP, the first entry shown in the table is sufficient. If you have the SAP ERP connected to multiple SAP SRM system clients for product master data transfer, then create multiple entries for each SAP SRM system client, as shown in Table 3.1.

User	Active	Description	Q_Prefix	Remarks
SRM	Select	SRM	R3A	Single SAP SRM system connection
SRDCLNT200	Select	SRM Client 200	S20	Multiple SAP SRM connections
SRMCLNT400	Select	SRM Client 400	S40	Multiple SAP SRM connections

Table 3.1 Sample CRMCONSUM Entries

The entry in the Q_prefix field is used as a prefix for a download queue, which can be used to select the queue in monitoring Transaction codes SMQ1 and SMQ2.

2. As shown in Table 3.2, maintain the entries in table CRMSUBTAB for each of the users defined for SAP SRM master data transfer in table CRMCONSUM. The sample entries in Table 3.2 are for one user, SAP SRM. If you have defined more users (e.g., SRDCLNT200, etc.), you need to maintain the entries for these users, also. Again, the **Remarks** column is included to describe each setting and is not part of the actual table.

User	U/D	Obj.Class	Funct.Name	Remarks
SRM	D-Download	CUSTOMIZING	S_CUSTOMIZING_EXTRACT	Keep the other fields blank
SRM	D-Download	MATERIAL	CRS_MATERIAL_EXTRACT	Keep the other fields blank
SRM	D-Download	SERVICE_MASTER	CRS_SERVICE_EXTRACT	Keep the other fields blank

Table 3.2 Sample CRMSUBTAB Entries

3. Maintain the entries in table CRMRFCPAR, as shown in Table 3.3, for each of the users you created in table CRMCONSUM. Table 3.3 shows sample settings for one user, SAP SRM.

User	Object	RFC Dest	Load Type	Info	Inqueue Flag	Send XML Flag
SRM	*	SRMCLNT100	I	Give any description here	X	X
SRM	*	SRMCLNT100	R	Give any description here	X	X
SRM	MATERIAL	SRMCLNT100	D	Give any description here	X	X
SRM	SERVICE_MASTER	SRMCLNT100	I	Give any description here	X	X

Table 3.3 Sample CRMRFCPAR Table Entries

4. Maintain filtering entries for the object MATERIAL in table CRMPAROLTP for each of the users you created in CRMCONSUM. Table 3.4 shows sample settings for one user, SAP SRM.

Parameter Name	Param. Name 2	Param. Name 3	User	Param. Value	Param. Value 2
CRM_FILTERING_ACTIVE	MATERIAL		SRM	X	

Table 3.4 Sample CRMPAROLTP Table Entries

5. Activate applications BC-MID and NDI in table TBE11. Note that activation of these applications may affect other SAP applications like SAP CRM, SAP NetWeaver BI, etc. Remember to coordinate with other consultants to test your configurations on any affected applications.

Deactivate CRM-Specific Middleware Settings in SAP SRM

Until SAP SRM 4.0, the same software component was used for both SAP SRM and SAP CRM applications. The middleware used for downloading products from SAP ERP (or SAP R/3) contains many CRM-related objects. In this setting, the CRM-related objects are deactivated. The settings described in this section should be configured in the SAP SRM system, using Transaction code BBP_PRODUCT_SETTINGS:

1. Read the documentation by clicking on the information icon.

2. Enter the user name you want to choose in the Consumer field (for example, SRM).

3. Activate or deactivate the service product. If you want to download the service master from SAP ERP, then select the Service Product Active radio button. If you do not want to download the service masters, then select the Service Product Inactive radio button.

4. Deselect the Test Mode checkbox and click on the execute icon. This will deactivate all CRM-specific middleware settings and set BBP as the active application in the SMOFAPPL table. The execution will take approximately 30 to 60 minutes. Download the objects MATERIAL (material master), DNL_CUST_PROD0 (material types, product number conversions), and DNL_CUST_PROD1 (material groups) are activated and all other CRM download objects are deactivated. If you activate a service product, then the download objects SERVICE_MASTER (service master) and DNL_CUST_SRVMAS (service categories) are also activated.

Set Up Filters for the Material Master for Replication in SAP SRM

Many customers may want to implement SAP SRM for only a few product categories. In such cases, you should replicate only the materials from the selected product categories. Also, the SAP material master consists of materials for all functions. However, you will only need materials with purchasing data in SAP

SRM. Therefore, it is recommended to maintain filters to replicate only required materials, using Transaction code R3AC1. Proceed as follows:

1. Click on the filter icon for the object MATERIAL.

2. Select the Source site name from the dropdown list and click on the pencil icon to move to edit mode. If you want to restrict the replication to materials with a purchasing view in SAP ERP, then maintain the settings as shown in Table 3.5.

Table/ Structure	Field	Op	Low	High	Incl/Excl
MARA	PSTAT	Contains Pattern	*E*		Inclusive

Table 3.5 Sample Settings for Material Filtering

You can also use any other table and field entry to restrict the materials to be replicated, and you can deactivate a specific set of materials for replication.

Downloading Customizing Objects and Products

In this section, you'll learn how to download customizing objects relevant for the product master and the download of materials and services, using Transaction code R3AS. The relevant customizing objects are UOMs, dimensions, currencies, material number conversions, material types, material groups, and service categories. Once the customizing objects are downloaded, you can download the materials and services. Follow these steps:

1. Enter "DNL_CUST_BASIS3" in the Load Object field and press the Enter key. The object DNL_CUST_BASIS3 downloads UOMs, dimensions, and currencies.

> **Note**
>
> Downloading the object DNL_CUST_BASIS3 is not required from SAP SRM 5.0 on.

2. The source site and receiver site information will be filled. If they are not filled, select the appropriate SAP R/3 system for the Source Site (Sender) and CRM for the Destination Site (Receiver). Click on the execute icon or press the F8 key.

3. Go to Transaction R3AM1 to monitor the download object. If you have a green light for DNL_CUST_BASIS3, return to Transaction R3AS. If you see a yellow light, click on the refresh icon. If there is no progress in the block number, then follow the steps in the section on product master download monitoring and troubleshooting that follows this section.

4. Repeat the previous steps to download DNL_CUST_PROD0 (material types and material number conversions) and DNL_CUST_PROD1 (product categories).

5. If you want to replicate the service master also, download object DNL_CUST_SRVMAS (service categories). With this step, downloading of customizing objects is completed.

6. Go to Transaction R3AS to download materials and services. The download object MATERIAL is used to replicate materials and SERVICE_MASTER is used to replicate services.

> **Note**
>
> The delta download of materials and services occur automatically whenever a new material or service conforming to your filter settings is created in SAP ERP, or when a material or service is changed.

Product Master Download Monitoring and Troubleshooting

Use the procedure given in this section to monitor and troubleshoot the download of customizing objects and products:

1. To start the download monitor, call Transaction R3AM1 and click on the execute icon. If all of the traffic lights are green, the download was successful. If a traffic light is yellow, click on the refresh icon and observe whether the block number increases. If so, the download is still in progress. If not, continue with the next step.

2. In the backend SAP R/3 system, check the outbound queue using Transaction code SMQ1. Enter the queue name as "R3A*" (or as defined in the CRMCONSUM table in SAP R/3) and click on the execute icon to display the queue. If the queue is locked, try to release the lock on it to activate it. If the queue disappears after a refresh, the download process has proceeded further.

3. Using Transaction SMQ2, check the inbound queues in the SAP SRM system. Double-click on any inbound queue line. Select the queue that appears next and click on the activate icon, if necessary.

4. Using Transaction codes SMWP and SMW01, you can obtain detailed information about the download progress. Start these transactions in the SAP SRM system. Look out for any error messages and correct the errors wherever possible.

5. After calling Transaction code SMW01, proceed as follows to get information about the download:

   ▸ Click on the execute icon.

   ▸ Select a row with an error flag in the State column and click on the 'Show BDoc Msg Errors/Receivers' icon.

▶ A list of errors is shown on the next screen. Click on the Longtext button to see a detailed description of the error.

6. After eliminating any errors, call Transaction SMQ2 and activate the inbound queue.

7. Now, to check whether the material types, material groups, and service categories have arrived in the SAP SRM system, call Transaction COMM_HIERARCHY. All of the required material groups should have been copied from SAP R/3 system to the SAP SRM system. If not, check the filter settings again and look at the data in the SAP R/3 backend system. Also, check whether the tables assigned to the objects contain the necessary data in the SAP R/3 backend system.

8. To check whether the materials and services are replicated to SAP SRM, call Transaction COMMPR01. You will find the materials and services that were replicated in this transaction.

9. If you use product hierarchy in the SAP R/3 material master, you may encounter an error message during the download of object DNL_CUST_PROD1. Refer to SAP Note 432339 to resolve the error.

Useful SAP Notes
872533: FAQ — Middleware
526980: How does the filtering for object MATERIAL work?
430980: CRM Server — Analysis of delta data exchange
429423: Analysis of errors in initial download
432339: Errors during customizing download DNL_CUST_PROD1

3.4.3 Product Master Data Maintenance in SAP SRM

Product master data can also be maintained in the SAP SRM system directly instead of replicating from the backend ERP system. It is required when customers do not have a backend system or when customers want to use the SAP SRM system as a standalone system. Some customers use the backend system for some of the categories and SAP SRM for others to reduce the burden of complex master data maintenance in the backend system. In such cases, categories and products that require integration with a backend system are replicated and products that are used only in the SAP SRM system are created directly. The following product master maintenance activities can be carried out:

▶ **Create or change product category**: Use Transaction COMM_HIERARCHY to maintain product categories.

▶ **Create or change product**: Use Transaction COMMPR01 to maintain product master.

▶ **Create or change product prices or product-vendor links**: Use Transaction COMMPR01 to maintain product prices and product-vendor links in the product master.

▶ **Delete a category**: Execute the COM_HIERARCHY_DELETE_SINGLE report to delete a hierarchy and category. If you want to delete all product hierarchy and category data, execute the COM_HIERARCHY_DELETE_ALL report.

▶ **Delete a product**: Execute the COM_PRODUCT_DELETE_SINGLE report to delete a product. If you want to delete all product master data, execute the COM_PRODUCT_DELETE_ALL report .

In this section, you have learned about product master data replication and maintenance. Before going ahead with vendor master replication, it is essential that we define an organizational plan in SAP SRM, which we will do next.

3.5 Defining the Organization

Defining the organization is a prerequisite for configuring business scenarios in SAP SRM. In this and the next section, we will explain designing and configuring the organizational structure in SAP SRM with the help of the Besttec Industries case study. As mentioned earlier in Section 3.1, Besttec Industries has global presence with operations in many countries. Besttec Industries has already implemented SAP R/3, including the Human Resources (HR) component. The organization has already been defined in SAP R/3 HR for the headquarters along with few of its subsidiaries. The purchasing team has two options for configuring the organizational plan in SAP SRM:

▶ Replicate the existing organizational structure from the HR implementation into the SAP SRM organization. This option is explained in Section 3.5.1.

▶ Define a new organizational structure in SAP SRM. This option is discussed in detail in Section 3.5.2.

3.5.1 Copy the SAP R/3 HR Organization to SAP SRM

In SAP R/3, each user is defined as an employee in the organizational plan. The functions defined for an employee are oriented toward the employee role, and attributes are assigned to control personnel-related activities. In the case of SAP SRM, users are typically defined as buyers and requesting employees, and attributes are assigned to users to control purchasing-related activity. Therefore, it is difficult to copy the HR organizational plan to SAP SRM. However, it can be done, using ALE, and both initial distribution and delta distribution are possible. This means that the complete organizational structure, consisting of organizational units, positions, and jobs, is made available in SAP SRM.

In addition, an SAP business partner is created for each organizational unit. This business partner is then referenced in individual processes. An SAP business partner for the employee is also created in SAP SRM, and it contains personal details, private address, business address, bank details (if required), different communication methods, employee number, and the corresponding user link. Ensure that the employee has the same user ID in both systems and that the user is assigned to the employee in the HR system (info type 0105/subtype 0001).

> **Note**
>
> For implementing SAP R/3 HR synchronization with the SAP SRM organizational plan, refer to the implementation steps in SAP Notes 550055 and 934372.

3.5.2 Define an Organizational Structure in SAP SRM

You can also define an organizational plan directly in SAP SRM. In SAP SRM, the organizational structure is more aligned with the procurement process, with organizational elements like purchasing organization, purchasing group, etc. Before defining the organizational plan, it is important to chart out different entities within the organization. We will take a look at this using our sample company, Besttec Industries.

As described in Section 3.1.1, Besttec Industries has presence in 12 countries. Each subsidiary is a separate legal entity with a different company code and organizational data. Table 3.6 shows a few of the countries in which Besttec Industries operates and the core business functions executed in these countries, along with the SAP ERP components implemented in each country.

Country	Core Functions	Company Code	Core Components Used
Germany Headquarters	Production, sales	1000	SD,PP,MM,PM, LE, HR, FI/CO
United States	Sales	2000	SD, MM,LE, FI/CO,HR
India	Raw material purchasing, component production	3000	MM, LE,PP, FI/CO
China	Raw material purchasing, component production	4000	MM, LE,PP, FI/CO
Singapore	Sales and production	5000	SD,PP,MM,PM, LE, FI/CO

Table 3.6 Besttec Industries Organizational Details for a Few of the Countries in Which It Operates

As you can see from Table 3.6, Besttec Industries has not implemented the HR component in some of countries in which it operates. Also, the Besttec Industries team wants to have a simplified organization in SAP SRM by defining only the required organizational entities and users. Hence, the Besttec Industries team has decided to define a new organizational plan in SAP SRM instead of importing the existing one from the SAP R/3 HR organization. Other important points that were considered while designing the Besttec Industries organizational plan include the following:

▶ Employees from production, sales, and purchasing departments create requests for procurement.

▶ Besttec Industries AG, Germany, has two purchasing organizations in SAP R/3 for raw materials and Maintenance, Repair, and Overhaul (MRO) item procurement.

▶ Besttec Industries wants to define and procure low-value indirect items in the SAP SRM system.

▶ Besttec Industries plans to use SAP SRM for plan-driven procurement and to procure direct materials as an extension of the current implementation. In the current implementation, Besttec Industries focusses on automating MRO item procurement.

In the next section, we will discuss, in detail, the configuration of the organizational plan in SAP SRM.

3.5.3 Organizational Plan Prerequisites

In this section, we will examine, in detail, the prerequisites for configuring the organizational plan, including defining business partner groupings and assigning number ranges, defining number ranges for business partners, maintaining address and person number ranges, defining partner functions, maintaining regions, downloading locations from SAP ERP, creating an EBP administrative user, creating a schedule for updating the business partner address, and configuring settings for creating an internal user.

Define Business Partner Groupings and Assign Number Ranges

This setting, using menu path **SPRO • Cross Application Components • SAP Business Partner • Business Partner • Basic Settings • Number Ranges and Groupings • Define Groupings and Assign Number Ranges**, is important for business partner creation and vendor replication from backend systems. Usually, SAP standard delivered settings are sufficient for this setting. However, it is important to check the number range assigned and change it as necessary.

Define Number Ranges for Business Partners

As with defining business partner groupings and assigning number ranges, defining number ranges for business partners is important for business partner creation and vendor replication from backend systems. Use menu path **SPRO • Cross Application Components • SAP Business Partner • Business Partner • Basic Settings • Number Ranges and Groupings • Define Number Ranges** to configure this setting. Again, typically, SAP standard delivered settings are sufficient. However, it is important to check the external number range and change it to synchronize with backend system number ranges.

> **Note**
>
> SAP SRM uses only one external number range during vendor replication from a backend system, while a backend system may have many number ranges based on account groups in the backend vendor master. You should define one external number range in SAP SRM that encompasses all vendor number ranges in a backend system.

Maintain Address and Person Number Range

This is an optional setting that you access using menu path **SPRO • SAP Web Application Server • Application Server • Basis Services • Address Management • Maintain Address and Person Number Ranges**. This setting is important because the system maintains an address master and person number for each business partner in the organizational plan. Again, typically, SAP standard delivered settings are sufficient. If you want to change the number ranges and provide your own number ranges, maintain the number ranges here.

Define Partner Functions

This is an optional setting that you access using menu path **SPRO • SAP Implementation Guide • Supplier Relationship Management • SRM Server • Cross Application Basic Settings • Define Partner Functions**. SAP delivers the standard partner functions like requester, bidder, etc. You can, however, change the texts for partner functions according to your organizational definitions. For example, you may want to change the description 'vendor' to 'supplier.'

Maintain Regions

This is an optional setting using menu path **SPRO • SAP Web Application Server • General Settings • Set Countries • Insert Regions**. Regions for many countries are delivered in the SAP standard. However, if you have defined your own regions in the backend SAP ERP system, then maintain them the same in SAP SRM, also.

Download Locations from SAP ERP

Before defining the organizational plan, SAP ERP plants and company codes should be replicated to SAP SRM as locations. Execute any of the following three programs using Transaction code SE38 to replicate the locations:

▸ **BBP_LOCATIONS_GET_ALL**
Get all locations from each backend system. Use this report if you have only one backend system defined in the *Define Backend Systems* configuration setting. You can also use it when you have many bakkend systems defined and you want to import plants from all backend systems.

▸ **BBP_LOCATIONS_GET_FROM_SYSTEM**
Get all locations from a selected backend system. Use this report if you have many backend systems defined in the *Define Backend Systems* configuration setting and you do not want to import locations from all backend systems.

▸ **BBP_LOCATIONS_GET_SELECTED**
Get selected locations from a selected backend system. Use this report if you do not want to import all locations from a backend system.

A business partner is created for each replicated location and you can view the mapping of the business partner with a backend plant in the table BBP_LOC-MAP. The business partner master can be viewed using Transaction code BP.

Troubleshooting Tip

▸ If you get an error message, "You have to execute XPRA BBP_ATTR_XPRA400 first!!," run the program BBP_ATTR_XPRA400 using Transaction code SE38.

▸ Importing plants is a mandatory activity. You will receive an error message in organizational plan maintenance (PPOMA_BBP) if you have not imported plants. However, in a standalone scenario implementation, you will not be able to import plants if you do not have any backend systems. Refer to SAP Note 563180 to solve this problem.

Create an EBP Administrator User

You also need to create an administrative user (for example, ADMIN) using Transaction code SU01. Assign the administrator role SAP_BBP_STAL_ADMIN-ISTRATOR to this user, and create the organizational plan using this user.

Create a Schedule for Updating the Business Partner Address

When an organizational unit is created in the organizational plan, the system creates a business partner. Whenever the address is updated for the organizational unit, the business partner address should also be updated. Use program HRALXSYNC to schedule a periodic comparison and update of addresses. It is recommended that you use Transaction code SM36 to schedule a job to run program HRALXSYNC and variant SAP&DEFAULT periodically. You can also use Transaction code BBP_BP_OM_INTEGRATE to synchronize the data whenever necessary.

Configuring Settings for Creating an Internal User

If you want to allow employee users to request a user ID that needs to be approved by the employee's manager, set the approval indicator using menu path **SPRO • SAP Implementation Guide • Supplier Relationship Management • SRM Server • Master Data • Create Users • Set Approval Indicator**. All user creation requests will then be routed for approval by the manager. Ensure that a manager is defined for each organizational unit.

3.6   Configuring an Organizational Plan

In this section, we will discuss the general steps for configuring an organizational plan in SAP SRM, how to design an SAP SRM organization for Besttec Industries, and how to maintain a vendor organizational plan. Structuring and defining an SAP SRM organizational plan is one of the most important tasks of an SAP SRM implementation. The organizational plan includes both organizational units and users. Administrators or consultants should define the organizational plan to represent all required organizational units and their attributes. This includes creating user master records for department managers using the Web application *Manage User Data*.

The remaining employee users and buyer users can be created by managers or administrators, or by the users themselves. Until SAP SRM 4.0, the organizational node for vendors is maintained along with the buying company's organizational plan. From SAP SRM 5.0 on, vendor organizations are separated from buyer organizations. In this section, we will discuss the general steps for maintaining an organizational plan, the organizational plan for Besttec Industries, the vendor organizational plan, and enhancements to the organization.

3.6.1   General Steps

The general steps to define an organizational plan are as follows:

1. Design the structure of the organizational plan based on your understanding of the current structure of the organization and process requirements.

2. Create a root organizational unit using Transaction PPOCA_BBP.

3. Create the remaining organizational units using Transaction PPOMA_BBP.

4. While defining a company, purchasing organization, or purchasing group, appropriate corresponding indicators have to be selected on the Function tab. Assign a backend SAP ERP organization when you create an organization representing a backend organization. For example, when you create a company code node, assign the backend company code of the respective SAP ERP system on the Function tab. When you create a local SAP SRM organization without reference to a backend organizational unit, then you do not need to assign a value. For example, when you create a local purchasing organization, just select the purchasing organization indicator on the Function tab without assigning a value.

5. Remember to maintain an address for all organizational units. If you do not maintain an address, the corresponding business partner will not be created and you will not be able to use the organizational unit.

6. Maintain the attributes and extended attributes for the organizational units. The attributes of the top-level node are inherited to lower level nodes. Hence, maintain the attributes used by all organizational units at the root level. Similarly, maintain attributes used by all organizational units in a company at the company code node level. For example, maintain all plants within a company as locations in extended attributes at the company code level. You should also maintain the attributes ACS (system alias for accounting systems), SYS (system alias), VENDOR_ACS (accounting system for vendor), VENDOR_SYS (system alias for vendor), and BUK (company code) at the company level. Similarly, maintain attributes for each organizational unit.

7. Specify the attributes. Important attributes for the self-service procurement scenario are Account Assignment Category (KNT) and related objects ACS, SYS, BUK, CAT, BSA, CUR, ADDR_SHIPT, VENDOR_ACS, and VENDOR_SYS, and product categories and locations in extended attributes. Typically, the logical system for SAP SRM and the backend SAP ERP system both are given as attribute values for SYS and VENDOR_SYS.

8. In SAP SRM, it is possible for an employee to shop on behalf of other employees. For example, a secretary can shop on behalf of managers so that managers have more time for strategic tasks. To facilitate this, the managers' user IDs should be maintained in the REQUESTER attribute in the position of secretary. You can also maintain the department's organizational unit in the REQUESTER attribute to facilitate the secretary to shop on behalf of all employees in the department. Note that maintaining a department with a large number of employees as REQUESTER adversely affects the system performance during shopping cart creation. The value in the REQUESTER attribute forms the basis for the F4 help in the Goods recipient field in the shopping cart. The shop-on-behalf-of functionality is only available in the extended shopping cart form available for purchasers.

9. You can also define responsibility for purchasing group nodes. A purchasing group represents a buyer or group of buyers responsible for procurement of products in specific product categories for specific requesting departments. Maintain the product categories and organizational units of requesting departments for which a purchasing group is responsible on the Responsibility tab of the purchasing group node.

10. Create user master records using the Web application Manage User Data, and assign users to the relevant organizational unit. Managers have to be represented as heads of organizational units and assigned the role of SAP_BBP_STAL_MANAGER.

11. Run Transaction code BBP_ATTR_CHECK or run program BBP_CHECK_CONSISTENCY to check whether the attributes were defined correctly with respect to the individual applications allowed for users.

12. If you use plan-driven procurement, maintain a node for each backend system as an external procurement channel to get purchase requisitions from the respective backend systems. All requirements from the backend systems will be routed through this external procurement channel node. An RFC logon user used in defining RFC destinations should be assigned to this node. The organizational unit should be included on the Responsibility tab of a local purchasing group.

Tips

▶ You can use Transaction USERS_GEN to create multiple users simultaneously by importing users from other SAP systems or from a file. You can also convert users created using Transaction code SU01 to EBP users by assigning an organizational unit in USERS_GEN. You should read the user documentation provided in the USERS_GEN transaction to understand its usage.

▶ You can use Transaction USERS_GEN to repair user master records when you have problems with the user master. Refer to SAP Note 785802 to repair defective user master records.

▶ A valid SAP SRM application user should have an organizational unit assigned. You can display valid users in Transaction PPOMA_BBP or PPOSA_BBP. SAP SRM–specific roles should be assigned to SAP SRM application users. Assigning profiles like SAP_ALL does not provide authorizations to execute SAP SRM transactions. You can search for SAP SRM roles with the search string SAP_EC_BBP* for single roles and SAP_BBP_STAL* for composite roles. The roles need no explanation here as the names indicate the nature of role.

▶ Note that performance problems can be encountered in Transaction PPOMA_BBP, if too many users are assigned to the same organizational unit. You should make sure that you do not assign more than 200 users to the same organizational unit.

▸ Useful Transactions include the following: PPOCA_BBP (create root organization), PPOMA_BBP (edit organizational plan), PPOSA_BBP (display organizational plan), PPOCV_BBP (create vendor root organization), PPOMV_BBP (edit vendor organizational plan), PPOSV_BBP (display vendor organizational plan), USERS_GEN (user master maintenance), BBP_BP_OM_INTEGRATE (synchronize business partners), and BBP_ATTR_CHECK (check consistency of attributes).

▸ You should read the help documentation on user attributes. The help documentation can be found at *http://help.sap.com* (launch the SAP SRM documentation and navigate to **Supplier Relationship Management** • **Architecture and Technology** • **Administration** • **Maintaining User Attributes**).

▸ You can change the properties of attributes by changing the properties in table T77OMATTR using Transaction code SM30.

Troubleshooting tip

If you get an error message "Attributes for user contains errors. Inform system admin" in any SAP SRM Web transaction, it means the user is not assigned to an organizational unit. Convert the user from an SU01 user to an EBP user in Transaction USERS_GEN.

Now, we will look at an organizational plan for our sample company, Besttec Industries.

3.6.2 Organizational Plan for Besttec Industries

Figure 3.7 represents a sample organizational plan for Besttec Industries, including a detailed organizational structure for Besttec Industries AG, Germany. Similar organizational units for other subsidiary companies can also be created. Although the structure defined in Figure 3.7 is self-explanatory, the following points need to be noted:

▸ Although there is only one local purchasing organization defined for Besttec Industries AG, it is possible to have multiple local purchasing organizations.

▸ **The Ext.Proc Channel** node is not required for the current self-service procurement project. It is, however, required for plan-driven procurement, which Besttec Industries plans to implement later. The responsibility of this node will be assigned to local purchasing group **L2**. The node is shown in Figure 3.7 to show the complete organizational plan in a typical implementation.

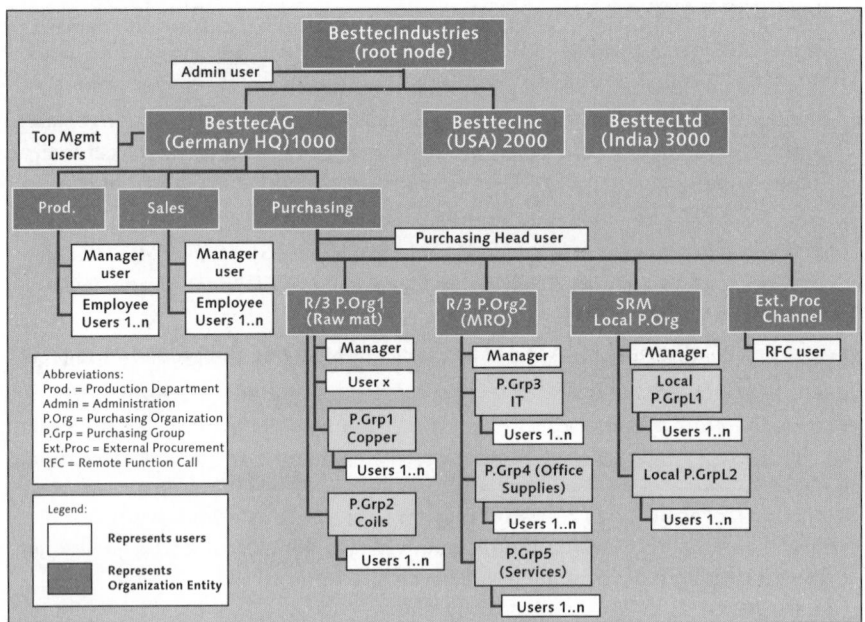

Figure 3.7 Sample Organizational Plan for Besttec Industries

3.6.3   Maintain the Vendor Organizational Structure

Until SAP SRM 4.0, the organizational node for vendors was maintained along with the buying company's organizational plan. From SAP SRM 5.0 on, the vendor organization is separated from the buyer organization. The settings described in this section are relevant from SAP SRM 5.0 on.

A root organization for vendors should exist before creating vendors in SAP SRM. Maintain this organization using Transaction PPOCV_BBP, and enter a name for it (for example, Besttec Industries Suppliers). Maintain the attributes VENDOR_ACS, VENDOR_SYS, and EXT_ITS at the root level. Any changes to the vendor organization structure should be made using Transaction PPOMV_BBP.

3.6.4   Enhancing the Organizational Plan

In SAP ERP, purchasing groups can be used with any purchasing organization without any restrictions. However, in SAP SRM, purchasing groups are assigned to a specific purchasing organization. Two BAdIs have been provided to make the connection between purchasing organizations and purchasing groups more flexible and lessen the hierarchical restrictions of the SAP SRM organizational plan. You can also link an employee user to a purchasing group using the "is purchaser of" relationship type. The BAdIs include the following:

▸ **BAdI BBP_F4_READ_ON_ENTRY**: Activate this BAdI to influence the input help and search help. Using this BAdI, you can display the purchasing groups that are not assigned to a purchasing organization in the organizational plan.

▸ **BAdI BBP_MSG_CTRL_CUST**: Activate this BAdI to influence the error messages in a transaction, for example, you can convert a warning message to an error message.

3.7 External Business Partners

Suppliers or vendors are called external business partners. Vendors can be replicated from the backend ERP system or created directly in SAP SRM using the Web transaction *Manage Business Partners*. Before replicating vendors from the backend SAP ERP system, payment terms data and QM systems data should also be imported, as explained in this section.

3.7.1 Upload Payment Terms

Execute the program BBP_UPLOAD_PAYMENT_TERMS to replicate payment terms from SAP ERP into the SAP SRM system. The payment terms from tables T052 and T052U from the backend SAP ERP system are uploaded into SAP SRM and stored in the tables BBP_PAYTERM and BBP_PAYTERM_TEXT respectively.

3.7.2 Upload QM Systems

Execute the program BBP_UPLOAD_QM_SYSTEMS to replicate QM systems from SAP ERP into the SAP SRM system.

3.7.3 Initial Download of Vendor Master Records from the Backend SAP ERP System

Vendor master records are replicated from the backend system into SAP SRM using Transaction /nBBPGETVD. Specify the logical system name of the backend system, the vendor range that needs to be replicated, and the vendor root node in SAP SRM, and execute the transfer to replicate the vendors. Use Transaction SLG1 to monitor the results of replication and to find errors, if any.

3.7.4 Add, Change, or Delete Purchasing Organizations in the Vendor Master

If a vendor belongs to many purchasing organizations, execute the program BBP_UPDATE_PORG to add, change, or delete the appropriate purchasing organizations. You can also maintain purchasing organizations for a vendor in the *Maintain Business Partners* Web transaction.

3.7.5 Mapping Vendors in a Multiple Backend System Scenario

If you have multiple backend systems and the vendor codes in all backend systems are the same, execute the program BBP_UPDATE_MAPPING to map the vendors across the backend systems. When you use the program BBP_UPDATE_MAPPING, vendors need to be replicated from one backend system only. You can also map the backend system and vendor code to a vendor in SAP SRM using the *Maintain Business Partners* Web transaction.

3.7.6 Vendor Master Update Synchronization

If you want to update the vendor master with the changes made in backend systems, then you need to maintain the settings described in this section.

Make Global Settings for Vendor Synchronization

To configure global settings for vendor synchronization, follow the menu path **SPRO · SAP Implementation Guide · Supplier Relationship Management · SRM Server · Technical Basic Settings · Settings for Supplier Synchronization · Make Global Settings**. Use the following guidelines for your configuration:

▶ Select Create New Vendors if you want to synchronize new vendors created in the backend system.

▶ Select Carry Out Address Check for Duplicates if you want the system to check for duplicates based on address data.

▶ Maintain the 8-digit vendor organizational unit in the Organizational Unit field in EBP for the Vendor.

▶ Select an option from the dropdown box in the Vendor Number Assignment Type field. For example, the option Only SAP R/3 numbers can be selected if you want the vendor number in the backend and SAP SRM to be the same.

Make Settings for Each Backend System

Maintain the settings for each backend system as described in the documentation for this setting using the menu path **SPRO · SAP Implementation Guide · Supplier Relationship Management · SRM Server · Technical Basic Settings · Settings for Supplier Synchronization · Make Settings for Each Backend System**.

3.7.7 Schedule the Synchronization Program

Schedule the periodic execution of the program BBP_VENDOR_SYNC using Transaction code SM36 to automatically synchronize vendor master data between the backend system and SAP SRM. You can view table entries in table BBP_VDSYNC_CUST to see when the last synchronization report ran. Table BBP_NEWVD_LOG or Transaction code BBP_SNEW_SYNCVD show new vendors added on a given date. Vendor synchronization can be monitored using Transaction code SLG1.

3.7.8 Customer Fields Replication in Vendor Master Data

If you have defined additional customer fields in the vendor master, you can use BAdI BBP_GET_VMDATA_CF to replicate additional fields from the backend system.

Note
For additional information on customer field replication, refer to the BAdI documentation.

3.7.9 Creating Vendor Contact Persons

Vendor contact persons and vendor users are required if you want to use the sourcing or supplier collaboration functionalities. Vendor contact persons are created using the "Maintain Business Partners" Web transaction. From SAP SRM 2007 on, the vendor users created in SAP SRM should be synchronized with portal user administration so that vendor users can access SAP SRM through the portal. The additional configuration required to synchronize with the portal is explained in Chapter 10, in Section 10.3 under the heading "New SAP SRM 2007 Settings for Business Partner Creation."

Let us now look into other common basic technical settings that are required in all SAP SRM implementations.

3.8 Common Basic Technical Settings

The settings described in this section are used in all SAP SRM scenarios and therefore are common basic technical settings. They include creating an Application Linking and Enabling (ALE) distribution model, generating partner profiles in the backend system, technical settings for email, setting control parameters, configuring jobs for scheduling reports, and starting application monitors.

3.8.1   Create an ALE Distribution Model

An ALE distribution model is defined to post goods, receipt documents, and invoices in the backend system using the menu path **SPRO • SAP Implementation Guide • Supplier Relationship Management • SRM Server • Technical Basic Settings • ALE Settings (Logical System) • Distribution (ALE) • Modelling and Implementing Business Processes • Maintain Distribution Model and Distribute Views**. For example, you can create a distribution model for sending documents between SAP SRM and the SAP ERP backend system. The following message types and BAPIs are used:

▶ **BBPCO**: Transfers commitments to the backend controlling component for local purchase orders.

▶ **BBPIV**: Transfers invoice information to the backend system.

▶ **MBGMCR**: Posts material documents for goods receipts.

▶ **ACC_GOODS_MOVEMENT**: Distributes procurement card charges to account assignment.

▶ **ACLPAY**: Posts invoice documents to pay the bank in a procurement card scenario.

▶ **BBP_PCSTAT**: Imports procurement card statements from the backend system to the SAP SRM system.

Follow these steps to create a distribution model:

1. Enter the edit mode by clicking on the pencil icon.
2. Click on the Create model view button. See screenshot 1 in Figure 3.8.
3. Enter a **Short text** and **Technical name** in the screen that appears and click on the enter icon.
4. Select your new model view by clicking on it and click on the **Add message type** button.
5. Select the SAP SRM system as the **Sender** and the SAP ERP system as the **Receiver**. Select Message Type **BBPCO** and click on the continue icon. See screenshot 2 in Figure 3.8.
6. Expand the arrow next to your model view. Click on the SAP ERP system line to select it (see screenshot 3 in Figure 3.8). Click on the **Add message type** button. In the screen that appears, Model view, the Sender and Receiver fields are filled with values automatically. Select the message type "BBPIV" and click on the continue icon.
7. Repeat the previous step to add the message type 'MBGMCR.'
8. If you want to use the procurement cards functionality, add message types 'ACLPAY' and 'ACC_GOODS_MOVEMENT.'

9. Click on the Add BAPI button. Select **BBP_PCSTAT** in the Obj. name/interface field and **Create** in the Method field and click on the continue icon. See screenshot 4 in Figure 3.8.

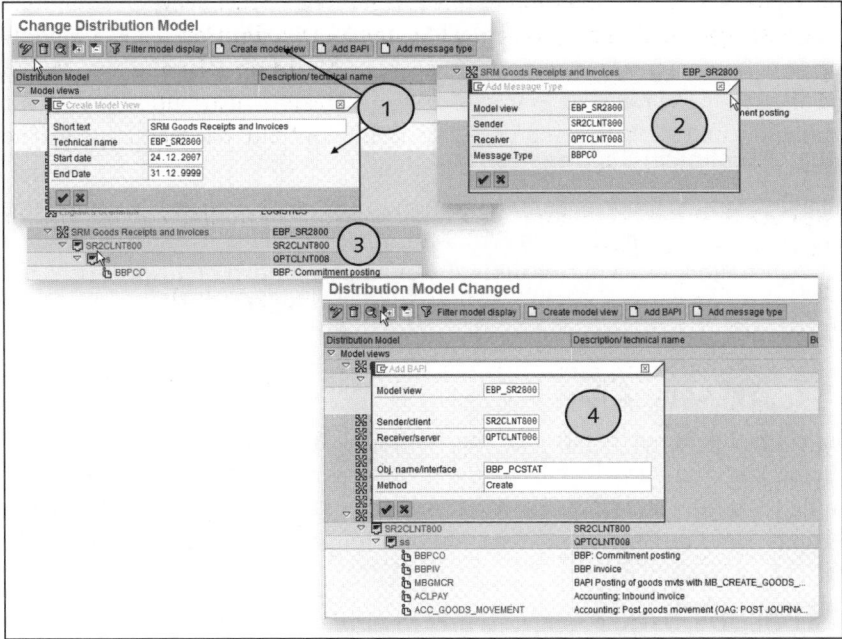

Figure 3.8 Create an ALE Distribution Model

10. Save the new model view by clicking on the save icon.

11. Select your model view by clicking on it and follow the menu path **Environment • Generate Partner Profiles**. Select 3 in the Version field and select the Transfer IDoc immediately radio button in the "Output Mode" section. Click on the execute icon to generate partner profiles.

12. To distribute the model to the backend system, select your model view and follow the menu path **Edit • Model View • Distribute**. Select the backend logical system name as the receiver of the model view and click on the continue icon.

3.8.2 Generate Partner Profiles in the Backend System

This setting is configured in the backend SAP ERP system using the menu path **SPRO • SAP Implementation Guide • SAP NetWeaver • SAP Web Application Server • IDoc Interface/Application Link Enabling (ALE) • Modelling and Implementing Business Processes • Maintain Distribution Model and Distribute Views**.

Follow these steps:

1. Select the model view transferred from the SAP SRM system and select **Environment · Generate partner profiles**.
2. Select the SAP SRM system as the Partner system, 3 as the Version, and Transfer IDoc immediately as the Output mode, and click on the execute icon.

3.8.3   Technical Settings for Email

Email is a normal mode of communication in SAP SRM. Hence, it is essential to configure sending emails from SAP SRM. In some scenarios, such as supplier self-registration, receiving emails is also an important part of the process. Refer to SAP Note 455140 to configure sending and receiving emails.

3.8.4   Set Control Parameters

The control parameters facilitate the communication to the backend SAP ERP system. You configure them using the menu path **SPRO · SAP Implementation Guide · Supplier Relationship Management · SRM Server · Technical Basic Settings · Set Control Parameters**. The control parameters include the following:

▸ **SPOOL_JOB_USER**: Configure a user to carry out the spool job.
▸ **SPOOL_LEAD_INTERVAL**: Specify a value of 60, indicating the time between two tries.
▸ **SPOOL_MAX_RETRY**: Specify a value of 10, indicating the maximum number of tries until the spool job is carried out.

3.8.5   Jobs for Scheduling Reports

Schedule background jobs for reports as described in Table 3.7.

Report Name	Description	Remarks
CLEAN_REQREQ_UP	Checks whether the backend documents (purchase requisitions, purchase orders, reservations) have been created in the backend system, deletes obsolete table entries in EBP, and updates document numbers in the shopping cart. You cannot process the shopping cart in SAP SRM until the update is completed.	Schedule the report to execute every few minutes.

Table 3.7 Important Reports to Schedule

Report Name	Description	Remarks
BBP_GET_STATUS_2	Ensures that the information on the back-end documents is up to date. Retrieves the updated information from the back-end system, for example, it retrieves a purchase order number after it was converted from a purchase requisition.	Schedule the report to execute every few minutes.

Table 3.7 Important Reports to Schedule (Cont.)

3.8.6 Start Application Monitors

Start application monitors using the menu path **SPRO • SAP Implementation Guide • Supplier Relationship Management • SRM Server • Cross Application Basic Settings • Start Application Monitors**. This ensures that any errors that occur in the SAP SRM system are displayed in application monitors.

3.8.7 Modifying the ITS Login Page

Many organizations modify the standard SAP SRM login page to incorporate their company logo and other useful links. Modification of the login page with company-specific communication guidelines should be planned during the design stage of the implementation. Refer to SAP Note 778488 to modify the ITS login page. However, you do not need to change the SAP SRM login page in SAP SRM 2007 because Enterprise Portal is the user interface in SAP SRM 2007.

3.9 Summary

In this chapter, you learned about the basic settings required for different SAP SRM scenarios. You also learned about the organizational structure and master data required for an SAP SRM implementation, with the help of a case study. While this chapter explained the basic technical settings required in all SAP SRM scenarios, Chapters 5 to 14 explain scenario-specific configurations. Next, in Chapter 4, we will discuss the deployment scenarios to explain the possible integration options with a backend SAP ERP system.

SAP SRM is flexibly integrated with backend planning, inventory, and accounting systems. In this chapter, we will discuss in detail the different deployment scenarios possible to enable different levels of integration with backend ERP systems.

4   SAP SRM Deployment Scenarios

SAP Supplier Relationship Management (SAP SRM) enables organizations to efficiently source and procure all categories of products, that is, direct materials, indirect materials, and services, and can be integrated with any backend planning, inventory, and accounting systems. SAP SRM provides four deployment scenarios, including the classic, extended classic, standalone, and decoupled scenario, and companies can decide on the level of integration with backend planning and accounting systems by implementing the appropriate deployment scenario. In this chapter, we will first provide you with an overview of the four possible deployment scenarios and then discuss them in detail.

SAP SRM provides an integrated enterprise procurement platform that enables integration of procurement with design, planning, inventory, and financial applications. SAP SRM is seamlessly integrated with the SAP ERP application and can be integrated with other non-SAP backend ERP applications as well. Depending on the system that you want to be the main purchasing application, there are four scenarios of integration with backend ERP applications. Remember, as an SAP SRM consultant you will play varied roles during a deployment: from a business process expert during the design phase to becoming a product expert during realization. We briefly reviewed these scenarios in Chapter 2 and will start with a brief recap of them in this chapter:

▸ **Local scenario or standalone scenario**
In the local or standalone scenario, all procurement documents are processed in the SAP SRM system itself. Procurement requisitions in the form of shopping carts and follow-on documents, such as purchase orders, goods receipts, and invoices, are processed in the SAP SRM system. Only the invoices are integrated with the backend financial accounting system and payments are made from the backend accounting system.

▸ **Classic scenario**
In the classic scenario, the shopping cart is processed in SAP SRM and the follow-on documents are processed in the backend ERP system. Goods receipts or invoices can be created either in SAP SRM or in the backend system.

▶ **Extended classic scenario**
In the extended classic scenario, the shopping cart and the follow-on documents are processed in SAP SRM. Purchase orders are replicated to the backend system. However, changes to purchase orders can be made only in SAP SRM. Goods receipts or invoices can be created either in SAP SRM or in the backend system.

▶ **Decoupled scenario**
Officially, SAP SRM does not have a scenario called decoupled. However, this scenario name is loosely used to indicate the ability to use all of the previous three scenarios in parallel. That is, you can run all of the previous scenarios in parallel based on product category. For example, you can specify that services are processed in SAP SRM and stock items are processed in the backend system. By using a Business Add-In (BAdI), you can define your rules on whether the purchase order should be created in SAP SRM or in the backend system.

We will now discuss the four deployment scenarios in more detail, examining for each the applicability of the scenario, the process flow, and, with the exception of the decoupled scenario, the important settings that determine the scenario.

4.1 The Standalone or Local Scenario

In a standalone scenario, all procurement processes are executed in SAP SRM, and shopping carts and other procurement documents are processed in SAP SRM. Only final invoice data is sent to the backend accounting system. Account assignments are checked locally with accounting data defined in SAP SRM. Figure 4.1 illustrates the standalone scenario.

4.1.1 Applicability of the Standalone Scenario

The standalone scenario is applicable for the following customer types:

▶ Customers who do not have an operational backend system for materials management and have only financial accounting systems.

▶ Customers who want to move all procurement activity for selected categories to the SAP SRM system. This also enables companies to reduce the load on the backend procurement system by transferring buyers who deal in these selected categories.

▶ Customers who do not have their own product data, those who want to maintain only minimal product data, and those who want to rely on supplier catalogs.

▶ Customers who want to use procurement card functionalities.

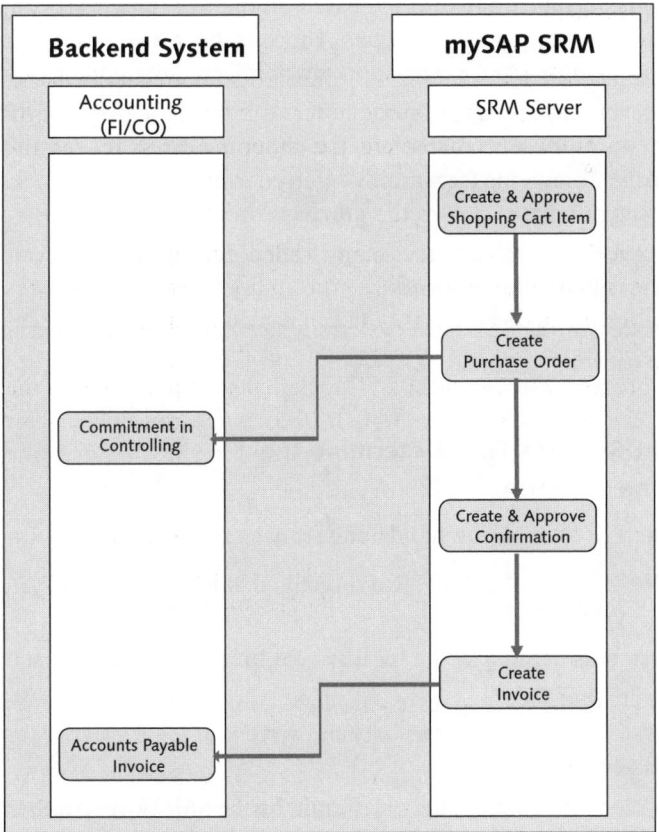

Figure 4.1 Standalone Scenario

▶ Customers who want to use all of the functionalities in the service procurement scenario.

▶ Customers who want to involve suppliers in procurement transactions using Supplier Self-Service (SUS) integration with SAP SRM.

Note

From SAP SRM 2007 on, the procurement card functionality is also available in the extended classic scenario.

4.1.2 Process Flow

Figure 4.1 also illustrates the standalone scenario process flow. The process is as follows:

1. An employee searches the catalogs and creates an online shopping cart for his requirements.

2. The system triggers an approval workflow based on the workflow start conditions defined in the configuration settings. The workflow is routed to the mailbox of the approving manager, who approves or rejects the shopping cart.

3. If the shopping cart is approved, the system creates a purchase order in the SAP SRM system. If the data is incomplete, the shopping cart is moved to a purchaser's worklist in sourcing (commonly referred to as the sourcing cockpit) from where the purchaser creates the purchase order.

4. The goods receipt for materials or service entry sheet for services is created in the SAP SRM sytem as confirmation.

5. An invoice is created in the SAP SRM system, which creates an accounting document in the backend system.

4.1.3 Important Settings That Determine the Standalone Scenario

The following settings determine the standalone scenario:

▶ Product categories are created in SAP SRM directly, that is, local product categories.

▶ The SAP SRM system is defined as the local system in the configuration setting *Define Backend Systems*.

▶ An accounting system is defined as the backend system in the configuration setting *Define Backend Systems*.

▶ The target system for the product category should be the SAP SRM system in the configuration setting *Define Backend System for Product Category*. You can also use the standalone scenario using backend product categories with this setting. Optionally, BAdI BBP_DETERMINE_LOGSYS is implemented to determine the target system as the SAP SRM system.

4.2 The Classic Scenario

In a classic scenario, the SAP SRM system is used mainly to capture procurement requisitions from employees in the form of shopping carts. All other procurement activities take place in the backend materials management system.

4.2.1 Applicability of the Classic Scenario

The classic scenario is applicable to customers who have a strong backend procurement system and where buyers do not want to use multiple systems for their operations. However, such customers may want to enable large numbers of employees to create requisitions with minimal or no training. If these customers want to use special purchase order features available in SAP ERP, such as one-time-vendor purchase order, partner functions, external services with many outline levels, and complex pricing with delivery costs, then the classic scenario is recommended. Classic scenario is also recommended for customers who want to involve suppliers in procurement transactions using SUS integration with Materials Management (MM).

4.2.2   Process Flow

Figure 4.2 illustrates the classic scenario process flow, which is as follows:

1. An employee searches the catalogs and creates an online shopping cart for his requirements. The employee can also view the stock status for the material.
2. The system triggers an approval workflow based on the workflow start conditions defined in the configuration settings. The workflow is routed to the mailbox of the approving manager, who approves or rejects the shopping cart.

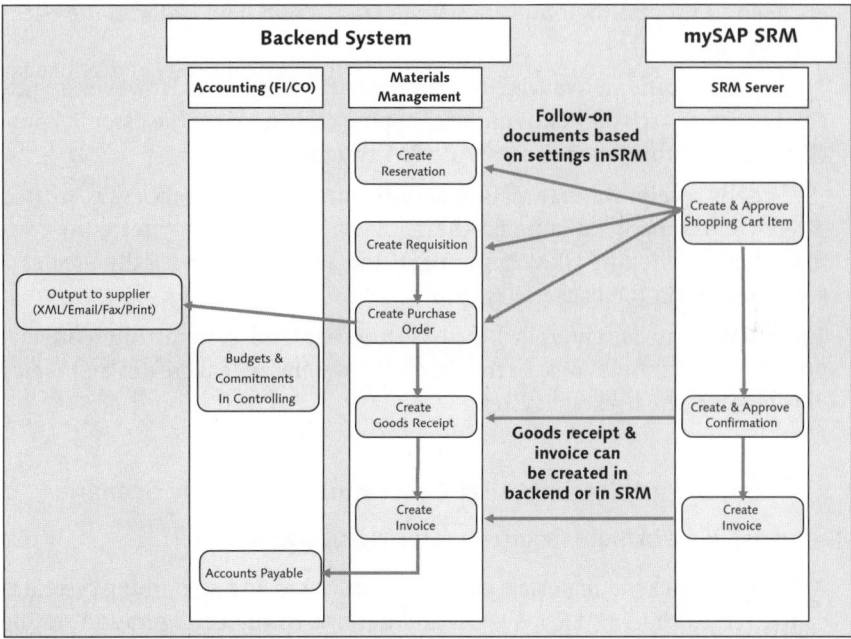

Figure 4.2 Classic Scenario

3. If the shopping cart is approved, the system creates a follow-on document in the backend system. The settings in the configuration setting *Define objects in backend system* determine the type of follow-on document. The following settings are possible for each product category:

   ▶ If stock for the material is available on the requested date in the backend system, you can specify that a reservation (material issue requisition) is created.

> ▶ Settings can be configured in such a way that the system always creates a reservation if the material belongs to a material type that is subjected to inventory management in the backend system.

- ▶ Settings can also be configured in such a way that the system never creates a reservation and always creates either a purchase requisition or purchase order.

  > ▶ Settings can be configured to always create purchase requisitions in the backend system.

  > ▶ The system can be configured to create a purchase order, if the shopping cart data is complete. If the data is not complete, the system creates a purchase requisition.

- ▶ Optionally, you can use customer-specific rules to determine the backend object by implementing BAdI BBP_TARGET_OBJTYPE.

4. If the system creates a purchase requisition in the backend system, purchasers need to process the requisition and create a purchase order in the backend system.

5. The purchase order is available only in the backend system. However, requisitioners can check the status of the shopping cart and view the essential purchase order information in the SAP SRM system, also.

6. The goods receipt for materials or service entry sheet for services is created directly in the backend system. Alternatively, users can also create the confirmations in the SAP SRM system and the system automatically creates a goods receipt in the backend system.

7. The invoice can be entered directly in the backend system. Alternatively, users can create an invoice in the SAP SRM system, which creates an invoice document in the backend system.

4.2.3   Important Settings that Determine the Classic Scenario

The following settings are required for the classic scenario:

- ▶ At least one backend materials management system and accounting system is connected to the SAP SRM system and defined in the configuration setting *Define Backend Systems.*

- ▶ Product categories from the backend procurement system are replicated and used in the SAP SRM system.

- ▶ The target system for each product category is the backend system in the configuration setting *Define Backend Systems for Product Category.* Optionally, BAdI BBP_DETERMINE_LOGSYS is implemented to determine the backend system based on shopping cart data.

▶ The extended classic scenario should not be activated in the configuration setting *Activate Extended Classic Scenario*. If the extended classic scenario is activated, then BAdI BBP_EXTLOCALPO_BADI should be implemented to enable the classic scenario based on customer-defined rules.

4.3   The Extended Classic Scenario

In an extended classic scenario, the procurement process takes place in the SAP SRM system. The purchase order is created in the SAP SRM system and a read-only copy of the purchase order is replicated to the backend system. Goods receipts and invoices can be entered either in the backend system or in the SAP SRM system.

4.3.1   Applicability of the Extended Classic Scenario

The extended classic scenario is applicable to customers who want sophisticated procurement functionalities in SAP SRM, such as the following:

▶ Purchase order response from the vendor can be captured in SAP SRM. Differences between purchase order and purchase order response, if any, can be approved by the purchaser in an interactive user interface.

▶ The full sourcing capabilities of SAP SRM are available in the extended classic scenario.

▶ Direct material procurement is enabled in the extended classic scenario only.

▶ Sophisticated workflow functionality is available in SAP SRM.

▶ Entry of confirmation is easier in SAP SRM compared to backend ERP. In SAP ERP, goods receipt for materials and service entry for services are done in two different transactions whereas in SAP SRM both goods receipts and service confirmations are done in the same transaction. In addition, SAP SRM also provides approval workflow for confirmations.

▶ Procurement card functionality is available in the extended classic and standalone scenarios only.

4.3.2   Process Flow

Figure 4.3 illustrates the extended classic scenario process flow, which is as follows:

1. An employee searches the catalogs and creates an online shopping cart for his requirements. The employee can also view the stock status, if the material used is a stock material.

2. The system triggers an approval workflow based on the workflow start conditions defined in the configuration settings. The workflow is routed to the mailbox of the approving manager, who approves or rejects the shopping cart.

3. If the shopping cart is approved, the system creates a purchase order in the SAP SRM system. If the data is incomplete, the shopping cart is moved to the sourcing cockpit for further action from the purchaser.

4. In the extended classic scenario, purchase orders can be created in the following ways:

   ▸ From a shopping cart

   ▸ From an external requirement created in the backend system and transferred to SAP SRM

   ▸ Directly in SAP SRM from the Transaction "Create purchase order"

   ▸ From the winning bid in a bidding or reverse auction process

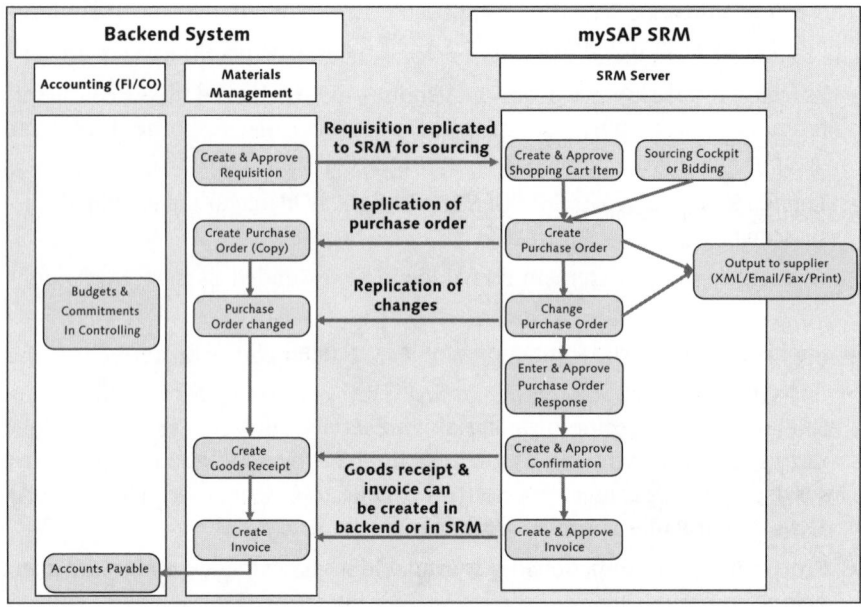

Figure 4.3 Extended Classic Scenario

5. The purchase order is created in the SAP SRM system. A copy of the purchase order is replicated to the backend system. The purchase order in SAP SRM is the leading purchase order, and any changes to the purchase order can only be made in SAP SRM. The data replicated to the backend system can be influenced by implementing BAdI BBP_ECS_PO_OUT_BADI. For example, a purchasing organization in SAP SRM can be mapped to a purchasing organization in SAP ERP using this BAdI.

6. The purchase order response from the supplier can be entered directly in SAP SRM or updated automatically via XML communication. The supplier may indicate a different delivery date or a different price in the response. The differences can be approved or rejected by the purchaser in an interactive user interface. A workflow can also be activated for purchase order response approvals.

7. The goods receipt for materials or service entry sheet for services is created directly in the backend system. Alternatively, users can also create the confirmations in the SAP SRM system and the system automatically creates a goods receipt in the backend system.

8. Invoices can be entered directly in the backend system. Alternatively, users can create invoices in the SAP SRM system, which in turn creates an invoice document in the backend system.

4.3.3 Important Settings that Determine the Extended Classic Scenario

The following settings are required for the extended classic scenario:

▸ At least one backend materials management system and accounting system is connected to the SAP SRM system and defined in the configuration setting *Define Backend Systems*.

▸ Product categories from the backend procurement system are replicated and used in the SAP SRM system.

▸ The target system for each product category is the backend system in the configuration setting *Define Backend Systems for Product Category*. Optionally, BAdI BBP_DETERMINE_LOGSYS is implemented to determine the backend system.

▸ The extended classic scenario is activated in the configuration setting *Activate Extended Classic Scenario*. Alternatively, BAdI BBP_EXTLOCALPO_BADI is implemented to control the extended classic scenario based on customer-defined rules.

▸ If the backend system is an SAP R/3 version lower than 4.6B, you must define local purchasing organizations and purchasing groups.

▸ If the backend system is an SAP R/3 version 4.6B or higher, you need to map the purchasing group used in the purchase order to the backend purchase group in one of the following ways:

  ▸ Use a backend purchasing organization and purchasing group in the shopping cart and purchase order.

  ▸ Use BAdI BBP_PGRP_FIND to determine a backend purchasing group in the shopping cart.

▶ If a local (created in SAP SRM without reference to a backend system) purchasing group and purchasing organization are used, then a valid backend purchasing group is assigned to the RFC user that created the backend purchase order. This assignment is made in the backend system using user parameter EKG in Transaction code SU01.

▶ Implement the user exit of the BAPIs BAPI_PO_CREATE1 (EXIT_SAPL2012_001 and EXIT_SAPL2012_003), and BAPI_PO_CHANGE (EXIT_SAPL2012_002 and EXIT_SAPL2012_004) to determine the purchasing group with a customer-specific logic.

4.4   The Decoupled Scenario

As mentioned earlier in this chapter, SAP SRM officially does not have a scenario called decoupled. However, as also mentioned earlier, this scenario name is loosely used to indicate the ability to use the other three scenarios in parallel. SAP recognizes that the procurement strategy for each category of purchases can be different and any procurement solution should offer flexibility during implementation to cater to all requirements. Hence, SAP SRM provides the flexibility to implement all three scenarios in parallel, based on customers' requirements.

4.4.1   Applicability of the Decoupled Scenario

Companies that wish to fully leverage the flexibility offered by SAP SRM use the decoupled scenario. For example, a company might want to use the stand-alone scenario for certain indirect materials and routine services, the classic scenario for stock materials so that inventory and planning capabilities of backend materials management system can be utilized, and the extended classic scenario for purchases where flexibility and greater collaboration with suppliers is required in purchase order responses.

4.4.2   Process Flow

Figure 4.4 illustrates the decoupled scenario process flow. The process is as follows:

1. An employee searches the catalogs and creates an online shopping cart for his requirements. The employee can also view the stock status for the material.

2. The system triggers an approval workflow based on the workflow start conditions defined in the configuration setting. The workflow is routed to the mailbox of the approving manager, who approves or rejects the shopping cart.

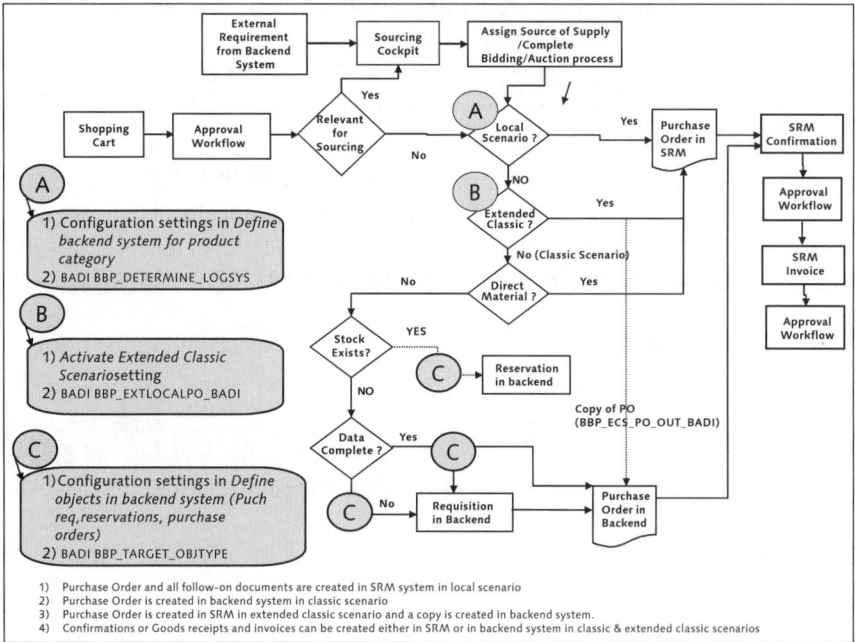

Figure 4.4 Decoupled Scenario

3. Alternatively, an external requirement from the backend system is received in the SAP SRM system.

4. The system verifies whether the product category used is a local SAP SRM product category. If the product category is a backend product category, the system verifies whether the target system defined in the configuration setting *Define backend system for product category* is a local SAP SRM system. Processing of such shopping cart items is handled in SAP SRM as a standalone scenario. On approval of such a shopping cart, the system creates a purchase order in the SAP SRM system. If the data is incomplete, the shopping cart is moved to the sourcing cockpit from where the purchaser creates the purchase order. Goods receipts or service confirmations and invoices are created in SAP SRM. Accounting documents from invoice postings are updated in the backend accounting system.

5. If the shopping cart does not belong to a standalone scenario, the system verifies whether the extended classic scenario is activated in the configuration setting *Activate extended classic scenario*. If the setting is activated, the system processes the shopping cart as described in the extended classic scenario.

6. If the extended classic scenario is not activated, the system checks whether the BAdI to control the extended classic scenario (BBP_EXTLOCALPO_BADI) is implemented. If the BAdI is implemented, then the system verifies the shopping cart data with the conditions specified in the BAdI. If the condi-

tions in the BAdI are met, then the system processes the shopping cart as described in the extended classic scenario.

7. If the extended classic scenario does not apply to the shopping cart, then the system processes the shopping cart as per the classic scenario process.

Let's now move on to learning about deployment scenarios.

4.5 Deployment Scenario Implementation Settings

For quick reference, Table 4.1 summarizes the settings that determine a deployment scenario in an implementation:

Scenario	Settings	Remarks
Standalone	▸ The product category used in the shopping cart should be local. ▸ In the configuration setting *Define backend systems for product category* OR in BAdI BBP_DETERMINE_LOGSYS, the target system should be the SAP SRM system.	If a product category is created in the SAP SRM system, then it is called local.
Classic	▸ The product category used in the shopping cart should be the backend product category. ▸ In the configuration setting *Define backend systems for product category* OR in BAdI BBP_DETERMINE_LOGSYS, the target system should be the backend system. ▸ The extended classic scenario should not be activated in the configuration setting *Activate Extended Classic Scenario*. ▸ If the extended classic scenario is activated in configuration setting *Activate Extended Classic Scenario*, then BAdI BBP_EXTLOCALPO_BADI should be implemented.	If a product category is replicated from the backend system into the SAP SRM system, then it is called the backend product category.
Extended classic	▸ The product category used in the shopping cart should be the backend. ▸ In the configuration setting *Define backend systems for product category*, the target system should be the backend system OR the target system determined in BAdI BBP_DETERMINE_LOGSYS should be the backend system.	

Table 4.1 Determination of Deployment Scenarios

Scenario	Settings	Remarks
Extended classic	▶ The extended classic scenario should be activated in the configuration setting *Activate Extended Classic Scenario*. ▶ If the extended classic scenario is not activated in the configuration setting *Activate Extended Classic Scenario*, then BAdI BBP_EXTLOCALPO_BADI should be implemented.	
Decoupled scenario	▶ BAdI BBP_EXTLOCALPO_BADI should be implemented along with the settings described for the previous scenarios.	

Table 4.1 Determination of Deployment Scenarios (Cont.)

Let's compare deployment scenarios now.

4.6 Comparison of Deployment Scenarios

A comparison of the deployment scenarios is given in Table 4.2.

Item	Classic	Extended Classic	Standalone
Indirect material procurement (requirement with account assignment)			
Shopping cart	Created in SAP SRM.	Created in SAP SRM.	Created in SAP SRM.
Shopping cart approval	Done in SAP SRM.	Done in SAP SRM.	Done in SAP SRM.
Shopping cart follow-on documents without sourcing	Purchase requisition, reservation, or purchase order in the backend system.	Purchase order in SAP SRM; purchase order copy is available in the backend system.	Purchase order in SAP SRM.
External requirements	Purchase requisition is created in the backend system and transferred to SAP SRM as a shopping cart in the sourcing cockpit.	Purchase requisition is created in the backend system and transferred to SAP SRM as a shopping cart in the sourcing cockpit.	Purchase requisition is created in the backend system and transferred to SAP SRM as a shopping cart in the sourcing cockpit.
Approval of external requirements	Only approved purchase requisitions are transferred from the backend. No approval in SAP SRM.	Only approved purchase requisitions are transferred from the backend. No approval in SAP SRM.	Only approved purchase requisitions are transferred from the backend. No approval in SAP SRM.

Table 4.2 Comparison of Deployment Scenarios

Item	Classic	Extended Classic	Standalone
Purchase order creation	Purchase order is created in the backend system from the shopping cart process or from the sourcing process.	Purchase order is created in SAP SRM from the shopping cart process, from the sourcing process, or directly from the "Create purchase order" transaction. A copy is created in the backend.	Purchase order is created in SAP SRM only.
Purchase order change	Purchase order is maintained only in the backend system.	Changes can be done only in SAP SRM.	Changes can be done only in SAP SRM.
Purchase order display	Complete document in the backend system and important data in the shopping cart follow-on documents.	Both SAP SRM and the backend system.	SAP SRM only.
Goods receipt or service entry	Backend system (can be entered as confirmation in SAP SRM also).	Backend system (can be entered as confirmation in SAP SRM also).	Confirmations are entered in SAP SRM only.
Invoice	Backend system (can be entered in SAP SRM also).	Backend system (can be entered in SAP SRM also).	Entered in SAP SRM only (accounting document is created in the backend).
Use of SUS	Use SUS with MM. (Refer to Chapter 13).	Not supported fully. Refer to SAP Note 543544.	Use SUS with SAP SRM (refer to Chapter 14).
Use of account assignment categories with special stocks in SAP ERP	Not supported (See SAP Note 586231).	Not supported (See SAP Note 586231).	Not supported (See SAP Note 586231).
Use of procurement cards	Not supported.	Supported from SAP SRM 2007. on.	Supported.

Table 4.2 Comparison of Deployment Scenarios (Cont.)

Item	Classic	Extended Classic	Standalone
Direct material procurement (requirement without account assignment i.e., order as direct material)			
Shopping cart	Created in SAP SRM with 'Order as Direct material.'	Created in SAP SRM with 'Order as Direct material.'	Not applicable.
Shopping cart follow-on documents without sourcing	Purchase order in SAP SRM; purchase order copy is available in the backend system.	Purchase order in SAP SRM; purchase order copy is available in the backend system.	Not applicable.
External require-ments	Purchase requisition is created in the back-end system and trans-ferred to SAP SRM as a shopping cart in sourcing.	Purchase requisition is created in the back-end system and trans-ferred to SAP SRM as a shopping cart in sourcing.	Not applicable.
Approval of external requirements	Only approved pur-chase requisitions are transferred from the backend. No approval in SAP SRM.	Only approved pur-chase requisitions are transferred from the backend. No approval in SAP SRM.	Not applicable.
Purchase order creation	Purchase order is cre-ated in SAP SRM. A copy is created in the backend.	Purchase order is cre-ated in SAP SRM. A copy is created in the backend.	Not applicable.
Purchase order change	Purchase order can be changed in SAP SRM only.	Purchase order can be changed in SAP SRM only.	Not applicable.
Use of SUS	Not supported fully. Refer to SAP Note 543544.	Not supported fully. Refer to SAP Note 543544.	Not applicable.

Table 4.2 Comparison of Deployment Scenarios (Cont.)

4.7   Summary

In this chapter, you learned that SAP SRM can be flexibly integrated with back-end ERP systems. Customers can choose the level of integration depending on their organization's requirements. This flexibility ensures that customers are not left with rigid rules in their procurement processes and they can choose the processes based on the requirements of each product category.

In Chapter 5, we will discuss scenarios in operational procurement and implementation of self-service procurement. Also, the configuration settings mentioned in this chapter are explained in detail in Chapter 5.

SAP SRM operational procurement enables companies to automate the requisition-to-pay process, and self-service procurement empowers all employees to procure their routine requirements with very little or no training while companies retain control on spend. In this chapter, you will learn about different scenarios in operational procurement and the implementation of self-service procurement.

5 Operational Procurement

A *requisition-to-pay cycle* — the requisition of goods, placement of a purchase order, order follow-up, receipt of goods ordered, receipt of invoice from suppliers, and payment to suppliers — is often called the *operational procurement cycle*. Toward the end of last millennium, many Business-to-Business (B2B) applications captured the imagination of large organizations by enabling employee self-service buying for indirect materials. Large enterprise resource planning (ERP) software vendors, like SAP, turned the heat on these B2B applications by providing a full suite of operational procurement tools to support all categories of spend, that is, direct materials, indirect materials, and services. SAP Supplier Relationship Management (SAP SRM) also supports integration with any backend ERP system for procurement of plan-driven requirements. Further, invoice management systems enable companies to manage exceptions and errors in invoices.

In this chapter, we will examine the various processes supported by SAP SRM in operational procurement, and the implementation of self-service procurement.

> **Note**
>
> Other operational procurement processes are discussed in later chapters. For example, plan-driven procurement is discussed in Chapter 6, invoice management and procurement cards are discussed in Chapter 7, and services procurement is discussed in Chapter 11.

5.1 Scenarios in Operational Procurement

SAP SRM is an integrated enterprise procurement platform that enables procurement of indirect materials, direct materials, and services. Requirements may be created manually in SAP SRM or generated automatically in a planning system. In addition, service requirements generated in plant maintenance or project systems applications in a backend ERP system can be routed to SAP SRM for determining sources of supply. The following scenarios are supported in SAP SRM operational procurement:

- **Self-service procurement**
  Self-service procurement enables all employees in an organization to requisition the goods and services they need to do their routine jobs with an easy-to-use browser-based user interface. Self-service procurement is discussed in detail in this chapter.

- **Service procurement**
  The *service procurement* scenario covers a wide range of services from routine housekeeping services to complex project services. By enabling services that are otherwise considered difficult and complex to be managed using information systems, SAP SRM helps companies to manage and control the entire procurement spend. Service procurement is described in more detail in Chapter 11.

- **Plan-driven procurement**
  Plan-driven procurement enables companies to transfer procurement demands generated from the operational backend systems, that is, planning, maintenance, and project systems, to SAP SRM for an efficient and streamlined centralized sourcing and procurement process. Plan-driven procurement is discussed in more detail in Chapter 6.

- **Invoice Management System (IMS)**
  IMS is an invoice management tool that enables companies to process supplier invoices and manage exceptions. IMS provides a collaborative platform with both internal employees and suppliers to process any discrepancies between invoices, thus addressing a major concern of both purchasers and suppliers. IMS is discussed in more detail in Chapter 7.

- **Procurement cards**
  Procurement cards are a payment method for low-value purchases in the self-service procurement scenario that enables automation of the invoicing and payment process, thus reducing the load on the invoicing department. Procurement cards have the potential to save 50%-60% on transaction costs for low-value purchases. The procurement cards process is discussed in more detail in Chapter 7.

5.2   An Introduction to Self-Service Procurement

As its name suggests, self-service procurement enables employees to create and manage their own procurement requisitions with easy-to-use catalogs in a browser-based user interface. This process lets a large number of employees directly procure goods and services using pre-negotiated contracts, while reducing the administrative burden on the purchasing department. It is easy to visualise the benefits of the self-service procurement process, including the following:

- Streamlines and standardizes the procurement process throughout the organization.

- Ensures contract compliance and reduces maverick buying.

- Encourages employees to use the system for all procurement requirements and bring all procurement spend online because of its easy-to-use and intuitive user interface.

- Reduces administrative burden on professional purchasers and frees up their time for more value-added activities, like strategic supplier development and sourcing. While traditional purchasers spend a lot of time 'chasing' supplies, modern purchasers are involved in making procurement a strategic function in the organization.

- Reduces overall procurement lead time by eliminating non-value-adding activities and increasing the speed of procurement.

We will now examine a case study of a software services company, which describes a real-life scenario where self-service procurement helped organizations improve procurement efficiency.

5.2.1 Case Study: Eprocurement at a Global Software Services Company

Jupiter Software Services (JSS) is a USD 2 billion software services company, providing software services to global fortune 500 customers. JSS has about 20,000 employees and is one of the fastest-growing software companies traded on NASDAQ. JSS operates from 56 countries with 90 offices globally. The company has plans to increase the number of employees to 75,000 over next three years. John, the Chief Procurement Officer (CPO), was asked to submit his plans to support the company's ambitious growth plans.

Currently, the procurement department regularly receives requests from employees to procure personal computers, laptops, computer accessories, software, and other office supplies necessary to perform their responsibilities, and each office has a buyer who ensures that employees' procurement requests are serviced promptly. John has identified the following procurement-related challenges that need to be addressed:

- Standardize the products offered to employees across offices.

- Build transparency into the procurement process and ensure compliance to the Sarbanes-Oxley (SOX) act.

- Negotiate central global contracts and ensure contract compliance.
- Standardize the procurement process.
- Reduce the burden of routine and numerous procurement transactions placed on the purchasing staff.

John recently attended a procurement conference and found that the challenges identified by him are not unique to his organization, and he was impressed with the capabilities of e-procurement software to meet these challenges. He learned that by using this software, employees can be empowered to buy their regular requirements without involvement of the purchasing department, thus reducing the burden on the procurement staff. Simultaneously, the procurement department can retain control over procurement by ensuring that online catalogs contain only prenegotiated items. The scalability of eprocurement software also lets the procurement department support the growth plans of the organization. John discussed his plans to implement eprocurement software with senior management and his request was approved.

After careful evaluation of eprocurement offerings, JSS selected SAP SRM for the flexibility it offers and the possibility of enhancing the use of the system for other procurement requirements, too. JSS is already familiar with SAP products as they currently use an SAP ERP solution. In the first phase of the implementation, it has been decided to implement a catalog-based self-service procurement scenario within the next three months.

The scope of the implementation is as follows:

- The software will enable publishing of supplier catalogs on an Internet portal.
- The software will also enable publishing of catalogs directly from prenegotiated contracts.
- The software will enable employees to search and order the required products on the portal.
- When the product is received, a confirmation will be entered by the respective employee.
- Users will be able to use the system with little or no training.
- The system will be integrated with the backend ERP system for inventory and financials.

The scope in terms of SAP SRM scenarios is as follows:

- Implementation of self-service procurement
- Implementation of catalog content management using SRM-MDM Catalog
- Implementation of contract management

In this chapter, you will learn about the implementation of self-service procurement. Implementation of catalog content management is explained in Chapter 9 and contract management in Chapter 12.

Now that we have outlined how customers can use self-service procurement to improve procurement efficiency, let us take a closer look at the actual self-service procurement process.

5.2.2 SAP SRM Self-Service Procurement — Overview of Functionalities

SAP SRM provides end users with an easy-to-use wizard interface to guide them through requisitioning and the automatic ordering process. This role-based intuitive interface enables even novice employees to do their tasks easily and with little or no training. Figure 5.1 illustrates a typical SAP SRM self-service procurement process, which includes the following general steps:

1. An employee searches the catalogs and creates an online shopping cart for his requirements. A wizard-based interface guides the employee through this process. Catalogs provide complete information on the goods and services available, thus enabling greater purchasing accuracy. The employee can check the status of his shopping cart at any time.

2. The system triggers a workflow based on the data in the shopping cart and criteria for approval defined in the workflow configuration. The workflow is routed to the mailbox of the approving manager, who receives the workflow request and verifies the shopping cart. Before approving the shopping cart, the manager can also display the budget details. The manager enters his remarks in an approval note and approves or rejects the shopping cart. What happens next depends on the status of the shopping cart:

   ▶ A rejected shopping cart is sent back to the requesting employee.

   ▶ If the information in the shopping cart is incomplete, it is routed to the professional purchaser's work area. The professional purchaser provides the missing information and assigns a source of supply. A purchase order is created and transmitted to the supplier. The purchaser can also indicate that a purchase order response from the supplier is required for the purchase order.

3. If the information in the shopping cart is complete, the system creates a purchase order and transmits the order to the supplier. A purchase order is created either in SAP SRM or in the backend system depending on the deployment scenario selected for the product category in the customizing settings. Depending on the deployment scenario, described in Chapter 4, the system can also create other documents, such as purchase requisitions or reservations, in the backend system.

4. The purchase order response from the supplier, acknowledging the receipt of the purchase order and confirming the terms and conditions, can be entered by the purchaser. If there is a discrepancy between the purchase order and the purchase order response, the discrepancy can be approved or rejected by the purchaser. For example, the supplier might indicate that ordered products will be supplied two days later than the requested delivery date in the purchase order response. The purchaser may accept the new delivery date, or insist on getting the delivery as per the purchase order. If the purchaser approves the date suggested by the supplier, the system updates the purchase order with the new delivery date. Purchase order response functionality is not available in classic deployment.

5. The goods receipt or services confirmation is created either by the requesting employee or by a stores officer. Goods receipt confirmation can also be submitted by the supplier via XML communication using supplier self-services (SUS) in a standalone deployment. If the confirmation is not entered by the employee, a workflow is triggered for the employee's confirmation of receipt of goods and services.

6. An employee or a central accountant records the supplier's invoice in the system. The invoice can also be submitted by the supplier via XML communication using SUS in a standalone deployment. Based on the settings, the employee may have to approve the invoice, if the invoice is recorded by an accountant or supplier. Once the invoice is approved, it is sent to the backend financial system where payment takes place.

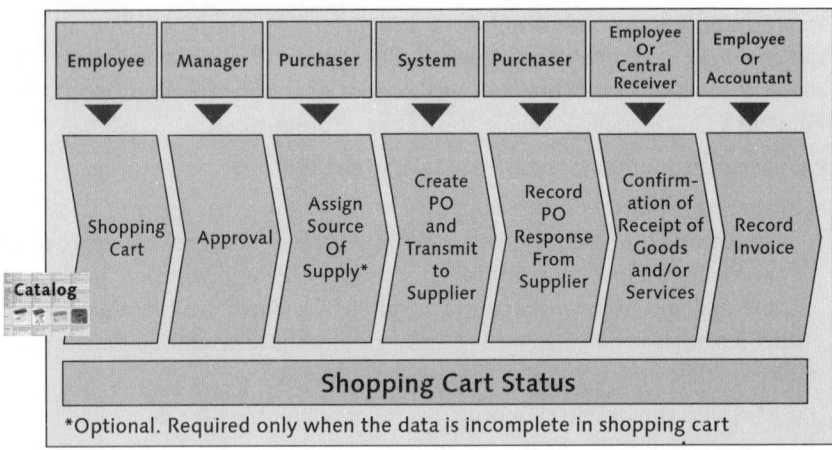

Figure 5.1 Self-Service Procurement

Additional functionalities, like account assignment validations, budget check, commitment update in the backend costing system, stock availability check from the backend inventory system, etc., are available depending on the product category and deployment scenario selected.

Data entry in each document is minimized to a great extent to make the complete process user friendly, as follows:

▸ In the shopping cart, most of the data is selected from the catalog and user settings.

▸ In a purchase order, most of the data is taken from the shopping cart, contracts, supplier master, and configuration settings.

▸ In a confirmation, most of the data is taken from the purchase order and only the received quantity and supplier's reference need to be entered manually. If the data is received via XML from the supplier, manual data entry is completely eliminated.

▸ In an invoice, most of the data is taken from the purchase order and confirmation. Only the invoiced quantity and supplier's reference need to be entered manually. If the data is received via XML from the supplier, manual data entry is completely eliminated.

We will now discuss in detail the configuration of the SAP SRM self-service procurement scenario.

5.3   Configuration of Self-Service Procurement

The required configuration settings to implement catalog-based self-service procurement at our case study company, JSS, are described in detail in this section, including menu paths to access the settings and transportability of the settings, if applicable. Note that unless otherwise stated, the settings should be configured in the Enterprise Buyer Professional client.

5.3.1   System Landscape

Refer to the system landscape described in Section 3.2.3 in Chapter 3.

5.3.2   Basic Settings for Enterprise Buyer Professional

All of the basic settings required for self-service procurement scenario should be configured, as follows:

▸ Basic technical settings to integrate with the backend systems

▸ Organizational plan setup

▸ Master data settings for suppliers, product categories, and products

▸ Other common technical settings

Detailed configuration of these settings is described in Sections 3.4, 3.5, 3.6, 3.7, and 3.8 in Chapter 3.

5.3.3 Business Workflow Setup

Maintain the settings as described in Chapter 8.

5.3.4 Catalog Content Management Setup

Maintain the settings as described in Chapter 9.

5.3.5 Define the Backend System for the Product Category

This setting determines whether the deployment scenario is standalone or classic/extended classic. For each product category you need to specify the system in which the purchasing documents are created when a shopping cart item is ordered. To do so, follow the menu path **SPRO • SAP Implementation Guide • Supplier Relationship Management • SRM Server • Technical Basic settings • Define backend system for product category**.

Figure 5.2 shows a screenshot of sample settings. What information you need to enter in the columns in this configuration setting is described in the following list:

▶ **Category ID**: Enter the product category or select from search help. The wild card character '*' can also be used.

Change View "Determination of Target System using Product Categories":

| New Entries | | | |

Determination of Target System using Product Categories			
Category ID	SourceSyst	Tgt system	
*	QW8CLNT250	QW8CLNT250	
*	QZBCLNT100	QZBCLNT100	
001	QPTCLNT100	QPTCLNT100	
00105		E6UCLNT300	
00105	E6UCLNT300	E6UCLNT300	
002	QPTCLNT100	QPTCLNT100	
LOC02	E6UCLNT300	E6UCLNT300	
LOCAL03	E6UCLNT300	E6UCLNT300	
LOCE6UCAT	E6UCLNT300	E6UCLNT300	
QPT01	QPTCLNT100	QPTCLNT100	
QPT02	QPTCLNT100	QPTCLNT100	
QPT06	QPTCLNT100	E6UCLNT300	
QPT07	QPTCLNT100	E6UCLNT300	
QPT08	QPTCLNT100	E6UCLNT300	
QPT09	QPTCLNT100	E6UCLNT300	

Figure 5.2 Define Backend Systems for Product Category

▶ **SourceSyst**: Enter the logical system to which the product category belongs. For example, if the product category is replicated from a backend ERP system, the logical system of this backend ERP system should be entered here.

If the product category is created within the SAP SRM system, then the logical system of the SAP SRM system is entered here.

▸ **Tgt system**: Enter the logical system in which the purchasing documents should be created. Enter the SAP SRM system's logical system ID here if you want to use a local standalone deployment. Enter the backend system's logical system ID if you want to use classic or extended classic deployment.

If you want to determine the target system based on customer-specific logic instead of the settings defined here, implement BAdI BBP_DETERMINE_LOGSYS.

Transportability of Settings

The settings are transportable. However, system names may have to be changed in the new system. Additional product categories in the new system, if any, should be configured.

5.3.6 Define Objects in the Backend System

This setting is relevant in the classic scenario to determine the follow-on document to be created in the backend system for a shopping cart item. You can define the backend document (purchase requisition, purchase order, or reservation) to be created for each purchasing group and product category combination. The number ranges for the backend documents are determined from the setting *Define number ranges for shopping carts*. If you want to determine the backend document based on customer-specific logic instead of the settings defined here, implement BAdI BBP_TARGET_OBJTYPE.

To define objects in the backend system, follow menu path **SPRO · SAP Implementation Guide · Supplier Relationship Management · SRM Server · Cross-Application Basic Settings · Define Objects in Backend System (Purch. Reqs, Reservations, Purch.Orders)**. Figure 5.3 shows a screenshot of sample settings. The columns in this customizing setting and the information you need to enter into them are described in the following list :

▸ **Purch.Grp**: Enter the purchasing group. The wild card character '*' can be used to represent all purchasing groups.

▸ **Category ID**: Enter the product category. The wild card character '*' can be used to represent all product categories. For example, 'AP*' represents all categories of names beginning with 'AP.'

▸ **SourceSyst**: Enter the logical system of the product category.

▸ **Int.Proc**: Determines whether a reservation or a procurement document should be created:

- Select **Always reservation for mat.types subject to inventory mgmt** if you want the system to always create reservations for stock materials. This is preferred when an organization wants to use material planning in the backend system for direct materials.
- Select **Reservn generated if stock available, otherwise ext.proc.** if you want the system to determine the creation of a reservation based on stock availability. If stock is available, a reservation is created. If stock is not available, a procurement document is created based on the settings in the corresponding field in the **Ext.Proc** column.
- Select **Always external procurement** if you do not want the system to create reservations. A procurement document is created based on the settings in the corresponding field in the **Ext.Proc** column.

- **Ext.Proc**: Determines whether a purchase requisition or purchase order should be created:
  - Select **Always purchase requisition** if you want to use the procurement process defined in the backend materials management. This is preferred when you use the SAP SRM system only for requisitioners and the purchasing department uses the backend system.
  - Select **Purchase order if item data complete, otherwise purch.req.** if you want the system to create a purchase order when all required data is available in a shopping cart item. If the data is incomplete, the system creates a purchase requisition in the backend system.

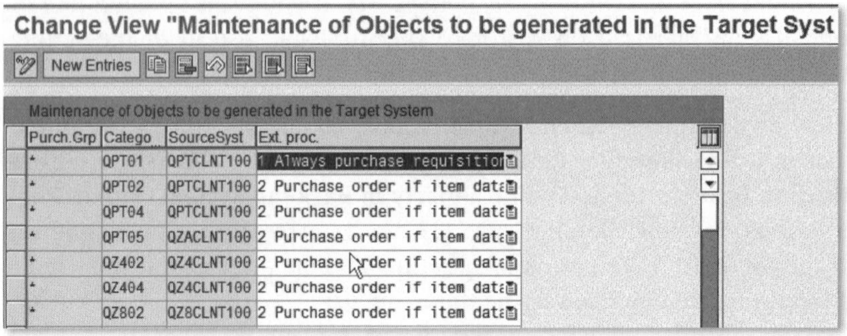
Change View "Maintenance of Objects to be generated in the Target Syst
New Entries
Maintenance of Objects to be generated in the Target System
Purch.Grp Catego SourceSyst Ext. proc.
* QPT01 QPTCLNT100 1 Always purchase requisitio
* QPT02 QPTCLNT100 2 Purchase order if item data
* QPT04 QPTCLNT100 2 Purchase order if item data
* QPT05 QZACLNT100 2 Purchase order if item data
* QZ402 QZ4CLNT100 2 Purchase order if item data
* QZ404 QZ4CLNT100 2 Purchase order if item data
* QZ802 QZ8CLNT100 2 Purchase order if item data

Figure 5.3 Define Objects in the Backend System

Transportability of the Settings

These settings can be transported, but remember that data might be different in the target system. For example, the business partner number for the purchasing group might be different in different systems.

5.3.7 Define External Web Services

In this setting you define the product catalogs and supplier directories, and vendor lists, etc. to be used in self-service procurement, using the menu path **SPRO • SAP Implementation Guide • Supplier Relationship Management • SRM Server • Master Data • Define External Web Services (Catalogs, Vendor Lists etc)**. The data given here is catalog-specific. Contact catalog provider(s) for details if you are connecting to external catalogs, also.

Figure 5.4 shows a sample screenshot of the screen **Web-Services:ID and Names** for the configuration of external Web services basic settings, which include the following:

- **New Entries**: Click on this button to create a new product catalog.
- **Web Service ID**: Enter the ID of the new catalog.

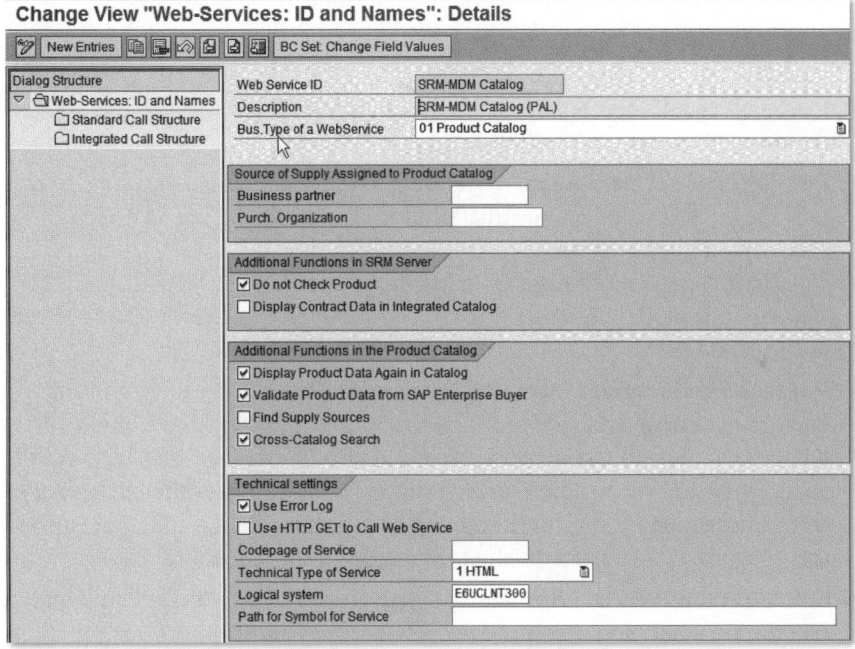

Figure 5.4 Define External Web Services

- **Description**: Enter an appropriate description to describe the catalog.
- **Bus. Type of a WebService**: This is a very important setting and determines the additional fields that are required to be customized. Select **Product Catalog** from the dropdown list to identify the new Web service as a product catalog.

- **Business Partner**: If the catalog belongs to one supplier, then the business partner number of the supplier can be entered here. If there is no business partner assigned to a catalog item, the system automatically assigns the business partner specified here. Keep it blank if the catalog items are supplied by multiple suppliers.

- **Do not Check Product:** If this flag is activated, the existence of products in the SAP SRM is not checked. In this case, there is no need to maintain or replicate products in SAP SRM. Activate the flag only when you do not want to maintain a product master and instead will completely rely on supplier catalogs. You can also activate this flag when you create a catalog with backend system product data and do not want to replicate the product data into SAP SRM in a classic scenario. In this case, you have to ensure that shopping carts are created only from catalogs as products are not checked in SAP SRM but chekked in the follow-on document created in the backend system. If you have a product master, it is recommended to not activate this flag.

- **Display Contract Data in Integrated Catalog**: If this flag is activated, contract data is displayed within the integrated catalog. This can only be activated when you define an integrated catalog (i.e., display the catalog data within the shopping cart window).

- **Display Product Data Again in Catalog**: Activate this flag if you want to display the detailed product information from the catalog in the SAP SRM shopping cart, too. This feature depends on the catalog and some catalogs do not support this. A prerequisite is mapping of the 'Global Id' and the NEW_ ITEM-EXT_PRODUCT_ID field in the Open Catalog Interface (OCI) settings in the catalog setup.

- **Validate Product Data from SAP Enterprise Buyer**: Activate this flag if you want to enable updating of product data in the shopping cart from the catalog. For example, if the shopping cart is created from a template, the system checks whether the product price is still valid and updates the changed data from the catalog item in the shopping cart. Some catalogs may not support this functionality. A prerequisite is mapping of the 'Global Id' in OCI.

- **Cross-Catalog Search**: Activate this flag if you want to do simultaneous searches in multiple catalogs. Some catalogs may not support this functionality.

- **Use Error Log**: It is recommended to activate this flag to maintain a log of all technical and business errors encountered during the transfer of data from the catalog to the shopping cart. This log can be displayed using Transaction SLG1 for object BBP_OCI.

- **Use HTTP GET to Call Web Service**: Activate this flag when you want to use the HTTP method GET to be used to call an external catalog. The recommended HTTP method is POST because it is more secure than GET, and you should not activate this flag if you want to use POST.

▶ **Logical system**: Specify the logical system of the Web service. If you are using SAP content integrator, then this is required to map product data.

To save your work, click on the save icon or press the <CTRL+S> key combination. To define a call structure, select either **Standard Call Structure** or **Integrated Call Structure** in the screen's **Dialog Structure** in the left pane. If an integrated call structure is defined for the catalog, the catalog is displayed in the same window as that of the shopping cart. In a standard call structure, the catalog is displayed in a new window. The call structures contain the URL for the catalog, logon information, and other required parameters to call the catalog from the shopping cart.

In Table 5.1, the necessary entries for SRM-MDM Catalog and SAP CCM catalog are shown. Please note that the **Remarks** column is not part of the setting but is there to provide you with additional information. Figure 5.5, Figure 5.6, and Figure 5.7 represent sample screen shots for an SRM-MDM Catalog, a CCM catalog, and an external catalog call structure settings, respectively.

Name	Content	Type	Remarks
	http://<HTTP_server>:<port> /sap/bc/bsp/ccm/srm_ cse/main.do http://<J2EE_server>:<J2EE_ port> /SRM-MDM/SRM_MDM	0 (URL)	Maintain the URL for catalog search. Sample URLs for CCM and MDM are given here.
CATALOGID	MASTER	2 (Fixed)	CCM
SAP-CLIENT	<Client in which search engine runs>	2	CCM
SAP-LANGUAGE	SY-LANGU	1 (SAP field)	CCM
locale	<Language in which you published the catalog>	2	CCM
ccm-user	<CCM user>	2	CCM
ccm-password	<CCM password>	2	CCM
username	<MDM user id>	2	For MDM
password	<MDM password>	2	For MDM
server	<MDM Server>	2	For MDM
catalog	<MDM catalog repository name>	2	For MDM
port	<port assigned to catalog repository in MDM console>	2	For MDM

Table 5.1 Configuration Entries for Catalog Call Structure

Name	Content	Type	Remarks
uilanguage	SY-LANGU	1	User interface language
datalanguage	SY_LANGU	1	Data language. You can also specify language code directly as fixed value (e.g., EN).
mask	<mask name>	2	Optional. For MDM.
namedsearch	<named search name>	2	Optional. For MDM.
sap-locale	<Language of catalog>	2	For MDM
HOOK_URL		4 (return URL)	Keep the value blank. All catalogs.
~OKCode	ADDI	2	For all. Optional from SAP SRM 5.0 on.
~target	_top	2	For all. Optional from SAP SRM 5.0 on.
~caller	CTLG	2	For all. Optional from SAP SRM 5.0 on.
returntarget	_parent		For external catalogs.

Table 5.1 Configuration Entries for Catalog Call Structure (Cont.)

Recommendation

It is recommended to use an SRM-MDM Catalog in all new implementations and upgrades.

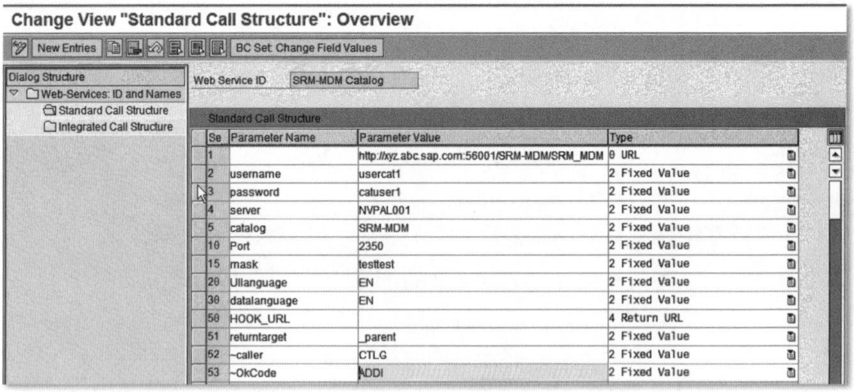

Figure 5.5 Standard Call Structure for SRM-MDM Catalog

Change View "Integrated Call Structure": Overview

New Entries | BC Set: Change Field Values

Dialog Structure
▽ ☐ Web-Services: ID and Names
 ☐ Standard Call Structure
 ☐ Integrated Call Structure

Web Service ID   GSC_AUSTRIA_EINKAUF

Integrated Call Structure

Se	Parameter Name	Parameter Value		Type	
10		http://xyz.wdf.sap.com:50017/sap/bc/bsp/ccm/srm_cse/main.do		0 URL	▲
20	SAP-CLIENT	200		2 Fixed Value	▼
30	CATALOGID	GSC_AUSTRIA_EINKAUF		2 Fixed Value	
40	SAP-LANGUAGE	SY-LANGU		1 SAP Field	
50	locale	EN		2 Fixed Value	
60	ccm-user	catuser7		2 Fixed Value	
70	ccm-password	usercat7		2 Fixed Value	
80	HOOK_URL			4 Return URL	
90	~OKCode	ADDI		2 Fixed Value	
100	~target	_top		2 Fixed Value	
110	~caller	CTLG		2 Fixed Value	

Figure 5.6 Integrated Call Structure for CCM Catalog

Change View "Standard Call Structure": Overview

New Entries | BC Set: Change Field Values

Dialog Structure
▽ ☐ Web-Services: ID and Na
 ☐ Standard Call Struct.
 ☐ Integrated Call Struct

Web Service ID   DELL

Standard Call Structure

Se	Parameter Name	Parameter Value	Type	
0		https://b2bpreview.us.dell.com/invoke/B2BDirect.Entry/processDocument	0 URL	▲
10	user_id	abcimn	2 Fixed Value	▼
20	password	xyz123	2 Fixed Value	
30	operation_type	create	2 Fixed Value	
40	b2bposturl	test	4 Return URL	
190	HOOK_URL		4 Return URL	
200	~target	_top	2 Fixed Value	
210	~caller	CTLG	2 Fixed Value	
220	~OKCode	ADDI	2 Fixed Value	

Figure 5.7 Sample Call Structure Settings for External Punchout Catalog

Assign External Web Service to Organizational Plan

Using Transaction PPOMA_BBP, assign an external Web service ID to the organizational plan attribute **CAT** at the appropriate organizational unit level or at the position level. Figure 5.8 shows a sample screenshot for the assignment. If you want to make a catalog Web service available to all users in a company, assign the Web service at the company node level. If you want to restrict access to a specific department or to a specific set of users, assign the Web service only to the department or set of users in question.

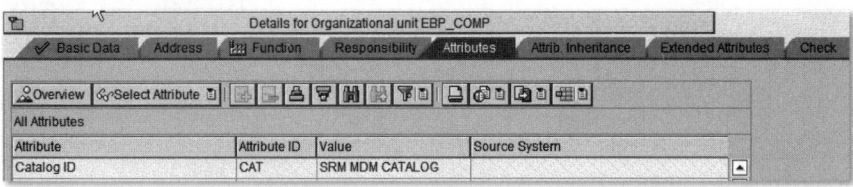

Details for Organizational unit EBP_COMP

Basic Data | Address | Function | Responsibility | Attributes | Attrib. Inheritance | Extended Attributes | Check

Overview | Select Attribute

All Attributes

Attribute	Attribute ID	Value	Source System
Catalog ID	CAT	SRM MDM CATALOG	

Figure 5.8 Assigning External Web Service to Organizational Plan

Transportability of Settings

These settings are transportable to other systems. However, the URLs and Business Partner number values may need to be changed after transportation according to new system settings.

5.3.8 Activate the Extended Classic Scenario

If you want to use the extended classic scenario in your implementation, activate the **Extended Classic Scenario Active** option in this configuration setting by following the menu path **SPRO · SAP Implementation Guide · Supplier Relationship Management · SRM Server · Cross-Application Basic Settings · Activate Extended Classic Scenario**. Figure 5.9 shows the screenshot for activating the extended classic scenario.

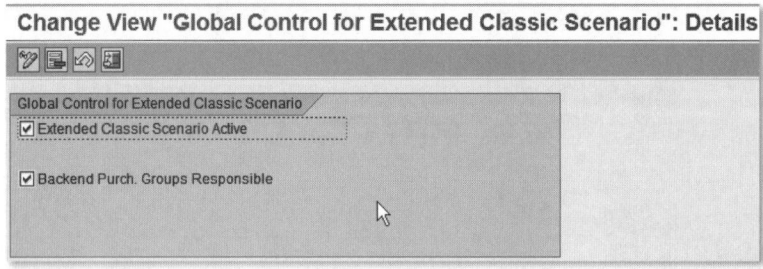

Figure 5.9 Activate the Extended Classic Scenario

When a shopping cart or purchase order is created in the extended classic scenario, the system determines a local purchasing group and purchasing organization. However, during transfer of a purchase order to the backend, the system needs a backend purchasing group. The following options are available:

- ▶ In SAP SRM 2007, activate the indicator for **Backend Purch.Groups Responsible**. However, this option is not available for SAP SRM 5.0 and lower versions.
- ▶ Use the backend purchasing group and purchasing organization in SAP SRM using BAdI BBP_PGRP_FIND.
- ▶ Set the purchasing group in the user exit in BAPIs BAPI_PO_CREATE1 (EXIT_SAPL2012_001 and EXIT_SAPL2012_003) and BAPI_PO_CHANGE (EXIT_SAPL2012_002 and EXIT_SAPL2012_004).
- ▶ Maintain a purchasing group for parameter EKG in the backend RFC user parameters in Transaction SU01. The purchasing organization is determined based on the plant.

If you want to use the extended classic scenario in general but use the classic scenario for a few product categories, then activate the extended classic scenario in this setting. Then, implement BAdI BBP_EXTLOCALPO_BADI to use the classic scenario for the few categories.

5.3.9 Define Number Ranges for Shopping Carts and Follow-On Documents

In this setting, the number ranges for both shopping carts and follow-on purchasing documents are defined. The follow-on purchasing documents are as follows:

▶ Local purchase orders (if you create purchase orders in SAP SRM from shopping carts)

▶ Backend purchase requisitions (classic scenario)

▶ Backend purchase orders (classic scenario)

▶ Backend reservations (classic scenario)

To set up number ranges for shopping carts, follow the menu path **SPRO • SAP Implementation Guide • Supplier Relationship Management • SRM Server • Cross-Application Basic Settings • Number Ranges • SRM Server Number Ranges • Define Number Ranges for Shopping Carts and Follow-on documents** or use Transaction code BBNU and then perform the following procedure:

1. Click on the **Change Intervals** button.

2. Click on the **Insert Interval** button.

3. The different columns in the screen that displays, as shown in Figure 5.10, and the information you can define, are as follows:

▶ **No**: Enter a number range number as follows:

   ▷ **01**:Used for shopping carts

   ▷ **LO**: Used for local purchase orders

   ▷ **PO**: Used for backend purchase orders

   ▷ **RQ**: Used for backend purchase requisitions

   ▷ **RS**: Used for backend reservations

▶ **From Number**: Enter the starting number of the number range.

▶ **To Number**: Enter the ending number of the number range.

▶ **Ext**: Not activating this checkbox indicates that the number range is internal.

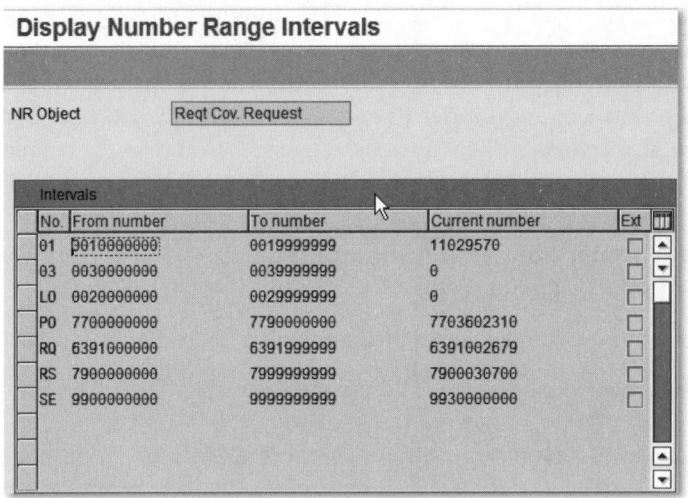

Display Number Range Intervals

NR Object   Reqt Cov. Request

Intervals

No.	From number	To number	Current number	Ext	
01	0010000000	0019999999	11029570	☐	▲
03	0030000000	0039999999	0	☐	▼
LO	0020000000	0029999999	0	☐	
PO	7700000000	7790000000	7703602310	☐	
RQ	6391000000	6391999999	6391002679	☐	
RS	7900000000	7999999999	7900030700	☐	
SE	9900000000	9999999999	9930000000	☐	

Figure 5.10 Number Ranges for Shopping Carts

Note the following:

▸ All of the number ranges should be internal number ranges (an internal range represents a system-generated number range).

▸ If multiple backend systems are connected, then define additional number ranges for backend purchasing documents as required. In this case, additional settings should be maintained in the setting *Define Number Ranges per Backend System for Follow-on Documents*.

▸ All number ranges defined here should be assigned to transaction types in the setting *Define Transaction Types*.

▸ Number ranges for backend system documents should also be defined in corresponding backend system as external number ranges.

▸ You can use BAdI BBP_BS_GROUP_BE (or BBP_SC_TRANSFER_BE) to define customer-specific logic for number ranges for backend documents.

Transportability

It is possible to transport number ranges. However, it is not recommended as it can lead to inconsistency in the target system. Make sure to read the warning message that appears while saving the number ranges for more details.

5.3.10 Define Number Ranges per Backend System for Follow-On Documents

If multiple backend systems are connected to the SAP SRM system, then the number ranges defined in the customizing setting *Defining number ranges for*

Shopping Carts and Follow-on Documents should be assigned to each backend system using the menu path **SPRO • SAP Implementation Guide • Supplier Relationship Management • SRM Server • Cross-Application Basic Settings • Number Ranges • SRM Server Number Ranges • Define Number Ranges per backend system for follow-on documents**. Figure 5.11 shows a sample screenshot for the settings. The settings are as follows:

▸ **New Entries**: Click on this button to define a number range.

▸ **LogSystem**: Logical system of the backend system.

▸ **Number Range POs**: Corresponding number range for backend purchase orders.

▸ **No. Range PReqs**: Corresponding number range for backend purchase requisitions.

▸ **No. Range Reservations**: Corresponding number range for backend reservations.

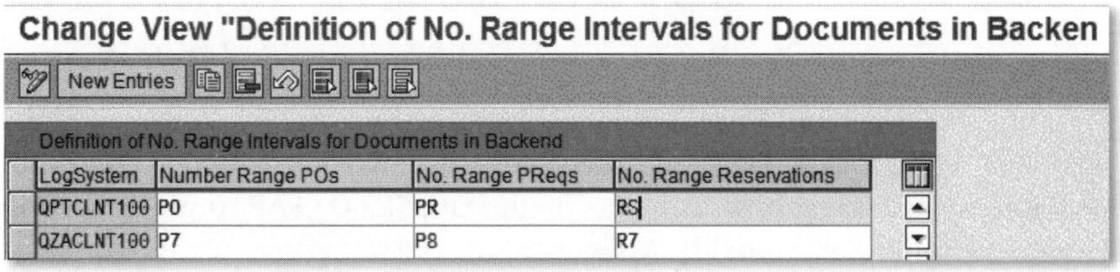

Change View "Definition of No. Range Intervals for Documents in Backen

New Entries						

Definition of No. Range Intervals for Documents in Backend

LogSystem	Number Range POs	No. Range PReqs	No. Range Reservations	
QPTCLNT100	PO	PR	RS	
QZACLNT100	P7	P8	R7	

Figure 5.11 Define Number Ranges per Backend System

5.3.11 Define Number Ranges for Local Purchase Orders

In this setting, you define number ranges if you want to create purchase orders in SAP SRM from the "Create/Process Purchase Order" transaction. To do so, follow the menu path **SPRO • SAP Implementation Guide • Supplier Relationship Management • SRM Server • Cross-Application Basic Settings • Number Ranges • SRM Server Number Ranges • Define Number Ranges for Local Purchase Orders**, or use Transaction code BBP_NUM_PO and then follow these steps, using Figure 5.12 for reference:

1. Define internal number ranges and external number ranges as required. If you wish to differentiate between different types of purchase orders in the organization, you should set up different number ranges.

2. All number ranges defined in this screen should be assigned to purchase order transaction types in the setting *Define Transaction Types*.

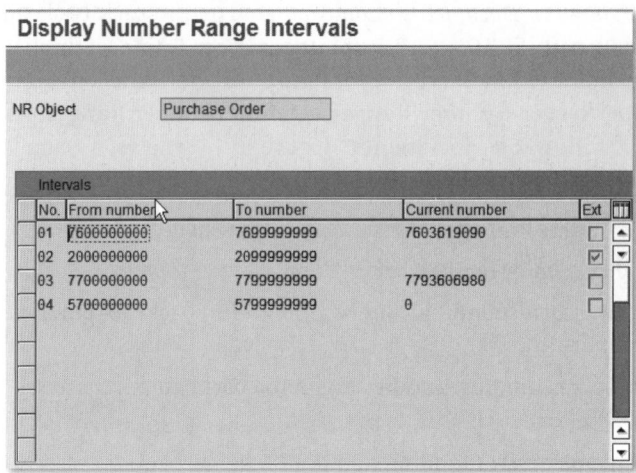

Figure 5.12 Maintain Number Ranges for Local Purchase Order

5.3.12 Define Number Ranges for Local Purchase Order Response

The purchase order response is used to capture the acknowledgement of the vendor on receipt of a purchase order and you define the number ranges for the purchase order response using the menu path **SPRO • SAP Implementation Guide • Supplier Relationship Management • SRM Server • Cross-Application Basic Settings • Number Ranges • SRM Server Number Ranges • Define Number Ranges for Local Purchase Order Response** or Transaction code BBP_NUM_PCO. Figure 5.13 shows a screenshot with sample settings, which you should configure as follows:

1. Define an internal number range and external number range as required.
2. The number ranges defined here should be assigned to the purchase order response transaction type in the setting *Define Transaction Types*.

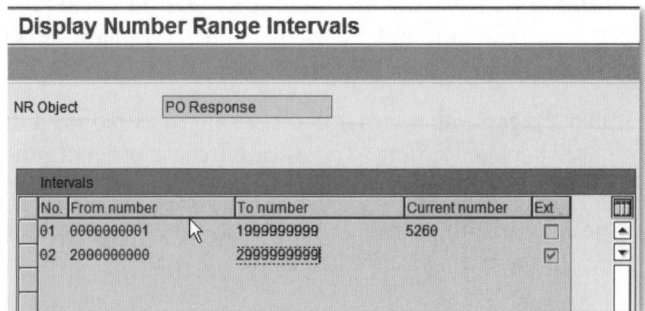

Figure 5.13 Maintain Number Ranges for Purchase Order Response

5.3.13 Define Number Ranges for Local Confirmations of Services and Goods Receipts

To configure this setting, you use the menu path **SPRO • SAP Implementation Guide • Supplier Relationship Management • SRM Server • Cross-Application Basic Settings • Number Ranges • SRM Server Number Ranges • Define Number Ranges for Local Confirmations of Services and Goods Receipts** or Transaction BBP_NUM_CONF. Figure 5.14 shows a screenshot with sample settings to maintain number ranges for confirmations, which you need to configure as follows:

1. Define internal number ranges and external number ranges as required.

2. All number ranges defined here should be assigned to confirmation transaction types in the setting *Define Transaction Types*.

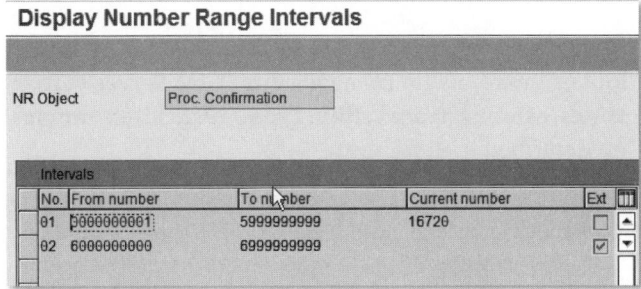

Figure 5.14 Maintain Number Ranges for Confirmations

5.3.14 Define Number Ranges for Local Invoices

You configure this setting using the menu path **SPRO • SAP Implementation Guide • Supplier Relationship Management • SRM Server • Cross-Application Basic Settings • Number Ranges • SRM Server Number Ranges • Define Number Ranges for Local Invoices** or Transaction BBP_NUM_INV. Figure 5.15 shows a screenshot with sample settings to maintain number ranges for invoices, as follows:

1. Define internal number ranges and external number ranges as required.

2. All number ranges defined here should be assigned to Invoice transaction types in the setting *Define Transaction Types*.

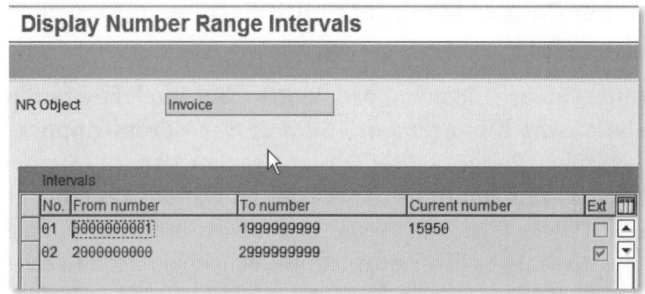

Figure 5.15 Maintain Number Ranges for Invoices

5.3.15 Define Transaction Types

Transaction types control basic parameters, like the number ranges of a purchasing document. Transaction types are similar to document types in SAP ERP. The parameters that can be controlled, using the menu path **SPRO • SAP Implementation Guide • Supplier Relationship Management • SRM Server • Cross-Application Basic Settings • Define Transaction Types**, depend on the purchase document and are described in detail next.

> **Note**
>
> Before configuring this setting, you should analyze customer requirements and decide on the transaction types to be defined. Also, consider the purchasing document types already defined in Materials Management.

Figure 5.16 shows a screenshot of the **Display View "Transaction Object Types": Overview** screen. The procedure to maintain transaction types is as follows:

1. From the list of **Transaction Object Types**, select a transaction category (e.g., **BUS2201 Purchase Order**) for which you want to define the transaction type.

2. Select **Transaction Types** in the **Dialog Structure** in the left pane (the screen that appears is shown later in Figure 5.17).

3. If you want to define new transaction types, click on the **New Entries** button. Maintain the entries in the screen that appears. You can also copy an existing transaction type to create a new one by clicking on the copy as icon and changing the values as required. This method of creating new transaction types is highly recommended.

4. Check the existing transaction types. If you want to change the details of any transaction type, double-click on it.

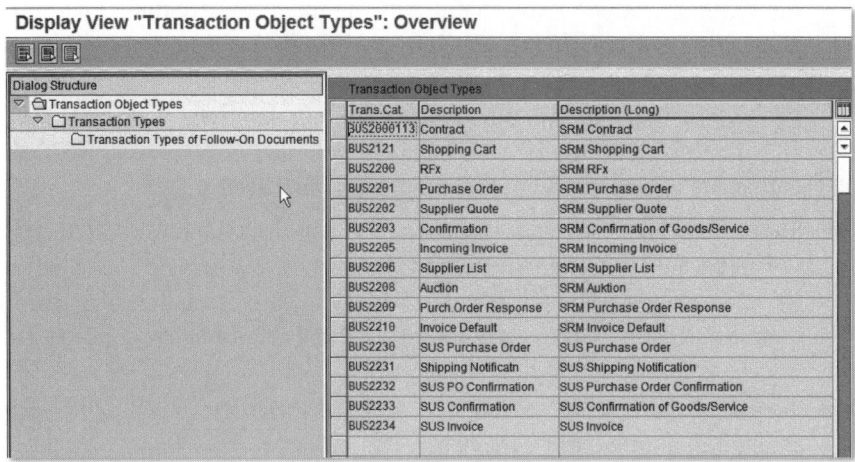

Figure 5.16 Transaction Types — Overview

Transaction Type Settings

The details of the common settings available for all objects are shown in Figure 5.17, with the help of settings for a shopping cart. Specific settings for each of the SAP SRM purchasing documents, shown in later figures, are described after the list of common settings:

- **Common Settings for all object types**
    - **Description**: Change the description as you wish. For example, if you create a new transaction type for service purchase orders, you can define the description as 'service order.'

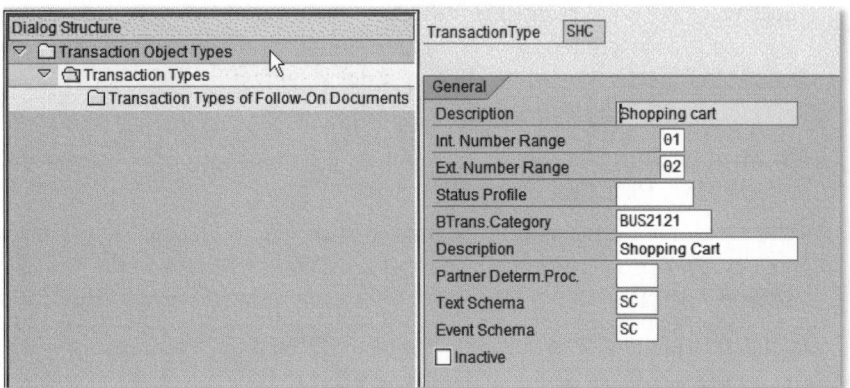

Figure 5.17 Transaction Types — Settings

▸ **Int. Number Range**: Enter the internal number range defined for shopping carts. You can use the search help to check the number range numbers defined for object REQREQ.

▸ **Ext. Number Range**: You can keep the number delivered in the standard. This number is not used in shopping cart transactions. However, you can define and use external number ranges for purchase orders.

▸ **Status Profile**: If you define a user status profile for the document, you can assign it to a transaction type here. Normally, this field is left blank.

▸ **BTrans.Category**: The transaction category for a given purchasing document is predefined in the standard (e.g., **BUS2121** for shopping cart). Do not change the given transaction category.

▸ **Partner Determ.Proc**: If you have defined a partner schema, you can assign it to a transaction type here.

▸ **Text Schema**: The text Schema defines the long texts (vendor text, internal note, etc.) you can have in a purchasing document. SAP delivers a standard text schema for each object type. You can also define your own text schema to cater to your requirements. Assign an appropriate text schema for the transaction type here. You can assign different text schema for different transaction types of the same object type. If you do not see long texts in any documents, then check the settings here and assign a text schema to the transaction type.

▸ **Event Schema**: An event schema enables sending alerts and messages for a transaction type using SRM Alert Management. If you want to use the alerts functionality, assign an appropriate event schema for the transaction type here.

▸ **Inactive**: If you do not wish to use a specific transaction type, you can deactivate it by selecting this indicator. Ensure that this indicator is not selected for all active transaction types. Only active transaction types are available for selection while creating a document.

▸ **Settings for shopping cart (object type BUS2121)**

  ▸ As mentioned earlier, Figure 5.17 shows a screenshot of the transaction type settings for a shopping cart.

  ▸ The predefined transaction type for shopping cart is **SHC** and you cannot create new transaction types. You can only make changes to the settings defined for SHC.

  ▸ External number range is not used in a shopping cart.

▸ **Settings for purchase order (object type BUS2201)**

  ▸ Figure 5.18 shows a screenshot for sample purchase order transaction type settings.

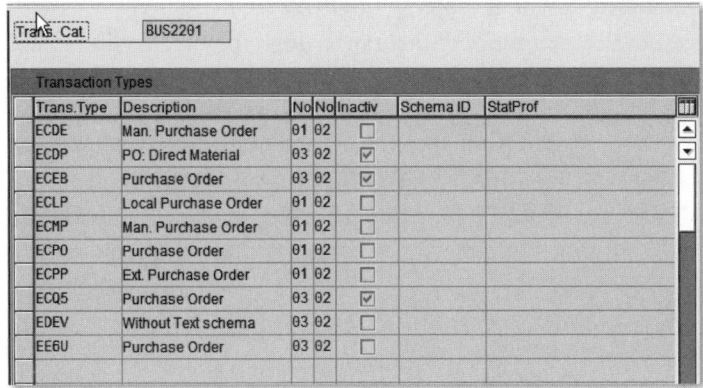

Figure 5.18 Sample Purchase Order Transaction Types

▶ You can also define new transaction types for purchase orders to cater to specific requirements. For example, you can define the transaction types to mimic the document types defined in MM or you can define separate document types for local purchase orders and extended classic orders.

▶ You can define both internal and external number ranges.

▶ **Settings for confirmations (object type BUS2203)**

  ▶ Figure 5.19 shows a screenshot of the transaction type for confirmations and return delivery.

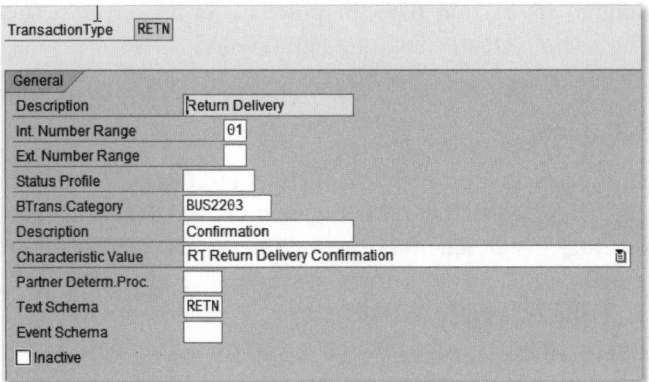

Figure 5.19 Transaction Type Settings for Confirmations

  ▶ CONF (confirmation) and **RETN** (return delivery) are pre-defined transaction types for confirmations and hence there is no need to create new transaction types.

  ▶ The field **Characteristic Value** determines whether the transaction type is a 'confirmation' or 'return delivery.'

143

▶ **Settings for incoming invoices (object type BUS2205)**

    ▶ Figure 5.20 shows a screenshot of the transaction type for a credit memo.

    ▶ **CRME** (credit memo) and INV (invoice) are predefined transaction types for incoming invoices and hence there is no need to create new transaction types.

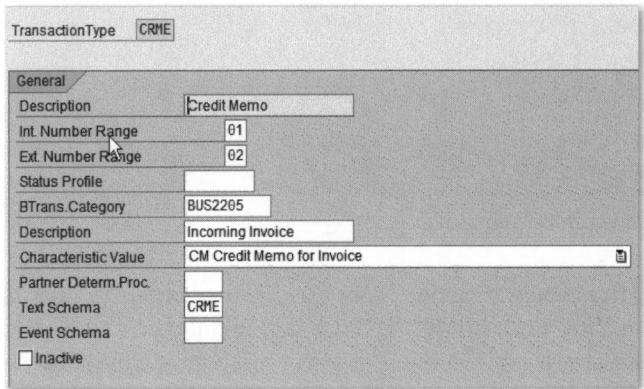

Figure 5.20 Transaction Type Settings for Invoices

    ▶ The field **Characteristic Value** is used to distinguish credit memos from invoices.

▶ **Settings for purchase order response (object type BUS2209)**

    ▶ PCO is a predefined transaction type for purchase order response and hence there is no need to create new transaction types.

5.3.16 Define Text Types

In this setting, which is accessible through the menu path **SPRO · SAP Implementation Guide · Supplier Relationship Management · SRM Server · Cross-Application Basic Settings · Text Schema · Define Text Types**, text type keys and descriptions are defined. There are many text types, such as "Header long text," "Item long text," "Internal note," etc., that are delivered in the standard. Customers can add more text types based on their specific requirements. Figure 5.21 shows a screenshot of sample settings for text types, which you define as follows:

1. Select the text object **BBP_PD** and double-click on **Text Type** in the **Dialog Structure** in the left pane.

2. Check the existing text types and change the description, if required.

3. To define new transaction types, click on the **New Entries** button. Maintain an **ID** and **Description**. Customer-defined text IDs should begin with 'Y' or

'Z'. For example, you can add **ZH01** (**General Terms and Conditions**), **ZH02** (**Specific Terms and Conditions**), and **ZI01** (**Special Service Requirements**) here.

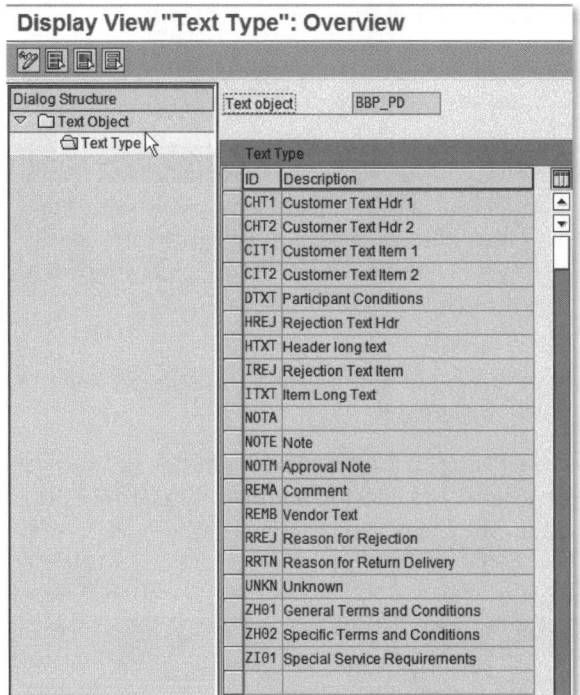

Figure 5.21 Text Types — Overview

Caution

This is a cross-client setting; that is, settings defined in one client will be applicable to all clients in the system.

5.3.17 Define Text Schema

A *text schema* consists of a set of text types and rules to define long texts in a document. This setting, accessible by following the menu path **SPRO • SAP Implementation Guide • Supplier Relationship Management • SRM Server • Cross-Application Basic Settings • Text Schema • Define Text Schema**, provides the flexibility to have customer-defined texts in a purchasing document. In this setting, you can create new text schemas as per your requirement. You can create different text schemas for a single object type (e.g., purchase order).

For example, if you want to have a set of long texts for local purchase order transaction types and a different set of long texts similar to MM purchase order long texts for extended classic order transaction types, you can define separate text schemas accordingly. For example, you may want to add 'Special service requirements' as item long text in shopping carts and purchase orders. You may also want to add 'General Terms and Conditions' and 'Specific Conditions' as long texts in contract and purchase order documents.

A text schema is assigned to a transaction type in the setting *Define Transaction Types*. Text schema functionality is available from SAP SRM 5.0 on.

Note

The text schema for each procurement object is delivered in the standard and changing the standard text schema is not recommend. If you want to have your own text schema for any object type, create a new text schema by copying a relevant text schema and modifying the newly created text schema.

Figure 5.22 shows a screenshot of sample settings for a text schema. The procedure to define the text schema is as follows:

1. Create a new text schema by clicking on the **New Entries** button or by selecting a relevant existing text schema and clicking on the copy as icon. Enter a text schema ID and description. The text schema ID should begin with 'Y' or 'Z.'

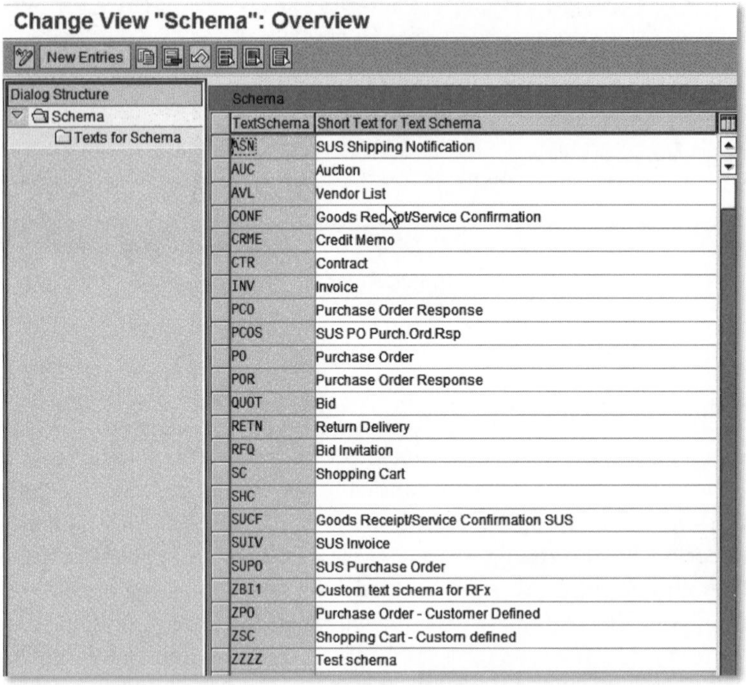
Change View "Schema": Overview
New Entries
Dialog Structure
Schema
Texts for Schema
Schema
TextSchema
Short Text for Text Schema
ASN
SUS Shipping Notification
AUC
Auction
AVL
Vendor List
CONF
Goods Receipt/Service Confirmation
CRME
Credit Memo
CTR
Contract
INV
Invoice
PCO
Purchase Order Response
PCOS
SUS PO Purch.Ord.Rsp
PO
Purchase Order
POR
Purchase Order Response
QUOT
Bid
RETN
Return Delivery
RFQ
Bid Invitation
SC
Shopping Cart
SHC
SUCF
Goods Receipt/Service Confirmation SUS
SUIV
SUS Invoice
SUPO
SUS Purchase Order
ZBI1
Custom text schema for RFx
ZPO
Purchase Order - Customer Defined
ZSC
Shopping Cart - Custom defined
ZZZZ
Test schema

Figure 5.22 Text Schema — Overview

2. Select the newly created schema ID and double-click on **Texts for Schema** in the left pane.

3. Assign all of the text types you want to include in the schema. Figure 5.23 shows a screenshot of sample settings for texts for a text schema called **ZPO**. A few guidelines are as follows:

   ▶ Note that text type 'NOTE' is proposed as the default long text in the first screen of the shopping cart in the shopping cart wizard. Hence it is recommended to maintain 'NOTE' as one of the text types in the schema for shopping cart.

   ▶ You should maintain text types 'RREJ' in the schema for invoice and text type 'RRTN' in the schema for return delivery. This is required if you want to run a check on a rejection or return delivery while approving a confirmation or invoice.

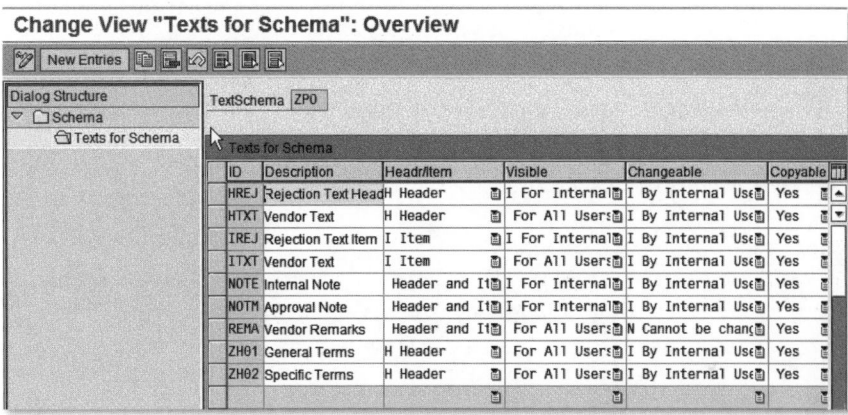

Figure 5.23 Texts for Text Schema

4. For each text type you need to maintain the following in the corresponding column:

   ▶ **Headr/Item**: Define whether the text type should appear in the **Header** or **Item** or both the **Header and Item** of the document. Note that in the text schema for shopping cart, all text types should belong to the item except NOTM (note for approval).

   ▶ **Visible**: Define whether the text type is visible to internal users only, to all users, or not visible to any users.

   ▶ **Changeable**: Define whether the text type is changeable by internal or external users, both internal and external users, or not changeable by any users. If you want the text to be changeable by workflow approving users, then select 'By workflow user in display mode.'

▸ **Copyable**: If you want the content of text type to be copied onto follow-on documents, select **Yes**. Ensure that the same text type exists in the follow-on document. Note that long texts for which fixed values have been defined cannot be copied. You can override this restriction by implementing BAdI BBP_LONGTEXT_BADI.

5. Remember to assign the text schema defined here to the relevant transaction type(s) in the setting *Define Transaction Types*.

5.3.18 Define Fixed Values for Texts

If you want users to select the text from a dropdown box, then maintain fixed values for transaction type, text schema, and text type combination, using the menu path **SPRO • SAP Implementation Guide • Supplier Relationship Management • SRM Server • Cross-Application Basic Settings • Text Schema • Define Fixed Values for Texts**. Figure 5.24 shows a screenshot of sample settings for fixed values for texts.

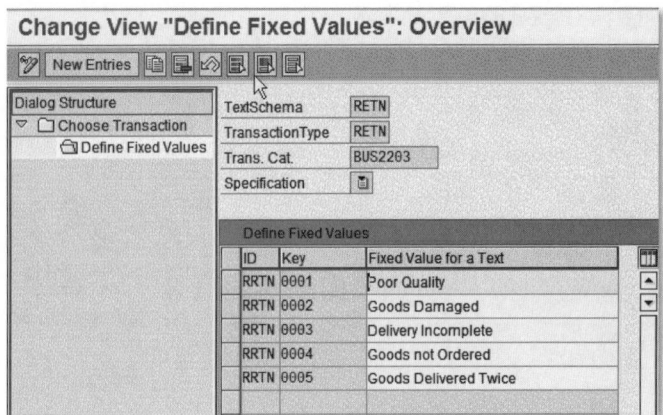

Figure 5.24 Define Fixed Values for Texts

To define fixed values for text, follow these steps:

1. In the list of transaction type and text schema combinations, select the combination for which you want to define fixed values. For example, you may want to predefine reasons for return delivery, so select the transaction type **RETN** and double-click on **Define Fixed Values** in the left pane.

2. Review the SAP standard delivered fixed values, if any. Change the values as appropriate for your organization. For return delivery, you may **Define Fixed Values** for text type **RRTN** (Reason for Return Delivery). You should define the keys and descriptions for return delivery according to the reasons for return delivery setting in MM.

5.3.19 Version Control

Using this setting, you can activate or deactivate version control for purchase orders, contracts, invoices, bid invitations, and bids, using the menu path **SPRO • SAP Implementation Guide • Supplier Relationship Management • SRM Server • Cross-Application Basic Settings • Switch on Version Control for Purchasing Documents**.

Note

Version control for bid invitations is available from SAP SRM 5.0 on, and for bids it is available from SAP SRM 6.0 on.

Figure 5.25 shows a screenshot of sample settings for activating version control. To activate version control, follow these steps:

1. Select the **Business Transaction Category** (**Purchase Order**, etc.) from the dropdown list.
2. Select the **On/off** checkbox for the appropriate category to activate version control, as shown in Figure 5.25.

You can use BAdI BBP_VERSION_CONTROL to determine when and under which circumstances the system creates a new version, and to circumvent the standard version creation logic.

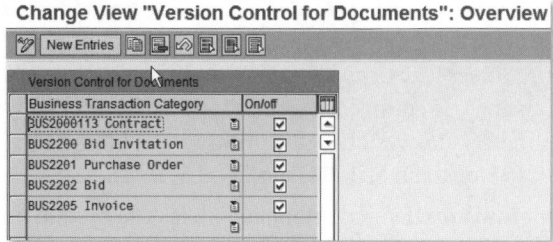

Figure 5.25 Version Control for Documents

5.3.20 Tax Calculation

Using the tax calculation settings, you can define tax calculation in purchasing documents. Tax calculation is used in shopping carts, purchase orders, invoices, credit memos, and Evaluated Receipt Settlements (ERS). We will describe the relevant settings in detail in this section.

Defining System for Tax Calculation

Using this setting, you define the system used for tax calculation, using the menu path **SPRO • SAP Implementation Guide • Supplier Relationship Man-**

agement • **SRM Server** • **Cross-Application Basic Settings** • **Tax Calculation** •
Determine System for Tax Calculation.

Figure 5.26 shows a screenshot of sample settings for determining the tax calculation system.

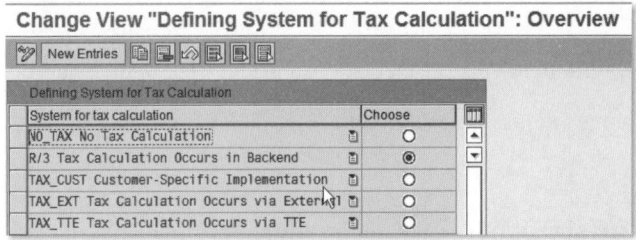

Figure 5.26 Define System for Tax Calculation

To define the system for tax calculation, specify the relevant option for your
organization by selecting the radio button next to the option, in the **Choose** column. The different options available include the following:

▶ **No Tax Calculation**: Select this option if you do not need any tax calculation
done in SAP SRM.

▶ **Tax Calculation Occurs in Backend**: Select this option if you have an SAP
system in the backend. In this case, tax calculation occurs via Remote Function Calls (RFCs) in the backend financial system. Ensure that tax codes in
SAP SRM and tax codes in the backend system are mapped in the configuration setting *Assign Enterprise Buyer Tax Code to FI System*. If an external tax
system, like Vertex® or Taxware®, is connected to the backend system, it is
automatically called from the backend system. This option is recommended
if you are connected to SAP R/3 or to an SAP ERP backend system.

▶ **Customer-Specific Implementation**: If you do not have a backend system or
tax system, you can use customer-specific tax calculation logic by developing
your own function module. To do so, replace the function module NOR3_
TAX_CALCULATION with your own function module in table BBP_
FUNCTION_MAP for object type 'Tax' and Method 'Calculate_NoR3.' The
interfaces of the new function module must be same as in NOR3_TAX_CAL-
CULATION.

▶ **Tax Calculation Occurs via External Tax System**: Tax calculation occurs in
Vertex or Taxware (only in USA and Canada). The logical system and destination of the external system should have been specified with system type
TAX_EXT in the configuration setting *Define Backend Systems*. Check the
function module EXT_TAX_CALCULATION if you encounter any problems.

▶ **Tax Calculation Occurs via TTE**: The Tax Transaction Engine (TTE) is part of
Internet Pricing Configurator (IPC) and is called via RFC. The logical system

and destination of the TTE should have been specified with system type **TAX_TTE** in the configuration setting *Define Backend Systems*. You also need to configure additional configuration settings for the TTE, which are not explained in this book. Check the function module TTE_TAX_CALCU-LATION_40 if you encounter any problems.

Note

If you do not select any option, the tax calculation is done in the backend financial system. Also, if you need to calculate tax for several countries, you have to use the TTE or backend system options.

Tax Codes in the Backend SAP ERP Financials System

We are describing this setting to introduce you to tax codes defined in the SAP ERP Financials application, however, you do not need to configure any settings here for your SAP SRM implementation. You access the setting using the menu path **SPRO • SAP Customizing Implementation Guide • Financial Accounting • Financial Accounting Global Settings • Tax on Sales/Purchases • Calculation • Define Tax Codes for Sales and Purchases**, or Transaction code FTXP.

Note

Contact your SAP ERP Financials consultant for more details on the tax code settings in your organization.

Figure 5.27 shows a screenshot of tax codes in a backend SAP ERP Financials system.

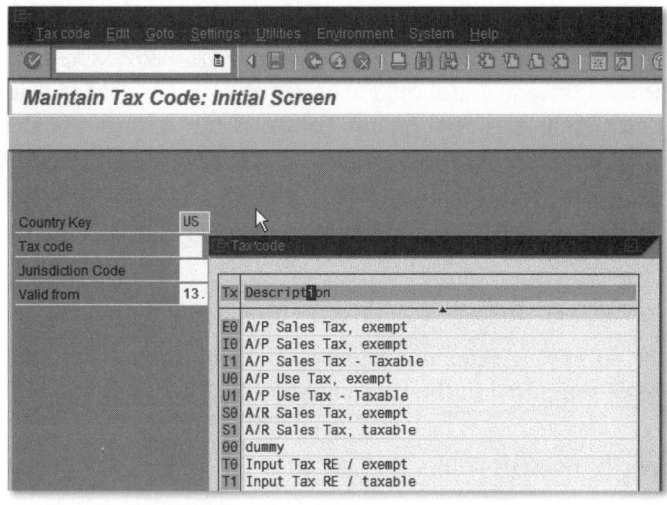

Figure 5.27 Tax Codes in Backend SAP ERP Financials

To configure tax codes in a backend SAP ERP Financials system, follow these steps:

1. **Country Key**: Enter the country key (code) for which tax codes need to be specified and click on the **Continue** button.
2. **Tax code**: Enter the appropriate tax code. You can click on search help for **Tax code** and you will see a list of tax codes that have been already defined, as shown in Figure 5.27. This list represents both input tax (used in purchasing) and output tax (used in sales). Consider input tax codes while defining tax codes in SAP SRM.

Assign Tax Codes for Nontaxable Transaction in SAP ERP Financial Accounting

We describe this setting to introduce you to nontaxable tax codes defined in the SAP ERP Financials application, however, you do not need to configure any settings here for your SAP SRM implementation. To access the setting, use the menu path **SPRO • SAP Customizing Implementation Guide • Financial Accounting • Financial Accounting Global Settings • Tax on Sales/Purchases • Posting • Assign Tax Codes for Non-taxable transaction**. Nontaxable Input tax code and Output Tax codes for each company code are defined in this setting.

> **Note**
>
> Contact your SAP ERP Financials consultant for more details on these settings in your organization.

Enter Tax Codes

In this setting, you define the tax codes to be used in your SAP SRM system. If you have an SAP backend system, you should maintain the same tax codes as in your backend SAP ERP Financials application. To access the setting, use the menu path **SPRO • SAP Implementation Guide • Supplier Relationship Management • SRM Server • Cross-Application Basic Settings • Tax Calculation • Enter Tax Code**. Figure 5.28 shows a screenshot of sample settings for tax codes in SAP SRM.

The columns in this screen are described in the following list:

▸ **Tax ind.**: Enter the tax code. As mentioned previously, you should enter the same codes as those configured in the backend SAP ERP Financials application.

▸ **Tax Descript.**: Specify a description of the tax code.

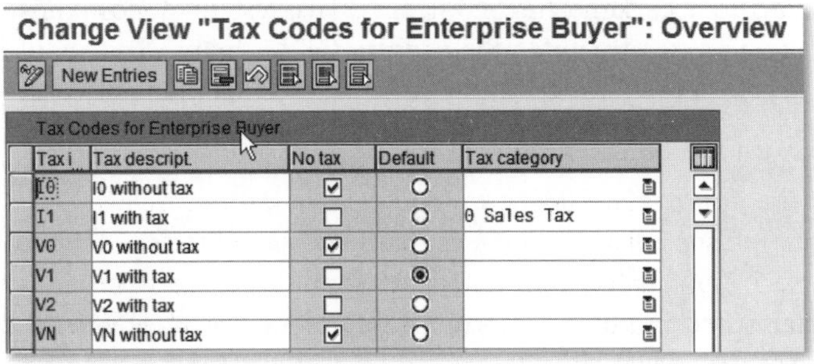

Tax i	Tax descript.	No tax	Default	Tax category
I0	I0 without tax	☑	○	
I1	I1 with tax	☐	○	0 Sales Tax
V0	V0 without tax	☑	○	
V1	V1 with tax	☐	◉	
V2	V2 with tax	☐	○	
VN	VN without tax	☑	○	

Figure 5.28 Tax Codes in SAP SRM

- **No tax**: Select this indicator if you want to use the tax code to indicate a 'no tax' transaction. Tax amounts for items with such tax codes are zero and cannot be maintained. If you have an SAP backend system, specify the tax codes assigned for nontaxable transactions in the backend system.
- **Default**: Define a default tax code. This is defaulted in the transactions and can be changed by users within the transaction.
- **Tax category**: Relevant only for USA, Canada, and Brazil. Keep this field blank for all other countries. Tax categories **Sales Tax** and **Consumer Use Tax** can be used for Brazil. When you use an external tax system, and for USA and Canada, you can use all tax categories.

Determine Tax Code for Country/Product Category

Using this optional setting, you assign a tax code for each country and product category. The system then automatically determines the tax code defined here in a transaction, depending on the country and product category. If you define tax codes for more than one country, you can specify the settings for each country here. If you have tax codes for only one country, then the 'default' tax code defined in configuration setting *Enter Tax Codes* is sufficient and you do not need to configure any settings here. When you configure these settings, the system produces an error if it cannot determine a tax code because settings for the country are not maintained.

Use the menu path **SPRO • SAP Implementation Guide • Supplier Relationship Management • SRM Server • Cross-Application Basic Settings • Tax Calculation • Determine Tax Code for Country/Product Category** to access the setting. The columns in this setting are as follows:

- **Domestic/Internat.ID**: Select Domestic or International from the dropdown list.
- **Country**: Enter the country ID, or leave the field blank.

▶ **Category ID**: Enter the product category ID, or leave the field blank. You cannot enter a product category when the country field is blank. You should maintain one entry with the Country and Category ID fields blank to determine the tax code when there is no specific entry for a country or product category combination.

▶ **Tax Code:** Enter the tax code for the given country and category combination.

You can use customer-specific rules to determine the tax code by implementing BAdI BBP_DET_TAXCODE_BADI.

Assign Enterprise Buyer Tax Code to the Financial Accounting System

Using this optional setting, tax codes in the SAP SRM system are mapped to a backend financial system. If there are no entries in this setting, the system assumes that tax codes in the SAP SRM system and the backend system are the same.

Use the menu path **SPRO • SAP Implementation Guide • Supplier Relationship Management • SRM Server • Cross-Application Basic Settings • Tax Calculation • Assign Enterprise Buyer Tax Code to FI System** to access the setting. Figure 5.29 shows a screenshot of sample settings for mapping of SAP SRM tax codes to backend tax codes. The columns are as follows:

▶ **EBP Tax Code**: Enter the tax code defined in SAP SRM

▶ **FI system**: Enter the logical system name of the backend system

▶ **FI tax code**: Enter the corresponding tax code in the given Financials system

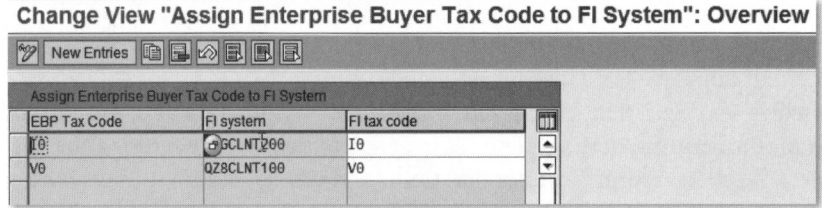

Figure 5.29 Assign SAP SRM Tax Codes to Tax Codes in Backend Financials

Determine Tax Calculation for Freight Costs

Using this setting, you define that freight costs are calculated in invoices with a separate tax code. Freight costs are normally distributed to individual items. However, you configure this setting when you do not wish to distribute freight costs to individual items.

Use the menu path **SPRO · SAP Implementation Guide · Supplier Relationship Management · SRM Server · Cross-Application Basic Settings · Tax Calculation · Determine Tax Calculation for Freight Costs** to access the setting.

Figure 5.30 shows a screenshot of sample settings for the freight costs tax calculation. Activate the **Freight Costs as Separate Item** indicator if you wish to calculate freight costs with a separate tax code and determine freight costs as a separate item. You can also use BAdI BBP_FREIGHT_BADI to calculate tax for freight costs.

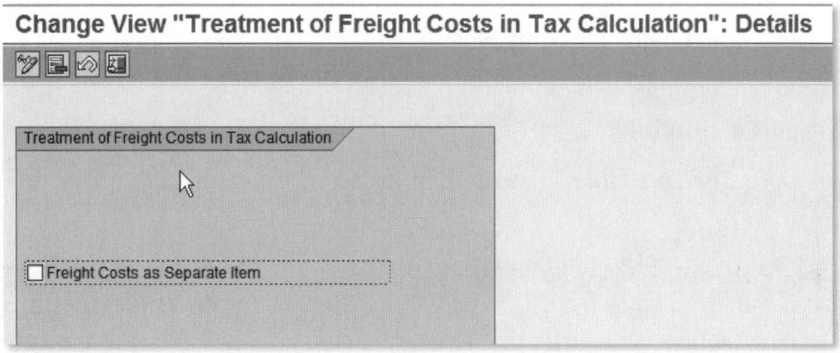

Change View "Treatment of Freight Costs in Tax Calculation": Details

Treatment of Freight Costs in Tax Calculation

☐ Freight Costs as Separate Item

Figure 5.30 Tax Calculation for Freight Costs

Activate Withholding Tax

Using this setting, you activate withholding tax for a supplier. Withholding tax functionality in SAP SRM is activated depending on the settings in the Financial Accounting system, company code, and supplier. You should maintain the settings in line with your backend SAP ERP Financials system. In MM or in the Financial Accounting component (FI) of SAP ERP, withholding tax is indicated in the vendor master.

Use the menu path **SPRO · SAP Implementation Guide · Supplier Relationship Management · SRM Server · Cross-Application Basic Settings · Tax Calculation · Activate Withholding Tax** to access this setting. Figure 5.31 shows a screenshot of sample settings for withholding tax.

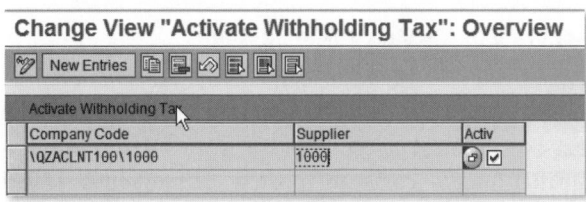

Figure 5.31 Activate Withholding Tax

The columns in the setting are described in the following list:

- **Company Code**: You should use search help to select the **Company Code**. The selected entry should be in the format *'LogicalSystem\companycode.'* For example, an entry of **QZACLNT100\1000**, as shown in Figure 5.31, would be correct, where QZACLNT100 represents the backend SAP ERP Financials system and 1000 represents the company code in the backend system.
- **Supplier**: Enter a supplier code or select one from search help. You can also enter '*' to specify that the data applies to all suppliers.
- **Active**: Activate this indicator to activate withholding tax or leave it blank to deactivate it for the given company code and supplier combination.

BAdIs in Tax Calculation

Two BAdIs are also available to further influence the tax calculation in SAP SRM:

- SAP ERP BAdI ME_TAX_FROM_ADDRESS is used in SAP ERP to determine the tax jurisdiction code from the delivery address. You can implement this BAdI when you face tax jurisdiction code–related errors while creating a purchase order in the backend system. For more information, refer to SAP Note 741822.
- BAdI BBP_TAX_MAP_BADI is used to change or supplement entries in the tables that are used for tax calculation. For example, you can determine a tax jurisdiction code from the delivery address transfer to the backend system. For more information, refer to SAP Note 436760.

5.3.21 Account Assignment

Account assignment settings enable procurement with cost object assignment. These settings are important for indirect material procurement and services procurement. You also configure settings to map SAP SRM account assignment categories to a backend MM application. In this section, we will look at each of the account assignment settings in more detail.

Account Assignment Categories in Materials Management

This setting is described to introduce you to account assignment categories defined in MM, however, you do not need to configure any settings here for your SAP SRM implementation. Account assignment categories determine the cost object to which the procurement costs are posted. These settings also determine whether a purchase order item is relevant for goods receipt and/or invoice receipt or whether goods receipt is valuated.

Note

Contact your MM consultant for more details.

Use the menu path **SPRO • SAP Customizing Implementation Guide • Materials Management • Purchasing • Account Assignment • Maintain Account Assignment Categories** to access the setting. A list of account assignment categories is displayed. To view more details of an account assignment category, including the fields to be maintained, double-click on it. The account assignment screen in transactions is presented based on the settings configured here.

Note

The account assignment category in MM is a single-digit key.

Define Account Assignment Categories in SAP SRM

Using this setting, you can define account assignment categories and map them to backend account assignment categories. You also define the fields available for each account assignment category. To access the setting, you use the menu path **SPRO • SAP Implementation Guide • Supplier Relationship Management • SRM Server • Cross-Application Basic Settings • Account Assignment • Define Account Assignment Categories**.

Most of the normally used account assignment categories and mappings to backend systems are delivered as standard settings, and you should keep these settings. You may, however, activate or deactivate any account assignment categories if necessary. Only active categories will be available for selection in transactions. You may create new entries according to your backend settings as required. Figure 5.32 shows a screenshot of account assignment categories.

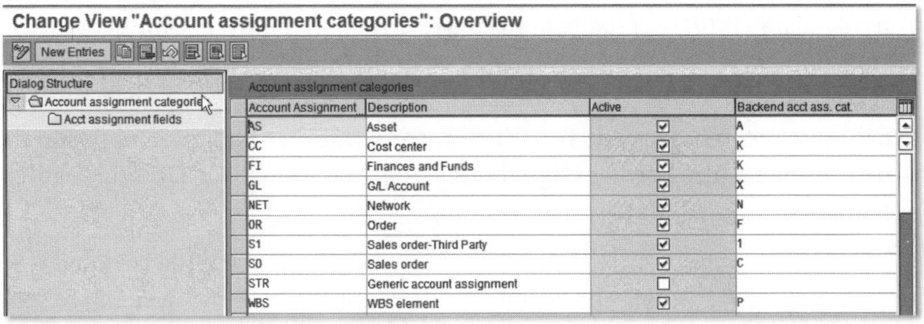

Figure 5.32 Account Assignment Categories — Overview

To create an account assignment category, follow these steps:

1. Copy an existing category by selecting it and clicking on the copy as icon, or by pressing F6.

2. Click on the **Copy all** button on the next screen. The columns in this screen are as follows:

   ▸ **Account assignment cat.**: Specify a key for the new account assignment category.

   ▸ **Description**: Specify a description to represent the new account assignment category.

   ▸ **Active**: Select this indicator to activate the new category and make it available in transactions.

   ▸ **Backend acct ass cat.**: Specify the relevant backend account assignment category.

3. Press the Enter key once to confirm the newly entered values.

4. Select the entry and double-click on **Acct assignment fields** in the left pane. This brings up a screen shown in Figure 5.33, which shows sample settings for account assignments fields. (The fields are also copied when you create a new category by copying an existing category.)

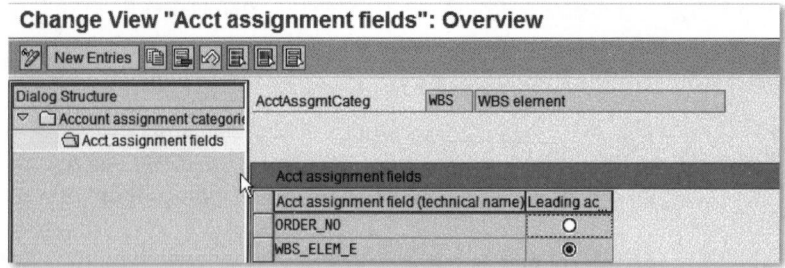

Figure 5.33 Account Assignment Fields

5. If you want additional fields in the entry screen in a transaction, click on the **New Entries** button. You can get an idea of the required field for any account assignment category from the backend settings. Select new fields from search help for **Acct assignment field (technical name)**. Maintain an appropriate field as the **Leading acct. assign. field**. For example, **COST_CTR** is the leading field for account assignment category CC.

The account assignment category 'STR' is normally used when the backend system is a non-SAP system. The required entries for the backend system are sent as a string. This has a length of 64 characters and is freely definable.

> **Note**
>
> SAP NetWeaver BI does not support the STR category as the length is too long.

You can also implement BAdI BBP_ACCCAT_MAP_EXP to achieve more complex mappings while creating backend documents from an SAP SRM shopping cart. For example, if you want to process third-party orders, you must implement this BAdI. You may also need to use this BAdI when the SAP SRM system is connected to multiple backend systems so that an account assignment category in SAP SRM can represent various account assignment categories in various backend systems.

Further, you can implement BAdI BBP_ACCCAT_MAP_IMP to achieve complex mappings when importing documents with reference to the backend system.

Define GL Account for Product Category and Account Assignment Category

In this setting, you specify GL accounts for a product category and account assignment category combination. You can also specify a default GL account. To access this setting, use the menu path **SPRO • SAP Implementation Guide • Supplier Relationship Management • SRM Server • Cross-Application Basic Settings • Account Assignment • Define GL Account for Product Category and Account Assignment Categories**.

> **Note**
>
> The ability to specify multiple GL accounts and a default GL account for a product category and account assignment category combination is available from SAP SRM 2007 on only. In SAP SRM 5.0 and earlier versions, you could specify only one GL account.

Figure 5.34 shows sample settings for the determination of the GL account in SAP SRM 2007.

The columns in this screen are described in the following list:

▶ **Category ID**: Enter a product category ID or select one from search help. When you select from search help, the source system is also copied from search help. You can also use the wild card '*.' For example, if you want to define an entry to represent all product categories with the first two letters 'AB,' then enter 'AB*' in this field.

▶ **SourceSyst**: Specify the logical system of the product category source system. If the product category is replicated from a backend system, then specify the logical system of the backend system.

▶ **AcctAssCat**: Enter or select the appropriate account assignment category.

▶ **GL Account**: Enter a valid GL Account. The GL account must be a valid GL account in the backend accounting system where the account postings are made.

▶ **Default**: If you specify multiple GL accounts for a product category and account assignment category combination, specify one of them as the default. This is defaulted into transactions and users can change the account within the transaction.

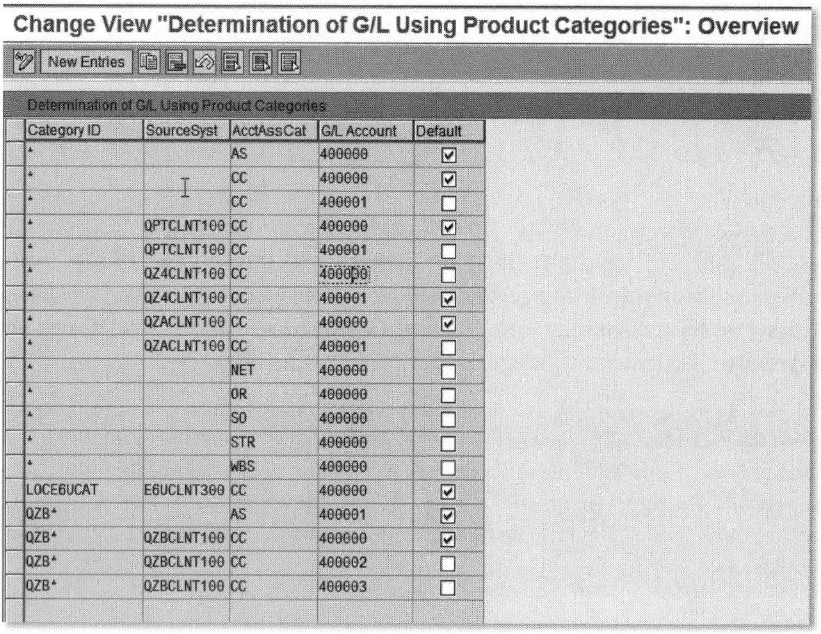

Category ID	SourceSyst	AcctAssCat	G/L Account	Default
*		AS	400000	☑
*		CC	400000	☑
*		CC	400001	☐
*	QPTCLNT100	CC	400000	☑
*	QPTCLNT100	CC	400001	☐
*	QZ4CLNT100	CC	400000	☐
*	QZ4CLNT100	CC	400001	☑
*	QZACLNT100	CC	400000	☑
*	QZACLNT100	CC	400001	☐
*		NET	400000	☐
*		OR	400000	☐
*		SO	400000	☐
*		STR	400000	☐
*		WBS	400000	☐
LOCE6UCAT	E6UCLNT300	CC	400000	☑
QZB*		AS	400001	☑
QZB*	QZBCLNT100	CC	400000	☑
QZB*	QZBCLNT100	CC	400002	☐
QZB*	QZBCLNT100	CC	400003	☐

Figure 5.34 Determination of GL Using Product Categories

You can also implement BAdI BBP_DETERMINE_ACCT if you wish to maintain your own logic for determining the GL account.

Note

If an item is ordered with a procurement card, the system uses the account assignment defined for the procurement card.

Maintain Local Accounting Data

Using this setting, you specify the account assignment data used for local validations. The validation is done based on the account assignment category, value, and validity period. Local validation is done if you specify a local validation in the *Define Backend Systems* configuration setting.

To access the setting, use the menu path **SPRO • SAP Implementation Guide • Supplier Relationship Management • SRM Server • Cross-Application Basic Settings • Account Assignment • Maintain Local Accounting Data**. Figure 5.35 shows sample settings for local accounting data.

Change View "Maint. of Acct Assgmt Obj. (Standalone w. Loc. Acct Assgm

New Entries

Maint. of Acct Assgmt Obj. (Standalone w. Loc. Acct Assgmt.)

LogSystem	AcctAss	A/AssgtVal	ValText	Valid From	Valid To
E6UCLNT300	ACCNO GL Acc	0000040000	Local Cost Data	01.01.2007	31.12.9999
E6UCLNT300	CC Cost Center	0000001000	Local Cost Data	01.01.2007	31.12.9999
E6UCLNT300	CC Cost Center	0000003000		01.03.2007	31.12.9999
E6UCLNT300	WBS Work Break	1000-2		10.10.2007	31.12.9999

Figure 5.35 Maintain Local Accounting Data

The columns in this screen are explained in the following list:

- **LogSystem**: Enter the logical system of the financial backend system.
- **AcctAss**: Select the account assignment object from the dropdown list, for example, Cost Center.
- **A/AssgtVal**: Specify the valid value for the given account assignment object. For example, specify a valid cost center here.
- **ValText**: Specify the description of the value. For example, specify the description of the cost center key given in the **A/AssgtVal** field.
- **Valid From**: Specify the validity start date.
- **Valid To**: Specify the validity end date.

5.3.22 Internet Pricing Configurator

Internet Pricing Configurator (IPC) is part of Web Application Server (WAS) 7.0 and hence does not require separate installation in SAP SRM 5.0 and SAP SRM 6.0. If you are using SAP SRM 4.0, or lower versions of SAP SRM, you need to install IPC separately. Note the following:

- **SAP SRM 5.0 and SAP SRM 6.0 implementations**: The Virtual Machine Container (VMC) should be enabled as per SAP Note 854170. To ascertain whether VMC is enabled, run the program RSVMCRT_HEALTH_CHECK in Transaction SE38. You should see four success messages. If there are any error messages, please contact a Basis expert to enable VMC. Refer to SAP Note 844817 for additional details.
- **SAP SRM 4.0 and below versions**: IPC should be installed separately. Always ensure that IPC is running. If you are using only the classic scenario and want to use simplified pricing, IPC is not required. Please refer to SAP

Note 539720 for the restrictions of simplified pricing and the procedure to activate simplified pricing.

> **Note**
>
> We do not recommend the activation of simplified pricing. Companies might activate simplified pricing initially but want to use complex pricing later. In SAP SRM 5.0 and later versions, IPC does not need to be installed separately and therefore does not involve additional IPC maintenance work. If you are using SAP SRM for direct materials, then simplified pricing will not work.

> **Troubleshooting Tip**
>
> If a short dump UNCAUGHT_EXCEPTION with exception CX_BBP_PD_ABORT occurs, check whether IPC is active. To do so, execute Transaction BBP_CND_CHECK_CUST. This transaction executes the program BBP_CND_CUSTOMIZING_CHECK. If there are any errors or warnings, take the appropriate action to address them. If there are no errors, execute program RSVMCRT_HEALTH_CHECK to check whether the VMC is running. Also, check VMC as per the instructions in SAP Note 844817.

5.3.23 Pricing

Configuring the settings in this section is optional because the standard settings delivered by SAP are sufficient for most customer requirements. You need to configure them only when you want to define additional condition types.

Process Condition Types

Using this setting, you can create new condition types, change existing condition types, and create group conditions. SAP delivers prices and discounts in the standard. You can also define new condition types to represent other pricing elements like surcharges, freight, etc.

> **Note**
>
> SAP SRM condition types do not offer the full flexibility they do in MM.

To access this setting, use the menu path **SPRO · SAP Implementation Guide · Supplier Relationship Management · SRM Server · Cross-Application Basic Settings · Pricing · Process Condition Types**. To work with condition types:

1. If you want to modify an existing condition type, double-click on the condition type to be modified.

2. If you want to create a new condition type, select an appropriate existing condition type and click on the copy as icon, or press F6. Remember to add

all new condition types defined here in the calculation schema 0100 in the *Process calculation schema* configuration setting.

Figure 5.36 shows sample settings for condition types.

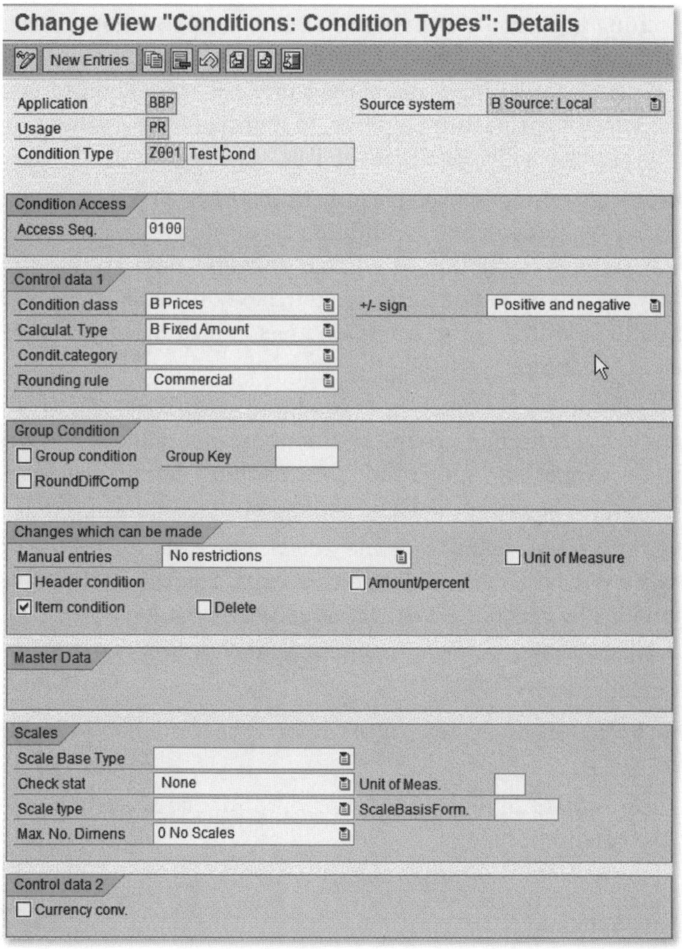

Figure 5.36 Condition Type Settings

The settings in this screen are described in detail in the following list:

▶ **Condition Type**: Enter a new condition type beginning with the number 8 or 9 or any letter from A to Z. Also, enter a description to identify the condition type. Condition type 0100 (Price) must exist for Enterprise Buyer 3.5, or lower versions, and if you are upgrading from Enterprise Buyer 3.5, or lower versions of SAP SRM.

▶ **Access Seq.**: Select the access sequence from the search help. This setting is optional.

- **Condition class**: Select the condition class from search help. It can be Prices, Discount, or Surcharge, or Tax.

- **Calculat. Type**: Select the appropriate value to specify how values are calculated. Typically used values are Percentage, Quantity, or Fixed amount.

- **+/- sign**: This setting is particularly important when the **Condition class** is Discount or Surcharge. Select Negative, if you are defining a discount, and select Positive if you are defining a surcharge condition type. For all other condition types, select **Positive and negative**, to indicate that the condition type value can be either positive or negative.

- **Group condition**: This setting is available only from SAP SRM 5.0 on. Select this indicator if you want to define a condition type as a group condition. *Group conditions* facilitate flexibility in volume discounts, and are used in contracts. Values or volumes of line items in a purchase order that are linked to a contract line item with a group condition are summed up for the purpose of scale determination.

  Remember to add the new condition type to condition group 0100 and to calculation schema 0100. Note that group conditions are not delivered in the standard and if you want to use group conditions, you must define them here.

- **Group Key**: You can use user exits for determining the basis for grouping in the group condition. If you want to define a new user exit, see SAP Note 809820. You will need Java skills to define user exits. You can see existing user exit assignments by executing Transaction /SAPCND/UEASS.

- **Header condition**: Select this indicator if you want the condition to be available in the document header.

- **Item condition**: Select this indicator if a condition type should be available at the item level.

- **Scales**: Define appropriate settings in this section to define scales (volume discounts) for the condition type.

Process Calculation Schema

Using this setting, you can check the settings in calculation schema 0100 and add any additional condition types to it. You cannot, however, define new schemas. IPC calculates the price based on the condition types and their order in this schema. Use the menu path **SPRO • SAP Implementation Guide • Supplier Relationship Management • SRM Server • Cross-Application Basic Settings • Pricing • Process Calculation Schema** to access this setting.

> **Note**
>
> We strongly recommend that you read the Implementation guide (IMG) documentation for this node before configuring any settings.

New condition types should be added in calculation schema 0100 at the appropriate level. Figure 5.37 shows sample settings for condition schema **0100**.

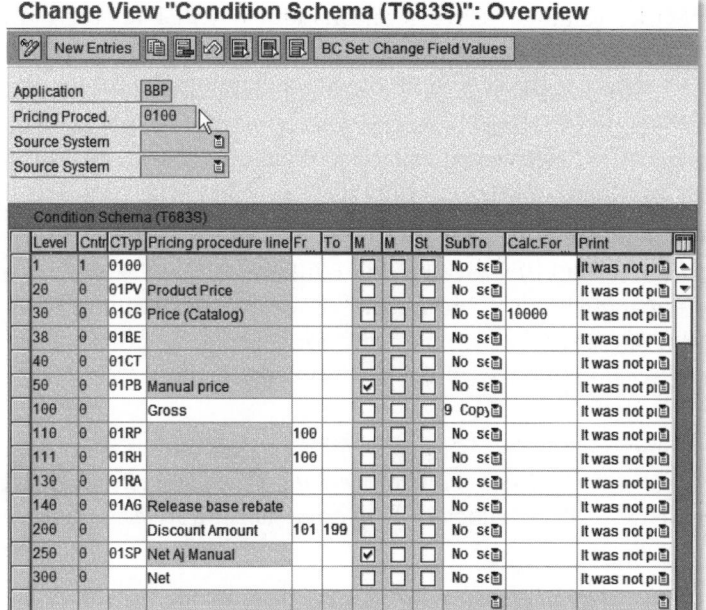

Figure 5.37 Condition Schema

Process Condition Groups

As mentioned earlier, condition groups define the condition types that will be available in a scenario. Condition groups are available for processing conditions in the product master, bid, contract, and global outline agreement. To access this setting, use the menu path **SPRO • SAP Implementation Guide • Supplier Relationship Management • SRM Server • Cross-Application Basic Settings • Pricing • Process Condition Groups**.

Condition groups delivered in the standard are described in the following list:

▶ **PRODUCTBBP**: Defines the condition types available for products and product linkages.

▶ **0100**: Defines the condition types available for a normal item in a contract. In a contract, you can have normal items and product category items. Condition types in this group are available for normal items.

▶ **01CO**: Defines the condition types available for product category items in a contract. Here, you should not maintain condition types of condition class "Prices" as they are normally not given at the product category level. SAP recommends that you assign only "Discount or surcharge" condition types.

- ▸ **01HD**: Defines the condition types available for the contract header. The condition types defined here are relevant for all items in a contract. SAP recommends that you do not use scales with these conditions.

- ▸ **01QU**: Defines the condition types available at the item level for bids. Remember that these are the conditions entered by the supplier. Condition types must be a subset of the conditions in the condition group for the follow-on document (contract or purchase order).

- ▸ **01HQ**: Defines the condition types available at the header level for bids.

- ▸ **01CC**: Defines the condition types available for a normal item in a global outline agreement.

- ▸ **01CP**: Defines the condition types available for product category items in a global outline agreement. Here, you should not maintain condition types of condition class "Prices" as they are normally not given at the product category level. SAP recommends assigning only "Discount or surcharge" condition types.

- ▸ **01CH**: Defines the condition types available for the global outline agreement header. The condition types defined here are relevant for all items in global outline agreements. SAP recommends that you do not use scales with these conditions.

Figure 5.38 shows sample settings for a condition group. You can modify the condition group settings as follows:

1. Select the condition group to be modified.

Change View "Condition Maintenance Group: Detail": Overview

| New Entries | | | | | | | | |

MaintenanceGrp   0100

Condition Maintenance Group: Detail

Counter	Ap	U	Conditio	Co	Description: Entry in Cond. Maint. Gro	Data Source System	
1	BBP	☺	SAP016	0100	old pricing	B Source: Local	
5	BBP	PR	SAP016	01CT	Contract		
7	BBP	PR	SAP068	01CT	Contract		
10	BBP	PR	SAP016	01RA	Absolute discount		
12	BBP	PR	SAP068	01RA	Absolute discount		
17	BBP	PR	SAP068	01RP	Percentage Discount		

Figure 5.38 Condition Groups

2. If you want to delete a condition type from the group, select it and click on the delete icon.

3. If you want to add a condition type to the group, click on the **New Entries** button. The columns available are:

- ▶ **Counter**: Enter a counter.
- ▶ **Application**: Enter "BBP." This condition technique is used in SAP for different purposes across SAP applications. For example, it is used in pricing and also in output determination. Application 'BBP' refers to the condition technique usage in SAP SRM and 'PR' represents its use in 'Pricing' (see the next bullet list item).
- ▶ **Usage**: Enter "PR."
- ▶ **Condition Table**: To be able to specify location-specific values for the condition, assign the condition table **SAP068**. For non-location-specific condition types, assign the condition table **SAP016**. Note that for each condition type, you can maintain two rows — one with SAP016 and another with SAP068.
- ▶ **Condition Type**: Enter the condition type.
- ▶ **Description**: Enter the description of the condition.

Check Technical and Customizing Settings for Conditions

You can execute this transaction at any time, for example, if you have any problems with pricing or if you encounter short dumps due to UNCAUGHT_EXCEPTION in purchasing documents, to verify pricing settings. On execution, the system checks whether IPC pricing is active and whether IPC is running. The system also checks the pricing settings and shows errors if any.

To access this transaction, use the menu path **SPRO · SAP Implementation Guide · Supplier Relationship Management · SRM Server · Cross-Application Basic Settings · Pricing · Check Technical and Customizing Settings for Conditions**, or Transaction code BBP_CND_CHECK_CUST.

5.3.24 Output Actions and Format

Using this setting, you define how different documents are output in SAP SRM. The settings in this section are optional as the standard settings are sufficient to take care of most requirements. However, if you encounter a problem in getting an output, you should check the settings shown here. You can also find the SmartForms or PDF forms (for SAP SRM 2007) used for output in this setting. To access this setting, use the menu path **SPRO · SAP Implementation Guide · Supplier Relationship Management · SRM Server · Cross-Application Basic Settings · Set Output Actions and Output Format · Condition-Dependent Document Output**, or Transaction code BBP_PO_ACTION_DEF.

To work with output actions and format settings, follow these steps:

1. Select an action profile and double-click on Action Definition in the left pane.

2. **Processing Time** on the **action definition** tab determines when an output is processed. Note that the value 'Immediate processing' is not supported in SAP SRM. If you see this value in the **Processing Time** field, you should change it to 'Processing when saving document.'

3. Check the setting in the field **Processing Times Not permitted**, too. We suggest selecting the option 'No Restrictions.'

4. Double-click on **Processing Types** in the left pane.

5. Select a **Permitted processing type** (e.g., Smartforms mail) and click on the **Set Processing** button. You can see the 'Form name,' etc., parameters on the **Document** tab. Note that 'Method Call' is used for XML communications. Processing type 'External Communication' uses PDF-based forms only, and is available from SAP SRM 2007 on.

6. If you want to use your own SmartForm instead of an SAP-delivered Smart-Form, copy the SAP-delivered SmartForm to create a new one and make your modifications to the copy. BAdI BBP_OUPUT_CHANGE_SF can be used to assign the changed SmartForm to the object. For example, if you want to use your own SmartForm for a purchase order, copy BBP_PO and create a new SmartForm, say ZBBP_PO in Transaction SMARTFORMS. You can define your own PDF form in Transaction PSF and assign it in method PERSONALIZE_PDF_DOC_PDFIF in BAdI DOC_PERSONALIZE_BCS.

5.3.25 Setting Up Attachments and Attachment Transfer

SAP recognizes that any procurement activity involves dealing with both structured data and unstructured data. Therefore, SAP SRM provides a functionality to attach documents (unstructured documents) to procurement documents to supplement the details furnished in various screen fields (structured data). This section describes the settings required to attach documents.

Perform the following series of steps to enable attachments:

1. Check that Profile parameters login/create_sso2_ticket and login/accept_sso2_ticket have value 1 in Transaction RZ11.

2. In Transaction SSO2, enter 'NONE' in the RFC destination field and execute.

3. Create a user of type 'Communication' in Transaction SU01. Maintain the user in each of the clients on the SAP SRM server.

4. Activate the service 'DOCSERVER' in Transaction SICF. The service can be found using the following path: **default_host • sap • ebp • docserver.**

5. Double-click on this service and maintain client, user, and password on the Logon data tab. The user specified here should be the communication user created in the previous step. If you have multiple clients on the SAP SRM server, create an external alias for each client as described in the next steps.

To create an external alias:

1. Click on the **External Alias** button in Transaction SICF. Select default_host and click on the "Create new external alias" icon.

2. Specify a name for the external alias, for example, "/attach100," and provide a description.

3. On the Trg Element tab, follow the path **default_host • sap • ebp • docserver** and double-click on docserver.

4. Select the Logon data tab, and specify the client, user, and password. Save the external alias by clicking on the save icon.

5. Repeat this process for all clients and create an external alias for each of the clients.

The following configurations are also required to enable attachments transfer to the backend system:

1. Implement BAdI BBP_CREATE_BE_PO_NEW (or BBP_CREATE_PO_BACK in older versions) for purchase order attachment transfer.

2. Implement BAdI BBP_CREATE_BE_RQ_NEW (or BBP_CREATE_REQ_BACK in older versions) for purchase requisition attachment transfer.

3. In addition to the above SRM BAdI implementations, document type 'SAP SRM' should be defined in the SAP ERP Document Management System (DMS) configuration.

Settings in the Backend SAP ERP System for Attachment Transfer

We will now look at the setting in the backend SAP ERP system for attachment transfer. DMS is used to manage documents and attachments in SAP ERP. Document types in DMS differentiate different types of documents used in different SAP components and control the basic document parameters, like number ranges for the document, status settings for the document, SAP objects with which a document can be linked, etc. When an attachment in SAP SRM is transferred to SAP ERP, a document record is created in DMS with document type 'SAP SRM' (or 'CTR' for contract attachments), which is linked to the relevant purchasing document. Use the menu path **SPRO • SAP Implementation Guide • Cross Application Components • Document Management • Define Document Types**, or Transaction code DC10.

Figure 5.39 shows the sample settings for the document type SAP SRM.

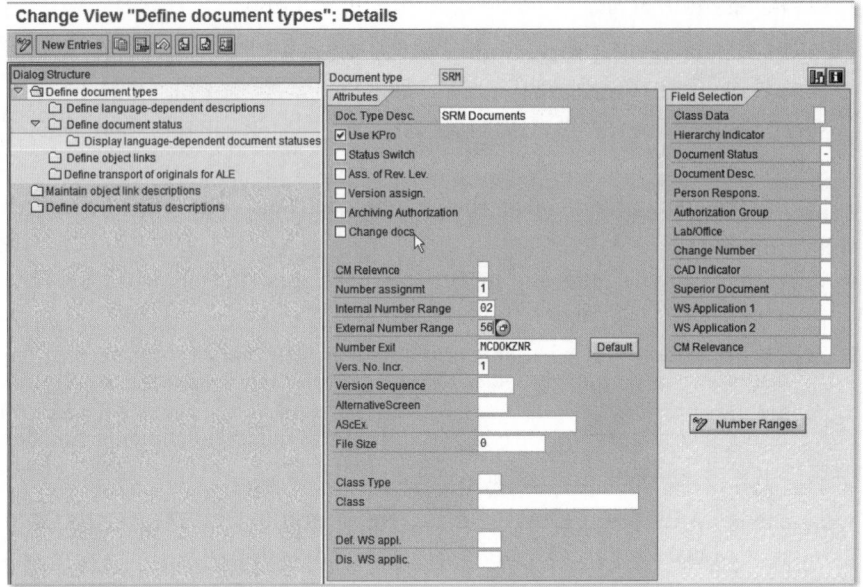

Figure 5.39 Define DMS Document Types

Configure the settings for document type SAP SRM as follows:

1. In the **Attributes** and **Field Selection** sections, configure the following settings:

   ▶ **Use Kpro**: Activate this indicator.

   ▶ **Number Assgmt**: Enter '1' (only internal number assignment).

   ▶ **Internal Number Range**: Select an internal number range using the search help. You can also create a new internal number range in Transaction CV90 if you want to assign a new number range for SAP SRM documents.

   ▶ **Number Exit**: Enter "MCDOKZNR." If you want to control the number assignment or version increment using a user exit, MCDOKZNR should be replaced with your own program.

   ▶ **Document Status**: Select '-' (suppress field) using search help.

2. Double-click on **Define object links** in the left pane.

3. Create **New Entries** for objects EBAN and EKPO. This means, the new document type 'SAP SRM' will be used to link documents in purchase requisitions (EBAN) and purchase order items (EKPO).

4. Specify the description and screen number for the objects EBAN (Purchase requisition item; Screen no 247) and EKPO (Purchase order item; Screen no. 248).

Processing and Transferring Attachments in SAP SRM

This is an optional setting, used for processing and transferring attachments. This configuration setting is available from SAP SRM 5.0 on. If you use SAP NetWeaver Exchange Infrastructure (SAP NetWeaver XI), then you do not need to configure settings for attachment transfer. Use the menu path **SPRO · SAP Implementation Guide · Supplier Relationship Management · SRM Server · Cross-Application Basic Settings · Define Settings for attachments** to access this setting.

Figure 5.40 shows a screenshot of sample settings for attachments. To create new entries, click on the New Entries button to maintain the settings as follows:

▸ **Deactivate Java Applet**: If you do not want to use the Java applet for attachments, then activate this indicator. If you activate this indicator, users will not be able to use checking in, checking out, and versioning functionalities.

▸ **Deactivate attachment versioning**: Attachment versioning is deactivated by activating this indicator.

▸ **Applet Timeout (Synchronization) in Seconds**: If the file upload applet is kept open for more than the time specified here, you will get a time out error. The default setting is 120 seconds.

▸ **Session Refresh (Checkout) in Seconds**: The default is 120 seconds. When you check out a document, the SAP SRM session is extended so that the session does not expire when you are processing a checked out document.

▸ **Also Transfer Attachments during Doc Output via Exchange Infrastructure**: If this is activated, attachments are transferred as SOAP attachments via SAP NetWeaver XI. In SAP SRM 5.0, this setting is referred to as 'Attachments in SOAP.'

▸ **Error Creating Attachment by URL Causes Termination**: This is linked to sending attachments via the SAP NetWeaver XI setting. Activating this setting indicates that sending attachments is critical and if there are any errors, the system causes a termination.

▸ **Incorrect Attachment Processing during Doc output Generated Output Errors**: If this is activated, any errors in attachments transfer cause an output error. If this is not activated, the output processing status will be successful even though there are errors in the attachments transfer.

▸ **C-Folder Settings**: There are three C-Folder-related settings. These are optional settings for the C-Folder attachment transfer when SUS is used.

▸ **Publish Internally, Publish Externally**: The settings in these two sections allow internal or external access to attachments. For example, vendors can access attachments through links in purchase orders that were transferred by XML. If publishing settings are the same for both internal users and external users, then the same Web server can be used for both settings.

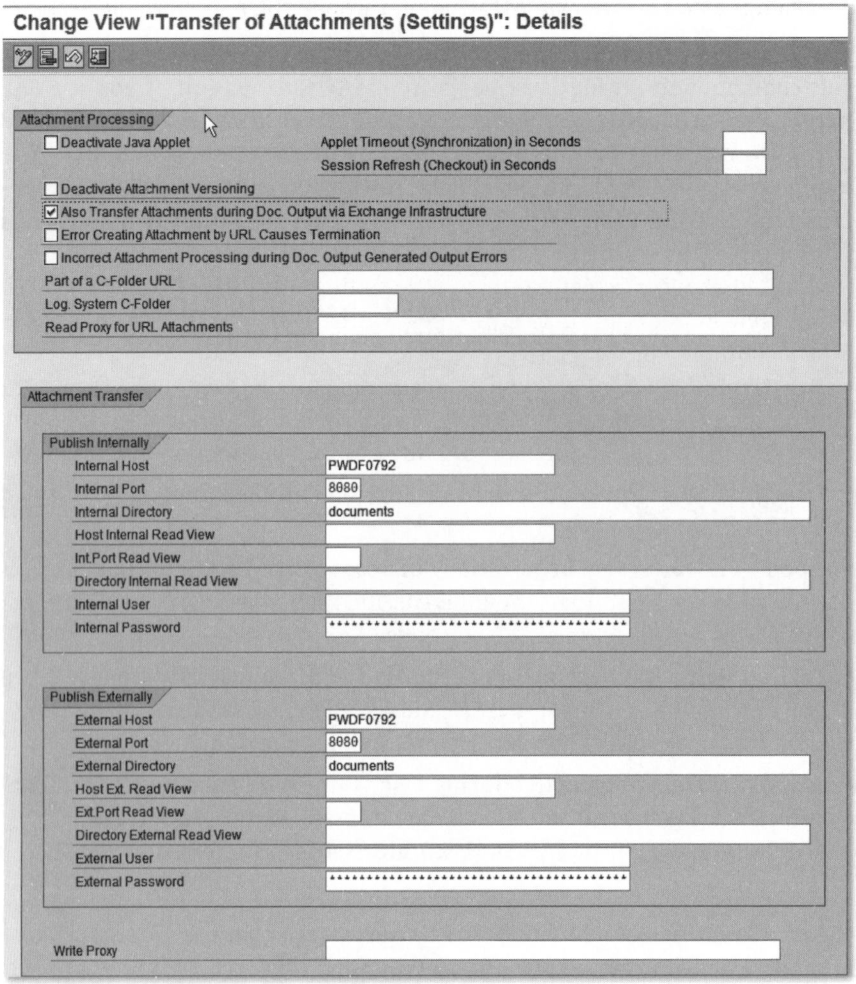

Figure 5.40 Setting Up Attachments and Attachments Transfer

5.3.26 Define Partner Functions and Partner Schema

This is an optional setting. The standard partner functions are sufficient for most customer requirements. However, you will need to configure these settings if you want to add to the already available partner functions and use them in purchasing documents. For example, if you want to add a new partner function, 'Lawyer,' to a purchase order, then you need to configure the following settings:

▶ Define Partner Functions
▶ Define Partner Schema

▶ Assign the new partner schema to a transaction type in the 'Define Transaction Types' settings

Define Partner Functions

New partner functions can be added in this setting, using the menu path **SPRO** • **SAP Implementation Guide** • **Supplier Relationship Management** • **SRM Server** • **Cross-Application Basic Settings** • **Define Partner Functions**.

Figure 5.41 shows a screenshot of sample settings for partner functions. Click on the **New Entries** button to create new entries and configure the settings as explained in the following list:

▶ **Function**: Enter a numeric key here. We suggest a key between 00000901 and 00000999.

▶ **Func. Type**: Select a function type from search help. The *function type* describes the type of partner. If you are not sure, select 0000 (undefined partner).

Change View "Partner Functions": Overview

New Entries 🗋 🗐 🖾 🖺 🗐 🖺

Partner Functions

Function	Func. Type	Usage	Description	Abbrev.	
00000016	0013	B2B	Requestor	RQ	
00000017	0007	B	Contact Person	CP	
00000018	0011	B2B	Bidder	BI	
00000019	0012	B2B	Supplier	SP	S
00000020	0002	B2B	Recipient	RP	
00000025	0014	B2B	Portal Provider	PP	
00000026	0008	B2B	Employee Responsible	ER	
00000027	0017	B2B	Ship-To Address	STA	
00000028	0003	B2B	Invoice Recipient	IR	
00000029	0015	B2B	Invoicing Party	IP	
00000030	0018	B2B	Ship-From Party	SFP	
00000034	0002	B2B	Plant	PLAN	
00000038	0001	B2B	Ordering Party	OP	
00000039	0026	B2B	Proposed Vendor	PV	S
00000051	0019	B2B	Authorizing Pur. Organisation	APO	
00000074	0025	B2B	Service Agent	SA	
00000075	0031	B2B	Location	LOCA	
00000097	0034	B2B	Invoicing Party Employee	IPEm	
00000098	0000	B2B	Customer Partner Function II	CPF2	
00000701	0501	B2B			
00000711	0501	B2B			
00000720	0505	B2B	Customer Contact Person	CUST	S
00009999	0505	B2B	MJ	CUST	

Figure 5.41 Partner Functions

- ▶ **Usage**: Select B2B. Partner functions functionality is used by many SAP components. B2B represents the partner functions functionality usage in SAP SRM.

- ▶ **Description:** Provide a description of the function, for example, Lawyer.

Define Partner Schema

Use this setting to add new partner functions to a schema. Do not add the standard partner functions in a new schema. Only add the new partner functions defined in your implementation. To access this setting, use the menu path **SPRO • SAP Implementation Guide • Supplier Relationship Management • SRM Server • Cross-Application Basic Settings • Define Partner Schema**.

Figure 5.42 shows a screenshot of sample settings for partner schema. To configure these settings, follow these steps:

1. Click on the **New Entries** button to create new entries. Configure the settings as explained in the following list:

   - ▶ **Schema ID**: Enter a 4-digit alphanumeric key to represent the schema, for example, PS02.

   - ▶ **Description**: Enter a description for the new schema.

2. Save the schema.

3. Select the new schema and double-click on **Partner Determination Procedure** in the left pane. Configure the following entries:

   - ▶ **Function**: Select the new partner function.

   - ▶ **Level**: Select the level at which the partner function will be used in procurement documents. Levels can be **Header**, **Item**, or **Header and Item**.

   - ▶ **Card.** (Cardinality): Select how often a partner function is used in the document.

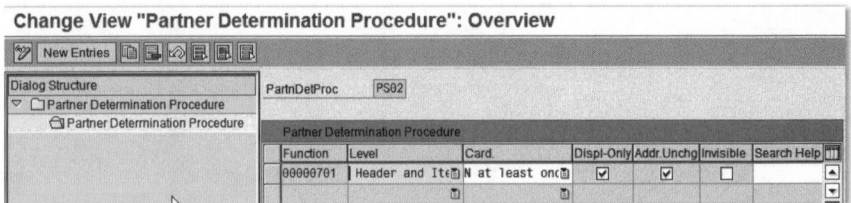

Figure 5.42 Partner Schema

- ▶ **Displ-Only**: Activating this indicator means that the partner function in the document is available in display mode only.

- ▶ **Addr.Unchg**: If you activate this indicator, address data for the partner cannot be changed in the document.

▶ **Invisible**: If you activate this indicator, the partner function will not be visible on the screen.

▶ **Search Help name**: Select a search help from F4 help. You can leave this blank.

5.3.27 Message Control

You can influence how system messages behave using message control settings. For example, you can convert warning messages into error messages, or suppress certain less-important informational or warning messages. Extra care should be taken when converting error messages into warning messages because this can affect the document processing. For example, users may not provide a value for a field that is required to process a document and save the document because the error message was converted into a warning message. You can also configure settings to ignore error messages in XML inbound. Messages generated during invoice simulation can also be controlled using these settings.

Influence Message Control

To influence message control, use the menu path **SPRO • SAP Implementation Guide • Supplier Relationship Management • SRM Server • Cross-Application Basic Settings • Message Control • Influence Message Control**. System messages can be controlled for the procurement objects shown in Table 5.2.

Procurement Object	Description
BUS2000113	Purchase Contract
BUS2121	EC Requirement Coverage Request
BUS2200	Bid Invitation EC
BUS2201	EC Purchase Order
BUS2202	EC Vendor Bid
BUS2203	EC Confirmation Goods/Services
BUS2205	EC Incoming Invoice
BUS2206	Vendor List EC
BUS2208	Auction EC
BUS2233	Confirmation in Supplier Self-Services
BUS2234	Invoice in Supplier Self-Services

Table 5.2 Procurement Objects Used to Control System Messages

To influence messages for particular procurement objects, select the object and double-click on message control. Figure 5.43 shows a screenshot of sample message control settings for a purchase order.

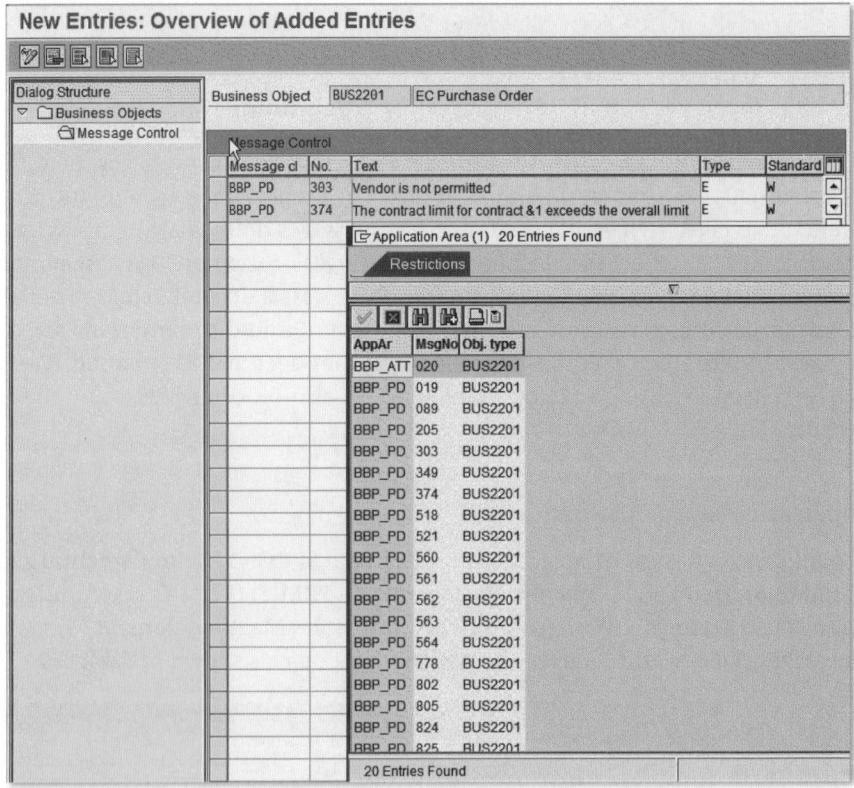

Figure 5.43 Message Control Settings for a Purchase Order

The messages that can be controlled are fixed and pre-determined. Click on the **New Entries** button to control messages as follows:

▸ **Message Id**: Use F4 search help and select the message to be controlled. You cannot input messages that do not appear in the F4 help results.

▸ **Type**: Specify the message attribute **E** (Error), **W** (Warning), or (Suppress).

> **Tip**
>
> In the standard, you cannot enter a return delivery if an invoice has already been entered. If you want to enter a return delivery after the invoice has been entered, suppress message BBP_PD 233.

Influence XML Message Control

Use this setting to configure that specific XML inbound error messages should be ignored. If such error messages occur, the document will still contain errors, but it is treated as an error-free document and approval workflow is triggered. The errors should be corrected, however, before the final approval to release the document.

Use the menu path **SPRO · SAP Implementation Guide · Supplier Relationship Management · SRM Server · Cross-Application Basic Settings · Message Control · Influence Incoming Message Control** to configure that XML error messages for the following objects should be ignored:

- ▸ **BUS2121**: EC requirement coverage request
- ▸ **BUS2203**: EC confirmation goods/services
- ▸ **BUS2205**: EC incoming invoice

Influence Invoice Simulation

Invoice simulation and messages during invoice simulation can be controlled using this setting. In addition, you can deactivate invoice simulation here. Use the menu path **SPRO · SAP Implementation Guide · Supplier Relationship Management · SRM Server · Cross-Application Basic Settings · Message Control · Influence Message Control for Invoice Simulation** to access this setting. Figure 5.44 shows a screenshot with sample settings for invoice simulation. The settings in the screenshot are self-explanatory.

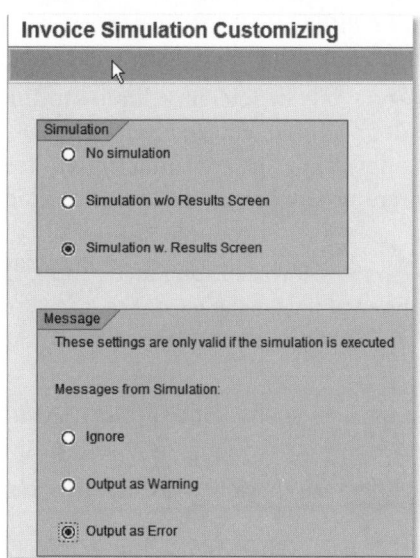

Figure 5.44 Invoice Simulation Settings

5.3.28 Set Tolerance Checks

This is an optional setting used to define tolerances for quantity or value over-runs for deliveries, invoices, or order responses. SAP delivers predefined tolerance keys to which tolerance values can be configured. You can also define tolerance groups, which consist of a set of tolerance keys. If you do not need tolerances, do not configure any settings here.

In confirmations and invoices, if variances are within the tolerances defined here, documents are posted. In the case of purchase order responses, the system uses these tolerances to automatically transfer the data from the purchase order response to the purchase order. The system does not take any tolerances into account when the data is transferred manually from a purchase order response. Automatic data transfer from purchase order response to purchase order is subject to the following conditions:

- Automatic transfer is possible only for the first purchase order response
- Data transfer is possible only if no contract exists for the purchase order item
- Variances are within the tolerance limits
- Workflow WS14500001 is active

If the purchase order response consists of multiple items, the system transfers the sum of all quantities, highest available price, and the latest available delivery date for the materials or the maximum period for services and limit items.

The implementation of tolerance checks involves the following steps:

1. Decide how tolerances will be applied in your organization. For example, the tolerance limits for different users can be different, that is, managers may have higher tolerance limits when compared to other employees.
2. Define tolerance groups to define different sets of tolerance limits. In the previous example, you would need to define one tolerance group for managers and another for employees. Remember to define a tolerance group for vendors, too. Vendor tolerance groups are used when an invoice is created using BAPI.
3. Maintain tolerance keys with tolerance values for each tolerance group. If you define both a percentage and absolute values for the tolerance, the system compares the variance with both and does not allow the document if it exceeds either of the tolerances.
4. Assign the appropriate tolerance group to users via tolerance group TOG in PPOMA_BBP.
5. Control the messages issued during the tolerance check in a document using the *Influence message control* settings.

To configure tolerance checks, use the menu path **SPRO • SAP Implementation Guide • Supplier Relationship Management • SRM Server • Cross-Applica-**

tion Basic Settings • Set Tolerance Checks. Figure 5.45 and Figure 5.46 show sample settings for tolerances.

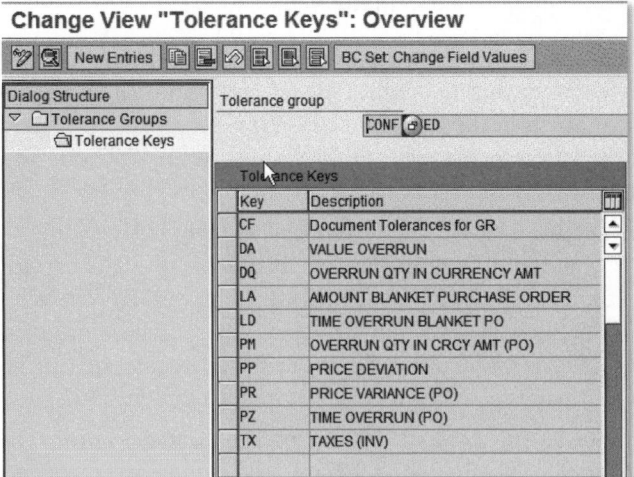

Figure 5.45 Tolerance Group and Tolerance Keys

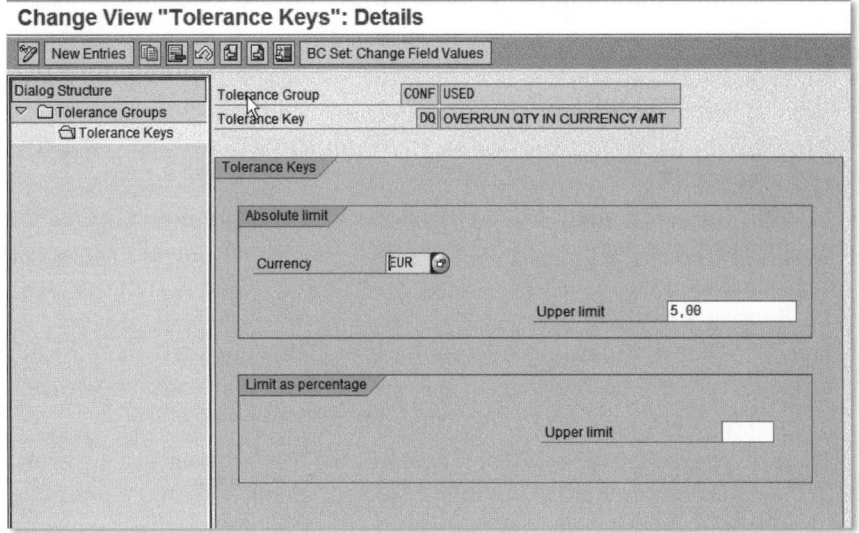

Figure 5.46 Sample Tolerance Settings for Quantity Overrun

Tolerance keys are delivered in the standard and assigned to documents as follows:

▸ **Purchase order response**: PM, PZ, and PR

▸ **Confirmation**: CF

- **Invoice**: PP and TX
- **Confirmations and Invoices**: DA, DQ, LA, LD

The tolerance keys are explained in detail in the following list:

- **CF (over deliver or under delivery tolerance)**: The system checks for over delivery and under delivery during confirmations. First, the system checks against the tolerances given in the purchase order. If none exist, the system checks the tolerances given in the relevant tolerance group. You can also specify 'Unlimited over delivery.'

- **DA (value overrun — cumulative)**: The system checks whether the cumulative invoice value (value of all previous invoice documents plus the current invoice document) or the cumulative confirmation value exceeds the purchase order value. The check is always made against the purchase order. If the variance is within the tolerance defined here, the document can be posted.

- **DQ (quantity variance in the defined currency)**: The tolerances are compared with the outcomes of the following formulas:
  - **If a confirmation is posted**: Net Order Price * [Quantity Invoiced – (total quantity delivered – total quantity invoiced)]
  - **If a confirmation is not expected**: Net Order Price * [Quantity Invoiced – (quantity ordered – total quantity invoiced)]

- **LA (amount of limit purchase order)**: The system compares the value limit in the purchase order with the cumulative invoice value (the sum of values invoiced so far plus current invoice value) for invoices and the cumulative confirmations value for confirmations.

- **LD (time overrun for limit purchase order)**: The system compares the number of days by which the invoice posting date is outside of the planned time interval. If the invoice posting date is before the validity start date, then the difference between start date and invoice posting date is taken as the variance. If the invoice posting date is after the validity end date, then the difference between end date and invoice posting date is taken as the variance. This variance is compared with the upper limit in number of days.

- **PP (price variance)**: The system compares the invoice item value (invoice item quantity * order price) with the expected value based on the preceding document (purchase order price or confirmation value).

- **TX (tax variance)**: The system compares the entered tax amounts with tax calculated by the system and if there is a variance, the variance is checked with tolerances set here.

- **PM (quantity variance converted to currency amount)**: The system compares the purchase order response quantity amount (purchase order response quantity * purchase order price) with the purchase order amount and checks the variance with the tolerances specified here. If percentage tolerances are specified, then the percentage variance from the expected quantity is calculated independent of the purchase order price.

▸ **PZ (time overrun)**: The system calculates the early or late delivery (purchase order delivery date ~ confirmation date) and compares the number of days in the tolerance setting.

▸ **PR (price variance)**: The system compares the purchase order response price with the price in the purchase order and checks the variance with the limits specified here.

5.3.29 Digitally Signed Version of Java Applet Usage in Approval Preview and Document History

Approval preview and document history in SAP SRM documents in earlier versions of SAP SRM use unsigned Java applets, however, SAP delivered a signed applet in SAP SRM 5.0. This confirms that the applet comes from SAP and is not malicious code. This setting is valid for SAP SRM 5.0 and is an optional setting.

To access the setting, use the menu path **SPRO • SAP Implementation Guide • Supplier Relationship Management • SRM Server • Cross-Application Basic Settings • SAP Business Workflow • Activate Signed Java Applet for Approval Preview and Document History**.

If you want to activate the signed applet, follow these steps:

1. Click on the **New Entries** button
2. Enter 'APPLET_SIGNED' in the **Key** field. (If you do not want to activate the signed applet, and the key 'APPLET_SIGNED' exists in this setting, select it and click on the delete icon.)
3. Do not enter anything in the **Value** field.

5.3.30 Define Reasons for Rejecting Supplier Invoices

Possible reasons for rejecting supplier invoices are defined in this setting. Use the menu path **SPRO • SAP Implementation Guide • Supplier Relationship Management • SRM Server • Confirmation and Invoice Verification • Invoice Management System • Define Reasons for Rejecting Supplier Invoices**, and define a reason code and description of the reason code.

5.4 Summary

In this chapter, you learned how SAP SRM helps companies automate their procurement processes. SAP SRM enables companies to empower their employees, without losing control on procurement spend. In this chapter you also learned how to configure self-service procurement in SAP SRM. Reading Chapter 6 on plan-driven procurement, which is coming up next, and Chapter 7 on advanced topics in invoicing, will provide you with a complete understanding of operational procurement capabilities in SAP SRM.

AP SRM plan-driven procurement enables companies to transfer pro-
curement requirements from external planning systems, like SAP ERP, to
SAP SRM to reap the benefits of centralized procurement.

6   SAP SRM Plan-Driven Procurement

The plan-driven procurement process is a classic case of an integrated supply
chain process facilitated by SAP solutions. Plan-driven procurement enables
companies to transfer procurement demands generated from the operational
backend systems, that is planning, maintenance, and project systems, into the
purchaser's work area or sourcing cockpit in SAP Supplier Relationship Management (SAP SRM) for an efficient and streamlined centralized procurement
process. By integrating with the core logistics operations, SAP SRM helps companies address direct materials procurement, which forms a significant percentage of procurement spend. A plan-driven procurement process is seamlessly
integrated with the organization's planning, plant maintenance, and project
management systems.

In this chapter, we will discuss the implementation of external requirements,
that is, requirements generated from systems other than SAP SRM, with specific focus on the requirements for SAP ERP. The integration of catalogs in
SAP's Plant Maintenance (PM) and Project Systems (PS) applications is also discussed in this chapter.

Note
SAP help documentation also refers to plan-driven procurement with the supplier integration scenario. This scenario is discussed in Chapter 13.

6.1   Case Study for Centralized Procurement: Automotive Industry

We will start this chapter with a case study for centralized procurement, using
a company in the automotive industry, Popular Automobile Inc. Popular Automobile Inc. is the market leader in A and B class cars. The company has grown
rapidly in the last five years and set up plants in multiple locations to cater to
customer demand. Each plant has its own procurement department to address
procurement-related requirements. A changing economic environment and the
abolition of protective government policies toward domestic industry have

forced the company to formulate new policies to remain competitive. A reputable management consulting firm was recruited to suggest policy and structural changes.

One of the recommendations was to set up a centralized procurement department and streamline procurement across the organization. The consultants also suggested launching two to three new models every two years to remain competitive in the market. Mr. Wisner has been appointed as head of the newly formed central procurement division at Popular Automobile Inc. He is also responsible for the procurement of all new product developments. His first major task is to consolidate the requirements of all locations for centralized procurement and at the same time increase the speed of procurement. Past efforts to consolidate demand across locations failed due to a considerable resulting increase in procurement lead time. Mr. Wisner knows that he needs to use an efficient information system to tackle these contradictory requirements.

Popular Automobile Inc. uses SAP ERP as its operational system to execute production and planning operations, maintenance activities, and also to execute and manage projects across locations. Mr. Wisner recently attended an SAP summit and was impressed with the capabilities of SAP SRM. He felt that the seamless integration of SAP SRM with SAP ERP could help him resolve the issue of his contradicting requirements. After speaking to SAP experts about SAP SRM, he decided to implement plan-driven procurement and sourcing scenarios to take care of the centralized procurement requirement. The SAP experts informed him that SAP SRM can also help increase the pace of new model development. It was also decided to use supplier catalogs in new model development projects by integrating them with SAP PS. This will help Popular Automobile Inc. use more standard components, leading to better design and reduced product development time. At the same time, integrating requirements from new model development projects with the online sourcing capabilities of SAP SRM is expected to reduce the sourcing lead times for nonstandard components.

The configuration settings required to implement the scenario described in this case study are explained later in this chapter, in Sections 6.3 and 6.4, and the configuration of sourcing is explained later in the book, in Chapter 10. Before starting the configuration, we will briefly look at the functionalities offered in SAP SRM plan-driven procurement.

6.2 Overview of Functionalities

SAP SRM plan-driven procurement helps companies integrate their operational systems with a purchasing platform to enable procurement of all categories of materials, that is, direct materials, indirect materials, and services. While the self-service procurement scenario lets an individual capture requirements, the plan-driven procurement scenario enables automatic order generation for requirements generated from supply chain plans and operational activities like maintenance and projects.

Figure 6.1 shows the plan-driven procurement process for external requirements. External requirements can be generated in the following ways:

▶ **Material Requirements Planning (MRP) integration**
Based on the production requirements and planning data, like safety stock, reorder level, etc., MRP generates the procurement requirements after netting off the stock and pending orders. These automatic requisitions are transferred to SAP SRM for further processing, thus streamlining the process from planning to fulfillment.

▶ **Materials Management (MM) integration**
Purchase requisitions can be created by professional users in the backend systems and transferred to SAP SRM for further processing.

▶ **PM integration**
Based on the components required in a maintenance order, purchase requisitions are generated in the backend system. These requisitions are in turn transferred to SAP SRM for further processing. The components in a maintenance order can also be selected by searching from external catalogs.

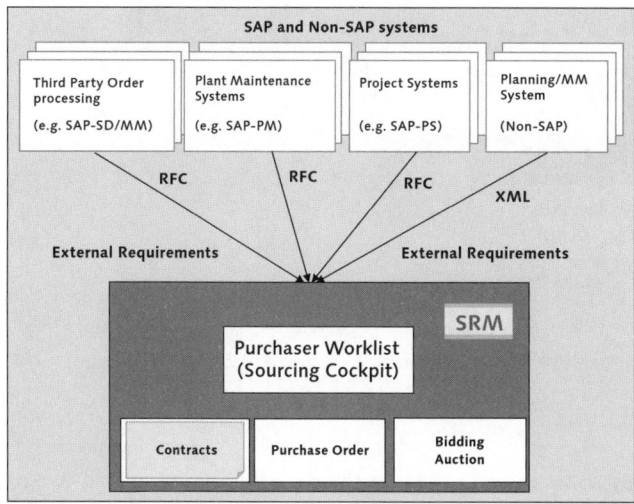

Figure 6.1 Plan-Driven Procurement with External Requirements

▶ **PS integration**
Based on the project requirements given in the project systems application, purchase requisitions are generated in the backend system. These requisitions are in turn transferred to SAP SRM for further processing. The compo-

nents in a project network can also be selected by searching from external catalogs.

▶ **Sales and Distribution (SD) integration for third-party order processing**
In a third-party order processing situation, organizations can send materials to customers directly from suppliers. In a highly integrated scenario, a requirement is generated from a sales order with all of the required information for the supplier to deliver goods to the customer directly. The requirement from the backend system is sent to SAP SRM for order processing.

In a manufacturing environment, demand from production is transferred to SAP SRM. If a contract exists for the material, then the contract is automatically assigned to the requirement and a purchase order is created and transmitted to the supplier. Depending on the settings configured in SAP SRM, human intervention can be minimized or eliminated. Alternatively, if no contract is available, a purchaser can initiate the necessary sourcing activities from the sourcing cockpit.

Figure 6.2 shows a more integrated scenario with PM and PS applications.

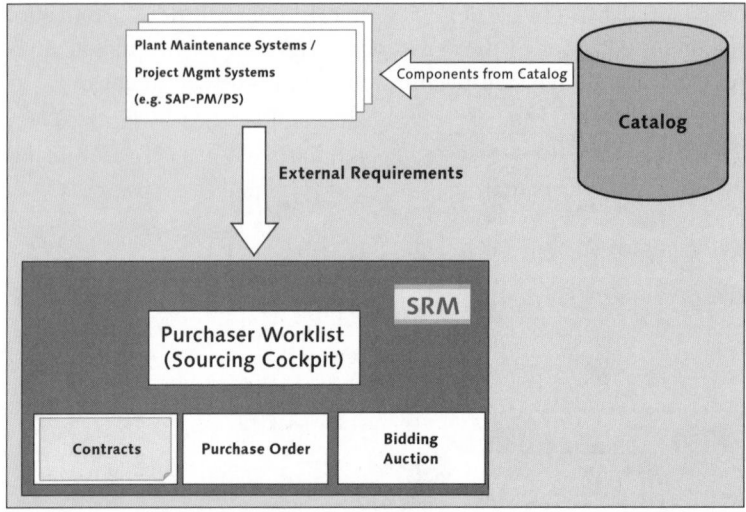

Figure 6.2 Plan-Driven Procurement Integration with PM and PS Applications

An SAP system enables companies to capture the data where the action is. For example, a maintenance engineer is the best person to indicate the components required for a maintenance job. Therefore, he captures all of the requirements in a maintenance order that is integrated with supplier catalogs to select the right components. Also, companies can negotiate organization-wide discounts on Original Equipment Manufacturer (OEM) supplier catalogs. These catalogs contain accurate and all necessary information to maintain the equipment, but this crucial information is normally not readily available to maintenance personnel when they need it. However, access to online supplier catalogs in maintenance applications enables engineers to obtain this information easily, and helps reduce overall maintenance lead time by engineers being able to quickly order the required materials. Once a maintenance engineer selects the required components and other services, he saves the maintenance order, which in turn generates procurement requirements in the form of a purchase requisition. The purchase requisition is automatically converted into a purchase order if a contract already exists. If there is no contract, the purchase requisition is transferred to the sourcing cockpit. A similar functionality for selecting components from a catalog is available from the PS component, also.

The backend system can be an SAP or non-SAP system. Requirements from SAP systems are transferred using Remote Function Calls (RFCs). Requirements from non-SAP systems are transferred using XML communication and thus require SAP NetWeaver Exchange Infrastructure (SAP NetWeaver XI).

Possible deployment scenarios for external requirements integration include the following:

▶ **Local or standalone scenario**
In this process, requirements are transferred from the backend system to SAP SRM. All follow-on processes (purchase order, goods receipts, and invoices) are executed in the SAP SRM system. The invoices posted in SAP SRM create an invoice in the account payables application in the backend system. This can also be integrated with Supplier Self-services (SUS) using EBP-SUS integration scenarios explained in Chapter 14. The local or standalone scenario in plan-driven procurement is normally used for requirements from non-SAP systems.

▶ **Extended classic scenario**
In this process, requirements are transferred from the backend system to SAP SRM. The purchase order is created in SAP SRM and a copy of the purchase order is available in the backend system, too. Goods receipts and invoices can be created either in the backend system or in the SAP SRM system. Direct material procurement is done using the extended classic scenario.

▶ **Classic scenario**
The classic scenario is supported only from SAP SRM version 3.0 on. However, direct material procurement is not supported in the classic scenario.

> **Note**
>
> For a listing of restrictions in external requirements integration, please refer to SAP note 505030. Also, read SAP Notes 441892 and 451245 for integration of requirements from MRP.

Now let's move on is a discussion about external requirements.

6.3 Configuration of External Requirements

In this section, we will explain the configuration settings required for the plan-driven procurement external requirements scenario.

6.3.1 Settings in the SAP SRM system

We will first look at the settings required in the SAP SRM system.

Basic Settings for the SAP SRM Server

All of the basic settings required for the self-service procurement scenario should be configured as follows:

▸ Basic technical settings to integrate with the backend systems
▸ Organizational plan setup
▸ Master data settings for suppliers, product categories, and products
▸ Other common technical settings

Detailed configurations of these settings are described in Sections 3.4, 3.5, 3.6, 3.7, and 3.8 in Chapter 3.

Define an Entry Channel in the Organizational Plan for the Backend System

In Transaction PPOMA_BBP, create a node in the organizational plan to act as an entry channel for external requirements. Figure 6.3 shows sample settings in an organizational plan. In this screenshot, external channel **EBP_EXT_CHANNEL** is defined to receive the external requirements. Maintain the attributes CUR (local currency), ACS (accounting system), and delivery address.

Create an RFC User in SAP SRM and Assign it to the Organizational Unit for the Entry Channel

Using the SAP SRM Web transaction to create users, create a user and assign it to the organizational unit for the entry channel. In Figure 6.3, user **EXTBBP** is assigned to organizational unit **EBP_EXT_CHANNEL**. This user should be assigned as an RFC user in the RFC destination for SAP SRM system in the backend system settings.

Define the Local Purchasing Group Responsible for the Organizational Unit for the Entry Channel

In Transaction PPOMA_BBP, define the local purchasing group(s) and assign the organizational responsibility for the entry channel and backend product categories. If you have different purchasing groups responsible for different product categories, maintain the local purchasing groups as required. In Figure 6.3, the local purchasing group **EBP_PG_LOC3** has the responsibility for organizational unit **EBP_EXT_CHANNEL** and backend product categories.

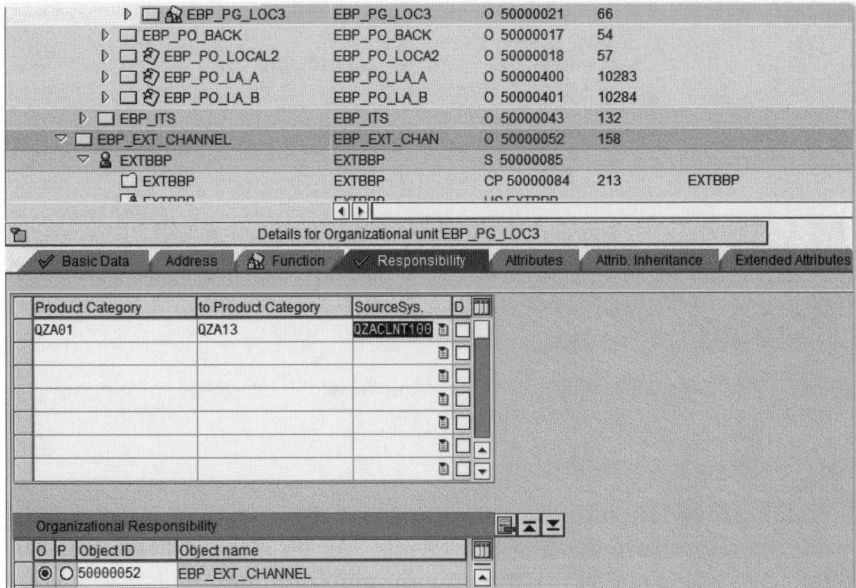

Figure 6.3 Organizational Plan Settings for External Requirements

Define Attribute DP_PROC_TY and Locations for the Purchasing Group

In Transaction PPOMA_BBP, maintain the attribute DP_PROC_TY (purchase order transaction type for direct material) for the local purchasing group(s) responsible for the entry channel. Also, maintain locations in extended attributes for the purchasing group(s). Ensure that you have created the purchase order document type with the same name as the transaction type specified for DP_PROC_TY and the same number range with external number assignment in the backend MM system.

Define Attributes BUK and BSA for the Purchasing Organizational Unit

Define the attributes BUK (company code) and BSA (document type in SAP ERP) for the local purchasing organization of the responsible purchasing group. Sample settings, where ERPCLNT100 is the backend system, are:

▸ **BUK**: ERPCLNT100\1000

▸ **BSA**: ERPCLNT100\ECQ5

6.3.2 Settings in the Backend System

We will now look at the settings you need to configure in the SAP ERP or SAP R/3 backend systems.

Maintain RFC Destination for the SAP SRM System

In Transaction SM59, maintain the RFC destination for the SAP SRM system. On the Logon tab, shown in Figure 6.4, maintain the RFC user assigned to the entry channel organizational unit as the logon user. In our example, RFC user **EXTBBP** is assigned as the logon user.

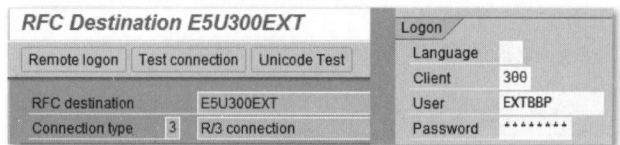

Figure 6.4 RFC Destination Settings in the Backend SAP ERP for the SAP SRM System

Maintain View V_T160PR

In Transaction SM30, maintain the settings for table view V_T160PR. Define profiles for all external procurement systems (SAP SRM systems) and assign the logical target systems. Figure 6.5 shows the sample settings.

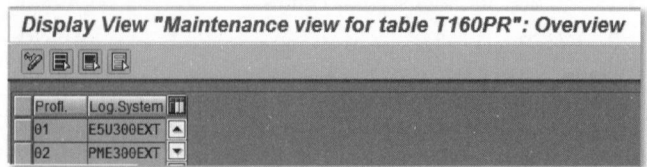

Figure 6.5 Maintain Profiles for External Systems

Maintain View V_T160EX

This is an important setting that determines the purchase requisitions that should be processed in the external procurement system (e.g., SAP SRM). The external procurement system is determined based on a combination of the material group and purchasing group. Some organizations define dedicated purchasing groups in SAP ERP for use in SAP SRM. In Transaction code SM30, maintain the settings for table view V_T160EX. Maintain the combinations of the material group and purchasing group and the profile for the external procurement system. From these settings, the system identifies the procurement system for the purchase requisitions. Figure 6.6 shows the sample settings.

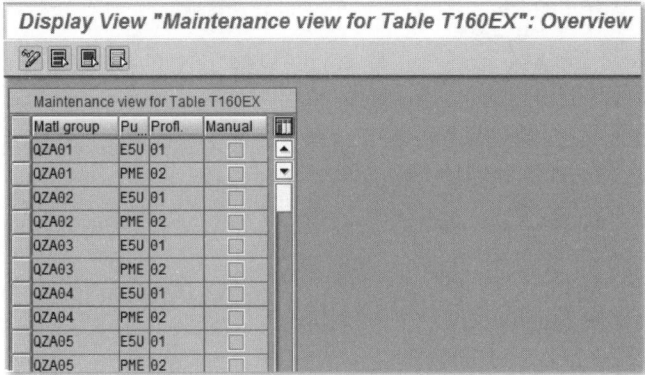

Figure 6.6 Maintain Settings in Table View V_T160EX

The settings are described in detail in the following list:

▶ **Matl group**: Enter the material group.

▶ **Purchasing group**: Enter the purchasing group.

▶ **Profile**: Enter the profile of the SAP SRM system to which requirements with the given material group and purchasing group combination will be sent for procurement. Profiles are defined in view V_T160PR.

▶ **Manual**: If you want to process the requirements that have a unique source of supply within the SAP ERP system, activate the **Manual** indicator. If this indicator is not set, the system automatically considers the requirements with the material group and purchasing group combination as external requirements. Refer to SAP Note 648074 for more details.

Note

User exit BBPK0001 can be used if you want to influence the profile determination (and hence requisitions to be sent to SAP SRM) with criteria other than the material group and purchasing group.

Schedule Report BBP_EXTREQ_TRANSFER

Program BBP_EXTREQ_TRANSFER is used for transferring the requirements from SAP ERP to the SAP SRM system. You can execute this program whenever required or schedule the program to run periodically so that requirements are transferred automatically.

> **Troubleshooting Tips for External Requirements**
>
> ▶ Requisition items marked as procurement in external systems will have the pro-file value in the EPROFILE field in the EBAN table.
>
> ▶ Requisition items to be transferred to the SAP SRM system are available in the EPRTRANS table.
>
> ▶ Sometimes, you may find items in the EPRTRANS table but when you execute the program BBP_EXTREQ_TRANSFER, no items are transferred. If so, check the transfer date given in the selection screen of BBP_EXTREQ_TRANSFER. The req-uisition items in the EPRTRANS table have a transfer date. You can transfer the items only on or after this transfer date. This is the Release Date on the purchase requisition Quantities/dates tab and is derived from the delivery date and pro-curement lead time.

6.4 Enable Catalogs with Plant Maintenance or Project Systems

The settings described in this section are required to enable catalogs in the Plant Maintenance (PM) and Project Systems (PS) applications. If you do not need to enable catalogs in SAP PM and SAP PS, the settings in this section are not required. This section is not related to SAP SRM implementations, but is provided to help consultants implementing catalog integration in PM and PS.

6.4.1 Prerequisites for Catalog Integration with Plant Maintenance and Project Systems

Prerequisites to integrate catalogs with the PM or PS applications are as follows:

▶ SAP R/3 Enterprise (release 4.7 or higher)

▶ Catalogs are SAP Open Catalog Interface (OCI) compliant

6.4.2 Configuration Settings to Enable Catalogs

The following settings are required in the the backend system to enable selec-tion of components from online catalogs in a maintenance order or task list.

Define Catalogs

You need to define all of the catalogs used in PM or PS applications using the menu path **SPRO • Plant Maintenance and Customer Service • Maintenance and Service Processing • Maintenance and Service Orders • Interface for Pro-curement Using Catalogs (OCI) • Define Catalogs**. Alternatively, you can use the menu path **Project System • Material • Interface for Procurement Using Catalogs (OCI) • Define Catalogs**. The data given here is catalog specific. Contact the catalog provider for details if you are connecting to external supplier catalogs, also.

In Table 6.1, the necessary entries for the SRM-MDM Catalog and the SAP CCM catalog are shown. Refer to Chapter 9 for more details on the SRM-MDM Catalog.

> **Note**
>
> The **Remarks** column in Table 6.1 is provided to describe the setting and is not part of the actual setting.

Parameter Name	Paremeter Value	Type	Remarks
	http://<HTTP_server>:<port>/sap/bc/bsp/ccm/srm_cse/main.do http://<HTTP_server>:<port>/SRM-MDM/SRM_MDM	0	Maintain the URL for catalog search. Samples for CCM and MDM are given here
CATALOGID	MASTER	2	Mandatory for CCM
SAP-CLIENT	<Client in which search engine runs>	2	Mandatory for CCM
SAP-LANGUAGE	SY-LANGU	1	Mandatory for CCM
Locale	<Language in which you published the catalog>	2	Mandatory for CCM
ccm-user	<CCM user>	2	Only for CCM
ccm-password	<CCM password>	2	Only for CCM
Username	<MDM user id>	2	For MDM
Password	<MDM password>	2	For MDM
Catalog	<MDM catalog name>	2	For MDM
sap-locale	<Language of catalog>	2	For MDM
HOOK_URL		4	Keep the value blank All catalogs
~OKCode	ADDI	2	For CCM, MDM
~target	_top	2	For CCM, MDM
~caller	CTLG	2	For MDM

Table 6.1 Configuration Entries for Catalogs

Assign Catalog to Order Type or Network Plan Type

Using the menu path **SPRO • Plant Maintenance and Customer Service • Maintenance and Service Processing • Maintenance and Service Orders • Interface for Procurement Using Catalogs (OCI) • Assign catalog to order type**, catalogs are assigned to maintenance order type and planning plant to make them available in the PM application.

Using the menu path **SPRO • Project System • Material • Interface for Procurement Using Catalogs (OCI) • Assign catalog to network plan type**, catalogs are assigned to the network plan type and planning plant to make them available in the PS application.

Convert HTML Fields to SAP Fields

In this configuration setting, HTML fields in the catalog and SAP fields are mapped using menu path **SPRO • Plant Maintenance and Customer Service • Maintenance and Service Processing • Maintenance and Service Orders • Interface for Procurement Using Catalogs (OCI) • Convert HTML fields to SAP fields**. Alternatively, you can use menu path **SPRO • Project System • Material • Interface for Procurement Using Catalogs (OCI) • Convert HTML fields to SAP fields**. Note that technical field names of the SAP fields are available in structure RIHFCOM_XL.

> **Tip**
>
> For more details on available SAP fields and HTML fields, please read the IMG documentation for this configuration setting.

Sample mappings are shown in Table 6.2.

Catalog ID	SeqNo	SAP Field	HTML Field
<catalog1>	1	MATERIAL	NEW_ITEM-VENDORMAT
<catalog1>	2	DESCRIPTION	NEW_ITEM-DESCRIPTION
<catalog1>	3	RIHFCOM_XL-MENGE	NEW_ITEM-QUANTITY
<catalog1>	4	MANUFACTCODE	NEW_ITEM-VENDOR
<catalog1>	5	RIHFCOM_XL-IDNLF	NEW_ITEM-VENDORMAT

Table 6.2 Convert HTML Fields to SAP Fields — Sample Settings

Convert HTML Field Values

In this configuration setting, you can specify how the catalog values should be changed prior to copying them into the SAP system. For example, you may want to change the unit of measure (UOM) to 'ST,' if the UOM in the catalog is 'pc.' Access the configuration using the menu path **SPRO** • **Plant Maintenance and Customer Service** • **Maintenance and Service Processing** • **Maintenance and Service Orders** • **Interface for Procurement Using Catalogs (OCI)** • **Convert HTML Field** Values.

> **Caution**
>
> The entries in the HTML value field and SAP value field are case sensitive.

Sample mappings are shown in Table 6.3.

Catalog ID	Seq No	HTML field	HTML Value	SAP Value
<catalog1>	1	NEW_ITEM-UNIT	ea	ST
<catalog1>	2	NEW_ITEM-UNIT	CT	CAR

Table 6.3 Convert HTML Field Values — Sample Settings

Define Conversion Components

Using this setting, you can define the conversion components used to convert catalog data into valid SAP ERP values. Access the settings using menu path **SPRO** • **Plant Maintenance and Customer Service** • **Maintenance and Service Processing** • **Maintenance and Service Orders** • **Interface for Procurement Using Catalogs (OCI)** • **Define Conversion Modules**. Sample settings are shown in Table 6.4.

> **Tip**
>
> The standard conversion components are listed in the IMG documentation. You can also use your own function components with the same interface as the function components IOCI_EXAMPLE_W.

Catalog ID	Seq No	Funct Name
<catalog1>	1	IOCI_DESCRIPTION_W
<catalog1>	2	IOCI_CONVERT_OLD_MAT_NO_W
<catalog1>	3	IOCI_SET_ITEM_CAT_W

Table 6.4 Define Conversion Component — Sample Settings

Implement BAdI PLM_CATALOG_IF

BAdI PLM_CATALOG_IF should be implemented to copy components from an external catalog into an order or task list.

Method COMPONENT_VIA_CATALOG_GET should be implemented. Sample coding is shown in Listing 6.1.

```
METHOD if_ex_plm_catalog_if~component_via_catalog_get .
 CALL FUNCTION 'IOCI_PLM_CATALOG_IF'
 EXPORTING
 caufvd_exp = caufvd_exp
 afvgd_exp = afvgd_exp
 plkod_exp = plkod_exp
 plpod_exp = plpod_exp
 TABLES
 fcom_xl_tab = fcom_xl_tab.
ENDMETHOD.
```

Listing 6.1 Sample BAdI PLM_CATALOG_IF Coding

6.5 Summary

In this chapter, you learned how the SAP SRM plan-driven procurement scenario enables companies to integrate the backend planning and operational systems with SAP SRM for direct material procurement. You also learned how to integrate catalogs with the PM and PS applications. In Chapter 7, we will discuss advanced invoicing functionalities in SAP SRM.

SAP SRM Invoice Management System (IMS) provides companies with advanced, collaborative, invoice exception-handling functionalities. Companies can also automate their invoicing and payment processes using procurement cards functionality in SAP SRM.

7   Advanced Topics in Invoicing

SAP Supplier Relationship Management (SAP SRM) provides two advanced functionalities to automate the invoicing and payments process — IMS and procurement cards. IMS, as its name suggests, is an invoice management tool that enables companies to process incoming invoices and manage exceptions. It provides a collaborative platform for both internal employees and suppliers to process any exceptions in the invoices, thus addressing a major concern of purchasers and suppliers. IMS is discussed in detail in Section 7.1.

Using a procurement card for low-value purchases in a self-service procurement scenario enables the automation of invoicing and payment processes, thus reducing the load on the invoicing department. Procurement cards have the potential to save 50-60% on transaction costs for low-value purchases. We will discuss procurement card functionality in detail in Section 7.2.

7.1   Invoice Management System

IMS provides a central platform for managing incoming supplier invoices. The invoices received from suppliers are entered in the system, mapped to the appropriate purchase orders, and posted in the relevant backend system — if there are no exceptions. Another useful feature in IMS is the collaborative exception handling. Invoices with exceptions are routed to the invoice monitor. An Adobe interactive form is generated for the exceptions, which can be forwarded through email to the appropriate processor, be it an internal employee or a supplier. The processor can correct the exceptions directly in the interactive form and submit it back to update the system. IMS also helps companies that wish to outsource the invoicing process or that wish to set up a central shared services model. The benefits of IMS include the following:

▶ A central platform for entry of incoming invoices with or without purchaser order reference. Invoices can be entered by means of XML, Electronic Data Interchange (EDI), or manually.

- An easy-to-use and standardized interface to facilitate entry of invoices in the system by users with very little training.
- The ability to streamline and standardize the invoice verification process regardless of the complexities in the backend system.
- A collaborative exception monitoring platform to resolve disputes faster.
- The ability to achieve better supplier relations by efficient processing of invoices and on-time payments.
- Efficient processing facilitates companies to obtain cash discounts offered by suppliers on early payments.
- A reduction in the overall invoice processing time.
- Support for new business models. like the shared services model or the outsourcing of invoice processing.

The case study we will look at in the next section will show a customer business scenario where IMS helps a diversified company handle centralized invoice processing and then distribute the final invoices to multiple backend accounting systems.

7.1.1 Case Study for Shared Services Invoicing: Diversified Group

Imperial Holdings Inc. is a well-known organization with interests in a variety of industries, including ready-made snacks, tobacco, paper, packaging, and software. Imperial Holdings Inc. has strategic business units (SBUs) in each of these industries. Each SBU is a market leader in its respective industry segment, is headed by a CEO, and all operations within an SBU are managed independent of the other SBUs. Furthermore, each of the SBUs has its own ERP system to manage operations. Imperial Holding Inc. has recently implemented a central SAP SRM system for indirect material procurement.

They have also recently formed a shared services department (SSD) to bring common services from all SBUs under one roof. This department has an aggressive target of saving $100 million annually. All SBUs have agreed to move the responsibility of supplier invoice processing to the newly formed SSD. The team analysing the invoicing processes at all SBUs has submitted the following key findings to Gerald, the head of the SSD:

- All invoices are received on paper and entered manually in the systems.
- About 15-30% of the invoices have exceptions and require extensive follow-up to resolve them.
- Around 70% of the invoice processing time is spent on dispute resolution, an entirely manual process, leading to inefficiency and high process cost.

▸ Almost 25% of the invoices do not have a purchase order reference.

▸ Any invoicing system deployed by the SSD should have a collaborative invoice dispute resolution management capability to reduce processing time. Processing time and errors can be reduced further if the system has capabilities to receive XML invoices from suppliers.

Gerald has recently attended an SAP event in Las Vegas and was impressed with the IMS functionality offered by SAP SRM. He noted that implementation of IMS should help his department in meeting their goals. SAP executives also demonstrated the supplier self services (SUS) capabilities of SAP SRM, which would enable Imperial Holding Inc.'s suppliers to send their invoices online without the need for any data entry by Imperial's SSD team. Gerald has decided to upgrade their SAP SRM system in two phases by implementing IMS in the first phase and SUS in the second phase.

We will now take a look at the functionalities of IMS in Section 7.1.2, before proceeding to discuss the configuration of IMS in Section 7.1.3.

7.1.2 Overview of Functionalities

IMS is a central platform for processing supplier invoices. IMS is built on SAP SRM's invoice verification functionality by providing exception handling capabilities. IMS takes care of the complete cycle of invoice processing: receipt of invoices, entry of invoices, matching invoices with purchase orders and goods or services receipts, dispute resolution, workflow approvals, and posting in the backend financial accounting system. IMS also enables a collaborative dispute management system to handle invoice disputes. It is essential for companies to process supplier invoices efficiently and ensure on-time payments to have effective relations with suppliers. IMS is available from SAP SRM version 5.0 on. You can also use IMS to manage invoices for purchases in SAP R/3 version 4.6C on.

IMS can be used with all SAP SRM deployment scenarios. Figure 7.1 illustrates invoice processing using IMS.

The process steps are described in more detail as follows:

1. Suppliers can send invoices via normal mail, courier, or fax (paper based invoices), EDI, or XML. Paper-based invoices are entered directly into SAP SRM. Invoices received via EDI can be converted into XML invoices using an appropriate adaptor in SAP NetWeaver Exchange Infrastructure (SAP NetWeaver XI). XML invoices from applications like SUS are processed in SAP NetWeaver XI and then posted in SAP SRM. Invoices can be created with or without reference to a purchase order.

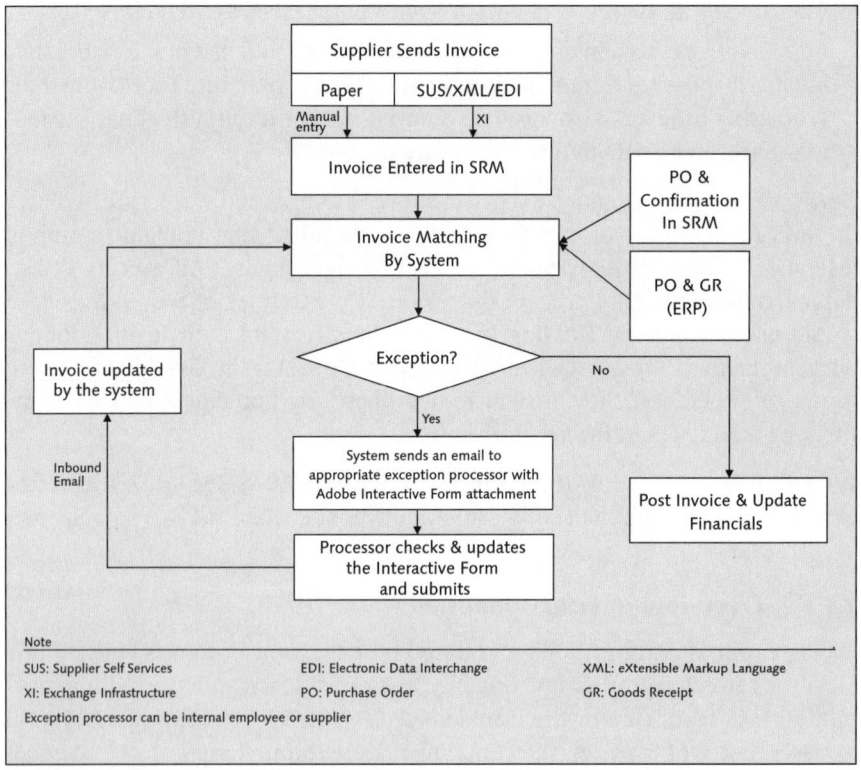

Figure 7.1 Supplier Invoice Processing Using IMS

2. Invoices are matched with purchase order information and goods or services receipt information from the relevant backend or SAP SRM system based on deployment scenario. Invoices are always created in SAP SRM when IMS is used. If there are no errors, the invoices are posted automatically and transferred to the backend financial accounting system.

3. If any errors exist, one or more exceptions are generated. Different types of exceptions are explained in Section 7.1.3. All invoices with exceptions are processed in the invoice monitor. If an exception needs to be resolved by internal employees, it can be forwarded to the relevant employee in the form of an interactive form. For example, if the exception is with regard to nonreceipt of goods, the exception can be forwarded to a store's clerk for verification.

4. The responsible employee receiving the exception email can verify the exception in the interactive form and update the form with a response. The submitted responses in the interactive form update the invoice automatically. Email is used to forward the exception and to receive the submitted response.

5. If the exception requires a response from the supplier, it can be forwarded to the supplier. For example, if the exception is related to supplier invoicing at a higher price, it can be forwarded to the supplier for correcting the price.

6. The supplier updates the form with a response, which updates the invoice automatically. For example, if the exception is related to a higher price, then the supplier may correct the price according to the purchase order. The supplier may also provide justification for the higher price in a note. The invoicing clerk can route this response to a purchaser who may confirm the higher price or reduce the price according to the purchase order and ask the supplier to provide a subsequent invoice for the difference in price.

7. The invoice is posted in the backend financial accounting system when all exceptions are resolved.

7.1.3   Configuration of an Invoice Management System

As mentioned previously, IMS is built on SAP SRM invoicing functionality and therefore all of the basic settings required for SAP SRM invoicing in self-service procurement are required for an IMS implementation. We'll look at this in more detail in this section.

Technical Components for IMS

Aside from SRM EBP, which facilitates the functionalities required for procurement and invoicing in SAP SRM, the following components are used in IMS for collaborative exception management:

▶ **Invoice Monitor**: Invoice monitor is used to manage exceptions in invoicing. It is available to users with the role SAP_EC_BBP_ACCOUNTANT.

▶ **Adobe Document Server**: The integration with adobe document server facilitates sending exceptions to an exception processor as an Adobe interactive form mail attachment.

▶ **Inbound and Outbound Email**: Email is used to send exceptions to exception processors and receive responses from processors.

▶ **TREX**: Optionally available to enable advanced duplicate searches.

Basic Configurations for an SRM Server

Maintain the settings as described in Chapter 3.

Configure Self-Service Procurement

Maintain the settings as described in Chapter 5.

Business Workflow Setup

Maintain the settings as described in Chapter 8.

Schedule Program BBP_IV_AUTO_COMPLETE

It is common practice at many companies that invoices are received and entered in the system before receiving the goods receipts. However, such invoices cannot be posted in SAP SRM until the corresponding goods receipts are posted. The BBP_IV_AUTO_COMPLETE program checks whether goods receipts have been posted in the system that correspond to pending invoices and tries to post such invoices automatically.

You should understand the following program selection screen fields:

▶ **Days for status change**: The system waits for goods receipt for the number of days mentioned here. After this time has elapsed, the system changes the status of the invoice from 'Waiting for preceding document' to 'To be corrected manually.'

▶ **Days for Email**: After the number of days mentioned here, an email is sent to the goods recipient to confirm the goods receipt.

You should schedule this program to run periodically (e.g., every 20 min.), using Transaction code SM36. Determine the frequency based on invoice volume and typical invoice entry timing in your organization.

Schedule Program RBBP_IMS_MAIL_PROCESS

When an interactive form is completed and submitted by a user via email, the system updates the invoice as soon as it receives the email. However, sometimes the system may not be able to update the invoice immediately, for example, if the document is locked by another user. Program RBBP_IMS_MAIL_PROCESS processes all such unprocessed emails periodically. It is recommended to schedule this program to run every few minutes (e.g., every 5 min.) using Transaction SM36.

> **Note**
>
> The field "Number of processing attempts" defines the number of times the system will try to process the email and update the invoice.

Assign Tasks of Approval Workflow

Using this setting, you can assign invoice approval workflow tasks that are relevant for triggering the *approval overdue* exception. To access this setting, use the menu path **SPRO • SAP Implementation Guide • Supplier Relationship Management • SRM server • Confirmation and Invoice Verification • Invoice Management System • Assign Tasks of Approval Workflow**. In the standard system, the following tasks are already assigned:

▸ **TS10407918**: Approval Task for IVApprFragm1

▸ **TS10407920**: Inv. Approval in 1 Step WF

▸ **TS10407921**: 1st Invoice in 2 Step WF

▸ **TS10407923**: 2nd Invoice Approval in 2 Step WF

▸ **TS10407925**: Approval Task in Admin-WF

▸ **TS14508056**: Correct Erroneous Invoice

If you define new workflows and wish to include them in the "approval overdue" exception, they need to be included here.

Define Exceptions

Using this setting, you define error messages that lead to the triggering of exceptions. Many exceptions are delivered as standard settings. Unless you want to define new exceptions or do not want certain errors as exceptions, you do not need to configure any settings here. Once an exception is triggered based on the settings made here, the processing of exceptions is performed based on the settings in the Web Transaction "Settings for Invoice Monitor."

To access this setting, use the menu path **SPRO • SAP Implementation Guide • Supplier Relationship Management • SRM server • Confirmation and Invoice Verification • Invoice Management System • Define exceptions**. Figure 7.2 shows sample settings for **Exception Error** and provides a list of typical exceptions.

The fields in the screen area **Exception -> Error** are as follows:

▸ **Event**: Select an exception category from search help.

▸ **Application Area**: Specify the application area of the error message. Alternatively, you can select a message number from search help in the MsgNo column and the application area will be automatically entered.

▸ **MsgNo**: Select an appropriate invoice error message from search help. The messages relevant for invoice errors are normally found in application areas BBP_IMS, BBP_PD, and BBP_IV.

▸ **By item**: If this flag is activated, exceptions are raised at the item level. An email with an interactive form can be sent for each item.

▸ **Inactive**: If this flag is activated, the error message is deactivated.

Change View "Exception -> Error": Overview

Event	Application Area	MsgNo	by item	Inactive	Message Text
DUPLICATE INVOICE			☐	☐	
DUPLICATE INVOICE	BBP_IMS	005	☑	☐	This invoice may have already been updated; check invoice &1
DUPLICATE INVOICE	BBP_PD	236	☑	☐	Invoice &1 has already been entered. Check your entries
DUPLICATE INVOICE	BBP_PD	811	☐	☐	Invoice has possible been posted; Compare with invoice &1
ERROR IN ACCOUNTING SYSTEM	BBP_IMS	008	☐	☐	
MISSING EXTERNAL INFO	BBP_PD	077	☑	☐	Enter an invoicing date
MISSING EXTERNAL INFO	BBP_PD	080	☐	☐	Enter an invoiced amount
MISSING EXTERNAL INFO	BBP_PD	112	☑	☐	Balance is not zero: &1
MISSING EXTERNAL INFO	BBP_PD	196	☑	☐	Enter a description
MISSING EXTERNAL INFO	BBP_PD	230	☑	☐	Please enter tax amount
MISSING EXTERNAL INFO	BBP_PD	235	☐	☐	Enter supplier invoice number
MISSING EXTERNAL INFO	BBP_PD	237	☑	☐	Enter an amount
MISSING EXTERNAL INFO	BBP_PD	711	☐	☐	The units of measure in the PO and invoice do not match
MISSING GR	BBP_IV	171	☑	☐	
MISSING GR	BBP_PD	713	☑	☐	Preceding document required for the invoice is not available
MISSING GR	BBP_PD	835	☑	☐	For item &1 there are no more open values for calculation
MISSING INTERNAL INFO	BBP_PD	822	☑	☐	Error in account assignment for item &
OTHER ERRORS	*		☐	☐	
PRICE TOLERANCE	BBP_IV	069	☑	☐	Average price too high: Tolerance limit of &1 and &2 exceeded
PRICE TOLERANCE	BBP_IV	070	☑	☐	
PRICE TOLERANCE	BBP_IV	071	☑	☐	Average price too low: below tolerance limit of &1 and &2
PRICE TOLERANCE	BBP_IV	072	☑	☐	
PRICE TOLERANCE	BBP_IV	078	☑	☐	Purchase order limit exceeded
PRICE TOLERANCE	BBP_IV	082	☑	☐	Value too high (tolerance limit of &1 and &2 exceeded)
PRICE TOLERANCE	BBP_IV	083	☑	☐	
QUANTITY TOLERANCE	BBP_IV	080	☑	☐	Quantity too high (tolerance limit of &1 and &2 exceeded)
QUANTITY TOLERANCE	BBP_IV	081	☑	☐	Error in currency translation
QUANTITY TOLERANCE	BBP_IV	127	☑	☐	Quantity too low: Below tolerance limit of & %
TAX TOLERANCE	BBP_IV	208	☑	☐	The entered tax amount is incorrect; correct amount is &
WRONG REFERENCE	BBP_IV	150	☑	☐	Collective invoice not possible for these purchase orders
WRONG REFERENCE	BBP_IV	170	☑	☐	At least one PO reference is incorrect, or you have no authorization

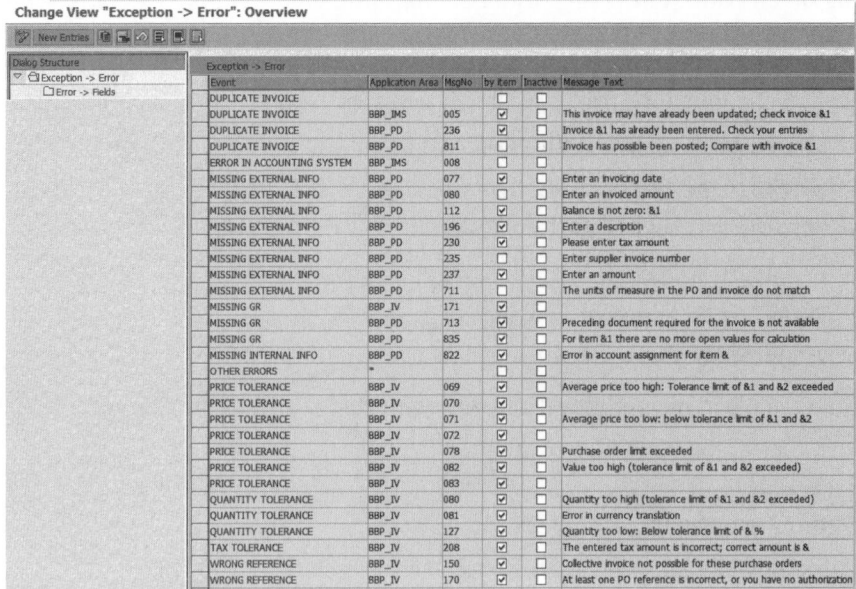

Figure 7.2 Sample Invoice Exception Error Settings

Figure 7.3 shows sample **Error -> Fields** settings for an exception. To access this screen and define which fields are input on the screen, and, in the interactive form to correct the error, in the left pane select an exception row and click on **Error -> Fields**.

Area: BBP_PD
Message: 112

Table Name	Field Name	Inactive
FREIGHT	AMOUNT	☐
HEADER	GROSS_AMOUNT	☐
TAX	TAX_AMOUNT	☐

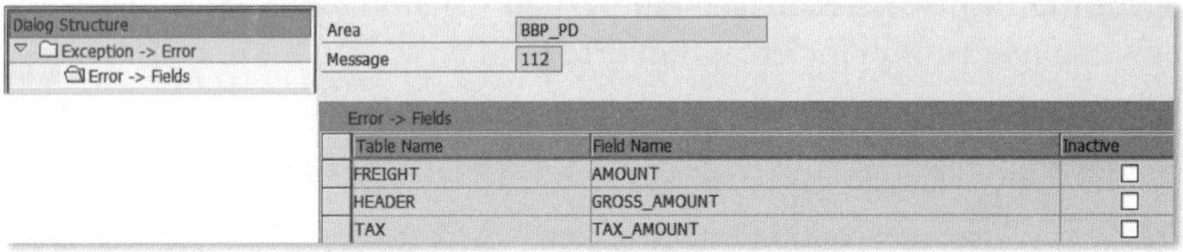

Figure 7.3 Sample Error Fields settings for an exception

The fields in this area are as follows:

- **Table Name, Field Name**: Select the field that is open for input using search help in the **Field Name** column. The table and fields that can be used are available in table BBPD_IV_ADB_FLDS.
- **Inactive**: If this flag is activated, then the corresponding field will not be available for input.

Set Up Authorizations for IMS

The authorization object for invoice verification in SAP SRM is BBP_PD_INV. Users can process invoices based on the activities (create, change, display, etc.) assigned under this authorization object. A new activity 36 'Extended Maintenance' is available in the authorization object. If this new activity is assigned to any users, then such users can use the invoice exception monitor.

The activity is assigned to role SAP_EC_BBP_ACCOUNTANT in the standard system. Users with this role can use the invoice exception monitor in addition to the normal invoicing functions. The role also has the additional menu options *Invoice monitor* and *Settings for invoice monitor*.

Activate Scenario-Specific Fields

Using this optional setting, additional fields in invoicing for planned delivery costs, one-time vendor are activated. This is necessary, if you want to use SAP SRM invoices for backend purchase orders. To access the setting, use the menu path **SPRO • SAP Implementation Guide • Supplier Relationship Management • SRM server • Cross Application Basic Settings • Personalization • Activate Scenario-specific fields**.

Scenario BBP_EXI (SAP SRM Extended Invoice Verification) is not activated in the standard. You may activate it by clicking on the checkbox in the Active column for scenario BBP_EXI.

Settings for Invoice Monitor to Configure Exceptions

Exceptions are triggered based on the settings in the configuration setting *Define Exceptions*. The triggered exceptions are processed based on the settings for each exception in the Web Transaction *Settings for Invoice Monitor*. This browser-based transaction is available to users who have the role SAP_EC_BBP_ ACCOUNTANT assigned. By maintaining appropriate settings, companies can ensure that most of the exception processing is done automatically by the system with very little manual intervention. The following 10 different types of exceptions can be configured:

► Duplicate invoice
► Missing internal information
► Missing external information
► Approval overdue
► Missing goods receipt
► Price variance
► Quantity variance

- Incorrect reference
- Other errors
- Tax variance

The following settings are available to be configured by customers for each of the listed exceptions:

- Whether the exception email is sent automatically by the system or manually.

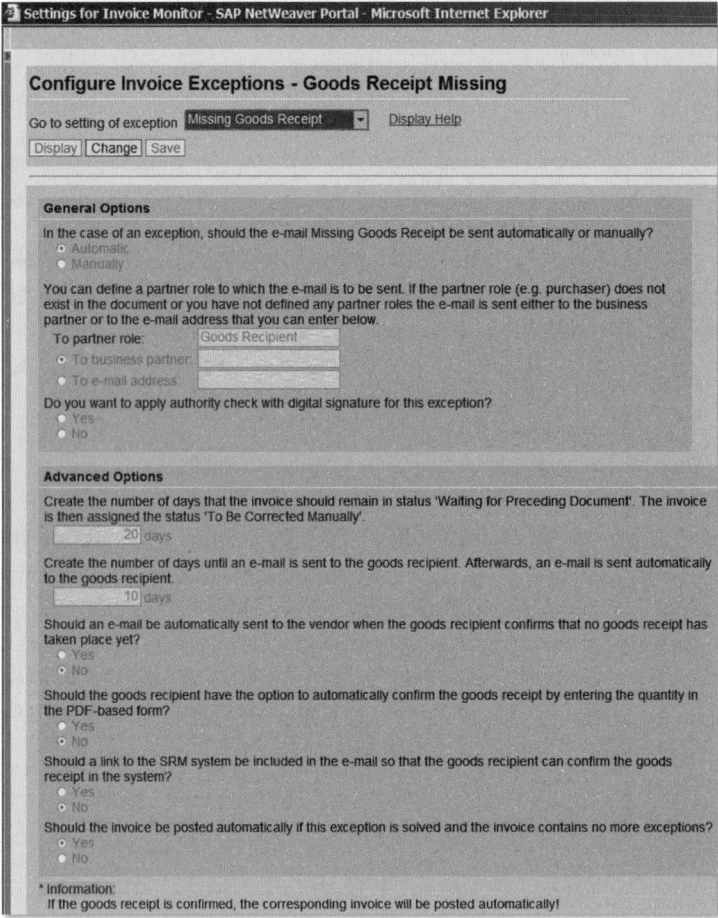

Figure 7.4 Sample Invoice Monitor Settings for Exception — Missing GR

- To which partner role the email should be sent. For example, for price variance, an email may be sent to the purchaser. For missing goods receipt, an email may be sent to the goods recipient. Customers can also maintain the business partner or email address to which an email is sent when the partner role does not exist in the document.

▸ To post the invoice automatically when the exception is corrected or approved and no other exceptions exist.

▸ Whether a link to the SAP SRM system is included in the email.

Figure 7.4 shows the sample settings for the **Missing Goods Receipt** exception.

To configure an exception, select it from the dropdown list and configure the appropriate settings. Settings for duplicate invoice checking are explained next.

Set up Duplicate Invoice Checking

TREX is used for advanced comparison capabilities to identify duplicate invoices. A duplicate invoice check can be done with or without a TREX connection to the SAP SRM system. When connected, the system always uses TREX. If TREX is not connected to the SAP SRM system, a standard duplicate invoice check is performed, based on the supplier's invoice number, the supplier, and the invoice date. Figure 7.5 shows a sample invoice monitor **General Settings** for duplicate invoice checking.

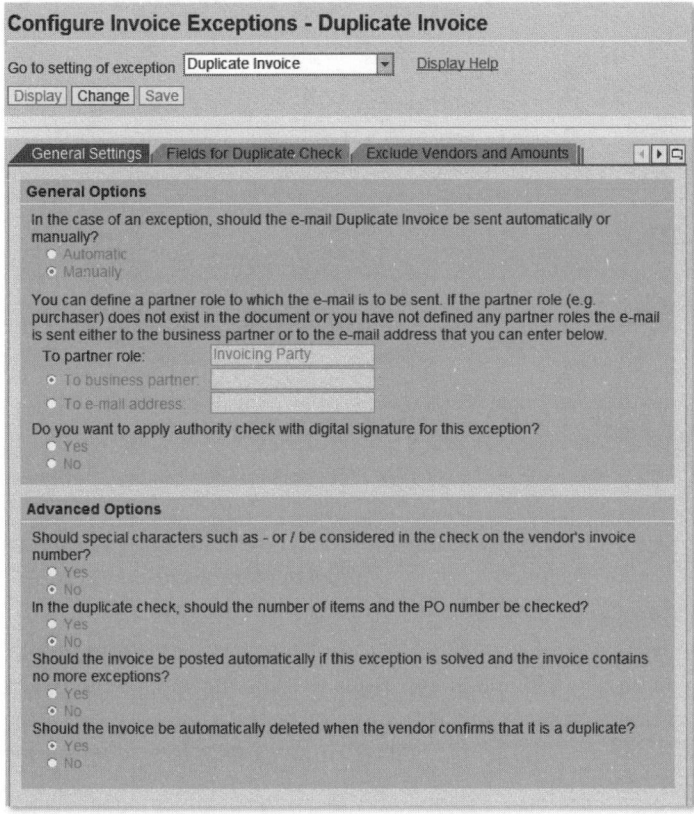

Figure 7.5 Settings for the Invoice Monitor — Settings for Duplicate Invoice Check

TREX facilitates the definition of advanced functionalities in Settings for Invoice Monitor, as follows:

▸ Invoices from multiple backend accounting systems can be compared.

▸ You can specify the fields to be compared to identify duplicate invoices. You can also define whether the comparison should be based on exact match or fuzzy logic with a defined percent of similarity or invoices within a range of number of days. Figure 7.6 shows sample settings on the **Fields for Duplicate Check** tab.

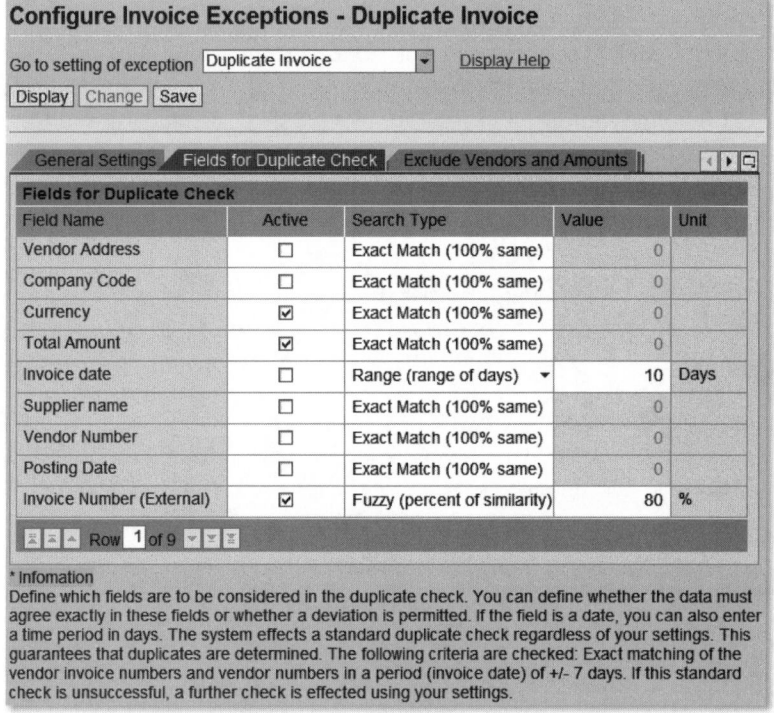

Configure Invoice Exceptions - Duplicate Invoice

Go to setting of exception [Duplicate Invoice ▾]   Display Help

[Display] [Change] [Save]

| General Settings | Fields for Duplicate Check | Exclude Vendors and Amounts |

Fields for Duplicate Check

Field Name	Active	Search Type	Value	Unit
Vendor Address	☐	Exact Match (100% same)	0	
Company Code	☐	Exact Match (100% same)	0	
Currency	☑	Exact Match (100% same)	0	
Total Amount	☑	Exact Match (100% same)	0	
Invoice date	☐	Range (range of days) ▾	10	Days
Supplier name	☐	Exact Match (100% same)	0	
Vendor Number	☐	Exact Match (100% same)	0	
Posting Date	☐	Exact Match (100% same)	0	
Invoice Number (External)	☑	Fuzzy (percent of similarity)	80	%

Row [1] of 9

* Infomation
Define which fields are to be considered in the duplicate check. You can define whether the data must agree exactly in these fields or whether a deviation is permitted. If the field is a date, you can also enter a time period in days. The system effects a standard duplicate check regardless of your settings. This guarantees that duplicates are determined. The following criteria are checked: Exact matching of the vendor invoice numbers and vendor numbers in a period (invoice date) of +/- 7 days. If this standard check is unsuccessful, a further check is effected using your settings.

Figure 7.6 Settings for the Invoice Monitor— Fields for Duplicate Check

▸ You can exclude specific suppliers and amounts. For example, invoices from supplier 2242 can be excluded from the duplicate invoice check. Figure 7.7 shows sample settings on the **Exclude Vendors and Amounts** tab.

▸ You can also group suppliers to check for duplicate invoices. For example, let's say supplier codes 1042 and 2041 belong to the same supplier company and hence invoices from both of these supplier codes are checked as if the supplier code is one and the same. Figure 7.8 shows sample settings on the **Grouping of Vendors** tab.

Figure 7.7 Settings for the Invoice Monitor — Exclude Vendors and Amount in Duplicate Invoice Checking

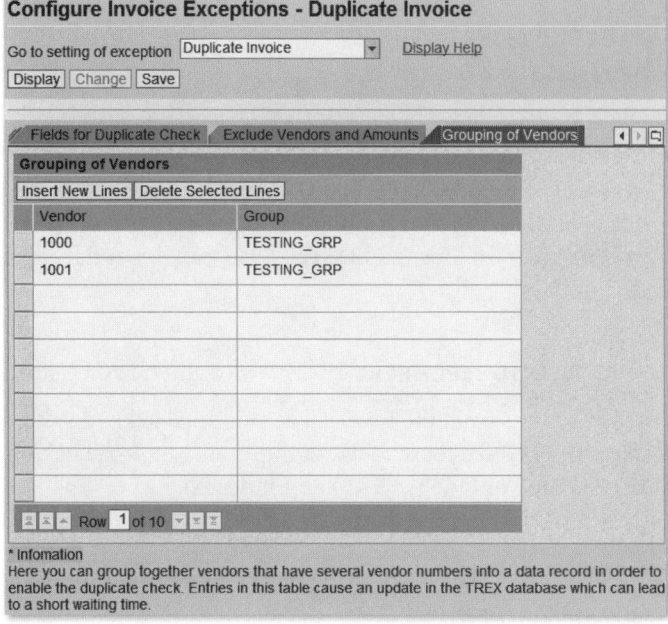

Figure 7.8 Settings for the Invoice Monitor —Grouping of Vendors in Duplicate Invoice Checking

Modify Message Control for Tax Exception

Access the message control configuration settings using the menu path **SPRO • SAP Implementation Guide • Supplier Relationship Management • SRM server • Cross Application Basic Settings • Message Control • Influence Message Control** and configure the message number BBP_IV 208 (specify "BBP_IV" in the Message Cl column and "208" in the No. column) as an error message (specify "E" in the Type column) for the Business Object BUS2205 (Invoice).

Define RFC Destination for TREX

The Remote Function Call (RFC) destination with the TREX server should be configured as described in Chapter 3.

Define Backend Systems

Maintain the settings with system type TREX in the configuration setting *Define Backend Systems*, as described in Chapter 3.

Execute Program BBP_TREX_INDEX_ADMIN

Execute program BBP_TREX_INDEX_ADMIN using Transaction SE38 to generate an index for invoices. Before doing so, you should read the program documentation once. The selection screen values for this program are as follows:

▸ **Business Object**: Enter "BUS2205"

▸ **Subtype business object**: Enter "IV"

▸ **Action for SRM TREX index**: Select the appropriate value from search help. For example, you would enter "A" for initial index generation.

▸ **Bundle size for indexing**: Enter "10." Bundle size indicates the number of documents that will be updated in one go. Bundle size affects performance. If there are a large number of documents, this size can be reduced to improve performance.

Schedule Program IMS_FI_DOUBLECHECK

This program selects the invoices from the financial accounting backend system and transfers them into the TREX database to use in duplicate invoice checking. This program must be executed only when TREX is connected.

Create a variant with the program selection screen fields as follows:

▸ **Last update**: Select the checkbox to ensure that only incremental invoices from the last update are transferred.

▸ **Logical System**: Enter the logical system of the backend system.

Create one variant for each backend system and create a separate job for each of the backend systems with a corresponding variant. Also, schedule this program to run daily. Ensure that the program CLEAN_REQREQ_UP is run before running this program.

Set Up Email Communication

IMS uses email extensively for collaborative dispute resolution. An exception is forwarded in the form of an interactive form to an internal user or a supplier using email. The response from the internal user or supplier is received using inbound email, which automatically updates the invoice based on the values in the interactive form.

The following steps are required to enable incoming and outbound email communication:

1. Configure the basic email settings as per SAP Note 455140. Normally, a NetWeaver Basis consultant configures these settings.

2. Create a role with specific settings required for the system user to automatically process invoices based on inbound email responses. To do so, execute Transaction PFCG and maintain a role Z_IMS_ROLE with authorization objects BBP_PD_INV and PLOG. Figure 7.9 shows the settings in the role.

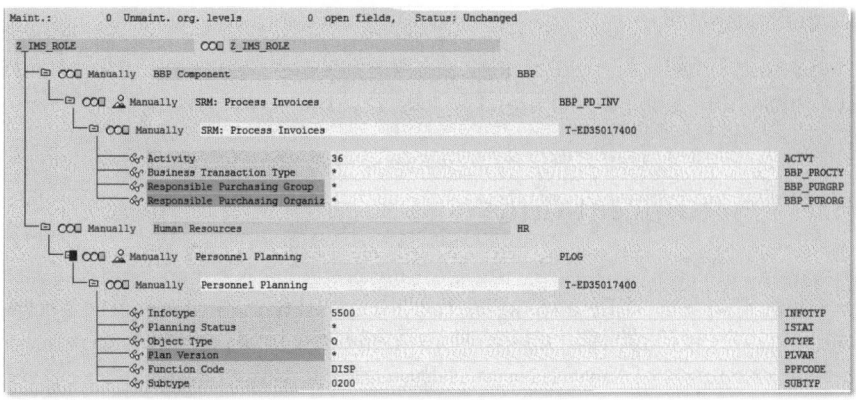

Figure 7.9 Role for Automatic Processing of Invoices

3. Using Transaction SU01, create a system user (for example, ADMINIMS) to be able to receive emails. Ensure that an email address is given in the address section. The email address is normally in the format *<user name>@<default domain>* (for example, *adminims@srm.imperial.com*). The default domain is defined in Transaction SCOT by your Basis expert. Assign the role Z_IMS_ ROLE created in the previous step to the system user. Also, assign profile S_ A.SCON to this user.

4. Maintain exit rules for inbound processing as follows:

- ▸ Execute Transaction SO50.
- ▸ Click on the insert row icon.
- ▸ Select, Internet Mail as the communication type.
- ▸ Enter the email address of the adminims user in the Recipient Address column (for example, adminims@srm.imperial.com).
- ▸ Enter '*' in the Document Class column.
- ▸ Enter 'CL_BBP_SMTP_INBOUND_INV' in the Exit Name column.
- ▸ Enter '1' in the Call Sequence column.

These inbound processing settings ensure that mails received at the email address provided here are processed using the user exit mentioned. The user exit ensures that invoices are automatically updated based on the values in interactive form in the email.

Adobe Document Server Settings

IMS uses Adobe interactive forms for collaborative exception resolution. Adobe document server (ADS) should be implemented for this purpose. The necessary installation and configuration needs to be done by a NetWeaver consultant. The latest configuration guide for ADS can be found at *http://service.sap.com/adobe*.

Let us now, in the next section, look into the role of procurement cards in purchasing and the implementation of procurement cards processing.

7.2 Procurement Cards

Procurement cards, or P-cards, are basically credit cards issued by credit card companies with the difference being that the monthly invoice is sent to a company. P-cards are given to employees or sometimes to departments to procure certain categories of low-value, over-the-counter, and emergency purchases. SAP SRM supports P-cards as a payment method in the standalone scenario. From SAP SRM version 2007 on, P-cards are supported in the extended classic scenario also.

We will now look at a case study that illustrates the use of P-cards.

7.2.1 Case Study for Procurement Card: Global Design Center

Innovative Products Inc. is the world leader in consumer appliances like refrigerators, air-conditioners etc. Innovative Products Inc. is very proud of its global design center (IGDC), which churns out new product designs at the rate of two new products per week. Much of Innovative Product Inc.'s market dominance is attributed to its superior design capabilities. The IGDC employs about 2500 design engineers and other staff. All of the procurement requirements for IGDC are handled by a 25-member procurement team headed by Norbert.

Norbert was disturbed by the fact that his team has to work an average of 11 hours a day to service the burgeoning demand from IGDC. Despite working so hard, the team seems to not be focusing on strategic procurement activities, such as sourcing or supplier development. He had recently commissioned a study of procurement activity analysis to see the possibility of realigning the activities. The analysis revealed that about 35% of the requirements were under $300 and they represented only 2% of the total spend. About 30% of the procurement department's time was spent on procuring these low-value requirements. It was also observed that sometimes the cost of procurement exceeds the value of the item being procured.

Norbert had recently attended a procurement conference in Zurich and was impressed with purchasing cards. To his pleasant surprise, the procurement cards demonstration at the SAP pavilion was led by Chandler, who is also an SAP SRM implementation project manager at IGDC. Norbert is the executive sponsor for SAP SRM implementation in IGDC. Norbert was told that purchasing cards functionality is supported by SAP SRM and can be included in the current implementation without altering project deadlines. The following benefits are expected on procurement card implementation:

▶ A 25% reduction in purchasing requests serviced by procurement department

▶ A 60% reduction in procurement costs (RFQs, purchase orders, processing, etc.) for low-value purchases

▶ A reduction in overall lead time, thus increasing employee satisfaction levels

The case study described explains a typical usage of procurement cards in business. Let us now look at the procurement cards process and configuration in SAP SRM.

7.2.2 Procurement Process with Procurement Cards

Procurement using procurement cards as the payment method significantly reduces the workload on purchasing and invoicing departments. Figure 7.10 shows the procurement process flow using a procurement card.

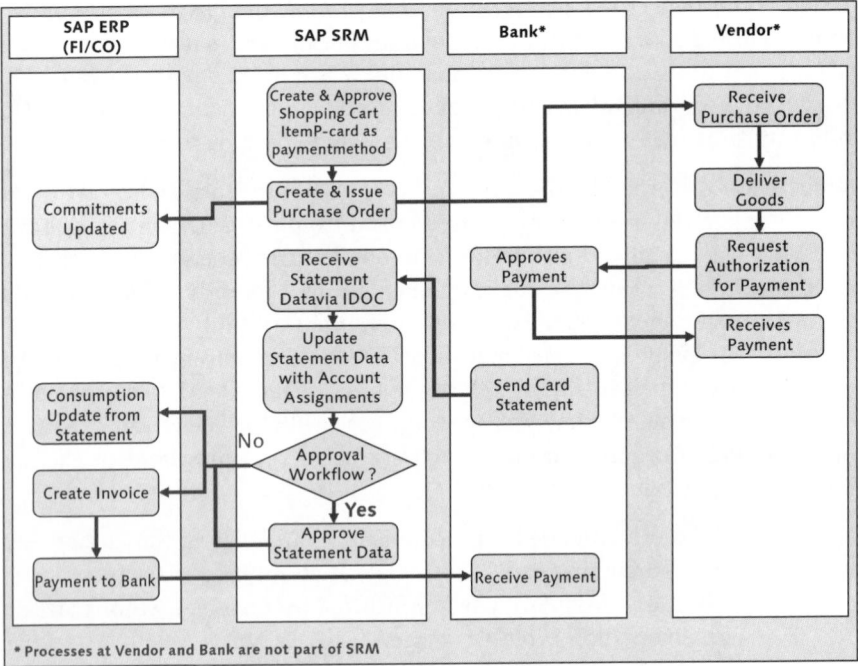

Figure 7.10 Procurement Card Process Flow

The detailed process is as follows:

1. The company provides P-cards to employees or departments.

2. An employee creates a shopping cart in SAP SRM and specifies the P-card as the payment method. On approval of the shopping cart, the order is placed and sent to the supplier.

3. The supplier supplies the ordered goods, requests payment authorization from the card company, and gets paid for the goods supplied.

4. The employee receives the goods. There is no need to create confirmations in SAP SRM for the goods receipt.

5. The card company (bank) sends the cardholder statement to the company every month. The card statement is imported into SAP SRM using IDoc BBP_PCSTAT01. There are three basic levels of bank statements:

   ▶ **Level 1**: Contains basic information, such as date of the transaction, supplier, and dollar amount

   ▶ **Level 2**: Contains Level 1 details, plus sales tax and a variable data field

   ▶ **Level 3**: Contains Level 2 details, plus product code, description, quantity, unit of measure, and unit price

6. SAP SRM updates the statement data supplied by the bank with an account assignment from the P-card configuration settings and generates an invoice.

7. If workflow approval is implemented, then workflow can be triggered. The employee receives the work item to verify the statement. He can change the account assignment details at the line item level. Once the reconciliation by the employee is completed, a work item is triggered for the employee's manager's approval. If the card holder does not complete the workflow within a specified duration, the invoices are automatically cleared by program BBPP-CRECN using the default account data and post accounting documents in the backend system. If you want to separate P-card invoices from other invoices, maintain a separate document type in the backend accounting system. Two accounting documents are generated in the backend system using the standard IDocs ACLPAY01 and ACC_GOODS_MOVEMENT02. as follows:

   ▶ **ACLPAY01**: Invoice to pay the bank. The accounts posted are normally 'card company' (supplier) account and card clearing account.

   ▶ **ACC_GOODS_MOVEMENT02**: Distribution of charges to the account assignment specified in the statement line items or the default account assignment for the card. The accounts posted are normally a card clearing account and a consumption account, as per account assignment.

8. Statements can be archived after a certain time period. Standard archiving object BBP_PC_ARC is available for archiving P-card statements.

7.2.3   Implementing Procurement Cards

Aside from the settings required for a standalone or extended classic scenario implementation, the additional settings described in this section are required for P-cards. Also, ensure that the card company is created as a vendor in the backend SAP ERP Financials system.

Define Number Ranges

Maintain number ranges for P-card statements for each year using the menu path **SPRO · SAP Implementation Guide · Supplier Relationship Management · SRM server · Procurement Card · Define Number Ranges**, or Transaction code PCNUM.

Define Card Company

Card issuing companies are maintained in this setting, using the menu path **SPRO · SAP Implementation Guide · Supplier Relationship Management · SRM server · Procurement Card · Define Card Company**, or Transaction code BBC1. Figure 7.11 shows sample settings for card companies.

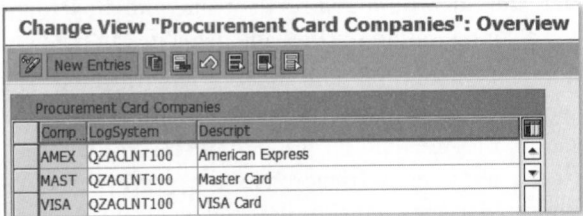

Figure 7.11 Define Card Company

The settings are explained in more detail in the following list:

- **Comp...**: The card issuing company
- **LogSystem**: Backend logical system for accounting entries
- **Descript**: Description of the card company

Allocate Company Code to Card Companies

Company codes, vendor codes, and document types in the backend system are assigned to the card company using this setting. To access the setting, use menu path **SPRO • SAP Implementation Guide • Supplier Relationship Management • SRM server • Procurement Card • Allocate Company Code**, or Transaction code BBC2. Figure 7.12 shows sample settings.

Comp	CoCo	G/L acc	Vendor	Type	Tax Acct	
AMEX	1000	261200	1001	RE	154001	
VISA	1000	261200	1000	RE	154001	

Figure 7.12 Allocate Company Code to Card Companies

The fields in this screen are explained in more detail in the following list:

- **Comp...**: The card issuing company.
- **CoCo**: Company code in the backend accounting system.
- **G/L acc**: Default consumption account for the card company. This is used in automatic reconciliations.
- **Vendor**: Vendor code for the card company in the backend accounting system.
- **Type**: Backend invoice document type used for bank invoice creation.
- **Tax Acct**: Tax account that P-card taxes are posted, if applicable.

Define Blocking Reasons

Blocking reasons indicate the reason for blocking a card. You can define a reason code and description in Transaction BBC3.

Process Procurement Card

The master data of cards issued to all employees is maintained in this setting using menu path **SPRO · SAP Implementation Guide · Supplier Relationship Management · SRM server · Procurement Card · Process Procurement Cards**, or Transaction code BBM1.

In the initial screen, follow these steps:

1. Configure the card company, card number, and company code to which the employee belongs. You can also refer to existing card data as reference to minimize data entry.

2. When you are finished, press the Enter key, and the screen shown in Figure 7.13 appears.

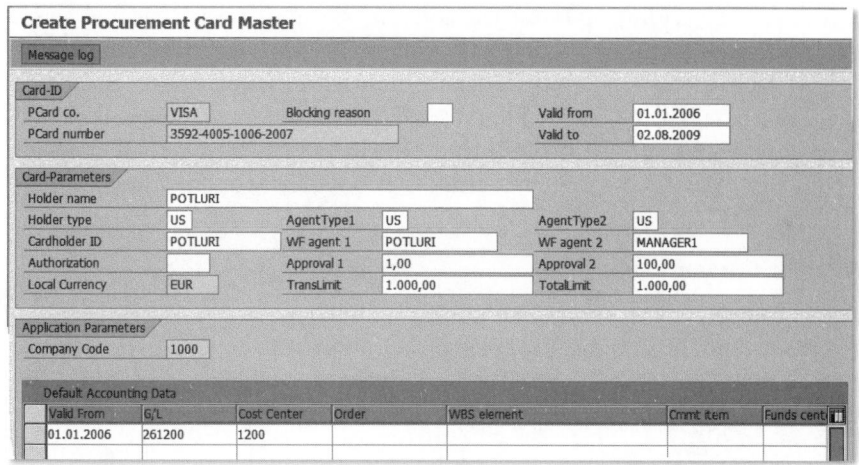

Figure 7.13 Procurement Card Master

Several key fields are described in more detail in the following list:

▸ **Blocking reason**: If you want to block the card, configure a reason here.

▸ **Holder name**: Enter the cardholder name as it appears on the card.

▸ **Holder type:** The cardholder can be a user (US) or a person (P).

▸ **Cardholder ID**: Enter the SAP SRM user ID of the cardholder if the holder type is user, or the personnel number, if the holder type is person.

- ▶ **Approval 1**: Specify an amount here. If the card statement line item value exceeds the amount given here, then a workflow is triggered to WF agent 1. Statement line items below this amount will be automatically reconciled.

- ▶ **WF agent 1**: If the card statement item amount exceeds the amount given in the **Approval 1** field, workflow is sent for approval by the user specified in WF agent 1.

- ▶ **Approval 2**: Specify an amount to be monitored, which requires manager's approval. If the card statement line item value exceeds the amount given here, then a second-level workflow is triggered. The second-level approval will be done by WF agent 2.

- ▶ **WF agent 2**: Specify a user ID of the manager of the employee who would approve the second-level workflow items.

- ▶ **TransLimit**: Specify an amount. An individual card transaction cannot exceed the amount configured in the transaction limit.

- ▶ **TotalLimit**: Specify an amount. Total spend on the card in a month cannot exceed the amount configured in the total limit.

- ▶ **Default Accounting Data**: The account assignment data specified here is defaulted into the shopping cart when a P-card is selected. Configure the default account assignment data to be used in automatic reconciliation. This data is also defaulted in the card statement sent for reconciliation or approval by WF agent 1. The user can change the default account assignment data in the statement before approving the workflow item.

Manage Commitments

If you want to create commitments for P-card purchase orders, select the option to create them. Ensure that purchase order number is supplied in the transaction file for IDoc BBP_PCSTAT01, if commitments creation is specified. The default setting is not to create commitments. Configure the settings in Transaction BBP_PCCOM.

Define Product Categories for Procurement Card

This setting is available in SAP SRM 2007 for the extended classic scenario. List the product categories for which a P-card field is enabled in the shopping cart. This helps restrict P-card usage to certain categories.

Maintain ALE Distribution Model

Set up an ALE distribution model to create accounting documents in the back-end systems using the menu path **SPRO · SAP Implementation Guide · Sup-**

plier Relationship Management · SRM server · Technical Basic Settings · ALE Settings (Logical System) · Distribution (ALE) · Modelling and Implementing Business Processes · Maintain Distribution Model and Distribute Views, or Transaction code BD64.

Set up a distribution model to the backend accounting system for ACLPAY and ACC_GOODS_MOVEMENT. Please refer to Chapter 3 for detailed instructions on how to set up an ALE distribution model.

Schedule Program BBPPCRECN

If you want to use automatic reconciliation, schedule a batch job for program BBPPCRECN in Transaction SM36. You can also perform automatic reconciliation for selected cards, for example, cards of senior management.

7.2.4 Enhancements to Procurement Card Functionality

In this section, we will discuss the standard enhancements provided for P-cards. Enabling P-cards in the classic scenario is also discussed.

Enhancements to Procurement Card Functionality

SAP provides the following BAdI and user exits to enhance P-card functionality:

▶ **BBP_PC_ACLPAY_BADI**: This SRM BAdI is used to fill ACLPAY segments from the P-card.

▶ **BBPPC001**: This is a user exit in SAP SRM for the P-card data feed.

▶ **ACCID001**: This is a user exit in SAP ERP for inbound IDocs. Function module exits EXIT_SAPLACC1_031, EXIT_SAPLACC1_032 and EXIT_SAPLACC1_033 are relevant for IDoc ACLPAY.

Enable P-cards in the Classic Scenario

Currently, SAP SRM does not support the classic scenario for P-cards. However, P-cards can be enabled in the classic scenario with the following enhancements in a customer implementation:

1. Create two customer fields in the shopping cart for card company and card number. To create customer fields, follow the instructions given in SAP Note 672960. Implementation of customer fields in SAP SRM is discussed in Chapter 17.

2. Implement BAdI BBP_CUF_BADI_2 to selectively enable the field for specific product categories and users. Note that this BAdI is obsolete in SAP SRM 2007. You need to maintain WebDynpro metadata configuration in view /SAPSRM/V_MDF_IC to selectively display the fields in SAP SRM 2007.

3. Implement BAdI BBP_DOC_CHANGE_BADI to default in the requester's procurement card.

4. Create similar customer fields in the backend requisition and purchase order. Enhancements MEREQ001 and MM06E005 can be used for this purpose. Refer to SAP Note 336692 for more information.

5. Transfer the customer fields from SAP SRM to the backend documents.

6. Refer to SAP Notes 336692, 870824, 867018, 752586, and 593366 for further information on transferring customer fields to the backend SAP ERP system.

7.3 Summary

In this chapter, you learned about implementing two advanced invoicing functionalities in SAP SRM. Collaborative invoice exception handling in IMS enables companies to facilitate faster resolution of invoice disputes. Procurement cards functionality has the potential to significantly reduce the transaction volume for low-value purchases and increase operational efficiency. In the next chapter, Chapter 8, we will discuss the workflow concept, an important technical feature of SAP SRM.

Workflow is defined as the systematic routing of documents to the users responsible for processing them. It is the way people, tasks, controls, and documents interact to ensure a smooth flow of business processes.

8 SAP SRM Business Workflow

While designing procurement processes, organizations have always struggled to achieve a balance between control, transparency, and efficiency. Approvals and authorizations are two key control elements in the procurement process in all organizations. Procurement documents are considered to be valid only when they are signed by authorized persons in the organization. In a manual process, organizations depend on people to ensure proper routing of documents for signing. This process is error prone and may even lead to corruption. As a result, organizations developed elaborate procedures and controls to eliminate errors, which in turn led to inefficiency in the procurement process and long cycle times. On the other hand, system-based workflow that automatically routes the documents to people according to the organization's approval process improves efficiency significantly. Workflow, thus, has become one of the most important features of any e-procurement application.

System-based workflow maintains an audit trail and transaction history that helps organizations conduct procurement transactions in a transparent manner without losing efficiency. Until SAP Supplier Relationship Management (SAP SRM) version 5.0, SAP SRM used the SAP Business Workflow concept, which is referred to as *old workflow* in this book. SAP SRM 2007 introduced a new workflow concept with SAP Business Rule Framework (BRF) and SAP Business Workflow. In this chapter, we will mainly discuss implementation of new workflow. First, however, we will briefly explain implementation of old workflow in Section 8.1.

8.1 Old SAP SRM Business Workflow

The SAP Business Workflow used with SAP SRM up to version 5.0 is illustrated in Figure 8.1 and the steps it contains are as follows:

1. The workflow process starts based on the occurrence of an event. Events are business object–specific (that is specific to, for example, a bid invitation, an

invoice, a shopping cart, etc.). Examples of events are "bid invitation published," "invoice saved," etc.

2. SAP delivers certain standard workflow templates for each business object. You can activate only the required workflows for a business object. Activated workflow templates for the business object are triggered when an event occurs, and the attributes of the business document are compared with the workflow start conditions defined for the object. Start conditions for workflow templates are defined in configuration Transaction SWB_PROCUREMENT.

3. If the start condition of any workflow meets the document values, the corresponding workflow is started. Other activated workflow templates for the business object, if any, are not started as start conditions except for these templates. If start conditions for two templates are valid, then the system gives the error 'Ambiguous workflow.'

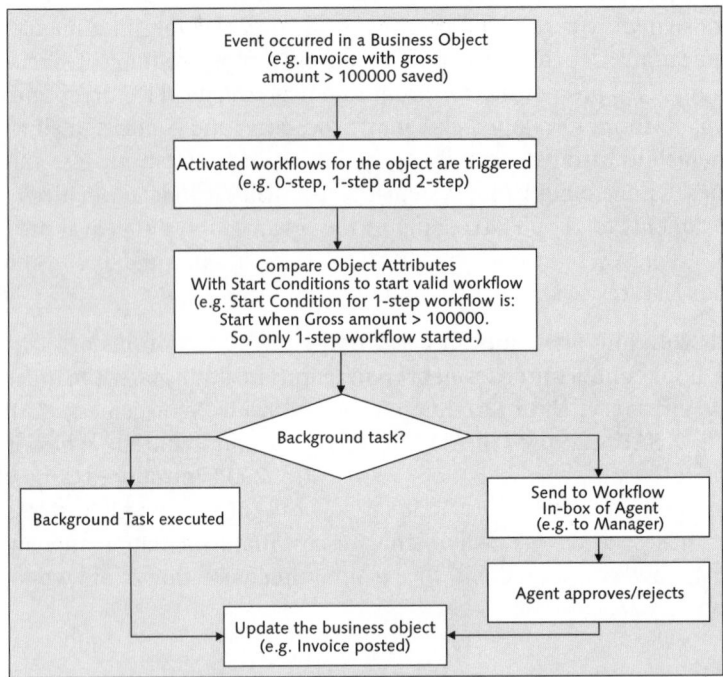

Figure 8.1 Old SAP SRM Business Workflow Process

4. The standard tasks can be background tasks or agent-driven dialog tasks. If the task is an agent-driven dialog task, the work item is sent to the inbox of the agent (e.g., a manager).

5. The user responsible checks the inbox, executes the work item, and approves or rejects the document.

6. The document is updated based on the result of work item execution.

Many business processes in SAP SRM are based on the workflow process. Some workflows are mandatory for executing SAP SRM transactions.

Note

The SAP SRM online help explains the standard workflows available for all business objects in detail. You should read the documentation at these links before venturing into implementing SRM Business Workflow:

▶ **SRM Business Workflow:** Explains all of the standard workflows available in SAP SRM.

▶ **Technical Information on Standard Workflows**: Provides a quick overview of the standard workflows and listings of mandatory workflows. This link is available below the SRM Business Workflow link.

▶ **Setting Up SAP Business Workflow**: Provides very useful information on workflow settings. This link is available below the SRM Business Workflow link.

To access these links, go to the URL *http://help.sap.com* and then follow this menu path: **SAP Business Suite • SAP Supplier Relationship Mgmt • SAP SRM 5.0 • Architecture and Technology • Administration**.

You need to identify the workflows required to be configured in your implementation, based on organizational requirements, and then follow the configuration settings explained next.

SAP provides a combination of automatic and manual configuration settings for workflow. Many standard technical settings can be configured automatically by the system. This leaves business process–specific configuration, like activating the required workflows for a business object, etc., for manual configuration.

8.1.1 Create System User WF-BATCH

Create a system user with the name WF-BATCH using Transaction SU01. Assign SAP_ALL and SAP_NEW profiles to this user. Remember the password created for the user. Specify a valid Internet email address for the user.

8.1.2 Maintain Standard Settings for SAP Business Workflow

Most of the technical workflow settings are configured automatically on execution of this transaction, using the menu path **SPRO • SAP Implementation Guide • Supplier Relationship Management • SRM Server • Cross-Application basic Settings • SAP Business Workflow • Maintain Standard Settings for SAP Business Workflow**, or Transaction code SWU3.

When you execute the transaction, the system provides a listing of all of the configured settings and also the settings that were not automatically configured. Figure 8.2 shows a screenshot with a listing of the automatically configured settings.

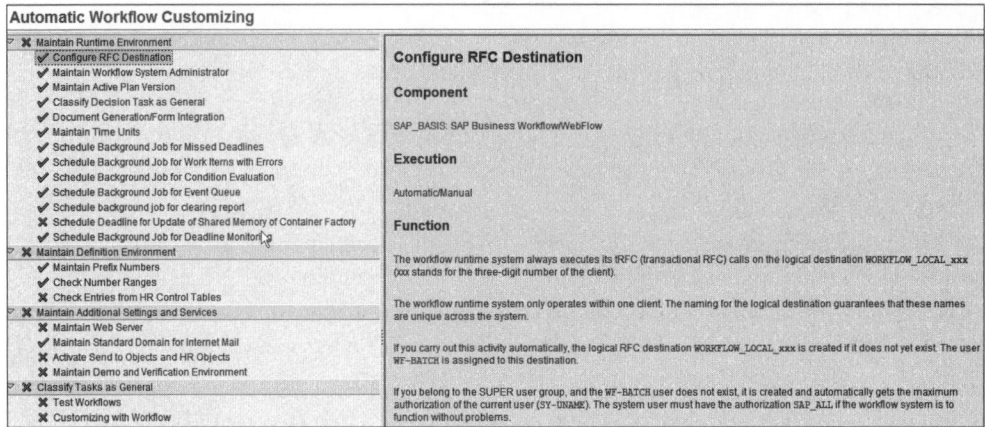

Figure 8.2 Sample Standard Settings for SAP Business Workflow

Documentation for each setting is shown in the right pane with clear instructions on the setting. To verify the settings that were configured for a node, select it and click on the execute icon. You should verify the following settings and change them, if required:

1. **Configure Remote Function Calls (RFC) Destination**: An RFC destination of type 'L' and name WORKFLOW_LOCAL_nnn (where 'nnn' is the SAP client) is created automatically. Verify that user WF-BATCH is assigned. Update the password with the password specified while defining the user.

2. **Maintain Workflow System Administrator**: Normally, automatic configuration assigns the user executing the standard workflow settings. So, you may see the user name as administrator. Replace it with the WF-BATCH user.

3. **Maintain Prefix Numbers**: Workflow templates and tasks are identified with an 8-digit number. The last five digits of this number are assigned automatically by the system. The prefix number defined in this setting is used for the first three digits of the 8-digit number. You should define a unique prefix number with nine as the starting number (e.g., 910) for each system ID and client.

4. **Maintain Standard Domain for Internet Mail**: Specify a standard domain (e.g., sap.com) for emails, according to your organization's email and domain policy.

5. **Maintain Demo and Verification Environment**: These optional settings are configured automatically. Press F9 to perform the auto-customizing, if

required. This setting will help you verify workflow settings with a verification workflow.

Once you have verified these settings, click on the start verification workflow icon or press F5. Follow the instructions given to verify that your workflow settings are correct.

8.1.3 Perform Task-Specific Customizing

In this step, you will activate events for required workflows. If you activate multiple workflows for any object in this setting, then you must carry out the configuration setting *Define Conditions for Starting Workflows* also.

To activate events for required workflows, use the menu path **SPRO • SAP Implementation Guide • Supplier Relationship Management • SRM Server • Cross-Application basic Settings • SAP Business Workflow • Perform Task Specific Customizing**, or Transaction code OOCU, and follow these steps:

1. Click on the arrow next to SAP SRM to expand the hierarchy

2. Click on the arrow next to SRM-EBP to expand the hierarchy

3. Scroll down to SRM-EBP-WFL and click on the **Activate Event Linking** button.

4. Locate the required workflow identified by you based on organizational requirements, and click on the arrow next to it to see the available events.

5. Click on the button next to the text **Deactivated**. The Properties of Event Linkage screen appears, as shown on the right of Figure 8.3. Select the Event linkage activated checkbox to activate the event.

6. Click on the checkmark icon to close the screen and now you should see the text **Activated** for the event, as also shown in Figure 8.3. Note that some workflows might have more than one event and you may want to activate all of the events.

7. If you want to deactivate an event, follow the same procedure and deselect Event linkage activated.

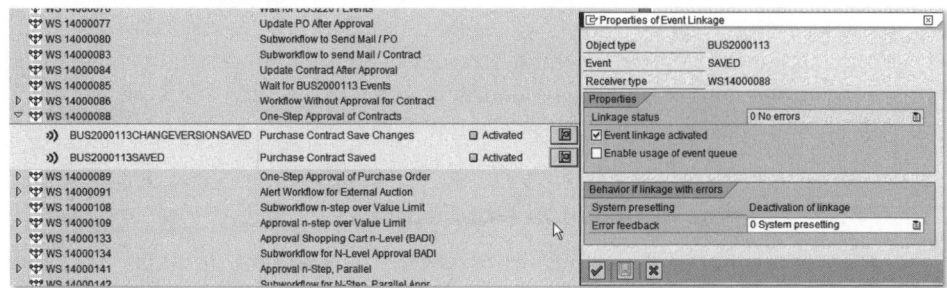

Figure 8.3 Activate Event Linkages for Workflow

8. If you want to use alert workflows for the monitoring of contracts or deadlines for approvals, activate the events for workflow WS14500051.

9. Click on the back icon to move to the previous screen. Click on the **Agent Assignment** button at the node SRM-EBL-WFL.

10. Select the standard task (TS*) required by you and click on the **Attributes** button. Select the **General Task** radio button and click on the **Transfer** button. This will ensure that the task can be processed by anybody and that the processor is controlled by the application. Repeat this step for all required standard tasks. You can also alternatively assign a role to the task to restrict the processing of standard tasks by users with specific roles only.

8.1.4   Define Conditions for Starting Workflows

If you have multiple workflow templates activated for any object, you must also define mutually exclusive, as well as all-inclusive start conditions for these workflows. If you do not define mutually exclusive conditions, the system may identify more than one workflow that satisfies the document attributes, and the error message 'Ambiguous Workflow' appears to the user processing the document (e.g., during purchase order processing). If you do not define all-inclusive conditions, then the workflow may not be triggered for some documents.

To proceed, use the menu path **SPRO • SAP Implementation Guide • Supplier Relationship Management • SRM Server • Cross-Application basic Settings • SAP Business Workflow • Define Conditions for Starting Workflows**, or Transaction code SWB_PROCUREMENT or SWB_COND, and follow these steps:

1. Click on the change start conditions icon to switch to change mode.

2. Select the business object for which you want to define start conditions for workflows.

3. Scroll down to the required workflow template and click on the **Activate** or **Deactivate** button to activate or deactivate a start condition.

4. To modify the start condition delivered by SAP with a customer-specific start condition, click on the white box where start conditions are defined. In the screen that appears, make changes to the start conditions. Normally, start conditions delivered in the standard SAP are sample conditions and hence, you should delete the start conditions given by SAP and add your own. It is best to make the conditions as simple as possible.

8.1.5   Define Recipient of Notifications

This is an optional setting but very is useful. Maintain settings in this task if you want to send notifications to specified recipients based on the processing of a standard task. For example, you may want to send a notification of workflow rejection to the initiator of the workflow. Figure 8.4 shows a screenshot with sample settings.

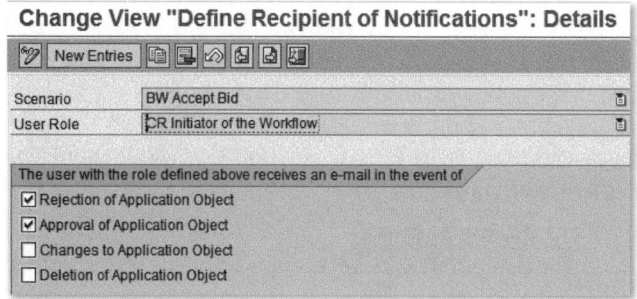

Figure 8.4 Sample Settings for Defining Receipient of Notifications

To access this setting use the menu path **SPRO • SAP Implementation Guide • Supplier Relationship Management • SRM Server • Cross-Application basic Settings • SAP Business Workflow • Define Recipient of Notifications**.

Configure the settings to receive notifications as per organizational requirements. For example, according to the settings shown in Figure 8.4, if the work item processor approves or rejects the work item for **Accept Bid**, the initiator of the workflow will receive a notification.

8.1.6 Special Features in Workflow

SAP SRM workflow supports many additional features. This section briefly describes these features:

▶ **Spending limit approval workflows**
The workflow starts when the shopping cart value exceeds an employee's spending limit. An approval limit can also be defined for approvers.

▶ **Purchasing budget workflow**
A workflow starts when the cumulative shopping cart value in a given period exceeds the budget specified for the user.

▶ **Completion workflow**
If an employee creates an incomplete shopping cart, the cart can be completed by a purchaser before submitting for final approval.

▶ **Line item level approval of shopping carts**
If you want to specify separate approvers for individual line items in a shopping cart, use workflow WS14500015 and implement BAdI BBP_WFL_ APPROV_BADI. Refer to SAP Note 731637 for detailed instructions on implementing the BAdI for line-item level approval.

▶ **Offline approval**
With offline approval, approvers can receive workflow items in an email and process the workflow item from the mail itself without logging on to SAP SRM. Approvers can also download these emails to mobile devices.

▶ **N-step workflow**
Most of the SAP SRM objects support no approval, single step, or 2-step approval workflows. Many organizations may have multiple levels of approval before a document is approved. N-step approval workflow facilitates multiple levels of approval. BAdI BBP_WFL_APPROV_BADI should be implemented to enable n-step workflow.

▶ **Changes to the document during approval**
You can define whether a document can be changed during the approval process, depending on personalization settings in the role. The personalization attribute BBP_WFL_SECURITY controls whether the changes can be made and the behavior of the approval process after the changes. BAdI BBP_WFL_SECURE_BADI can be used to further influence the behavior.

▶ **Creating approval workflow**
If you want to define a new workflow, you should always copy a standard workflow template and modify it.

Note

For a detailed explanation of these features, follow the online documentation for SRM Business Workflow at *http://help.sap.com* and then follow the menu path: **SAP Business Suite • SAP Supplier Relationship Mgmt • SAP SRM 5.0 • Architecture and Technology • Administration • SRM Business Workflow**.

Troubleshooting Tips

▶ A useful SAP Note for analysis of workflow problems is SAP Note 322526.

▶ The workflow work item number can be found using Transaction BBP_PD. Use the work item number for workflow log and further analysis in Transaction SWI1 or SWI2_FREQ.

▶ If the workflow is not running, clean or synchronize the buffer using Transaction PPWFBUF or SWU_OBUF.

▶ If a purchase order hangs with the status 'In Approval' due to a problem in output conditions, refer to SAP Note 886606.

▶ If the workflow hangs, the document status remains as 'Awaiting Approval,' even after the workflow item is approved. If you encounter this problem, check whether the WF_BATCH user has a valid email ID. Alternatively, the password may have been specified incorrectly for this user in configuration.

▶ Check whether the workflow is stuck in the queue using Transaction SWU2 or SM58 and clear the queue.

▸ If you want to enable the manager to approve or reject a work item directly from the inbox overview, execute Transaction SWL1. Maintain EC_DECISION in the column "Expression (first attr.)" for the task and user combination.

▸ Useful Transactions: SWU3 (automatic customizing), SWB_PROCUREMENT (start conditions), OOCU (task customizing), SWETYPEV (event type linkages), SWDD (Workflow Builder), PFTC (tasks), SWELS (event trace), SWEL (display trace), SWU2 (workflow tRFC monitor), SWI2_DIAG (diagnosis of workflows with errors), SWI2_ADM1(work items without agents), SWI1 (work items), SWI6 (workflows for object), and SWIA (process work items as administrator). Some of these transactions need a work item number, which you can find using Transaction BBP_PD.

8.2   The New SAP SRM Business Workflow

From SAP SRM 2007 on, SAP SRM introduced a new workflow with BRF. In this section, we will explain the new workflow, compare the new workflow with the old workflow, and the configuration of the new workflow.

8.2.1   Overview of the New Workflow

The new workflow combines the SAP Business Workflow with the BRF capabilities to offer a more flexible and freely configurable SAP SRM workflow. In this section, we will discuss BRF and how BRF it is used in the new SRM Business Workflow, along with a few new features of SRM Business Workflow.

BRF — An Introduction

BRF is an event-controlled runtime environment for processing rules. BRF consists of events, rules, expressions, and actions. Every application that uses BRF has an application class assigned. The application class for SAP SRM workflow is SRM_WF. A BRF event forms a connection between the application and BRF. You can implement a BRF event at a technical or business event in an application. If a technical or business event is reached in the application, the BRF event is triggered along with the processing of the associated rules. In the event settings, one or more rules are assigned to BRF events. A rule consists of expressions and actions. In an SAP SRM workflow, actions are not used, only expressions. *Expressions* are BRF objects that return results. Expressions can also be nested, that is, one expression accesses results of another expression. Expressions can be of many types from a simple 'constant' type to a more flexible 'call function component' type.

> **Tip**
>
> For more details on BRF, refer to the online help documentation for SAP ERP Central Component at *http://help.sap.com*. Then follow the path **SAP ERP** • **ERP Central Component** • **SAP ERP Central Component** • **Cross-Application Services** • **Business Rule Framework (BRF)**.

New SRM Business Workflow Concept

The new SRM Business Workflow is as follows, and as illustrated in Figure 8.5:

1. An employee user creates a shopping cart and orders. This event triggers the workflow template associated with the shopping cart.

2. The system checks the process schema evaluation settings and finds the evaluation ID (BRF event) assigned to the shopping cart business object.

3. The rules and expressions associated with the event are processed and return a result. All of the possible results for the event have been configured in the process schema settings. For example, the expressions can be based on shopping cart value. If the shopping cart value is less than $100,000, the result is 'process schema 1,' otherwise the result is 'process schema 2.' In this example, let us assume 'process schema 2' is the result. If the process schema evaluation returns a valid process schema, workflow template WS 40000014 is started. In the new workflow, only one workflow template WS 40000014 is used for all SAP SRM business objects.

4. Each process schema is similar to a workflow template. The process levels are configured for each process schema. Process levels represent the levels in an approval process. For example, 'process schema 1' can have single level approval configured where as 'process schema 2' can have two levels of approval.

5. Each process level configuration setting determines the responsible agent to carry out the approval processing, type of approval, decision type, standard task to be executed, and the evaluation ID (BRF event). The system starts with the first process level. If the expression associated with the event returns a Boolean result 'true,' the standard task is triggered. If the result is false, then the next process level is processed.

   For example, if the product category in the shopping cart is 'Electronics,' then the task in the process level is executed. If it is not 'Electronics,' then this specific process level is not processed and the system evaluates the next process level. The responsible agent or approver is determined based on the implementation of BAdI /SAPSRM/BD_WF_RESP_RESOLVER. The approval type can be 'completion' or 'approval.' The completion approval type can be used to change an incomplete document. The decision type is explained next.

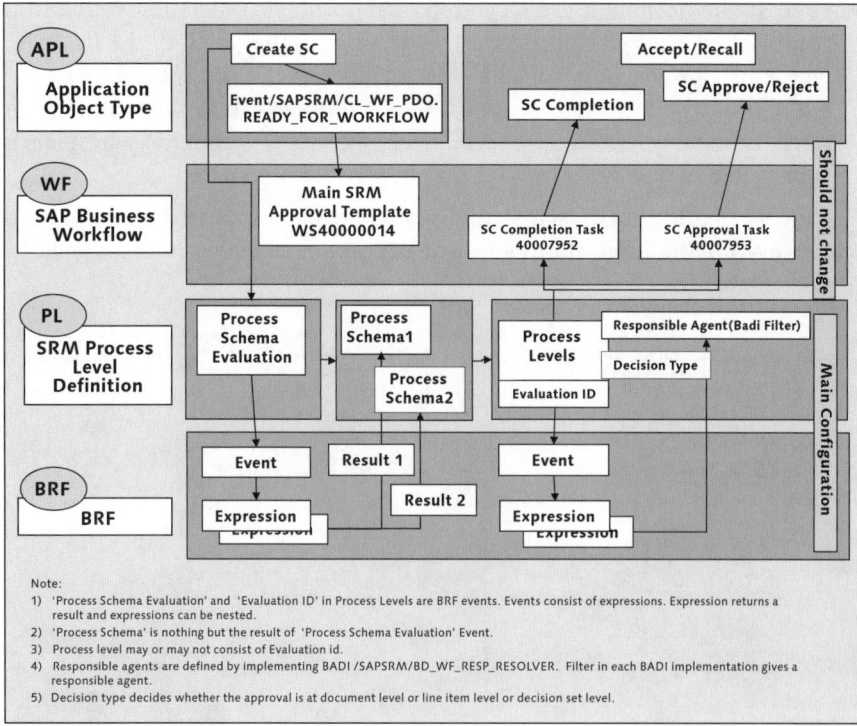

Note:
1) 'Process Schema Evaluation' and 'Evaluation ID' in Process Levels are BRF events. Events consist of expressions. Expression returns a result and expressions can be nested.
2) 'Process Schema' is nothing but the result of 'Process Schema Evaluation' Event.
3) Process level may or may not consist of Evaluation id.
4) Responsible agents are defined by implementing BADI /SAPSRM/BD_WF_RESP_RESOLVER. Filter in each BADI implementation gives a responsible agent.
5) Decision type decides whether the approval is at document level or line item level or decision set level.

Figure 8.5 Overview of the New SRM Business Workflow

Decision Type

The *decision type* determines the level at which the approval decision is made. It can be made at the document header level, at the item level, or at the decision set level. During the approval process, an area of responsibility is assigned to each item. All items with the same area of responsibility form a *decision set*. An area of responsibility can be, for example, a department, a product category, or a cost center. For each decision set, a new subworkflow is started. Method GET_AREA_TO_ITEM_MAP in BAdI BBP_WF_RESP_RESOLVER assigns areas of responsibility to the items in a document. This method is called in the approval workflow when the document is split into decision sets. A decision set can contain all items in a document or only a subset of items (i.e., partial documents). There are four decision types supported in the SAP SRM new workflow, as shown in Figure 8.6, and outlined as follows:

▶ **Type 1**: The document is approved or rejected by an approver. In this case, all line items in the document get approved or rejected.

▶ **Type 2**: The document is approved by a single approver but the decision is made at the item level. This means, the approver may approve some items and reject other items in a single document.

▸ **Type 3**: The document is split into partial documents (decision sets) and is approved by multiple approvers. The decision applies to all of the items for which an approver is responsible. For example, the document can be sent to multiple category managers, based on the product category of the item. A category manager can approve or reject all of the items for which he is responsible.

▸ **Type 4**: The document is split into partial documents (decision sets) and is approved by multiple approvers. The decision is made at the item level by each approver.

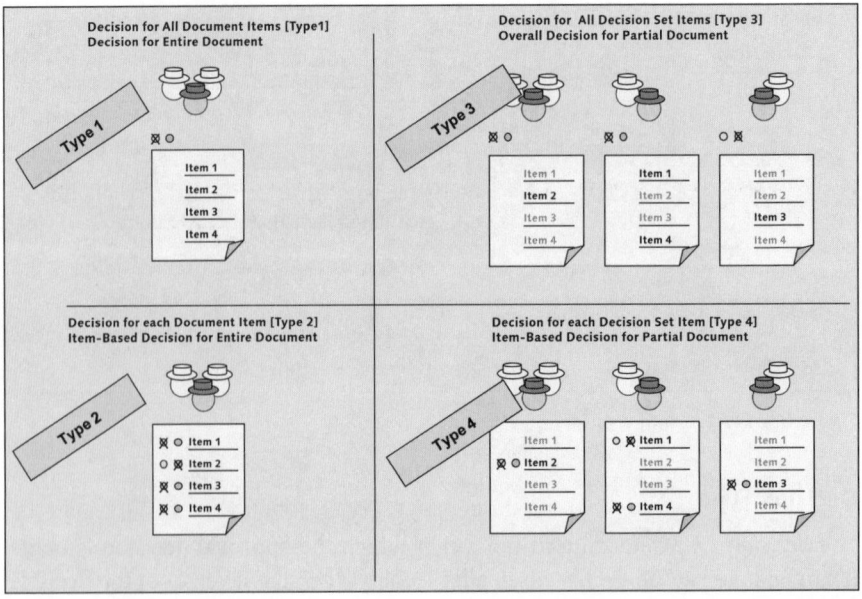

Figure 8.6 Decision Types

8.2.2 Comparison of the New Workflow with the Old Workflow

For single-step approval workflows, the new workflow is more complex to set up than the old workflow. However, for defining complex workflows, the new workflow will be much easier. Table 8.1 shows a comparison of features between the old workflow and the new workflow. Certain new features and changes to the existing features are also described in this table.

Feature	Old Workflow	New Workflow
Workflow template	One template is used for each workflow. Thus, each SAP SRM object may have multiple workflow templates (SC single-step approval, two-step approval, etc.)	One workflow template is used for all SAP SRM objects. Multiple workflows in SAP SRM are achieved through multiple process schema in process level configuration. Each process schema in the new workflow is equivalent to a workflow template in old workflow.
Completion process	Separate workflow in the shopping cart. Not available for other SAP SRM documents.	Part of configuration and available for all documents. Approval in the new workflow is of two types: completion and approval
Decision options available to approver in completion process	Approval and rejection.	Approval, rejection and inquire. Inquire option facilitates 'back and forth' processing.
Back and forth processing	Available only with n-step dynamic approval workflows using BAdI BBP_WFL_APPROV_BADI	Available as the 'Inquire' functionality in the completion process, which is configurable.
User interface	Graphical view with Java applet or tabular view. This view has nice graphics, but also has performance issues.	New enhanced tabular view with improved performance.
Changes to documents during approval	Based on attribute BBP_WFL_SECURITY in the personalization settings in user master or role.	Possible in approval type 'completion,' based on process level configuration. Changes are not possible during approval type 'approval.' Requester needs to recall the document to change it to avoid inconsistencies in approval.
N-step workflow	Available with BAdI BBP_WFL_APPROV_BADI only.	Part of the process level configuration
Offline Approval	Email-based offline approval is available.	Both email-based offline approval and duet-based offline approval are available.
Ad-hoc approvers	Can be added at every level	Can be added at every next level

Table 8.1 Comparison of Workflow Features Between Old and New Workflows

Feature	Old Workflow	New Workflow
Add reviewers	Reviewers can be added at every level an a reviewer can add an ad-hoc approver.	Reviewers can be added at every level. Reviewers cannot add ad-hoc approvers. Rules can be configured to determine reviewers.
Retain functionality	Is possible. Facilitates temporary saving of work item without completing the approval.	Is possible.
Change of approver	Possible in the approval pre-view.	Not possible. However, work items can be forwarded to another approver. Approver can also set a substitute. Administrator can reassign approvers using Transaction SWIA.
Budget workflow	Notifies the user with a pop up if the budget is exceeded.	Pop up notification not available. Instead, a warning message is issued.
Decision sets	Not available.	Available. Enable assigning areas of responsibility within a document and approval of each area of responsibility by a different approver.
Line item level approval	Available with BAdI BBP_WFL_APPROV_BADI. See SAP note 731637.	Available, based on configuration.
Approver	Dependent on the organizational plan in most of the workflows.	Flexible, and based on configuration.
Workflow log	SAP Business Workflow log using Transaction SWI1.	Application log (Transaction SLG1) provides the complete log of BRF evaluation.
BAdIs	BBP_WFL_APPROV_BADI, BBP_CHNG_AGNT_GET, and BBP_WFL_ADMIN_APPROV are used to enhance the standard workflow.	BBP_WFL_APPROV_BADI, BBP_CHNG_AGNT_GET, and BBP_WFL_ADMIN_APPROV are obsolete. BAdIs in the new workflow are explained in Section 8.2.4.
Workflow Inbox	Work items, alerts, and notifications are received in SAP Business Workplace Inbox.	Work items and alerts are received in Universal Worklist (UWL). For receiving notifications (e.g., workflow deadlines notifications) in UWL, refer to SAP Note 1051787.

Table 8.1 Comparison of Workflow Features Between Old and New Workflows (Cont.)

Feature	Old Workflow	New Workflow
Objects using old SAP Business Workflow	All objects	Purchase order response, procurement card, and business partner still use old workflow.
Objects using new BRF workflow	None	Shopping cart, RFQ, quotation, contract, purchase order, confirmation, and invoice.
New workflow creation	Requires copying an existing template and modifying it. Technical expertise in workflow is required.	Can be created using the process-level configuration with appropriate changes to BRF event and expressions.
Skill required	Complex SAP Business Workflow knowledge	BRF knowledge, which can be easy for an ABAP consultant.

Table 8.1 Comparison of Workflow Features Between Old and New Workflows (Cont.)

8.2.3 Designing Approval Workflows Using the New Workflow

The new workflow configuration involves configuring settings in workflow, configuring process levels, defining BRF events and expressions, and implementing BAdI for agents. Before you start configuring the new workflow, you should design approval workflows using the following steps:

1. Identify the objects (e.g., purchase order, contract) requiring approval workflows.

2. Identify the events triggering the workflow for each object. Also, identify the number of workflows required for each object and conditions that determine each workflow. For example, a purchase order with a value of less than $100,000 may require a one-step workflow. If the purchase order value exceeds $100,000, it may require a two-step workflow. Based on the design in this step, define BRF events for the process schema evaluation and expression results for the process schema definition.

3. Identify the approval steps and approvers for each workflow. For example, if you decide to have a two-step workflow for a purchase order, you need to determine the approver for the first step and the approver for the second step. Verify whether the agents delivered in the standard will suffice for your approver requirements. If not, you need to implement BAdI /SAPSRM/BD_WF_RESP_RESOLVER to define new agents. The processing of each level and the approving agents may also depend on additional conditions, like product category. For example, critical categories may have to be sent for a senior manager's approval while noncritical categories may be sent for a manager's approval. Based on the design in this step, process levels are configured.

235

Once the design of approval workflows is complete, you can start configuring the workflows, as you will learn how to in the next section.

> **Note**
>
> BAdI /SAPSRM/BD_WF_RESP_RESOLVER can be used to define default agents, which are used when no approving agent could be found from configuration settings.

8.2.4 Configuring the New SRM Business Workflow

New SRM Business Workflow configuration involves maintaining standard settings for SAP Business Workflow and BRF configuration. We will look at the settings you need to configure for the new SRM Business Workflow in this section.

Create System User WF-BATCH

Maintain the settings as described in Section 8.1.1.

Maintain Standard Settings for SAP Business Workflow

Maintain the settings as described in section 8.1.2. Also, ensure that active plan version is set as '01' in the setting *Maintain Active Plan Version.*

Copy BRF Objects

Using this setting, you copy BRF objects from client 000 into your current client using the menu path **SPRO • SAP Implementation Guide • Supplier Relationship Management • SRM Server • Cross-Application basic Settings • SAP Business Workflow (New) • Basis Workflow Settings • Copy BRF Objects**, or Transaction code /SAPSRM/BRFTRANSPORT. Complete the fields in this screen as shown in Figure 8.7 and execute. You can also use this transaction to transport the BRF settings.

Activate Workflow

In this step, the SAP SRM workflow is activated and SAP SRM tasks are set as general tasks using the menu path **SPRO • SAP Implementation Guide • Supplier Relationship Management • SRM Server • Cross-Application basic Settings • SAP Business Workflow (New) • SRM Workflow Settings • Workflow Settings • Activate Workflow**:

1. In the "Choose Activity" screen that appears, double-click on the "Task Customizing" row.
2. Click on "Activate Event Linking" for application component "SRM".

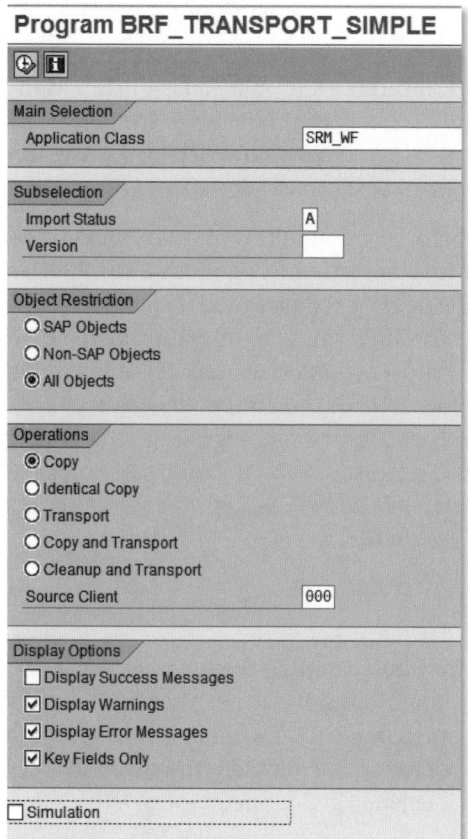

Figure 8.7 Copy BRF Objects

3. Click on the arrow next to "WS 40000014" to expand and click on the button next to the text "Deactivated" (if the event linkage has already been configured, you will see the text "Activated"). In the screen that appears, select the "Event linkage activated" checkbox.

4. Return to the "Choose Activity" screen. Double-click on the row "Generalize Tasks".

5. Select "Workflow Template" in the Task Type field and enter "40000014" in the Task field.

6. Click on the execute icon.

7. Select the tasks with status "Undefined:Action Required" and click on the "Generalize" button. This action will set the SAP SRM tasks as general tasks so that any approver determined by the process levels configuration settings can execute the standard task.

Migrate Workflows to BRF

This setting is relevant for upgrade customers. To access this setting, use the menu path **SPRO • SAP Implementation Guide • Supplier Relationship Management • SRM Server • Cross-Application basic Settings • SAP Business Workflow (New) • SRM Workflow Settings • Workflow Settings • Migrate Workflows to BRF,** or Transaction code /SAPSRM/WF_COND_MAPP.

You should read the documentation before executing this transaction. On execution, the start conditions defined in Transaction SWB_PROCUREMENT in the old workflow are transferred to the new workflow as BRF expressions. The system also creates process schemas for all active and relevant old standard workflows with associated process levels. If errors occur during the migration of the start conditions, refer to SAP Note 1015211 to correct the errors. Verify the process schemas and process levels created by the migration program for correctness, and manually correct the process levels, if required. Note that there is no migration available for n-step workflows. N-step workflows should be configured in the *Define Process Levels* setting.

Define Process Levels

Define process levels is the main configuration setting for the new workflow. Before defining process levels, you should ensure that necessary BRF events and expressions are defined using Transaction BRF. Defining BRF events and expressions is explained later in this chapter. You should also ensure that the required responsibility resolver names (agents) are defined in the *Define Filter Values for Business Add-In* setting.

To define process levels, use the menu path **SPRO • SAP Implementation Guide • Supplier Relationship Management • SRM Server • Cross-Application basic Settings • SAP Business Workflow (New) • SRM Workflow Settings • Workflow Settings • Define Process Levels,** or Transaction code /SAPSRM/WF_PROCESS. Figure 8.8 shows a screenshot with an overview of the settings that can be configured in this configuration transaction.

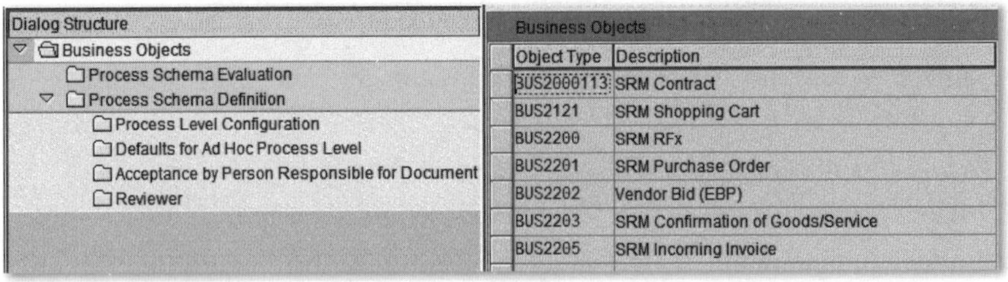

Dialog Structure	Business Objects	
▽ 🗀 Business Objects	Object Type	Description
🗀 Process Schema Evaluation	BUS2000113	SRM Contract
▽ 🗀 Process Schema Definition	BUS2121	SRM Shopping Cart
🗀 Process Level Configuration	BUS2200	SRM RFx
🗀 Defaults for Ad Hoc Process Level	BUS2201	SRM Purchase Order
🗀 Acceptance by Person Responsible for Document	BUS2202	Vendor Bid (EBP)
🗀 Reviewer	BUS2203	SRM Confirmation of Goods/Service
	BUS2205	SRM Incoming Invoice

Figure 8.8 Overview of Define Process Levels Setting

Table 8.2 provides a brief overview of each setting shown in Figure 8.8 .

Step	Dialog Structure	Description	Pre-requisite(s)
1	Business Objects	Select the business object for which workflows need to be set up (see Figure 8.9).	Identify requirements and design workflow as explained in Section 8.2.3.
2	Process Schema Evaluation	Configure the event that triggers the required workflows (see Figure 8.10).	BRF event to be defined.
3	Process Schema Definition	Specify workflows associated with the business object. These are technically the result of a process schema evaluation event (see Figure 8.11).	Process schema evaluation event should be set up to provide these results.
4	Process Level Configuration	Define the levels in each process schema, the approver for each level, and the type of decision (see Figure 8.12).	Responsibility resolver set up, BRF events defined, and BAdI implemented for /SAPSRM/BD_ WF_RESP_ RESOLVER.
5	Defaults for Ad Hoc Process Level	Will be used in future support packs and versions.	BRF event defined.
6	Acceptance by Person Responsible for Document	Configure to send the work item back to requestor based on rules, e.g., on rejection of document.	BRF event defined.
7	Reviewer	Configure settings for the reviewer determination.	BRF event defined, and BAdI implemented for /SAP-SRM/BD_WF_ REVIEWER_RULE.

Table 8.2 Overview and Order of Settings in Define Process Levels

We will discuss these settings in more detail in the following list.

▶ **Business Objects**

The SAP SRM business objects are listed as shown in Figure 8.8. Select the object for which you want to set up a workflow.

▶ **Process Schema Evaluation**

A BRF event that triggers a workflow for the business object is defined in this setting. Figure 8.9 illustrates sample settings for a shopping cart. In this example, BRF event **9EV_SC_00S** has been defined as an event in Transaction BRF.

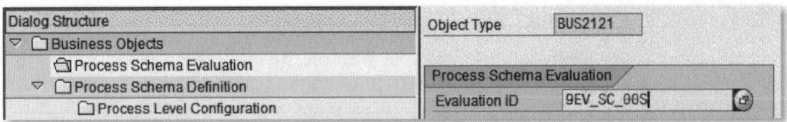

Figure 8.9 Sample Settings for Process Schema Evaluation

▶ **Process Schema Definition**

The results of the event defined in the process schema evaluation form the basis for different workflows triggered for the SAP SRM object. Figure 8.10 illustrates sample settings, and the process schema shown in this figure is the final result of the event "9EV_SC_00S" used in the **Process Schema Evaluation** setting. Each of the process schemas here represents a workflow. The event results are not available in this setting as search help and hence you need to ensure that the entry here represents the event result.

Dialog Structure	Process Schema Definition	
▽ ☐ Business Objects	Obj. Type	Process Schema
☐ Process Schema Evaluation	BUS2121	9C_BUS2121_EX01
▽ ☐ Process Schema Definition	BUS2121	9C_BUS2121_EX02
☐ Process Level Configuration	BUS2121	9C_BUS2121_EX03
☐ Defaults for Ad Hoc Process Level		

Figure 8.10 Sample Settings for Process Schema Definition

▶ **Process Level Configuration**

Process levels for each process schema are defined in this setting. You can also add additional process levels and ad-hoc agents using BAdI /SAP-SRM/BD_WF_PROCESS_CONFIG. Figure 8.11 shows a screenshot with sample settings for process schema **9C_BUS2121_EX01**.

Object Type BUS2121
Process Schema 9C_BUS2121_EX01

Process Level Configuration

No	Level Type	Resp. Resolver Name	Resp. Resolver Parame	Eval. ID	Evaluati	Task ID	Decision Type		Changeable
100	C Approval with Completion	RR_ROLE	SAP_EC_BBP_SECRETARY	9EV_SC_001	Check Pr	40007952	2 Decision for each Document Item		☑
200	C Approval with Completion	SC_RR_PURCHASING_GROUP		9EV_SC_002	Check Pr	40007952	2 Decision for each Document Item		☑
300	A Approval	RR_MANAGER		9EV_SC_003	Check Pr	40007953	4 Decision for each Decision Set Item		☐
400	A Approval	RR_MANAGER		9EV_SC_004	Check Pr	40007953	4 Decision for each Decision Set Item		☐
500	A Approval	RR_MANAGER_OF_MANAGER		9EV_SC_005	Check Pr	40007953	4 Decision for each Decision Set Item		☐
600	A Approval	SC_RR_PURCHASING_GROUP		0EV000	Standard	40007953	4 Decision for each Decision Set Item		☐
999	S Automatic (System User)			0EV999	Check Ne	40007989	1 Decision for all Document Items		☐

Figure 8.11 Sample Settings for Process Level Configuration

The settings shown in Figure 8.11 are explained in Table 8.3.

Field	Description	Remarks
No	Sequence number of the process levels indicating the step in the workflow. The workflow processes process levels sequentially.	
Level Type	Allowed values are as follows: ▸ **Approval with Completion** (Used to complete the document. The document can be changed during this process.) ▸ **Approval** (Used for approval by user.) ▸ **Automatic (System User)** (Used when there is no approval required, or in zero-step approval; in either case, the document will be approved automatically by the system.)	You should configure **Automatic** approval as the last process level (e.g., you may use sequence number 999 for the automatic approval).
Resp. Resolver Name	This entry determines the approving agent. You can select a value from search help. Many preconfigured agents, such as employee, purchase manager, purchasing group, etc., are delivered in the standard. For spending limit approval workflow, use predefined agent RR_SPENDING_LIMIT_APPROVER.	Customer-specific agents can be configured by implementing BAdI /SAPSRM/BD_WF_RESP_RESOLVER. BAdI filters should be set up in the setting *Define Filter Values for Business Add-In*.
Resp. Resolver Parameter	The parameter values for certain responsibility resolver names can be specified here. For example, if the responsibility resolver is a role, you can specify the role here.	
Eval. ID	Maintain a BRF event here. Determines whether the step is valid or not. The execution of a step depends on the Boolean result of the expression linked to this event. If the result is true, a work item is generated. If the result is false, then the next level is executed. For example, if you want to execute this level for free text items only, then specify an event that can check for free text items.	BRF event should have been defined in Transaction BRF.
Evaluation Description	A description of the event specified in the Eval.ID column is automatically filled in.	

Table 8.3 Explanation of Process Level Configuration Settings

Field	Description	Remarks
Task ID	Select the appropriate task from the search help. The new standard tasks typically have a prefix of 400. The task given here contains the text for the work item received by the agent. All standard workflow tasks are assigned to package /SAPSRM/WF_CFG.	
Decision Type	Select the decision type from the four options given.	Decision types are explained in Section 8.2.1
Changeable	This indicator determines whether the document can be changed during approval. Relevant only when the level type is Approval with Completion.	

Table 8.3 Explanation of Process Level Configuration Settings (Cont.)

Note

For spending limit approval workflow, use the predefined agent RR_SPENDING_LIMIT_APPROVER. You need to define only one process level, even if it requires n-step spending limit approvals. When an employee's spending limit (the value above which a shopping cart requires approval) is exceeded, the system determines the first approver. If the first approver's approval limit is exceeded, further approvers will be determined until the last approver has been found with an approval limit that is high enough. All approvers in this process have to approve sequentially and hence it is a sequential n-step workflow. The n-step spending limit workflows in the shopping cart and purchase order are achieved by providing standard implementations for the BAdI /SAPSRM/BD_WF_PROCESS_CONFIG.

▸ **Reviewer**

The settings here determine the reviewer for a given process schema. Figure 8.12 shows a screenshot with sample settings.

Figure 8.12 Sample Settings for Reviewer

Select an entry for the **Rule** from search help. The entries available in rule search help are configured in the setting *Define Filter Values for BAdI Define Reviewer*. SAP delivers role, employee, department, and document responsible as predefined values for the reviewer role. You can also define your own values by implementing BAdI /SAPSRM/BD_WF_REVIEWER_RULE. Specify the return value for the BAdI filter in **Rule Parameter**. Specify a BRF event to determine whether the reviewer step should be executed or not in **Evaluation ID**. Specify a workflow task in **Task ID**.

Define Filter Values for Business Add-In

Use this setting, which can be accessed at **SPRO • SAP Implementation Guide • Supplier Relationship Management • SRM Server • Cross-Application basic Settings • SAP Business Workflow (New) • SRM Workflow Settings • Workflow Settings • Define Filter Values for Business Add-In**, to specify the filters for BAdI /SAPSRM/BD_WF_RESP_RESOLVER. These filter values are used in the field "Resp. Resolver Name" in the process levels configuration. The BAdI uses these filters to determine the user responsible to execute a workflow task.

Define Filter Values for BAdI, Define Reviewer'

Use this setting, which can be accessed at **SPRO • SAP Implementation Guide • Supplier Relationship Management • SRM Server • Cross-Application basic Settings • SAP Business Workflow (New) • SRM Workflow Settings • Workflow Settings • Define Filter Values for BADI 'Define Reviewer'**, to specify the filters for BAdI /SAPSRM/BD_WF_REVIEWER_RULE. These filter values are used in the field "Reviewer Rule" in the reviewer configuration of the process schema. The BAdI uses these filters to determine the user responsible to execute a standard task as reviewer.

Convert Workflows

In this activity, old workflows are deactivated and new workflows are activated using the menu path **SPRO • SAP Implementation Guide • Supplier Relationship Management • SRM Server • Cross-Application basic Settings • SAP Business Workflow (New) • SRM Workflow Settings • Workflow Settings • Convert Workflows**, or Transaction code /SAPSRM/PRWFMIGCFG.

There are three steps in this setting. To execute the first step, select the Set toggle indicator and click on the execute icon. The new workflows are then activated for all objects. The column "NEW_WF_ACTIVE" in table /SAPSRM/D_WF_001 is set to "X" for all business objects. If you encounter an error in the new workflow, check this table and verify whether the new workflow is active.

Upgrade customers should also execute step two (Test new workflow concept manually) and three (Stop open work items and start new work items) in this transaction to stop open work items from an old workflow, if any, and start new work items.

Note

It is highly recommended that you read the IMG documentation for this setting.

Define BRF Groups

Define BRF groups to group together the events and expressions used in your implementation. These groups are used in Transaction BRF. Use the menu path **SPRO • SAP Implementation Guide • Supplier Relationship Management • SRM Server • Cross-Application basic Settings • SAP Business Workflow (New) • SRM Workflow Settings • BRF Settings • Define Groups** to access this setting.

Figure 8.13 illustrates sample settings for BRF groupings. You should create one top-level group (e.g., **Z_BESTTEC** in Figure 8.13) and different subgroups for each object. You can also define one subgroup to define the events used for process schema.

Application Class	Group	Short Text	Higher Node
SRM_WF	Z_BESTTEC	Top Level	
SRM_WF	ZRFQ	RFx - BUS2200–Process Levels	Z_BESTTEC
SRM_WF	ZSC	Shopping Cart - BUS2121-Process Levels	Z_BESTTEC
SRM_WF	Z0SCHEMA	Process Schema	Z_BESTTEC

BRF: Groups

Figure 8.13 Sample BRF Groupings

Define BRF Events and Expressions

BRF events and expressions are defined using Transaction BRF. You should define all of your events and expressions under the new group created in the setting *Define BRF Groups*. Events are used in process levels configuration, process schema evaluation, and process level settings. The process level and BRF linkages are explained in Figure 8.14, and the complete processing of process level settings shown earlier in Figure 8.11 is explained with the help of Figure 8.14. Process level 400 is configured so that department manager approves shopping carts with a value of more than 1,000:

1. Process level 400 has BRF event **9EV_SC_004** assigned.

2. Event **9_EV_SC_004** is configured in Transaction BRF as shown in step 2 in Figure 8.14. An expression **9B_SC_LEVEL_004** is assigned to this event.

3. The expression **9B_SC_LEVEL_004** is a Boolean-type expression with a formula **0V_SC_TOTALVALUE > 1000**, as shown in step 3. This means if the result of expression **0V_SC_TOTALVALUE** is greater than 1000, then it is TRUE, otherwise it is FALSE. The process level will be processed if the expression result is TRUE. The expression **0V_SC_TOTALVALUE** is one of many expressions delivered by SAP.

4. Step 4 shows the setting for expression **0V_SC_TOTALVALUE**. This expression executes the standard function module /SAPSRM/WF_BRF_0EXP000 with the parameters shown on the screen. Each of these parameters in turn are expressions with constant values.

5. As shown in step 5 in Figure 8.14, for example, parameter **0C_C3_C_TOTAL-VALUE** is an expression which has the Constant value **TOTALVALUE**.

Thus, the event **9EV_SC_004** returns a result that is a Boolean value based on the value of the shopping cart. If the result is TRUE, the standard task **40007953** is executed by the manager. If the result is FALSE, the next process level 500 is processed in a similar way.

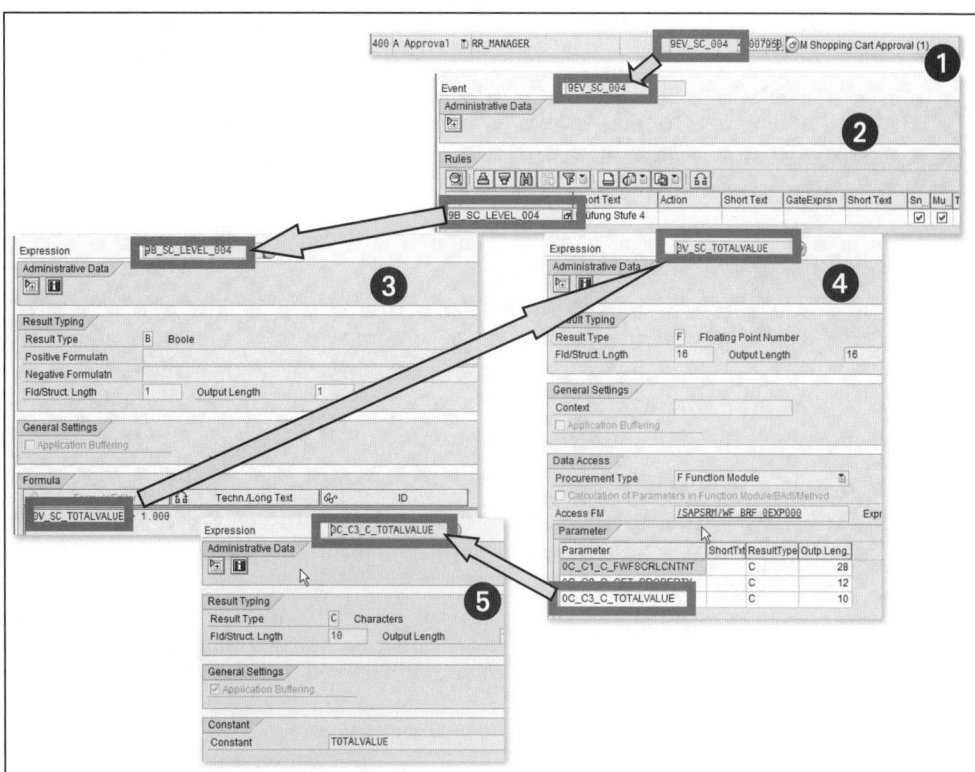

Figure 8.14 Process Level and BRF Linkage

Tip

When defining your own expressions, verify whether SAP has already delivered the expression you need. SAP delivers more than 230 standard BRF expressions. You can access more details on standard BRF expressions for SAP SRM, refer to SAP service marketplace at *http://service.sap.com/srm-inst* and then follow the path **Using SAP SRM Server 6.0 • Workflow in SAP SRM 2007**. You can also use the formula editor to create a new expression by combining multiple expressions. Formula Editor is a powerful tool with many standard expressions that can be used with a variety of formulas.

Offline Approval

In offline approval, approvers process approval work items from their emails without logging on to the SAP SRM system. The system sends the work items to approvers by email and updates the status of the workflow by processing the reply emails from the approvers. The offline approval process is briefly explained in the following steps:

1. The program /SAPSRM/OFFLINEAPPROVALSEND sends the work items to the approvers by email. Schedule the program to run periodically using Transaction SM36. BAdI BBP_OFFLINE_APP_BADI can be implemented to influence outbound processing, for example, to determine the recipients of email or to change the email content.

2. The email contains two buttons for the approver to approve or reject the work item. The system sends a reply email when the approver approves or rejects the work item.

3. When the system receives the reply email, the class (exit name) entered in inbound processing setting is triggered to process the work item. The processing parameters in inbound processing can be overridden by implementing BAdI BBP_OFFLINE_APP_BADI. The following inbound processing settings should be made using Transaction SO50:

   ▶ **Communication Type**: Select "Internet Email."

   ▶ **Recipient Address**: Specify the email address of WF_BATCH user. Ensure that user WF_BATCH has authorization profile S_A.SCON assigned in user master.

   ▶ **Document**: Enter "*."

   ▶ **Exit Name** : Enter "/SAPSRM/CL_OFFLINEAPP_INBOUND."

   ▶ **Call Sequence**: Enter "1."

8.2.5 Troubleshooting Tips and Tricks

The following are some troubleshooting tips and tricks, should you run into problems:

- Check the application log using Transaction SLG1 and search for object /SAP-SRM/ to analyze any BRF-related issues.
- You can use programs /SAPSRM/WF_CFG_ANALYSIS_001 and /SAP-SRM/WF_CFG_ANALYSIS_002 to analyse the workflow.
- For analysing SAP business workflow issues, use workflow Transactions SWI1, SWI6, or SWI2_FREQ. You can also use Transactions SWUS (test workflow) and SWF_DEBUG (debug workflow).
- The troubleshooting tips identified in Section 8.1 are applicable for the new workflow, also.
- SAP SRM–related workflow tasks should be defined as 'general task' using Transaction code /SAPSRM/WF_GEN.
- Check Transaction SM13 for any update errors.
- Check for lock entries in Transaction SM12.
- If a document cannot be approved because of illness on the part of an approver, work items can be reassigned to different approvers by administrators using Transaction SWIA.

8.3 Summary

Workflow is one of the most important e-procurement features and is used in all SAP SRM scenarios. In this chapter, you learned how workflow is implemented in SAP SRM, including the new workflow introduced in SAP SRM 2007. The comparison of features between the old workflow and new workflow equip you to design a good workflow solution for your company or customers with the understanding of new or improved features as well as the limitations in new workflow. In Chapter 9, we will discuss the functionality that revolutionized the way businesses operate in the internet world — catalogs.

Catalog items are considered master data by many organizations and are now an integral part of the master data management strategy. SRM-MDM Catalog enables consistent product master data between SRM-MDM Catalog, SAP SRM, and SAP ERP, and supports consolidation of catalog data from suppliers and procurement systems.

— David Marchand, Product Manager for SRM Catalog

9 Catalog Management

The existence of electronic product catalogs is one of the main contributors to the proliferation of e-commerce in the late 1990s. The search capabilities of catalogs make selecting required products by sifting through thousands of products an easy and enjoyable experience, rather than a long and tedious one, plus the skill to do so requires no training. Catalogs are also the main component in many e-procurement software offerings. Many software vendors, like SAP, launched their e-procurement applications with third-party catalog providers. However, SAP soon realized that their customers expect more integration with ERP and procurement applications than a simple catalog solution can provide.

Therefore, SAP's current catalog solution is a strategic shift from SAP's earlier catalog solutions and enables organizations to integrate catalog management with their master data management strategies. You will learn more about the evolution of SAP Supplier Relationship Management (SAP SRM) catalog solutions in Section 9.1, however, in this chapter, we will mainly discuss SAP's latest offering, the SRM-MDM Catalog. The functionalities of the SRM-MDM Catalog are discussed in Section 9.2 and implementing the SRM-MDM Catalog in Section 9.3.

9.1 Evolution of SAP SRM Catalog Solutions

Innovation and keeping pace with customer requirements and expectations has been the cornerstone of SAP's strategy in the SAP SRM area. In its approximately 10 years of existence, SAP SRM has used three different catalogs, with SRM-MDM Catalog being the latest offering. Figure 9.1 summarizes the three catalog solutions used in SAP SRM to date and suggested catalog strategies for customers.

In the early versions of SAP SRM, SAP bundled a third-party catalog software with its software. The third-party catalog provided the functionalities to upload supplier catalogs easily. The third-party catalog was integrated with the SAP SRM shopping cart using SAP Open Catalog Interface (OCI). This served customer requirements well in the early stages of e-procurement. Integration being a core strength of SAP's software, customers started expecting a better and more integrated catalog solution from SAP. Hence, SAP launched the SAP Catalog Content Management (CCM) solution in 2003, which replaced the third-party catalogs. SAP CCM enabled organizations to integrate product masters and procurement contracts from SAP SRM with CCM catalogs.

However, customers expected a much more deeply integrated product from SAP, which treats catalogs on par with other master data and enables them to adopt a consistent master data management strategy for catalogs, also. This prompted SAP to release a new strategic catalog solution based on SAP NetWeaver Master Data Management (MDM) technology within two years of releasing SAP CCM.

Evolution of SAP Catalog Solutions

	1999-2003	2004-2006	December 2006-onwards
Catalog Solution	Requisite Technology	**SAP CCM**	**SRM-MDM Catalog**
SRM Version	B2B 1.0 to SRM 4.0	SRM 3.0 to SRM 5.0	**SRM 3.0 onwards (Standard from SRM2007)**
Strategy	Publish Supplier Catalogs	More integration with Procurement Processes	Catalog part of Master Data Strategy and deep integration with ERP and SRM
SAP Maintenance & Support	Requisite Products - Till Dec end 2006	SAP CCM 2.0 - Till Dec end 2013	Migrate to SRM-MDM / SRM MDM 1.0 - Till Dec end 2013

Suggested Implementation Strategy for SAP SRM Customers

New SRM Customers	Implement SRM-MDM Catalog*
SRM Upgrade Customers	Implement SRM-MDM Catalog* or Migrate to SRM-MDM Catalog from existing catalog
SRM Customers with Requisite / CCM1.0 Catalog	Migrate to SRM-MDM Catalog* (No need to upgrade SRM)

* SAP MDM license is not required for SRM-MDM Catalog. SRM scenario licensing covers SRM-MDM Catalog license also

Figure 9.1 Evolution of SAP Catalog Solutions and Suggested Strategy

SRM-MDM Catalog is a functionality of SAP NetWeaver MDM, which runs on the platform layer and is therefore available to all applications shared by the platform. This means that SRM-MDM Catalog is deeply integrated with products and processes in SAP ERP and SAP SRM. David Marchand, SAP product manager for SAP SRM catalogs, asserts that SRM-MDM Catalog offers important functionality that is much better than SAP CCM and most of the third-party catalog solutions available on the market. We will discuss the SRM-MDM Catalog functionalities in more detail in Section 9.2. Customers who are currently implementing SAP CCM as part of their SAP SRM implementation may ask local SAP advisors to decide whether to switch to SRM-MDM Catalog or not.

> **Note**
>
> You may also want to read the article "Master Data Management with SAP SRM" by David Marchand at *https://www.sdn.sap.com/irj/sdn/bpx-srm*.

9.2 SRM-MDM Catalog Overview

In addition to normal product expectations, all SAP products must meet integration expectations from users. For example, SRM-MDM Catalog needs to not only meet the expectations of typical catalog users and content managers, but also the integration expectations of SAP ERP and SAP SRM users. The SRM-MDM Catalog content management process is described in Figure 9.2. We will now take a look at the typical requirements of catalog users and content managers and see how SRM-MDM fulfils these requirements:

▶ The fundamental requirement of any catalog is a great search experience for end users. The search should be easy and return relevant results very fast. Users should be able to get as much information as possible about the products they are looking for. Different search methods, like advanced search, drilldown search, keyword search, memory-based search (enables faster searches), hierarchy search, etc., are available in SRM-MDM Catalog. The search user interface is provided with WebDynpro Java technology. Searching is described in the **Search for Items** step shown in Figure 9.2.

▶ From a content manager's perspective, a catalog should be able to support the product schema used in the organization. It should support both the standard schema (UNSPSC, eClass, etc.) and customer-specific schemas. This is managed with the MDM Console and described in the **Manage Repository** step in Figure 9.2. SRM-MDM Catalog version 2.0 also includes MDM CLIX to facilitate a command line interface for most operational MDM console commands.

▶ Importing catalogs should be easy. Suppliers may provide catalogs in the form of spreadsheets or in XML format. Content managers should be able to upload catalogs in a variety of formats. The application should also enable mapping of different supplier catalogs to the organization's product schema. Importing catalogs and mapping imported catalogs to the product schema can be done manually in MDM Import Manager or automatically as a background job in MDM Import Server. The process is described in the **Import and Map** step in Figure 9.2. An advanced key mapping technique enables SAP NetWeaver MDM to store a matrix of systems and values as key mappings, facilitating data harmonization. With this technique, a product that has different keys in different systems (e.g., product code 1000 in ERP1 and 3342 in ERP2) can be mapped to a catalog item. Another feature is the ability to save a mapping and reuse it later. For example, while mapping a supplier catalog with a product schema for the first time, you can save the mappings. These mappings can be reused when another catalog from the same supplier is imported, saving time and effort.

▶ Content managers should be able to add information to enrich the catalog item information. For example, images and attachments, such as, product specification brochures, help users select the right products. MDM Data Manager facilitates this task and is described in the **Enrich Product Content** step in Figure 9.2. You can also add new items or make mass changes using this process.

▶ Some organizations may need an approval process before content is available for users. MDM Data Manager enables designing workflows for approval using the Microsoft Visio Pro plug-in. Workflows for new and changed items and for price deviations are predefined. Approval tasks can be assigned to users or a group of users. This process is described in the **Approve Product Content** step in Figure 9.2.

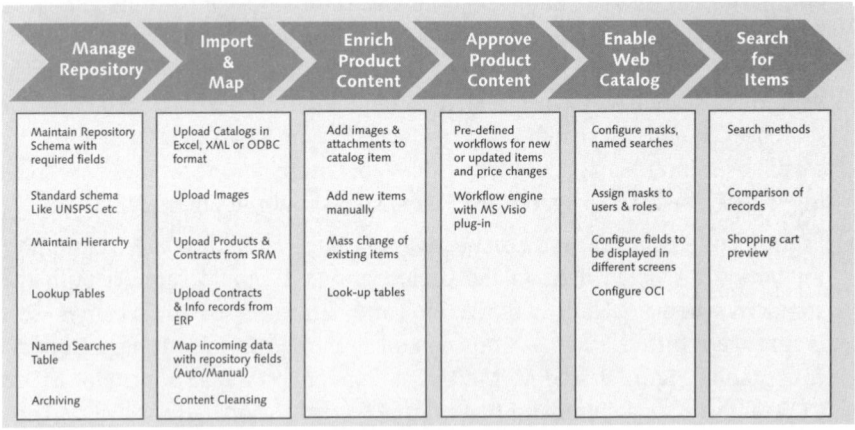

Manage Repository	Import & Map	Enrich Product Content	Approve Product Content	Enable Web Catalog	Search for Items
Maintain Repository Schema with required fields	Upload Catalogs in Excel, XML or ODBC format	Add images & attachments to catalog item	Pre-defined workflows for new or updated items and price changes	Configure masks, named searches	Search methods
Standard schema Like UNSPSC etc	Upload Images	Add new items manually	Workflow engine with MS Visio plug-in	Assign masks to users & roles	Comparison of records
Maintain Hierarchy	Upload Products & Contracts from SRM	Mass change of existing items		Configure fields to be displayed in different screens	Shopping cart preview
Lookup Tables	Upload Contracts & Info records from ERP	Look-up tables		Configure OCI	
Named Searches Table	Map incoming data with repository fields (Auto/Manual)				
Archiving	Content Cleansing				

Figure 9.2 SRM-MDM Catalog Content Management Process

▶ Content managers should be able to predefine the look of different catalog screens for end users with all required and useful fields. Content managers should also be able to create different views of catalogs for different sets of users. For example, if different departments in the organization are authorized to procure different sets of items, then different views are created to ensure that only authorized sets of items are displayed for a particular department's users. This process is described in the **Enable Web Catalog** step in Figure 9.2. Display settings for fields in catalog screens, like the item details screen, search results screen, product comparison screen, shopping cart preview screen, etc., are defined in this step. Masks and named searches can be configured to facilitate different views to different sets of users. You can also configure OCI field mapping to facilitate integration with procurement applications.

As mentioned, aside from these normal catalog functionalities, SAP users also expect integration capabilities from SAP products. Some of these expectations, which are fulfilled in SRM-MDM Catalog, include the following:

▶ The catalog should be integrated with other SAP applications, like SAP SRM and SAP ERP so that these applications can use catalog items.

▶ The catalog should be able to import purchasing info records from SAP ERP, so that requesters can create requisitions using standard master data with the convenience of catalogs.

▶ The catalog should be able to import products and contract items from SAP ERP and SAP SRM. This will facilitate linking of contracts with catalog items. This is also a procurement governance requirement in some organizations.

As explained earlier, SAP NetWeaver MDM runs on the platform layer and therefore all applications can share the data across the platform. The importing of master data into SRM-MDM Catalog from SAP SRM and SAP ERP is achieved with standard interface mappings provided in SAP NetWeaver Exchange Infrastructure (XI). SAP ERP 6.0 users can call the catalog, search for items, and transfer the selected items to a purchase requisition, purchase order, maintenance order, or network. Similarly, SAP SRM users can use the catalog from all procurement documents. This integration is achieved using OCI. The integration with SAP ERP and SAP SRM and the interaction between various MDM components is explained later in the chapter, in Figure 9.4. Note that importing contracts and info records from SAP ERP is available from SAP ERP 6.0 on.

Interesting Blogs
▶ SAP SRM and MDM Episode #1 by David Marchand *https://www.sdn.sap.com/irj/sdn/weblogs?blog=/pub/wlg/7172* ▶ Previewing SRM-MDM Catalog 2.0 by Vijayasarathy Raghunandan *https://www.sdn.sap.com/irj/sdn/weblogs?blog=/pub/wlg/7246*

9.3 Implementing SRM-MDM Catalog

The implementation of SRM-MDM Catalog involves setting up the following:

- ▶ **Initializing the SRM-MDM Catalog repository**: Discussed in Section 9.3.2.
- ▶ **Configuring SAP NetWeaver XI settings**: Explained in Section 9.3.3
- ▶ **Processing customizing in SRM or SAP ERP**: Explained in Section 9.3.4
- ▶ **Configuring the search user interface**: Explained in Section 9.3.5

However, before we dive into these configuration details, let us take a brief look at the technical architecture of SRM-MDM Catalog.

9.3.1 SRM-MDM Catalog Technical Architecture

The SRM-MDM Catalog is built on SAP MDM 5.5. The architecture of SRM-MDM Catalog is illustrated in Figure 9.3. The architecture consists of server components, client components, and a WebDynpro Java-based search user interface. Tasks performed by each of the components are also outlined in Figure 9.3.

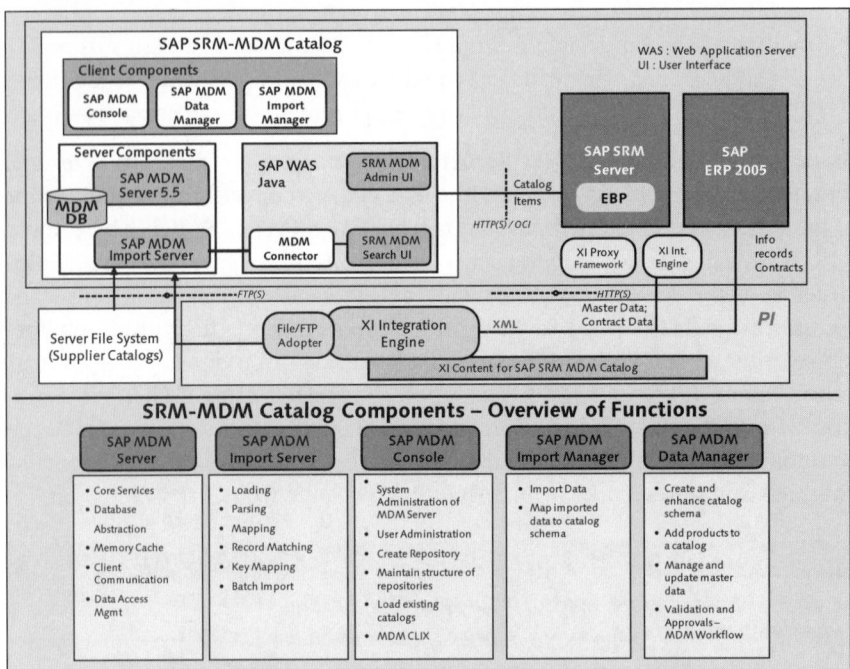

Figure 9.3 SRM-MDM Catalog Architecture

The data is typically imported using Import Manager. The imported data is managed and updated using Data Manager. Finally, the data is accessed by end users of procurement applications through the search user interface. The client components mentioned in Figure 9.3 are required only on the computers of catalog and content managers and system administrators. End users of a catalog need not have any additional components installed on their computers.

Catalog data imports from SAP SRM and SAP ERP are performed using SAP NetWeaver XI. You will need to install SAP NetWeaver XI if you need to import master data and contracts from SAP SRM or SAP ERP. The SRM-MDM Catalog user interface is based on WebDynpro Java technology, and you can install all server components and the user interface on one server. You also need to install SAP Web Application Server (WAS) Java for the user interface. Alternatively, you can also configure a distributed deployment using three servers — one for the MDM database, one for the MDM Server and MDM import server, and another one for the user interface.

Figure 9.4 illustrates in detail the integration between SRM-MDM Catalog, SAP ERP, and SAP SRM and the activities performed in each of the SRM-MDM Catalog components.

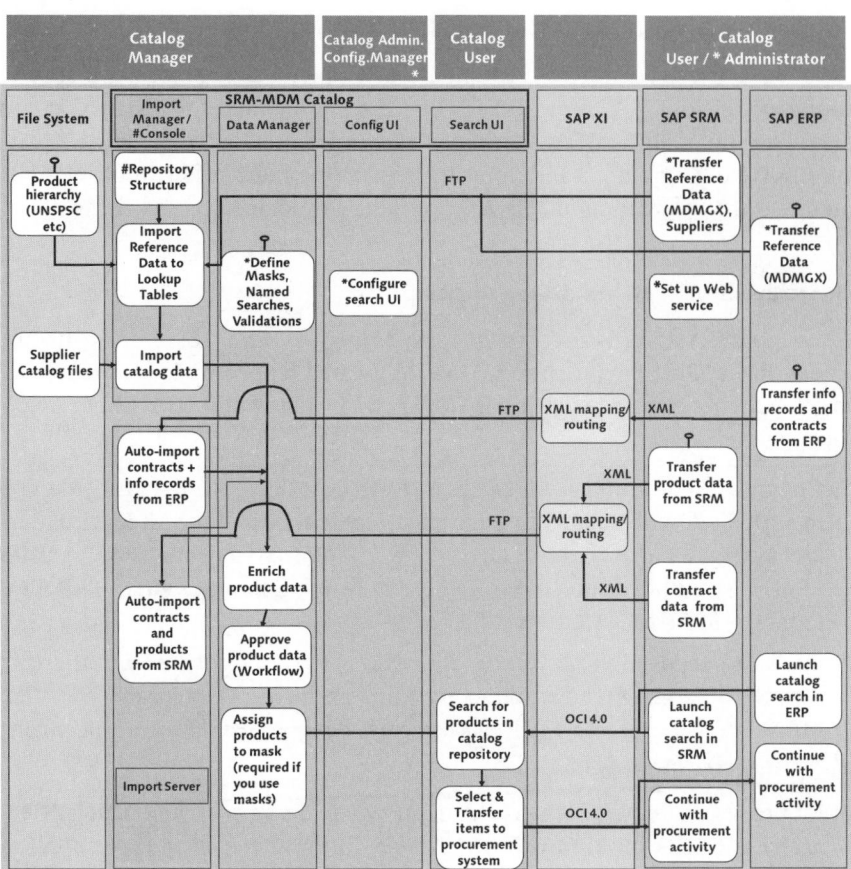

Figure 9.4 SRM-MDM Catalog Processes — Component View

> **Note**
>
> You do not need TREX installed for a catalog item search. SRM-MDM Catalog has a memory-based search capability, which provides much faster search results.

9.3.2 SAP NetWeaver Master Data Management Settings

In this section, we will explain the settings required in SAP NetWeaver MDM so you can import master data from SAP SRM and SAP ERP and maintain catalogs as master data in SAP NetWeaver MDM. We will also discuss some important SAP NetWeaver MDM settings required in a typical implementation.

> **Note**
>
> MDM generic extractor settings are required in SAP SRM and SAP ERP systems, but not in SAP NetWeaver MDM.

Ensure Implementation of Notes 964991 and 1057316

SAP Notes 1057316 and 964991 should be implemented before you start to configure settings. SAP Note 1057316 is the master note for installation and configuration of SRM-MDM Catalog 2.0. Download the text file MDMGX_Catalog.TXT from this note and copy it in your local drive. SAP note 964991 describes the installation of MDM 5.5 generic extractor for customizing data.

Unarchive SRM-MDM Catalog Repository

Although this setting is also explained in SAP Note 1057316, it is worthwhile explaining it. Unarchiving the SRM-MDM Catalog repository loads the repository template delivered by SAP for SRM-MDM Catalog and consists of the following steps:

1. Obtain the repository .a2a file (e.g., SRMMDMCAT20_SP01_2.a2a) either on the installation CD in directory Business_Content or on the SAP Service Marketplace under *http://service.sap.com/swdc*, **SAP Installations and Upgrades • Entry by Application Group • SAP Application Components • SAP SRM Catalog • SRM-MDM Catalog 2.0**.

2. Store the repository a2a file in the *<SAP_NetWeaver_MDM_installation_directory>\Server\Archives* directory (for example, C:\Program Files\SAP MDM 5.5\Server\Archives). If this directory does not exist, create it manually.

3. Open MDM Console.

4. Mount MDM Server: Right-click on **SAP MDM Servers** in the **Console Hierarchy** and click on **Mount MDM Server**. In the screen that appears, select the relevant MDM server from the list or enter the server name. Click on **OK**.

You will now see the MDM server in the **Console Hierarchy**. The setting is shown in step 1 in Figure 9.5.

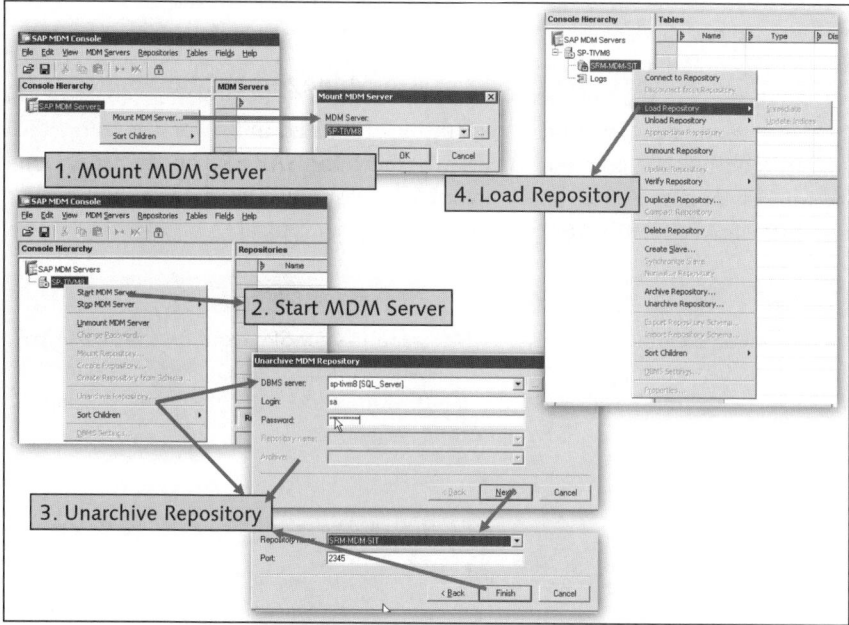

Figure 9.5 Unarchive SRM-MDM Catalog Repository

5. Start MDM Server: Select the MDM server and right-click to see the context menu. Click on **Start MDM Server**. The setting is shown in step 2 in Figure 9.5.

6. Unarchive repository: Right-click on the MDM server and select **Unarchive Repository**. In the screen that appears, specify the database server, login, and password. Specify the repository name, for example, SRM_MDM_CAT-ALOG. Select the archive file, which is the name of the .a2a file. The setting is shown in step 3 in Figure 9.5.

7. Load the repository and update indices: The repository should be loaded before it can be accessed by MDM clients on the network. Righ-click on the repository, select **Load Repository**, and then click on **Update Indices**. The setting is shown in step 4 in Figure 9.5.

MDM Generic Extractor for Importing Reference Data

The repository template delivered by SAP consists of a main table — **Catalog Items** — and a number of additional subtables. Figure 9.6 shows a sample screenshot of the SRM-MDM Catalog standard repository. For example, **Cata-**

log Items has a field **Unit of Measure**. The valid values for this field are contained in a subtable called UOM ISO Code.

These subtables are also called lookup tables. The data in these tables is normally customizing data in your SAP SRM or SAP ERP system. You can import the customizing data into these tables using the MDM generic extractor for reference data. The generic extractor hands over the customizing tables to the MDM server in XML format. From there, the data can be loaded into MDM lookup tables either automatically using the Import Server or manually using the Import Manager. The generic extractor is imported to SAP SRM or SAP ERP systems using SAP Note 964991.

Note

For more information on the SAP MDM generic extractor, refer to the MDM reference guides section in the SAP Service Marketplace. You can set up and extract the data using Transaction MDMGX in SAP SRM or SAP ERP. Note that the generic extractor is applicable for SAP applications only.

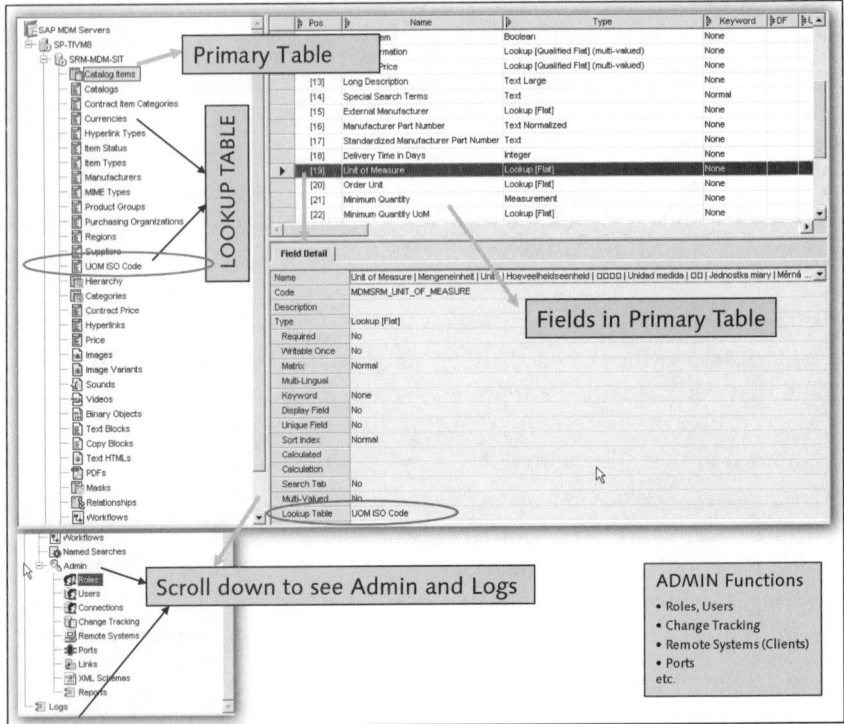

Figure 9.6 SRM-MDM Catalog Standard Repository

Setting the Home Directory for the FTP Server

Before you configure the MDM generic extractor, you have to configure the home directory of your FTP server to the directory name of your MDM Server installation.

To do so, on the MDM Server (Windows server) use the menu path **Settings • Control Panel • Administrative Tools • Computer Management • Services and Application • Internet Information Services • FTP Sites • Default FTP Site** and proceed as follows:

1. Right-click on the Default FTP Site folder and select Properties.
2. Select the Home Directory tab.
3. Check the entry in the FTP Site Directory Local Path field. A sample entry is D:\Program Files\SAP MDM 5.5\Server\Distributions. If you have changed the Distribution Root Dir. setting in the mds.ini file on the MDM Server, specify the corresponding setting for the distribution directory in the home directory.

**Setting up the MDM Generic Extractor for Reference Data
and Extracting Reference Data**

You need to set up the MDM generic extractor in your SAP SRM or SAP ERP system to import reference customizing data into the MDM system from SAP SRM or SAP ERP. Decide which system to use based on your integration needs. If you want to use SRM-MDM Catalog with your SAP SRM system, then select SAP SRM. If you want to use it with your SAP ERP system, then select ERP. If you want to import data from both systems, you need to set up the generic extractor in both SAP SRM and SAP ERP systems. If you are importing the same data (for example, UOM) from different systems, then MDM Import Manager provides several methods of matching incoming data with existing data. In such cases, refer to the setting for "Merging Reference Data" in this section.

> **Note**
>
> In this section, we will only discuss predefined template data. For additional data and objects, you should read the MDM generic extractor reference guide available in SAP note 964991.

Execute Transaction code MDMGX in your SAP SRM or SAP ERP system, and follow these steps to set up and execute the extraction.

1. Click on **Upload Ports and Check-Tables** to upload the standard SAP NetWeaver MDM ports and check table data into table MDMGXC1. Select "Catalog" as the **Object Type** and select the downloaded file "MDMGX_Catalog.txt" from your local drive. If you do not have this file, you can download

it from SAP note 1053716. Select **Remove Header Line** and click on the execute icon.

2. Click on **Maintain Ports and Check-Tables** to check the entries in the MDMGXC1 table. Select "Catalog" as the **Object Type** and execute. Verify the entries. You should see five entries for system type "R3" and five entries for system type "SRM." Currencies, product groups, purchasing organizations, and UOMs are available in the predefined templates. Note that purchasing organizations are only imported from system type R3.

3. Click on **Define Repositories and FTP servers**. You will see two entries. Copy the entry "SAP_SP4_PRODUCT" and create a new entry for the MDM repository. Configure the settings according to sample settings shown in Figure 9.7. Ensure that the **Reposit. Name (Code)** field value is identical to the SRM-MDM Catalog repository name in MDM. In the field **FTP Server**, enter the URL to your FTP server that contains the home directory. In **MDM Root**, enter the root folder of your home directory. The **Clnt Code** should be "SRM" or "ERP" depending on the **Remote System Type** selected. Save your entries.

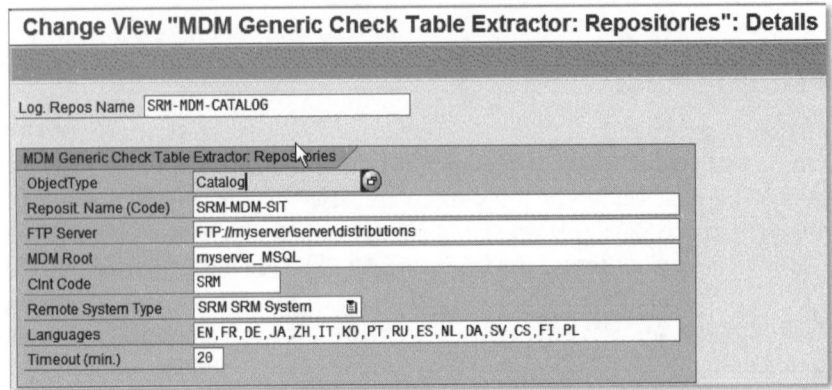

Figure 9.7 Define Repositories and FTP Servers

4. Click on **Start Extraction** to extract the data. Select the **Reposit. Name (Code)** from the list of available repositories. You can download the reference data to the FTP server or download it locally to your PC.

Verify the Replication Result in SAP NetWeaver MDM

The data extracted using the SAP NetWeaver MDM generic extractor updates the lookup tables in the SRM-MDM Catalog repository. You can verify the data and check for errors, if any, in SAP NetWeaver MDM Import Manager or SAP NetWeaver MDM Data Manager. If you use SAP NetWeaver MDM Import Manager, check for the ports LT_Currencies, LT_ProductGroups, LT_UOM_ISO_Code, and LT_PurchasingOrganization. If you use SAP NetWeaver MDM

Data Manager, check for the entries in Currencies, Product Groups, UOM ISO Code, and Purchasing Organizations. Note that purchasing organizations will be available only when data is replicated from SAP ERP.

Merging Reference Data

When you import data from multiple systems, it is necessary to consolidate the incoming information to one single set of data with the corresponding key mapping information to the remote systems (e.g., SAP ERP or SAP SRM). It is also possible that the same information may be represented with different keys in different systems. The SAP NetWeaver MDM Import Manager provides several methods to match incoming data with the already imported data. The Import Manager automatically matches and merges records that are exactly the same, and creates a key mapping entry to the data record for each remote system. If this does not work, check the configuration option in Import Manager "Do not update record matching field value" and set it to "No." If the records matched are slightly different, then Import Manager will create new records for incoming data. You should match the data and merge it after the import, using Data Manager, to ensure quality data in the lookup tables.

Modify the Repository Schema

This is an optional step. However, if your organization's catalog data model requires you to modify the standard repository schema delivered by SAP, then you need this step. For example, you may want to add additional fields or modify the properties of existing fields in the Catalog Items table. You may want to add lookup tables for the additional fields. You can modify the repository schema in MDM Console. To do so, select the repository you want to modify and perform the necessary modifications. Note that you need to unload the repository before making any modifications.

> **Note**
>
> Repository schema and repository structure are used interchangeably in this book.

Repository Security, Users, and Roles

The SAP NetWeaver MDM Console features a flexible multidimensional security scheme that controls which users can access a repository, which repository functions users can perform, and which records or fields users can access or modify. SRM-SAP NetWeaver MDM Catalog delivers a set of predefined roles and users, which meet the requirements of most organizations. Predefined users do not have passwords configured in the standard, and you should add passwords to all predefined users in the production system. You may also create additional users as required and assign roles.

If you use workflows, you should configure email addresses in the user master to receive notifications. For user interface configuration, a predefined user Master is delivered in the standard. You can maintain users and roles from the **Admin** area for the repository in MDM Console (see Figure 9.6).

Set Up Change Tracking

This is an optional, but useful setting. Some organizations want an audit trail of changes made to important fields in the catalog. You can set up change tracking from the **Admin** area for the repository in MDM Console (see Figure 9.6). For each field, you can specify whether to track changes (add, modify, delete). For each change, MDM records the date, time, and user who made the changes, the old value, and the new value. Tracking changes can degrade system performance and you should set change tracking only for very important fields (for example, price).

Product Masks and Named Searches

This setting is optional but useful. If you want to set up different repositories of data for different sets of users, then here is good news for you. You do not need to have different repositories! You can have a single repository of all of the data but set up different views to show only a subset of the data in repository. You may want to create different views based on your organization's requirements. Typically, department-, company-, or role-specific views are created. SRM-MDM Catalog Data Manager provides two options for this:

1. **Product masks**: Using this option, you can search for the required product records, select them from the search results, and add them to a mask. You can create any number of masks, thus creating many virtual repositories. Note that when a new relevant item is added in repository, you need to add it to the relevant masks, too.

2. **Named searches**: With this option, you store the search criteria in a named search. Every item you add to the repository that matches the criteria will be added to the results list whenever you restore the named search. If you do not see the named searches table in your repository, add it manually.

You should use named searches. The process of defining named searches and assigning them to users involves the following steps:

1. (This step is valid only in SRM-MDM Catalog version 1.0. You do not need this step in version 2.0). Verify whether a named searches table exists, and, if required, create it using MDM Console. To be able to add a table of type Named Searches, you need to add a specific registry entry in your Microsoft Windows system using the command RegEdit. In RegEdit, go to HKEY_CURRENT_USER\Software\SAP\MDM5.5\Console\Development. Add the

parameter **Enable Named Searches** with a value of **True** and save the registration.

2. Create a named search by opening MDM Data Manager, changing to Record mode, runing a search to create search results, opening the Search menu, selecting the **Set Named Search** option, and selecting an entry.

3. While defining External Web Services for catalogs in SAP SRM, add named search as the OCI parameter. Create different catalogs (i. e., different external Web services) with different named searches here. Each external Web service has a unique ID.

4. Assign the appropriate external Web service ID to attribute **CAT** in the organizational plan (Transaction PPOMA_BBP) at the company, department, or user position level as required.

Tip

You can pass the named search parameter dynamically using BAdI BBP_CAT_CALL_ENRICH. This BAdI can be used instead of passing the named search parameter in the external Web services setting.

Enable Multiple Languages

This setting is relevant if you want to use multiple languages in the SRM-MDM Catalog. SAP Note 1057316 contains information on the languages supported with different databases. The SRM-MDM Catalog offers three different types of multilanguage support: user interface (screens, menus, etc.), metadata (table headers, field descriptions, etc.), and record language (for all text objects in data).

Also, two-layer inheritance can be configured for each language. This means that you can define a primary and secondary inheritance language for all languages. For example, you can define English and French as the inheritance languages for German in MDM Console in repository settings. In this case, while showing data, if the system cannot find a translation text in German, it checks whether translation text exists in English (primary inheritance language) and shows the text in English. If it does not find text in English, it shows the text in French.

To configure this, you define "English (EN)###French(FR)" for the German language in the repository settings in the MDM Console. You can assign *uilanguage* (language for user interface) and *datalanguage* (language for data) as OCI parameters while defining external Web service settings in SAP SRM.

Slave Repository

This is an optional but useful setting. You can create *slave repositories* as a read-only copy of the master repository using MDM Console. The reason why you would want to create slave repositories is that a master repository cannot be used by end users when an administrator makes changes to it. Instead, if they exist, slave repositories can be used during such times. Once the changes to the master repository are complete, and it is stable, slave repositories can be synchronized with the master. Slave repositories can be part of the same database or part of a dedicated slave database. You should use slave repositories in your production environment.

Configuring a Role for Data Import via the MDM Import Server

If you use the MDM Import Server for an automatic upload of contract data, you can also configure the optional External Integration role. In the standard, the system user has this role assigned. But, by default, the Import Server uses the user Admin to upload the external data through an XML inbound interface and file system. The External Integration role allows you to differentiate between imports performed by the Administrator and those done by the system user. In this setting, you will change the import user from Admin to System, as follows:

1. In the MDM Console, check whether you have changed the default password for user System. The default password for user System is system. It is recommended that you change the password.

2. Shut down the Import Server and MDM Server.

3. In the installation directory, open the mdis.ini file.

4. Enter the appropriate name for the Server setting.

5. Start the MDM Server and then start the Import Server.

6. In the MDM Console, load the catalog repository. This initiates the system creation of a database-specific entry for your catalog repository in the mdis.ini file. In the next step, we will change this entry.

7. Shut down the Import Server and modify the repository section of mdis.ini. Change the entry "login = Admin" to "login = System." Change the entry "password =" to "password = *<your new password for user System>*."

9.3.3 SAP NetWeaver Exchange Infrastructure Settings

You will need SAP NetWeaver XI only when you want to import catalog data into SRM-MDM Catalog from an SAP SRM or ERP system. You can import suppliers, contracts, and products from SAP SRM into SRM-MDM Catalog. Similarly, you can import info records and contracts from SAP ERP. You do not need SAP NetWeaver XI if you do not import data into SRM-MDM Catalog from SAP SRM or ERP.

Before you start configuring the settings required to accomplish this integration, ensure that SAP NetWeaver XI content for SRM Server and SRM-MDM Catalog 2.0 has been imported into SAP NetWeaver XI.

Define RFC Destination for SAP NetWeaver XI in SAP SRM

You should configure these settings in the SAP SRM system using Transaction code SM59:

1. Define a Remote Function Calls (RFC) destination for the SAP NetWeaver XI system with connection type H (HTTP connection to ABAP system).

2. Configure an RFC destination name (e.g., XI_INTEGRATION_SERVER). In the Target host field, specify an SAP NetWeaver XI system host name (e.g., XID01.besttec.com) and specify a port number in the Service No. field.

3. Configure /sap/xi/engine?type=entry in the path prefix field.

4. On the Logon/Security tab, configure the client, logon user, (e.g., XIAP-PLUSER) and password in the SAP NetWeaver XI system. The logon user should have role SAP_XI_APPL_SERV_USER assigned.

5. For connecting to SAP NetWeaver XI, two additional RFC destinations, LCRS-APRFC and SAPSLDAPI, are defined with connection type T (TCP/IP connection). For LCRSAPRFC, maintain LCRSAPRFC_XID (or LCRSAPRFC_UNI-CODE) as the registered server program ID, where XID is the system ID of the SAP NetWeaver XI server.

6. Similarly, maintain SAPSLDAPI_XID (or SAPSLDAPI_UNICODE) as the registered server program ID for SAPSLDAPI. Configure the gateway host and gateway service for both connections. These two registered server programs are defined on the SAP J2EE RFC engine of the SAP NetWeaver XI server. The gateway host and service can be obtained using Transaction SMGW in your SAP NetWeaver XI system.

Define the RFC Destination for SAP NetWeaver XI in SAP ERP

You should configure these settings in the SAP ERP system (necessary only if you want to import contract data or info records from SAP ERP). Use Transaction code SM59 and proceed as follows:

1. Define an RFC destination for the SAP NetWeaver XI system with connection type 3 (SAP R/3 connection).

2. Specify an RFC destination name (e.g., XI_INTEGRATION_SERVER).

3. In the Target host field, specify the SAP NetWeaver XI system host name (e.g., XID01.besttec.com) and configure the system number of the SAP NetWeaver XI system in the System Number field.

4. On the Logon/Security tab, maintain the client, logon user, and password in the SAP NetWeaver XI system. The logon user should have profiles SAP_ALL and SAP_NEW assigned.

Maintain Logical System for Catalog in the SAP SRM system

You should specify a logical system name for your SRM-MDM Catalog system (e.g., CATALOGSRD) in your SAP SRM system using the menu path **SPRO · SAP Implementation Guide · Supplier Relationship Management · SRM Server · Technical Basic Settings · ALE Settings · Distribution · Basic Settings · Logical Systems · Define Logical System**.

Enable Use of SAP NetWeaver XI in SAP SRM

You should enable SAP NetWeaver XI in SAP SRM to enable XML communication through SAP NetWeaver XI using the menu path **SPRO · SAP Implementation Guide · Supplier Relationship Management · SRM Server · Cross Application Basic Settings · Enable use of Exchange Infrastructure**. Then, click on **New Entries** and select the checkbox for the Use Application Integration Infrastructure field.

Activate Service for SAP NetWeaver XI in the SAP SRM System

You should configure these settings in your SAP SRM system to activate the services for SAP NetWeaver XI. Use Transaction code SICF, and follow these steps:

1. Click on the execute icon.
2. Expand Default_host.
3. Expand SAP.
4. Right-click on xi, and select Activate Service.

Integration Engine Configuration

You should configure these settings in your SAP SRM system as follows, using Transaction code SXMB_ADM:

1. In the Integration Engine: Administration screen, execute the Integration Engine Configuration option.
2. Select **Edit · Change Global Configuration Data**.
3. In the field Role of Business System, select Application System.
4. In the corresponding Integ. Server field, enter "dest://<HTTP Destination>" where <HTTP Destination> is the RFC destination name for the SAP NetWeaver XI system. Save the settings.
5. Return to the Integration Engine: Administration screen. Execute the Manage Queues option.
6. Select all of the available options and click on the Register Queues button. Then click on the **Activate Queues** button.

Maintain SLD Access Data

You should configure these settings in your SAP SRM system to define the access to System Landscape Directory (SLD) in SAP NetWeaver XI. To do so, use Transaction code SLDAPICUST, and refer to Figure 9.8 for sample settings:

1. Maintain the **Alias Name** (for example, **PI_XID**).
2. Select the checkbox in the **Prim.** Column.
3. Maintain the **Host Name** and **Port** for SLD.
4. Enter a logon **User** and **Password**.

Alias Name	Prim.	Host Name	Port	User	Password
PI_XID	☑	p123456 wdf.sap.corp	50100	xisuper	🖉

Figure 9.8 Sample SLD Access Data Settings

Verify the settings using Transaction SLDCHECK.

Maintain Technical Systems in SLD

You should configure these settings in your SAP NetWeaver XI system. Verify whether you already have SAP SRM, ERP, and SRM-MDM Catalog business systems defined. If they do not exist, maintain the technical systems for SAP SRM, ERP, and SRM-MDM Catalog as outlined in this activity.

Use Transaction code SXMB_IFR to launch the SAP NetWeaver XI tool for configuration in your browser window, and then follow these steps:

1. Click on the **SLD** link.
2. Click on the **Technical Systems** link.
3. Click on the **New Technical System...** button.
4. Select the option **Web AS ABAP**. Click on **Next**.
5. Specify the System ID, 10-digit Installation Number, and Database Host Name. (You can get all of this information from your SAP SRM system by selecting **System • Status**.) Click on Next.
6. Specify the Message Server Port. (This will be the 3600 + system number of your SAP SRM system.) Also, specify the Central Application Server Host name and Instance Number (this is the System number of the SAP SRM system). Click on Next.
7. If you have multiple application servers, add them. Click on **Next**.
8. Add the Clients and Logical System Names of your SAP SRM system. Click on **Next**.

9. In the Installed Products screen, select the appropriate installed applications (e.g., SAP SRM 6.0). You can use the filter to quickly select the required products.

10. Click on the **Finish** button.

Configure the technical system for your ERP system in a similar manner. Then, configure the technical system for SRM-MDM Catalog as follows:

1. Click on the **New Technical System...** button.

2. Select the option **Third-Party**. Click on **Next**.

3. Specify the System name (e.g., SRM_MDM_CATALOG_SRD) and Database Host Name of the MDM system. Click on **Next**.

4. In the Installed Products screen, select the appropriate installed MDM application version (e.g., SAP MDM 5.5). You can use the filter to quickly select the required products.

5. Click on the **Finish** button.

Tip

You can create technical systems for SAP SRM in SLD automatically from your SAP SRM system using Transaction RZ70. Configure the SLD Bridge Gateway and host. Click on the proposal icon in the bottom right corner. Then click on the activate icon. Next, click on the start data collection and job scheduling icon. The system will create a technical system for SAP SRM in SAP NetWeaver XI SLD.

Maintain Business Systems in SLD

You should configure these settings in your SAP NetWeaver XI system. Verify whether you already have SAP SRM, ERP, and SRM-MDM Catalog business systems defined. If they do not exist, configure them in this activity. Configure your business system for SAP NetWeaver XI also, if you have not done so already.

Use Transaction code SXMB_IFR to launch the SAP NetWeaver XI tools for configuration in your browser window, then follow these steps:

1. Click on the System Landscape Directory (SLD) link, then click on the Business Systems link.

2. Click on the **New Business System...** button.

3. Select the option Web AS ABAP. Click on **Next**.

4. Select the System and Client of the SAP SRM system from the dropdown list. Click on **Next**.

5. Enter a Business System Name (e.g., "SRD_100"). Click on **Next**.

6. The Installed Products screen appears. Click on **Next**.

7. In the step Integration, select Application System as the Business System Role from the dropdown list.

8. In the Related Integration Server field, select the SAP NetWeaver XI business system from the dropdown list.

9. Click on the **Finish** button.

Define the business system for your SAP ERP system in a similar fashion. If you are defining an SAP NetWeaver XI business system, the settings in step "Integration" will be different from that of other business systems. Here, you will select Integration Server as the Business System Role and configure a Pipeline URL in the format *http://HOST:PORT/sap/xi/engine?type=entry*.

Define the business system for the SRM-MDM Catalog as follows:

1. Click on the **New Business System...** button.

2. Select the option Third-Party. Click on **Next**.

3. Select the Technical System SRM-MDM Catalog in the system dropdown list and specify a Logical System Name for SRM-MDM Catalog (e.g., CATALOGSRD). You should specify the same logical system name for the catalog as the one you defined in the SAP SRM system.

4. Enter a Business System Name (e.g., SRM_MDM_CATALOG_SRD). Click on **Next**.

5. In the Installed Products screen, click on **Next**.

6. In the step Integration, select Application System as the Business System Role from the dropdown list. Select the SAP NetWeaver XI business system from the dropdown list in the Related Integration Server field.

7. Click on the **Finish** button.

Set Up Integration Scenarios

You should configure these settings in your SAP NetWeaver XI system, using Transaction code SXMB_IFR. The SAP NetWeaver XI tools for configuration in your browser window are launched. Follow these sets of steps:

1. Click on the **Integration Directory** link.

2. Enter the user ID and password. The Configuration: Integration Builder window appears.

3. This step is optional but recommended. Select **Environment • Clear SLD Data Cache**. You can also perform this step if you cannot find the business systems you created previously.

To assign a business system:

1. Click on the **Objects** tab.

2. Expand **Service Without Party**, then expand **Business System**.

3. Check whether the business systems of SAP SRM, ERP, and SRM- MDM Catalog already exist. If they do not exist, then right-click on Business System and select **Assign Business System**. The Assign Business System wizard screen appears.

4. Click on the **Continue** button twice. Do not enter anything in the Party field.

5. Select the business system for SRM- MDM Catalog from the list shown. Do not select the checkbox Create Communication Channels Automatically.

6. Click on the **Finish** button. You may see a pop up to select the language. If so, select the language. The business system is then assigned. Repeat this set of steps for SAP SRM and ERP systems, too.

To transfer an integration scenario from the repository:

1. Select **Tools • Transfer Integration Scenario from Integration Repository**.

2. Select the scenario **SRM_MDM_Catalog** with the appropriate version (e.g., SRM- MDM CATALOG 2.0) from the search list in the **Name** field. See step 1 in Figure 9.9. Note that you may have more than one entry for a scenario.

3. Click on the **Continue** button. You'll now have to create a configuration scenario.

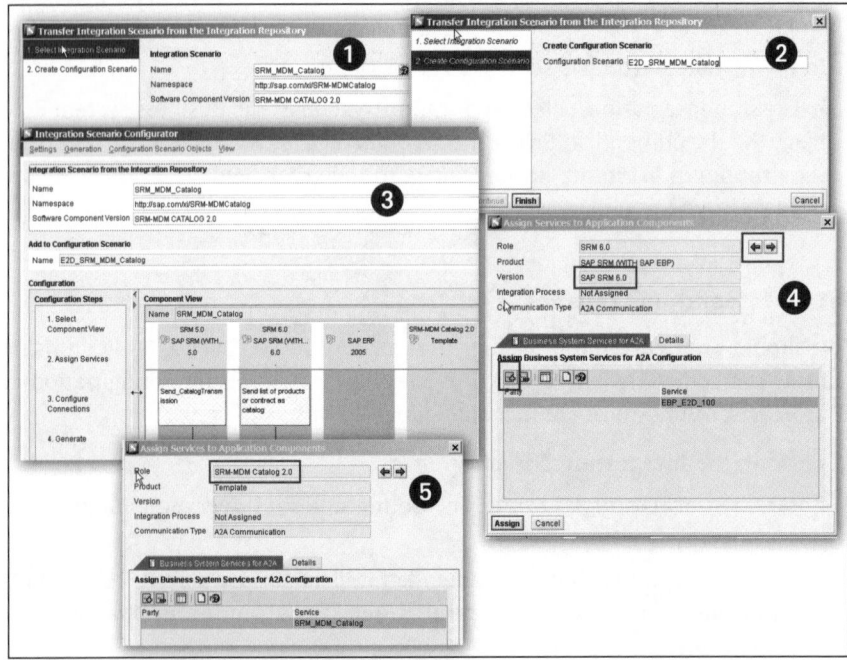

Figure 9.9 Integration Scenario Configuration

4. Enter a name for the **Configuration Scenario**, such as "E2D_SRM_MDM_ CATALOG." See step 2 in Figure 9.9. You should use a consistent nomencla-

ture for naming configuration scenarios. For example, you could use the system ID of the SAP SRM system as a prefix for the scenario name.

5. Click on the **Finish** button.

6. In the next screen that appears, click on the **Close** button.

Assign services to application components as follows:

1. In the **Integration Scenario Configurator** wizard that appears, click on **Component View**. See step 3 in Figure 9.9.

2. In the next screen, click on the **Apply** button.

3. In the **Assign Services to Application Components** screen, verify the **Role** and **Version**. If the version is not appropriate, click on the right arrow next to the **Role** field. Click on the "insert" icon (icon with a + sign). In the Service Selection screen, select the relevant business system. Assign services for SAP SRM and SRM-MDM Catalog as shown in steps 4 and 5 in Figure 9.9.

Next, configure the connections as follows:

1. Click on **Configure Connections** in the left pane of the wizard. The integration scenario includes actions for the upload of products and contracts from SAP SRM and/or ERP.

2. In the next screen, click on the right arrow icon until you get the right components in both the **From Action** and **To Action** areas (step 1 in Figure 9.10).

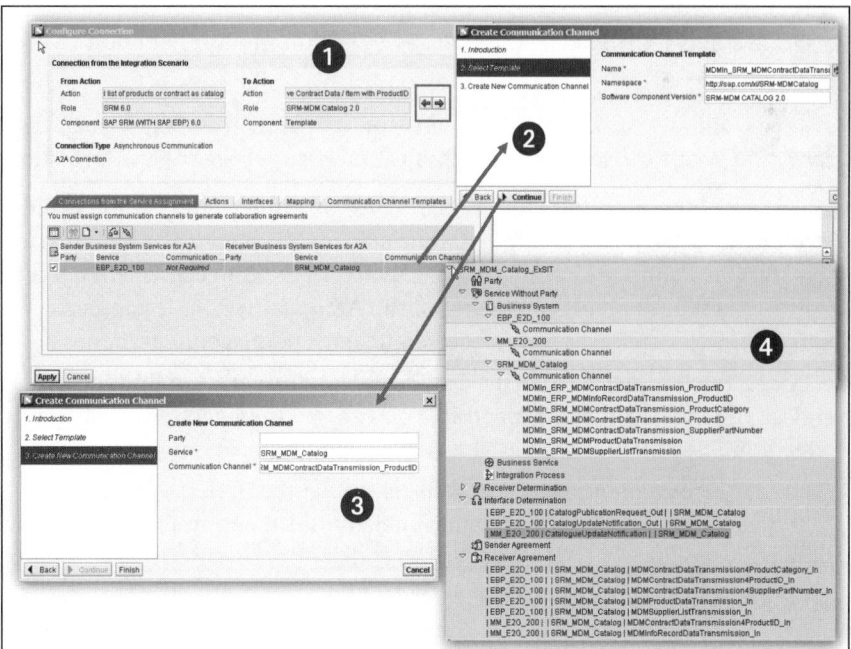

Figure 9.10 Configuration of Connections

3. Right-click on the **Communication Channel** field and select **Create Communication Channel**.

4. Select **Create Communication Channel with Template**.

5. Click on **Continue** in the next screen.

6. Check the template **Name, Namespace,** and **Software Component Version** and click on the **Continue** button (step 2 in Figure 9.10).

7. Check the **Service** and **Communication Channel**, and click on the **Finish** button. (step 3 in Figure 9.10)

8. In the **Configure Connection** screen, click on the right arrow icon, select the next relevant action for your scenario, and repeat the steps to create a communication channel. The screenshots shown in Figure 9.10 illustrate the configuration with sample settings.

Next, you're ready to generate the scenario configuration:

1. Select **Generate** in the left pane of the wizard (see Figure 9.9). You can simulate the generation by selecting the **Generation Simulation** radio button.

2. Verify the simulation results. If there are no errors, select the **Generation** radio button and click on the **Start** button to generate the scenario configuration. Close the results log screen.

3. In the Integration Scenario Configurator main screen, select **Settings • Apply Changes and Save Configuration Scenario**.

4. Close the **Integration Scenario Configurator** screen. If you receive a message "Do you want to keep the changes," click on the **Apply** button to keep the changes.

Now, you will see how to activate the configuration from the change lists screen, and access scenario and communication channel overview information:

1. Select the **Change Lists** tab in the **Configuration: Integration Builder** screen. All of the newly configured (or changed) objects are listed. Right-click on **Standard Change List** and select **Activate**. In the **Objects** screen, select all of the configured objects and click on the **Activate** button. If you make any changes, this step needs to be repeated to activate the configuration.

2. Click on the **Scenarios** tab in the **Configuration: Integration Builder** screen. Select your scenario and expand it. You can see the overview as shown in step 4 in Figure 9.10.

3. You can see the communication channels configured in step 4 in Figure 9.10. The settings in a communication channel are illustrated in Figure 9.11. The link between the FTP folder and the target directory specified in the communication channel is also shown Figure 9.11.

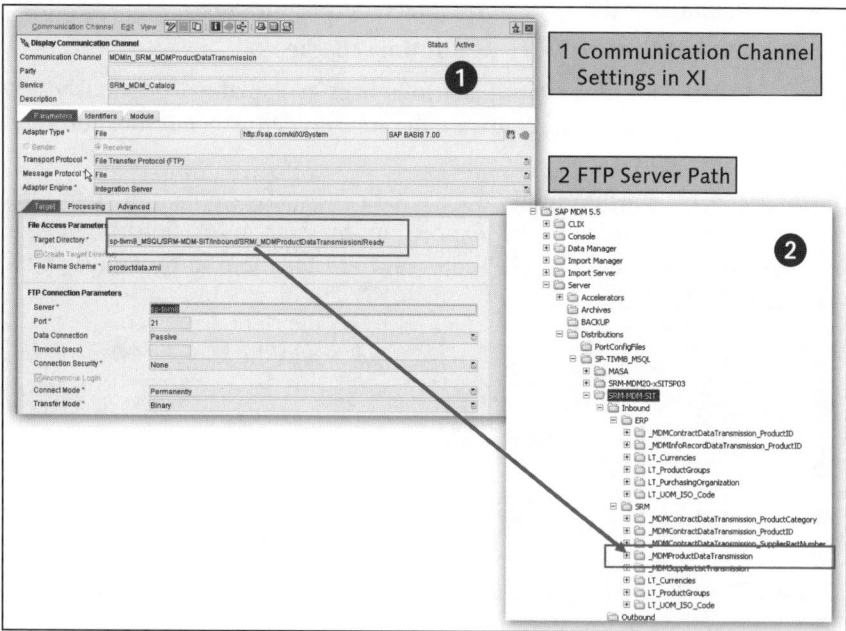

Figure 9.11 Communication Channel Settings

The next step is editing the interface determination to ensure that the upload of product and contract data uses the proper interfaces:

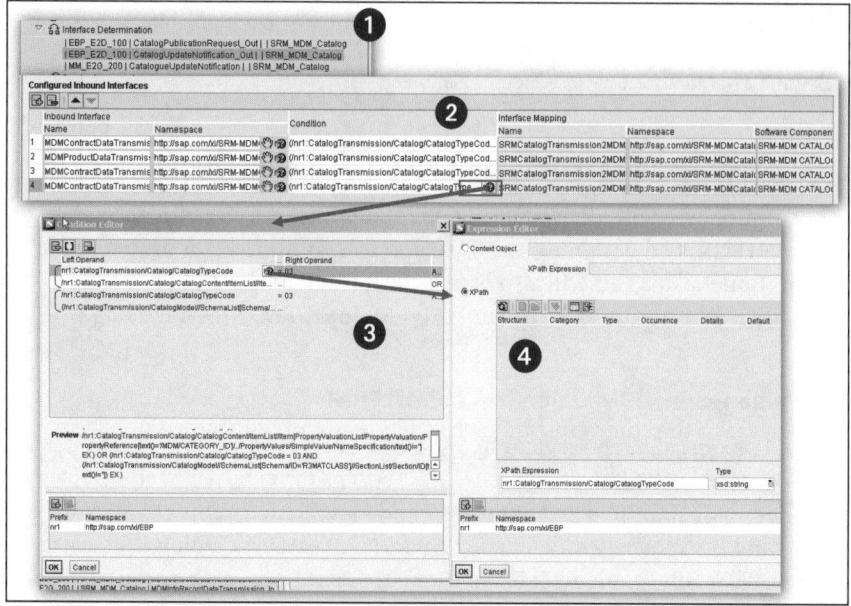

Figure 9.12 Maintaining Condition in Interface Determination

1. Select **Standard** as the **Type of Interface Determination**.

2. Deselect the **Maintain Order At Runtime** checkbox.

3. Edit the condition for each of the interfaces as explained previously. The screenshots in Figure 9.12 illustrate the steps to define conditions for interface determination.

The interfaces for which conditions need to be maintained are outlined in Table 9.1. The condition syntax (Xpath expression) for each interface is provided in SAP Note 1057316. Refer to SAP note 1057316 for more information on the Xpath expression.

Interface	Inbound Interface	Condition (See Note)
CatalogUpdateNotification_Out	MDMContractDataTransmission4Supplier-PartNumber_In	1057316
CatalogUpdateNotification_Out	MDMProductDataTransmission_In	1057316
CatalogUpdateNotification_Out	MDMContractDataTransmission4Product-ID_In	1057316
CatalogUpdateNotification_Out	MDMContractDataTransmission4Product-Category_In	1057316
CatalogueUpdate-Notification	MDMInfoRecordDataTransmission_In	1057316
CatalogueUpdate-Notification	MDMContractDataTransmission4Product-ID_In	1057316

Table 9.1 Conditions for Interface Determination

9.3.4 Process Customizing in SAP SRM and/or SAP ERP

In this section, we will discuss setting up catalog Web services for accessing catalogs via URLs, and assigning the Web services to users or departments in an organizational plan. You will also learn which transactions and programs to use to replicate data from SAP SRM and SAP ERP into SRM-MDM Catalog.

Setting up External Web Services in SAP SRM

Configure external Web services in SAP SRM to access the SRM-MDM Catalog via a URL from SAP SRM documents. The settings for external Web services are explained in Chapter 5, using Figure 5.5 and Figure 5.6. In this chapter, we will define only the *Integrated Call Structure* for SRM-MDM Catalog Web services. If you have many named searches or masks, define a Web service for each named search or mask so that you can assign them to different users or departments in an organizational plan.

To perform this configuration, use the menu path **SPRO · SAP Implementation Guide · Supplier Relationship Management · SRM Server · Master Data · Define External Web Services (Catalogs, Vendor Lists etc)**. The parameters in the Integrated Call Structure are explained in Table 9.2.

Name	Content	Type	Remarks
	Syntax for the URL: http://<J2EE server>:<J2EE port>/SRM-MDM/SRM_MDM	URL	Required. Maintain the URL for catalog search.
username	<MDM user id>	Fixed	Required.
password	<MDM Password>	Fixed	Required.
server	<MDM Server> e.g., smwdf001	Fixed	Required. Host on which MDM server is installed.
catalog	<MDM Catalog repository name> e.g., SRM_MDM_CATALOG	Fixed	Required. Name of the catalog repository in MDM.
port	<Port assigned to catalog repository in MDM Console>	Fixed	Required. Port assigned to the catalog repository in MDM Console.
uilanguage	SY-LANGU	SAP field	Required. User interface language.
datalanguage	For example: SY-LANGU or <EN>	Fixed or SAP field	Required. Data language.
mask	<mask_name>	Fixed	Optional.
namedsearch	<named_search_name>	Fixed	Optional.
HOOK_URL		Return URL	Required. Keep the value blank.

Table 9.2 Integrated Call Structure Parameters for SRM-MDM Catalog

Assign External Web Service to an Organizational Plan

Assign external Web service ID to organizational plan attribute CAT at the appropriate organizational unit level or at the position level using Transaction

PPOMA_BBP. If you want to make a catalog Web service available to all users in a company, assign the Web service at the company node level. If you want to restrict access to a specific department or to a specific set of users, assign the Web service only to the department or set of users in question.

Setting up External Web Services in SAP ERP

You need to set up external Web services in SAP ERP using the menu path **SPRO • SAP Implementation Guide • Materials Management • Purchasing • Environment Data • Web Services • ID and Description** if you want to use the catalogs in SAP ERP transactions, such as purchase requisition, purchase order, plant maintenance, or project network. Integration of catalogs with purchase requisitions and purchase orders is only available from SAP ERP 6.0 on. Integration of catalogs with maintenance orders and project networks is available from SAP R/3 4.7 on and you can refer to Chapter 6 for more details. The settings in this section will be similar to the settings described in the section *Setting up External Web Services in SAP SRM*.

Contract Replication from SAP SRM

Contract items in SAP SRM can be distributed to SRM-MDM Catalog as catalog items. You can send the contract data to catalog by selecting the checkbox Distribute Contract to Catalog in the contract. The data is sent to SRM-MDM Catalog using SAP NetWeaver XI. The fields product ID, supplier ID, supplier part number and category, price and price unit, contract and contract item ID are transferred to the catalog. You can enrich the contract data using BAdI BBP_SAPXML1_OUT_BADI. If you want to transfer discounts and price scales to SRM-MDM Catalog, you should implement this BAdI.

Product Master Data Replication from SAP SRM

You can transfer product master data in SAP SRM to SRM-MDM Catalog using Transaction BBP_CCM_TRANSFER.

Supplier Master Data Replication from SAP SRM

You can transfer supplier master data in SAP SRM to SRM-MDM Catalog by executing the program ROS_SUPPLIER_SEND_TO_CATALOG using Transaction SE38. The program sends the data using XML interface CatalogPublicationRequest_Out and Inbound XML interface MDMSupplierListTransmission_In.

Contract and Info Records Replication from SAP ERP

Contracts and info records from SAP ERP can be replicated to SRM-MDM Catalog using Transaction MECCM. This capability is available only from SAP ERP 6.0 on.

9.3.5 Search User Interface Overview

SRM-MDM Catalog uses WebDynpro Java-based user interface (UI). Catalog users use this UI to search for required items from available catalogs. The success of a catalog largely depends on the user experience while searching for items. Therefore, the search UI is very important. Users with the role UI Configuration Manager can configure the search interface to influence the following:

▸ General behavior, for example, availability of a shopping cart preview.

▸ Search behavior, for example, the use of advanced search, or tree and selection list search.

▸ Availability of content, for example, which fields are available to which users.

▸ OCI mapping.

▸ User configuration. The standard UI configuration is assigned to the **Default User**, as shown later in Figure 9.13. The settings for the **Default User** are used for all search users who have not been assigned specific UI configuration settings.

Configure the Search User Interface

You can access the UI configuration by accessing the URL *http://<J2EE Server:J2EE Port>/SRM-MDM/SRM_MDM*. Then proceed as follows:

1. In the Server Name field, specify the host on which the MDM server is installed, and also specify the Server Password.

2. Select the relevant Repository and enter a user name and password for the repository. The user must have the role UI Configuration Manager assigned in MDM Console. In the standard, the user Master is delivered with this role assignment. Click on the Login button.

3. Select the catalog user for whom the UI needs to be defined from the User dropdown list. The default is Default User.

Configure the settings on the **General** tab, shown in Figure 9.13, as follows:

1. If you select the **Shopping Cart** radio button, under **Shopping Options**, then the shopping cart preview is not shown before transferring items to the shopping cart.

2. If you select **Yes** for **Context view is available**, the system enables the display of items with an enlarged image size along with multiple configurable user fields.

3. If you select **Yes** for **Show Price Base Quantity**, the system compares the items based on the quantity entered so that the right scale price is calculated. (If pricing scales are maintained, prices are dependent on the quantity.)

4. If you select **Yes** for **Manage your current Shopping Lists**, then the user is authorized to create, modify, and delete their own shopping lists.

5. The options for **Other Shopping Lists** enable users to modify or delete the shopping lists of others.

6. Click on the **OCI Mapping** button to map the fields in the catalog repository with SAP OCI structure to transfer the fields to SAP SRM shopping cart. OCI mapping is explained later in the *OCI Mapping* section.

The remainder of the options on the **General** tab are self-explanatory.

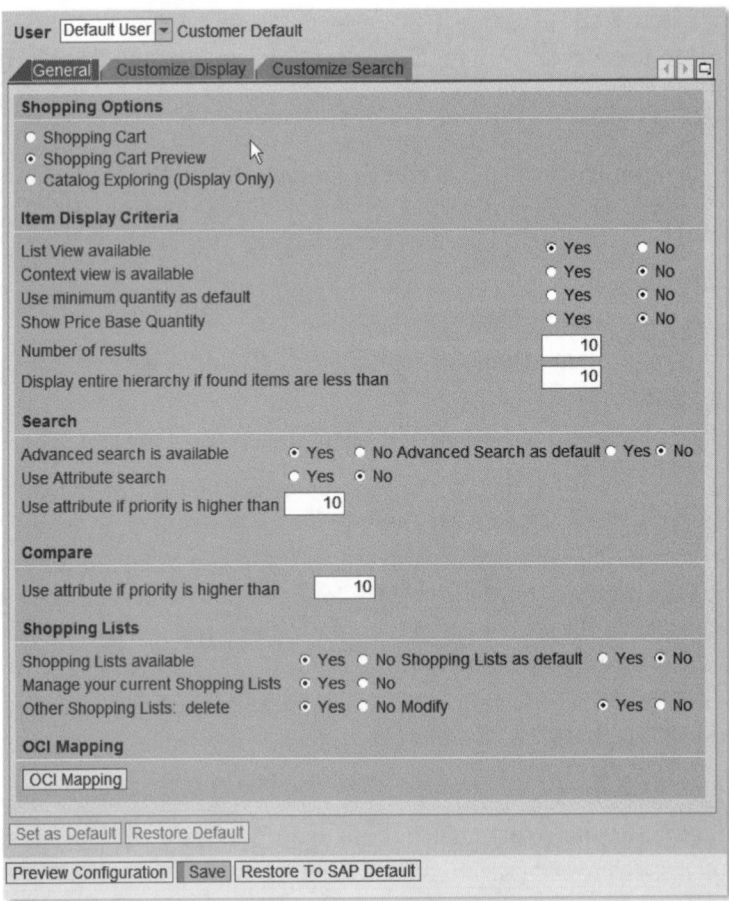

Figure 9.13 User Interface Configuration — General Tab

Configure the settings on the **Customize Display** tab shown in Figure 9.14 as follows:

1. You can customize the available fields, the order of the fields, and the default sorting field for the screens in UI. The screens in UI available for configuration are **Item Lists**, **Shopping Cart Preview**, **Compare**, **Item Details**, and **Context View**.

2. If you want to use the same settings for all screens, configure the settings for one screen and click on the **Copy To All** button.

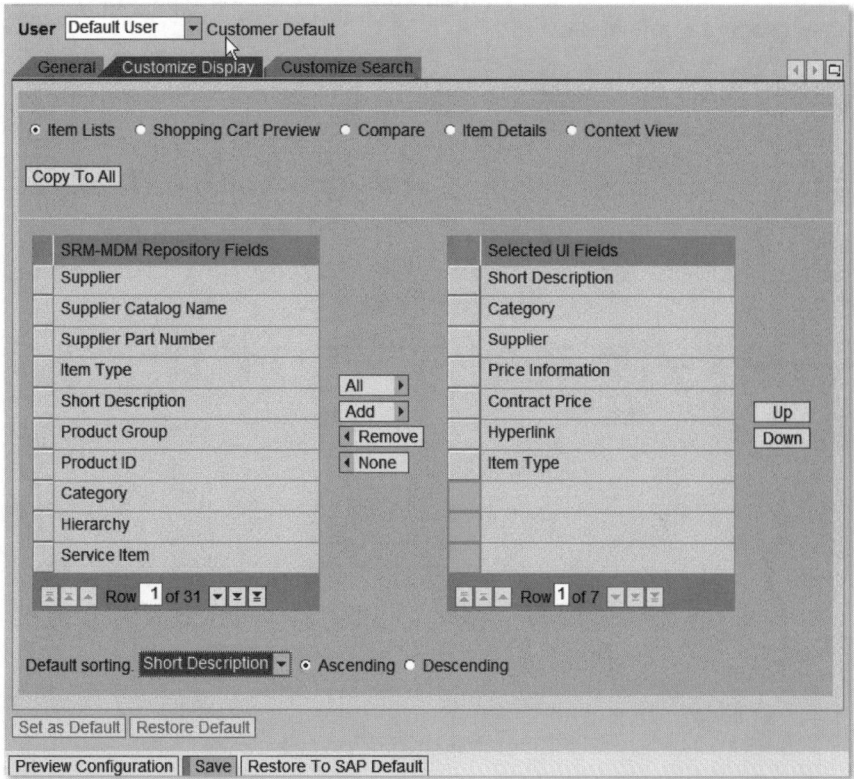

Figure 9.14 UI Configuration — Customize Display

Configure the settings on the **Customize Search** tab, shown in Figure 9.15 as follows:

1. You can configure various search options and fields available in Advanced Search, as illustrated in Figure 9.15. To configure a field, select the appropriate checkmark(s) for the **Field Name**. The selected fields will be available for use in an advanced search.

▶ If the **Dropdown Box** column is selected for any field, the field is displayed with its values in a dropdown box. Users can select a value to filter the search.

▶ If the **Free Text Search** column is selected for any field, users can enter free text in the field to search the catalog.

▶ If **Range** is selected, then users can enter a range of values for the field to search in the catalog.

2. Specify the **Operators** you want to use.

3. If you want to use **Search via Attributes**, select the value **Category** in the **Hierarchy** dropdown box.

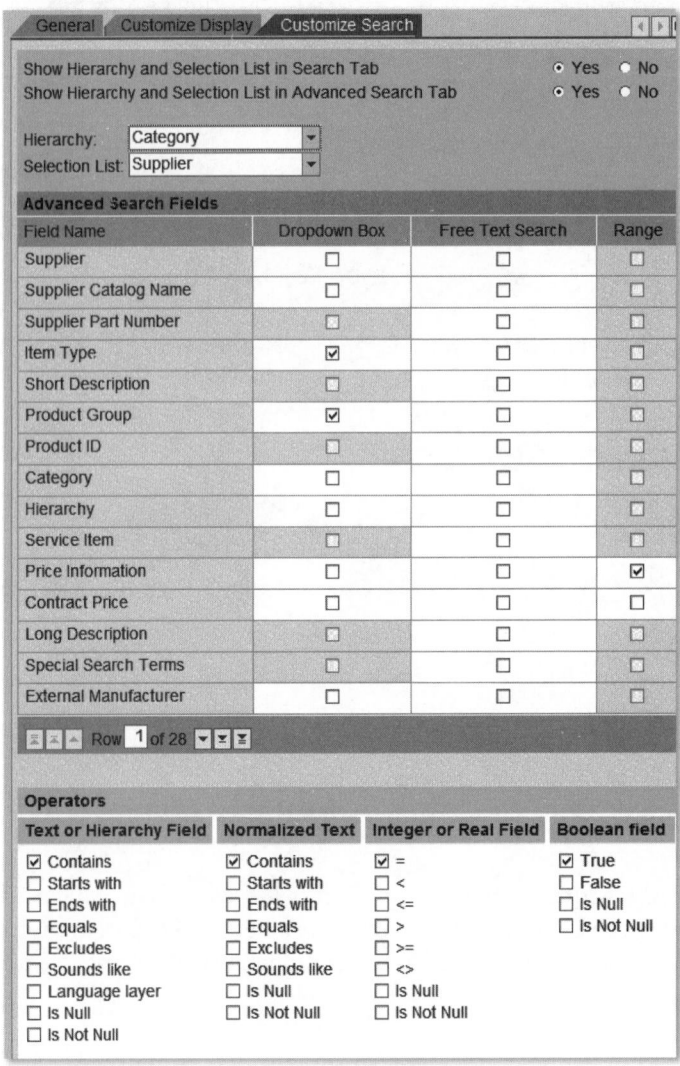

Figure 9.15 UI Configuration — Customize Search

OCI Mapping

This setting is optional. OCI mapping maps the SRM-MDM Catalog repository fields to fields in SAP OCI. The OCI mapping configuration is available on the General Data tab of UI configuration. If you have added any fields to the SRM-MDM repository, then you can map the new fields to OCI fields. SAP OCI has five predefined customer fields that can be used to map additional repository fields.

Extending OCI Fields

This procedure allows you to define your own OCI fields by accessing *http://<J2EE Server:J2EE Port>/SRM-MDM/SRM_MDM*. Then, proceed as follows:

1. In the Server Name field, specify the host on which the MDM server is installed and specify the Server Password.
2. Select the relevant Repository and enter a user name and password for the repository. The user must have role UI Configuration Manager assigned in MDM Console. In the standard, user Master is delivered with this role assignment. Click on the Transport Configuration button.
3. Click on the Export link. Edit the XML structure that appears.
4. Using the format <field Name="NEW_ITEM-ZZ_CUSTOM_FIELD1" />, add your own OCI field at the end within the tag OCIFields.
5. Save the changed XML file.
6. Import the changed XML file.

9.4 Summary

In this chapter, you learned about the evolution of SAP SRM catalog solutions, and how SAP has proactively responded to fast-changing customer expectations with its next-generation catalog solution, the SRM-MDM Catalog. Consultants should be able to implement the new SRM-MDM Catalog comfortably with the exhaustive details provided in this chapter. We have now covered all of the aspects of implementing operational procurement. Next, we will move on to strategic supply management topics starting with Sourcing in Chapter 10.

Sourcing refers to a number of procurement practices, aimed at finding, evaluating, and engaging suppliers of goods and services. Global sourcing is a procurement strategy aimed at exploiting global efficiencies in production.

— *Wikipedia*

10 Sourcing

Negotiation is considered an essential competence of a purchaser, and globalization, competitive cost pressures, and the increasing need for transparency are driving organizations to adopt Information Technology (IT) applications in sourcing. Electronic Request for Quotation/Proposal (eRFx) and reverse auctions have become regular tools of trade in the era of global sourcing. Also, modern purchasers do not want to settle with suppliers from their region or country. They want to achieve sourcing excellence by sourcing their goods and services from the best suppliers in the world. While the shrinking globe provides many sourcing opportunities, it has also increased sourcing-related risks. Selection and evaluation of suppliers has become more complex as purchasers need to evaluate geographical, political, and cultural risks before selecting a supplier.

Although eRFx and reverse auction are the most commonly used sourcing tools, the sourcing process comprises many subprocesses that enable purchasers to identify and assign sources of supply for procurement requirements. A good sourcing and procurement application ensures that negotiated contracts are used as supply sources for procurement requirements, and ensures automatic contract compliance.

SAP Supplier Relationship Management (SAP SRM) facilitates purchasers to analyze spend, determine sourcing strategies for each category, and execute the sourcing strategy. It also ensures that the benefits of the best negotiated prices are realized in procurement. Other important functionalities in SAP SRM that help sourcing professionals are supplier self-registration and supplier qualification, supplier evaluation, demand aggregation, and automatic source of supply identification.

We will discuss the sourcing functionalities offered by SAP SRM in detail in Section 10.2. The implementation of sourcing functionalities in SAP SRM is explained in section 10.3. In Section 10.1, we are using a case study of a fictitious oil and gas company, called OBECO Oil and Gas Corporation, to explain the sourcing needs in an asset-intensive industry.

10.1 Case Study: OBECO Oil and Gas Corporation

OBECO Oil and Gas Corporation is one of the top 10 global oil and gas firms in the world with interests in both upstream (exploration) and downstream (refinery) activities. OBECO has operations in 185 locations across the world. The oil and gas business is an asset-intensive business with assets such as off-shore platforms, drilling rigs and other large equipment used in daily activities. OBECO spends a large part of its nonhydrocarbon spend for purchasing and maintenance of assets. OBECO implemented SAP ERP to streamline the business processes in the organization, which helped the company standardize business processes across locations and businesses.

The success of ERP prompted OBECO to look at the next wave of integration, because currently, suppliers and customers are not integrated into OBECO's processes. For this purpose, OBECO set up two teams, one for procurement processes and another for sales processes, comprised of its best procurement and sales managers and IT professionals to identify gaps and suggest solutions to becoming a truly collaborative enterprise (note that we will only discuss procurement processes in this case study). The procurement team came up with the following high-level findings and suggestions:

- **Supplier Registration**: A supplier registration process to register new potential suppliers is not available in ERP. OBECO should have an online supplier self-registration capability to encourage potential suppliers to register themselves.

- **Sourcing Strategy**: There is no evidence that sourcing strategies for each category are being determined and executed in a scientific manner. OBECO should implement a category management tool to determine and execute sourcing strategies.

- **Tendering**: ERP facilitates request for quotation processing, but suppliers are not integrated in the process. OBECO should implement an online tendering solution.

- **Design Collaboration**: Like other asset-intensive organizations, OBECO collaborates with design consultants and Original Equipment Manufacturer (OEM) suppliers in finalizing technical specifications for new equipment purchases. Technical evaluation of tenders is also done in collaboration with internal and external experts. OBECO should implement a tendering solution that lets them finalize the design and specifications in collaboration with suppliers.

- **Reverse Auctions**: Reverse auctions have the potential to reduce the cost of certain categories of goods and services where competition is high. OBECO should conduct reverse auctions periodically.

- **Sourcing Hub**: Currently, demands from individual businesses and locations are sourced in their respective locations. OBECO should follow a sourcing hub model for certain categories of spend where demand from across locations can be aggregated and sourced to leverage the consolidated spend.

- **Catalog Buying**: OBECO negotiates discounts on OEM catalogs for equipment spares and expert services. However, the company is unable to benefit from these negotiated discounts, as there is no easy mechanism in place to distribute catalogs to all of the maintenance engineers. OBECO should implement a catalog management solution and integrate it with ERP. It was also observed that currently not all OBECO employees have access to the requisitioning process in ERP. Therefore, OBECO should implement online shopping capabilities for all employees using the catalogs for the most frequently used goods and services.

- **Supplier Collaboration**: Purchasers spend a lot of their time chasing suppliers after placing an order. Activities like order confirmation, dispatch confirmation, and invoice receipt require integration with suppliers. OBECO uses Electronic Data Interchange (EDI) with a few top suppliers, but most of the suppliers are not integrated. OBECO should implement a browser-based solution to integrate with all suppliers.

- **Software**: All of the previous features should be available in a single software application and it should be able to readily integrate with SAP ERP.

As a result of these observations and recommendations, OBECO decided to implement SAP SRM as it is the only application that has all of the functionalities required by OBECO and that will also readily integrate with SAP ERP. With the help of SAP experts, OBECO finalized the following scenarios for implementation:

- Plan-driven procurement for external requirements
- Self-service procurement
- SRM-MDM Catalog integration with SAP ERP
- Category management to determine and execute the sourcing strategy
- Sourcing cockpit
- Sourcing with RFx and live auction
- Bidding with collaboration
- Supplier self-registration
- Supplier Self-Services (SUS), to integrate 25 vendors initially during go-live, and roll out to 1,000 vendors within six months of go-live.

Note

Some of these items are explained in other chapters, as follows:

▶ The implementation of plan-driven procurement and catalog integration with SAP ERP were explained in Chapter 6.

▶ The implementation of SUS will be explained in Chapters 13 and 14.

▶ Self-service procurement was explained in Chapter 5.

The implementation of the sourcing cockpit, sourcing with RFx and live auction, tendering with collaboration, and supplier self-registration will be explained in Section 10.3. However, before we delve into the configuration settings, in Section 10.2, we will briefly look at the functionalities offered in SAP SRM sourcing.

10.2   SAP SRM Sourcing — A Brief Overview of Functionalities

SRM Sourcing contains several subprocesses or tools:

▶ Demand consolidation using the sourcing cockpit.

▶ Automatic and manual source of supply identification and assignment.

▶ Vendor lists and quota arrangement.

▶ Supplier registration and qualification.

▶ Online RFx and live auction, including tendering with collaboration process.

We will discuss all these tools and associated processes in detail in this section.

10.2.1   Sourcing Cockpit

The *sourcing cockpit* is a purchaser's work list where a purchaser can process purchasing requirements. The requirements from backend ERP systems and shopping carts from SAP SRM that require a purchaser's action are shown in the sourcing cockpit. Figure 10.1 illustrates the sourcing cockpit functions, which are as follows:

▶ Aggregate requirements from backend ERP systems and SAP SRM.

▶ Let users view shopping carts created from external requirements.

▶ Let users change SAP SRM shopping carts

▶ Act as a central tool for purchasers to process all requirements. Based on the configuration settings, the system can carry out sourcing activity automatically, or the purchaser can select and move the requirements into a work

area and use any of the following functions to process the selected requirements:

- ▶ **Propose Sources of Supply**: Used to get help from the system to assign
  sources of supply. The system can also automatically assign the sources of
  supply for a requirement. This automatic determination will be based on
  the cheapest contract item or product-vendor linkage.

- ▶ **Take Vendor from an External List**: Used to search for and select vendors from an external supplier directory.

- ▶ **Create Purchase Order**: Used to create purchase orders with reference to
  selected requirements. The system creates separate purchase orders for
  requirements with different goods recipients.

- ▶ **Create Contract**: Used to create contracts with reference to selected
  requirements. The system creates a contract in SAP SRM for each vendor
  and purchasing organization combination. You can also create a backend
  contract by implementing BAdI BBP_DETERMINE_LOGSYS. You can
  implement BBP_SOURCING_BADI to ensure that the requirement is still
  open and available in the sourcing cockpit even after creating the contract.

- ▶ **Create Bid Invitation**: Used to create bid invitations with reference to
  selected requirements. If you want to influence the bid invitation data,
  you need to implement BAdI BBP_CREAT_RFQ_IN_DPE.

- ▶ **Create Auction**: Used to create live auctions with reference to selected
  requirements

- ▶ **Submit to Grouping**: Used to submit selected requirements to the grouping program BBP_SC_TRANSFER_GROUPED to create a purchase order or
  bid invitation for the consolidated requirements.

- ▶ **Replace Item with Catalog Item**: Used to replace free text items with catalog items. This function is available from SAP SRM 2007 on.

- ▶ Provide purchasers with the following capabilities to obtain information to
  support decision making:

  - ▶ Branch to *Vendor list* to see the list of sources

  - ▶ Branch to contract details

  - ▶ Branch to catalog for requirement items that originate from catalog

  - ▶ Branch to vendor evaluation reports

  - ▶ Compare prices of different sources of supply

  - ▶ Display priority for each source of supply, if the priority is maintained in
    the vendor list

- ▶ Create purchase orders, contracts, RFx or auctions using background
  processing (this functionality is available starting with SAP SRM 2007). You
  can define the number of shopping cart items, above which the sourcing

cockpit follow-on documents are processed in the background. If the background processing fails, the system sends an alert email with the problematic shopping cart details to the person who started the background process. Refer to SAP Note 896296 to learn how to control the email notification.

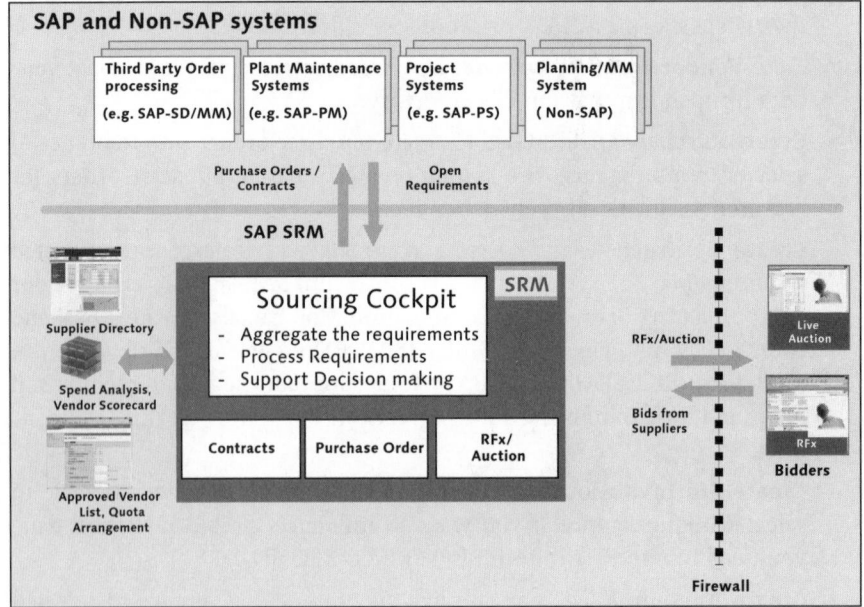

Figure 10.1 Sourcing Cokpit Functions

Let us now look at how to determine sources of supply and automatic sourcing.

Source of Supply Determination Rules

The "propose sources of supply" functionality in the sourcing cockpit is used for processing requirements and optimizing the source of supply for individual items. It identifies savings opportunities by evaluating the ability of suppliers to provide materials and services at low cost, high quality, and according to schedule. Sources of supply are determined based on the following rules:

▸ Assign sources proposed by the system to items automatically. We will discuss this in more detail in the *Automatic Sourcing* section.

▸ Match the product category or product in the requirement with the following data:

  ▸ Quota arrangement

  ▸ Vendor list

  ▸ Operational contracts in SAP SRM

  ▸ Product-vendor linkages (vendor-specific prices defined in the product master)

- ▸ Backend SAP ERP contracts (only in the classic scenario for account assigned requirements)
- ▸ Info records in the relevant backend SAP ERP system (only in the classic scenario for account assigned requirements)

- ▸ Check the validity of the following primary sourcing criteria (the check is performed by the system):
  - ▸ The product must be identical in the requirement and the contract.
  - ▸ The product category must be identical in the requirement and the contract.
  - ▸ The vendor must be identical in the requirement and the contract.
  - ▸ Procurement takes place for the same company with which the contract exists.
  - ▸ The purchasing organization responsible for the requirement is authorized to use the contract.
  - ▸ The location specified in the requirement is release-authorized for the contract.
  - ▸ The goods recipient has not been deleted and has not been excluded from a goods delivery for this contract.
- ▸ Define criteria in addition to the primary sourcing criteria described in this list using BAdI BBP_SRC_DETERMINE in method DETERMINE_SOURCING.

> **Note**
>
> If sourcing is turned off in the configuration item *Define sourcing for product categories*, the system creates a purchase order in SAP SRM for all requirements.

Automatic Sourcing

SAP SRM sourcing automatically determines sources of supply for a requirement depending on the configuration settings defined for the product category. Based on the configuration settings for the product category, the following sourcing activities are performed automatically without the need for purchasers to process the requirements in the sourcing cockpit:

- ▸ A valid source of supply is assigned in the shopping cart and a purchase order is created on approval of the shopping cart.
- ▸ A bid invitation is created for all requirements without a source of supply.
- ▸ Requirements are grouped together by vendor and a complete or incomplete purchase order is created. Incomplete purchase orders have to be processed further by the purchaser.
- ▸ Requirements that do not have a source of supply are grouped together and a bid invitation is created.

You can check sources of supply according to your own rules using BAdI BBP_SOS_BADI.

10.2.2 Quota Arrangements

If you have multiple suppliers for a product, you can assign business volumes to different suppliers using quota arrangements. *Quota Arrangements* are used in both manual sourcing processes and automated sourcing processes to generate purchase orders. They allow you to define target percentages and distribute them between two or more purchasing contracts. Quota arrangements ensure that a contract is guaranteed both a minimum sales volume and a percent of the total purchasing volume of a product category or product. Quota arrangements have the highest priority in the sourcing process.

During the validity period of a quota arrangement there are two phases:

▶ **Fulfillment of guaranteed minimums**: Before the system assigns contracts based on target percentages, the quota arrangement ensures that all guaranteed minimums of contracts participating in that quota arrangement are fulfilled. The sequence in which the guaranteed minimums are fulfilled is determined by the target percentages defined in the quota arrangement. Guaranteed minimums are defined in the contract.

▶ **Assignment of contracts based on target percentages**: Once all of the guaranteed minimums of contracts participating in a quota arrangement have been fulfilled, the system continues to automatically assign contracts based on the target percentages defined in that quota arrangement. The winning contract is then determined by the relative difference between the actual release value and the target value of the quota arrangement.

The following features are available:

▶ The system allows the source of supply to be selected automatically, based on the fulfillment of guaranteed minimums and target percentages defined in the quota arrangement.

▶ When a purchase order is created against a contract that is part of a quota arrangement, the system automatically updates the release values for each contract line item.

▶ The system shows the winning contract for a quota arrangement in the manual sourcing process.

▶ During manual sourcing, the system displays up-to-date quota arrangement data, including the release quantity for each contract line item, percentages of each contract line item, and participating vendors and contract line items.

Quota arrangement uses standard rules to determine the winning contract in the sourcing process. However alternative logic can be implemented using BAdI BBP_QA_REDETERM_CTR.

10.2.3 Vendor List

The *vendor list* represents the preferred list of suppliers and contracts for a product or product category. This is similar to a *sourcing list* in SAP ERP. Using Open Partner Interface (OPI), sourcing can be extended to cover external vendor lists (or supplier directories), too. The vendor list is integrated into all SAP SRM applications that contain a vendor search help and in which sources of supply can be displayed.

You can deactivate certain vendors or backend contracts in the vendor list to block the release of purchase orders for these vendors. To facilitate decision making, from SAP SRM 5.0 on, you can also configure a priority for each entry in the vendor list that appears in the sourcing cockpit. You can also trigger a vendor evaluation questionnaire from the vendor list to evaluate vendors. In addition, you can configure the system to allow sources of supply only from vendor list. In this case, you must maintain vendor lists for all product categories and products.

10.2.4 Supplier Self-Registration and Qualification

You can let suppliers all over the world register themselves as your suppliers using supplier self-registration. This process is illustrated in Figure 10.2 and consists of the following steps:

1. Interested suppliers click on a link provided on the company website for self-registration.

2. On the registration page, suppliers specify basic address details — including an email address that should be a valid email address — and categories in which they are interested. They must also accept the data privacy statement and then submit the registration details. You can change the welcome text on the registration page by implementing BAdI ROS_CUST_WEL_TXT. You can also define mandatory fields to be filled out by suppliers using BAdI ROS_REQ_CUF. The values entered in these fields can be checked using BAdI ROS_BUPA_DATA_CHECK.

3. The system then sends an email to suppliers with one or more questionnaires, depending on the categories selected. The questionnaires will be sent either as a link in the email or as an attachment, depending on the configuration setting for the questionnaire.

4. Suppliers need to open the attachment, or click on the link, in the email, fill out the questionnaire and submit it. If the questionnaire is received as an attachment, the filled-in questionnaire will be sent from the supplier's email software.

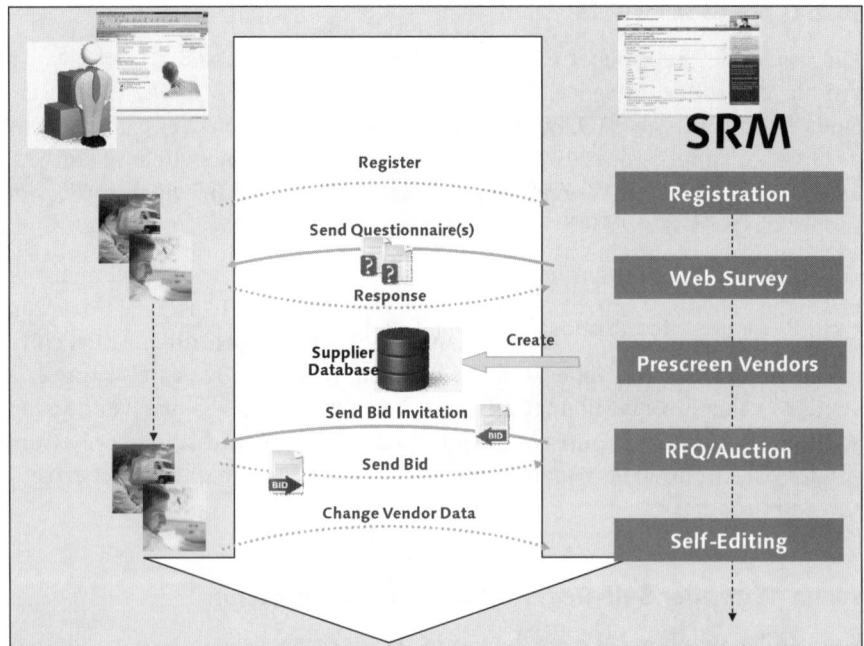

Figure 10.2 Supplier Self-Registration Process

5. The questionnaire is received by the system and automatically updates the supplier registration information. The filled-out questionnaire is available as a link and can be accessed by the purchaser from the supplier prescreening application.

6. The purchaser accesses the Prescreen Suppliers application from Enterprise Buyer Professional (EBP) and verifies the responses from suppliers. Purchasers may also carry out additional verifications, like vendor site visits, verifying the data with independent supplier data base systems, such as Dun and Bradstreet, etc. If the purchaser is satisfied with the supplier information, the registration will be approved.

7. The approved supplier data can then be transferred to EBP and a business partner in EBP can be created. Purchasers may initially want to create the new suppliers as bidders. If the new supplier wins a bid, then the bidder can be converted into a vendor and a purchase order is created for the new vendor.

8. If a backend SAP ERP is connected, you should also create a vendor master in SAP ERP.

10.2.5 Sourcing with RFx (Tendering or Bidding) using the SRM Bidding Engine

RFx is a general term used to represent different types of bid invitations:

▶ **RFQ (Request for Quotation)**: Typically used for standard items and services where both buyer and supplier are clear about the specifications of the product.

▶ **RFI (Request for Information) or EOI (Expression of Interest)**: Typically used to elicit information from the market on a requirement. It is also used when the buyer has only broad parameters of the requirement and wants to evaluate different options and technologies before finalizing the specifications of the requirement. This is also used to gather information about suppliers. Purchaser does not seek prices in this case.

▶ **RFP (Request for Proposal)**: Normally used for complex requirements and project purchases where the buyer outlines the requirement in an RFP and the supplier submits a detailed proposal for the requirement.

The Sourcing with RFx process is integrated with the following other processes in SAP SRM to provide a fully integrated purchasing application:

▶ **Sourcing Cockpit**: You can consolidate the requirements from all systems and process bid invitations.

▶ **Contract Management**: A contract can be created from the winning bid. You can also create bid invitations to renew or renegotiate a shortly expiring contract.

▶ **Procurement**: Purchase orders can be created from the winning bid to ensure that the best negotiated prices are used in procurement.

A typical bidding or tendering process involves the following three steps:

1. **Process Bid Invitations**: A bid invitation represents an invitation to bidders to submit their prices, terms, and conditions for given procurement requirements. A bid invitation is created with reference to the shopping cart(s) or backend purchase requisition(s), either automatically or manually from the sourcing cockpit. You can create a bid invitation directly without reference to shopping carts or purchase requisitions. You can create a bid invitation using a template. A bid invitation can also be created from a shortly expiring contract.

   Bid invitations can be of type *restricted* or *public*. Only specific bidders are invited to submit their bids in restricted bid invitations. Public bid invitations do not have any restriction and any vendor can submit a bid. Bid invitations contain various dates, such as submission deadline, opening date, etc., to ensure that the bidding activity is transparently completed within a given time frame.

2. **Submit Responses**: Vendors submit their prices, terms, and conditions for a bid invitation online. These responses are usually called quotations, offers, or bids.

3. **Bid Evaluation and Follow-on Document Creation**: All of the bids from vendors are viewed and a comparison report is prepared after the opening date to evaluate bids. SAP SRM displays an automatic comparison report with scores for each bid immediately after the opening date and time, to facilitate the decision making by the purchaser. SAP SRM also delivers standard content for bid evaluation using SAP NetWeaver Business Intelligence (SAP NetWeaver BI). Based on the comparison reports, purchasers decide the winning bid. A purchase order or contract can be created in SAP SRM from the winning bid.

From SAP SRM 5.0 on, it is possible to create a purchase order in the backend ERP system, if the bid invitation was created with reference to an account-assigned external requirement. It is also possible to create a contract in the backend system by implementing BAdI BBP_DETERMINE_LOGSYS.

Additional features in the bidding engine are as follows:

▸ Aside from bidders being invited from the SAP SRM vendor master, bidders can also be invited from external supplier directories.

▸ Entering internal notes or a vendor text, and creating attachments by uploading documents, is supported. Collaborative document management functionalities of SAP cFolders can also be made available for managing both internal and external documents. Refer to the information under *Bidding with Collaboration* in Section 10.2.6 for more details.

▸ A variety of pricing elements (or pricing conditions) can be used to provide a complete break-up of pricing for each item. Purchasers can indicate the pricing conditions that need to be filled in by suppliers. Discounts or surcharges can also be maintained at the header level. SAP SRM calculates the net price for each item from the given price break-up.

▸ Purchasers can add fields in each bid invitation as dynamic attributes at both the header and item level to elicit additional information from suppliers.

▸ Multiple currency bidding is supported. Purchasers can indicate the acceptable currencies and also the base currency for the document. Bidders can bid in the currency of their choice. The system compares the bids by converting prices to the base currency using the exchange rate master.

▸ Weighting and ranking can be used to evaluate and compare different bids that are submitted in response to a bid invitation. This functionality helps purchasers incorporate nonprice factors in the bid evaluation. To use this function, dynamic attributes or standard fields should be assigned weights, according to how important they are for the requirements, using a weighting factor. The sum of the weighting factors must be 100% per item. The sum of the weighting factors of all items must be 100%. Depending on the settings in the bid invitation, bidders can view the weightings and can make their offers accordingly. The following four valuation functions are used to calculate valuation factors:

▶ **Linear**: This function is especially suitable for parameters of amount fields. The parameters of this function are minimum and maximum attribute values, together with minimum and maximum function values. If a bidder enters a value that is outside of the defined range, the minimum or maximum value is taken as the score value accordingly.

▶ **Step**: This function can be used for parameters such as delivery times. You can define intervals of values and scores for each interval. When you are entering the intervals, you must ensure that a new interval begins where the previous one ends, for example, 1-10 and 10-20.

▶ **Fixed**: This function is especially suitable for attributes with determined fixed values. If fixed values are defined for an attribute, the score values can be assigned to particular fixed values.

▶ **Manual**: This function is especially suitable for attributes with no fixed values. In this case, the purchaser manually valuates the contents of the parameters in the bid document once this has been received from the bidder.

▶ Bid invitations can be structured hierarchically with outline levels. Outlines for bid invitations can be created by entering a description, an internal note, or a vendor text. Items are added to each level.

▶ You can also create lots that group together related items. Bidders must have bid on every item in a lot before they can submit their bid. Bid prices that are entered at the item level are aggregated at the lot level.

▶ A live auction can be created from a bid invitation. In this case, the bidding process helps shortlist vendors for a reverse auction.

▶ SAP SRM also supports surrogate bidding where purchasers can enter a bid on behalf of a bidder. If the bidder is not able to access the system, they can contact the purchaser, who then enters the bid on their behalf. You can maintain in the vendor master whether surrogate bidding is allowed.

▶ SAP SRM supports multiround bidding. It is possible to create a bid invitation as a follow-on document for another bid invitation. In this case the system closes the original bid invitation and creates a new bid invitation. The original bid invitation remains in the document history for further reference.

10.2.6 Bidding with Collaboration

SAP SRM supports integration with SAP Product Lifecycle Management (SAP PLM) cFolders in the bidding process. Purchasers can use the document collaboration functions of cFolders to finalize specifications and prepare RFP documents. Bidders can store information about their offer in a private area. The bidder's documents are available only to purchasers and cannot be viewed by other bidders. Confidentiality is assured as the information is accessible only to the purchaser. Purchasers can also invite technical and financial experts to review the technical and commercial documents submitted by bidders without sharing the price information. Figure 10.3 illustrates the integration between SAP PLM cFolders and SAP SRM.

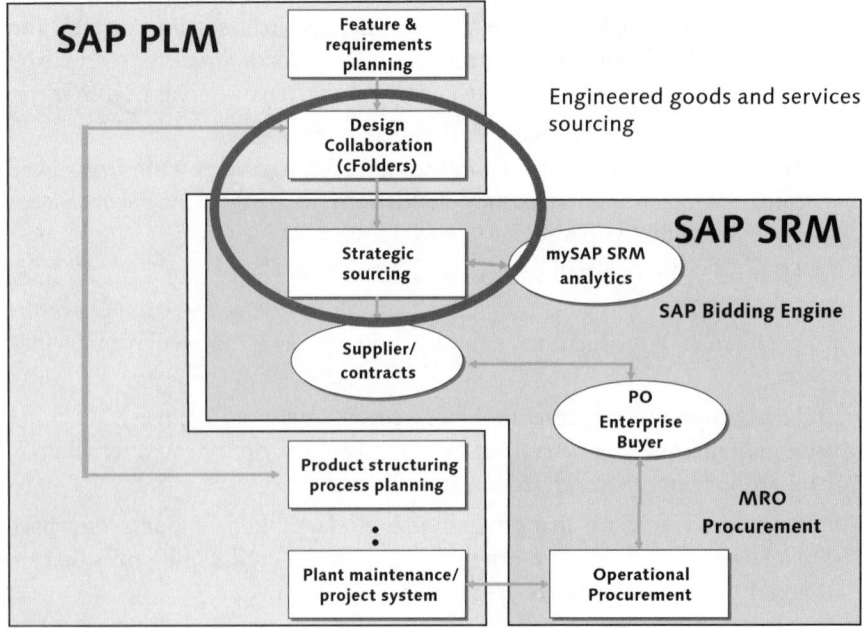

Figure 10.3 SAP PLM cFolders and SAP SRM Integration

Bidding with collaboration process is explained as follows:

► A purchaser creates a bid invitation and then creates a collaboration for the bid invitation. The purchaser can do this on the documents tab of bid invitation. When the purchaser creates the collaboration, a folder is set up automatically in a public area in cFolders under competitive collaboration.

► The purchaser goes to the collaboration area in cFolders and invites the engineers on the purchasing side to place all relevant design and specification information in the folder for potential bidders to view. Only the purchasing side can make changes to the public area of the folder.

► When potential bidders access a bid invitation, they can also access the collaboration, view the documents, and decide whether they wish to submit a bid.

► When a bidder creates a bid, a private area is created automatically in cFolders. Bidders can upload all of their technical documents into the private area as part of their bid.

▸ All project participants on both the purchasing and supplier sides can access the work area in cFolders, and add to and correct the data until all parties have agreed on the final and binding specifications.

▸ The link to cFolders is included in the bid and also in the follow-on purchase order or contract. The collaboration area remains open, allowing the purchaser and the supplier to fine-tune the design documents even after the winning bid has been determined.

Recommendation

We strongly recommend using the bidding with collaboration process for project purchases, equipment purchases, and all other purchases where requirements are finalized collaboratively. We also recommend this scenario for public sector organizations where there is a need to have a single case file with all tender information.

10.2.7 Live Auction (Reverse Auction)

SAP SRM provides the Live Auction Cockpit (LAC) interface, which allows conducting reverse auctions in a real-time environment that mimics the activity and process of an actual auction floor. Reverse auctions enable bidders to compete with each other for the business and helps the purchaser get the most competitive prices. An auction can be created in the following ways:

▸ Directly, by using the *Process Auction* Transaction

▸ By using an auction template

▸ By copying an auction

▸ By converting a bid invitation

▸ From the sourcing cockpit

Types of Live Auctions

Auction types comprise auction rules to validate incoming bids and information disclosure rules for the bidder. The following predefined auction types are available as transaction types:

▸ English auction

▸ Blind bidding auction

▸ Rank-only auction

▸ Company best-bid auction

▸ Dutch auction (from SAP SRM 2007 on)

You can also configure additional auction types in the auction transaction types configuration. Each transaction type is associated with certain information disclosure rules that control the level of information displayed to bidders. You should refer to the SAP online help documentation for more details on auction types.

Functional Highlights of Live Auctions in SAP SRM

Functional highlights of live auctions in SAP SRM include the following:

▶ **Multi-currency bidding**: By default, the bid currency for an auction is the auction currency defined by the purchaser. Purchasers can also indicate additional currencies allowed and bidders can bid in any allowed currency. The system automatically converts the incoming bid prices to the currency of the bidder to enable easy bidding.

▶ **Lotting**: It is possible to create lots to group-related line items to structure complex auctions by first creating an outline. Item start price, reserve price, and bid decrement can be defined at the lot level, and reference price at the individual item level.

▶ **Cascading line item auctions**: In a cascading line item auction, the auction closing time for each item or lot can be defined with a time gap, for example, the auction closing time of the second line item can be 10 minutes after closing the first line item and so on. This facilitates bidders to focus their attention on a single lot or line item at a time, rather than monitoring and bidding on all lots and line items simultaneously.

▶ **Factored-cost bidding**: Factored cost bidding enables purchasers to consider nonprice factors during evaluation of bids. A purchaser can assign factors to each bidder based on their past performance and other qualitative criteria. Factors can be assigned both at the header and item level. If factors exist at both the header and item levels, the values assigned at the item level have precedence over those at the header level.

In auctions with lotting, factors cannot be assigned to line items included in lots, but are instead assigned at the lot level and header level; any lot-level factors take precedence over those defined at the auction header. The system normalizes the incoming bid prices based on the factors. Factors are not visible to bidders, nor are the effects of factored-cost bidding. The bidders can only see the normalized next valid bid price and their own raw bid prices. Purchasers can view both raw prices and normalized prices.

▶ **Proxy bidding**: If proxy bidding is selected, the system acts as a proxy agent and automatically bids on line items on a bidder's behalf during the auction. The system places bids according to bidding parameters, such as bid decrement and reserve price, to maintain the bidder's leading position in an active auction until the auction ends or the bidder's minimum bid is reached. The following restrictions apply:

  ▶ Proxy bidding can only be enabled for auctions that use the overall best-bid validation.

▸ Proxy bidding can only be enabled if bid decrements greater than zero have been defined for all line items.

▸ Proxy bidding is not available in auctions with lots.

- **Conversion of bid invitations into auctions**: An auction can be created by converting a bid invitation into an auction, enabling purchasers to process converted auctions more efficiently and use bids copied from a bid invitation to drive competitive bidding. Full-quantity bids can be copied without attributes from the bid invitation to the auction.

- **Charts**: Bidding activity for each item can be displayed in graphical form during the auction. You can double-click on a chart to open it in a separate window, which enables you to do a side-by-side comparison of multiple line items. The charts are instantly updated with each new bid. Bar charts and line graphs for prices and a line chart for bid volume can be displayed.

- **Banning and reinstating bidders**: Purchasers can ban a bidder or reinstate a bidder during the auction.

- **Auction activity control**: Purchasers can pause, stop, or extend an auction. This helps purchasers act appropriately when they face connectivity or technical issues.

- **Surrogate Bidding**: By logging on as a bidder, a purchaser can submit a bid on the bidder's behalf when a bidder faces technical issues submitting bids. This does not affect the bidder's connection status or ability to access the cockpit. The bid history table, visible to both purchasers and bidders, indicates which bids are surrogate bids.

Live Auction Technical Definition

Figure 10.4 illustrates the technical landscape of the LAC until SAP SRM 5.0. From SAP SRM 2007 on, the Internet Transaction Server (ITS) interface was replaced with WebDynpro. It has two layers as described here:

- **Business Logic Layer**: The auction process is defined in the SRM Bidding Engine. Process definitions, control logic, data definition and tables, etc., exist in this layer. This can also be referred to as the *definition layer*.

- **Presentation Layer**: The presentation layer consists of two parts. The first part, in which auctions are set up and bids are processed, uses the ITS (SAP SRM 5.0 and lower) or WebDynpro (SAP SRM 2007 on) user interface. The second part, in which the auction is conducted, uses the Java-based LAC, which is deployed on the SAP J2EE Engine. It is a pure front-end logic layer with limited business process logic for live auction activities. The business logic layer and live auction cockpit are connected using the Java Connector (JCo). It can be referred to as the *run-time layer*.

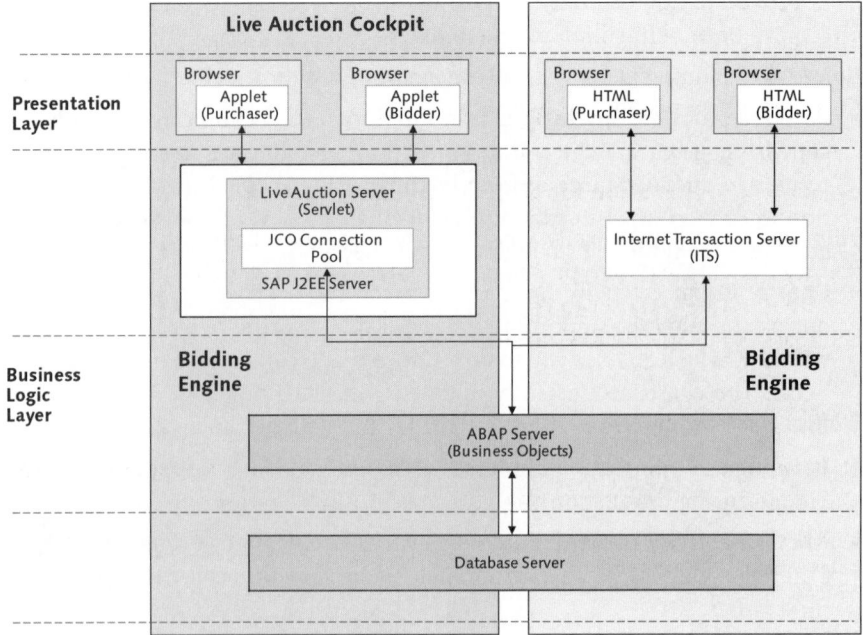

Figure 10.4 Live Auction Technical Details

10.3 Implementing Sourcing Functionalities

The implementation of the sourcing processes described in the case study in Section 10.1 is explained in this section. Figure 3.3 in Chapter 3 illustrates the landscape required for implementing all of the scenarios described in the case study. We would suggest that you have a separate client for cFolders in the SAP SRM server. Let us now look at the configuration settings required.

Basic Settings for the SAP SRM Server

All of the basic settings required for the self-service procurement scenario should be configured, including:

- Basic technical settings to integrate with backend systems
- Organizational plan setup
- Master data settings for suppliers, product categories, and products
- Other common technical settings

Detailed configurations of all of these settings are described in Sections 3.4, 3.5, 3.6, 3.7, and 3.8 in Chapter 3.

Define Logical System

This setting is required only if you want to use cFolders or live auction. In addition to the settings configured as described in Chapter 3, define logical systems for the cFolders system and live auction.

Create RFC Destination for cFolders and Live Auction

This setting is required only when you want to use cFolders or live auction. Specify RFC destination type 3 for the cFolders system using Transaction SM59. Ensure that the RFC user to connect to the cFolders system has role SAP_CFX_USER assigned. Specify RFC destination type G for the live auction Java service.

Define Backend Systems

Use the menu path **SPRO • SAP Implementation Guide • Supplier Relationship Management • SRM Server • Technical Basic Settings • Define Backend Systems** to maintain an entry for the cFolders client (with CFOLDERS as the system type) and an entry for live auction (with SRM_AUC as the system type).

Define Transaction Types

In addition to the transaction types delivered in the standard system, which are sufficient to take care of most requirements, you can define transaction types for bid invitations and auctions using this setting. Determine the number ranges for each transaction type. You should have different number ranges for each transaction type so that the documents can be easily differentiated.

Maintain the number ranges using the menu path **SPRO • SAP Implementation Guide • Supplier Relationship Management • SRM Server • Cross-Application Basic Settings • Number Ranges • SRM Server Number Ranges** for each bid invitation transaction type. Similarly, define number ranges for bids, auctions, and vendor lists, too.

Maintain transaction types using menu path **SPRO • SAP Implementation Guide • Supplier Relationship Management • SRM Server • Cross-Application Basic Settings • Define Transaction Types** for objects BUS2200 (bid invitation) and BUS2208 (auction). You cannot define new transaction types for bids. If you have defined a new number range for bids, then assign the number range for object BUS2202 (bid). Refer to Chapter 5 for a detailed explanation of the fields in this setting.

Activate Version Control for Documents

Version control enables purchasers to keep track of changes made to documents. This is an optional setting but it is recommended. Use the menu path

SPRO · SAP Implementation Guide · Supplier Relationship Management · SRM Server · Cross-Application Basic Settings · Switch on Version Control for Purchasing Documents to turn on the version control for bid invitations. You can also turn on version control for bids from SAP SRM 2007 on. You can also use BAdI BBP_VERSION_CONTROL to influence the version control.

Settings for Text Schema

You can maintain different long texts in bid invitations, bids, and auctions. You can define custom text types, bundle them in a text schema and assign the text schema to the transaction type. For a detailed discussion on defining and using text schemas, refer to Chapter 5.

Pricing

The SRM Pricing configuration is explained in detail in Chapter 5. If you define additional condition types to be used in bidding, remember to assign these additional condition types to condition groups 01QU and 01HQ.

Workflows for Bid Invitation, Auction, and Bids

Refer to Chapter 8 for workflow settings.

Define Sourcing for Product Categories

Sourcing rules applicable for each product category are defined in this setting using the menu path **SPRO · SAP Implementation Guide · Supplier Relationship Management · SRM Server · Sourcing · Define Sourcing for Product Categories**. You can use "*" as a wild card entry for product category (e.g., "1*" to represent all product categories with the first character as 1). If you selected the product category from search help, the source system is filled automatically. If you enter the product category manually, then enter the logical system of the product category (backend ERP or SAP SRM) also.

The sourcing rules defined in this setting can be further influenced with additional rules by implementing BAdI BBP_SRC_DETERMINE. The following sourcing rules are available in this setting:

► **Sourcing is never carried out**: This is the default setting at delivery. The requirements are not transferred to the sourcing cockpit. Instead, a purchase order is created in SAP SRM for the requirement. If the source of the supply does not exist in the requirement, then an incomplete purchase order is created.

► **Sourcing is always carried out**: The system transfers all requirements to the sourcing cockpit.

- ▶ **Sourcing is carried out for items without a source of supply**: If a unique source of supply is not assigned in the shopping cart, then the requirement is transferred to the sourcing cockpit.

- ▶ **Sourcing via automatic bid invitation for items without a source of supply**: System creates a bid invitation for all requirements that do not have a source of supply.

- ▶ **Automatic requirement grouping; sourcing for items without an assigned source of supply**: If the source of supply is assigned to a requirement, then the grouping report BBP_SC_TRANSFER_GROUPED groups several requirements and attempts to create purchase orders automatically. If it is unable to do this, the requirement is displayed so that you can assign it manually in the sourcing cockpit. Once you have assigned a source of supply, you can submit the requirement to the grouping report.

- ▶ **Automatic requirement grouping; sourcing is never carried out**: If the source of supply is assigned to the requirement, then the grouping report BBP_SC_TRANSFER_GROUPED groups several requirements and attempts to create purchase orders automatically. If it is unable to do this, the system creates an incomplete purchase order for the requirement.

- ▶ **Automatic grouping and creation of a bid invitation in the case of items without an assigned source of supply**: If a source of supply is not assigned to the requirement, then the grouping report BBP_SC_TRANSFER_GROUPED automatically attempts to create a bid invitation from several requirement items. If it is unable to do so, this is recorded in the error log of the report.

- ▶ **Automatic grouping of requirements into purchase orders**: The program BBP_SC_TRANSFER_GROUPED selects all requirements that have a unique valid source of supply and have been set up for grouping. It groups together all of the requirements that can be sent to the same vendor and creates a purchase order. To create the requirements in separate local purchase orders, BAdI BBP_GROUP_LOC_PO can be used.

- ▶ **Automatic grouping of requirements into bid invitations**: The program BBP_SC_TRANSFER_GROUPED selects all requirements that have been set up for grouping. A source of supply is not required. Selection criteria are used to further restrict the requirements that are selected. BAdI BBP_TRANSFER_GROUP should be used to split the grouped bid invitation up on the basis of your own customer-specific criteria. BAdI BBP_SAVE_BID_ON_HOLD should be used to determine whether a bid invitation should be published automatically.

Schedule Report BBP_SC_TRANSFER_GROUPED

Schedule the program BBP_SC_TRANSFER_GROUPED to run periodically using Transaction SM36. The program is run separately for each object (purchase order and bid invitation).

Activate Temporary Contact Person Creation

This functionality became available from SAP SRM 2007 on and is useful when you want to use a supplier from an external supplier directory to source transactions via OPI. If you activate a temporary contact person creation in this setting, the system automatically creates a contact person when you transfer a supplier from a supplier directory into SAP SRM via the OPI interface.

Use the menu path **SPRO • SAP Implementation Guide • Supplier Relationship Management • SRM Server • Bid Invitation • Activate Temporary Contact Person Creation** to work with this functionality. If you want to create a temporary contact person while transferring a supplier from an external directory, set the indicator.

You can influence the input values for contact person creation by implementing BAdI FILL_DUMMY_CONTACTPERSON. Also, refer to the new configuration settings required to synchronize with the portal in SAP SRM 2007. The new settings are described under the heading "New SAP SRM 2007 Settings for Business Partner Creation" in this chapter.

Define Sourcing Via Vendor List Only

You can ensure that a source of supply is assigned only from the sources given in an approved vendor list. You can further influence the setting by implementing BAdI BBP_AVL_DETERMINE. Use the menu path **SPRO • SAP Implementation Guide • Supplier Relationship Management • SRM Server • Sourcing • Define Sourcing Via Vendor List Only** to configure this setting.

Define Dynamic Attributes

You can define data types and groups for the dynamic attributes using the menu path **SPRO • SAP Implementation Guide • Supplier Relationship Management • SRM Server • Bid Invitation • Dynamic Attributes**. The following settings are available:

▸ **Define Data Types for Dynamic Attributes**: This is an optional setting. Five data types are available: MENG13 for quantity, WERT7 for amount, BBP_YESNO for a yes or no type of field, CUF_VALUE for text of 130 characters, and DATUM for dates.

▸ **Define Groups**: The dynamic attributes created in the bid invitations can be saved by purchasers for use in future bid invitations. These attributes should be grouped by logical grouping. The groupings can be defined in this setting.

Valuation Factors for Weighting

Standard fields like inco term, item price, etc., can be included in the valuation process in this setting. Specify the fields to be included for valuation using the menu path **SPRO · SAP Implementation Guide · Supplier Relationship Management · SRM Server · Bid Invitation · Valuation · Default for Valuation Records**.

Define SAP NetWeaver BI Template Names

You can use bid evaluation and vendor evaluation reports from SAP NetWeaver BI in SAP SRM sourcing transactions. Use the menu path **SPRO · SAP Implementation Guide · Supplier Relationship Management · SRM Server · Cross-Application Basic Settings · Define Logical Systems and Template Names for BW Reports** to access a listing of SAP NetWeaver BI reports used in SAP SRM. Maintain the logical system for SAP NetWeaver BI and assign SAP Business Warehouse (BW) template names used for each report. The standard template names are delivered in standard settings. However, it is very common practice to modify the templates during the implementation. Therefore, you should ensure assigning final BW templates in this setting.

Email Notification SmartForm

The system sends an email to bidders whenever a bid invitation or an auction is published. Email notifications are also sent when a bid is accepted or rejected by the buyer. The email content is specified in SmartForm BBP_BIDINV_BID. If you want to modify the content, copy this SmartForm and create your own. Implement BAdI BBP_CHANGE_SF_BID to assign the new SmartForm.

Live Auction Configuration

Business logic for a live auction is defined in the SRM Bidding Engine in the ABAP layer, and runtime logic is defined in the live auction Java layer. Both layers need to be integrated to exchange information. The following configuration is required for this connectivity:

1. Install the LAC and carry out the post-installation steps according to the installation guide instructions. These steps are part of the installation and ensure that your Basis consultant carried out all of the settings as specified in the installation guide.
   - Enable security library
   - Set up HTTP connection
   - Adjust server name and IP address
   - Start SAP J2EE engine on Microsoft Windows
   - Configure SAP J2EE engine as a Microsoft Windows service
   - Conduct a live auction smoke test to determine if installation is successful
2. Define the logical system for the live auction.

3. Define the RFC destination of type G for the live auction.

4. Maintain an entry for live auction in the setting *Define Backend Systems*.

5. Maintain the live auction applet properties in view BBPV_LA_PROP. Maintain applet properties, if required, using Transaction SM30.

6. Configure live auction background jobs. To start, end, or publish an auction in SAP SRM, event triggering is necessary. These events are triggered in the background based on the dates entered in the auction. Schedule a class A job for background processing in Transaction RZ04 to effect the activation, closing, and extension of auctions during auction cycles. Background jobs are also used to create bids at the end of a live auction from the price data in the live auction applet.

Configuration in SAP SRM to integrate with cFolders

The required configuration items for this integration have already been explained in this chapter under the headings "Define Logical System," "Create RFC Destination for cFolders and Live Auction," and "Define Backend Systems."

Configuration in cFolders to Integrate cFolders with SAP SRM

These settings should be configured in the cFolders system:

▸ **RFC destination**: Create an RFC destination of type 3 for the SAP SRM system using Transaction SM59.

▸ **Generate roles**: Using the mass generation option in Transaction PFCG, generate all cFolders standard roles (SAP_CFX*).

▸ **Maintain time zone settings**: Maintain the time zone settings in the cFolders system using Transaction STZAC. Keep them the same as the settings in SAP SRM.

▸ **Activate services**: Activate the following services using Transaction SICF:

   ▸ Default_host – sap – bc – bsp – sap

   ▸ Default_host – sap – bc - kw

▸ **cFolders URL**: The default cFolders URL is *http://<server>:<port>/sap/bc/bsp/sap/cfx_rfc_ui/default.htm*. If you want to have a shorter URL, you should create an external alias for the path (default_host/sap/bc/bsp/sap) in Transaction SICF. The URL in such cases will be *http://<server>:<port>/<external alias name>/cfx_rfc_ui/default.htm*. Do not maintain any logon data in the cFolders external alias.

▸ **Create an Administrator User**: Create an administrator user to carry out configurations in cFolders using Transaction SU01. The user should have roles SAP_CFX_ADMINISTRATOR, SAP_CFX_CFOLDERS_ADMINISTRATOR, SAP_

CFX_NETWORK_ADMINISTRATOR, and SAP_CFX_USER_ADMINISTRATOR. You should take a look at the roles starting with SAP_CFX to understand other standard roles available.

▶ **Absolute URL:** This setting should be configured in the cFolders browser interface. The absolute URL will be used by SAP SRM to create the link for cFolders in bid invitations. Launch the cFolders URL. Click on the Network Administration link and select the Network tab. Click on the **Determine Application URL** button for automatic settings. Click on the **Test HTTP connection** button to test the connection. If you encounter problems, also maintain a proxy server name and port.

▶ **Create System User:** Launch the cFolders URL. Click on the User Administration link. In the area Functions for local user administration, click on the **Create System User** button. A system user CFXEMAILBTCH is created automatically.

▶ **Maintain Users:** Ensure that all SAP SRM users who need to access cFolders have a user ID in cFolders. The user id for these users should be the same in both SAP SRM and cFolders. You only need to assign role SAP_CFX_USER to these users; no other role is required for standard users. Remember that you also need to create users in cFolders for supplier users.

▶ **Configure Single Sign-On (SSO):** Configure SSO between SAP SRM and cFolders.

Supplier Self-Registration (ROS) Settings in the ROS client

The settings described in this section should be carried out in the ROS client:

▶ **Create product categories**
You can replicate material groups from the backend SAP ERP system to SAP SRM, as explained in Chapter 3. However, many organizations follow a different set of categories while registering suppliers. Therefore, we recommend that you create product categories directly for supplier registration instead of replicating them from the backend. Create a product category hierarchy and categories for supplier registration using Transaction COMM_HIERARCHY.

▶ **Assign category hierarchy to applications**
Assign the new category hierarchy to the "Purchasing" application in Transaction COMM_PRAPPLCAT.

▶ **Create/change questionnaire**
Define the survey questionnaires for the supplier registration. You can define as many questionnaires as you want. You can also define separate questionnaires for each category to obtain category-specific details from suppliers. Use the menu path **SPRO • SAP Implementation Guide • Supplier Relationship Management • Supplier Registration • Basic Settings • Create/Change Questionnaire**, or Transaction code ROS_QSTN_SURVEY.

In the standard, a survey with two questionnaires is delivered as a template. You should copy the delivered survey and create your own, one for each language. Then you should create one general questionnaire to get basic details about the vendor, and also create other category-specific questionnaires. Assign the required questionnaires to each survey. You can assign one questionnaire to multiple surveys.

Questionnaires can be sent as an attachment or as a link to the suppliers. The settings for both cases are described here:

▶ **Questionnaire as attachment**
This functionality lets suppliers fill out the survey questionnaire without connecting to the Internet. While defining a questionnaire, if you do not select the checkbox Direct Update into Application in the questionnaire header data, it is sent as an email attachment. You should also ensure that the appropriate configuration is performed to receive inbound emails (in the ROS client) according to SAP Note 455140 in this case. In the standard, when a questionnaire is sent as an attachment in the mail, the body of the mail also contains the questionnaire. This is confusing and some suppliers may fill out the questionnaire in the mail body and reply to the mail. We recommend that you modify the mail body for the survey by providing appropriate text. You can modify the mail body as follows:

  ▶ Open the survey in edit mode.

  ▶ Select the active questionnaire in the right pane.

  ▶ In the left pane, click on the edit letter icon. This icon is next to status icon.

  ▶ In the standard, you will see an entry /URL/ here. Delete this entry and type your own mail body text.

Repeat these steps for all questionnaires in the survey.

▶ **Questionnaire as link**
While defining a questionnaire, if you select the checkbox Direct Update into Application in the questionnaire header data, a link for the questionnaire is sent in the email to suppliers. You do not need to configure inbound email in this case. However, suppliers need an Internet connection to access the link and fill out the survey questionnaire. Suppliers can click on the link and fill out the questionnaire, which will directly update the supplier registration database. You can also change the mail body as explained under Questionnaire as attachment, but make sure that /URL/ exists in the mail body. Sometimes, you might encounter a problem opening the questionnaire link as uws_forms_service is not available. The following settings are required to ensure a trouble-free configuration:

  ▶ The checkbox Direct Update into application should be selected in the questionnaire header data

- ▶ Ensure that the entry /URL/ exists in the mail body for the questionnaire
- ▶ Implement SAP Notes 1046522 and 1078545
- ▶ Assign a service user and password in the logon data of service UWS_ FORMSERVICE using Transaction SICF.

- ▶ **Language selection for questionnaire**
  Maintain the default language for questionnaire.

- ▶ **Select product categories for registration**
  The categories defined in this setting are visible to suppliers when they register using the self-registration page. Select the product categories defined for supplier self-registration, and select the respective checkboxes in the Display and Active columns. If you do not want certain product categories to be displayed on the registration page, do not select their checkboxes in the Display column.

- ▶ **Assign questionnaire and language to product category**
  Specify a questionnaire in each of the required languages for the product categories. When, during registration, a new supplier selects the categories in which he is interested, the system determines the questionnaires to be sent to the supplier from this setting. Use the **New Entries** button to create new entries. For each product category and required language, configure the Web Survey ID and Web Survey Questionnaire ID.

- ▶ **Create anonymous User ID for supplier registration**
  Create a service user in Transaction SU01 and assign the following roles:

  - ▶ SAP_EC_BBP_CREATEVENDOR
  - ▶ SAP_EC_BBP_CREATEUSER

  If you want to use this user as a supplier administrator user in SUS, then assign the following additional roles:

  - ▶ SAP_BC_BASIS_MONITORING
  - ▶ SAP_EC_SUS_ADMIN_VENDOR

- ▶ **Assign anonymous User ID to self-registration service**
  When a new supplier launches the self-registration page, the system should not ask for a user ID and password. But when a new supplier submits the registration information, a temporary business partner is created in the ROS client. To facilitate this, you assign an anonymous user ID with appropriate authorizations to the self-registration service in Transaction SICF. To do so, go to service ROS_SELF_REG by expanding the hierarchy default_host – sap – bc – bsp – sap – ros_self_reg. Double-click on the ros_self_reg service and enter the client, the anonymous user defined in the previous step, and password on the Logon data tab.

- ▶ **Activate services**

  Activate the following BSP services for supplier self-registration using Transaction SICF:

  - ▶ default_host – sap – bc – bsp – sap – ros_self_reg
  - ▶ default_host – sap – bc – bsp – sap – ros_self_edit
  - ▶ default_host – sap – bc – bsp – sap – ros_prescreen

- ▶ **Define organizational plan for buyer and vendor**

  If you use the SUS client for supplier self-registration also, and have already configured the settings for SUS, then you do not need to configure any additional settings here. Create an organization node for the purchasing organization using Transaction PPOCA_BBP. Also, create a supplier root organization using Transaction PPOCV_BBP. Refer to the settings described under Create Purchasing Organization and Create Supplier Root Organization in Chapter 13 for more details.

- ▶ **Maintain BBP_MARKETP_INFO table**

  Maintain the following table entries in table BBP_MARKETP_INFO using Transaction SM30:

  - ▶ **Vendor Root**: Enter the vendor root organization ID, for example, VG50000020. You can get this value using Transaction PPOMV_BBP.
  - ▶ **Std.Purch.Org**: Enter the purchasing organization ID, for example, O 50000010. You can get this ID using Transaction PPOMA_BBP.
  - ▶ **CURR**: Maintain the default currency code.

  You can keep the rest of the columns blank.

- ▶ **Specify data privacy settings for suppliers**

  A data privacy statement is shown when a new supplier registers. The supplier must accept the data privacy statement before completing the registration process. Use the menu path **SPRO • SAP Implementation Guide • Supplier Relationship Management • Supplier Self-Services • Settings for User Interface • Specify Data Privacy Settings for Suppliers** to configure the data privacy settings.

  In this setting, you will define whether a data privacy statement is required during supplier self-registration. You will also define which text should be displayed as the privacy statement. The following six keys are used to define the settings:

  - ▶ **PRIVACY_STMNT_PERS_USED**: Valid values include TRUE or FALSE. Indicates whether a data privacy statement should be activated for self-registration. The value TRUE indicates activation of the privacy statement.
  - ▶ **PRIVACY_STMNT_PERS**: By default, the text ID BBP_PRIV_STMNT_EXTERNAL is assigned. This text ID contains text for the data privacy statement used during self-registration.

- ▶ **PRIVACY_STMNT_PERS_HD**: By default, the text ID BBP_PRIV_STMNT_ EXTERNAL_HEAD is assigned. This text ID contains text for data privacy acceptance. Replace this default text ID with your own text ID.

We suggest the following actions during implementation:

- ▶ Determine the privacy statement and acceptance texts based on the organization's policy.

- ▶ Maintain your own texts using Transaction SE61. For example, copy the general text ID BBP_PRIV_STMNT_EXTERNAL and create your own text ID (e.g., ZBBP_PRIV_STMNT_EXTERNAL). Maintain the privacy statement text as determined previously. Also, maintain other text (BBP_PRIV_ STMNT_EXTERNAL_HEAD).

- ▶ In the configuration setting Specify Data Privacy Settings for Suppliers, replace the default text IDs with your new text ids.

▶ **Maintain outbound and inbound email integration**
Ensure that your Basis consultant configures email integration with your ROS client. If you want to receive questionnaires as email attachments, you should make sure that the inbound email settings have been configured to receive emails in the ROS client. Obtain the inbound email address at which to receive questionnaires from your Basis or mail expert. Refer to SAP Note 455140 for configuring email integration.

▶ **Inbound mail processing**
When a questionnaire is received through email, the system triggers a user exit that processes the email attachment automatically and updates the supplier registration data with the received questionnare. Refer to SAP Note 779972 for more details. Maintain an entry in Transaction SO50 with the following settings:

- ▶ **Communication Type**: Select Internet Mail

- ▶ **Recipient Address**: Enter the inbound email address. The email address should be of a user that has profile S_A.SCON assigned.

- ▶ **Docu**: Enter '*'

- ▶ **Exit Name**: Enter "CL_UWS_FORM_RUNTIME_MAIL"

- ▶ **Call Sequence**: Enter "1"

▶ **Verify table entry in UXB_APPL**
Verify whether an entry exists for application ROS_QUESTIONNAIRES and application type 02.

▶ **Configure SSO**
Configure SSO between the ROS client and the SRM EBP client so that purchasers can access the ros_prescreen service from the EBP client without logging on to the ROS client.

- **Delete rejected business partners**
  You should periodically run the ROS_DELETE_REJECTED_BP report to delete rejected suppliers' data.

- **Dump while submitting self-registration**
  You might encounter dumps when self-registrations are submitted. This is a very common problem faced by many customers. For example, you might receive an ABAP dump Message_Type_X with message class UWS_FORMS. You can resolve this problem by executing the program UXS_ADD_MISSING_XSLT_NAME. Enter the application ROS_QUESTIONNAIRES and execute.

- **Attachments in supplier self-registration**
  Purchasers can add attachments to the supplier data in supplier prescreening. Sometimes, however, the attachments may not get saved. To resolve this, execute program REPAIR_BDS_OC1 as per SAP Note 798605. Remember that the purchaser should have authorization object S_BDS_DS assigned. This object exists in the role SAP_BBP_STAL_STRAT_PURCHASER.

- **SAP NetWeaver BI integration of survey data**
  If you want to bring survey data into SAP NetWeaver BI, you can find the data source for survey 0CA_SUR under the PI_BASIS node in Transaction RSA5 (in the ROS client). You can get the extraction structures by searching in SE11 with string UWS_S_BW*.

Supplier Self-Registration Settings in SRM EBP Client

The settings described in this section should be carried out in the EBP client:

- **Maintain BBP_MARKETP_INFO table**
  Maintain the following table entries in table BBP_MARKETP_INFO using Transaction SM30:
  - **Vendor Root**: Enter the vendor root organization ID, for example, VG50000020. You can get this value using Transaction PPOMV_BBP.
  - **Std.Purch.Org**: Enter the purchasing organization ID, for example, O 50000010. You can get this ID using Transaction PPOMA_BBP.
  - **CURR**: Specify the default currency code.

  You can keep rest of the columns blank.

- **Define external Web services for supplier directory**
  The potential suppliers registered in the supplier registration act as the supplier directory in the EBP client until they are transferred to EBP as business partners. You can search for suppliers from the supplier directory in all sourcing transactions. This setting is also required to access the vendor screening application from the EBP purchaser menu without logging on to the ROS client. The supplier directory can be accessed using OPI in the EBP client.

▶ Use the menu path **SPRO · SAP Implementation Guide · Supplier Relationship Management · SRM Server · Master Data · Define External Web Services (Catalogs, Vendor Lists etc)** and proceed as follows:

1. Click on the New Entries button to create a new Web service.

2. Enter a Web service ID, for example, "ROS_SUP_Dir", and description, for example, "ROS Supplier Directory".

3. Select List of Vendors as **Bus.Type** of a Web service.

4. In the left pane, double-click on **Standard Call Structure**.

5. Click on the **New Entries** button and maintain the parameter settings provided in Table 10.1.

Parameter Name	Parameter Value	Type	Remarks
	http://<HTTP_ server>:<port>/sap/bc/bsp/sap/ros_ prescreen/main.do Where <HTTP server> and <port> are of your SUS/ROS system	0 (URL)	URL for the supplier prescreening
sap-client	xxx Where xxx is your ROS client number	2 (fixed value)	
sap-language	Sy_langu	1 (SAP field)	
sap-sessioncmd	Open	2 (fixed value)	

Table 10.1 Call Structure for ROS Supplier Directory

▶ **Maintain catalog attribute**
Maintain attribute CAT with the Web service ID defined for the supplier directory in the organizational plan using Transaction PPOMA_BBP. You should maintain the attribute for the required purchasing groups in the organizational plan.

▶ **Role adjustment**
This setting is also required to access the vendor screening application from the EBP purchaser menu. The following roles need to be modified:

▶ SAP_EC_BBP_OP_PURCHASER

▶ SAP_EC_BBP_ST_PURCHASER

▶ Any other role where you have the menu option Preselect vendors

Modify the roles as follows:

▶ Open the role in edit mode using Transaction PFCG.

▶ Go to menu option Preselect vendors and double-click it to edit.

▶ Enter ROS_PRESCREEN in the field BSP Application.

▶ In the parameters, maintain the parameter name sap-client and value <ROS client> (e.g., 200).

▶ **Configure SSO**
Configure SSO between the ROS client and the SRM EBP client so that purchasers can access the ros_prescreen service from the EBP client without logging on to the ROS client.

Maintain the Supplier Self-Registration Link on the Company Website

The supplier self-registration URL should be provided on the company website for potential suppliers to register themselves. Provide this URL to the company website maintenance team to do this. You should plan this activity in your implementation. The self-registration URL is *http://<server>:<port>/sap/ bc/bsp/sap/ros_self_reg/main.htm*. You can find the supplier self-registration URL as follows:

1. Open the BSP application ROS_SELF_REG in Transaction SE80 in ROS client.

2. Expand the node Pages with flow logic and then double-click on main.htm.

3. You can see the URL on the Properties tab at the bottom.

New SAP SRM 2007 Settings for Business Partner Creation

In SAP SRM 2007, using the SAP NetWeaver Enterprise Portal is mandatory. Whenever a new business partner contact person is created in SRM EBP, the new user should also be synchronized with the portal. The following settings ensure this synchronization:

1. In the SRM EBP client, create an RFC destination of type G with the name SPML for the portal server. On the **Technical Settings** tab, specify the **Target Host** and **Service No** of the portal server. Leave the **Path Prefix** field blank.

2. Activate UME-SPML connection using the menu path **SPRO • SAP Implementation Guide • Supplier Relationship Management • SRM Server • Master Data • Create Users • Activate UME-SPML Connector** and enter "SPML" in the field RFC destination and select the Activate SPML checkbox.

3. Map the portal role to an SAP SRM role. All business partner roles should be mapped with corresponding portal roles. The following standard roles, in addition to custom roles, if any, should be mapped:

▶ SAP_EC_BBP_VENDOR

▶ SAP_EC_BBP_BIDDER

▶ SAP_BBP_STAL_VENDOR

▶ SAP_BBP_STAL_BIDDER

The mapping can be configured by following these steps:

▸ Execute Transaction PFCG and open the SAP SRM role in edit mode.

▸ Select the **Personalization** tab.

▸ Double-click on the key **/SAPSRM/SRM_ROLES**.

▸ Add the relevant portal role unique ID for the given SAP SRM role.

▸ Repeat these steps for other SAP SRM roles.

4. Verify the SAPJSF user and role assignment. Ensure that user SAPJSF exists and the roles SAP_BC_JSF_COMMUNICATION and SAP_BC_JSF_ COMMUNICATION_RO are assigned to the user.

Useful Tables for Survey Data in Supplier Registration

The following tables contain survey data that you can use in custom reports, if any:

▸ TUWS_SURVEY

▸ TUWS_SURVEY_LOG

▸ TUWS_TAROBJ_ATTR

▸ Others

10.4 Summary

The sourcing strategy used by purchasers may vary based on the characteristics of the products being procured. In this chapter, you have learned how SAP SRM helps purchasers with different sourcing strategies. In summary, a few scenarios are as follows:

▸ If there is an established supply base, automated sourcing can be used.

▸ To establish a new source or to source a new product, an online bidding process can be followed.

▸ If a vendor has to be identified along with the best price in a competitive market, a bidding process can be used together with a reverse auction.

▸ In case of complex procurement, project procurements, etc., bidding with cFolders collaboration will offer value.

You have also seen how SAP SRM facilitates Web-based supplier self-registration. In Chapter 11, we will discuss service procurement in SAP SRM.

Procurement of services differs significantly from procurement of materials and is more complex. Requirements for services are largely undefined at the time of requisition — the scope is not fully known until the service is actually performed. SAP SRM supports the services procurement with flexible, collaborative capabilities for managing the cost constraints and variability associated with procuring services such as temporary labor, consulting, maintenance, marketing, printing, and facility management.

— Source: mySAP SRM Statement of Direction 2003

11 Service Procurement

Procurement experts agree that services procurement is more complex than materials procurement for the simple reason that there is more uncertainty in the requirements and often the buying organization may not be able to clearly specify the requirements. More often than not, it is the supplier who determines the services to be performed. "It is the subjectivity in the services procurement that frightens me," says a procurement expert. Most of the procurement applications focus on materials procurement and ignore services procurement. In many organizations, services procurement is handled by the department that uses the services and typically is not computerized due to its complexity.

SAP recognizes the complex nature of services procurement, thanks to its popular *External Services Management (MM-SRV)* functionality in SAP ERP. SAP introduced special collaborative services procurement scenarios, such as *Temporary labor and consulting,* in its SAP SRM application way back in 2003. Service agents can submit their time sheets and expenses using an Internet browser, thus providing project managers who manage resource-intensive projects with a much-needed, real-time, actual, project resource cost-monitoring capability. SAP SRM also helps companies put a lid on unplanned service costs by providing capabilities to define and enforce spending limits. Companies can also reduce the uncertainty in services being performed by defining service catalogs with prenegotiated rates and enabling service agents to pick unplanned services from catalogs.

We will discuss the SAP SRM service procurement functionalities in Section 11.2 and implementation of service procurement in Section 11.3. The case study in Section 11.1 describes the requirements of a growing professional services organization and how they selected and implemented a service procurement application.

11.1 Case Study: Techedge Inc.

Techedge Inc. is a California-based technology services provider. The company prides itself in providing cost-effective solutions to its customers, using a multishore delivery model. Techedge Inc. employs about 400 full-time consultants. It also uses the services of an additional 700 consultants on a temporary contract from India, the Philippines, and Ireland. Every month Techedge Inc.'s operations team and project managers have to reconcile and approve hundreds of time sheets and expense reports submitted by the contract consultants. If Techedge continues current growth rates of 50% per annum, in the next few years, it will employ 800 full-time consultants, and 2,000 consultants on contract.

In a management planning workshop, the operations team estimated that managing the growth would not be possible without deploying an Information Technology (IT) application to manage the external service providers. They argued that services constitute almost 80% of its external spend and a good procurement application to manage this spend is essential. Automation of the routine work will improve the operational efficiency and will help project managers and the operations team focus on delivering projects. Project managers demanded a more robust system to hire consultants based on required skill sets, and a system to help them evaluate consultants. Techedge Inc.'s management decided to implement a service procurement application and appointed Masa, a veteran in the company, to select and implement a world class application.

Masa wasted no time, he conducted a series of meetings with all stakeholders in the organization, and listed the following capabilities required by the new procurement system:

▸ Techedge Inc. should be able to manage the procurement of services from external consultants.

▸ Consultants should be able to record their time sheets and expenses that require approval from project managers. The system should be able to match the expenses claimed with purchase order limits.

▸ Suppliers should be able to maintain a pool of available consultants with them.

▸ Project managers should be able to request specific consultants from the pool or request consultants by specifying skills required.

▸ The system should be able to cater to other services, such as facilities management, maintenance of office, and IT equipment, etc.

- The system should facilitate evaluation of suppliers and consultants.
- The system should be able to integrate with SAP ERP Financials for project budget control and expense recording.

Masa invited the top four software vendors to give demos to his team. After going through the demos and presentations from all of the vendors, the Techedge Inc. team selected SAP SRM for the following reasons:

- SAP SRM meets all of their current requirements.
- SAP SRM is seamlessly integrated with SAP ERP Financials. Techedge Inc. uses SAP's internal order-based budget controls and SAP SRM enables this readily without additional interfacing effort. Also, SAP Accounts Payables is seamlessly integrated with SAP SRM invoices.
- SAP SRM also supports highly mobile project managers with its offline workflow approval process using mobile phones.
- SAP's solution roadmap indicates substantial investments in services procurement.

The implementation at Techedge, Inc., led by Yeu Sheng, an SAP SRM expert, took about five months and they successfully went live two months ago. The initial feedback is very positive and Masa intends to carry out a return on investment (ROI) study after 10 months. Masa is sure that the ROI study will show a large positive ROI, if emails from happy project managers are any indication.

We will discuss the implementation of service procurement for the previous scenario in Section 11.3. First, however, we will briefly look at the functionalities offered by SAP SRM service procurement.

11.2 SAP SRM Service Procurement — A Brief Overview of Functionalities

As stated in the introductory statement, SAP SRM supports procuring services, such as temporary labor, consulting, maintenance, marketing, legal, printing, and facility management. Based on the underlying process, all services can be broadly categorized under the following three types:

- **Simple Services**
  Procurement of simple services is similar to indirect materials procurement. For example, changing a light bulb or providing a new decorative plant are simple facility management services. These services are normally known and therefore can be clearly specified without ambiguity in the service requisition or order. You can also maintain service catalogs for many commonly used services. Self-service procurement, explained in Chapter 5, covers sim-

ple services, too. If you are using the classic or extended classic scenario, note that the system groups multiple service items in a shopping cart and creates a single line item with item category *D* and multiple service specifications in the follow-on document in the backend SAP ERP system.

▶ **Unplanned services**
Sometimes it is difficult to clearly specify the services to be performed during the requisition or order stage. During service confirmation, a supplier gives an account of services performed. For example, when a laptop needs to be repaired, the requisitioner can only state the problem being faced with the laptop. The service provider takes the laptop, identifies the work to be done, and gives an estimate. The service provider provides a list of tasks actually performed only after the repair is done. It's the same with vehicle servicing. To address this issue, SAP SRM supports unplanned services with a functionality called *limits*. That is, the requisitioner or purchaser can specify a value limit for jobs that require unplanned services. During service confirmation, the system warns the approver if the value of actual services performed given by the supplier exceeds the limit specified. If you are using the classic or extended classic scenario, the system creates the backend SAP ERP document with item category *B*.

▶ **Staffing services (temporary labor and consulting)**
Almost all companies use third-party staffing services. Third-party services contracts can be *deliverable-based* or *time- and material-based*. In a deliverable-based contract, the buyer clearly specifies the deliverable and the supplier deploys the labor or consultants to deliver the deliverable as per the specifications. This type of third-party services can be handled as simple services. In time- and material-based contracts, the buyer manages the project or works with staffing from the supplier to achieve an end objective. Effective project management and resource management are essential to control costs and schedule in this case. In this case, the buyer enters into an agreement with the supplier to provide staff with the required skill sets and hourly or daily rates for each skill are pre-negotiated. Actual expenses for the staff, such as travel, lodging, per diem, telephone, etc., will be reimbursed by the buyer based on actual expenses. There may be a limit on the maximum expenses that can be claimed, also. Service providers (consultants, temporary labor, etc.) will have to submit time sheets regularly to claim payment for their services. Hence, time- and material-based staffing contracts usually have a fixed service component (time) and unplanned services components (expense reimbursement and overtime).

We will mainly discuss the implementation of staffing services and unplanned services in this chapter. Staffing services procurement is a combination of the self-service procurement, sourcing, and supplier collaboration (EBP-SUS) scenarios. The service procurement process for staffing services is illustrated in Figure 11.1 and explained as follows:

1. A special entry screen for a shopping cart is provided in SAP SRM for creating a *request for external staff* or *order for external staff*. Note that an order for external staff is available to users with the purchaser role only. An employee creates the shopping cart requesting third-party services. In addition to normal shopping cart entries, the purchaser will be able to specify the number of service providers required, search and specify the favored service agents from each supplier, and create a skills profile using a PDF form. Service agents are employees of the supplier maintained as service agents in SRM Supplier Self-Service (SUS) by the supplier.

You can define limits for a specific purpose for each service unit (e.g., stay costs per day) or limits for unplanned expenses, which will be determined during service confirmation. All of the items in a request are displayed in a hierarchical form to ensure that related items are always shown together. Note that you can create a request for external staff only when there is a source of supply for the given service master or product category. The source of supply can be a contract, product vendor linkage, or vendor list.

In an order for external staff, the purchaser can manually specify a supplier when there is no source of supply found for the requested service. The shopping cart is sent for approval based on the workflow settings. On approval of the shopping cart, a purchase order is created if the request is an order for external staff, or a bid invitation is created if the request is for external staff.

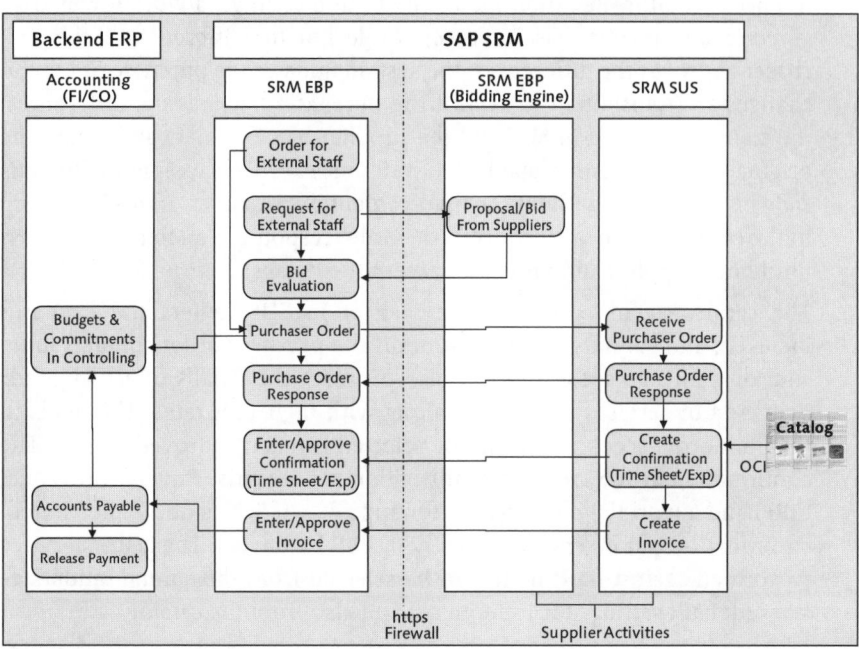

Figure 11.1 Service Procurement for Staffing Services

2. The system creates a bid invitation based on the request and sends a notification to the suppliers specified in the request. Suppliers access the bid invitation on the Web, verify the skills requested, verify the availability of the service agents being requested, and submit their response. Depending on the configuration settings for transaction type, suppliers can submit availability of service agents and prices or just the availability of service agents. If the transaction type does not allow submission of prices, then prices will be determined based on the source of supply (contract, or product and vendor linkage, or price in product master). If the requested service agents are not available, the supplier can propose other available service agents for the requested skill sets.

3. The purchaser evaluates the bids received and determines the winner. A purchase order is created from the winning bid. Note that the purchaser verifies the bids received using the *check shopping cart status* transaction.

4. A purchase order is either created from the order for external staff or from a winning bid. The purchase order is transmitted to SUS and almost instantly visible to the supplier on their browser. The order values also update budgets and commitments in the backend SAP ERP Financials system.

5. The supplier verifies the order and confirms it by accepting it after making the necessary changes, if any. If there are differences between the purchase order and the order response sent by supplier, the system activates the differences monitor. Based on the configuration settings, a workflow is triggered to alert the purchaser to accept or decline the differences. If the purchaser approves the differences, the system updates the purchase order and changes are transmitted to SUS. If the purchaser declines the differences, the status is updated in SUS and the supplier has to review and accept the original purchase order again. The differences can be accepted automatically by the system without the involvement of purchaser, if this is allowed in the configuration settings. Thus the order response is an iterative process until both supplier and purchaser accept the details.

6. The service agent enters the time sheet in SUS, enters the expenses incurred, and submits a confirmation. If the purchase order contains lump sum or limit items, the supplier also provides the details of actual goods delivered or services performed, along with their unit rates. The items in the limit order scenario can also be selected from an approved catalog. The confirmation in SUS creates a confirmation in Enterprise Buyer Professional (EBP) and a workflow is triggered for approval. If SUS is not implemented, confirmation can be entered directly in EBP by buyers. The actual services performed against limit items can be selected from the configuration settings (default settings for limit items) and also from the catalog.

7. The approver verifies the time sheets and expenses, and approves or rejects the confirmation. The approval or rejection status is updated in SUS. If the

confirmation is rejected, the supplier can correct the details and send it again. Thus the confirmation is an iterative process until both supplier and purchaser accept the details.

8. Invoices in SUS can be created with reference to purchase orders or confirmations. In service procurement, invoices can be created with reference to contact persons, too. You can also select multiple documents belonging to the same company code, currency, and logical system and create a collective invoice. Suppliers can also create credit memos with reference to existing invoices. The invoices created in SUS are sent to EBP via SAP NetWeaver XI and the system creates an invoice in EBP. This invoice is sent for approval.

9. The approver verifies the invoice and accepts or rejects it. The system updates the status of the SUS invoice based on this decision. If the invoice is rejected, the supplier can correct it and send it again. The approved invoice creates an invoice in the backend SAP ERP Financials system. The invoice also updates the budgets and commitments. If SUS is not implemented, invoices can be entered directly in EBP by buyers and approved.

10. Periodic payment jobs in backend SAP ERP Financials ensure that the vendor is paid on the appropriate due date.

All of the functionalities described in this section are possible when you deploy a standalone scenario. You will not be able to use SUS scenario fully, however, if you want to deploy a classic or extended classic scenario. In these cases, confirmations and invoices in SUS cannot be used, and confirmation of time sheets, expenses, and invoices will have to be entered in EBP by buyers.

Next, in Section 11.3, we will discuss the implementation of a services procurement scenario in the standalone deployment mode.

11.3   Implementation of Service Procurement

Implementation of the business case described in Section 11.1 requires a standalone deployment of the service procurement scenario. SUS should be implemented to ensure the operational efficiency demands in the business case. In Section 11.3.1, we will explain the landscape requirements and then in Section 11.3.2, discuss the configuration settings required.

11.3.1   System Landscape

The sample system landscape shown in Figure 11.2 illustrates the required system landscape when both EBP and SUS are implemented in SAP SRM Server 5.5. If you are implementing SAP SRM 2007, you should also implement SAP NetWeaver Portal. The following software components are required, assuming that SAP SRM version is 5.0:

- ▶ SAP SRM 5.0

- ▶ SAP NetWeaver XI 7.0 (PI 7.0) from SAP NetWeaver 7.0

- ▶ SAP Web Dispatcher as an Application Gateway outside the firewall. Alternatively, you can also have a reverse proxy.

- ▶ SAP NetWeaver Portal 7.0 (Optional)

- ▶ SRM-MDM Catalog (Optional. Required if you want to implement catalogs in EBP or SUS, also.)

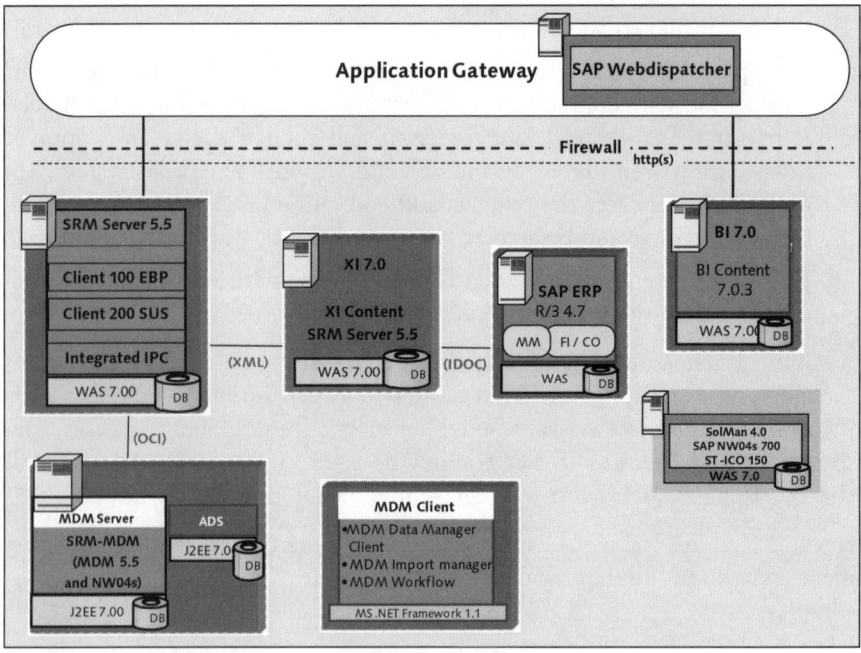

Figure 11.2 Sample System Landscape for Service Procurement

> **Note**
>
> Always refer to the SAP Master Guide for the relevant SAP SRM version before deciding on the final system landscape, installation sequence, and other important information.

11.3.2 Configuring the Service Procurement Scenario

In this section, we will discuss only the implementation of additional settings required for services procurement. We will also explain the additional settings required — if you are implementing SAP SRM 2007. Other required settings are explained in other chapters, as also outlined in this section.

Settings for Self-Service Procurement

Refer to Chapter 5.

Settings for EBP-SUS Scenario

Refer to Chapter 14.

Create Skills Profile

This is an optional setting that you will need when you want to use a skills profile PDF form in your request. You need to install Adobe Document Server and use Adobe reader 6.0.2 or higher for this functionality. The skills profile is defined and activated by implementing BAdI BBP_SKILLS. This BAdI has two methods. You can define a list of skills using the PREPARE_SKILLS method, or you can activate or deactivate skills profile in the request for external staff screen based on product category using the SKILLS_ACTIVE method. A sample implementation is delivered in the standard.

Define Message Control for Limit Purchase Orders

If you want to receive confirmations for limit purchase orders from SUS in EBP, then you must configure this setting. If you do not, a confirmation is not created in EBP and is automatically set to *rejected* status in SUS. To configure this setting, use the menu path **SPRO • SAP Implementation Guide • Supplier Relationship Management • SRM Server • Cross-Application Basic Settings • Message Control • Influence XML Message Control**. Select BUS2203 and double-click on XML Message Control in the left pane. For the message number 217 (Enter the product category), select the checkbox in the Ignore column.

Configure Link to Service Agent List in EBP

This setting is required to obtain SUS service agent search help in EBP, and is relevant for SAP SRM version 5.0 or lower. Use the menu path **SPRO • SAP Implementation Guide • Supplier Relationship Management • SRM Server • Master Data • Define External Web Services (Catalogs, Vendor Lists etc)** and proceed as follows:

1. Click on the **New Entries** button to create a new Web service.
2. Enter a Web service ID, for example, "SERVICE_AGENT," and Description, for example, "SUS Service Agents".
3. Select Service Provider List as **Bus.Type of a WebService**.
4. In the left pane, double-click on **Standard Call Structure**.
5. Click on the **New Entries** button and maintain the parameter settings as provided in Table 11.1.

Parameter Name	Parameter Value	Type
	https://<HTTP_server>:<port>/sap/bc/bsp/sap/bbp_sus_sagent/sus_serviceagent_f4.htm Where <HTTP server> and <port> are the http server and port of your SUS system	0 (URL)
Sap-client	Xxx Where xxx is your client number	2 (Fixed Value)

Table 11.1 Call Structure for SUS Service Agents Search Help

Assign Service Agent External Web Service to an Organizational Plan

Using Transaction PPOMA_BBP, assign the service agent external Web service ID to the organizational plan attribute CAT at the appropriate organizational unit level or at the position level. If you want to make the service agent Web service available to all users in a company, assign the Web service ID at the company node level. If you want to restrict access to a specific department or to a specific set of users, assign the Web service ID only to the department or set of users in question.

Settings in SAP SRM 2007 for SUS Service Agent Search Help in EBP

The following settings are required to get search help for service agents in request or order for external staff in SAP SRM 2007:

- **Configure Web service for SUS**
  Use Transaction code WSCONFIG. This setting should be configured in the SUS client. Enter SAPSRM_CH_WS_SUS in the fields Service definition and Variant and click on the create icon. In the next screen, click on the ICF Details button. Activate the service SAPSRM_CH_WS_SUS.

- **Create a Web service user in the SUS client**
  This setting should be configured in the SUS client. Create a user (e.g., WS_SUS) using Transaction SU01.

- **Create an RFC destination for SUS Web service**
  Create an RFC destination with name WS_SUS of type H (HTTP connection to ABAP system). Maintain the SUS host as Target Host and enter "/sap/bc/srt/rfc/sap" in the field Path Prefix. On the Logon & Security tab, specify the Web service user (e.g., WS_SUS) created in SUS as the logon user and password.

- **Logical Port Configuration in EBP Client**
  Configure this setting in the EBP client using Transaction code LPCONFIG. Enter "CO_SAPSRM_CH_WS_SUS" in Proxy Class, "LP_SUS" in Logical Port

and select the checkbox Default Port. Click on the create icon. On the Call Parameters tab, enter "WS_SUS" in the field HTTP_DESTINATION and "SAPSRM_CH_WS_SUS" in the field Path Suffix. Click on the activate icon.

▶ **Define Defaults for Time Recording**
These settings are optional. If you want to default in times while recording time sheets, then carry out the settings described here. You can create multiple default entries using versions but only one version can be active at any point of time.

Use the menu path **SPRO • SAP Implementation Guide • Supplier Relationship Management • SRM Server • Confirmation and Invoice Verification • Define Defaults for Time Recording** to define start and end times, real working units, unit of time (e.g., hours or days), and number of weekdays worked. If you do not configure any settings here, then no values will be defaulted during time sheet recording and you will have to maintain all entries every time. We recommend you maintain defaults here to ease the data entry. If you want multiple active versions, implement BAdI BBP_TREX_BADI to modify the version used for default values during time recording.

▶ **Define Default Setting for Limit Items**
The default settings defined in this activity will appear as buttons in the confirmation screen while entering actual services performed against limit item, making data entry easier. This is an optional setting.

Use the menu path **SPRO • SAP Implementation Guide • Supplier Relationship Management • SRM Server • Confirmation and Invoice Verification • Define Default Settings for Limit Items**. Click on the **New Entries** button and configure a preset group for BUS2203 (confirmation). You can define multiple versions of preset groups and make one version active with value X in the Active column. Select a preset group and double-click on the **Preset** button to maintain the default actual items. For example, you may define *Telephone*, *Conveyance*, *Flight*, *Per Diem*, and *Mineral Water* as the default actual items during confirmation for limit items. You can also use product(s) from the product master. Configure the unit of measure, category, and applicable tax code for each item. If you want multiple active versions, implement BAdI BBP_UNPLAN_ITEM_BADI to modify the version used for limit items during confirmation.

▶ **Business Partner Maintenance in EBP**
You can define service agents for a supplier in EBP by configuring contact persons for the supplier and selecting the checkbox for service agent.

▶ **Activate SICF services in SUS**
Activate the service bbp_sus_sagent using Transaction SICF.

▶ **Roles in SUS**
  Service agent users in SUS should have role SAP_EC_SUS_SERVICE_AGENT assigned.

11.4 Summary

Service procurement is more complex than materials procurement due to the 'unknown' factors in defining the requirements. Monitoring and controlling procurement costs becomes more difficult in such cases. In this chapter you learned that SAP SRM addresses the complexities in service procurement and provides a solution that includes supplier collaboration. You have seen that by enabling a collaborative request-to-pay process with service agents, SAP SRM facilitates more efficient external staffing services procurement. Limit items functionality facilitates managing unplanned services without losing control on the costs. Next, in Chapter 12, we will discuss how contract management in SAP SRM helps companies manage a central repository of contracts and ensure contract compliance.

Globalization, failure of several high-profile corporations in the early years of this century, and SOX compliance have been some of the key drivers for Contract Management. Maintaining a central repository of contracts and ensuring contract compliance across the organization are essential in today's business.

12 Contract Management

Experienced purchasers are aware that the benefits of some of the best negotiations are often squandered by weakly drafted contracts and poor contract execution and monitoring. Globalization has led companies to move out of their comfort zones and seek supply bases from countries across the globe. This has made purchasers' task more complex as they now need to learn contractual clauses applicable in various countries and interpretation of local contractual terms in other countries. Contract authoring with appropriate clauses has become a specialized task and many companies set up contract creation, review, and approval processes to mitigate risks. The contract creation and approval process includes involvement of legal, technical, and financial teams, depending on the contract type. This in turn increases the contract creation cycle times dramatically.

Globalization also opened up many opportunities. Purchasers in large multinational companies (MNC) have realized the potential opportunities in entering into global supply contracts with other MNC suppliers. This required purchasers to aggregate the demand across the globe for identified categories of goods and services and leverage it by getting large discounts. However, making these global contracts available to all locations and businesses is another daunting task. Many independent Supply Relationship Management (SRM) vendors came out with contract management solutions that help companies maintain central contract repositories that are instantly available to all businesses across the globe. This helped companies realize some of the benefits of global negotiations. Central contract repositories also offered a bonus in the form of a large knowledgebase on contracts, the benefits of which cannot be underestimated.

But, leaders have already realized that it is not enough to have a central repository of contracts unless you link these contracts to your negotiating and executing systems. This is where SAP's solutions outperform other contract management software vendors' solutions, with its end-to-end Contract Lifecycle Management (CLM) applications. SAP offers a variety of contract management solutions that are integrated with sourcing and executing applications. They currently offer procurement contract management functionalities in the following applications:

- Operational contracts in SAP ERP
- Global contracts and operational contracts in SAP SRM
- SAP xCLM to manage contracts in all SAP applications (also available as part of SAP E-Sourcing for procurement contracts)

We will discuss SAP contract management solutions in Section 12.1. We will also look at the centralized contract management requirements of a large company in the mineral resources industry in our case study in Section 12.2. An overview of contract management functionalities in SAP SRM is described in Section 12.3. Finally, we will look at implementation aspects in Section 12.4.

12.1   SAP Contract Management Applications

SAP caters to customer requirements in contract management in all of its procurement applications. While some SAP applications, like SAP ERP, cater to customer requirements for contract execution, some applications, like xCLM, offer end-to-end CLM functionalities.

Before looking at the functionalities offered by SAP applications, you need to understand the typical structure of an electronic contract. A contract consists of structured data (e.g., dates, item codes, quantities, price, etc.) and a physical contract document, which will be signed by both supplier and purchaser. The term *contract authoring* in this chapter refers to authoring of the physical contract document. If an application only supports contracts with structured data, then we refer to it as a *basic* contract.

In Sections 12.1.1 through 12.1.3, we will take a look at the SAP applications that offer contract management. In Section 12.1.4, we will compare these applications with one another.

12.1.1   Outline Agreements in SAP ERP

Outline agreements in SAP ERP have been the most popular basic contract repositories used by all SAP customers. Outline agreements represent long-term agreements with suppliers for regularly procured materials and services. Long-term agreements reduce procurement lead time by eliminating the need for sourcing activity whenever a new requirement for regularly used materials or services arises. Different types of contracts, such as value contracts, quantity contracts, and scheduling agreements, are supported in SAP ERP. Scheduling agreements are used by all manufacturing customers because of their ability to integrate with the planning run (MRP run in SAP ERP or advanced planning in SAP APO). The MRP run generates and dispatches delivery schedules to suppliers automatically, thus reducing the workload of the purchasing department considerably.

12.1.2 Contract Management in SAP SRM

SAP SRM offers central contract management functionalities for the entire organization across its businesses and locations. Contracts in SAP SRM can be negotiated using SAP SRM sourcing functionalities, like bidding and reverse auctions. Purchasers are alerted on shortly expiring contracts to start the renegotiation process. Purchasers can maintain two types of basic contracts depending on the requirements:

▶ **Operational Contracts**
An operational contract is a purchasing contract within SRM EBP that represent a long-term agreement negotiated by a strategic purchaser. It can be used for fulfilling the requirements sourced in SAP SRM. The contract can also be published as a catalog to make it available to all employees.

▶ **Global Outline Agreement (GOA):**
A GOA is a contract centrally negotiated by a purchasing department and can be used by all businesses and locations across the company, even if they use different procurement systems. A GOA is distributed to all executing procurement systems as contracts. For example, a GOA from SAP SRM can be distributed to multiple ERP systems in the organization as backend contracts or outline agreements. Call-offs from such backend contracts in turn update GOA usage status in SAP SRM.

Note
SAP SRM contracts are our focus in this chapter.

12.1.3 Contracts in SAP E-Sourcing

Refer to Section 12.1.4 for information on contracts in SAP E-Sourcing.

12.1.4 Contract Lifecycle Management using xCLM

xCLM 1.0 is based on SAP E-Sourcing contract management capabilities. SAP E-Sourcing 5.0 offers full contract management capabilities, including contract creation and authoring, contract creation integrated with sourcing, contract terms negotiation, contract performance management, and compliance monitoring. Once a contract is approved, it can be transferred to SAP ERP for use in requirements fulfillment. xCLM supports all of the tools necessary for contract authoring, such as a standard clause library, master templates, and Microsoft Word integration to facilitate quick draft contract generation. Collaboration and negotiation capabilities enable users to finalize contracts much faster than would otherwise be possible. xCLM is also available in a hosted deployment model. In future versions, xCLM is slated to provide functionalities to support sales contracts and other types of contracts. Future plans also include Duet-based contract authoring, SAP SRM integration, and many other key enhancements.

12.1.5 Comparison of SAP Applications in Contract Management

Table 12.1 provides a comparison of the SAP contract management applications. Note that SAP SRM contract management is integrated with SAP R/3 from version 4.6B on. However, other functionalities of SAP SRM can be integrated with SAP R/3 version 3.1 on.

Feature	SAP ERP	SAP SRM	xCLM
Basic contracts	Yes	Yes	Yes
Contract authoring	No	No	Yes
Attachments	Yes (with Document Management System (DMS))	Yes	Yes
Clause library	No	No	Yes
Contract templates	No	Basic only	Yes
Contract performance reporting	Yes	Yes	Yes
Contract compliance reporting	Yes (limited)	Yes	Yes
Integrated sourcing	No	Yes	Yes (SAP E-Sourcing)
Standard integration with other sourcing systems	SAP SRM	No	E-Sourcing
Integrated procurement	Yes	Yes	No
Standard integration with other procurement systems	SAP SRM sourcing cockpit in the classic scenario	From SAP R/3 4.6b on.	From SAP R/3 4.6c on
Central contract distribution to backend systems	No	Yes	No
Contracts other than procurement contracts	Basic sales contracts	No	Planned in future versions
Hosted deployment	No	No	Yes

Table 12.1 Comparison of SAP Applications in Contract Management

12.2 Case Study: Centralized Contract Management

Minerals and Metals International Inc. (MMI) is a global resources company with business operations in 15 countries. MMI employs around 20,000 employees operating from 100 locations. The company manages its estimated USD nine billion spend using nine SAP R/3 systems. In mid-2000, MMI set up a centralized procurement department to carry out global sourcing, serving all of its locations. Ruediger, a seasoned professional in procurement, was appointed as the department head. Over the next six months, Ruediger and his team poured over the data coming from the nine SAP systems. They quickly realized that it's not easy to get any meaningful output without harmonizing the data. Based on the high-level data analysis, Ruediger sensed that it's possible to start global sourcing for a few spend categories. However, he worried about executing global sourcing contracts in the absence of a central procurement system. Ruediger's team listed the following capabilities required in a central procurement system that would address his department's needs:

▶ Should be able to consolidate spend data from nine SAP systems and provide spend analysis reports with harmonized data

▶ Should have online sourcing tools like bidding and reverse auctions

▶ Should provide the ability to negotiate central contracts applicable for all locations

▶ Should be able to distribute central contracts to nine executing SAP systems

▶ Should continuously monitor contract usage in all systems

Ruediger approached SAP with these requirements and was told that SAP SRM meets all of them. The SAP team advised him to implement the strategic sourcing and contract management functionalities of SAP SRM. Therefore, over the next nine months, MMI implemented SAP SRM and once it was up and running, Ruediger could already see some of the benefits in the form of a central spend analysis report lying in front of him. Before SAP SRM was implemented, it took more than six man-months for him to get such a report. Now, he can get this report at any time. Most importantly, MMI can now negotiate central contracts and distribute them to all procurement systems, and the first three central contracts negotiated for consolidated requirements of all locations resulted in an estimated savings of USD 12 million. Ruediger has already identified other opportunities that would result in further significant savings for the organization.

We will discuss the implementation of contract management for the preceding scenario in Section 12.4. Before we learn how to implement it, however, let us take a look at the functionalities offered in SAP SRM contract management.

> **Note**
>
> The implementation of sourcing was explained in Chapter 10 and spend analysis will be covered in Chapter 15.

12.3 SAP SRM Contract Management — A Brief Overview of Functionalities

Figure 12.1 illustrates the following contract management processes that are supported by SAP SRM and that are explained in this section:

- Contract Creation
- Contract Fulfillment
- Contract Monitoring

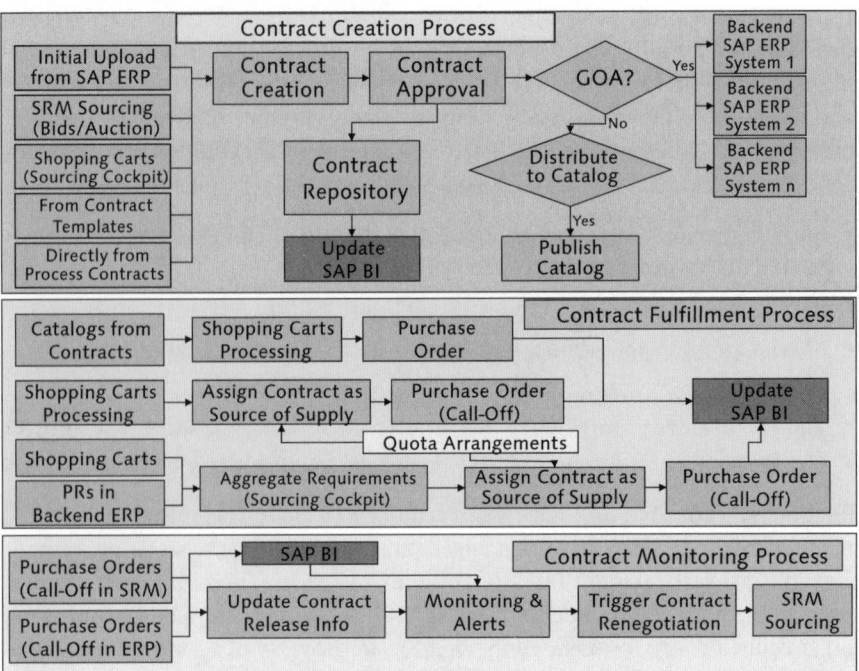

Figure 12.1 SAP SRM Contract Management Processes

12.3.1 Contract Creation Process

A typical contract creation process in SAP SRM involves the following steps, as shown in Figure 12.1:

1. Contract creation
2. Contract approval
3. Special contract processes in SAP SRM, if applicable

We will now discuss these processes in more detail.

Contract Creation in SAP SRM

As explained in Section 12.1.2, you can maintain two types of contracts in SAP SRM, that is, operational contracts and GOAs. Contracts in SAP SRM can be created in any of the following ways:

▶ **Initial upload from backend SAP ERP**
If you want to use SAP SRM as the central contract repository system, you can use the program BBP_CONTRACT_INITIAL_UPLOAD to upload the backend SAP R/3 or SAP ERP contracts into SAP SRM during SAP SRM go-live. This is recommended if you want to use backend ERP contracts for requirements fulfillment in SAP SRM. Note that backend ERP contracts can still be used in the ERP system and there will be no link between backend contracts and SAP SRM contracts after the upload. The changes in either system will not update the contract in the other system. If you do not want to use contracts anymore in the backend ERP system, you should block the items from further usage.

▶ **Contract creation from sourcing**
Contracts can be created as follow-on documents from the bidding or reverse auction process. The negotiated terms and conditions from winning bids are copied into such contracts. You can also configure settings to create backend contracts from sourcing.

▶ **Contract creation from sourcing cockpit**
You can select shopping carts in the SAP SRM sourcing cockpit and process contracts with reference to these shopping carts. The item data from the shopping carts is copied into such contracts. You can also configure settings to create backend contracts.

▶ **Contract creation using contract templates**
You can create templates for frequently used contracts and then create contracts from these templates.

▶ **Directly from process contracts**
You can also use the process contracts Web Transaction in SAP SRM to create contracts from scratch. In this case, you need to enter all of the data in a contract.

> **Note**
>
> Using configuration settings and BAdI implementations, you can influence the system in which a contract is created and the type of contract. We will explain the configuration options in Section 12.4.2.

A typical contract consists of header data that is applicable for the entire document and item data. You can maintain specific contract terms and conditions in the form of long texts. You can also include the physical contract documents as attachments. SAP SRM provides the ability to use attachments at both the header and item level. Some special features of SAP SRM contracts are:

▶ **GOA**: As defined earlier, a GOA is a centrally negotiated contract by the central purchasing department and can be used by all businesses and locations across the company, even if they use different procurement systems. A GOA is especially useful for central procurement departments in an organization that uses the center-led procurement model explained in Chapter 1. Note that GOAs cannot be distributed to the SAP SRM system itself and you cannot use GOAs in SAP SRM for requirements fulfillment.

▶ **Contract hierarchies**: Related contracts can be linked together with a parent-child relationship, forming contract hierarchies. This feature is especially useful when you negotiate with global suppliers for special prices and discounts, based on an aggregated global business relationship. That is, you can negotiate global terms and conditions in a global contract with a global supplier, define region-specific terms in a regional contract with the regional subsidiary of the global vendor, and then enter into more specific contracts with local conditions in a local contract with a local subsidiary of the vendor. You can then link all of these contracts using contract hierarchy and vendor hierarchy functionality in SAP SRM. The hierarchies can be used to define discounts based on aggregated release values for contracts within a hierarchy. The system automatically updates the aggregated release values at each hierarchy level. You can also define some contracts as header level contracts only, by selecting the Basic contract checkbox in the header. This feature facilitates defining only broad terms and conditions without specifying the items at a global level. The contract hierarchies functionality is available for operational contracts from SAP SRM 5.0 on.

▶ **Contract confidentiality**: You can define a contract as a confidential contract. Only users with specific authorization to view confidential contracts can view such contracts. This functionality is useful when you have very sensitive contracts that are accessible by only a few people in the organization. The purchaser can also authorize specific users to view or change certain parts of a contract. For example, you may authorize a technical officer to review the attachments specifying technical terms in a contract or you can authorize a finance colleague to verify the entire contract. These colleagues will have access to only the contract to which they are authorized. This functionality is available from SAP SRM 5.0 on.

▶ **Contract mass changes**: Contract mass change functionality allows purchasers to easily carry out changes in multiple contracts. You can also change all of the contracts in a hierarchy using this functionality. This functionality is available from SAP SRM 5.0 on.

▶ **Exchange rate thresholds**: You can specify the current exchange rate between the contract currency and additional purchase order currencies.

You can also specify lower and upper thresholds for these exchange rates. When a purchase order is created with reference to a contract, the system checks whether the current exchange rate in the purchase order is within the thresholds defined in the contract. If the exchange rate is not within the thresholds, the system issues a message to the user warning him of the exchange rate risk. This functionality is available from SAP SRM 2007 on.

▸ **Alerts at the contract level**: Predefined alerts regarding expiring contracts alert purchasers to renegotiate or renew contracts in a planned manner. The alerts were defined generically in SAP SRM 5.0 for all contracts. For example, an alert is triggered for contracts with release values exceeding 95% of the contract value. From SAP SRM 2007 on, purchasers can also define alert thresholds at the contract level. For example, they can define a 90% release value as the threshold for some contracts, and contracts expiring within next three months as the threshold for other contracts.

▸ **Advanced Search**: You can enable a full text search in the attachments and long texts in contracts using TREX from SAP SRM 5.0 on.

▸ **Novation:** Novation refers to the transfer of some or all of the contracts and purchase orders from one vendor to another due to a merger or buyout. It allows you to change the vendor number in a contract and define the new validity period of that contract.

Contract Approval

Based on the workflow configuration settings, once a contract is released, it is sent for approval by the responsible approver(s). The approver(s) receive a workflow notification for approval. Once all approvers approve, the contract is released for follow-on activities. Released contracts are stored in SAP SRM and can be used by purchasers to create purchase orders or process invoices. If the contract is a GOA, then it is distributed to backend systems according to the given distribution in the contract.

Special Contract Processes in SAP SRM

SAP SRM, being a complete procurement solution, offers the following special follow-on processes for contracts:

▸ **Distribution of GOA to backend procurement systems**
If the contract is of a GOA, then it is distributed to backend systems as specified in the GOA distribution. In this case, backend systems are used for procurement and assigning contracts to requirements for fulfillment.

▸ **Distribution of contract items to catalog**
If you want to facilitate easy usage of contracts for all users, you can distribute contract items as catalogs via SAP NetWeaver XI. To do so, you need to

select the checkbox in the contract header for distributing the contract items to the catalog. From SAP SRM 2007 on, you also have the option to select the items to be distributed at the contract item level.

12.3.2 Contract Fulfillment

Contract fulfillment refers to the fulfillment of procurement requirements using contracts. Figure 12.1 illustrates various contract fulfillment processes. In addition to the processes in Figure 12.1, fulfillment of GOAs actually occurs in the backend procurement systems to which a GOA is distributed. We will discuss fulfillment of requirements by assigning contracts within SAP SRM in this section. Contracts are used to fulfill requirements within SAP SRM in several ways, as follows:

▸ **Assignment within shopping cart**: Whenever a shopping cart is created for a product, the system determines all of the available contracts as sources of supply in the shopping cart. The requester can select one of the contracts and assign it. On ordering the shopping cart, a purchase order is created with reference to the contract.

▸ **Sourcing cockpit**: Purchase requisitions from backend ERP systems and shopping carts from SAP SRM are aggregated in the sourcing cockpit. The system proposes the available contracts for the requirements and purchasers can assign the most suitable contract. The contract can also be automatically assigned to requirements, creating a purchase order without the involvement of a purchaser. If there are multiple contracts, quota arrangements can be used to automatically assign contracts to requirements based on predefined quotas.

▸ **Catalogs from contracts**: Contract items can be distributed to SRM-MDM Catalog via SAP NetWeaver XI as catalogs. Requesters can simply search items in the catalog and order while ensuring contract compliance automatically.

12.3.3 Contract Monitoring

Contract monitoring refers to the monitoring of contract compliance to avoid noncontract maverick buying. While the fulfillment functionalities in SAP SRM takes care of automatic or semiautomatic contract compliance, monitoring reports alert purchasers of any other maverick spending in the organization. Alerts can also be configured to inform purchasers of shortly expiring contracts so that contracts are renegotiated on time. As sourcing is integrated with contracts in SAP SRM, you can create bid invitations or trigger a reverse auction directly from the contract for renegotiation. Integration with SAP NetWeaver Business Intelligence (SAP NetWeaver BI) provides purchasers with many predefined reports. You can also easily add other compliance reports to the predefined queries in SAP NetWeaver BI, and you can monitor the usage of GOAs across multiple backend procurement systems and drive compliance.

12.4 Implementation of Contract Management

In this section, the implementation of the business case described in the case study in Section 12.2 is explained. The business case requires implementation of the following scenarios:

- Plan-driven procurement for external requirements
- Sourcing
- Contract management

Implementation of external requirements and sourcing are described in Chapters 6 and 10 respectively. In addition to the previous scenarios, you can refer to Chapter 9 for the integration of SRM-MDM Catalog with SAP SRM contracts. In this section, we will discuss the implementation of contract management.

12.4.1 System Landscape

The suggested landscape for implementing the MMI case study is shown in Figure 12.2. The following components are part of a typical contract management implementation:

- SAP SRM 2007
- SAP NetWeaver BI 7.0: Optional. (Required for advanced contract compliance reports.)
- SAP NetWeaver Portal 7.0
- TREX 7.0: Optional. (Required for advanced search functionalities.)
- SAP NetWeaver XI 7.0: Optional. (Required for integration with SRM-MDM Catalog.)
- SRM-MDM Catalog 2.0: Optional. (Required when you want to distribute contract items to SRM-MDM Catalog.)
- SAP Solution Manager 4.0
- SAP Web Dispatcher
- SAP R/3 4.6B on (or SAP ERP): Backend ERP systems are required for GOA implementation.

> **Note**
>
> Always refer to the SAP Master Guide for the relevant SAP SRM version before deciding upon the final system landscape, installation sequence, and other important information.

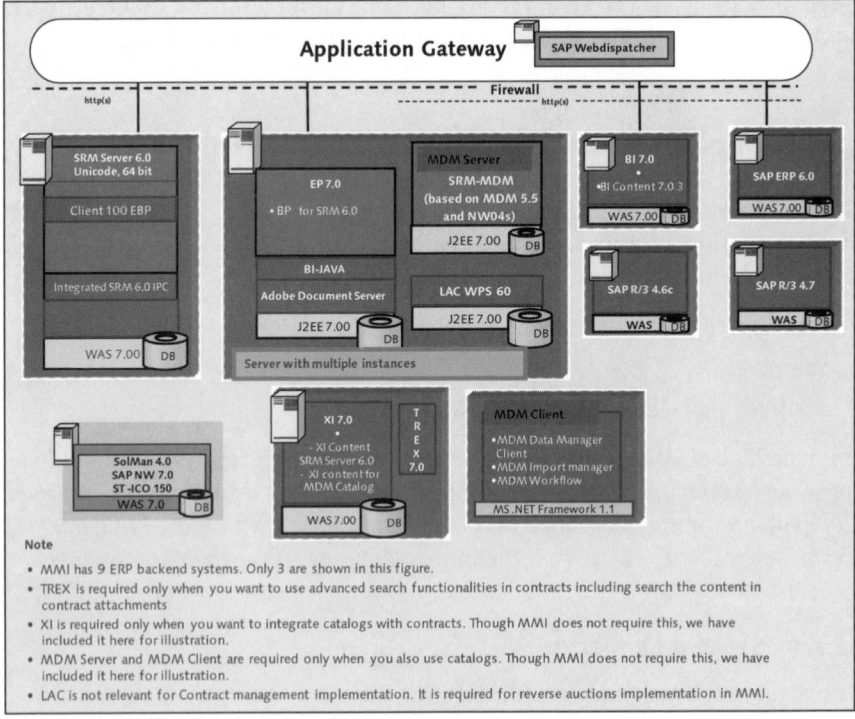

Note

- MMI has 9 ERP backend systems. Only 3 are shown in this figure.
- TREX is required only when you want to use advanced search functionalities in contracts including search the content in contract attachments
- XI is required only when you want to integrate catalogs with contracts. Though MMI does not require this, we have included it here for illustration.
- MDM Server and MDM Client are required only when you also use catalogs. Though MMI does not require this, we have included it here for illustration.
- LAC is not relevant for Contract management implementation. It is required for reverse auctions implementation in MMI.

Figure 12.2 Sample System Landscape for Contract Management at MMI

12.4.2 Configuration Options in Contract Management

In this section, we will explain the configuration options for processing contracts. Figure 12.3 illustrates the four process variants available in processing contracts:

1. **Contract/GOA from Sourcing**: A contract in SAP SRM can be created from the sourcing cockpit or from a winning bid. The contract created can be an operational contract or a GOA, depending on the transaction type. The transaction type is determined as follows:

   ▸ The system checks the value in the CT_PROC_TY attribute in the organizational plan. This value determines the transaction type for the contract.

   ▸ If no value exists in the attribute, the system checks whether follow-on document settings are configured in the transaction type settings. For example, you can configure a contract transaction type as a follow-on document in the bid invitation transaction type Request for Quotation (RFQ) settings.

   ▸ If no value exists in the previous two options, the system picks the first transaction type available for contracts in table BBPC_PROC_TYPE.

GOAs are distributed to one or more backend systems as a contract or scheduling agreement. The backend system should be SAP R/3 version 4.6B or higher. The document type in the backend system determines whether a contract or scheduling agreement should be created. You can map the SAP SRM contract data with the backend contract data or influence the contract data being distributed to the backend system using BAdI BBP_CTR_BE_CRE-ATE in SAP SRM or BADI BBP_CTR in SAP ERP.

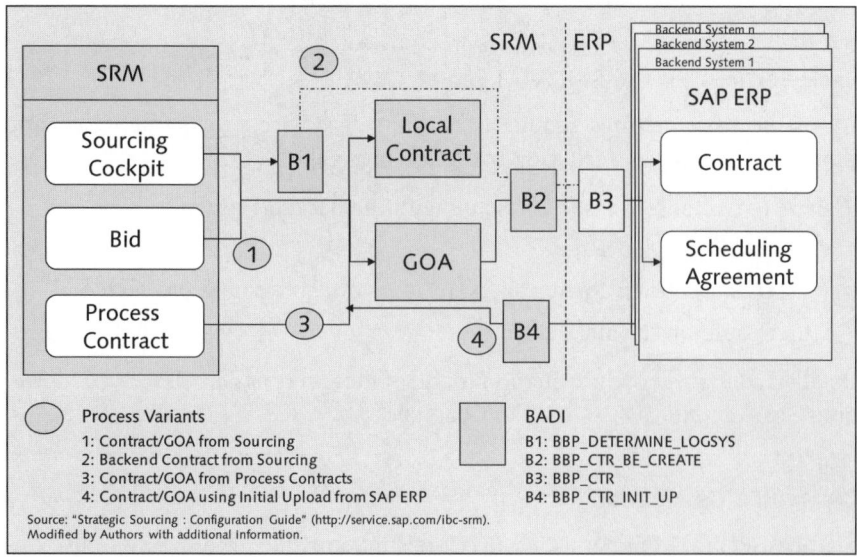

Figure 12.3 Configuration Options in Processing Contracts

2. **Backend Contract from Sourcing**: In the standard, the system creates only local SAP SRM contracts or GOAs. If you want to create a contract in the backend system when the contract data meets specific criteria, for example, for a backend purchasing organization, you need to implement BAdI BBP_DETERMINE_LOGSYS. If you implement the BAdI, the system checks the conditions in the BAdI before deciding whether the backend contract or local contract should be created. You can change the contract data before creating a contract in the backend system using BAdI BBP_CTR_BE_CREATE in SAP SRM or BAdI BBP_CTR in SAP ERP.

3. **Contract Creation Directly**: You can create a contract in SAP SRM directly using the Transaction 'Process Contracts.' The transaction type selected while creating the contract determines the contract type. GOAs are distributed to the backend systems as explained previously.

4. **Initial Upload from SAP ERP**: SAP provides the program BBP_CONTRACT_INITIAL_UPLOAD to upload the backend SAP R/3 contracts into SAP SRM during SAP SRM go-live. You can use BAdI BBP_CTR_INIT_UP in SAP SRM to

influence the contract data. Alternatively, you can also use BAdI BBP_CTR_INIT_UP_PI in SAP ERP. Note that this option should ideally be used for initial upload only.

12.4.3 Configuring the Contract Management Scenario

We will discuss the configuration settings required for contract management in this section.

Basic Settings for the SAP SRM Server

All of the basic settings required for the self-service procurement scenario should be configured, including the following:

- Basic technical settings to integrate with the backend systems
- Organizational plan setup
- Master data settings for suppliers, product categories, and products
- Other common technical settings

Detailed configuration information for all of these settings are described in Sections 3.4, 3.5, 3.6, 3.7, and 3.8 in Chapter 3.

Create RFC Destination

Maintain Remote Function Call (RFC) destinations for all other systems connected to SAP SRM using Transaction SM59, as follows:

- Create an RFC destination of type 3 for your backend ERP systems using Transaction SM59.
- Create an RFC destination of type TCP/IP for the TREX server, if you want to use TREX search.
- Create an RFC destination of type H for the SAP NetWeaver XI system, if you want to integrate catalogs with contracts.

> **Note**
>
> Refer to Chapter 3 for more details on these settings.

Define Backend Systems

Using the menu path **SPRO • SAP Implementation Guide • Supplier Relationship Management • SRM Server • Technical Basic Settings • Define Backend Systems**, perform the following:

1. Configure your backend ERP systems.

2. Configure an entry for TREX in the backend systems. In the Logical System column, you can enter a dummy entry, for example, TREX. Enter the RFC destination for the TREX server and select the system type for TREX using search help.

3. If you want to distribute contract items to a catalog, configure an entry for the catalog. Specify a dummy logical system, for example, CATALOG, and in the field System type, select CATALOG from search help. You can keep the RFC destination field blank.

Transaction Types

Transaction types in SAP SRM are similar to document types in SAP ERP. You can use transaction types to differentiate different types of contracts (e.g., project contracts, normal contracts, global contracts, global scheduling, agreements etc.). Companies use transaction types for the following reasons:

- To differentiate different types of contracts
- To define different number ranges
- As a basis for setting up authorizations
- As search criteria
- To categorize contracts in reports and analyses
- To synchronize with contract document types in SAP ERP

SAP delivers two transaction types in the standard — PCTR for operational contracts and GCTR for GOAs. Transaction type configuration involves the following steps:

1. Determine the transaction types required. If you want to do an initial upload of contracts, ensure that contract document types in SAP ERP are created as transaction types in SAP SRM. If you do not want to create SAP ERP document types in SAP SRM, then you need to implement BAdI BBP_CTR_INIT_UP in SAP SRM or BBP_CTR_INIT_UP_PI in SAP ERP.

2. If you want to use the contract renegotiation functionality, determine the bid invitation document type to be used for calling tenders for renegotiation.

3. Configure number ranges using the menu path **SPRO • SAP Implementation Guide • Supplier Relationship Management • SRM Server • Cross-Application Basic Settings • Number Ranges • SRM Server Number Ranges • Define Number Ranges for Purchase Contracts** or Transaction code BBP_NUM_PC. Configure number ranges for each contract transaction type.

4. Configure transaction types using the menu path **SPRO • SAP Implementation Guide • Supplier Relationship Management • SRM Server • Cross-Application Basic Settings • Define Transaction Types**.

Configure transaction types for object BUS2000113. Refer to Chapter 5 for a detailed explanation of the fields in this setting. Configure bid invitation transaction types to be used for renegotiation in "Transaction Types of Follow-on Documents." Note that GOAs can be distributed to SAP ERP as either contract or scheduling agreements. If you want to use GOA to create both contracts and scheduling agreements, you should create at least two transaction types for the GOA.

5. If you want to create the backend contracts using BAdI BBP_DETERMINE_LOGSYS or if the transaction type is of type GOA, then configure similar transaction types in the backend SAP ERP system as document types. Ensure that backend external number ranges for the document type and internal number ranges specified in the SAP SRM transaction type are the same.

You should configure these settings in backend SAP ERP system. In SAP ERP, contracts can be defined as contracts or scheduling agreements. Maintain the document types as required. If you want to use these contracts for service items also, ensure that item category 'D' is allowed for the document type.

To define document types for contracts, use the menu path **SPRO • Materials Management • Purchasing • Contract • Define Document Types**. To define document types for scheduling agreements, use the menu path **SPRO • Materials Management • Purchasing • Scheduling Agreement • Define Document Types**.

Activate Version Control for Documents

Version control enables purchasers to keep track of changes made to documents. This is an optional but recommended setting. Use the menu path **SPRO • SAP Implementation Guide • Supplier Relationship Management • SRM Server • Cross-Application Basic Settings • Switch on Version Control for Purchasing Documents** to turn on version control for contracts. You can also use BAdI BBP_VERSION_CONTROL to influence version control.

Settings for Text Schema

You can maintain contract clauses as long texts in SAP SRM contracts. You can define custom text types, bundle them in a text schema, and assign the text schema to a contract transaction type. For a detailed discussion on defining and using text schemas, refer to Chapter 5. If you want to distribute the long texts in GOAs to the backend ERP system, you need to implement BAdI BBP_LONGTEXT_BADI to provide mapping of SAP SRM text IDs to ERP text IDs.

Pricing

SAP SRM pricing configuration is explained in detail in Chapter 5. In this section, we will discuss a few recommended settings for contracts:

▶ **Discount on aggregated release value**
If you want to use discounts based on aggregated release value, ensure that condition type 01AG exists. If you use contract hierarchies, the system determines the discounts according to the aggregated release value within the contract hierarchy up to seven hierarchy levels. This functionality is available only from SAP SRM 5.0 on. The field Access Sequence should have value 01HI defined, and the field Scale Basis Formula should have a value of 15000 defined. Include condition type 01AG in calculation schema 0100 and condition group 0100. If you want to define new aggregated release value discounts, you should copy condition type 01AG. Note that this functionality is not applicable for GOAs.

▶ **SAP ERP condition types in SAP SRM**
If you want to perform an initial contract upload from SAP ERP, you need to map the ERP condition types to SAP SRM condition types. You can either create the same condition types in SAP SRM or implement BAdI BBP_CTR_INIT_UP. You can also implement BAdI BBP_CTR_INIT_UP_PI in the SAP ERP system. For example, you can create condition types P000 and PRS in SAP SRM by copying 01CT. Remember to include condition type 01AG in calculation schema 0100 and condition group 0100.

▶ **New condition types**
If you define new condition types, ensure that they are included in the appropriate condition groups. Condition groups relevant for operational contracts are 0100, 01CO, and 01HD. Condition groups relevant for GOAs are 01CC, 01CP, and 01CH. Remember to use condition table SAP016 if you want to define location-dependent conditions. You should refer to the IMG documentation for condition groups for more details.

▶ **SAP SRM condition types in SAP ERP**
This setting should be configured in the backend SAP ERP system. If you are using GOAs, you should create SAP SRM condition types (e.g., 01CT, 01RH, 01RA, etc.) in the SAP ERP system also, using Transaction M/06. If you want to use services in GOAs, create these conditions in services pricing, too, using Transaction M/10. Configure the new conditions in the relevant pricing procedures in SAP ERP using Transactions M/08 and M/12.

We strongly recommend that you test the new conditions by creating contracts directly in SAP ERP with the same conditions that you use in SRM GOAs. Also, test creating a purchase order with reference to such contracts. Alternatively, you can map SAP SRM condition types to SAP ERP condition types in BAdI BBP_CTR in SAP ERP or BAdI-BBP_CTR_BE_CREATE in SAP SRM.

Contract Alerts

Contract alerts are used to proactively send messages to a purchaser when a predefined event occurs. Alerts can be configured to send messages for shortly expiring contracts or expired contracts. In SAP SRM 4.0, these alert notifications are sent using workflow WS10400022. From SAP SRM 5.0 on, these alerts are processed by SRM Alert Management. In this section, we will explain the settings for contract alerts using SRM Alert Management:

> **Note**
>
> SRM Alert Management is a generic alert framework that can be used with any SAP SRM object to trigger alerts on specific events. Although we explain the settings here with reference to contracts, you can explore the predefined alerts for other objects and trigger them as required.

- **Define event schema**

  For all SAP SRM business objects multiple events are delivered in the standard. In this setting, you can bundle the events for which notifications or alerts need to be sent and create an *event schema*. You can also use an SAP-delivered event schema, in which case you do not need to configure any additional settings here. You can refer to the IMG documentation for more details on event schemas.

  To define an event schema, follow the menu path **SPRO • SAP Implementation Guide • Supplier Relationship Management • SRM Server • Cross-Application Basic Settings • Event and Event Schema for Alert Management • Define Event Schema** and select the business object BUS2000113 for contracts. Click on Event Schema. Copy the schema CTR to create your own schema. Select your new schema and click on Event Control to see the events in your schema. Delete events that are not required and save the settings. If you want to create multiple event schemas, repeat the steps to define additional schemas.

> **Note**
>
> - You can only use SAP-delivered events in event schemas. If you define new events, they will be considered modifications by the SAP system. You can activate the new events using BAdI BBP_ALERTING. Implement SAP Note 984184 to activate the BAdI. Also, see SAP Note 865249 for important information on new alerts.
> - You can change alert long texts in Transaction ALRTCATDEF.

- **Assign event schema to transaction types**

  The event schema will be active only when you assign it to a transaction type. In the IMG setting Define Transaction Types, select the contract transaction type and assign the event schema defined for contracts. If you have defined multiple event schemas, then you can assign different schemas to different transaction types.

▸ **Schedule program BBP_CONTRACT_CHECK**
Program BBP_CONTRACT_CHECK checks the expiration of the contract validity date and overrun of the target quantity or value thresholds to provide the events GOING_TO_EXPIRE and THRESHOLD_EXCEEDED. Schedule this program to run periodically, for example, every 15 minutes, using Transaction SM36.

▸ **Enter alert threshold data for contracts**
This setting is available from SAP SRM 2007 on. The threshold values to trigger expiring contracts and contract overspend can be defined for each contract transaction type. You can define multiple thresholds for each transaction type. The threshold values defined here are used to trigger alerts. These values can be overwritten for a particular contract by entering the thresholds directly in the contract document.

Setting up TREX Search

You need TREX set up only if you want to enable full text search for long texts and attachments in contracts. You need to install the TREX Server and configure the settings in this section to enable advanced search functionality:

1. Create an RFC Destination of type TCP/IP for TREX Server using Transaction SM59

2. Maintain an entry for TREX in the Define Backend Systems setting.

3. Activate full text search by executing the program BBP_TREX_INDEX_ ADMIN using Transaction SE38. You need authorization from S_TREX_ADM to execute this program. We strongly recommend that you read the program documentation at least once. The selection screen values for this program are as follows:

   ▸ **Business object**: Enter "BUS2000113."

   ▸ **Subtype business object**: Enter "CC" (for GOAs) or " " (blank for operational contracts)

   ▸ **Action for SRM TREX index**: Select the appropriate value from search help. For example, you would specify "A" for the initial index generation.

   ▸ **Bundle size for indexing**: Enter "10." Bundle size affects performance. The size indicates the number of documents that will be updated in one pass. If there are a large number of documents, then this size may be reduced to improve performance.

Workflows in Contract Management

Please refer to Chapter 8 for workflow settings.

Settings to Create Backend Contracts

You can create contracts in the backend ERP system from SAP SRM by implementing BAdI BBP_DETERMINE_LOGSYS or by distributing GOA. The backend ERP system should be SAP R/3 version 4.6B or higher.

► **Settings in the SAP SRM System to Create Backend Contracts**
The following steps have to be performed to configure the required settings in the SAP SRM system to create backend contracts:

 ► Configure an RFC destination for the backend system.

 ► Configure transaction types and number ranges for contracts.

 ► Ensure that you have downloaded the master data from the backend SAP ERP system for materials, services, material groups, vendors, currencies, and payment terms. Master data replication is explained in Chapter 3.

 ► Ensure that the organizational plan contains backend purchasing organizations and backend purchasing groups.

 ► Assign the transaction type for contracts to attribute CT_PROC_TY in the organizational plan for the responsible purchasing group node.

 ► Ensure that you have used the same condition types and text IDs as in the backend system. Alternatively, the data should be mapped using BAdI BBP_CTR in SAP ERP or BBP_CTR_BE_CREATE in SAP SRM. Text IDs can be mapped by implementing BBP_LONGTEXT_BADI.

 ► Implement BAdI BBP_DETERMINE_LOGSYS to create backend contracts from the sourcing cockpit or a winning bid.

 ► To receive contract release order information from the backend system in the case of GOAs, you need to perform two steps in SAP SRM. You need to create a port of type tRFC and assign an RFC destination of the backend system using Transaction WE21, and you need to specify inbound parameter BLAREL with process code BLAR in the partner profile for the backend system using Transaction WE20.

 ► Activate grouping logic for locations in GOAs using the menu path **SPRO • SAP Implementation Guide • Supplier Relationship Management • SRM Server • Cross-Application Basic Settings • Activate Grouping Logic for Locations in GOA**. Click on the **New Entries** button and select the checkbox for **Activate grouping logic for locations in GOA**. This setting enables creation of a single backend contract for all GOA items with the same release purchasing organization but different locations. This is available only from SAP SRM 2007 on. In earlier versions, the system used to create multiple backend contracts, if the locations are different in GOAs.

▶ **Settings in the Backend SAP ERP System to Create Backend Contracts**
The following steps need to be performed to configure the required settings
in the backend SAP ERP system to create backend contracts:

  ▶ Configure document types for contracts and scheduling agreements. The
  document type should be same as that of the SAP SRM transaction type.
  Alternatively, use BAdI BBP_CTR in SAP ERP to map the SAP ERP document types to SAP SRM transaction types. Refer to the settings described
  under 'Transaction types' in this chapter.

  ▶ Ensure that the external number ranges for contracts are the same as the
  internal number ranges used with SAP SRM contracts.

  ▶ Configure the pricing configuration for purchasing and external services
  as described in 'Pricing' in this chapter.

  ▶ If you want to use services, configure an internal number range for
  number range object BBP_SRV using Transaction SNRO.

  ▶ Ensure that you use the same master data in both systems for materials,
  services, material groups, vendors, currencies, condition types, payment
  terms, and text IDs. Alternatively, the data should be mapped using BAdI
  BBP_CTR in SAP ERP or BBP_CTR_BE_CREATE in SAP SRM.

  ▶ Assign message type BLAORD to process code BLAO using Transaction
  WE42.

  ▶ Assign message type COND_A to process code COND using Transaction
  WE42.

  ▶ Using Transaction WE20, create an ALE partner profile for partner type
  LS with the logical system being the sending SAP SRM system. Configure
  inbound parameters for message type BLAORD with process code BLAO
  and message type COND_A with process code COND.

  ▶ To update GOA release data in SAP SRM, the backend SAP ERP system
  should send the contract release order information to SAP SRM. You need
  to configure two settings in SAP ERP to achieve this. You need to create a
  port of type tRFC and assign the RFC destination of the SAP SRM system
  using Transaction WE21. You also need to configure outbound parameter
  BLAREL with IDoc basis type BLAREL02 in the partner profile for the SAP
  SRM system using Transaction WE20. Under Outbound Options, select
  the receiver port that refers to the SAP SRM system.

  ▶ Implement SAP Note 641919.

  ▶ If you are creating backend contracts from external requirements, then
  some restrictions apply. First, contract limits are not supported, and second, backend sources of supply (info records and backend contracts) cannot be assigned.

> **Troubleshooting Tip**
>
> ► You might see the message 'Contract xxxxxx was created' in SAP SRM, but the contract was not actually created in SAP R/3 or SAP ERP. Follow the instructions in SAP Note 609222 to identify and resolve the problem.
>
> ► You can use Transaction BBP_CTR_MON to monitor errors in the distribution of contracts to the backend system.

Settings for Global Outline Agreements

See Settings for Creating Backend Contracts for more information on GOAs. Also, refer to SAP Note 646903 for tips and tricks on GOA.

Lock an Expired Contract

Implement BAdI BBP_CTR_STAT to lock an expired contract. In the BAdI, you can define when exactly an expired contract or shortly expiring contract should be locked. Locked contracts will not be available as a source of supply in sourcing.

Maintain Log Object for Initial Upload of Controls

This functionality is available only from SAP SRM 5.0 on. Configure the setting if you want to use initial upload of contracts from SAP ERP. Maintain log object BBP_CTR_INIT_UPLOAD using Transaction SLG0. This will facilitate the error reporting during upload in Transaction SLG1.

Contract-Enhanced Authorizations for Purchasers

This functionality is available only from SAP SRM 5.0 on. Contract-enhanced authorizations allow specific purchasers to perform the following special tasks:

► Authorize other users, who generally do not have authorization to contracts or GOAs, to modify or display certain sections of a contract.

► Process confidential contracts.

Regular operational purchasers will not have authorizations to perform these functions. Perform the following steps to configure the settings to authorize specific purchasers with enhanced authorizations:

1. Activate enhanced authorizations for contracts using the menu path **SPRO · SAP Implementation Guide · Supplier Relationship Management · SRM Server · Cross-Application Basic Settings · Activate Enhanced Authorizations for Contracts**. Click on the **New Entries** button and select the **Authorization Object BBP_CTR_2 Act** checkbox to activate enhanced authorizations.

2. Create new roles using Transaction PFCG. Configure authorizations for authorization object BBP_CTR_2 as required. You can create multiple roles with different sets of authorizations. For example, you can create a role to process confidential contracts and another role to process normal contracts.

3. Assign the new roles to selected contract users (purchasers).

Assign Role to Users

Assign the role SAP_BBP_STAL_STRAT_PURCHASER to all users who process contracts. If you want to restrict authorizations by transaction type, purchasing group, etc., copy the role SAP_EC_BBP_ST_PURCHASER and create your own roles using Transaction PFCG. Assign the new role and SAP_EC_BBP_ EMPLOYEE to contract users.

Contract-Enhanced Authorizations for Employees

This functionality is available only from SAP SRM 5.0 on. Purchasers with contract-enhanced authorizations can authorize employees who do not have authorization to contracts or GOAs to display or change certain sections in a specific contract. This functionality is provided to let expert employees review contracts without compromising confidentiality. To do so, perform the following steps:

1. Create and assign new roles in SAP SRM 5.0. Employee users normally have only the role SAP_BBP_STAL_EMPLOYEE assigned and will not be able to see contract transactions in the SAP SRM browser menu. Therefore, create a new role that has only menu options for processing contracts using Transaction PFCG. To do so, on the Menu tab (while creating the new role in PFCG), insert Transactions BBP_CTR_MAINCC and BBP_CTR_MAIN. On the Authorizations tab, ensure that you do not give authorizations to any authorization objects. Generate the role and assign it to the selected employee users. These employees can now see transactions to process contracts in the SAP SRM browser menu.

2. Assign portal roles in SAP SRM 2007. In SAP SRM 2007, you do not need to create new roles to see menu entries for processing contracts. Simply assign the strategic purchaser portal role to the employee users. In the portal, they can then see the menu options to process contracts.

3. Authorize users to change conditions. A normal employee user can be authorized to change conditions in a specific contract by the purchaser. However, the employee will not be able to process the contracts as condition changes require authorizations for authorization object /SAPCND/CM. Create a role with authorizations for this object and assign it to the appropriate employee users.

Define Hierarchies

You can activate contract hierarchies, vendor hierarchies, and product category hierarchies in this setting. To activate hierarchies, you use the contract hierarchy functionality using the menu path **SPRO • SAP Implementation Guide • Supplier Relationship Management • SRM Server • Cross-Application Basic Settings • Activate Hierarchies for Product Categories, Vendors and Contracts**. Note that the setting should not be reset once activated. Select the checkboxes to activate contract hierarchies, product category hierarchies, and vendor hierarchies.

Delete Mass Change Work Packages

If you use the mass change functionality, we strongly recommend that you schedule program BBP_CONTRACT_MASS_UPDATE to archive and delete mass change work packages periodically. For example, you can schedule this program to run weekly and delete work packages older than 10 days. Use Transaction SM36 to schedule the program.

Transfer Contract Attachments to SAP ERP

You can transfer attachments in GOAs to the backend SAP ERP as documents. You need to follow these steps to configure the Document Management System (DMS) settings:

1. Define document type CTR using the menu path **SPRO • Cross-Application Components • Document Management • Control Data • Define Document Types**, or Transaction code DC10. Verify whether document type CTR exists. If it does not exist, create a new entry by clicking on the **New Entries** button.

2. Enter a description.

3. Select the checkbox Use KPro.

4. Configure an external number range. Ensure that the number range contains the number range of contracts. You can click on the **Number Ranges** button to configure new number ranges.

5. In the field Number Exit, enter "MCDOKZNR."

6. In the field Vers.No.Incr., enter "1," to indicate that the new document versions will be incremented by 1.

7. In the Field Selection section, for Document Status, select **Suppress Field** from search help.

8. Save the new document type.

9. Select the new document type and click on **Define Object Links** in the left pane. Click on the **New Entries** button.

10. Enter the Object as "EKPO," and the Screen Number as "248."

11. Save the entries.

12. Define the workstation application. Configure the settings to define the type of attachments (e.g., Microsoft Word) and the workstation application to read the attachments. If they do not exist, you should configure entries for workstation applications WRD, URL, and XLS.

Settings for Contract Renegotiation

Contract renegotiation involves the creation of a bid invitation from the contract. Once the bidding process is completed, a winner is determined. You can either update the existing contract (renewal) or create a new contract from the winning bid. You need to maintain follow-on transaction types in transaction type settings for both bid invitation and contract. In the standard system, RFCR is given as the follow-on transaction type for contract type PCTR, and PCTR is given as the follow-on transaction type in bid invitation type RFCR.

12.5 Summary

In this chapter, you learned about the importance of contract management and the features of SAP SRM contract management. SAP SRM GOAs facilitate maintaining a central contract repository for organizations with global operations. SAP SRM enables organizations to ensure contract compliance in a variety of ways, thanks to the integration with backend execution systems. In this chapter, you also learned how to implement contract management in SAP SRM and how to integrate SAP SRM contracts with backend SAP ERP systems. With this chapter, we have completed all of the purchaser-side scenarios supported by SRM EBP. In Chapters 13 and 14, we will discuss supplier enablement using SRM SUS.

SAP SRM Supplier Self-Services (SUS) offers collaboration capabilities that support and enhance relationships while making integration with suppliers of all sizes economical and easy to manage.

— mySAP SRM Statement of Direction 2004

13   Supplier Self-Services with Materials Management Integration

Maintaining a mutually beneficial long-term relationship with suppliers is the dream of every purchaser. Having successful long-term relationships not only reduces transaction costs but also provides an opportunity to tap the innovation capabilities of suppliers. Companies in industries like automotive and high tech, which depend on suppliers to provide the majority of components and systems, nurture strong relationships with their suppliers. Furthermore, the pace with which a company can launch new products has become a competitive differentiator in many industries. Companies have realized that they need to collaborate and co-innovate with their suppliers to service the ever-increasing demands of customers. Traditionally, phone, fax, courier, and email are the most common tools used for collaboration with suppliers. A few large organizations use a more efficient Electronic Data Interchange (EDI) to connect to their large suppliers. However, EDI is expensive and suitable only for large organizations. SAP Supplier Enablement provides a simple and economical way to connect to suppliers of all sizes and the technical capabilities for real-time collaboration.

Supplier enablement enables collaboration with suppliers in all supplier-facing activities starting with supplier self-registration, design collaboration, collaborative replenishment, and order collaboration. The focus of this chapter is order collaboration using Supplier Relationship Management (SRM) Supplier Self-Services (SUS). We will discuss supplier enablement briefly in Section 13.1. In Section 13.2, the customer case study will describe the collaboration challenges faced by an automotive manufacturer and how SRM SUS helps companies with supplier enablement. In Section 13.3, we will provide an overview of the functionalities of SRM SUS in more detail, before discussing the implementation of SUS in Section 13.4. We have also included a mapping of special enhanced scenarios that are relevant to many customers in Section 13.4.5.

13.1 Supplier Enablement Overview

Most, if not all, organizations have part of their processes fulfilled by supplier organizations. For example, in a sourcing process, requests for quotation are received by suppliers and bids are submitted by suppliers. In a traditional procurement system, requests for quotation are sent by fax or mail and suppliers in turn submit their bids using fax or mail. Then these bids have to be entered into the procurement system by procurement staff. This means two to three layers of inefficiency are built into the process. Fax or mail communication is error prone, time consuming and environment unfriendly. Bids are entered twice in the system — once by suppliers and again by buyers. Supplier enablement eliminates these inefficiencies by enabling suppliers to perform their respective activities in the procurement system of buyers. This paves the way for real-time collaboration and has the potential to reduce cycle times drastically. The supplier activities enabled by SAP applications are:

- ▶ **Supplier self-registration**: Organizations can provide a link on their websites for new potential suppliers across the globe to register. Interested suppliers register themselves by filling an online form and associated category-specific questionnaire. Purchasers verify the details provided by potential suppliers and approve suitable suppliers. Accepted suppliers can then participate in sourcing activities of the organization. Supplier self-registration is explained in detail in Chapter 10.

- ▶ **Design collaboration**: Design collaboration enables companies to involve suppliers in the early stages of design, minimizing risk and improving the success rate of new designs. With the help of the SAP Product Lifecycle Management (PLM) cFolders application, teams across organizations share design documents online, mark up and redline 2D and 3D drawings, and manage versions easily. We briefly discussed bidding with collaboration using cFolders in Chapter 10, but a detailed explanation of an implementation of design collaboration is beyond the scope of this book.

- ▶ **Collaborative project management**: Using SAP PLM cProjects, companies can also extend the project management processes to their suppliers, ensuring that projects are completed on time. This enables companies to work closely with their trusted suppliers in a new product design project, helping them launch new products more quickly. Integration of cProjects with SAP SRM is discussed briefly in Chapter 17. A detailed discussion of collaborative project management, however, is beyond the scope of this book. Readers are encouraged to learn more by visiting the SAP help portal at *http://help.sap.com*.

- ▶ **Sourcing collaboration**: The SAP SRM bidding process enables suppliers to receive requests for quotation (or requests for proposal) and auction information online. Suppliers can also submit their bids online. The bidding process is explained in detail in Chapter 10.

▶ **Collaborative replenishment**: Companies can pursue Supplier Managed Inventory (SMI) initiatives using SAP Supply Chain Management (SCM) so that purchasers can provide inventory, demand, and consumption data to suppliers. Suppliers take the responsibility of maintaining the stock levels based on this information and according to predefined agreements.

▶ **Order Collaboration**: It is a well-known fact that a typical purchaser spends most of his time performing follow-up tasks, which include order acknowledgement, delivery confirmation, invoice receipt, and payment. Order collaboration using SRM SUS facilitates real-time exchange of documents between purchasers and suppliers. Order collaboration can also be achieved by connecting the procurement system with the supplier's system using SAP NetWeaver XI. It can also be achieved by using the SAP Supplier Network, if your supplier is part of the network. SRM SUS is integrated with the organization's procurement system and behaves like a supplier's Customer Relationship Management (CRM) system hosted by the organization. In this chapter, we will discuss the implementation of SRM SUS with Materials Management (MM) as the procurement system. We will discuss the implementation of SRM SUS with SRM EBP as the procurement system in Chapter 14.

▶ **Invoicing exception collaboration**: Invoicing exceptions and collaborative invoice exception management have been explained in Chapter 7.

Let us now look at a customer case study to explain the business problems addressed by SRM SUS.

13.2 Case Study: Supplier Collaboration

Concept Auto Inc. is a leading automobile producer in India with annual revenues of USD 2 billion. Like all automotive companies, Concept Auto Inc. finds that nurturing collaborative relationships with suppliers is crucial to success in the fiercely competitive auto industry. Long-term relationships help increase productivity, efficiency, and reliability along with lowering costs and improving quality. Concept Auto Inc. takes pride in being a leader in deploying the latest technologies to effectively collaborate with suppliers. The company introduced an in-house developed portal in its attempts to connect to suppliers. The portal provided information on orders, schedules, and payment status to suppliers based on the data extracted from the company's four SAP ERP systems. Although this is a step toward collaboration with suppliers using the Internet, Concept Auto Inc. wanted to do more. They realized that the following problems still needed to be addressed:

▶ Purchasers still spend a lot of time chasing suppliers for order confirmations and delivery information. The use of phone and fax communication to get order status is still very high.

▶ Better information on deliveries reduces the uncertainty in planning of direct materials. Better planning helps the company reduce inventories with a direct positive impact on the bottom line.

▶ Errors in data entry during goods receipts and invoices are detrimental to healthy supplier relationships. Purchasers and suppliers also spend significant time in resolving such disputes.

▶ Non-receipt of invoices in time results in delays in payments to suppliers.

▶ Concept Auto Inc. wants to take advantage of cash discounts offered by suppliers for early payments.

▶ Concept Auto Inc. wants to have real-time bi-directional information flow between purchasers and suppliers and they want their suppliers to perform transactions on the system that update Concept Auto Inc.'s SAP ERP systems in real time.

The indicated challenges can be eliminated if suppliers can transmit order acknowledgements, delivery confirmations, and invoices online that directly update the respective transactions in SAP ERP. After scouting the market for a suitable solution, Concept Auto Inc. zeroed in on SAP SRM SUS for the following reasons:

▶ SAP is a tried and trusted vendor.

▶ SRM SUS integrates seamlessly with SAP ERP. Moreover, SRM SUS provides a single user interface for suppliers with order details from all four ERP systems.

▶ Suppliers can perform transactions to update order status with relevant details, which in turn updates the SAP ERP system relevant for the order.

▶ SRM SUS is easy to implement and scalable. SAP consultants informed Concept Auto Inc. that the solution can be implemented within three months for the first set of vendors. Concept Auto Inc. wants to start with 50 top vendors and then scale the system up to 1,200 suppliers within 3-4 months.

▶ SRM SUS is flexible and customizable. Concept Auto Inc. liked the fact that they can very easily add more fields, as they need about 20 additional fields to capture delivery and tax details.

The implementation of the business scenario described in this case study is explained in Section 13.4. In Section 13.3, we will take a look at the functionalities offered by SRM SUS.

13.3 SRM SUS with SAP Materials Management — Overview of Functionalities

SRM SUS helps companies publish orders from SAP Materials Management (MM) to a system accessible via an Internet browser interface where suppliers can access the orders and perform follow-up activities. Suppliers just need an Internet connection and a computer with a browser to access the buying company's orders and perform order follow-up tasks. Figure 13.1 illustrates the order collaboration process using SRM SUS with SAP MM as the procurement system. This process is commonly referred to as the MM-SUS scenario.

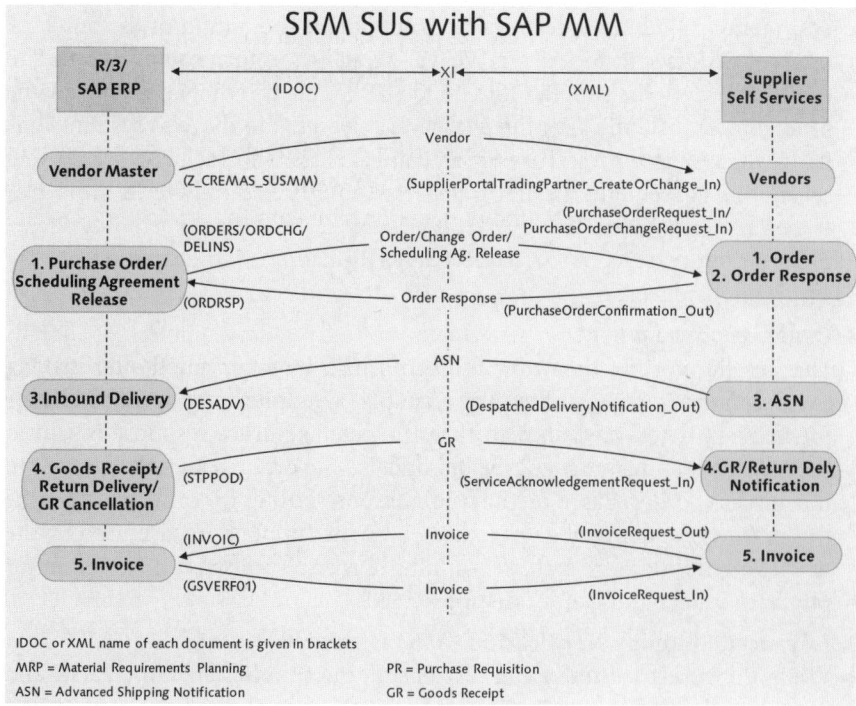

Figure 13.1 MM-SUS Scenario

As you can see in Figure 13.1, the document exchange between SAP SRM and MM is achieved via SAP NetWeaver Exchange Infrastructure (XI). SAP MM sends out documents to SAP NetWeaver XI in IDoc form. SAP NetWeaver XI converts the IDocs into XML and sends them to SUS. Similarly, SUS sends documents to SAP NetWeaver XI in XML form and SAP NetWeaver XI converts the documents to IDoc form before sending them to SAP MM.

> **Note**
>
> The MM-SUS scenario is used only for materials. If you want to use the scenario for services, refer to SAP Note 868192.

The MM-SUS scenario involves the following steps:

1. **Purchase order or Scheduling Agreement Release (SAR) is created**
   A purchase order is created and approved in SAP MM. The purchase order can be created directly or with reference to a purchase requisition. Alternatively, Material Requirements Planning (MRP) creates a SAR (delivery schedule based on scheduling agreement). A confirmation control key (say, 0001) is assigned to the purchase order item to ensure receipt of order acknowledgement and inbound delivery from suppliers. The output of the purchase order or SAR is sent to SAP NetWeaver XI, which in turn routes it to SUS to create an order. The supplier logs on to SUS via the Internet and can view the order almost instantly after the purchaser released it in the MM system. Similarly, changes to the purchase order, if any, are transmitted to SUS. Note that scheduling agreements are not transferred to SUS and only SARs are transferred in the standard. However, it is possible to configure scheduling agreement output and custom SAP NetWeaver XI mappings to enable scheduling agreement transfer.

2. **Order response is sent**
   The supplier verifies the order and confirms it by accepting it after making the necessary changes, if any. For example, a supplier may want to change the delivery date based on realistic estimates. The order response is sent to the MM system instantaneously and updates the order acknowledgement in the purchase order. Based on the configuration settings for confirmation control in MM, the delivery dates indicated by the supplier are also used by the next MRP run for more realistic planning. Order response is only relevant for purchase orders and is not relevant for SAR.

3. **Advanced Shipping Notification (ASN) is created**
   When the goods are ready and dispatched, the supplier creates an ASN and provides all delivery details. The ASN creates the inbound delivery in SAP MM, thus informing the purchaser of the incoming receipts.

> **Note**
>
> If you implement the SUS India Localization add-on, the supplier can also intimate the excise tax details, which update the excise invoice details in SAP MM. SUS India Localization is only relevant for India-based companies and is currently available for SAP SRM version 5.0 only and from SAP R/3 version 4.7 on. More details on India Localization can be found in SAP Note 906672.

4. **Goods Receipt (GR) is created**
   A goods receipt is created with reference to the inbound delivery when the goods arrive at the buying company's stores. All of the details from inbound delivery are copied to the GR document, making data entry easier. If the goods are rejected in quality inspection, a return delivery is created to return the goods to the supplier. GR or return delivery information is sent to SUS as GR notification. The GR notification feature is available from SAP SRM version 5.0

on and SAP ERP 6.0 (formerly ERP 2005). You can refer to consulting note 1026638 to enable GR notifications in SAP ERP versions below ERP 2005.

5. **Invoice is created**

An invoice can be created either in SUS by the supplier or captured in SAP MM by the purchaser. Invoices created by suppliers in SUS are transferred to SAP MM as logistics invoices and verification is done by the system. Suppliers can create invoices with reference to ASN or GR notification or purchase order. If an invoice is created by the buyer in SAP MM, it is transferred to SUS, providing visibility to the supplier. Note that in the standard, invoice creation in SUS is not supported for SAR. However, you can customize this in a customer implementation.

In addition to the aforementioned, SUS analytics facilitates sharing of a variety of reports, such as account status with suppliers using SAP NetWeaver Business Intelligence (SAP NetWeaver BI). The following reports are delivered in the standard:

- **Contracts**: Suppliers can display a list of contracts that will expire shortly. This list enables them to proactively start discussion on renewal of contracts. Suppliers can also display the status of their contracts and release values against each contract.

- **Procurement values**: Provides suppliers with the history of different order values from different perspectives.

- **Supplier evaluation**: Suppliers can see their own performance and scores for various evaluation criteria. This helps suppliers take corrective action and improve their performance.

- **Consignment stocks**: Suppliers can view their stock at the customer's location as consignment stock. Suppliers can use this information to check and control stock levels.

You can also define additional reports in SAP NetWeaver BI and share them with your supplier.

Useful Notes
586466: Follow-on document control as per confirmation control key.
756472 and 1068470: MM-SUS processing of purchase order response for rejected items.
793669: FAQ SUS in SAP SRM 4.0 with SAP NetWeaver XI 3.0.
800866: SUS-MM invoice with delivery costs.
886307: Creating follow-on documents.
858662: Report RPODDELVRY to synchronize goods receipts in SUS.
1026638: GR notifications in SUS with ERP versions < ERP 2005.
921368: Different price unit of measure in MM-SUS.

Useful Notes
830705: Customer texts in SUS and XML mapping.
1075345: User exit information.
780923: Transferring attachments in SAP MM to SUS.
1028264: Consulting solutions in SUS.
868192: Consulting solution for SUS-MM service procurement.
906672: SRM SUS India Localization.
1073400: Tax Calculation in Invoice for SUS India Localization.
456127: FAQ: EDI in Purchasing
Also, check other notes under component XX-CSC-IN-SRM for SUS-India localization-specific problem resolution.

Let us now look at the implementation of the MM-SUS scenario at Concept Auto Inc.

13.4   Implementation of Supplier Self-Services with Materials Management Integration

In this section, we will explain the implementation of the MM-SUS scenario as outlined in our case study company Concept Auto Inc. The implementation will be done in two phases and follows the ASAP implementation methodology:

▶ **Phase 1**: Pilot implementation with the top 50 vendors in the first 4-5 months, including one month post go-live support.

▶ **Phase 2**: Roll out of implementation to 1,200 more vendors over a period of 3-6 months.

The vendors for collaboration using SUS will be selected based on the following five criteria:

▶ Number of transactions per year.

▶ Value of annual spend.

▶ Criticality of the material.

▶ Distance of vendor's location from Concept Auto Inc.'s plants.

▶ All of these factors will be weighed against the cost of maintaining the vendor in the SUS system.

13.4.1   System Landscape

The following components are part of a typical MM-SUS scenario implementation:

- SAP SRM 5.0
- SAP NetWeaver XI 7.0 (PI 7.0)
- SAP Web Dispatcher as the application gateway outside of the firewall
- SAP NetWeaver BI 7.0 (optional)
- SAP NetWeaver Portal 7.0 (optional)

> **Tip**
>
> Always refer to the Master Guide for your SAP SRM version to understand the components required for your scenario, the installation sequence, and other important information.

Concept Auto Inc. has decided not to go for an EP implementation. However, they may implement EP as a separate project at a later date. Concept Auto Inc. has already implemented SAP NetWeaver BI and the same server will be used for SUS analytics. As mentioned previously, Concept Auto Inc. has four SAP ERP implementations in different locations. The proposed landscape for Concept Auto Inc. is shown in Figure 13.2.

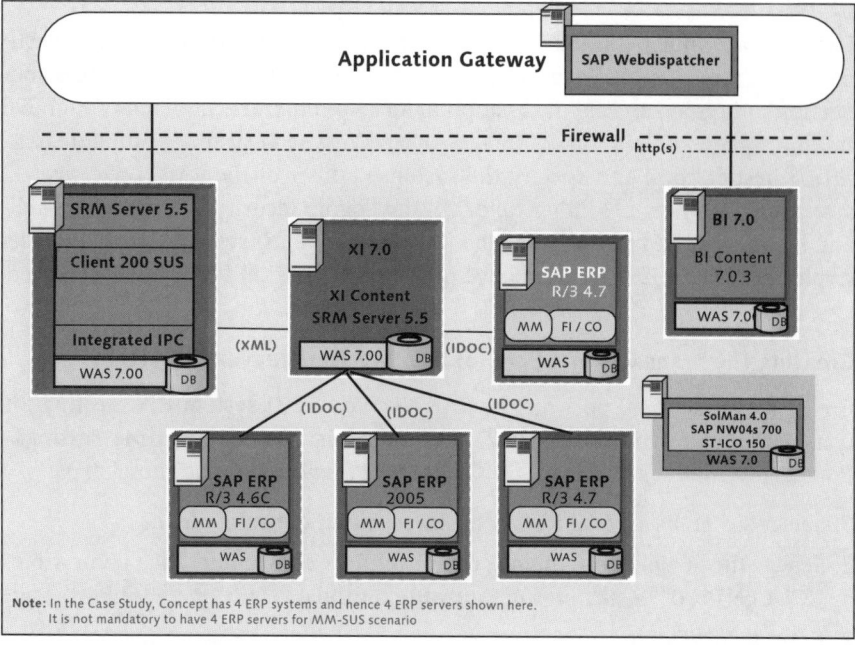

Figure 13.2 Proposed Landscape for Concept Auto Inc.'s MM-SUS Scenario Implementation

Note that the SUS analytics implementation is outside the scope of this book. There will, however, be a brief explanation of SAP NetWeaver BI integration in Chapter 15.

Notes

► Although we have taken SAP SRM 5.0 as the basis for this implementation, the same settings are also valid in SAP SRM 2007. We have mentioned the basic differences in the settings for SAP SRM 5.0 and SAP SRM 2007 wherever applicable.

► Unlike SRM Enterprise Buyer Professional (EBP), which uses Internet Transaction Server (ITS) in SAP SRM 5.0 and WebDynpro in SAP SRM 2007, SUS uses the Business Server Page (BSP) user interface.

13.4.2 Settings in the Materials Management system

In this section, we will explain the settings that need to be configured in the MM system for the MM-SUS scenario. All of the settings in this section should be performed in the MM system unless otherwise stated.

Define Logical System

Define the logical systems for both the MM and SUS systems.

Define the RFC Destination for the SAP NetWeaver XI System

Use Transaction code SM59 and define an Remote Function Calls (RFC) destination for the SAP NetWeaver XI system with connection type 3 (SAP R/3 connection). Maintain an RFC destination name (e.g., XI_INTEGRATION_SERVER). In the Target host field, maintain an SAP NetWeaver XI system host name (e.g., XID01.besttec.com) and specify the system number of the SAP NetWeaver XI system in the System Number field. On the Logon/Security tab, specify the client, logon user, and password in the SAP NetWeaver XI system. The logon user (typically XIAPPLUSER) should have profiles SAP_ALL and SAP_NEW assigned.

Creating the Transactional Port for the SAP NetWeaver XI System

Create a transactional port for the SAP NetWeaver XI system RFC destination using the menu path **Tools • ALE • ALE Administration • Runtime Settings • Port Maintenance**, or Transaction code WE21, and following these steps:

1. Select the Transactional RFC node and click on the create icon.
2. Select the Own Port name radio button and enter the name (e.g., "XIDCLNT100"). Click on the **Continue** button.
3. Enter a Port Description.
4. Ensure that the IDOC record types SAP Release 4.x radio button is selected.
5. Specify the RFC destination for the SAP NetWeaver XI system.

Note

This setting is not transportable.

Setting Up IDocs: Creating Reduced Message Type

A reduced message type is defined to distribute only relevant vendor master data from MM to the SUS system. Use Transaction code BD53 and follow these steps:

1. Enter the reduced message type as "Z_CREMAS_SUSMM" and click on the **Create** button.

2. Enter Message type reference as "CREMAS" and click on the **Continue** button

3. Enter a description of "SUS Vendor master data" and click on the **Continue** button.

4. Select the segment E1LFA1M (segment for general vendor data) and click on the **Select** button. Similarly, select segments E1LFA1A and E1LFM1M, too.

5. Double-click on the segment E1LFA1M and select the checkbox next to the following fields: **NAME2, ORT02, PFACH, REGIO, STCD1, STCD2, STRAS, TELF1, TELFX, ADRNR**, and **TXJCD**.

6. Double-click on the segment E1LFA1A and select the checkbox next to the field **LFURL**.

7. Click on the save icon and then click on the back icon.

8. Click on the **Activate change pointers** button to enable subsequent synchronization of the vendor master data.

Setting up IDocs: Checking Change Relevant Fields

Ensure that field ADRNR is deleted from the change relevant fields list of the reduced message type defined for vendor master distribution. Use Transaction code BD52 and enter the message type as "Z_CREMAS_SUSMM." Verify if ADRNR exists. If ADRNR exists, delete the entry.

Defining an Object Class for Master Data Distribution

In this activity, create a class type ALV for vendor master and a class under this class type. Use the menu path **SPRO • IMG • Cross-Application Components • Classification System • Classes • Maintain Object Types and Class Types**, and follow these steps:

1. Select object table LFA1 and double-click on **Class Types** in the left pane.

2. Copy the class type 010 to ALV.

3. Enter the class type description as "Lists for SUS vendor distribution."

4. In the Functions section, select the **Multiple classification and Distr. Class** type.

5. Save the settings.

Now, using Transaction code CL01, perform these steps:

1. Select class type ALV.
2. Enter a class name of "Z_CRED_SUSMM_*xxx*" where *xxx* is the system ID of the SUS system.
3. Click on the create icon.
4. Enter a description of "SUS Vendor List in xxx," and set the status as Released.
5. Save the class.

Assigning the Message Type and Distribution Object Class to the SUS Logical System

To assign a message type and distribution object class to the SUS logical system, use Transaction code BD68 and follow these steps:

1. Enter the SUS Logical system.
2. Click on the New Entries button.
3. Enter a record with the data outlined in Table 13.1.

Message Type	Class	PoP
Z_CREMAS_SUSMM	Z_CRED_SUSMM_xxx	2 (Push)

Table 13.1 Assign Message Type and Distribution Object Class to the SUS Logical System

Creating a Distribution Model

Create a distribution model to distribute vendor master data from MM to the SUS system. Use Transaction code BD64, and follow these steps:

1. Press F9 to switch to change mode.
2. Click on the **Create Model View** button.
3. Enter a name in the Short text field, for example, "MM-SUS Vendor Master."
4. In the Technical name field, enter the name of the distribution model, for example, "MM-SUS," and press the Enter key.
5. Select the newly created node and click on the **Add message type** button.
6. Enter the logical system of MM as the Sender, the logical system of the SUS system as the Receiver, and "Z_CREMAS_SUSMM" as the Message Type, and press the Enter key. The logical systems for MM and SUS systems were defined in the configuration setting *Define Logical Systems*.
7. Expand the new MM-SUS model view and double-click on **No filter set**.

8. In the filter editor, click on "Create filter group" and select the "Dependent on class membership" attribute.
9. Press the Enter key.
10. Save the settings.

Note

This setting is not transportable.

Configure User Exit VSV00001

Activate user exit VSV00001 to enable the transfer of supplier email address via IDoc to the SUS system. Use Transaction code CMOD, and follow these steps:

1. Enter an enhancement project name, for example, "ZPSMM" and click on the Create button.
2. Enter a short text for the user exit project and click on the save icon.
3. Click on Enhancement assignments and assign enhancement VSV00001.
4. Click on the Components button.
5. Double-click on the component EXIT_SAPLKD01_001.
6. Double-click on the include program ZXVSVU03 and add the code shown in Listing 13.1:

```
data: ls_data_a type E1LFA1A,
ls_data_m type E1LFA1M,
ls_idoc_data type edidd,
lv_index type sy-tabix.
if segment_name = 'E1LFA1A'.
 read table idoc_data into ls_idoc_data with key segnam = 'E1LFA1M'.
 ls_data_m = ls_idoc_data-sdata.
 clear ls_idoc_data.
 read table idoc_data into ls_idoc_data with key segnam = segment_name.
 ls_data_a = ls_idoc_data-sdata.
 lv_index = sy-tabix.
 select single smtp_addr from adr6 into ls_data_a-lfurl
 where addrnumber = ls_data_m-ADRNR
 and flgdefault = 'X'.
 ls_idoc_data-sdata = ls_data_a.
 modify idoc_data from ls_idoc_data index lv_index.
endif.
```

Listing 13.1 User Exit VSV00001

7. Activate the code and activate the enhancement project.

Configure User Exit MM06E001

This is an optional setting. If you want to process order responses for rejected items, activate user exit MM06E001 according to the instructions in SAP Note 756472.

Setting Up Purchase Order Output

Purchase orders are transmitted to SUS from MM using the output medium EDI. This section explains the settings required to define the output for purchase orders.

Fine-tune the message type for purchase order output by setting up a new output message type and assign it in the message schema. To do so, use the menu path **SPRO · IMG · Materials Management · Purchasing · Messages · Output Control · Message Types · Define Message Types for Purchase order**, and follow these steps:

1. Double-click on **Maintain Message Types** for PO.
2. Copy output type NEU and create a new output type, for example, "ZSUS."
3. In Processing Routines, specify an entry for transmission medium EDI with the processing program RSNASTED and Form routine EDI_PROCESSING.
4. In Partner Roles, specify an entry for EDI as the medium and LS (logical system) as the function.
5. Save the entries and click on the exit icon.
6. Double-click on **Fine-Tuned Control: Purchase Order**.
7. Maintain the new output type ZSUS for operations 1 (new) and 2 (change).

Now, using the menu path **SPRO · IMG · Materials Management · Purchasing · Messages · Output Control · Message Determination Schema · Define Message Schema for Purchase order**, follow these steps:

1. Double-click on Maintain Message Determination Schema: Purchase Order.
2. Select RMBEF1 and double-click on Control Data.
3. Create a new entry for output type ZSUS and assign requirement 101 to it.
4. Save the entries.

Define Message Conditions for Purchase Order

This is master data and needs to be configured whenever a new vendor is introduced to the SUS system. This setting ensures that the purchase orders released to the vendor are transmitted to the SUS system. Use the menu path **Logistics · Materials Management · Purchasing · Master Data · Messages · Purchase Order · Create**, or Transaction code MN04.

1. Enter output type "ZSUS" and press the Enter key.
2. Select Key Combination Purchasing Output Determination: Purch.Org/Vendor for EDI.
3. Configure the entries for each purchasing organization and vendor combination. Specify LS in the PartF field and SUS logical system in the Partner field. Select the output medium as 6 (EDI).

Setting Up Outline Agreement Output

Use the menu path **SPRO · IMG · Materials Management · Purchasing · Messages · Output Control · Message Types · Define Message Types for Outline Agreements** to set up outline agreement output. This setting is required if you want to transfer scheduling agreements to SUS as a project solution, also.

The settings are similar to the ones explained in the section "Setting up Purchase Order Output." Copy output type NEU and create a new output type ZSUS. Also, assign the new output type in the message determination schema for outline agreement RMBEV1 with requirement 101.

Setting Up Scheduling Agreement Release Output

These settings are configured to transfer scheduling agreement releases to SUS. Also, assign the new output type in the message determination schema for scheduling agreement release RMBEL1 with requirement 105.

Use the menu path **SPRO · IMG · Materials Management · Purchasing · Messages · Output Control · Message Types · Define Message Types for Scheduling Agreements Release/Expediter**. The settings are similar to the ones explained under the section "Setting up Purchase Order Output." Copy output type LPET and create a new output type ZSET. In fine-tune control, enter the new output type "ZSET" for operations 5 (new) and 8 (change).

Define Message Conditions for Scheduling Agreement Delivery Schedules

This is master data and needs to be maintained whenever a new vendor is introduced to the SUS system. This setting ensures that the delivery schedules released to the vendor are transmitted to the SUS system. Use the menu path **Logistics · Materials Management · Purchasing · Master Data · Messages · Scheduling Agreement Delivery Schedule · Create**, or Transaction code MN10. The settings are similar to the ones described for purchase order. Maintain the settings for new output type ZSET.

Define Message Conditions for Evaluated Receipt Settlement (ERS) Invoice Output

This is master data and needs to be maintained whenever a new vendor is introduced to the SUS system. This is an optional setting. Configure the settings if you want to use an ERS invoice for the vendor and want to transmit ERS invoices to the SUS system.

Use the menu path **SPRO • IMG • Materials Management • Logistics Invoice Verification • Message Determination • Create Condition : Invoice Verification**, or Transaction code MRM1. Select the output type as ERS6, and the key combination as CoCode, Vendor. The settings are similar to the ones described for a purchase order.

Implement User Exit MEETA001

Implement user exit MEETA001 to calculate open quantities in SARs. The code shown in Listing 13.2 should be added in the enhancement component EXIT_SAPLEINL_001. Include ZXM06U27:

```
data: ls_ekeh like i_ekeh,
 lv_menge like i_ekeh-menge.
loop at i_ekeh into ls_ekeh.
 *check not ls_ekeh-updkz is initial.
 lv_menge = ls_ekeh-menge - ls_ekeh-dabmg.
 if lv_menge eq 0.
 clear ls_ekeh-updkz.
 else.
 ls_ekeh-menge = lv_menge.
 endif.
 modify i_ekeh from ls_ekeh.
endloop.
```

Listing 13.2 User Exit MEETA001

Setting Up a Partner Profile for Connectivity

In this section, configure the ALE partner profile settings necessary to determine the documents to be exchanged between MM and SUS. Use the menu path **Tools • ALE • ALE Administration • Runtime Settings • Partner Profiles**, or Transaction code WE20 to create a partner profile for the SUS logical system under Partn.Type **LS**. Specify an RFC user as the post processing agent. Figure 13.3 shows sample settings for Partner Profiles.

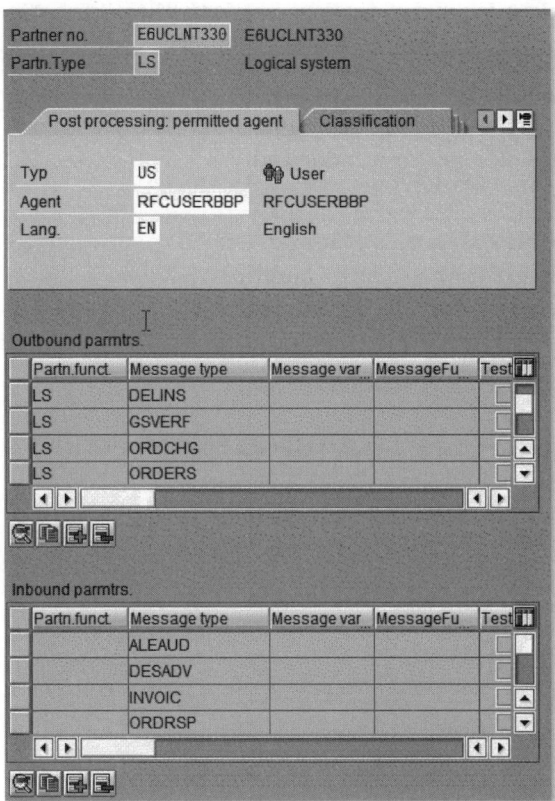

Figure 13.3 Sample Partner Profile Settings

Configure the message types in the **Outbound parmtrs.** (outbound parameters) and **Inbound parmtrs.** (inbound parameters) sections according to the information provided in Table 13.2. Click on the icon with the '**+**' sign below the outbound parameters or inbound parameters table to add a message type. The **Remarks** column in Table 13.2 indicates the document exchanged by each message type.

Outbound/ Inbound	Partner Role	Message Type	Message Function	Remarks
Out	LS	Z_CREMAS_SUSMM		Vendor master
Out	LS	DELINS		Delivery schedule
Out	LS	GSVERF		ERS invoice/credit memo
Out	LS	STPPOD	GRN	GR notifications In SAP ERP 6.0

Table 13.2 Outbound/Inbound Parameters in Partner Profile

Outbound/ Inbound	Partner Role	Message Type	Message Function	Remarks
Out	LS	ORDCHG		Order change
Out	LS	ORDERS		Purchase order
In	LS	ALEAUD		Credit memo
In	LS	DESADV		ASN
In	LS	INVOIC		Invoice
In	LS	ORDRSP		Order response

Table 13.2 Outbound/Inbound Parameters in Partner Profile (Cont.)

The following common settings are made for all outbound parameters:

▶ Specify the SAP NetWeaver XI Port as the **Receiver port**.

▶ Select the output mode **Transfer Idoc immed**.

Figure 13.3 shows screenshots for sample outbound parameter settings.

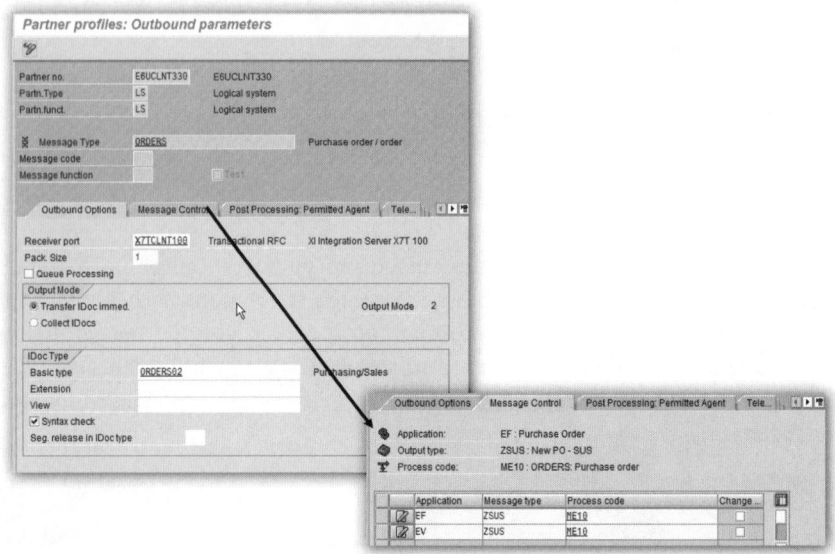

Figure 13.4 Sample Outbound Parameters Settings

Configure the detailed parameter settings according to Table 13.3. Note that the fields Application, Message type, and Change message are relevant for outbound parameters only.

Message Type	Basic Type	Application	Message Type	Process Code	Change Message
Z_CREMAS_SUSMM	CREMAS03				
DELINS	DELFOR02	EL	ZSET	ME14	
GSVERF	GSVERF01	MR	ERS6	MRRL	
STPPOD	DELVRY03				
ORDCHG	ORDERS02	EF	ZSUS	ME11	X
ORDCHG	ORDERS02	EV	ZSUS	ME11	X
ORDERS	ORDERS02	EF	ZSUS	ME10	
ORDERS	ORDERS02	EV	ZSUS	ME10	
ALEAUD				AUD1	
DESADV				DELS	
INVOIC				INVL	
ORDRSP				ORDR	

Table 13.3 Detailed Parameter settings

Setting Up Invoice Verification

In this section, you configure the EDI settings required for the logistics invoice verification:

▸ **Assign partner data to company code**
Specify the company codes relevant for invoice verification and assign them to the SUS Logical system. Use the menu path **SPRO · IMG · Materials Management · Logistics Invoice Verification · EDI · Assign Company Code**, or Transaction code OBCA. Enter a record for each of the company codes relevant for SUS transactions. Figure 13.5 shows sample settings. Specify the **Partn.Type** as **LS**. Specify the SUS logical system in the partner type and assign the company code(s).

Partn.Type	PartnerNo	Comp.code name in the invoice	Co
LS	UCLNT330	0000001000	1000
LS	E6UCLNT330	3000	3000

Figure 13.5 Assign Partner Data to Company Code

▸ **Assign tax codes**
Map the tax codes of the SUS system to the respective tax codes in MM. Use menu path **SPRO · IMG · Materials Management · Logistics Invoice Verifi-**

cation · EDI · Assign Tax Codes, or Transaction code OBCD. Configure LS as the partner type. Specify the SUS logical system in the field PartnerNo. Specify SUS tax codes in the tax type field and assign MM tax codes in the Tx field.

▶ **Define program parameters**
Assign the document types for the invoice and credit memo to the SUS logical system and company code. Use the menu path **SPRO · IMG · Materials Management · Logistics Invoice Verification · EDI · Enter Program Parameters**, or Transaction code OMRY. It is recommended to assign document type RE.

Goods Receipt Notifications

Goods receipt (GR) information from MM is transmitted to SUS as GR notifications. This functionality is available only from ERP version SAP ERP 6.0 (formerly ERP 2005) on. Please refer to consulting note 1026638 to enable GR notifications in ERP versions below SAP ERP 6.0. The settings described in this section are relevant for SAP ERP 6.0:

▶ **Implement user exit MM06E001**
Implement the user exit MM06E001 and component EXIT_SAPLEINM_002 according to the code given in note 888725.

▶ **Schedule background report RPODDELVRY**
The RPODDELVRY report selects all goods receipts for purchase orders of vendors in the SUS system in accordance with the selected vendor class, including respective cancellations and return deliveries that were not yet synchronized with SRM SUS. The selected goods receipts are transferred to the respective SRM SUS system using IDoc STPPOD.DELVRY03. Create a variant for the report RPODDELVRY in Transaction SE38 and schedule a background job to run periodically in Transaction SM36.

Tip
You can enable GR notifications in ERP versions lower than SAP ERP 6.0 by following the steps in SAP Note 1026638. Alternatively, if your ERP version is >= 4.7, you can configure settings as in SAP ERP 6.0, copy the report RPODDELVRY, and use it to transfer GR notifications.

13.4.3 Settings in the SRM SUS System

All of the settings in this section should be configured in the SRM SUS system, unless otherwise stated.

Set Up SUS User Management

In this section, we will generate the profiles for roles in the SUS system and create an administrator user. Follow these steps:

1. **Perform mass generation of profile for roles**
   Use the menu path **SPRO • SAP Implementation Guide • Supplier Relationship Management • SRM Server • Cross Application basic Settings • Roles • Define Roles**, or Transaction code PFCG. Select the Mass generation option from the Utilities menu. Select the All Roles radio button. Enter "SAP_EC_SUS_*" in the Role field. Click on the execute icon. Also, generate profiles for role SAP_BC_BASIS_MONITORING. If you want to create your own roles, we suggest that you use the IMG documentation for reference.

2. **Create SUS Administrator**
   Using Transaction SU01, create a Dialog user, for example, SUS_ADMIN. Specify a valid email address for the user. Assign the following roles to the user:
   - SAP_EC_SUS_ADMIN_PURCHASER
   - SAP_EC_SUS_ADMIN_VENDOR
   - SAP_BC_BASIS_MONITORING

3. **Create Service User**
   Using Transaction SU01, create a Service user, for example, SUS_SERVICE. Configure a valid email address for the user. Assign the role SAP_EC_SUS_ADMIN_VENDOR and save. This service user is used as the anonymous logon user for self-registration.

4. **Create XIAPPLUSER (or PIAPPLUSER)**
   Using Transaction SU01, create user XIAPPLUSER as a Communications user. Assign roles SAP_EC_SUS_ADMIN_VENDOR and SAP_XI_APPL_SERV_USER to the user.

SUS-Specific Role Attributes

Activate the SUS-specific role attributes using personalization settings in Transaction PFCG. For a detailed explanation of the settings, refer to Chapter 14, Section 14.2.2.

Check Unit of Measure (UOM) Settings

Ensure that UOM settings are synchronized with your MM system settings. Verify the UOMs using Transaction CUNI.

Set Up SUS Self-Registration Services

In this section, you configure settings to use the Business Server Pages (BSP) as the user interface and start self-registration. You also assign the user to be used for anonymous login for self-registration:

1. **Activate Services**
   Use Transaction code SICF and click on the execute icon. Select each of the following services, right-click it, and choose **Activate Service**:
   - Default_host – sap – bc – bsp – sap – system
   - Default_host – sap – bc – bsp – sap – public
   - Default_host – sap – bc – bsp – sap – srmsus
   - Default_host – sap – bc – bsp – sap – srmsus_selfreg
   - Default_host – sap – public – bsp – sap – htmlb
   - Default_host – sap – public – bc
   - Default_host – sap – xi

   Select the **Yes** button (the button with a hierarchy graphic) to activate all of the nodes below the node being activated.

2. **Maintain Log on Data in SRMSUS_Selfreg service**
   Select the service SRMSUS_Selfreg in Transaction SICF. Double-click on the service and select the **Logon Data** tab. Select the Standard logon procedure and specify the SUS client, service user for anonymous logon and password. If you use https, select the SSL radio button in the Security Requirement section.

3. **Create external alias for SRMSUS_Selfreg**
   This step is optional. If you want a shorter URL for the SUS self-registration page, then you can create an external alias for SRMSUS_Selfreg service. Click on the External Aliases button in Transaction SICF. Right-click on default_host and click on Create External Alias. Enter a name in the External Alias field, for example, "/sus_selfreg." Enter a description for the external alias, for example, "SUS self-registration." On the logon data tab, enter the SUS client, the service user for anonymous logon and password. On the Trg Element tab, select the node srmsus_selfreg (navigate default_host – sap – bc – bsp – sap – srmsus_selfreg) and double-click on it. Save your external alias. Test the external alias by right-clicking on it and choosing Test Ext.Alias.

Configure RFC Destinations

Before you configure RFC destination settings, ensure that you have RFC users created in the SUS, SAP NetWeaver BI, and ERP systems and the user XIAPPLUSER (or PIAPPLUSER) in the SAP NetWeaver XI system. You need to set up the following RFC destinations:

- Type 3 for the SUS system
- Type 3 for the backend SAP ERP system
- Type 3 for the SAP NetWeaver BI system (optional)
- Type T for LCRSAPRFC

▸ Type T for SAPSLDAPI

▸ Type H for SAP NetWeaver XI system

Use Transaction code SM59 to define RFC destinations of type 3 (ABAP connection) for the SUS, SAP ERP, and SAP NetWeaver BI systems. Specify the target host and system number on the Technical settings tab. Maintain the client, RFC user, and password on the Logon Data tab. Test the connection and remote logon in each RFC destination. If the remote logon is successful, you should be logged on to the corresponding system to which you tried to connect.

Define an RFC destination for the SAP NetWeaver XI system with connection type H (HTTP connection to ABAP system). Specify an RFC destination name (e.g., XI_INTEGRATION_SERVER). In the Target host field, specify an SAP NetWeaver XI system host name (e.g., XID01.besttec.com) and specify the port number in the Service No. field. Enter "/sap/xi/engine?type=entry" in the path prefix field. On the Logon/Security tab, specify the client, logon user (e.g., XIAPPLUSER), and password in the SAP NetWeaver XI system. The logon user should have the role SAP_XI_APPL_SERV_USER assigned.

For connecting to SAP NetWeaver XI, two additional RFC destinations LCRS-APRFC and SAPSLDAPI are defined with connection type T (TCP/IP connection). For LCRSAPRFC, configure LCRSAPRFC_*XID* (or LCRSAPRFC_UNICODE) as the registered server program ID, where *XID* is the system ID of the SAP NetWeaver XI server. Similarly, configure SAPSLDAPI_*XID* (or SAPSLDAPI_UNICODE) as the registered server program ID for SAPSLDAPI. Specify the gateway host and gateway service for both connections. These two registered server programs are defined on the SAP J2EE RFC engine of the SAP NetWeaver XI server. Gateway host and service information can be obtained using Transaction SMGW in your SAP NetWeaver XI system.

Enable Use of SAP NetWeaver XI in SAP SRM

NetWeaver XI should be enabled in SAP SRM to enable XML communication through SAP NetWeaver XI. Use the menu path **SPRO • SAP Implementation Guide • Supplier Relationship Management • SRM Server • Cross Application Basic Settings • Enable use of Exchange Infrastructure**, click on **New Entries**, and select the checkbox for the **Use Application Integration Infrastructure field**.

Integration Engine Configuration

You should perform these settings in your SAP SRM system using Transaction code SXMB_ADM:

1. In the Integration Engine: Administration screen, execute the option Integration Engine Configuration.

2. Select **Edit • Change Global Configuration Data**.

3. Select Application System in the field Role of Business System.

4. In the field Corresponding Integ.Server, enter "dest://<*HTTP Destination*>" where <*HTTP Destination*> is the RFC destination name for the SAP NetWeaver XI system.

5. Save the settings.

6. Return to the Integration Engine: Administration screen. Execute the option **Manage Queues**.

7. Select all of the options and click on Register Queues. Then click on **Activate Queues**.

Maintain SLD Access Data

You should configure these settings in your SAP SRM system to define access to the System Landscape Directory (SLD) in SAP NetWeaver XI. Use Transaction code SLDAPICUST and follow these steps:

1. Maintain the alias name (for example, PI_XID).

2. Select the checkbox in the Prim. column.

3. Specify the Host Name and Port for SLD.

4. Enter a logon user and password.

5. Verify the settings using Transaction SLDCHECK.

Defining Technical Settings for Email

These settings are usually configured by a Basis or NetWeaver consultant:

1. **Activate the SAPCONNECT service in SICF**
Contact your Basis consultant to configure the settings as relevant to your email system.

2. **Create the email service**
Contact your Basis consultant to configure the settings as per SAP Note 455140 to send email via SMTP.

3. **Create the Job for the email service**
Configure a job to periodically send SMTP email from the SUS system. To do so, in Transaction SCOT, select **View • Jobs**. Click on the create icon. Enter a job name and press the Enter key. Enter the ABAP program "RSCONN01." Select the variant SAP&CONNECTALL. Select Schedule job. Select Schedule Periodically. Enter a duration time between jobs and click on Create.

Define the Backend Systems

Using this setting, you configure the backend systems for the SUS, SAP NetWeaver BI, and ERP systems. This enables linkage of the logical system and

RFC destinations. Use the menu path **SPRO • SAP Implementation Guide • Supplier Relationship Management • SRM Server • Technical Basic Settings • Define Backend Systems**. Select the checkbox in the RFC column for the ERP and SAP NetWeaver BI systems. You do not need to select a checkbox for the SUS system entry. Specify a System Landscape Directory (SLD) name for each system as defined in the SAP NetWeaver XI SLD settings. (We have not yet discussed SAP NetWeaver XI SLD settings.) Refer to the SAP NetWeaver XI configuration section for more details.

Define the Organizational Plan

In this section you will learn how to define a root node for the purchasing organization and a root node for the supplier organization:

> **Note**
>
> You do not need to set up a complete organizational plan as in SRM EBP.

1. **Create a purchasing organization**
   Create an organization node using Transaction PPOCA_BBP. Select the validity dates in the screen that appears and press the Enter key. On the basic data tab of the new organizational unit, replace the name and description with your entries, for example, "SUS_PORG" and "Concept SUS Purchasing Org." On the **Function** tab, select the purchasing organization indicator. Specify the address data. Write down the business partner ID created by the system for the node. This will be used as the default purchasing organization in "Make Settings for Business Partners."

2. **Create supplier root organization**
   Create a root supplier organization node using Transaction PPOCV_BBP. Select the validity dates in the screen that appears and press the Enter key. On the basic data tab of the new organizational unit, replace the name and description with your entries, for example, "SUS_Vendor" and "Concept SUS Vendor Root Org." Specify the ERP logical system for attributes VENDOR_ACS and VENDOR_SYS. Write down the business partner ID created by the system for the node. This will be used as the default vendor organization in "Make Settings for Business Partners."

> **Note**
>
> The supplier organization is defined using Transactions PPOCA_BBP through SAP SRM version 4.0. From SAP SRM 5.0 on, it is defined using Transaction PPOCV_BBP.

3. **Replicate buying company data**
   Using this setting, you replicate the company codes that you use in SUS from

379

your MM system to SUS. Log on as the SUS administrator user (for example, SUS_ADMIN) that has the SAP_EC_SUS_ADMIN_PURCHASER role assigned. Then, use Transaction code BBP_SUS_BP_ADM and double-click on Business Partner as Company Code. Enter the required company code in the Company Code field. Select the ERP logical system in the Logical System field. Enter the address information for the company code and click on the execute icon. The system replicates the given company code and creates an entry in the organizational plan. You can view the company details using Transaction PPOSA_BBP.

4. **Adjust attributes for the company organizational unit**

   Verify the replicated company codes using Transaction PPOMA_BBP and adjust the following entries as required:

   ▶ The Function tab should have the Company checkbox selected and the company code of the ERP system assigned.

   ▶ Configure attributes BUK, ACS, and SYS.

Make Settings for Business Partners

Using this setting, you define the basic settings for business partners maintenance using the menu path **SPRO • SAP Implementation Guide • Supplier Relationship Management • Supplier Self-Services • Master Data • Make Settings for Business Partners**. If there are no entries, click on the New Entries button to create an entry. Figure 13.6 shows a screenshot with sample settings. The fields are as follows:

▶ **Administrator**: This user is used in all notifications. Specify the SUS administration user (for example, SUS_ADMIN). This user should have a valid Internet email address specified in user master.

▶ **Docu Object for Email**: Specify **BBP_SUS_BP_REG_CREATION**. The text entered in this text object is used as the email text when a vendor registration mail is sent.

▶ **URL for UM**: This URL is sent to the vendor administrator for self-registration and creation of additional users when you replicate a vendor from ERP or SRM EBP. The URL will be of the format *https://<host:port>/ sap/bc/bsp/sap/srmsus_selfreg* (or *https://<host:port>/sus_selfreg* if you have configured an external alias for the srmsus_selfreg service). The host and port can be obtained from Transaction SMICM. Select **Goto • Services** to identify the host and port.

▶ **URL for Notification**: This URL is used in emails sent for document receipt notifications. The format of the URL is *https://<host:port>/sap/bc/bsp/ sap/srmsus/default.htm*.

▶ **No Notification of Registration**: If you do not want to send the notification of registration to your supplier, select this checkbox. In this case, you will have to maintain supplier users yourself.

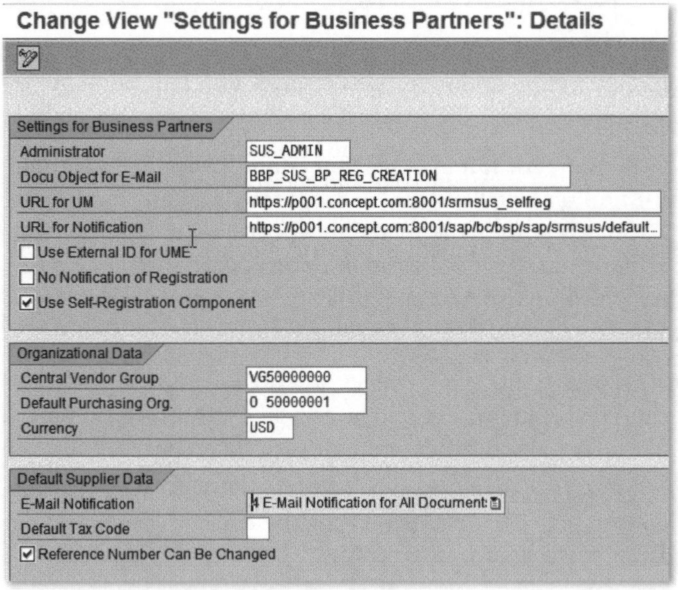

Figure 13.6 Sample Settings for Business Partners

- **Use Self-Registration Component**: If you use the supplier self-registration scenario, select this checkbox.
- **Central Vendor Group**: Enter the ID from your vendor's root organization as seen in PPOMV_BBP. The format should be "VGnnnnnnnn," where nnnnnnnn is the vendor root organization ID.
- **Default Purchasing Org.**: Enter the ID from your purchasing organization as seen in PPOMA_BBP. The format should be "O nnnnnnnn," where nnnnnnnn is the purchasing organization ID.
- **Currency:** Specify the default currency.
- **E-Mail Notification**: Select the relevant option from the dropdown list. If you do not want to send an email notification when a document is created, you can also select the relevant option here.
- **Reference Number Can Be Changed**: If you select this indicator, vendor document numbers are created automatically and vendors can change the number.

Specify Data Privacy Settings for Suppliers

A data privacy statement is shown whenever a supplier user is created in SUS. The person creating the supplier user must accept the data privacy statement before completing the user creation process. A supplier user is created in one of two ways:

381

▶ Using self-registration (srmsus_selfreg). Refer to step 4 in Figure 13.8, shown later in this chapter.

▶ From the user administration option in SUS (srmsus). Refer to step 6 in Figure 13.8.

Use the menu path **SPRO • SAP Implementation Guide • Supplier Relationship Management • Supplier Self-Services • Settings for User Interface • Specify Data Privacy Settings for Suppliers** to define whether a data privacy statement is required in both supplier user creation options described previously. You will also define which text should be displayed as the privacy statement. The following six keys are used to define the settings:

▶ **PRIVACY_STMNT_PERS_USED**: Valid values are TRUE or FALSE. Indicates whether the data privacy statement should be activated in self-registration. A value of TRUE indicates the activation of the privacy statement.

▶ **PRIVACY_STMNT_PERS**: By default, the text ID BBP_PRIV_STMNT_EXTERNAL is assigned. This text ID contains text for the data privacy statement used during self-registration.

▶ **PRIVACY_STMNT_PERS_HD**: By default, the text ID BBP_PRIV_STMNT_EXTERNAL_HEAD is assigned. This text ID contains text for data privacy statement acceptance. Replace this default text ID with your own text ID.

▶ **PRIVACY_STMNT_OTHER_USED**: Valid values are TRUE or FALSE. Indicates whether data privacy statement should be activated while creating a user from the user administration option. Value TRUE indicates activation of the privacy statement.

▶ **PRIVACY_STMNT_OTHER**: By default, the text ID BBP_PRIV_STMNT_INTERNAL is assigned. This text ID contains text for the data privacy statement used during self-registration. Replace this default text ID with your own text ID.

▶ **PRIVACY_STMNT_OTHER_HD**: By default, the text ID BBP_PRIV_STMNT_INTERNAL_HEAD is assigned. This text ID contains text for data privacy acceptance. Replace this default text ID with your own text ID.

We suggest the following actions during implementation:

1. Determine the privacy statement and acceptance texts based on your organization's policy.

2. Maintain your own texts using Transaction SE61. For example, copy the general text ID BBP_PRIV_STMNT_EXTERNAL and create your own text ID (for example, ZBBP_PRIV_STMNT_EXTERNAL). Specify the privacy statement text as determined in step 1. Similarly, maintain other data privacy texts explained in this section (for example, BBP_PRIV_STMNT_EXTERNAL_HEAD), also.

3. In the configuration setting **Specify Data Privacy Settings for Suppliers**, replace the default text IDs with your new text IDs.

> **Tip**
>
> You can also configure a few other settings for the SUS user interface in this setting. For example, you can specify the number of documents to be shown per page in a list against key LIST_ENTRIES_PER_PAGE. IMG documentation about other keys is available at the IMG node Customer Settings, which can be accessed using the menu path **SPRO • SAP Implementation Guide • Supplier Relationship Management • Supplier Self-Services • Settings for User Interface • Customer Settings**. You can also define whether payment status of an SUS invoice can be obtained from the backend SAP ERP Financials system, if the SAP ERP version is SAP ERP 2005 or higher.

Define Number Ranges

Configure the number ranges for the following SUS documents:

- SUS purchase orders
- SUS purchase order responses
- SUS shipping notifications (ASNs)
- SUS confirmations
- SUS invoices

Use the menu path **SPRO • SAP Implementation Guide • Supplier Relationship Management • Supplier Self-Services • Cross-Application Basic Settings • Settings for Documents • Number Ranges** to configure the number ranges for all SUS documents.

Specify Means of Transport

Different means of transport (e.g., ship, truck, train, etc.) can be specified in this setting. These are used while creating ASNs. Use the menu path **SPRO • SAP Implementation Guide • Supplier Relationship Management • Supplier Self-Services • Cross-Application Basic Settings • Settings for Documents • Specify Means of Transport** to configure this setting. We suggest that you create the entries to match those in your backend ERP system.

Define Tax Calculation

The tax calculation settings in SUS are the same as the tax calculation settings in SRM EBP. Therefore, please refer to the settings described in Chapter 5.

Set Values for the Session Manager/Profile Generator

These settings, accessible using the menu path **SPRO • SAP Implementation Guide • Supplier Relationship Management • Supplier Self- Services • Settings for User Interface • Set Values for the Session Manager/Profile Generator**, are optional, but some, such as CONDENSE_MENU, are quite useful. Here you specify the settings for the SAP Easy Access menu and the settings for managing roles in the SUS browser user interface. If a transaction is assigned to several roles, a user with many roles assigned will see the same transaction appearing many times in the screen. You can avoid this redundancy by setting the parameter CONDENSE_MENU value to Yes. Refer to SAP Notes 772904, 203994, 380029, 498074, 504006, and 357693 for other useful options available in this setting.

13.4.4 Settings in the SAP NetWeaver XI System

Documents are exchanged between SAP MM and SUS via SAP NetWeaver XI. The settings you will learn about in this section enable the document exchange between the systems. You should configure the settings described in this section in the SAP NetWeaver XI system unless stated otherwise.

Ensure SAP NetWeaver XI Content and Apply Important Notes

Contact your NetWeaver consultant and ensure that appropriate SAP NetWeaver XI content for your SAP SRM version has been imported. The procedure to import SAP NetWeaver XI content is explained in SAP Note 705541. Also, ensure that the following notes are applied to correct errors in SAP NetWeaver XI content:

▶ 1025763: If the value of field SORTL is missing.
▶ 1028132, 1032505: If there is no order acknowledgment in SAP R/3 for a purchase order response from SUS for n items.
▶ 1032506: If a schedule line agreement with multiple schedule lines is not transferred.
▶ 1061076: If the means of transport and transport ID values are swapped.
▶ 1064135: To process purchase order responses for rejected items.

Set Up RFC Destinations

You need to set up the following RFC destinations:

▶ Type 3 for the backend ERP system
▶ Type T for LCRSAPRFC
▶ Type T for SAPSLDAPI

Use Transaction code SM59 to configure the settings. They will be similar to those described in the RFC destination settings in Section 13.4.3.

Set Up a Port for the SAP ERP System and the SAP NetWeaver XI System

To set up a port for the SAP ERP system, use Transaction code IDX1. Then, click on the create icon to create a port. Enter a Port (for example, "SAPERD" where ERD is the system ID of the SAP ERP system), client of the ERP system, and a description. Specify the RFC destination of the ERP system. Similarly, create a port for the SAP NetWeaver XI system, if it does not exist. Enter a Port (for example, "SAPXID"), client of the SAP NetWeaver XI system, and a description. Specify "NONE" as the RFC destination.

> **Note**
>
> Remember to maintain the ERP port in the communication channel in SAP NetWeaver XI in the Integration Builder Configuration, also. The port in GeneratedReceiverChannel_IDoc for MM business system should be changed to specify the ERP port as defined here.

Maintain Technical Systems in SLD

You should configure these settings in your SAP NetWeaver XI system. Verify whether you already have SAP SRM and ERP technical systems defined. If they do not exist, maintain the technical systems for SRM SUS and ERP as shown in this activity using Transaction code SXMB_IFR.

1. In the SAP NetWeaver XI tools that are launched for configuration in your browser window, click on the **SLD** link, then click on the **Technical Systems** link.
2. Click on the **New Technical System** button.
3. Select the option Web AS ABAP. Click on **Next**.
4. Specify the System ID, 10-digit Installation Number, and Database Host Name. (You can get all of this information from your SUS system by selecting **System • Status**.) Click on **Next**.
5. Specify the Message Server Port. (This will be 3600 + the system number of your SUS system.) Also specify the Central Application Server Host name and the Instance Number. (This is the system number of the SRM SUS system.) Click on Next.
6. If you have multiple application servers, add them. Click on **Next**.
7. Add the Clients and Logical System Names of your SAP SRM system. Click on **Next**.

8. In the Installed Products screen, select the appropriate installed applications (e.g. SAP SRM 6.0). You can use the filter to quickly select the required products. Click on the Finish button.

9. Maintain the technical systems for your ERP system in a similar way.

Tip
You can create a technical system for SAP SRM in SLD automatically from your SAP SRM system using Transaction RZ70. To do so, configure an SLD bridge gateway and host. Click on the proposal icon at the bottom right corner. Then click on the activate icon. Click on the start data collection and job scheduling icons. The system will then create a technical system for SAP SRM in SAP NetWeaver XI SLD.

Maintain Business Systems in SLD

You should configure these settings in your SAP NetWeaver XI system. Verify whether you already have SRM SUS and ERP business systems defined. If they do not exist, configure the business systems for SRM SUS and ERP as explained in this activity. Configure a business system for SAP NetWeaver XI also, if you do not have one already. Use Transaction code SXMB_IFR and follow these steps:

1. In the SAP NetWeaver XI tools that launch in your browser window for configuration, click on the System Landscape Directory (SLD) link, then click on the **Business Systems** link.

2. Click on the **New Business System** button.

3. Select the option **Web AS ABAP**. Click on **Next**.

4. Select the System and Client of the SRM SUS system from the dropdown list. Click on **Next**.

5. Enter a Business System Name (e.g., "SRD_200"). Click on **Next**.

6. In the Installed Products screen, click on **Next**.

7. In the step Integration, select **Application System** from the Business System Role dropdown list.

8. In the Related Integration Server field, select the **SAP NetWeaver XI business system** from the dropdown list.

9. Click on the **Finish** button.

Define a business system for SAP ERP in a similar way. If you are defining an SAP NetWeaver XI business system, the settings in the step Integration will be different from that of other business systems. Here, you will select Integration Server as the Business System Role and specify a Pipeline URL in the format of *http://HOST:PORT/sap/xi/engine?type=entry*.

Set Up Integration Scenarios

You should configure these settings in your SAP NetWeaver XI system. The steps are similar to those described in Chapter 9, Section 9.3.3, except for the step Configure Connections. Use Transaction code SXMB_IFR, and follow these steps:

1. In the SAP NetWeaver XI tools that launch in your browser window for configuration, click on the Integration Directory link.

2. Enter the user ID and password. The Configuration: Integration Builder window appears.

3. This step is optional but recommended. Select **Environment -> Clear SLD Data Cache**. You can also perform this step if you do not see the business systems created by you in the assign business system step (which we'll discuss next).

4. To assign a business system: Select the **Objects** tab. Expand **Service Without Party**. Expand **Business System**. Check whether the business systems of SUS and ERP already exist. If they do not exist, right-click on Business System and select Assign Business System. The Assign Business System wizard screen appears. Click on the **Continue** button twice. Do not enter anything in the Party field. Select the business system for SUS from the list shown. Select the checkbox **Create Communication Channels Automatically**. Click on the **Finish** button. You may get a pop up to select the language. If so, select the language. The business system is now assigned. Repeat this step for the SAP ERP system.

5. Modify the IDoc communication channel generated for the ERP (GeneratedReceiverChannel_IDoc) system. Change the Port with the port defined in Transaction IDX1 (e.g., SAPERD). Specify the RFC destination of the SAP ERP system. Specify the SAP Release (e.g., 620). Select the Queue Processing checkbox. Note that the system creates four communication channels for the ERP system but only an IDoc channel is required. The other three communication channels can be deleted.

6. Verify the settings in the SAP NetWeaver XI communication channel generated for the SUS system (GeneratedReceiverChannel_XI). If the Addressing Type is URL Address, the following should be verified:

   ▶ Verify that Target Host is the host of the SUS system.

   ▶ Verify that Service Number belongs to the SUS system.

   ▶ Verify that the Path field contains */sap/xi/engine?type=receiver*.

   ▶ Verify that Authentication Type contains the value Use Logon Data for SAP System.

   ▶ Verify the user name (say, XIAPPLUSER), password, and client. Ensure that these values exist in your SUS system.

Alternatively, the Addressing Type can be changed to the HTTP destination. In this case, only the HTTP destination of the SUS system should be specified. The HTTP destination for the SUS system should have been specified as an RFC destination of type H in the SAP NetWeaver XI system. The entries in the RFC destination settings will be similar to those verified with Address Type as URL Address.

To transfer the integration scenario from the repository, select **Tools • Transfer Integration Scenario from Integration Repository** and proceed as follows:

1. **Select Integration Scenario**: Select the scenario Plan_Driven_Procurement_ SupplierEnablement of the appropriate version (e.g., SAP SRM SERVER 5.5) from the search list in the Name field. Note that you may have more than one entry for a scenario. Click on **Continue**.

2. **Create Configuration Scenario**: Enter a name for the configuration scenario. You should have a consistent nomenclature for naming the configured scenario. For example, you can use the system ID of the SAP SRM system as the prefix for the scenario name (for example, SRD_Plan_Driven- Procurement_ SupplierEnablement). Click on the **Finish** button. In the next screen that appears, click on the **Close** button.

In the Integration Scenario Configurator wizard that appears, click on **Component View**. In the next screen, click on the **Apply** button and perform these steps:

1. **Assign Services**: Verify the role and version. If the version is not appropriate, click on the right arrow next to the Role field. Click on the insert icon (icon with a + sign). In the Service Selection screen, select the relevant business system. Assign services for SUS and MM.

2. **Configure Connections**: Click on **Configure Connections** in the wizard. The integration scenario includes actions for the exchange of documents between SUS and MM systems, as shown previously in Figure 13.1. In the next screen, click on the right arrow icon until you have the correct components specified in both the From Action and To Action areas. Right- click on the Communication Channel field and select the appropriate communication channel for each document exchange action. For example, if you need to select a communication channel for SUS, select SAP NetWeaver XI, and for MM, select IDoc. Click on the right arrow icon, select the next relevant action for your scenario, and repeat the steps to assign the communication channel.

3. **Generate**: Click on the **Generate** option in the wizard. You can simulate the generation by selecting Generation Simulation. Verify the simulation results, and if there are no errors, select the Generation radio button and click on the Start button to generate the scenario configuration. Close the results log screen.

4. In the Integration Scenario Configurator main screen, select the menu option Settings and then click on **Apply Changes and Save Configuration Scenario**.

After saving the settings, close the configurator screen. If you get a message "Do you want to keep the changes," click on the **Apply** button to keep the changes.

In the Configuration: Integration Builder screen, perform the following steps:

1. **Change Lists**: Select the **Change Lists** tab. Right-click on **Standard Change List** and select **Activate**. In the Objects screen, select all of the objects configured above and click on the **Activate** button. This step needs to repeated to activate the configuration, if you make any changes.

2. **Scenario Overview**: Select the **Scenarios** tab, then select your scenario and expand it. You can see the overview with nine document exchanges mapped, as shown in Figure 13.7. If you do not see nine document exchanges after configuring SAP NetWeaver XI, refer to Section 13.4.5 for troubleshooting. Note that GR notification (STPPOD) is available from SAP SRM 5.0 on only and therefore the number of document exchanges in SAP SRM 4.0 and lower versions will be eight or less.

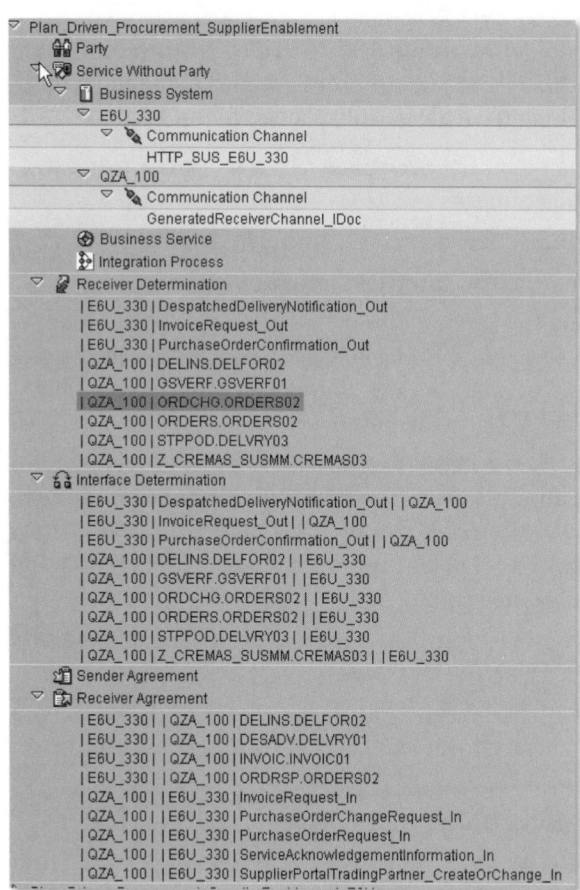

Figure 13.7 MM SUS Integration Scenario in SAP NetWeaver XI

13.4.5   Special Scenarios Mapping in SAP NetWeaver XI

In this section we will cover the following special scenarios where additional mapping is required in SAP NetWeaver XI:

▶ All nine document exchanges are not mapped when you finish the standard wizard-based SAP NetWeaver XI scenario configuration. In such cases, you need to map the missed document exchanges.

▶ If your MM system is connected to multiple SUS systems, you need to configure additional conditions to ensure that documents are exchanged correctly.

▶ If your SUS system is connected to both MM and SRM EBP systems (or to multiple MM systems), you need to configure additional conditions to ensure that documents are exchanged correctly.

Mapping of Missed Document Exchanges

In some SAP SRM and SAP NetWeaver XI content versions, you will observe that purchase order change document exchange (IDoc ORDCHG) is not configured when you perform SAP NetWeaver XI scenario configuration using the wizard. You can add the missed document exchange as explained in this section:

1. Click on your scenario name on the **Scenarios** tab to select the scenario to which you want to add mappings.

2. Select **Tools · Configuration Wizard**.

3. In the screen that appears, click on **Internal Communication**.

4. **Inbound Message- Specify the Sender**: You should select the values from the search list. Select Business System as Service Type. In the Service field, select the business system for MM. In the Interface field, select ORD-CHG.ORDERS02. Click on the Continue button.

5. **Outbound Message–Specify the Receiver**: You should select the values from the search list. Select Business System as Service Type. In the Service field, select the business system for SUS. In the Interface field, select PurchaseOrderChangeRequest_In of the appropriate SAP SRM version and scenario. Click on the **Continue** button.

6. **Sender Agreement**: Click on the **Continue** button as no sender agreement is required in this case

7. **Receiver Determination**: If the receiver determination already exists, you can select the radio box **Reuse Object** and click on the **Continue** button.

8. **Interface Determination**: If the interface determination already exist, you can select the radio box **Reuse Object** and click on the **Continue** button.

9. **Receiver Agreement**: If the receiver agreement already exists, you can select the radio box **Reuse Object** and click on the **Continue** button.

10. **Generate Objects**: Select the scenario to which this configuration should be added and click on the **Finish** button.

11. Activate the Change Lists as explained in the Set up Integration Scenario section.

SAP NetWeaver XI Mapping when One MM System Is Connected to N SUS Systems

If you have multiple SUS systems connected to one MM system, you need to configure conditions to determine the correct receiver (SUS system) for all of the following outbound messages from the MM system:

▸ Z_CREMAS_SUSMM.CREMAS03

▸ STPPOD.DELVRY03 (Only from SAP SRM 5.0 on)

▸ ORDERS.ORDERS02

▸ ORDCHG.ORDERS02

▸ GSVERF.GSVERF01

▸ DELINS.DELFOR02

Proceed as follows:

1. On the scenarios tab in the Receiver Determination section, expand your scenario and select Z_CREMAS_SUSMM.CREMAS03. The receiver determination settings are displayed on the right side of the window. Click on the pencil icon to switch to change mode.

2. In the Configured Receivers section, you will see as many entries as there are SUS systems.

3. Click on the search list icon in the Condition field for Service (SUS system). Select the search list icon in the Left Operand field. Enter "RCVPRN" in the Xpath expression and click on the **OK** button. Enter the appropriate SUS business system name (e.g., "SRD_200") in the Right Operand field. Repeat this step to define conditions for all SUS systems.

4. Select ORDERS.ORDERS02 in the Receiver Determination section of your scenario. Add a condition for each SUS system. Select the search list icon in the Left Operand field. Expand ORDERS02, IDOC, EDI_DC40, select RCVPRN, and click on the OK button. Enter the appropriate SUS logical system (e.g., "SRDCLNT200") name in the Right Operand field. Repeat this step for all SUS systems.

   Repeat this step for all other messages from MM. The condition determination is the same as that of ORDERS.ORDERS02 for other documents, also.

5. Activate the Change Lists as explained in the section "Set up Integration Scenarios."

SAP NetWeaver XI Mapping when One SUS System is Connected to Multiple Procurement Systems

One example of connecting multiple procurement systems to SUS is when you connect both MM and SRM EBP to your SUS system. Another example is our case study company Concept Auto Inc., where SUS is connected to four SAP ERP systems. If you have multiple procurement systems connected to one SUS system, you need to configure conditions to determine the correct receiver (the MM or SRM EBP system) for all of the following outbound messages from the SUS system:

- DespatchedDeliveryNotification_Out
- InvoiceRequest_Out
- PurchasOrderConfirmation_Out

Now follow these steps:

1. Expand your scenario on the **Scenarios** tab and select **PurchaseOrder-Confirmation_Out** in the section Receiver Determination. The receiver determination settings are displayed on the right-side of the window. Click on the pencil icon to switch to change mode.

2. In the section **Configured Receivers**, you will see as many entries as there are procurement systems.

3. Click on the search list icon in the Condition field for a Service (procurement system). Select the appropriate software version. Click on the search list icon in the Left Operand field. Expand **PurchaseOrderConfirmation • Message-Header • RecipientParty • InternalID**, select SchemeAgencyID, and click on the OK button. Enter the appropriate Procurement Business system (e.g., "ERD_100") name in the Right Operand field. Repeat this step for all procurement systems.

4. Repeat the previous step for all other messages sent from SUS.

5. Activate the Change Lists as explained in the section "Set up Integration Scenarios."

13.4.6 Master Data

You need to replicate only vendor master data from the procurement system. You do not need to replicate material master to the SUS system. In this section, you will learn about replicating vendor data from the MM system.

Modify Vendor Master Data to Add SUS-Specific Data

This should be done in the MM system. Determine the vendors to be collaborated with using the SUS system as part of the implementation plan. Modify the master data of these vendors using Transaction XK02 in the MM system. The following changes should be made:

1. **Address Data**: Maintain a valid email address in this field. The SUS self-registration information will be sent to this email address.

2. **Classification**: Assign the class Z_CRED_SUSMM_xxx created in Section 13.4.2 to the vendor. You can assign the class by selecting **Environment -> Classification**.

3. **Correspondence**: In the Correspondence screen, enter the company code in the field Acct w/ vendor.

4. **Purchasing Data**: This setting is optional. These settings will be defaulted in purchase orders. Alternatively, you can directly maintain these settings in each purchase order. Select the checkbox **Acknowledgement reqd**. Enter "0001" in the Confirmation control field. The confirmation control key 0001 is delivered in the SAP standard. If you made any changes, you should provide a different confirmation control key. The confirmation control key setting should have order acknowledgement and shipping notification keys assigned to it.

Replicate Vendor Master Data from the MM System to the SUS System

The process of replicating vendor master data from the MM system is shown in Figure 13.8 and explained as follows:

1. The purchaser executes Transaction BD14 in the SAP ERP system (see step 1 in Figure 13.8). He enters the vendor class, message type (e.g., "Z_CREMAS_SUSMM"), and target SUS system. The purchaser can also specify specific vendor codes in the selection screen and click on the execute icon to send data.

2. If there are no problems with the data transfer, the vendor receives an email with a registration user ID, password, and self-registration URL (see step 2 in Figure 13.8). Note that in SAP SRM 2007, registration user ID and password are sent in two separate emails to ensure enhanced security. The email is sent to the address in the vendor master data. The purchaser can also find the registration user and password information using Transaction SLG1 in SUS. The self-registration URL is taken from the Settings for Business Partners settings in SUS. This registration user ID can be used only for vendor self-registration and initial vendor user creation.

3. The vendor's administrator clicks on the URL in the email. In the screen that appears, the vendor enters the registration user ID and password from the email and submits it (see step 3 in Figure 13.8).

4. A self-registration screen (srmsus_selfreg service) will appear. The vendor's administrator should maintain the registration details, new user ID, initial

password, accept the data privacy statement, and create an administrator user (see step 4 in Figure 13.8).

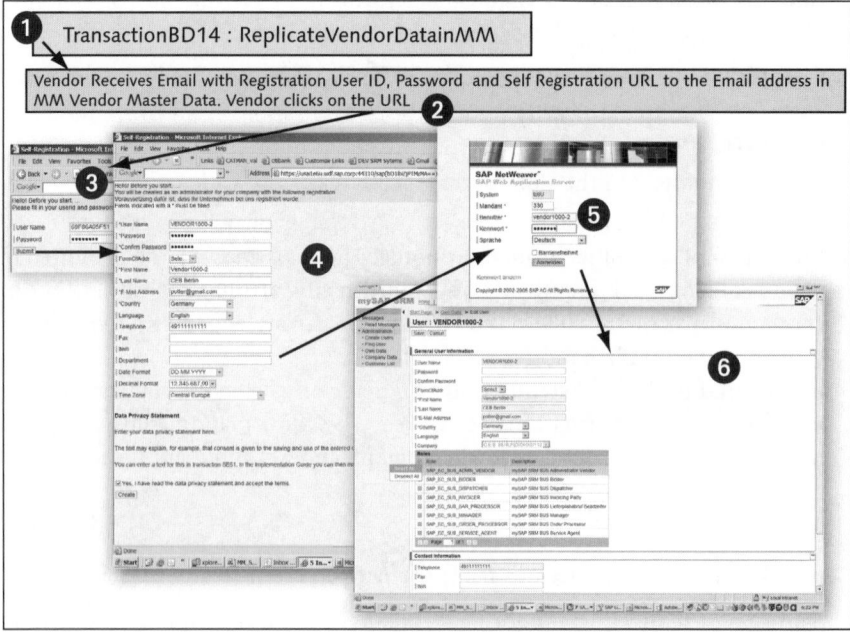

Figure 13.8 Replicate Vendor Data from MM to SUS

5. In the SUS logon screen, the vendor's administrator enters the new user ID and password to logon to the SUS system (see step 5 in Figure 13.8).

6. The SUS browser window is launched. The vendor's administrator can maintain new users or adjust the roles of users from the **User Administration** menu option in the SUS browser (see step 6 in Figure 13.8).

Tips

▶ The newly replicated vendor and vendor users can be displayed from Transaction PPOSV_BBP. A business partner is created when a vendor is replicated, and vendor users are displayed on the Contact person tab. Note that the relevant Transaction in SAP SRM 4.0 is PPOSA_BBP.

▶ The mapping of the business partner GUID (unique key for the business partner), vendor code in the source system (for example, the MM system), and the logical system of the source system are available in table VENMAP in SUS.

13.4.7 Troubleshooting and Tips for the MM-SUS Scenario

In this section, we will provide you with several common troubleshooting tips.

Monitoring of Document Exchange in MM-SUS Scenario for Troubleshooting

The following steps will help you trace any errors when a document is sent from MM to SUS in a document exchange process:

1. Verify whether the output is successfully sent through the EDI medium. You can check the status of the message from the message output in the document. For example, to verify purchase order output status, click on the Messages button in Transaction ME23n. This step is not relevant for vendor master replication.

2. Check the IDoc monitor in SAP ERP (MM system) using Transaction BD87 (or WE02). If the status is 03, then IDoc generation was successful and there is no problem in ALE layer. If no IDoc message is created, check the partner profile settings using Transaction WE20.

3. Verify the status of the XML message(s) in the SAP NetWeaver XI system using the Transaction SXMB_MONI or SXI_MONITOR.

4. If the status in the SAP NetWeaver XI system is successful, verify the status of the XML message in the SUS system using Transaction SXMB_MONI or SXI_MONITOR.

5. Check the tRFC monitor in SAP ERP using Transaction SM58. The problem could be as simple as the logon user defined for the SAP NetWeaver XI connection in the SM59 settings (in the ERP system) not having sufficient RFC authorizations. It could also be due to wrong entries in the SAP NetWeaver XI port definition (Transaction IDX1 in the SAP NetWeaver XI system).

6. You can also verify the application logs in the SUS system using Transaction SLG1.

7. You can also use a debugger with the incorrect message to find the reason for the error using Transaction SXI_SUPPORT. Refer to SAP Note 793669 for more details on troubleshooting.

You can also use the previous steps to trace document exchanges from SUS to MM.

Avoid Duplication of Business Partner in SUS for the Same Vendor

If you have multiple vendor codes for the same vendor in the MM system (e.g., different locations of the same vendor will be created as different vendor codes in MM), then the system creates multiple business partners in the SUS system when you replicate these vendors. This is also true when you have vendors replicated from multiple procurement systems (e.g., n number of MM systems or a combination of MM and SRM EBP systems). This would also mean that the vendor needs to have multiple user IDs to access all documents. This duplication can be avoided as follows:

1. Execute Transaction SE16. Enter table VENMAP and press the Enter key.

2. Enter all of the vendor codes of the same vendor in the selection screen and execute.

3. You will see the list of vendors selected and their Partner GUID.

4. If you are sure that all of these vendors actually belong to one vendor, click on the pencil icon to switch to the Change (or Edit) mode. Copy the Partner GUID from the first entry (or select any Partner GUID) and paste it in all other entries. You should take one of the source systems as the anchor system and use the Partner GUID from this source system entry.

5. You should now see that the same GUID exists in all entries.

6. Create the users for the vendor business partner. Documents of all of these vendor codes can now be accessed from the same vendor user ID.

> **Note**
>
> Alternatively, you can write a custom program to have the previous steps performed automatically by the system, based on certain selections and conditions.

Online Documentation for the MM-SUS Scenario

You will not find documentation for the MM-SUS scenario in the SAP help portal (*http://help.sap.com*). This is because the documentation for the MM-SUS scenario is maintained under the heading Plan-Driven procurement with Supplier Integration. For example, you can access the MM-SUS documentation for SAP SRM 2007 at *http://help.sap.com* and then follow the path **SAP Business Suite • SAP Supplier Relationship Management • SAP SRM 2007 SP03 • Business Scenarios • Plan-Driven Procurement • Plan-Driven Procurement with Supplier Integration**.

Customer Fields in SUS

Customer fields let you add fields in SUS documents as required by the organization. To enable customer fields in SUS documents, refer to SAP Notes 672960 and 762984.

Modify Screen Fields Display in SUS

If you want to modify the display of SUS screen fields, configure table BBPC_SUS_TABDEF. For example, you can configure a field to be a display-only field, whereas it is editable on the screen in standard SUS.

Useful BAdIs and User Exits

The following are useful BAdIs and user exits:

- If you want to modify the mapping of incoming or outgoing XML messages in SUS, you can use BAdI BBP_SAPXML1_OUT_BADI or BBP_SAPXML1_IN_BADI.

- Document BAdIs, such as BBP_DOC_CHANGE_BADI, BBP_DOC_CHECK_BADI, and BBP_DOC_SAVE_BADI, are very useful to modify any SUS document.

- The concept of *customer fields* is also widely used to add fields in SUS documents. Refer to SAP Notes 672960, 762984, and 458591, if you want to use customer fields. You need to configure table BBPC_SUS_TABDEF to make the new fields visible in SUS documents.

- You can use user Exits in the MM system. If you want to modify the incoming or outgoing IDoc data for purchasing documents in SAP MM, use user exit MM06E001. Similarly, if you want to modify incoming IDocs for LIV, use user exit MRMH0002. Use user exit V55K0004 to modify incoming IDocs for inbound delivery. Use user exit VSV00001 to modify outgoing vendor master IDocs.

Transfer Scheduling Agreement to SUS

In standard SUS, scheduling agreements from SAP MM are not transmitted to the SUS system. The basic structure of the scheduling agreement is similar to a purchase order, except that you will not have delivery dates at the item level. If you want to transmit scheduling agreements, you need to do the following:

1. Configure a new output type for outline agreements in SAP MM. This step is explained in Section 13.4.2

2. Configure message conditions for scheduling agreements using Transaction MN07 in SAP MM.

3. Implement BAdI BBP_SAPXML1_IN_BADI in SUS system. In this BAdI implementation, if the date is blank, default a date (e.g., current date plus one year) as the item delivery date. You may also want to change the header description as 'Scheduling Agreement' instead of 'Purchase Order.' For this, you need to identify that the incoming document is a scheduling agreement. One idea is to identify this based on the document number (e.g., in the MM system, configure different number ranges for purchase orders and scheduling agreements).

4. If you want to receive order acknowledgements for scheduling agreement items in SAP ERP, please refer to SAP Note 810340.

Creation of Invoice Based on ASN for a Scheduling Agreement Release

In the standard system, invoices are not allowed for SARs in SUS. Only the transfer of ERS invoices from SAP R/3 to SUS is supported. This is because price details for SAR are not available in SUS. If you want your supplier to create invoices based on ASN for SAR, do the following:

1. Implement BAdI BBP_DOC_CHANGE_BADI method BBP_SUSPO_CHANGE to get a price at the item level from the scheduling agreement to the SAR. Ensure that these changes only update DELINS XML in your code.
2. Implement BAdI BBP_DOC_CHANGE_BADI method BBP_SUSINV_CHANGE to get the currency from the scheduling agreement.

Change Email Text for Supplier Self-Registration Email and Document Notifications Email to Suppliers

When a supplier is replicated from the MM system to SUS, the system sends an email to the email address in vendor master. This email contains text as per text object BBP_SUS_BP_REG_CREATION. You can also see this in the IMG node Settings for Business Partners. If you want to change the email text, follow these steps:

1. Execute Transaction SE61.
2. Copy the general text ID BBP_SUS_BP_REG_CREATION and create your own text ID ZBBP_SUS_BP_REG_CREATION. Modify the text as per your requirement. If you are implementing SAP SRM 2007, two emails (one with the user ID and another with the password) are sent from SAP SRM 2007 on. The text of both emails is contained in the same text id. The BREAK command in the text separates both the email texts.
3. Update the text ID provided in the IMG node Settings for Business Partners with the new text ID.

When a document is transmitted to SUS from the MM system, a notification is sent to the supplier (only if you allow to send notifications in Settings for Business Partners). The email contains text as per text ID BBP_SUS_SUP_NOTIFICA-TION. If you want to add your own text, then modify the text in this text ID in Transaction SE61.

SUS Upgrade to SAP SRM 5.0 Problem

You might encounter the following SUS-related problems when upgrading to SAP SRM 5.0:

► When you upgrade from SAP SRM 4.0 to SAP SRM 5.0, you may face problems processing open purchase order items. This is due to changes in structures in SUS of SAP SRM 5.0, where follow-up document control is changed from header to item. Run the program BBP_COPY_FI_INFO_TO_ITEM to update the document flow.

▶ The programs in the following list are not available in SAP SRM 5.0. If you have used them in any customer-specific developments, then you may copy them from SAP SRM 4.0 and create them in the SAP SRM 5.0 system:

   ▶ BBP_VENDOR_READ_DETAIL

   ▶ BBP_ORGANIZATION_GETDETAIL

   ▶ BBP_GET_VENDOR_MAPPING

Problems During Vendor Replication from SAP ERP

If you have SUS and ROS in the same client, you may face problems replicating vendors from SAP ERP. You may get an error "Vendor with e-mail address xxxxxx not found;process monitor." In this case, you should read the long text to better understand the problem. The easiest workaround to eliminate the problem is to deselect the checkbox Use Self registration component in the IMG node Settings for Business Partners.

13.5   Summary

SAP SRM SUS enables organizations to collaborate with suppliers of all sizes economically and easily. Suppliers do not need to install expensive software or do extensive mappings to achieve the collaboration, thus facilitating even small suppliers to collaborate effectively. In this chapter, we have discussed the integration of the MM procurement system with SUS to enable collaboration for direct materials. Implementation of the MM-SUS scenario is explained comprehensively based on in-depth experience with numerous customer implementations. We have also explained the enhancements and troubleshooting in additional detail as there are no standard training courses for this scenario.

In Chapter 14, we will discuss the integration of the SRM EBP procurement system with SUS, which is referred to as the EBP-SUS scenario. This scenario is used mainly for indirect materials and services.

*Supplier Self-Services with SRM enables organizations to exchange docu-
ments with suppliers easily. While SUS with Materials Management
(MM) facilitates collaboration with direct material suppliers, SUS with
SRM EBP facilitates collaboration with indirect materials suppliers and
service providers.*

— *Enterprise Buyer Professional (EBP)*

14 Supplier Self-Services with SRM Enterprise Buyer Professional Integration

SAP Supplier Relationship Management (SRM) Supplier Self-Services (SUS)
facilitates order collaboration with suppliers of all types of procurement. SRM
SUS with SAP Enterprise Buyer Professional (EBP) effectively enables collaboration with direct materials and indirect materials suppliers. If you have implemented SRM EBP as your procurement system, then you can integrate with SRM
SUS to include your suppliers in the order management process. This integration
complements the MM-SUS scenario by enabling service providers and other
indirect materials suppliers. In the service procurement scenario, you can enable
service providers to submit their time sheets and expense details online, eliminating the drudgery of manual data entry and the tedious reconciliation process.
Consulting and staffing suppliers can also maintain their consultants and staff
details in the SUS system, which can be accessed by the requesters in the SRM
EBP system to select the right people for the jobs on hand.

In this chapter, we will discuss the implementation of SUS when the procurement
system is SRM EBP. We will refer to this as the EBP-SUS scenario. We will provide
you with an overview of the functionalities supported in the EBP-SUS scenario
in Section 14.1 before addressing the implementation details in Section 14.2.

14.1 EBP-SUS Scenario — A Brief Overview of Functionalities

The EBP-SUS scenario is officially part of the service procurement scenario in
the SAP online documentation. However, the scenario supports materials procurement, also. In this section, we will discuss a typical order collaboration
process with EBP as the procurement system and the applicability of the EBP-
SUS scenario.

14.1.1 Order Collaboration in the EBP-SUS Scenario

Figure 14.1 illustrates the document exchange process between EBP and SUS. While the process is similar to that explained in the MM-SUS scenario, EBP offers more flexibility in response processing in the procurement system. As you can see from Figure 14.1, documents are exchanged between EBP and SUS via SAP NetWeaver XI using XML communication. The XML messages that correspond to each of the documents are shown in parentheses in Figure 14.1. The required mappings between both systems are delivered as standard SAP NetWeaver XI content.

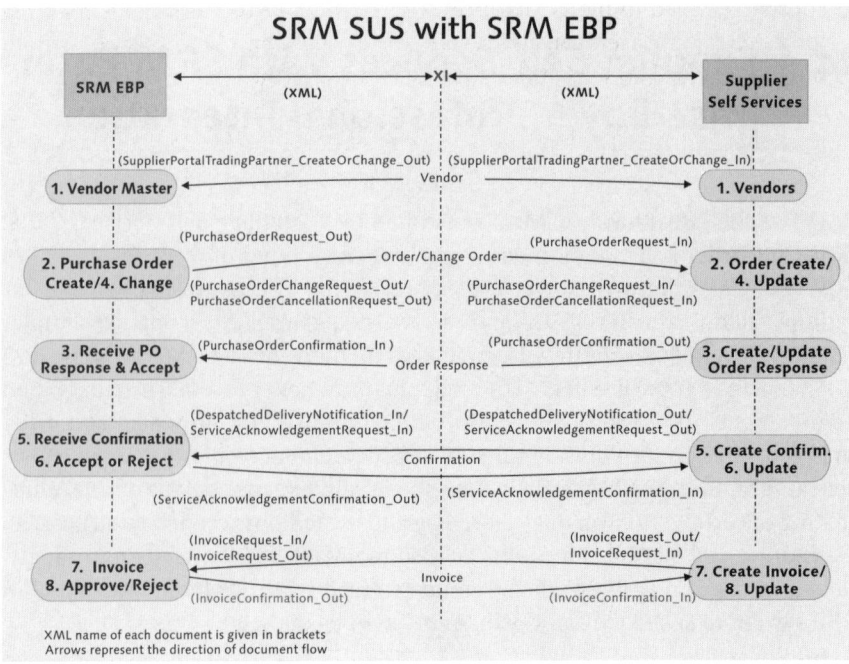

Figure 14.1 Order Collaboration Process in the EBP-SUS Scenario

The steps in the EBP-SUS scenario illustrated in Figure 14.1 are as follows:

1. **Vendor Master**: Any vendor designated as portal vendor in EBP is replicated to the SUS system. In the EBP business partner master, an external business partner can be designated as vendor, bidder, portal vendor, etc. The output medium should be selected as SAP NetWeaver XI/XML for the required purchasing organizations. You can also configure default settings for follow-on document control for each purchasing organization. For example, you may specify that order response and invoice are required as follow-on documents for the EBP purchasing organization. If a business partner is designated as vendor and portal vendor, then the master data is also replicated to the con-

nected SUS system. Suppliers can maintain their employees (goods dispatchers, order receivers) and service agents (consultants, staff) as users in SUS. Based on the configuration for synchronizations of users, these users can be created automatically in EBP. If a supplier makes changes to his own data in the SUS system, these changes are replicated in the EBP system, also.

2. **Purchase Order**: A purchase order (PO) is created and approved in SRM EBP. The PO can be created directly or with reference to a shopping cart or bid. The PO can also contain lumpsum or limit service items in which the purchaser only specifies a value limit, and actual services performed can be entered by the supplier in the SUS confirmation. The follow-on document control assigned to the PO item controls the follow-on documents required for the PO. Purchasers can also search for service agents of the suppliers from the SUS system and select the right consultants for the job being ordered. The output of the PO is sent to SAP NetWeaver XI, which in turn routes it to SUS to create an order. The supplier logs on to SUS via the Internet and can view the order almost instantly after the purchaser releases it in the EBP system.

3. **Order Response**: The supplier verifies and confirms the order by accepting it after making the necessary changes, if any. For example, the supplier may want to change the delivery date based on realistic estimates or the supplier may suggest updated prices. The *order response* (which is also sometimes called the *PO confirmation*) is immediately sent to the EBP system, and a PO response document is then created. Unlike a PO acknowledgement in MM — which is a confirmation in a PO document — the PO response in EBP is a different document. If there are differences between the PO and the order response sent by the supplier, the system activates the differences monitor. Based on the configuration settings, a workflow is triggered to alert the purchaser to accept or decline the differences. If the purchaser approves the differences, the system updates the PO and PO changes are transmitted to SUS. If the purchaser declines the differences, the status is updated in SUS and the supplier has to review and accept the original PO again. The differences can be accepted automatically by the system without the involvement of the purchaser, if this is allowed in the configuration settings. Thus the order response is an iterative process until both supplier and purchaser accept the details.

4. **PO Change**: A PO in EBP may be changed automatically by the system, if the purchaser accepts the changes sent by supplier. Alternatively, the purchaser may amend the PO at any time to reflect newly negotiated terms with suppliers, if any. The changes are transmitted instantly to the SUS system once they are approved. Note that even a PO cancellation is transmitted to SUS.

5. **Confirmation or Shipping Notification**: When the goods are ready and dispatched, the supplier creates a confirmation or shipping notification and provides all delivery details. The document created depends on the follow-on

document settings in the EBP PO. Similarly, a confirmation is created for services performed. In case of consulting or staffing services, the respective consultants or staff can provide their time sheets and incidental expenses in the confirmation. If the PO contains lumpsum or limit items, the supplier also provides the details of actual goods delivered or services performed, along with their unit rates. The items in the limit order scenario can also be selected from an approved catalog. The confirmation in SUS creates a confirmation in EBP and a workflow is triggered for approval.

6. **Accept or Reject Confirmation**: The approver verifies the goods received or services rendered, and received time sheets, and approves or rejects these items. The approval or rejection status is updated in SUS. If the confirmation is rejected, the supplier can correct the details and send it again. Thus the confirmation is an iterative process until both supplier and purchaser accept the details. Note that return delivery or cancellation of confirmation in EBP does not update SUS. However, cancellation of confirmation in SUS updates EBP.

7. **Invoice**: An invoice can be created either in SUS by the supplier or in EBP using the Evaluated Receipt Settlement (ERS) invoice functionality. Invoices in SUS can be created with reference to purchase orders or confirmations. In service procurement, invoices can be created with reference to contact persons, also. You can also select multiple documents belonging to the same company code, currency, and logical system and create a collective invoice. The supplier can also create credit memos with reference to an existing invoice. The invoices created in SUS are sent to EBP via SAP NetWeaver XI and the system creates an invoice in EBP. This invoice is sent for approval. If the ERS indicator is selected in the business partner master and in the PO, then the system automatically creates ERS invoices in EBP, based on approved confirmations. These ERS invoices are transmitted to SUS as accepted credit memos.

8. **Accept or Reject Invoice**: The approver verifies the invoice and accepts or rejects it. The system updates the status of the SUS invoice based on this decision. If the invoice is rejected, the supplier can correct it and send it again. Thus the invoice processing is an iterative process until the supplier and purchaser agree on the details. Note that this iteration is not applicable for ERS invoices.

Some other highlights of the EBP-SUS scenario include the following:

▶ The supplier can add attachments in confirmations, invoices, or credit memos.

▶ Based on the configuration settings, the supplier can request the payment status of an invoice from the SAP ERP Financials application. This facility is available if your backend SAP system version is SAP ERP 2005 or above, and is based on the the IMG setting *Customer Settings in SUS*.

▸ If SUS Analytics is implemented, then the supplier's users that have role SAP_EC_SUS_MANAGER can view different analyses. In addition to the reports listed in Chapter 13, Section 13.3, an additional report 'Evaluation of Service Agents' is delivered in the standard for the EBP-SUS scenario.

14.1.2 Applicability of the EBP-SUS Scenario

Before you implement the EBP-SUS scenario, it is important to see whether your EBP implementation is compatible with SUS. You need to consider the following points before designing your EBP-SUS scenario:

▸ All processes in the EBP-SUS scenario are fully supported when the deployment mode in EBP is standalone.

▸ SUS confirmations and invoices are not supported when you use the extended classic scenario in EBP. In an extended classic scenario, only POs, PO changes, and PO response are supported in SUS. Refer to SAP Note 543544 for more details.

▸ In case of a plan-driven procurement scenario in EBP, SUS processes are supported when the deployment mode is classic. Note that only materials procurement is supported in this case. Procurement of services and confirmations is not supported. You need to implement the MM-SUS scenario in this case.

▸ In case of a self-service procurement scenario in EBP, EBP-SUS processes are not supported when the deployment mode is classic.

Note
Refer to SAP Note 700350 for additional details.

14.2 Implementing the EBP-SUS Scenario

In this section, we will discuss in detail how to implement the EBP-SUS scenario, assuming that MM-SUS has already been implemented. We also assume that EBP has been implemented, including settings for service procurement in EBP.

The sample system landscape shown in Figure 14.2 illustrates the required system landscape when both EBP and SUS are implemented in SRM Server 5.5. If you are implementing SAP SRM 2007, you should also implement SAP NetWeaver Portal.

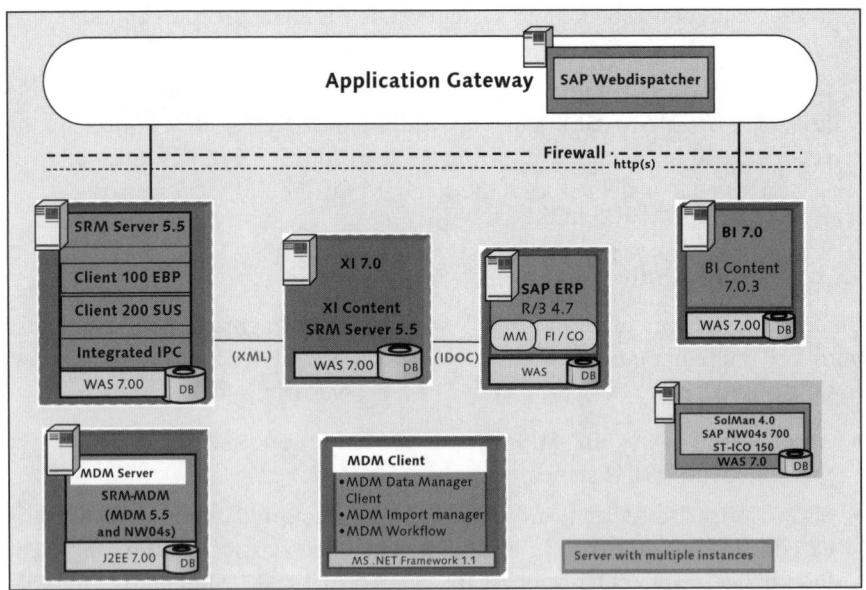

Figure 14.2 Sample System Landscape for the EBP-SUS Scenario

The following software components are required (assuming that SAP SRM version is 5.0):

▶ SAP SRM 5.0

▶ SAP NetWeaver XI 7.0 (PI 7.0)

▶ SAP Web Dispatcher as the Application gateway outside of the firewall. Alternatively, you can also have a reverse proxy.

Optionally, you might also have the following components as part of your implementation:

▶ SAP NetWeaver BI 7.0

▶ SAP NetWeaver Portal 7.0

▶ SRM-MDM Catalog (required if you want to implement catalogs in EBP or SUS, also)

> **Note**
>
> Refer to SAP Note 573383 for more details on single-client EBP and SUS implementation. However, we do not recommend implementing EBP and SUS in the same client as vendors will have technical access to your procurement system. Although the authorizations prevent vendors from accessing your purchasing data, any unintended errors in role assignment may provide them with additional access.

In the system landscape shown in Figure 14.2, EBP and SUS are implemented on the same server in separate clients. You can also implement both EBP and SUS in the same client.

Also, please refer to the following important SAP Notes before you start configuring the EBP-SUS scenario:

- **573383**: EBP and SUS in the same client
- **836200 and 705541**: Importing SAP NetWeaver XI content
- **884695**: Configuration of several integration scenarios
- **573383**: EBP and SUS in one client
- **1028264**: Consulting solutions in SUS
- **700350**: EBP SUS — deployment scenarios
- **793669**: FAQ — SUS in SAP SRM 4.0 with SAP NetWeaver XI 3.0

Once you have read these notes, you can proceed with the configuration settings required for the EBP-SUS scenario.

14.2.1 Settings in the SRM EBP system

You should configure the settings described in this section in the SRM EBP system.

Define Logical System

Define the logical systems for both the EBP and SUS system. This is normally done by a NetWeaver consultant. Refer to Chapter 3 for more details, if required.

Assign Client to Logical System

Assign the logical systems to the respective clients of the EBP system and SUS system. This is normally done by a NetWeaver consultant. Refer to Chapter 3 for more details, if required.

Define the Remote Function Call Destinations

Before you configure Remote Function Call (RFC) destination settings, ensure that you have RFC users created in the SUS and SAP NetWeaver BI systems and that the XIAPPLUSER (or PIAPPLUSER) exists in the SAP NetWeaver XI system. You need to set up the following RFC destinations, using Transaction code SM59:

- Type 3 for the SUS system
- Type 3 for the SAP NetWeaver BI system (optional)
- Type T for LCRSAPRFC

- ▸ Type T for SAPSLDAPI
- ▸ Type H for the SAP NetWeaver XI system

All required RFC destinations were configured while implementing the MM-SUS scenario. This is a client-independent setting and hence you can see the settings configured in Chapter 13 here. Refer to Chapter 13 for more details.

Define Backend Systems

Configure the backend system details for the SUS system as follows, using the menu path **SPRO • IMG • Supplier Relationship Management • Technical Basic Settings • Define Backend Systems**:

- ▸ Configure the SUS system as a backend system with system type as SUS_1.0. Select the checkbox in the RFC column.
- ▸ The System Landscape Directory (SLD) name should be entered according to SAP NetWeaver XI SLD settings for the SUS business system (e.g., "SRD_200").
- ▸ Also, configure the RFC destination of the SUS system that has the dialog user assigned.

Enable Use of Exchange Infrastructure

Enable the use of the exchange infrastructure using the menu path **SPRO • IMG • Supplier Relationship Management • Cross-Application Basic Settings • Enable Use of Exchange Infrastructure**. Click on **New Entries** and select the checkbox for the **Use Application Integration Infrastructure** field.

Create XIAPPLUSER

Using Transaction SU01, create a service user with the role SAP_XI_APPL_SERV_USER (e.g., XIAPPLUSER) in the EBP client.

Configure the Integration Engine

To configure the integration engine, use Transaction code SXMB_ADM, and proceed as follows:

1. In the Integration Engine: Administration screen, execute the option Integration Engine Configuration.
2. Select **Edit • Change Global Configuration Data**.
3. Select Application System in the field **Role of Business System**.
4. In the field Corresponding Integ.Server, enter "*dest://<HTTP Destination>*," where <HTTP Destination> is the RFC destination name for the SAP NetWeaver XI system.

5. Save the settings.

6. Return to the Integration Engine : Administration screen. Execute the option **Manage Queues**.

7. Select all of the options and click on **Register Queues**.

8. Click on **Activate Queues**.

Configure SLD Access Data

Configure the connection settings for SAP NetWeaver XI SLD as follows, using Transaction code SLDAPICUST:

1. Specify the alias name (for example, "PI_XID").

2. Select the checkbox in the **Prim.** Column.

3. Maintain the Host Name and Port for SLD.

4. Enter the logon user and password.

Test the Connection between SAP SRM and SAP NetWeaver XI SLD

Execute the Transaction SLDCHECK. The system will try to launch SLD in a browser window and will prompt you to enter the user ID and password. Enter the user ID and password specified in Transaction SLDAPICUST. Verify the report shown; all messages should be green.

Replicate Company Data to SUS

To replicate company data to SUS use Transaction code BBP_SP_COMP_INI. Decide on the companies that will be using SUS. Then, select the respective SAP SRM company using search help and click on the Replicate button. Although you can replicate both companies and employees, we suggest that you replicate the companies only as you do not need employee users in SUS.

Replication of EBP Vendors to the SUS system

Vendors are replicated to the SUS system from EBP automatically when you create them in SAP SRM using the *Manage Business Partners* Web transaction. Ensure that you select the Portal Vendor checkbox while creating the vendor. Also, ensure that the communication protocol XML/XI is selected, because SAP NetWeaver XI is used to send purchasing documents to SUS vendors.

When a vendor is replicated to SUS, the system sends an email with a registration ID, password, and registration URL to the vendor. The registration URL is taken from the *Settings for Business Partners* configuration in SUS. From SAP SRM 2007 on, the system sends two emails, one with a registration ID and

URL, and another with a password. The vendor can log on using the registration data in the email and create an administrator user who in turn can create other required users to process SUS documents. This is explained in detail in Chapter 13, Figure 13.8 steps 2 to 6 (step 1 in Figure 13.8 is relevant only for the MM-SUS scenario). You should refer to Section 13.4.7 to avoid duplication of business partners in SUS when you replicate vendors from both EBP and MM.

Define XML Message Control for Limit POs

Define the settings here to ensure that confirmations for limit POs from SUS are sent to EBP and create a confirmation in EBP. If you do not configure this setting, the confirmation is not created in EBP and is automatically set to Rejected status in SUS. Use the menu path **SPRO • IMG • Supplier Relationship Management • SRM Server • Cross-Application Basic Settings • Message Control • Influence XML Message Control** and proceed as follows:

1. Select BUS2203 (EC Confirmation for Goods/Services).

2. In the left pane, double-click on **XML Message Control**.

3. If an entry for message number 217 does not exist, click on the New Entries button and add an entry (where Message class is "BBP_PD," No. is "217," and Text is "Enter the Product Category"). Also, select the checkbox **Ignore**.

Configure Link to Service Agent List

In the shopping cart for consulting or staffing services, you can also request specific service agents from a vendor. The service agents (consultants or staff at a vendor) are maintained by the vendor in SUS and the list of service agents in the EBP shopping cart or purchase order is provided from the SUS system. Use the menu path **SPRO • IMG • Supplier Relationship Management • SRM Server • Master Data • Define External Web Services (Catalogs, Supplier Lists and so on)**, and click on the **New Entries** button. Configure the following settings:

▶ **Web Service Id**: Enter a short name, for example, "SUS_Service_Agent"

▶ **Description**: Enter a name, for example, "SUS Service Agents List"

▶ **Bus.Type of a Web Service:** Select Service Provider List from the dropdown list.

Then, perform these steps:

1. In the left pane, click on **Standard Call Structure**.

2. In the first row, enter "10" in the Seq. column. Keep the Parameter Name column blank. Enter *"https://<SUS Host:Port>/sap/ bc/bsp/sap/bbp_sus_sagent/sus_serviceagent_f4.htm"* in the Parameter value column.

3. Select URL as the Type. Replace SUS Host ad Port with your SUS host name (e.g., "Concept.srd.com") and Port (e.g., "8001").

4. In the second row, Enter "20" in the Seq. column. Enter "sap-client" in the Parameter Name column. Enter the SUS client number (e.g., "200") in the Parameter Value.

5. Select **Fixed Value** as **Type**.

14.2.2 Settings in the SRM-SUS System

Settings in the SRM-SUS system are similar to those configured for connecting the SAP-MM system as explained in Chapter 13. Table 14.1 lists the configuration settings required in the SUS system for connecting to the SRM EBP system.

> **Note**
>
> If you are connecting SUS with both SAP-MM and EBP systems, then you need to configure most of the settings only once.

The **Settings** column in Table 14.1 explains the settings to be made in the EBP-SUS scenario. The **Remarks** column explains the differences or additional settings to be made in SUS to connect to SAP SRM compared to the settings explained in Chapter 13.

Settings	Remarks
Set up SUS User Management Mass Generation of Profiles for Roles Create SUS Administrator Create Service User	Same as in Chapter 13. Also, verify SUS-specific role attributes and modify them as required.
Setup SUS Self-Registration Services Activate Services in SICF Create alias for SRMSUS_selfreg	Same as in Chapter 13 Activate service sap – bc – bsp – sap – bbp_sus_sagent in SICF.
Configure RFC Destinations for: SUS EBP LCRSAPRFC SAPSLDAPI SAP NetWeaver XI SAP NetWeaver BI (Optional)	Same as in Chapter 13 except the following: You need to set up RFC destination of type 3 for the EBP system, also.

Table 14.1 Settings in the SUS System

Settings	Remarks
Configure XI communication and security Configure SLDAPICUST Configure SUS Integration Engine Register and Activate Queues Enable Use of Exchange Infrastructure Check SUS communication to SAP NetWeaver XI	Same as in Chapter 13
Define settings for Email Activate SAPCONNECT service Create the Mail Service Create the Job for Mail Service	Same as in Chapter 13
Define Backend Systems Configure settings for: SUS EBP SAP NetWeaver BI (Optional)	Same as in Chapter 13 You also need to configure settings for the EBP system as the backend system.
Create Organizational Plan Create Purchasing Organization Create Supplier Root Organization Adjust Attributes for Company Organizational Unit	Same as in Chapter 13
Replicate Buying Company Code	Not required
Adjust Attributes for Company Organizational Unit	Not required
Configure settings for Business Partners	Same as in Chapter 13
Specify Data Privacy Settings for Suppliers	Same as in Chapter 13
Define Number Ranges	Same as in Chapter 13
Specify Means of Transport	Same as in Chapter 13
Set Values for the Session Manager/Profile Generator	Same as in Chapter 13

Table 14.1 Settings in the SUS System (Cont.)

SUS-Specific Role Attributes

To configure SUS-specific role attributes, execute Transaction PFCG. Here, you can define new roles or modify existing roles. SUS roles normally have the prefix SAP_EC_SUS. SUS role attributes are illustrated in Figure 14.3 with a screenshot of the role **SAP_EC_SUS_ORDER_PROCESSOR**.

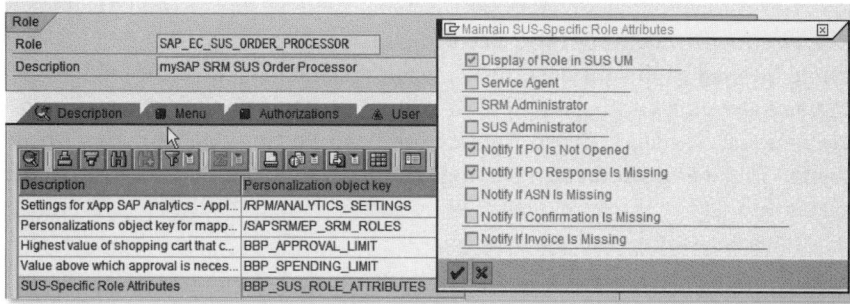

Figure 14.3 Sample Settings for SUS Role Attributes

After you execute the PFCG transaction, select an SUS role. Select the Personalization tab and double-click on Personalization object key BBP_SUS_ROLE_ATTRIBUTES. The following attributes can be activated here:

▸ **Display of Role in SUS UM**: If selected, the role is displayed for assignment during user creation in the SUS browser. If you create a Z-role, you need to select this. You should not select this for role SAP_EC_SUS_ADMIN_PURCHASER as supplier users should not be assigned this role.

▸ **Service Agent**: If selected, the user with this role can be displayed as the service agent for the buyer.

▸ **SRM Administrator**: If selected, users with this role can maintain any supplier user data. Do not select this for any role other than SAP_EC_SUS_ADMIN_PURCHASER.

▸ **SUS Administrator**: If selected, users with this role will become supplier administrator. In the standard, this is selected for SAP_EC_SUS_ADMIN_VENDOR.

▸ **Notify if PO is Not Opened**: If selected, users with this role are sent notifications of new POs.

The remaining attributes are self-explanatory and are used for notifications of various documents.

> **Note**
>
> The SUS-specific role attributes configuration setting is also relevant in the MM-SUS scenario.

Follow-On Documents in SUS for SUS POs with Deviation

This is applicable when there is a discrepancy between an SUS PO and a PO confirmation (i.e., PO response). If you want to allow follow-on documents (i.e., confirmations or invoices) even when there are discrepancies, select the checkbox Allow Follow-on Docs for Discrepancy between PO and PCO item. If you selected the checkbox, you need to also specify whether PO or PCO data should be used as default data in follow-on documents. To configure this setting, use the menu path **SPRO · IMG · Supplier Relationship Management · Supplier Self-Services · Cross-Application Basic Settings · Settings for Documents · Make Follow-on Doc.Settings for SUS Purchase Orders with Status "Deviation."**

Alert Notifications

This is an optional setting, but is required if you want to send alert notifications to users based on certain events (e.g., when a PO is received in SUS). The alert configuration settings are generic in both EBP and SUS, and can be used for any document in EBP or SUS. Alert notifications are configured in two steps as illustrated in the screenshots in Figure 14.4. We suggest that you read the detailed documentation provided in the IMG for event schema. Two steps are involved in configuring alert notifications, as follows:

1. **Define Event Schema for Alert Notifications**
   Use the menu path **SPRO · IMG · Supplier Relationship Management · SRM Server · Cross-Application Basic Settings · Events and Event Schema for Alert Management · Define Event Schema**, then define events required for each business object, as follows, and as shown in Figure 14.4:

   1a) Select a business ObjectType (e.g., BUS2230 - SUS Purchase Order) for which you want to assign events. In the left pane, double-click on **Event Schema**.

   1b) Click on the **New Entries** button and enter an event schema name to identify your new event schema. Alternatively, you can copy an existing schema to create a new one. Select the new Event Schema row.

   1c) In the left pane, double-click on **Event Control**. Click on **New Entries** and select the events as required in the **Event** column. Select an Event Category from the dropdown list for each event. Select an appropriate **Subcategory of Event**, if the event category is **ALERT**. Keep the **Event Deadline in** column blank.

   Repeat steps 1a, 1b, and 1c for other business objects as required.

2. **Assign Event Schema to Transaction Type**
   Use the menu path **SPRO · IMG · Supplier Relationship Management · SRM Server · Cross-Application Basic Settings · Define Transaction Types**. Then, select the Business Object (for example, BUS2230 - SUS PO) and double-click on **Transaction Types** in the left pane. Enter your new event schema in the **Event Schema** field.

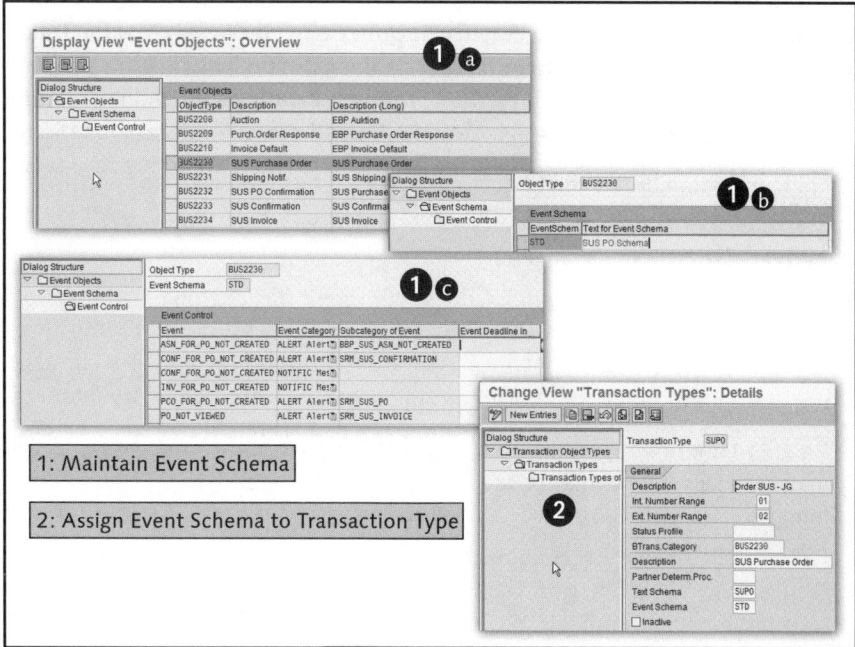

Figure 14.4 Alert Notifications Configuration

Customer Settings in SUS

These settings are optional, and are relevant for both MM-SUS and EBP-SUS scenarios. Some of these settings are very useful and we strongly recommend that you read through the IMG documentation for more information on these settings. Use the menu path **SPRO • IMG • Supplier Relationship Management • Supplier Self-Services • Settings for User Interface • Customer Settings**, and proceed as follows:

1. Define URLs for the bidding system and the SAP NetWeaver BI system.
2. Define the number of documents and the number of items to be displayed per page.
3. Define whether payment status of an SUS invoice can be obtained from the the backend SAP ERP Financials systems, if the SAP ERP version is SAP ERP 2005 or above.

User Synchronization

You can synchronize SUS supplier users with other systems, for example, the EBP system for bidders or service agents, and the SAP NetWeaver BI system for reporting. If you allow your suppliers to create users in the SUS system, then we suggest that you configure settings here to create contact persons in the EBP system automatically. Use the menu path **SPRO • SAP Implementation Guide • Supplier Relationship Management • Supplier Self-Services • Master Data • Maintain Systems for Synchronization of User Data**, then click on the New Entries button to create an entry. See F1 help for each of the fields for more details. The entries for EBP and SAP NetWeaver BI are as follows:

▸ **Logical System**: Enter the target system with which you want to synchronize users. In our case, enter the EBP logical system.

▸ **Activated**: Select the checkbox.

▸ **System Name**: Enter a name of the system here (for example, "EBP system SRD Client 100").

▸ **FM BPID**: Keep this field blank for EBP. Enter "RS_BW_BCT_SRM_SUS_USER_BPID" for the SAP NetWeaver BI system.

▸ **Role**: Enter a role that must be assigned to the user in the target system. You may keep this field blank for the EBP system. For the SAP NetWeaver BI system, enter "SAP_BWC_SRM_SUPPLIER."

▸ **F.Mod:Create User**: Enter a function module name used to create user. Enter "BBP_USER_VENDOR_CREATE" for EBP. Keep the field blank for the SAP NetWeaver BI system.

▸ **F.Mod:Change User**: Enter a function module name used to change the user. Enter "BBP_USER_VENDOR_CHANGE" for EBP. Keep this field blank for the SAP NetWeaver BI system.

▸ **F.Mod:Delete User**: Enter a function module name used to delete the user. Enter "BBP_SUS_USER_DELETE" for EBP. Keep this field blank for the SAP NetWeaver BI system.

▸ **Use Procurement BPID**: Select this checkbox for EBP.

In the left pane, click on **Roles in External Systems**. Map the SUS role with the corresponding role in the EBP system. For example, role SAP_EC_SUS_BIDDER can be mapped to EBP role SAP_EC_BBP_BIDDER.

Tolerance Checks

This is an optional but recommended setting. If you have many invoices created for a PO, rounding differences may lead to exceeding the PO value during final invoice creation, resulting in errors. Hence, you should configure tolerance settings. The procedure involves three steps:

1. Set tolerance checks and create and configure tolerance group SINV in the IMG. The required settings are explained later in this section.

2. In Transaction PPOMV_BBP, assign the tolerance group SINV to attribute TOG. You will use Transaction PPOMA_BBP in SAP SRM version 4.0, as Transaction PPOMV_BBP is available only from SAP SRM 5.0 on.

3. Implement the corrections in SAP Note 835073, if applicable for your SAP SRM version.

To create and configure tolerance group SINV, use the menu path **SPRO · IMG · Supplier Relationship Management · SRM Server · Cross-Application Basic Settings · Set Tolerance Checks**, and proceed as follows:

1. Click on the **New Entries** button and create tolerance group SINV. Enter a description, for example, "SUS Confirmation/Invoice."
2. Select the newly create tolerance group and, in the left pane, double-click on **Tolerance Keys**.
3. Configure tolerance keys DA (Value Overrun), DQ (Quantity Overrun in Currency Amount), and PP (Price Deviation). Specify the limits for each of the tolerance keys as per your organization policy.

Enable Prices from Catalogs for Limit POs

A *limit PO* in EBP is used when the purchaser is not sure of the actual goods or services required for a particular task, e.g., for repair work. In a limit PO, a value limit is given to execute the task without specifying details of the goods and services involved. Actual goods and services details are provided during confirmation and invoice processing. In the EBP-SUS scenario, suppliers can enter the actual goods and services performed in the SUS confirmations or invoices. The items can be entered directly or by selecting from catalogs, ensuring contract compliance for the items and prices.

Use the menu path **SPRO · IMG · Supplier Relationship Management · SRM Server · Master Data · Define External Web Services (Catalogs, Supplier Lists and so on)**. Then configure the settings as explained in Section 5.3.7, *Define External Web Services (Catalogs)*, in Chapter 5. Refer to Figures 5.4. and 5.5 for screenshots of sample settings.

To ensure that you show only items of a specific supplier without compromising confidentiality, you should perform the following steps :

1. Configure unique named searches for each supplier's catalogs.
2. Define the catalogs as external Web services in the SUS client. Ensure that you configure the namedsearch parameter in the settings. Configure a unique catalog Web service ID for each supplier for whom you want to enable catalogs.
3. For each supplier, create a unique vendor group node under the vendor root node in Transaction PPOMV_BBP. This is required because you can configure attributes only at the vendor group level. Configure the attribute CAT with the appropriate catalog Web service at the vendor group node.

417

14.2.3 Settings in SAP NetWeaver XI

The documents between SRM EBP and SUS are exchanged via SAP NetWeaver XI. The settings discussed in this section enable the document exchange between the systems. You should maintain the settings described in this section in the SAP NetWeaver XI system unless stated otherwise. The procedure to configure the settings in SAP NetWeaver XI is similar to the SAP NetWeaver XI settings explained in Chapter 13, Section 13.4.4. Hence, we will only briefly explain the settings here.

Table 14.2 lists the configuration settings required in the SAP NetWeaver XI system for the EBP-SUS scenario. If you are connecting SUS with both SAP-MM and EBP systems, you need to make most of the settings only once. Assuming that you have already configured the **Settings** for MM-SUS scenario, the **Remarks** column explains the differences or additional settings to be configured in SUS to connect to SAP SRM.

Settings	Remarks
Ensure SAP NetWeaver XI content	Same as in Chapter 13, Section 13.4.4.
Set up RFC destination for: EBP (optional) SUS (optional) LCRSAPRFC SAPSLDAPI SAP NetWeaver BI (optional)	Same as in Chapter 13, Section 13.4.4. Set up RFC destination of type H for EBP and SUS. This setting is optional as you can define communication channel settings in SAP NetWeaver XI as an alternative. If you define HTTP destination, the path should be /sap/xi/engine/?type=receiver.
Maintain technical systems in SLD for: SRM EBP SRM SUS SAP NetWeaver XI	Same as in Chapter 13, Section 13.4.4. If both SRM EBP and SUS are in the same system as different clients, you do not need to configure any additional settings. If EBP and SUS are in different systems, configure settings for the EBP system, also.
Maintain business systems in SLD for: SRM EBP SRM SUS SAP NetWeaver XI	Same as in Chapter 13, Section 13.4.4. Configure business system for SRM EBP.
Set up integration scenarios	The procedure is similar to the one explained in Chapter 13, Section 13.4.4, with the following differences: a) Settings for ERP are not required. b) Verify the settings for SAP NetWeaver XI communication channel generated for EBP, also.

Table 14.2 SAP NetWeaver XI Settings for EBP-SUS Scenario

Settings	Remarks
	c) The integration scenario should be Service_ Procurement_SupplierEnablement of the appropriate SAP SRM version (e.g., SAP SRM SERVER 5.5) with namespace *http://sap.com/xi/SRM/Basis/Global*.
	d) Assigning services: instead of assigning services for MM, assign services for EBP.
	e) Configure connections: connections for EBP and SUS should be defined for document exchange as shown earlier in Figure 14.1.
	f) Scenario overview: The document exchanges are mapped as shown in Figure 14.5.
SAP NetWeaver XI mappings when one SUS is connected to multiple procurement systems	Make the settings as explained in Chapter 13, Section 13.4.5, if you have both MM_SUS and EBP-SUS scenarios implemented.

Table 14.2 SAP NetWeaver XI Settings for EBP-SUS Scenario (Cont.)

Figure 14.5 shows the overview of the integration scenario configuration. In this screenshot, an example of communication channel settings is shown when you have RFC Destinations of type H defined for your EBP and SUS systems.

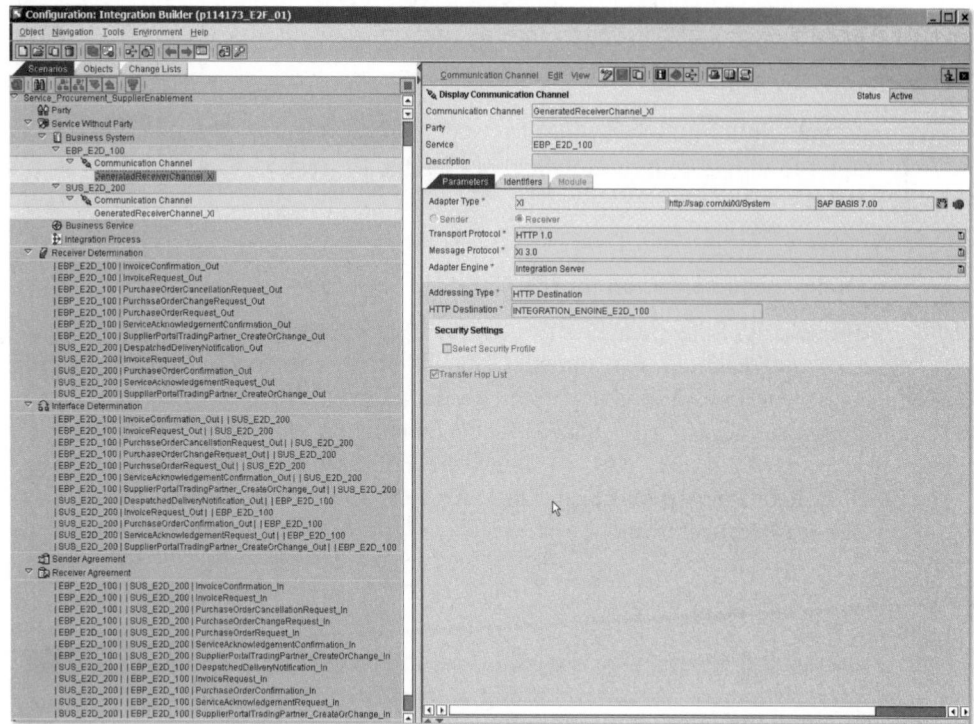

Figure 14.5 Overview of Integration Scenario Configuration

14.2.4 Troubleshooting and Tips for the EBP-SUS Scenario

Most of the troubleshooting tips explained in Chapter 13 Section 13.4.7 are applicable here, too. In this section, we will cover additional troubleshooting and tips that apply to the EBP-SUS scenario.

Monitoring of Document Exchange in the EBP-SUS Scenario for Troubleshooting

Important transactions to monitor document exchange in EBP-SUS scenario are as follows:

- SXMB_MONI or SXI_MONITOR to monitor XML messages
- SXI_SUPPORT
- SLG1
- SM58
- SMQ1
- SMQ2

SAP NetWeaver XI Debugging

SAP Note 793669 explains the SAP NetWeaver XI debugging procedure and FAQ on SAP NetWeaver XI.

Avoid Duplication of Business Partner in SUS for the Same Vendor

Refer to the procedure explained in Chapter 13, Section 13.4.7 to address this issue.

Online documentation for the EBP-SUS Scenario

You will not find documentation for the EBP-SUS scenario in the SAP help portal (*http://help.sap.com*) directly. This is because the documentation for EBP-SUS scenario is located under the heading Service Procurement. For example, you can access the EBP-SUS documentation for SAP SRM 2007 at *http://help.sap.com* and then follow the path **SAP Business Suite • SAP Supplier Relationship Management • SAP SRM 2007 SP03 • Business Scenarios • Service Procurement**.

Customer Fields in SUS

Customer fields enable you to add fields in SUS documents as required by your organization. To do so, refer to SAP Notes 672960 and 762984.

Modify Screen Fields Display in SUS

If you want to modify the display of SUS screen fields, configure table BBPC_ SUS_TABDEF. For example, you can configure a field as a display-only field, whereas it is editable on the screen in standard SUS.

Useful BAdIs and User Exits

Useful BAdIs and user exits include the following:

▶ If you want to modify the mapping of incoming or outgoing XML messages in SUS, you can use BAdI BBP_SAPXML1_OUT_BADI or BBP_SAPXML1_IN_ BADI.

▶ Document BAdIs such as BBP_DOC_CHANGE_BADI, BBP_DOC_CHECK_ BADI, and BBP_DOC_SAVE_BADI are very useful to modify any SUS document.

Changing Email Text

Change email text for the supplier self-registration email and document notifications email to suppliers. To do so, modify the text BBP_SUS_BP_REG_CREA- TION and BBP_SUS_SUP_NOTIFICATION using Transaction SE61 as explained in Chapter 13, Section 13.4.7.

14.3   Summary

The EBP-SUS scenario facilitates collaboration with suppliers for document exchange when your procurement system is SRM EBP. In this chapter, you have learned that the EBP-SUS scenario facilitates service providers to submit time sheets and expense details in a staffing or consulting project. If you have already implemented EBP and MM-SUS scenarios in your organization, the EBP-SUS scenario can be implemented with little additional effort.

Next, in Chapter 15, we will discuss how SAP SRM leverages the SAP NetWeaver technology platform to provide integrated procurement, sourcing, and supplier collaboration functionalities.

SAP NetWeaver is the technical foundation for all SAP applications. It is a comprehensive integration and application platform that works with a customer's existing IT infrastructure to enable and manage change. SAP SRM provides innovative applications to customers by leveraging the strengths of the NetWeaver platform.

15 SAP NetWeaver for SAP SRM

SAP Supplier Relationship Management (SRM) runs on the SAP NetWeaver platform for integrating people, information, and business processes across technologies and organizations. The platform ensures that mission-critical business processes are reliable, secure, and scalable. It also helps companies get more from their current software and systems by extending the purchasing process to meet their needs. SAP NetWeaver enables upgrades from one release of SAP SRM to the next to be implemented effectively. It also unifies disparate integration technologies and provides preconfigured business content, which reduces the need for custom integration. Based on industry-standard technology, the platform can be extended with commonly used development tools, such as Java 2 Enterprise Edition (J2EE), Microsoft .NET, and IBM WebSphere.

SAP NetWeaver, together with the service-enabled SAP Business Suite, provides the environment needed for adopting Enterprise Services Architecture (ESA). As companies adopt this service-oriented architecture, they enable faster and cheaper changes to their integrated system landscape and increase reuse of existing technology. Within SAP SRM, ESA provides the blueprint by which an empowered workforce can implement effective, sustainable purchasing practices that can be changed easily over time.

SAP SRM provides innovative applications by effectively utilizing the NetWeaver components. SAP SRM users can access all procurement-related transactions from all underlying systems (e.g., SRM EBP, ERP, PLM, etc.) with a single sign-on access using SAP NetWeaver Portal. The global spend analysis, supplier evaluation, and advanced analytics functionalities in SAP SRM are provided using SAP NetWeaver Business Intelligence (SAP NetWeaver BI). SAP NetWeaver Master Data Management (SAP NetWeaver MDM) integration provides functionalities like master data harmonization for global spend analysis and the advanced catalog and content management tool SRM-MDM Catalog. The SAP NetWeaver Exchange Infrastructure (SAP NetWeaver XI) is used to enable cross-system processes, integrating both SAP and non-SAP systems. In this chapter, we will look into the roles of SAP NetWeaver Portal, SAP NetWeaver BI, and SAP NetWeaver XI in SAP SRM and the implementation of these NetWeaver components.

15.1 SAP SRM on SAP NetWeaver — A Brief Overview

SAP NetWeaver enables flexible deployment of SAP SRM scenarios in the organization. Figure 15.1 illustrates how SAP SRM leverages SAP NetWeaver. The following components of NetWeaver are used in SAP SRM scenarios:

▶ **SAP NetWeaver Portal**
SAP NetWeaver Portal is the main component for role-based access to different processes in SAP SRM. It makes single sign on (SSO) access to integrated procurement processes enabled by SAP SRM and other applications like ERP, PLM, etc., possible. With unified roles across all applications it enables users to access information across systems and different processes. Note that SAP NetWeaver Portal is commonly referred to by consultants using the term Enterprise Portal (EP).

▶ **SAP NetWeaver BI**
Information integration from different processes and systems is crucial for strategic analysis. Depending on the process setup of the customer, purchasing and associated data can be stored in different systems. To make things even more complex, some of this data is stored in non-SAP systems or in external directories. Depending on the nature of the purchasing analysis, it is important for purchasers to access data within the SAP SRM system and also from other external systems. SAP NetWeaver BI allows reporting across different systems by extracting data and presenting them through standard reporting tools. Note that SAP NetWeaver BI is commonly referred to by consultants with different acronyms such as SAP NetWeaver BI, BW, or BIW.

▶ **SAP NetWeaver XI**
SAP NetWeaver XI enables implementation of cross-system processes. With SAP NetWeaver XI, it is possible to connect systems, both non-SAP and SAP, and of different versions, to each other. SAP NetWeaver XI is based on open architecture and standards, in particular those from the XML and Java environments. It offers services that are essential in a heterogeneous and complex system landscape. With SAP NetWeaver XI, process integration can be achieved across different processes.

▶ **SAP NetWeaver Application Platform**
SAP NetWeaver Application Server (AS) (also sometimes referred to as Web Application Server (WAS) in this book) is the Basis foundation layer for all SAP SRM (and also SAP) applications. All of the application components are installed on SAP NetWeaver AS. SAP SRM utilizes both ABAP and the Java

foundation of SAP NetWeaver AS. The SRM Server is deployed on the ABAP Engine. The SRM Live Auction Cockpit (LAC) is deployed on the J2EE Server. On top of that the WAS also serves as a database (DB) and operating system (OS) abstraction layer.

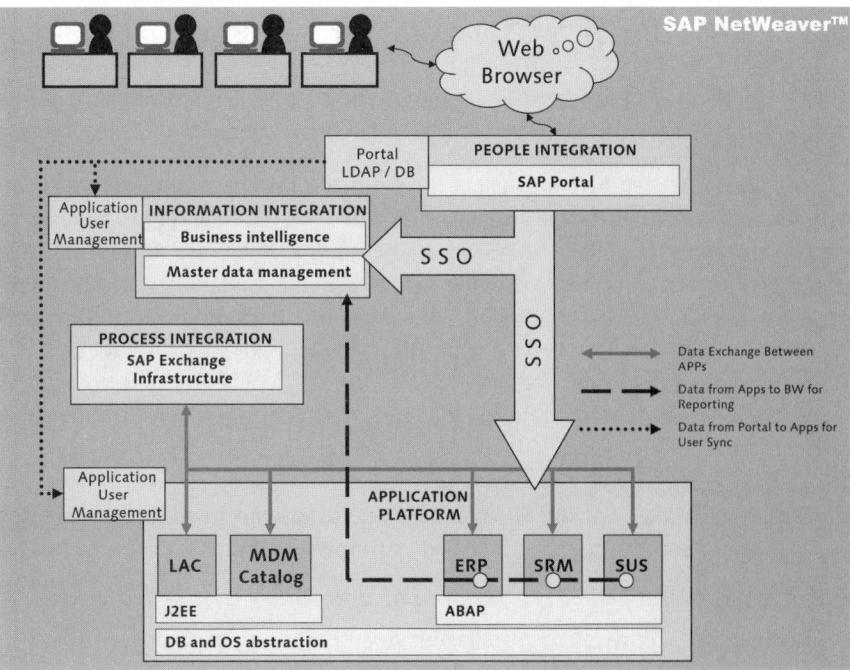

Figure 15.1 SAP SRM on SAP NetWeaver

▶ **SAP NetWeaver MDM**

SAP NetWeaver MDM is used for cleaning up and harmonizing master data. The typical challenges for analyzing spend data and making good use of this data are well known. The challenges include inaccurate and duplicated master data (e.g., supplier and product data) residing in many systems, incomplete data records, several classification schemas, and uncoordinated policies for changing master data records. In such an environment, purchasers and commodity managers have to struggle with manual efforts to get an integrated and harmonized data for making decisions. The SAP SRM purchasing platform addresses the challenges related to content consolidation through SAP NetWeaver MDM and SAP NetWeaver BI. SAP SRM also uses catalog content management solution based on MDM. The SRM-MDM Catalog is explained in more detail in Chapter 9.

In Sections 15.1.1 through 15.1.3, we will explain how these NetWeaver components can be used to extend the purchasing processes for maximum benefit.

15.1.1 SAP NetWeaver Portal

The SAP NetWeaver Portal (commonly referred to and known as the Enterprise Portal) provides users with role-based access to the following services of the SAP SRM components:

- Enterprise Buyer Professional (EBP)
- Supplier Self-Services (SUS)
- SAP NetWeaver BI reports (for evaluation and analysis of SAP SRM applications)

The business package provides users (on both the purchaser and vendor side) with an integrated workplace and user-friendly role-based access to all tasks of the procurement process in SAP SRM via iViews in Enterprise Portal. All integrated SAP SRM components provide logon-free access via SSO. Two business packages are delivered in the standard — Business Package for SAP SRM and Business Package for Supplier Collaboration. Let us take a closer look at these business packages next.

Business Package for SAP SRM

The Business Package for SAP SRM focuses on the support of all functional roles in purchasing. Some roles are described as follows:

- Employee, for employee self-service procurement
- Manager, for approval of purchasing documents in employee self-service procurement
- Employee and manager, in professional procurement covering operational and strategic purchasing
- Operational and strategic purchaser, for procure-to-pay and sourcing activities
- Accountant, purchasing assistant, and recipient, for procurement-related activities like receiving and invoicing
- Content manager, catalog manager, and catalog approver, for catalog and content management
- Component planner, for project system- and plant maintenance-related activities
- SAP SRM administrator, for administration- and system monitoring-related activities.

Business Package for Supplier Collaboration

The Business Package for Supplier Collaboration runs on the SAP NetWeaver Portal to create a self-service, collaborative environment for supplier companies. Suppliers have access to various supplier-managed transactions, analyses, and processes related to purchasing through a Web-based interactive gateway. This business package can be connected to SAP ERP backend systems, SAP SRM, SAP Product Lifecycle Management (PLM), Collaboration Folders (cFolders), and SAP Supply Chain Management (SCM). This provides access to collaborative planning, sourcing, procurement, content management, and design processes. This business package supports the following roles:

▶ Planner (supplier): Allows the supplier user to single sign on to SAP SCM Application to view and maintain planning data.

▶ Engineer (supplier): The supplier can exchange design documents with purchasers in a collaborative environment.

▶ Sales manager (supplier): Allows order management capabilities.

▶ Purchase administrator: The purchaser is allowed to maintain supplier data.

> **Note**
>
> There are constraints related to the version compatibility between different software components. Refer to the SAP online help documentation for more details.

15.1.2 SAP NetWeaver XI

Exchange Infrastructure with SAP NetWeaver XI enables customers to implement cross-system processes. It connects systems from different vendors (non-SAP and SAP) of different versions and implemented in different programming languages (Java, ABAP, and so on) to each other. As mentioned earlier, SAP NetWeaver XI is based on an open architecture and uses open standards (in particular those from the XML and Java environments). SAP NetWeaver XI differentiates itself from other middleware offerings in the market with its readily available content on business processes from all SAP applications. It offers the following services that are essential in a heterogeneous and complex system landscape:

▶ Modeling and design of messages, transformations, and cross-component integration processes

▶ Configuration options for managing collaborative processes and message flow

▶ Runtime environment for message and process management

▶ Adapter engine for integrating heterogeneous system components

▶ Central monitoring for monitoring message flow and processes

SAP NetWeaver XI supports internal and cross-company scenarios.

Elements of SAP NetWeaver XI

Important elements of SAP NetWeaver XI are illustrated in Figure 15.2 and are explained as follows:

▸ **System Landscape Directory (SLD)**
SLD is the main tool used to represent the system landscape. SLD enables you to describe products, software components, logical systems, and technical systems in the landscape.

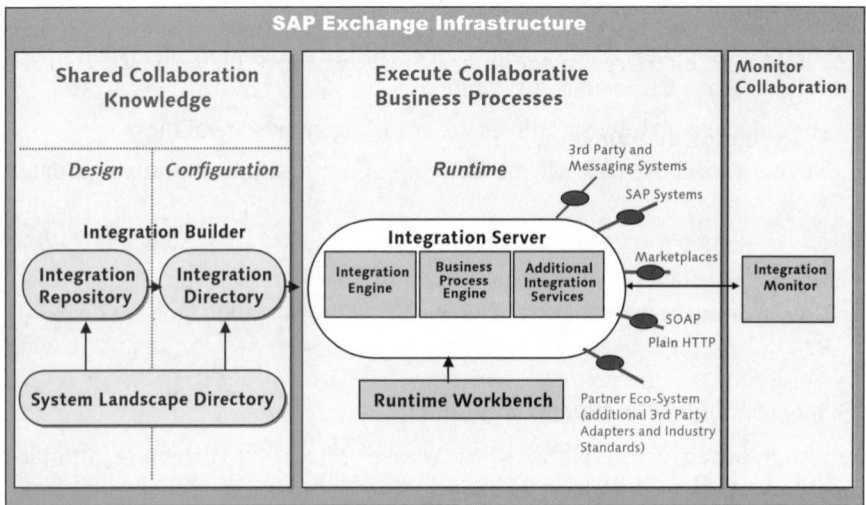

Figure 15.2 SAP Exchange Infrastructure

▸ **Integration Builder**
Integration Builder is the central tool for the design and configuration of the collaborative process. It contains two main components:

  ▸ Integration Repository

  ▸ Integration Directory

The content of the Integration Repository and Integration Directory is known as collaboration knowledge.

Before continuing with the remaining main SAP NetWeaver XI components, let's look at the Integration Repository and Integration Directory in more detail:

▸ **Integration Repository**
Interface definitions and mappings are stored in the Integration Repository, and different interfaces are defined and linked using mappings in this repository. You will find process definitions and mappings for processes in many SAP applications in the Integration Repository. Further, it is a tool for the following design tasks:

▶ **Designing integration scenarios**
In the Integration Builder, integration scenarios are used as the central point for understanding the relationships between the objects involved (interfaces, mappings, integration processes). The design of integration scenarios is also used at configuration time to map the collaborative process to the current system landscape.

▶ **Designing interfaces and proxy generation**
Interfaces are defined in the Integration Repository and used for proxy generation to generate executable proxies in SAP application systems. Furthermore, Integration Builder can be used to import message schemas and SAP interfaces to the Integration Repository for further use in the design process.

▶ **Designing mappings**
The design of graphical message mappings and the import of Java and XSLT mappings is maintained in the Integration Repository. A description of how to register these mapping programs for the source and target interface is also maintained here.

▶ **Integration Directory**
Relationships between interfaces, and physical and logical routing details are stored in the Integration Directory. This directory also stores the link between the logical destination, physical destination, and mode of communication protocol that should be used to connect to the systems. The Integration Directory is used to configure cross-system processes as described below:

▶ **Defining collaboration profiles**
The Integration Directory is used for the description of the technical sender and receiver options (and how to identify them) using communication parties, services, and communication channels.

▶ **Defining receiver determinations**
The definition at a logical level identifying which service a message should be sent to is configured in the Integration Directory. The service can be a business system, an integration process, or a service for a Business to Business (B2B) communication.

▶ **Defining interface determination**
Assignment of a receiver interface to a sender interface is defined in the Integration Directory. Also, mapping programs that need to be executed from the Integration Repository for the corresponding sending and receiving interface pair is registered in the Integration Directory.

▶ **Defining collaboration agreements**
In a collaboration agreement, a communication channel that should be used to process messages for a particular combination of senders and

receivers is defined. The collaboration agreements are defined in the Integration Directory.

▶ **Defining configuration scenarios**
Grouping of all configuration objects by the scenario is needed for easy maintenance. This is done in the Integration Directory using configuration scenarios.

We will now look at the remaining main elements of SAP NetWeaver XI:

▶ **Runtime Integration Engine**
The Integration Engine is the runtime component of SAP NetWeaver XI for processing XML messages that are exchanged between applications in heterogeneous landscapes. The important elements include the following:

▶ **Integration server**
The integration server is the central runtime component for receiving, processing, and forwarding messages. SAP NetWeaver XI supports direct communication using proxies and communication using adapters.

▶ **Proxy runtime**
Proxy runtime is the runtime component for proxy communication between the integration server and application systems based on SAP NetWeaver AS (or WAS).

▶ **Adapter engine**
The adapter engine is the runtime component that uses adapters to connect external systems and SAP systems to the integration server. The IDoc adapter and the plain HTTP adapter run independent of the adapter engine.

▶ **Central Monitoring**
The Central Monitoring element of SAP NetWeaver XI lets you monitor the SAP NetWeaver XI components, the message processing by one or more components, and the performance of message processing. The transaction SXMB_MONI offers you these central monitoring functionalities and is one of the most used transactions.

Integration Scenarios with SAP SRM

SAP SRM uses the SAP NetWeaver XI for communication with other applications and components. Some integration scenarios are listed below:

▶ **Integration between SAP SRM and SAP ERP systems**:

▶ By default, the integration between SAP SRM and ERP uses Remote Function Calls (RFCs), mainly due to the fact that both solutions are deployed behind the firewall and it is secure to use RFCs.

▶ If there is a firewall between the SRM Server and the ERP system, it is necessary to use SAP NetWeaver XI. In this case, the SRM Server communicates with SAP NetWeaver XI using proxy XML communication through the HTTP protocol. The ERP system communicates with SAP NetWeaver XI using native interfaces, like RFC or IDoc using adapters.

▶ A mapping is needed between the SAP SRM proxy XML and traditional SAP interfaces.

▶ **Integration between SAP SRM and non-SAP ERP systems**:

▶ If the ERP system is not an SAP ERP system, it is not possible for SAP SRM to exchange data directly using RFCs. SAP NetWeaver XI is used together with non-SAP adapters to make this integration possible. In this case, the SRM Server communicates with SAP NetWeaver XI using proxy XML communication through the HTTP protocol. The non-SAP systems communicate with SAP NetWeaver XI using application or technical adapters that will support the native protocols of non-SAP systems.

▶ Mapping is needed between the formats supported by the SAP SRM system and the non-SAP system.

▶ **Integration between SAP SRM EBP and SAP SRM SUS applications**.

▶ SAP SRM EBP and SAP SRM SUS have a similar proxy interface model. Because the SRM SUS solution is accessed by suppliers, SAP SRM and SAP SRM SUS are usually deployed with a firewall in between. In such cases, SAP NetWeaver XI is needed for communication between the solutions. In this case, both solutions communicate with SAP NetWeaver XI using proxy XML communication through the HTTP protocol.

▶ **Integration between SAP ERP and SAP SRM SUS applications**:

▶ SAP ERP is usually deployed behind a firewall and hence it is necessary to use SAP NetWeaver XI. In this case, the SRM SUS Server communicates with SAP NetWeaver XI using proxy XML communications through the HTTP protocol. SAP ERP communicates with SAP NetWeaver XI using native interfaces, such as RFCs or IDoc using adapters.

▶ A mapping is required between the SUS proxy XML and SAP traditional interfaces.

▶ **B2B communication to external suppliers**:

▶ In this case, the SRM Server communicates directly with the supplier CRM system or sales system.

▶ The SAP SRM Server communicates with SAP NetWeaver XI using proxy XML communication through the HTTP protocol. The SAP NetWeaver XI B2B adapter ensures that the data is sent to the supplier Web server using the HTTPS protocol.

▸ On the supplier side, the SAP NetWeaver XI B2B connector is used to receive the data and send it to the supplier integration server. This can be either another SAP NetWeaver XI server, or a non-SAP integration server.

15.1.3 SAP NetWeaver BI

SAP NetWeaver BI provides structured analyses for SRM. SAP NetWeaver BI is used for both operational and strategic analysis, as follows:

▸ For operational analysis, the data is provided on an individual document level with document header and document item information. Operation data storage (ODS) objects for purchase orders, confirmations, invoices, contracts, bid invitations, and bids have been defined on the basis of the ODS technology of SAP NetWeaver BI.

▸ Data is provided on an aggregated level for strategic analysis. It is possible to analyze data aggregated according to time, vendor, product, and product category, as well as according to account assignments. The InfoCubes defined for this are supplied with the information from the ODS objects. Global spend analysis and supplier evaluation are examples of strategic analysis.

Note
An InfoCube is a set of relational tables that are created in accordance with the star schema and used in SAP NetWeaver BI queries.

Analytical functionality within SAP SRM relies on the SAP NetWeaver BI component. Analytical information is presented within the context of business processes, so users can react immediately to the information and take the necessary steps to correct or optimize work processes.

Next, we will look at global spend analysis, supplier evaluation and transactional analysis, which are the mostly used types of analysis in procurement.

Global Spend Analysis

Global spend analysis is the foundation for strategic sourcing initiatives. Using this analysis, a company can identify corporate spend on an enterprise-wide level to gain a clear and accurate view of the corporate spend. Global spend analysis enables discovering of sourcing opportunities with substantial savings potential for different product categories and suppliers. It serves as the starting point to develop, execute, and monitor corporate sourcing strategies. With global spend analysis, customers can optimize their supplier base, improving bottom-line results. With global spend analysis, a company also gets better visibility to contractual terms and can strengthen their negotiation position. SAP SRM comes with predelivered content for spend analysis, as follows:

▶ There are ready-to-plug-in extractors to SAP EBP and SAP ERP, for immediate use without much implementation effort.

▶ SAP NetWeaver BI has extensive reporting capability. The data is collected and combined from the entire enterprise, across geographical and functional boundaries. This data is then aggregated and turned into information, delivered specifically to the role of the strategic sourcing professional.

▶ The tool comes delivered with many standard InfoCubes and hundreds of attributes reflecting dimensions such as market, suppliers, products, and the internal organization.

▶ There are predefined reports for spend analysis. Data can be structured in hierarchies to analyze, for example, spend on different aggregated levels of the organization. Multiple parallel hierarchies are also possible.

▶ Customers can also add their own company-specific attributes and InfoCubes. Predelivered reports are available not only for spend analysis but also for supplier performance analysis, supplier segmentation, bid analysis, compliance analysis (e.g., maverick spend), contract management, purchasing controlling, etc., giving more substance and a broader view of the spend reporting. And as mentioned, in addition, users can easily create their own reports and queries, based on existing or customer specific InfoCubes.

▶ Data can be presented and visualized in a number of different ways, including the following:

  ▶ Graphical presentation

  ▶ Dashboard with personalized information

  ▶ Tables

  ▶ Maps

  ▶ Download to Microsoft Excel

Supplier Evaluation

Vendor evaluation can support the process on both a strategic and operational level. It contains two parts:

▶ Automatically calculated key figures. For example, on-time delivery and correctness in goods receipt.

▶ Surveys or questionnaires measuring "soft" factors (SoftFacts) or qualitative criteria.

  SAP SRM has developed a solution for the SoftFacts, using Web surveys. SAP ERP vendor evaluation calculates vendor scores from automatically calculated key figures. Both types of key figures are aggregated and reported in SAP NetWeaver BI. In this section, we will focus on the Web surveys for SoftFacts.

SAP vendor evaluation measures performance both qualitatively and quantitatively. Qualitative measures can be collected via Web surveys, distributed to internal buyers or other internal parties. They can be configured to appear for multiple events based on certain parameters, such as every 100th invoice for material XYZ. The answers translate into scores. In addition, key performance indicators (KPIs) are automatically calculated from the procurement process. Some highlights of vendor evaluation functionalities include the following:

▶ Users can create hierarchies, grouping KPIs that go together, such as quality, price and delivery related. All KPIs can be summarized to one single number with an overall score for all KPIs. KPIs can be given different weighs, which can be adapted depending on the product category or other characteristics.

▶ The Web surveys can be event-triggered by, for example, a goods receipt. When users enter a goods receipt in the system, they are required to fill out a questionnaire related to receipts, quality, service, etc. Web survey triggering can also be scheduled so that, for example, only every tenth goods receipt will be evaluated.

▶ The Web surveys can be created either in SAP SRM or in SAP NetWeaver BI. However, SAP NetWeaver BI–based surveys are not event driven.

▶ Grouping and weighting of criteria is supported and done in SAP NetWeaver BI. This includes both automatically calculated key figures from SAP ERP as well as Web surveys.

Transactional Analysis

In addition to the strategic analysis we just discussed, SAP SRM and SAP NetWeaver BI provide content for analysis of operational data. Data is extracted from the SAP SRM and ERP systems for the integrated analysis. Some examples include the following:

▶ **Contract management analytics**
Monitoring contracts is an integratal part of contract management. Standard SAP NetWeaver BI content for SAP SRM provides several central reports, such as expiring contracts, contract call off and utilization, contracts per category, releases volume per contract, invoices per contract, contract alerts, maverick buying, etc.

▶ **Bidding analytics**
For both request for quotations (RFQs) and reverse auctions, SAP SRM supports sophisticated analysis that helps companies weigh price concerns along with other important factors. Some of these factors include quality of materials and services, delivery times, past experience, dependability, ability to meet growing demand, and so on. To enable this level of analysis, SAP SRM provides a toolset with capabilities for complex multiparametric analysis.

Purchasing professionals can easily generate insightful bidding statistics and perform side-by-side comparisons of individual bids and vendors. An easy-to-use Web template with a preconfigured analysis scenario keeps customization to a minimum and helps buyers make the kind of decisions that provide their companies with the most benefit in the long term. Some of the standard reports include analysis of responses, weighted score analysis, bidder past history, supplier evaluation analysis, etc.

We will now move on to our discussion of how to implement the SAP NetWeaver components for SAP SRM.

15.2 Implementing SAP NetWeaver Components for SAP SRM

In this section, we will provide you with a checklist of configuration settings for SAP NetWeaver Portal, XI, and BI. Detailed implementation information for each of these SAP NetWeaver components is beyond the scope of the book and you should refer to the respective application guides for more details.

15.2.1 Implementing SAP NetWeaver Portal

In this section, we will look at the implementation of the SAP NetWeaver Portal, including prerequisites and implementation considerations.

Prerequisites

The following prerequisites should be considered for SAP NetWeaver Portal implementations:

- ▶ Prerequisites for installing the Business Package for SAP SRM:
  - ▶ SAP SRM Server is installed.
  - ▶ SSO for SAP SRM is configured.
  - ▶ Configuration of required SAP SRM scenarios has been carried out.
- ▶ Pre-requisites for installing the Business Package for Supplier Collaboration:
  - ▶ Basic SAP NetWeaver Portal and Server components have been installed.
  - ▶ All SAP application components are optional.

You should refer to the relevant SAP SRM version's master guide for supported version details between the SAP NetWeaver Portal, SAP SRM, PLM, SAP ERP, etc.

Implementation Considerations

You should keep the following considerations in mind while implementing Business Packages:

- **SSO**: SSO must be configured for SAP EP and for each backend system to be integrated with the business package. Identical user IDs must exist on the portal and the backend systems.

- **User data persistence**: The users created for the business package must have a business partner, central person, and organizational unit relationship designated within the EBP system. Besides its own user store, the portal can be configured for the SRM Server system's user management, LDAP, or EBP Central User Management Administration (CUA) ABAP client.

- **User synchronization and replication**: User synchronization and replication can be achieved by using CUA.

- **The following sequence should be followed for installation**:
  - Install SAP NetWeaver Portal 7.0.
  - Download the Business Package for Supplier Collaboration 2.0 from the Service Marketplace at *http://service.sap.com*.
  - Use Software Deployment Manager (SDM) to install the EPA or SCA file in which the business package is delivered.
  - Assign the purchaser administrator role to the user performing the configuration of the business package.

For additional configuration details refer to the Solution Manager. The documentation can be found in the Solution Manager at **SAP Solution Manger • Configuration • SAP SRM • Basic Settings for SAP SRM • Business Package for Supplier Collaboration (or Business Package for SRM Server)**.

15.2.2 Implementing SAP NetWeaver XI

The following prerequisites should be considered for your SAP NetWeaver XI implementation:

- PI content for the SRM Server should have been imported.

- Enable SAP NetWeaver XI on the SRM Server using the menu path **SPRO • SAP Implementation Guide • Supplier Relationship Management • SRM Server • Cross-Application Basic Settings • Enable use of Exchange Infrastructure**.

- Download and install the latest SLD content from the SAP Service Marketplace at *https://service.sap.com/swdc*. Then follow the path **Download • Support Packages and Patches • Entry by Application Group • Additional Components • SAP Master Data for SLD**.

▸ On the SAP Exchange Infrastructure host (Integration Builder), create the directory called *<systemdir>/xi/repository_server/import* if it does not already exist. Then proceed as follows:

 ▸ Copy all *.tpt files from *<SRM-XI Content CD>/TPT* to the directory *<systemdir>/xi/repository_server/import*.

 ▸ Download all *.TPZ files from the SAP Service Marketplace at *https://service.sap.com/swdc*, then follow the path **Download · Support Packages and Patches · Entry by Application Group · SAP Application Components · SAP SRM (with EBP) · SAP SRM 5.0 · XI Content**.

 ▸ Copy the downloaded *.TPZ files to the directory *<systemdir>/xi/repository_server/import*.

 ▸ Start the Integration Repository (Design) tool of the Integration Builder.

 ▸ Select **Object · Import XI 3.0 Development Object**.

 ▸ Select all *.TPT files that are copied to the import directory.

 ▸ The SAP SRM–specific integration content will be loaded into the repository and can be used.

▸ Refer to Chapter 9 for more details on configuring SRM-MDM Catalog scenarios.

▸ Refer to Chapters 13 and 14 for more details on configuring SUS scenarios.

15.2.3 Implementing SAP NetWeaver BI Content for SAP SRM

In this section, we will discuss the prerequisites and implementation considerations involved in implementing SAP NetWeaver BI for SAP SRM.

Prerequisites

Before SAP NetWeaver BI can be used for reporting with SAP SRM, the following prerequisites should be considered:

▸ Installation of SAP NetWeaver BI: For a minimal system landscape SAP NetWeaver BI can be installed on the SAP SRM Server, if data volumes are not high. The following installation activities should be completed:

 ▸ Install SAP NetWeaver AS ABAP, which includes SAP NetWeaver BI 7.0 and PI_BASIS.

 ▸ Configure the database of SAP NetWeaver AS for SAP NetWeaver BI.

 ▸ Install SAP NetWeaver BI Business Content Add-On BI_CONT on the SAP NetWeaver AS ABAP system.

▸ Connect the source system (e.g., SAP SRM and ERP systems) to the SAP NetWeaver BI system.

▸ Activate the SAP NetWeaver BI DataSources in SAP SRM.

► Activate the SAP NetWeaver BI Business Content for SAP SRM in SAP NetWeaver BI.

► Integrate the SAP NetWeaver BI roles for SAP SRM into the SAP SRM composite roles.

Implementation Considerations

The following implementation steps are needed to activate the SAP NetWeaver BI content for usage in SAP SRM scenarios:

► **Preparation of operational system**
All data and transactions that are later passed to SAP NetWeaver BI for analysis are created in the operational system (or transactional system, OLTP-System). The operational system has to be prepared so that it can send the correct data:

  ► **Activating Data Sources**: Business content includes the metamodels that hold the data and reports for scenarios. In the transactional system, data sources define the structures and the data that are provided for reporting. These data sources must be activated.

  ► **Installing Data Sources**: To load data for reporting from the SAP Bidding Engine into SAP NetWeaver BI, the relevant data sources must be activated in EBP.

► **Configuration of SAP NetWeaver BI**
Business content includes the metamodels that hold the data and reports for the scenarios. Customers can extend the delivered structures, modify them, or use them as is. Perform the following steps:

  ► Define the source systems in SAP NetWeaver BI

  ► Transfer global settings to SAP NetWeaver BI

  ► Install Business Content

  ► Enable Web reporting

  ► Set up authorizations (optional)

► **Data load**
Data has to be loaded from the transactional system into SAP NetWeaver BI to carry out the analysis. The following steps need to be performed for loading data:

  ► **Maintain system IDs**: The systems and system ID enables SAP NetWeaver BI to uniquely identify objects. Therefore, transactional systems and their system IDs have to be maintained in SAP NetWeaver BI.

▶ **Load master data**: Master data contains the texts, attributes, and hierarchies of characteristics for display and should be loaded before loading transaction data.

▶ **Load transaction data**: Transaction data holds all of the information for which the user wants to generate reports.

15.3 Summary

In this chapter, we have learned how SAP SRM leverages the capabilities of the SAP NetWeaver platform effectively to provide innovative and user-friendly applications. SAP NetWeaver allows companies to benefit from using the existing IT infrastructure by adding customer-specific processes to the standard SAP SRM processes. SAP NetWeaver allows procurement professionals to extend their procurement processes beyond SAP SRM scenarios by integrating them with other business applications. SAP NetWeaver plays an important role in enabling services-based integration of business applications with cross-system process flows.

With this chapter, we have completed explaining the implementation of all SAP SRM scenarios. In Chapters 16 and 17, we will discuss frequently answered questions, troubleshooting tips and tricks, and the implementation of a few customer-specific scenarios with enhancements.

Progress comes from the intelligent use of experience.

— Elbert Hubbard

16   FAQs, Troubleshooting Tips and Tricks in SAP SRM

We have compiled the contents of this chapter from our in-depth experience in numerous customer implementations. We invite you to learn from our experience to help you ensure successful and quick SAP SRM implementations. In Section 16.1, you will find frequently asked questions, and their answers. In Section 16.2, we provide you with many troubleshooting tips and tricks. In Section 16.3, you will find a list of useful SAP Notes and consulting notes. Although the information in these notes is available to consultants in the service marketplace (*http://service.sap.com/notes*), we have observed that they are often ignored. Always refer to this list of notes before jumping to the conclusion that a customer's requirement cannot be supported in SAP SRM. Being able to draw upon the information in this chapter enhances an SAP SRM consultant's value for his/her clients.

16.1   Frequently Asked Questions (FAQs)

In this section, we will discuss questions asked recently by consultants:

▶ **What are the new features in SAP SRM 2007?**
The main changes in SAP SRM 2007 when compared to SAP SRM 5.0 are as follows:

  ▶ Enhanced user interface using WebDynpro and SAP NetWeaver Portal (the new user interface screenshots are shown in Figure 16.1 and Figure 16.2).

  ▶ New workflow based on the Business Rule Framework (BRF).

  ▶ Enhanced features in bidding, which include expressive bidding.

  ▶ Enhancements in contracts, including alerts definition at the document level.

  ▶ Integration with Duet for shopping cart approvals and reporting.

▸ There are a few changes in terminology. For example, the term 'Vendor' is replaced with 'Supplier'; 'Bid invitation' with 'RFx'; and 'Bid' with 'RFx Response.'

The detailed delta functionalities in SAP SRM 2007 can be accessed in the SAP SRM wiki section in the SAP Developer Network (SDN) at *http://sdn.sap.com.*

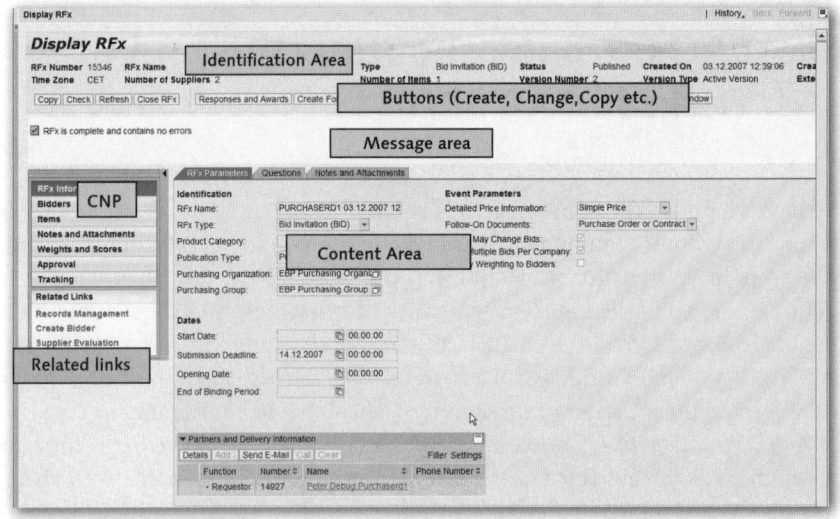

CNP: Control Navigation Panel

Figure 16.1 New User Interface in SAP SRM 2007

▸ **What are the high-level technology changes in SAP SRM 2007?**
The high-level technology changes are as follows:

▸ As mentioned previously, the Internet Transaction Server (ITS) user interface has been replaced with the WebDynpro user interface (refer to Figure 16.1 for new document screens).

▸ As mentioned previously, there is a new workflow using the BRF.

▸ The SAP Catalog Content Management (CCM) catalog has been replaced with the SRM-MDM Catalog, which is based on SAP NetWeaver Master Data Management (MDM) 5.5. The user interface for catalog searches uses WebDynpro-Java technology.

▸ The SAP NetWeaver Portal features, like Universal Worklist (UWL) and Personal Object Work List (POWL) have been added. Figure 16.2 shows a sample screenshot of the portal and POWL.

▸ The SAP NetWeaver Portal is a mandatory component in the SAP SRM landscape.

There are no changes to the Businee Server Page (BSP) user interfaces of supplier self-registration (ROS) and Supplier Self-Services (SUS).

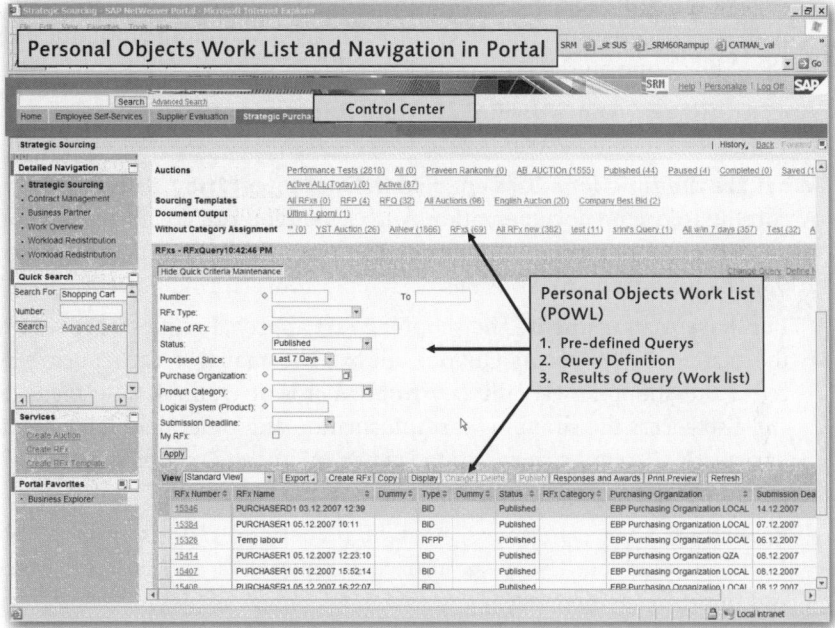

Figure 16.2 POWL and Navigation in SAP NetWeaver Portal

▶ **I have SAP SRM 4.0 and SAP SRM 5.0 implementation experience. What should I learn and what should I unlearn to implement SAP SRM 2007?**
You should learn the following:

▶ How to implement the new workflow

▶ WebDynpro-ABAP and WebDynpro-Java programming

▶ How to configure WebDynpro metadata

▶ How to configure an Enterprise Portal integration

You should unlearn the following:

▶ Many of the ITS-specific user interface features and BAdIs have become obsolete. For example, the BAdIs BBP_UI_CONTROL_BADI, BBP_CUF_BADI_2, etc., have become obsolete. Even in other BAdIs, you will not be able to use certain commands, such as "sy_ucomm."

▶ Some of the old workflow configuration settings, like *Workflow Start Conditions,* are no longer required. If you activate old workflows, you will need to convert them to new BRF workflows. Please refer to Chapter 8, Section 8.2.4 for more details on converting workflows.

▸ Many SAP SRM implementations will involve logon page changes, also. For example, beautification of the logon page with customer-specific communication guidelines is a common task. However, you do not need to change the SAP SRM logon page anymore as the Enterprise Portal is the main user interface in SAP SRM 2007. Therefore, all of the beautification should be done on the Enterprise Portal logon page.

▸ **Are SAP SRM 6.0 and SAP SRM 2007 different versions?**
No, they are the same versions.

▸ **What are the functionalities enabled in Duet integration with SAP SRM?**
According to online documentation, with Duet, you can access and interact with SAP processes using Microsoft Outlook 2003 and Microsoft Excel 2003. The following SAP SRM business applications are supported:

  ▸ **Purchase Management**: The shopping cart approval requests are sent to the manager's Microsoft Outlook inbox. The manager can approve or reject the shopping cart directly from Microsoft Outlook. The manager can also access the shopping cart information and other decision support information from the Duet Action Pane in Microsoft Outlook without logging on to the SAP SRM system.

  ▸ **Reporting**: Users can access a set of predefined reports from within Microsoft Outlook. Users can also view report data in Microsoft Excel, and to run related reports.

▸ **I have heard that SAP E-Sourcing offers advanced sourcing functionalities. Does the bidding engine in SAP SRM still exist ? Will it be continued in future versions?**
The bidding engine is an integral part of SAP SRM and we expect that it will continue to exist to protect current bidding engine customers. However, while the bidding engine takes care of most of the sourcing requirements, SAP E-Sourcing provides more advanced sourcing and project management capabilities.

▸ **Is there integration between SAP E-Sourcing and SAP SRM?**
Currently, SAP E-Sourcing and SAP SRM are not integrated. SAP E-Sourcing is integrated with SAP ERP, however. We expect that both E-Sourcing and SAP SRM will be integrated in the future.

▸ **Does xCLM replace contract management in SAP SRM?**
No. xCLM offers advanced contract authoring capabilities while SAP SRM contract management provides operational contract capabilities.

▸ **Can we deploy SUS and EBP in the same client?**
Yes, this is possible. Please refer to SAP Note 573383, which explains Enterprise Buyer Professional (EBP) and SUS deployment variants. SAP Note 1095018 describes the important settings for this scenario.

However, we do not recommend implementing EBP and SUS in the same client as vendors will have technical access to your procurement system.

Although the authorizations prevent vendors from accessing your purchasing data, any unintended errors in role assignment may provide them with additional access.

▶ **Can we have ROS and EBP in the same client?**
Yes, this is possible. However, we strongly recommend that you implement ROS and EBP in different clients. You may implement ROS and SUS in the same client.

▶ **Can we have ERP, EBP, and SUS in the same client? If yes, do we have any restrictions using all SAP SRM functionality?**
SRM@ERP2005 facilitates the implementation of SAP SRM as an add-on to ERP 2005. You can use self-service procurement and SUS in this case. You will not be able to use sourcing functionalities. Please refer to SAP online help documentation for more details.

▶ **Can we use SUS with EBP as a backend procurement system without any restrictions?**
You can use SUS with EBP as a backend procurement system. Please refer to Chapter 14 for more details. The following SAP Notes explain some restrictions that do exist, depending on the deployment scenario:

  ▶ **543544**: SUS not supported in the extended classic scenario (ECS)

  ▶ **700350**: SUS with various EBP deployment scenarios

▶ **Can we use same SUS client for both MM-SUS and EBP-SUS scenarios? Can we use '1' SUS client with 'n' procurement systems (1:n)?**
Yes, you can use 1:n deployment, where each SUS system is connected to 'n' procurement systems. You can also use n:n deployment where each procurement system may be connected to 'n' SUS systems and each SUS system to 'n' procurement systems. In both cases, the receiver determination in some SAP NetWeaver XI mappings need to be adjusted to determine the correct receiver for each message. Please refer to Chapters 13 and 14 for more details. SAP Note 884695 indicates the additional receiver determination settings.

▶ **When do we need SAP NetWeaver XI in SAP SRM?**
SAP NetWeaver XI is required when you want to implement the following SAP SRM scenarios:

  ▶ SUS: Both MM-SUS and EBP-SUS require SAP NetWeaver XI.

  ▶ CCM (both SAP CCM and SRM-MDM Catalog): If you want to load products from SAP SRM into a catalog or if you want to distribute contract items into a catalog, you will need SAP NetWeaver XI.

  ▶ SAP NetWeaver XI is required when you use distributed landscape for SAP CCM (for example, catalog authoring in one server instance and catalog search in another server instance). However, you will not need SAP NetWeaver XI, when SAP CCM catalog authoring and catalog search are installed in the same server instance.

▸ If you want to integrate any SAP SRM scenario with a non-SAP backend system, you will require SAP NetWeaver XI.

▸ **When do we need TREX in SAP SRM?**
TREX enables advanced text search and is required in the following scenarios:

  ▸ If you use SAP CCM as your catalog, you will need TREX for the catalog search engine. However, SAP CCM is now obsolete and we recommend implementing SRM-MDM Catalog, which does not require TREX.

  ▸ If you want to use advanced text search functionality in SAP SRM contracts, you will need to install TREX. Advanced search functionality enables you to search in contract attachments and contract long texts as well.

  ▸ If you are using advanced duplicate search in the invoice management system, you will need TREX.

▸ **Are SAP SRM and SRM Server the same thing?**
SRM Server is the main software component of the SAP SRM application. The version numbers of SAP SRM and SRM Server might not match, however. Table 16.1 shows the various SAP SRM versions and the corresponding SRM Server versions:

SAP SRM Name and Version	Software Component Name and Version
SAP SRM 2007	SRM Server 6.0
mySAP SRM 5.0	SRM Server 5.5
mySAP SRM 4.0	SRM Server 5.0

Table 16.1 SAP SRM and Underlying Software Component (SRM Server) Versions

▸ **Can we use special stocks in SAP SRM?**
In SAP ERP, the concept of *special stocks* is used to represent project stock, sales order stock, etc. Procurement of special stocks is done using special account assignment categories. SAP SRM does not support the creation of documents with account assignment categories that are linked to special stocks. Please also refer to SAP Note 586231.

▸ **Why don't we see cFolders collaboration in contracts?**
cFolders collaboration in contracts is possible only when the contract is created from a bid that has cFolders collaboration. If you directly create a contract, you will not see cFolders collaboration.

▸ **Why don't we see cFolders collaboration in bid invitations?**
Check whether a cFolders entry exists in the backend system settings in the configuration node *Define Backend Systems*. Verify your configuration with the prerequisites given in Chapter 10.

▸ **Can we have goods receipt notifications in MM-SUS scenario when our ERP version is SAP R/3 4.6C?**
Consulting note 1026638 explains the necessary configuration settings and procedure to transfer goods receipt information to SUS from SAP R/3 versions 4.7 and lower.

▸ **Are there SAP SRM country versions to handle country-specific taxation?**
Yes. There is SAP SRM country-specific functionality for Brazil from EBP 3.0 on. India-specific SUS functionalities are available on SAP SRM 5.0. Please refer to SAP Notes 504773, 970320, and 980659 for Brazil-specific EBP functionalities and SAP Note 906672 for SUS localization for India.

▸ **Where can we get SAP SRM configuration guides?**
You can generate SAP SRM configuration guides from Solution Manager. If you have not yet installed Solution Manager, you can also get SAP SRM configuration guides in the SAP SRM wiki section in SDN (*http://sdn.sap.com*).

▸ **Can you suggest some good references to learn and implement SAP SRM?**
The following links provide good documentation on SAP SRM and are very useful:

   ▸ *https://www.sdn.sap.com/irj/sdn/wiki*: This is the SAP SRM page in the SDN wiki, which has many useful links that include BAdI sample codes. You can also get links to other references here.

   ▸ *http://www.sap.com/srm*: This is the official SAP SRM site.

   ▸ *http://service.sap.com/srm*: This is the official SAP SRM site in the SAP Service Marketplace.

   ▸ *http://service.sap.com/ibc-srm*: This link will take you to SAP SRM 4.0 configuration guides, documentation, etc.

   ▸ *http://service.sap.com/srm-inst*: This link provides access to master guides, installation guides, upgrade guides, security guides, etc.

   ▸ *http://help.sap.com*: Here you will find SAP online help documentation

   ▸ *http://service.sap.com/releasenotes*: This link takes you to release notes of different SAP SRM versions.

   ▸ *http://service.sap.com/pam*: Here you will find a product availability matrix. If you want to know which operating systems, databases, languages, browsers, etc., are supported for a specific SAP SRM version, you should visit this link.

   ▸ *https://www.sdn.sap.com/irj/sdn/wiki?path=/display/SRM/Blogs&*: SAP SRM and MDM blogs in SDN.

   ▸ SAP SRM forum in SDN.

Additionally, you can also refer to Sachin Sethi's book *Enhancing Supplier Relationship Management Using SAP SRM* published by SAP PRESS.

Now let's move on to some troubleshooting tips and tricks for SAP SRM.

16.2   Troubleshooting Tips and Tricks

In this section, we will show you a few troubleshooting tips and tricks in addition to the tips provided in other chapters. However, this is not an exhaustive list. For further assistance, note that the SDN forum for SAP SRM is very active and we recommend that you make use of this forum. We also urge you to contribute by sharing your experiences in this forum.

SAP Remote Support during SAP SRM Implementation

We strongly recommend that you set up SAP remote connection services early in your implementation. If you face any problem during your implementation, the SAP support team may want to connect to your system to verify the problem and provide a resolution. Unlike with ERP support, where SAP personnel can log on to the sapgui and debug the system, you need to provide both browser access and sapgui access for your SAP SRM implementation. PC-Anywhere, Windows Terminal Server, HTTP, or other such connections can be used for this purpose. Please refer to SAP Note 984434 for connection types and other hints to speed up support message processing.

Understanding SAP SRM Tables and Function Components

In this section, we will provide you with a few hints regarding SAP SRM tables and function modules. Note that most of the SAP SRM tables have GUID as the key field. We have also provided tables and function modules for cFolders here.

▸ You can get the complete details of any document by any of the following methods:

  ▸ Execute function module BBP_PD_xxx_GETDETAIL, where xxx is the short ID of the object (e.g, BID for the bid invitation, CTR for the contract). You can get a list of function modules by using search key BBP_PD_*_GETDETAIL in Transaction SE37. You can also get function groups for each of the documents and use these function groups to see associated other function modules, for example, function modules for creating or checking a document.

  ▸ Execute Transaction BBP_PD. Select the required Object Type, enter the Object ID, and execute to see all of the details of the document.

▸ Important tables and relations in SAP SRM are shown in Figure 16.3. Most of the tables that contain procurement document data have the prefix BBP_PD. You can search for other tables in Transaction SE16 using search key BBP_PD*.

▸ Business partner data table names normally start with BUT. You can search for the tables with search key BUT* in Transaction SE16.

▸ Supplier registration survey-related tables can be found with search key TUWS* in Transaction SE16.

▶ cFolders provides API function modules to process areas, collaborations, folders, or documents. You can use search key CFX_API* to find the available APIs in Transaction SE37.

▶ Some useful tables in cFolders are: CFX_COL, CFX_FOL, CFX_ASSIGN-MENTS, CFF_PHF, ACO_GROUP, and ACO_GROUP_USER. You can use search keys CFX_* or ACO_* in Transaction SE37 for other tables.

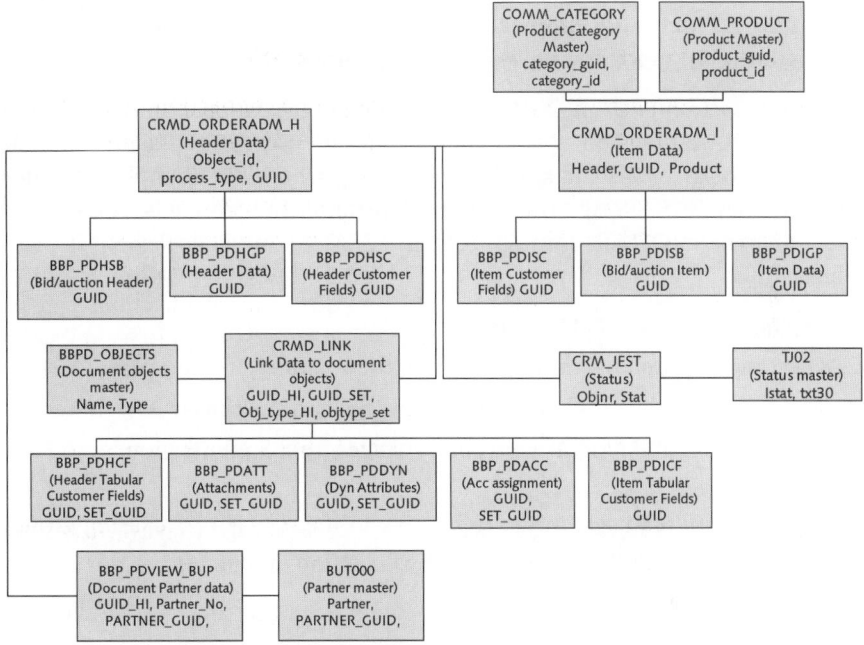

Figure 16.3 SAP SRM Tables

Setup, Transport, and Copy in SAP SRM

To perform any of the following tasks, download the document "Transporting SAP EBP Systems Ver 1.4" from the service marketplace as explained in SAP Note 447651:

▶ Transport the SAP EBP system

▶ Perform a system copy of an SAP EBP system landscape

▶ Distribute the organization model between an SAP HR and an SRM EBP system or between two SRM EBP systems

▶ Transport the attributes in the organization model from one EBP system to another

▶ Transport product categories from one SAP EBP system to another

Other useful notes on these topics include the following:

▶ **995771**: Contains information on copying the SAP SRM system landscape

▶ **418886**: Product download and GUIDs

▶ **338588**: Product GUIDs

▶ **390380**: Composite note on HR/ALE distribution to EBP

▶ **312090**: Consulting note for the integration of HR and EBP/SAP SRM

Assigning a Purchasing Group to a User without Changing the Organization of Users ('Is Purchaser Of' Relation)

Using Transaction PPOMA_BBP, you can assign organizational units and assign users to organizational units. Sometimes, you want users to be assigned to their respective departments and also to a purchasing group. For example, a finance manager may also be responsible for administrative procurement. You can use the "Is Purchaser Of" relationship from SAP SRM 4.0 on. Follow these steps to achieve this:

1. Execute Transaction PPOMA_BBP.

2. Select the required purchasing group in the bottom left-hand pane.

3. Right-click on the purchasing group and click on **Purchaser Assignment**.

4. You will see that the right-hand pane changes from Staff Assignment to **Purchaser Assignment**.

5. Link the required users in the right pane to the selected purchasing group. This assignment will not change their staff assignment.

Translation-Related Issues

While creating a purchase order, if you do not see any long text descriptions but see an error message that you should maintain text types, you've run into a translation-related problem. If you are working in a multi-language environment, text entries (names or descriptions) in master data and configuration settings should be translated into multiple languages. In the master data, you will see an option to enter a description in multiple languages while maintaining data. While maintaining configuration settings in the IMG, you can maintain translations in multiple languages by following the menu path **Goto • Translation**. For the problem described here, maintain the translations in your language for text types in IMG setting **SPRO • SRM Server • Cross Application Basic Settings • Text Schema • Define Text Types**. Also, verify whether a text schema is assigned to the purchase order transaction type.

Identifying Valid Namespaces

While configuring settings, you might encounter a message that you are violating name space rules. SAP reserves certain naming conventions for customer-specific configuration entries. The remaining name spaces are reserved for SAP to use in future versions. For example, it is a common practice to prefix the customer settings with 'Y' or 'Z.' These rules are defined to ensure smooth upgrades. Follow these steps to identify the allowed name space:

1. Identify the table or view of the required configuration entry. You can find it by clicking F1 in a field and then clicking on the technical information icon.
2. Execute program RDDKOR54 using Transaction SE38.
3. Enter the table or view name and execute to see a list of the reserved name spaces.

Viewing Engineering Drawings Attachments from cFolders and Other SAP Applications without Installing CAD Software

SAP provides ECLViewer, which can be used to view, review, and redline drawings, etc. Using this tool, you can add attachments of any type, including drawings in cFolders, and view them without installing the associated CAD software on your computer. Please refer to SAP Notes 494146 to install ECLViewer. You can also refer to SAP Note 551319 for a FAQ on ECLViewer.

Attachment Problems

In this section, we will discuss common attachments problems in SAP SRM:

▸ **You try to attach a file but the system does not save the file**
You may see this problem, especially in the prescreen suppliers transaction in ROS. You can resolve this by executing program REPAIR_BDS_OC1. If you do not have this program in your system, implement SAP Note 798605.

▸ **You try to attach a file but the system does not seem to be saving the file**
In some cases, the system might be saving the file but you are unable to view this as you do not have sufficient authorizations. Ensure that authorization object S_BDS_DS is assigned to you.

▸ **You encounter problems due to an incompatibility of virtual machines with a Java applet**
Please refer to SAP Note 889701 to resolve this problem.

Configuration File Names Inside the SAP J2EE Engine for Live Auction Cockpit

The names of configuration files inside the SAP J2EE engine for Live Auction Cockpit (LAC) are as follows:

▸ **srmla.properties**: Contains Jco parameters for the Java-to-ABAP connection
▸ **srmlaClient.properties**: Lets you change the applets look and feel

- **log.properties**: Enables error logging into a local file
- **mySAP.properties**: Contains Java user management settings

Problems with Auction Batch Jobs

You may face problems with batch jobs that are supposed to start, publish, or end an auction, such as auctions starting correctly but not ending. One or more of the following solutions should help in such situations:

- Implement SAP Note 811180 and execute program BBP_LA_CREATE_QUOTATION, if quotations are not created at the end of the auction.
- The user creating an auction may not have authorization to release batch jobs. Ensure that the user has authorization object S_BTCH_JOB assigned.
- You should have at least one of the batch processors configured to run class 'A' jobs. Contact your Basis consultant to ensure this.

Dealing with Invoice Number Range Problems When You Use Both Extended Classic and Standalone Scenarios

If you use both the extended classic scenario and the standalone scenario, you may see that invoices from the standalone scenario do not get posted in backend SAP ERP. In Transaction WE02, you can see that the invoice IDoc resulted in the error "Number range not found.' In the backend ERP, the number ranges for Logistics Invoice Verification (LIV) and accounting documents may be set as the same. It is a normal practice to set the internal number range for LIV and the external number range to accounting document type 'RE.' This setting should work fine, if you have defined the same number range for invoices in SAP SRM, also.

If you have a different invoice number range in SAP SRM, the standalone invoice from SAP SRM cannot create accounting documents in SAP ERP as SAP ERP expects a valid number (a number in the external number range for 'RE') to be sent from SAP SRM. Logistics invoices will not have any problem as an internal number range is defined for them. The solution is to synchronize the number ranges in SAP SRM and SAP ERP or define an internal number range for the accounting document 'RE,' too.

Generate Mass Data to Analyze Performance

You can use program BBP_ANALYSE_PERFORMANCE to copy a document line item and mass generate line items (for example, 500, 1000, etc.) to test performance.

Business Partner- and User-Related Issues

If, when you move users in PPOMA_BBP to a different organization using drag-and-drop functionality, the Business Partner relations become inconsistent, implement SAP Note 1045813. Please also refer to other useful SAP Notes provided for component SRM-EBP-ADM-USR in this chapter, in Section 16.3.

Finding the Open Catalog Interface (OCI) Parameters Passed from SAP CCM to EBP

To find the OCI parameters passed from SAP CCM to EBP, implement Note 847229.

Setting Up and Troubleshooting OCI

Please refer to the SDN blog by Masayuki Sekihara on OCI settings and trouble-shooting. The link for the blog is *https://www.sdn.sap.com/irj/sdn/ weblogs?blog=/pub/wlg/7780*.

Budget Check in EBP

If you are implementing the budget check functionality in SAP SRM, you should refer to the following SAP notes:

- ▸ **520717**: Budget check in EBP — consulting note
- ▸ **828231**: Commitments and SAP SRM
- ▸ **524670**: Budget display in EBP
- ▸ **633107**: EBP — funds management budget display
- ▸ **752983**: Budget display does not display any data
- ▸ **1081758**: FAQ: Budget check/display
- ▸ **1068860**: Budget check errors on trying to change purchase order
- ▸ **919378**: Duplicate commitment for purchase orders from SAP SRM

BAdI BBP_SC_VALUE_GET can be used to determine the shopping cart value for user budget.

You can also use component SRM-EBP-CA-BUD to search for messages or notes for budget checking in the service marketplace.

Using Pricing Scales in SAP CCM

If you maintain pricing scales (i.e., volume discounts) in CCM, then maintain the quantity in the catalog and transfer the items to the shopping cart. Note that you will not see scale price during an item search but the price transferred to shopping cart will be in line with the scale price. The scale price is transferred based on the quantity if you activate implementation /CCM/CSE_OCISCALEPRI for BADI /CCM/CSE_ENRICHMENT.

Catalog Publishing Issues

If you are trying to publish a catalog but the publishing process seems to be hanging, and you have run program /CCM/CLEANUP_CATALOG to remove lock entries and the status is still "being published," check the publishing status in table /CCM/D_PUB_ST. If the status is "R," create an OSS message for support. You can also change the publishing status in the table directly to "E" using Transaction SE16.

Replication Problems in the Standalone Scenario Without Backend Integration

If you are implementing SAP SRM in a standalone scenario without integrating to a backend system, you will, while maintaining the organizational plan using Transaction PPOMA_BBP, receive an error that locations or plants are not replicated using the program BBP_LOCATIONS_GET_ALL. Read SAP Note 563180 carefully and implement the solution suggested in this note.

Publish Several Internet Services

You can use program W3_PUBLISH_SERVICES to publish all ITS services and Internet application components (IACs). Refer to SAP Notes 629784 and 399578. SAP Note 629784 also explains changing Java script files.

Sourcing Cockpit ITS Screens in German

You might find that some sourcing cockpit ITS screen options are in German. Please refer to SAP Note 632982 for a solution. If the problem still exists, perform the following steps:

1. Log on in your language and execute Transaction SE80.

2. Choose Function Group BBP_SOCO_UI_ITS.

3. Drill down to Screens. Select screen 0301, then select the tab **Element List**. Select the subtab **Texts I/O templates**. Check whether the field descriptions are in your logon language. Write down the screen number if it is not in your logon language.

4. Repeat step 3 for screens 0011, 0021, and 0201.

5. Execute program RSSCRPINT001. Enter the program name as "SAPLBBP_ SOCO_UI_ITS." Enter the problematic screen numbers in the field Dynpro

number, and enter your logon language in the field Language. Repeat the step for all problematic screens.

6. Repeat step 3 and activate the Dynpro screens.

SAP WebDynpro Metadata Configuration

Many customers would like to modify the screen field behavior (hide or display, editable or not editable, and required or optional). The field behavior in WebDynpro screens can be changed by configuring WebDynpro metadata. For example, if you want to change an optional field in the purchase order screen into a required field, proceed as follows:

1. Find the technical field name as follows:
   - In the purchase order screen, right-click in the field to be changed and select "More Field Help."
   - The technical details of the field will appear in a new screen.
   - Write down the Field ID.

2. Verify the standard properties of the field in table view /SAPSRM/V_MDF_HD. (Properties of header fields can be displayed in table view /SAPSRM/V_MDF_HD and item fields in table view /SAPSRM/V_MDF_IT).

3. Change the field properties of the field as required in table view /SAPSRM/V_MDF_HC (for header fields) or in table view /SAPSRM/V_MDF_IC (for item fields).

4. During run time, WebDynpro gets the metadata details from the look up tables (/SAPSRM/V_MDF_HL or /SAPSRM/V_MDF_IL). In case of conflicting entries in standard properties tables and customer-specific properties, the more restrictive entry is valid. For example, if the field property is 'required' in the standard tables and 'optional' in the customer tables, the more restrictive entry will be 'required.'

5. If you want to change the field behavior only in certain cases (for example, based on some other field value), you need to implement dynamic customer classes and methods and include it in table view /SAPSRM/V_MDF_HC (for header fields) or in table view /SAPSRM/V_MDF_IC (for item fields). The implemented classes have to inherit the interface /SAPSRM/IF_MDx_yyy_DYN_CONTROL (where x can be "F" for fields and "A" for actions, and yyy can be "HDR" for header and "ITM" for item).

If you define customer fields for any SAP SRM document, you will need to configure the screen field behavior in table view /SAPSRM/V_MDF_HC (for header fields) or in table view /SAPSRM/V_MDF_IC (for item fields).

Using the enhancement framework, developers can extend the WebDynpro screens according to customer requirements. Please refer to SAP Notes 1115579 and 1103956 for more details.

Making Customer-Specific Roles (Z-Roles) Available in the Create Users or Create Business Partner Web Applications

If you have defined new roles in SUS, then the key BBP_SUS_ROLE_ATTRIBUTES on the Personalization tab in Transaction PFCG should have the value Display of Role in SUS UM selected.

If you have defined new roles in EBP, then configure the attribute ROLE in Transaction PPOMA_BBP with all of the roles you want to use on the Web application.

Short Dump During Supplier Self Registration

If a short dump MESSAGE_TYPE_X occurs when the system tries to send questionnaires to a vendor after he fills out the supplier self-registration general details and clicks on the **Submit** button, generate the XSLT for questionnaires by executing program UXS_ADD_MISSING_XSLT_NAME for application ROS_QUESTIONNAIRES to resolve the problem. The short text of the error message is "Name of generated XSLT program is initial."

Workflow Troubleshooting

The following are tips to help you resolve workflow problems:

- ▶ Use Transaction BBP_PD to see if the workflow was triggered and to get the workflow item number. Then you can use Transaction SWI1 or SWI2_FREQ to analyse the work item.
- ▶ If the workflow is not running, clean or synchronize the buffer using Transaction PPWFBUF or SWU_OBUF.
- ▶ Check whether the WF_BATCH user has a valid email ID assigned in the user master.
- ▶ Check whether the WF_BATCH user password was provided incorrectly in the workflow configuration.
- ▶ Check whether the workflow is stuck in the queue using Transaction SM58 (or SWU2) and clear the queue.
- ▶ Sometimes a purchase order hangs in status 'in approval' due to a problem in output conditions. Check the output conditions configuration according to SAP Note 886606.
- ▶ Check entries in Transaction SM13 for any update errors.
- ▶ Check for lock entries in Transaction SM12.
- ▶ A useful SAP Note for the anaysis of workflow problems is SAP Note 322526.

▸ Useful transactions for workflow troubleshooting include SWI1, SWI6, SWIA, SWU2, SWI2_DIAG, SWI2_ADM1. OOCU, SWETYPEV, PFTC, SWELS, SWEL, and SWB_PROCUREMENT.

▸ Check the application logs using Transaction SLG1 and search for object /SAPSRM/ to analyze any BRF related issues in SAP SRM 2007.

▸ Analyze new workflows using programs /SAPSRM/WF_CFG_ANALYSIS_ 001 and /SAPSRM/WF_CFG_ANALYSIS_002.

▸ Use Transaction SWIA to reassign approvers for a work item.

Useful Transactions in SAP SRM, XI, ERP for Troubleshooting

A list of useful transactions for troubleshooting SAP SRM, SAP NetWeaver XI, and SAP ERP are provided in Table 16.2. If you are new to any of these transactions, you should familiarize yourself by executing them once.

Transaction Code	Description/Remark
SXMB_MONI or SXI_MONITOR	SAP NetWeaver XI message (Integration Engine) monitoring
SXI_CACHE	SAP NetWeaver XI directory cache
SXMB_IFR	Start Integration Builder to configure SAP NetWeaver XI
SPROXY	ABAP proxy generation
SLDCHECK	Test SLD connection
RZ70	SLD administration
SM59	RFC destination
ALRTCATDEF	Define alert category
ALRTDISP	Display alerts
SU01	User maintenance
R3AM1	Monitor data exchange (e.g., master data exchange)
SMQ1	Outbound queue monitoring
SMQ2	Inbound queue monitoring
SMW01	Display BDoc messages
SWELS	Switch event trace on/off
BD83	Process outbound IDocs with errors again
BD87	Status monitor for ALE messages
WE02	ALE IDoc list display

Table 16.2 Useful Transactions for Troubleshooting

Transaction Code	Description/Remark
WE05	ALE IDoc list display
WE19	ALE IDoc test tool
SOST	Mail transmission status check
ST22	ABAP short dumps monitoring and analysis
SM12	Lock entries
SM13	Update monitoring
SM21	System log to display problem messages
SM58	Transactional RFC monitoring
RZ20	Application monitors
SLG1	Application logs
SU53	Identify a missing authorization
SU22	Identify authorizations checked for a transaction
SWI1	Workflow item selection
SWI2_ADM1	Work items without agents
SWI2_DIAG	Diagnosis of workflows with errors
SWI30	Unlock workflows
SWU2	Workflow RFC monitor
PFWFBUF or SWU_OBUF	Clean workflow buffer
BBP_CND_CHECK_CUST	Pricing check / Check IPC
BBP_PD	SAP SRM documents details

Table 16.2 Useful Transactions for Troubleshooting (Cont.)

Useful Programs

A list of useful programs (or reports) and their explanation is provided in the SAP SRM online documentation at *http://help.sap.com*. From there, follow the path **SAP Business Suite • SAP Supplier Relationship Management • SAP SRM 5.0 • Architecture and Technology • Administration • Reports**.

SAP SRM Testing Strategy

Many SAP SRM implementations simply adapt the testing strategy used in their ERP implementation. However, we strongly recommend that you include the following additional testing in your SAP SRM testing strategy:

- Test all processes in the company's network (intranet).
- Test all processes from the external network (e.g., from the implementation partner's network), if your processes require access from the Internet.
- If you implement bidding or SUS where your vendors need to access the SAP SRM application, you should test from at least one of your vendor's network. You may also want to invite a few selected vendors for a test run of the new application.
- Create one or two dummy vendors in your production system and test run the processes in the production system before going live.
- If you use both HTTP and HTTPS protocols, we recommend that you test all processes using both protocols.
- If you use the Enterprise Portal to access SAP SRM, then test your processes from the portal environment.
- Test SSO between applications (e.g., between ROS and EBP for prescreening vendors or between SAP SRM and cFolders during bidding).
- Always test with actual end user roles. It is a common practice to test with administrator rights and we strongly recommend that you avoid this. Always separate administrator users from application users and test only with application users.

16.3 Useful SAP Notes

Table 16.3 provides many very useful SAP SRM–related SAP notes. We have selected the notes that we have used in many of our implementations. These notes can help you while designing and configuring SAP SRM scenarios. We strongly recommend that you check this list during your implementation(s).

Component	Note	Note Description
BC	654982	URL requirements due to Internet standards
BC-FES-ITS	742048	Integrated ITS memory requirements
BC-SRV-COM	455140, 455127	Configuration of email, fax, paging, or SMS using SMTP
BC-SRV-COM	607108	Problem analysis when you send or receive emails
BC-SEC	550742, 817529, 138498	FAQ: Single sign on (SSO), SSO configuration checklist, and SSO solutions
BC-SEC	23611	Security in SAP products (Collective note)

Table 16.3 Useful SAP Notes for SAP SRM

Component	Note	Note Description
BC-BSP	616900	FAQ: BSP
BC-MID-RFC	369007	FAQ: qRFC scheduler
CRM-IPC	844816	Upgrade from IPC 4.0 to SAP AP 7.00 — Composite note
SRM-BW-EBP	614940	BW data sources for EBP/SRM Server
SRM-CAT	890553	CCM FAQ — General problems
SRM-CAT	973594	Cross-catalog search configuration — Consulting note
SRM-CAT	395312	Catalog data not copied to shopping cart — OCI troubleshooting note
SRM-CAT	487917	BAdI BBP_CATALOG_TRANSFER implementation for OCI troubleshooting
SRM-CAT-MDM	1077701	SRM-MDM Catalog FAQ
SRM-CAT-MDM	1084526	How to upload translations into an MDM repository
SRM-EBP	312090	EBP-HR integration
SRM-EBP	390380	HR/ALE distribution in EBP/CRM — Composite note
SRM-EBP	110909	Generic attributes (PPOMA_BBP) — Composite note
SRM-EBP	564826	Customizing for output of EBP documents
SRM-EBP	171113	Problems with Cleaner Job (Report CLEAN_REQREQ_UP)
SRM-EBP	874589	SRM 4.0 connection to an SAP ERP 2005 system
SRM-EBP	931020	SRM 4.0 connection to an SAP ERP 2004 system
SRM-EBP	334563	SRM with non-SAP backend system
SRM-EBP	673372	Short dump UNCAUGHT_EXCEPTION analysis and resolution
SRM-EBP-ADM-ORG	548796	FAQ:Organizational management in EBP
SRM-EBP-ADM-USR	548862	FAQ: EBP user administration
SRM-EBP-ADM-USR	642202	RFC User profile in backend system
SRM-EBP-ADM-USR	656633	Search help requires dialog users
SRM-EBP-ADM-USR	644124	Copy or delete access rights to attributes per user role with report BBP_ATTR_COPY_ACCESS_RIGHTS

Table 16.3 Useful SAP Notes for SAP SRM (Cont.)

Component	Note	Note Description
SRM-EBP-ADM-USR	785802, 419423	Repairing incorrect EBP users
SRM-EBP-ADM-USR	683782	Position assignment of employees and users
SRM-EBP-ADM-USR	385928	Deletion of inconsistent users
SRM-EBP-ADM-USR	402592	EBP in Central User Administration (CUA)
SRM-EBP-APM	396102	Alert Monitor (RZ20) does not work
SRM-EBP-BID	770902	Setup of SSO between bid invitations and cFolders
SRM-EBP-BID	730158	Bid invitation mail to bidder does not contain URL link with client
SRM-EBP-BID	811595, 828558, 855069	Dynamic attributes with 255 characters (ITS) instead of standard 60 characters — Consulting note
SRM-EBP-BID	943988	Using bid comparison BAdI BBP_BID_EVAL_DISPLAY — Consulting note
SRM_EBP-BID	790860	FAQ: Microsoft Excel upload and download
SRM-EBP	812884	Change fields in Microsoft Excel upload and download — Consulting note
SRM-EBP-CA-ACC	815849	FAQ: Account assignment
SRM-EBP-CA-DEX	1103956	SRM 2007 — WebDypro meta data handling — Consulting note
SRM-EBP-CA-DEX	1115579	How to create SRM 2007 WebDynpro field enhancements
SRM-EBP-CA-DEX	672960	Customer fields in SRM (Most frequently used SRM-related note. Also check all related notes in this note)
SRM-EBP-CA-DEX	675800	Customer fields in business partner master
SRM-EBP-CA-DEX	752586	Transfer customer fields to backend system
SRM-EBP-CA-PRC	850008, 850335	Incorrect prices with different currencies
SRM-EBP-CA-UI	1109666	How to activate WebDynpro customizing in SRM 2007
SRM-EBP-CGS	549846	FAQ: Goods receipt confirmation EBP
SRM-EBP-CON	1097230	Contract conditions problems (after upgrade)

Table 16.3 Useful SAP Notes for SAP SRM (Cont.)

Component	Note	Note Description
SRM-EBP-CON	904025	Sample code in BAdI BBP_CTR_INIT_UP (initial contracts upload) for text ID mapping
SRM-EBP-CON	646903	Global Outline Agreement: Tips and Tricks
SRM-EBP-CON	609222	Sourcing: Create SAP R/3 contract, tricks, and hints
SRM-EBP-EXR	505030	External Requirements — Restrictions — Consulting note
SRM-EBP-EXR	441892	Integrating external requirements — Composite note
SRM-EBP-EXR	648074	Extended transfer of PRs to SRM with manual flag in V_T160EX
SRM-EBP-EXR	656597	External requirements not transferred to SRM due to missing settings
SRM-EBP-EXR	746769	Determination of company code with external requirements
SRM-EBP-EXR	783383	Analysis of errors in external requirements
SRM-EBP-EXR	787426	Mapping backend purchasing group to SRM purchasing group
SRM-EBP-EXR	899646	Restrictions in external requirements for services
SRM-EBP-EXR	947032	SRM, APO and ERP integration
SRM-EBP-INV	548734	FAQ: EBP Invoice
SRM-EBP-POR	1079525, 850165	Select company code when creating a purchase order manually — Consulting note
SRM-EBP-POR	861889	Limitations on limit and service purchase orders in the extended classic scenario
SRM-EBP-POR	907564, 904960	One-time vendor in SRM purchase order — Consulting note
SRM-EBP-POR	918169	Program BBP_SC_Transfer_Grouped cannot use BAdI BBP_GROUP_LOC_PO — Consulting note
SRM-EBP-POR	635703	Document status check in BAdI BBP_DOC_CHECK_BADI — Consulting note
SRM-EBP-SHP	550071	FAQ: EBP Shopping cart
SRM-EBP-SHP	1057932	FAQ: Attachment transfer to backend ERP, required configurations
SRM-EBP-SHP	767461	Transfer of ship-to-address from shopping cart to backend system

Table 16.3 Useful SAP Notes for SAP SRM (Cont.)

Component	Note	Note Description
SRM-EBP-SHP	891924	Create reservation in backend system from shopping cart
SRM-EBP-SOC	1064325	SRM 2007 sourcing cockpit: Creating follow-on documents in the background
SRM-EBP-TEC-INS	1095175	Missing or incorrect translations in SRM menu (ITS)
SRM-EBP-TEC-INS	995771	SRM system landscape copy — Consulting note
SRM-EBP-TEC-ITS	546748	FAQ: ITS in EBP
SRM-EBP-TEC-ITS	778488	Modifying logon page in internal ITS (SRM 5.0)
SRM-EBP-TEC-ITS	451292, 389806, 114119	How to use the external ITS debugger Enabling the ITS debugger
SRM-EBP-TEC-ITS	722735	Debugging IAC tasks in integrated ITS
SRM-EBP-TEC-ITS	595266	Debugging ITS services with endless loop in ABAP code
SRM-EBP-TEC-MW	872533	FAQ: Middleware
SRM-EBP-TEC-MW	429423	CRM middleware: General analysis of initial upload
SRM-EBP-TEC-MW	430980	CRM middleware: Analysis of delta exchange from SAP R/3
SRM-EBP-TEC-MW	519794	Replication of materials with purchasing view only
SRM-EBP-TEC-MW	757212	CRM middleware: Download objects remain in status "wait"
SRM-EBP-TEC-PM	549208	FAQ: Resubmitting rejected shopping carts
SRM-EBP-TEC-PM	549206	FAQ: Development requests for new functionality
SRM-EBP-TEC-PFM	1095895	Slow response times for many SRM transactions: Improve performance consulting note
SRM-EBP-TEC-UPG	826487	Additions to upgrade on SRM Server 5.5
SRM-EBP-WFL	322526	Analysis of workflow problems
SRM-LA	890391	SSO between LAC and portals
SRM-LA-UI	666849	Running LAC in non-US locales
SRM-ROS	779972	Survey: Configuration required to receive emails
SRM-ROS	859304	ROS: Vendor master record synchronization
SRM-SUS	793669	FAQ: XI in SUS troubleshooting

Table 16.3 Useful SAP Notes for SAP SRM (Cont.)

Component	Note	Note Description
SRM-SUS	958273	FAQ: Taxes in SRM SUS
SRM-SUS	848164	FAQ:Logic of tax calculation in SUS
SRM-SUS	1026638	GR notifications in SUS from SAP R/3 version 4.7 and below — Consulting note
SRM-SUS	1095018	EBP and SUS in one client — Important settings — Consulting note
SRM-SUS	1063504	Default correct invoice quantity in SUS — Consulting note
SRM-SUS	780923	Transferring attachments in SAP MM to SUS
SRM-SUS	830705	Customer specific long texts in SUS and enhancements to XML communication
SRM-SUS	798272	Email address change in MM vendor master not transferred to SUS
SRM-SUS	800866	SUS invoice with delivery costs to MM
SRM-SUS	861578	SUS-MM: Usage of free text items without material master
SRM-SUS	586466	SUS follow-on document control with confirmation control key in SAP ERP
SRM-SUS	756472	SUS-MM: Purchase order response for rejected items
SRM-SUS	835073	Enhancement of tolerance checks in SUS invoice
SRM-SUS	886307, 888725	Creating follow-on documents in MM-SUS scenario
SRM-SUS	762984	Customer fields in SUS
XX-SER-GEN	192194	Tips for problem analysis and note search
Consulting Services	1012010	SRM add-on on ERP2005 implementation consulting service
Consulting Services	1028264	Consulting solutions in SUS
Consulting Services	868192	SUS-MM service procurement — Consulting solution
PLM-CFO	595989	General procedure with cFolders support

Table 16.3 Useful SAP Notes for SAP SRM (Cont.)

16.4   Summary

In this chapter, you have seen answers to frequently asked questions and learned some troubleshooting tips and tricks. We have also provided you with a list of SAP consulting and FAQ notes, which should help you in your implementation. Some of the notes are extremely useful and we have always felt that if we had known of the existence of even a few of these notes, we could have provided more solutions to our customers.

Also, you might be pleasantly surprised to get a consulting note to a seemingly difficult problem. Always remember to search for an SAP Note for any problem you may encounter. You can also use the SDN forum to post a problem or provide a solution to somebody else's problem. Next, in Chapter 17, we will examine several little known SAP SRM scenarios as well as a few customer scenarios with enhanced functionalities.

Any packaged application can satisfy only 60%—80% of a customer's requirements. However, applications built on open and flexible technologies can be molded to satisfy all customer requirements. To that end, SAP SRM is built on the SAP NetWeaver platform and provides great flexibility to define customer processes.

17 Customer Scenarios and Enhancements

Until now in this book, we have discussed the business scenarios supported by SAP SRM and the implementation of these scenarios. SAP SRM is one of the main applications in the SAP Business Suite and it effectively leverages this association to provide many integrated business processes. For example, we discussed the integration with SAP ERP and SAP PLM cFolders in the earlier chapters, and in this chapter, we will discuss several other little-known scenarios that we feel are extremely useful to customers. Bringing the knowledge of your experience, as well as knowing about varied scenarios and enhancements makes you a valued SAP SRM consultant.

In our opinion, no packaged application can claim to satisfy 100% of customer requirements. But the technology of the application should enable the implementation team to extend the package with customer-specific enhancements, and the enhancements should not endanger the upgradeability of the application to the next version. In our experience, SAP SRM is highly flexible and enables easy implementation of customer-specific procurement processes. The only limiting factor is the experience and willingness of the implementation team (both the customer team and the consulting team). Many consultants and customers believe that SAP applications are rigid and that you should not make any changes to SAP processes. We feel that this is a myth and, through several customer scenarios, want to break this myth to prove that SAP SRM can be enhanced to meet stringent customer requirements.

In Section 17.1, we will discuss these little-known SAP SRM scenarios. In Section 17.2, we will briefly explain the enhancement framework. In Section 17.3, we will explain several critical BAdI implementations using customer process examples. Later, in Section 17.4, we will look into the implementation of more complex customer scenarios such as 2-Envelope Bidding, and so on.

17.1   Little-Known SAP SRM Scenarios

In this section, we will examine the following SAP SRM scenarios, enabled by integrating with other SAP Business Suite applications:

▸ Lease Asset Management (LAM)

▸ Ordering materials and recources for projects from cProjects

▸ Customer service outsourcing

▸ Design collaboration with SAP PLM cFolders

Most of the information for these scenarios is based on the SAP SRM online help documentation. We will discuss the LAM scenario first in Section 17.1.1.

17.1.1   Lease Asset Management

SAP leasing is one of the main business scenarios supported by SAP Customer Relationship Management (CRM). LAM is a scenario that leverages the functionalities in SAP SRM, SAP CRM, SAP ERP, and SAP NetWeaver XI. Using this scenario, you can order leased items from a manufacturer or vendor in accordance with the requirements of the lessee. We will learn the LAM process and implementation of the LAM scenario in this section.

LAM Process Overview

The LAM scenario is illustrated in Figure 17.1 and its steps are explained in this subsection, as follows:

1. A lease quotation is processed in the CRM system. The CRM system then sends a purchase requisition to SAP SRM using SAP NetWeaver XI when the quotation has reached a certain status. You can define in the CRM configuration which quotation status triggers the purchase requisition. You can also trigger the purchase requisition manually or from a lease contract. The quotation item is assigned the status "Requirement requested." Changes, if any, to the lease quotation or contract are transferred to an external requirement in SAP SRM.

2. An external requirement (shopping cart) is created in SAP SRM. It contains the references to the CRM quotation or contract. These references are also forwarded to follow-on documents in SAP SRM. When the shopping cart is created in SAP SRM, a confirmation is sent to CRM, which updates the status of the lease quotation to "Requirement confirmed." If the status for the leasing document item is set as "Cancel Requirement" the external requirement is sent again to SAP SRM without the cancelled item.

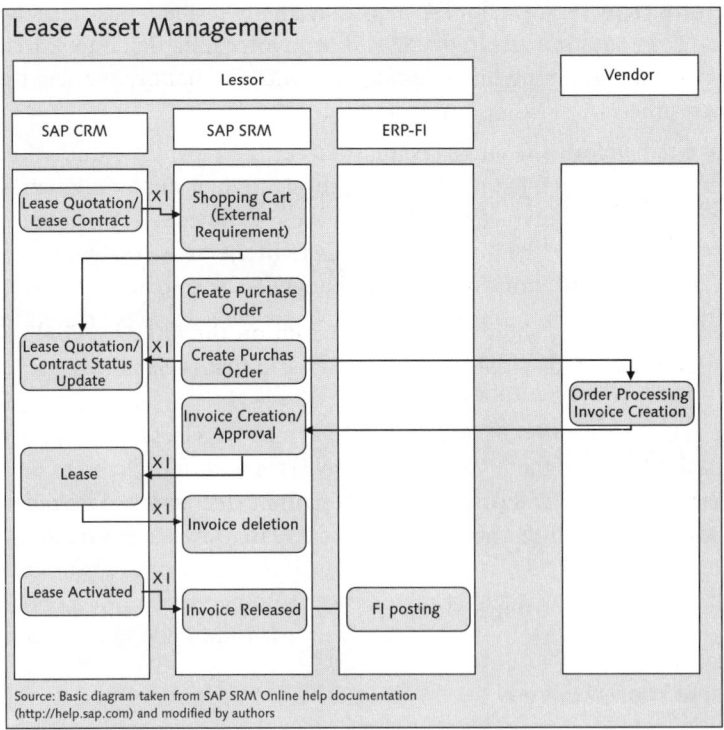

Figure 17.1 Lease Asset Management Scenario

3. Depending on the sourcing settings in SAP SRM, a purchase order is created automatically or manually from the sourcing cockpit. You can also use the bidding process to determine the source of supply and create a purchase order, if required. You can also activate a workflow to process the purchase order approval. Once the purchase order is approved, a confirmation is sent to CRM, which updates the status of the lease quotation to "Requirement ordered." The document flow in the lease quotation is also updated. In some cases, ordering may not be required from SAP SRM. In such cases, CRM sends an external reference to the field "Assumption of purchase order ID" in the external requirement, and invoices in SAP SRM are entered without reference to the purchase order. A purchase order in SAP SRM can be changed or cancelled from the CRM system based on the changes to the lease quotation. If the purchase order cannot be changed or cancelled due to the existence of follow-on documents, the purchaser receives a message that advises him of this situation.

4. The vendor processes the order, supplies the goods, and sends an invoice.

5. The vendor's invoice is entered with reference to the purchase order. The vendor's invoice can also be entered without reference to a purchase order, but the lease quotation or lease contract number should be entered as an

external reference. A search help (F4 help) is available in the fields "Leasing Quote" and "Leasing Contract" in the SAP SRM invoice item detail to search for CRM leasing documents while entering an invoice without reference to a purchase order.

6. The invoice entry in SAP SRM updates the status of the CRM lease quotation to "Supplier Invoice Posted Externally" If a contract item or quotation item is cancelled, the associated invoices in SAP SRM are also deleted. If the invoice is already posted to SAP ERP Financials, then a credit memo is created. However, purchase orders are not cancelled or changed. The purchaser receives an appropriate message to modify the purchase order. A lease is created in the CRM system.

7. The lessee confirms the receipt of goods (outside the system).

8. During the action 'Inception,' CRM sends a message to release the supplier invoice in SAP SRM, and the invoice is then released and transferred to SAP ERP Financials. However, if a customer wants to use a different release process, they can implement it without waiting for release instructions from the CRM system.

9. The necessary financial postings are carried out in SAP ERP Financials.

LAM Implementation Overview

We will mainly discuss SAP SRM integration-specific settings in this section. You can refer to the CRM online documentation for detailed leasing process implementation information in CRM. Prerequisites for the scenario and the settings required in SAP SRM are as follows:

▶ The CRM and SAP SRM systems should use the same backend ERP system.

▶ The vendor should exist in the backend ERP system and be replicated from ERP to SAP SRM.

▶ Product categories should be replicated from ERP to SAP SRM and CRM.

▶ SAP SRM Self-Service Procurement settings for a standalone deployment scenario should be maintained. The LAM process is enabled in the standalone deployment only.

▶ Activate LAM in IMG setting **SPRO • SRM Server • Cross Application Basic Settings • Personalization • Activate Scenario-specific Fields**.

▶ Maintain Remote Function Call (RFC) destination for the CRM system using Transaction SM59.

▶ Make an entry for the CRM system with system type as LAM in IMG setting **SPRO • SRM Server • Technical Basic Settings • Define Backend Systems**.

▶ Define the target system for product categories in IMG setting **SPRO • SRM Server • Technical Basic Settings • Define Backend Systems for Product Category**.

▸ Verify that the enhancement spot implementations LAM_BBP_SAPXML1_OUT_ICC and LAM_BBP_SAPXML1_IN_ICC are active for enhancement spot BBP_BDI_MAPPING_SAPXML1. If the enhancement spot implementations are active, the checkbox in the fields "Implementation is active" and "Implementation is activated in current client with switch BBP_LAM_MAIN" should be selected. The implementation LAM_BBP_SAPXML1_OUT_ICC generates a long text that is used in CRM to link the leasing quote to the invoice.

▸ Activate the BAdI implementation BBP_INV_SEND_XML for BAdI EXEC_METHODCALL_PPF to send an invoice in XML format.

▸ The SAP NetWeaver XI configuration necessary for the Leasing Integration scenario should be carried out.

Next, we will discuss the SAP SRM scenario "Ordering Materials and Resources from SAP PLM cProjects."

17.1.2 Ordering Materials and External Staff from SAP PLM cProjects

You can order external materials and resources directly from cProjects using SAP SRM. We will briefly discuss the process and implementation of this integration in this section.

Process Overview

The cProjects and SAP SRM integration for external materials and staffing process is as follows:

1. You can create material or external resource requests from the Shopping Cart tab in a cProjects project. If you request external staff for a project role, the system automatically transfers the qualifications of the project role to the description of the shopping cart. The system also creates a resource assignment on the Staffing tab in the project. The requirement is transferred to SAP SRM using SAP NetWeaver XI. The shopping cart status in cProjects shows as In Preparation.

2. A shopping cart for the external requirement is created in SAP SRM and a confirmation is transmitted back to cProjects using SAP NetWeaver XI. The status of the shopping cart in cProjects is changed to In Process.

3. The purchaser processes the shopping cart and creates a purchase order. The purchaser may use bidding functions to process the shopping cart. The purchase order and purchase order item number are sent to cProjects.

4. The goods receipt information is recorded in SAP SRM and sent to cProjects. In case of external staffing requests, the time recording and expenses incurred are recorded in SAP SRM and sent to cProjects.

Now let us discuss the configuration settings required for this integration.

Implementation Overview

An overview of the configuration settings required for ordering materials and external staff from cProjects using SAP SRM are briefly explained in this section:

▶ Activate Shopping in SAP SRM for the required project types in cProjects IMG setting **SPRO • Collaboration Projects • Structure • Define Project Types**. If you want to order external staff, then configure settings in the Confirmation section, also.

▶ Maintain an RFC destination for the SAP SRM system in cProjects using Transaction SM59.

▶ Select the RFC destination for SAP SRM as the source system for SAP SRM categories in cProjects IMG setting **SPRO • Collaboration Projects • Connection to External Systems • SRM Integration • Specify Source System for SRM Categories**.

▶ Maintain product categories in SAP SRM using Transaction COMM_HIERARCHY.

▶ Maintain SAP SRM Self-Service Procurement and Service Procurement settings for the standalone deployment scenario. The cProjects integration process is enabled in standalone deployments.

▶ Maintain an RFC destination for the cProjects system using Transaction SM59.

▶ Create an entry for the cProjects system with system type XISAPXML1 in IMG setting **SPRO • SRM Server • Technical Basic Settings • Define Backend Systems**.

▶ Define the target system for product categories in IMG setting **SPRO • SRM Server • Technical Basic Settings • Define Backend Systems for Product Category**.

▶ Perform the SAP NetWeaver XI configuration necessary for the "SAP SRM Integration with cProjects." Refer to SAP Note 960237 for more details.

You can also refer to the online help documentation for more details on cProjects settings.

17.1.3 Customer Service Outsourcing

The customer service outsourcing scenario is the result of the integration between the Customer Service component in SAP ERP and SAP SRM. In this process, a customer service request is outsourced to an external contractor. Ordering and execution of the job by an external contractor are performed in

SAP SRM. At the end of the process, a customer bill is created based on an actual invoice from the external contractor. The scenario is also described as "Third-Party Rebilling" in the SAP SRM online documentation. We will briefly describe the process and the implementation of the scenario in the next two subsections.

Process Overview

The process starts with a request from a customer for a servicing an item or equipment. The process steps are as follows:

1. Create a service order for the customer request in the Customer Service component of SAP ERP. Select the materials or external services required in the service order and release the order.

2. A purchase requisition is created in SAP ERP, which is automatically transferred to the SAP SRM system for sourcing.

3. The purchaser carries out the necessary sourcing activities in SAP SRM and creates a purchase order for the external requirement.

4. The purchase order follow-on activities, such as confirmation and invoicing, are performed in SAP SRM. You can also allow the supplier or service agent to perform these activities using SUS. If the servicing requires any additional materials, the supplier indicates this during time sheet recording and expense confirmation.

5. The invoice is approved in SAP SRM and sent to SAP ERP Financials for payment to the supplier.

6. A resource-related billing document is created based on the supplier invoice details using Transaction DP90. The bill is sent to the customer and monitored in the Accounts Receivables component of SAP ERP.

Implementation Overview

An overview of the required settings for this scenario is provided in this section.

1. Configure the Customer Service component in SAP ERP. We suggest that you configure a separate order type for SAP SRM integration and configure the necessary settings for resource-related billing. Assign the customer service order type to a sales order type.

2. The sales order type should be assigned to all required sales areas in the Sales and Distribution (SD) component configuration.

3. If you assign a dummy service material (of material type DIEN) to be used during billing in IMG setting Profiles for **Quotation Creation · Billing · Results Analysis**, then extend this material to all required sales areas.

4. Maintain the settings required for plan-driven procurement with external requirements and Supplier Self-Services (SUS).

Detailed customer service settings are beyond the scope of this book.

Tip

You can use a similar process in the insurance industry to settle claims. When an insurer calls claiming damages, the replacement or repair of the damaged item can be arranged by the claim handler using SAP SRM.

In the next section, we will discuss design collaboration, another very useful scenario.

17.1.4 Design Collaboration with SAP PLM cFolders

This scenario is extremely useful in asset-intensive industries where high cost and complex product or service purchases are very common. Some scenarios where design collaboration is useful include the following:

▶ When preparing Request for Proposal (RFP) documents during sourcing of engineered goods and services.

▶ When purchasing equipment, for example, a utlities company searching for an ash-handling plant supplier.

▶ When purchasing new products, for example, a car manufacturer collaborating with suppliers to design and supply a new fuel-injection system for their new model car.

▶ During project subcontracting, for example, a construction company collaborating with a subcontractor for a central air-conditioning and heating system.

We will discuss an overview of the design collaboration process and its implementation in the next two subsections.

Overview of the Design Collaboration Process

The design collaboration process with cFolders can be initiated either from an SAP SRM bid invitation or from cFolders. The bidding with collaboration process explained in Chapter 10, Section 10.2.6 is initiated from an SAP SRM bid invitation. We will discuss the process initiated from cFolders in this section:

1. An internal engineer or project manager initiates a competitive collaboration in cFolders. The project manager adds design ideas and provides authorization to other design team members in the organization to add technical documents.

2. Design engineers review the design idea and post technical documents.

3. Design engineers and the project manager review the technical documents and finalize the technical documents for sourcing.

4. The project manager (or an engineer) creates a shopping cart from the collaboration in cFolders. The shopping cart will have free text items only.

5. The system creates a shopping cart in SAP SRM and adds a URL link to the SAP SRM shopping cart in collaboration.

6. The purchaser carries out sourcing for the shopping cart in the sourcing cockpit. If the purchaser creates a bid invitation from the sourcing cockpit, the bid invitation contains the collaboration. The rest of the process is the same as the Bidding with Collaboration process explained in Chapter 10, Section 10.2.6.

Overview of Implementation of Design Collaboration Process

Integrating cFolders with SAP SRM is explained in Chapter 10, Section 10.3. We will discuss the additional requirements to implement a cFolders initiated process here:

▶ The user creating the shopping cart from cFolders should have administration authorization on collaboration (competitive scenario).

▶ The user creating the shopping cart should have a valid product category ID in user settings.

▶ The deployment scenario in SAP SRM is standalone only.

▶ The SAP SRM system user used in the RFC connection for SAP SRM should have authorization to create shopping carts.

▶ You can implement BAdI CFX_SRM_SC to modify the shopping cart creation.

Let us now move on to building enhanced functionalities in SAP SRM. The enhancement framework explained in Section 17.2 is the technical foundation for this.

17.2 Enhancement Framework

According to SAP online help documentation, the *enhancement framework* of the SAP ABAP Workbench enables the integration of different concepts for modifying and enhancing development objects in SAP. The enhancement framework enables customers to enhance SAP source code without making modifications and thus ensuring upgradeability of SAP applications.

The following basic technologies can be used through the enhancement framework:

- **ABAP source code enhancements**: As part of the enhancement concept, it is possible to enhance ABAP source code, without modifications, using source code plug-ins.
- **Function module enhancements**: Function module enhancements can be separated into the following categories:
  - **Source code enhancements**: Enhancements to the source code are carried out through ABAP source code enhancements.
  - **Parameter interface enhancements**: You can enhance the parameter interface of a function module with new, optional formal parameters as enhancement implementation elements.
- **Global Class Enhancements**: The enhancements to global classes and interfaces can be separated into the following:
  - Enhancements to the source code of methods, local classes, etc. These enhancements are carried out through ABAP source code enhancements.
  - Enhancements to components of classes and interfaces.
- **Business Add-Ins (BAdIs)**: SAP Business Add-Ins (BAdIs) are one of the most important technologies used to adapt SAP software to specific requirements. BAdIs were introduced with Basis release 4.6 and have replaced the function module user exits. In various SAP applications, BAdI calls are implemented at places where enhancements are appropriate. SAP SRM provides more than 250 BAdIs as of release SAP SRM 2007. SAP provides explanations of BAdIs in the BAdI documentation which can be accessed from Transaction SE18. You can implement a BAdI using Transaction SE19.

> **Note**
>
> For a detailed explanation of the enhancement framework and enhancement technologies, refer to the SAP NetWeaver online help documentation. You can also get more details in the SDN (*https://www.sdn.sap.com/irj/sdn/devguide*).

SAP SRM also provides a flexible *customer fields* concept to add customer-specific fields to any SAP SRM business object (shopping cart, purchase order, etc). We will discuss the concept of customer fields in more detail in Section 17.3. We will also discuss several critical BAdI implementations in SAP SRM with specific customer processes in that section.

17.3   BAdI Implementations and Customer Fields

Some of the most commonly used BAdIs in SAP SRM are as follows:

- **BBP_DOC_CHECK_BADI**: BAdI to perform customer-specific checks in any SAP SRM document.

- **BBP_ITEM_CHECK_BADI**: BAdI to perform customer-specific checks at the item level in SAP SRM documents. If you want to perform any item-level checks in edit mode of the document, you should use this BAdI instead of BBP_DOC_CHECK_BADI.

- **BBP_DOC_CHANGE_BADI**: BAdI to make customer-specific changes in SAP SRM documents.

- **BBP_DOC_SAVE_BADI**: BAdI to modify the data while saving a document.

- **BBP_WFL_APPROV_BADI**: BAdI to implement customer specific workflow functionalities, such as n-level workflow. This BAdI is not used in SAP SRM 2007.

- **BBP_CUF_BADI or BBP_CUF_BADI_2**: BAdI to modify customer-specific fields.

- **BBP_CATALOG_TRANSFER**: BAdI to enrich the catalog data before creating a shopping cart by transferring items from the catalog.

- **BBP_UI_CONTROL_BADI**: BAdI to influence Internet Transaction Server (ITS) screens. This BAdI is not available in SAP SRM 2007. SAP SRM 2007 uses the WebDynpro user interface, which requires metadata configuration to control the user interface. Refer to SAP Notes 1103956 and 1115579 for more information on WebDynpro meta data configuration.

- **BBP_PGRP_FIND**: BAdI to determine the responsible purchasing group in a shopping cart and external requirement.

- **BBP_DETERMINE_LOGSYS**: BAdI to override the settings configured in "Define Backend System for Product Category.". You can incorporate customer-specific logic to determine the backend system for creating follow-on documents from a shopping cart. If you want to create contracts in the backend system from the sourcing cockpit or bidding, then implement this BAdI.

- **BBP_WF_LIST**: BAdI to influence work lists and search lists, for example, you can ensure that only orders from certain product categories are displayed for a particular user.

As these are the most commonly used BAdIs , you will find use cases and sample codes on various SAP sites, for example, in SDN. SAP provides good documentation for all BAdIs to help implementation consultants. You can list most of the BAdIs by using search query "BBP*" in Transaction SE18. You can also list enhancement spots in SAP SRM 2007 using search query "/SAPSRM/*" in Transaction SE18.

17.3.1 Customer Fields

Customer fields is one of the most often used features of SAP SRM. You can add any number of fields to any SAP SRM business object (purchase order, contract, etc.) using this functionality. Even functional consultants can add customer fields easily. There is no need to perform any screen coding for customer fields. Some of the notable features of customer fields are as follows:

► ITS screens are automatically generated for customer fields through SAP SRM 5.0.

► WebDynpro screens are automatically generated in SAP SRM 2007 and the customer field display can be modified using WebDynpro metadata configuration. Refer to SAP Notes 1103956 and 1115579 for more details on WebDynpro meta data configuration.

► Customer fields can be enabled in both the header and the item of any document.

► Tabular custom fields can be created, if you want to have multiple values for each customer field.

► Customer fields have an inheritance property. That means that if you have the same customer field defined in multiple business objects, the values of original document flows into the follow-on document. For example, assume that you have defined the same customer field in the shopping cart object, as well as the purchase order object. When you create a purchase order with reference to a shopping cart, the value in the shopping cart customer field is copied into the purchase order customer field.

The following are a few examples of customer requirements where customer fields are useful:

► A customer wants to link all procurement documents to the appropriate project. The additional fields Project Id, Project short description, and Project manager are created in the shopping cart and purchase order using customer fields. Requesters assign the appropriate project while creating a shopping cart. When a purchase order is created with reference to shopping cart, the project details are also copied into the purchase order.

► A customer wants to add additional details, such as Estimated value, Tender fee, and Caution deposit in bid invitations. The fields Tender fee and Caution deposit should be visible to bidders and Estimated value should not be visible to bidders. All three fields have been defined as customer fields in bid invitations. In a bid, only the Tender fee and Caution deposit fields are added so that only these two fields can be visible to bidders.

► A customer wants to aggregate requirements from multiple locations for an item and carry out the bidding process. In a normal process, requirements from each location will have one line item in a bid invitation. However, the customer wants to have only one line item for the aggregated demand and subitems showing requirements for each location. The solution is to have tabular customer fields at the line-item level to represent location requirements whereas the line-item quantity represents the aggregated quantity.

▶ Many customers want their suppliers to provide a lot of delivery details, such as vehicle numbers, taxation document numbers, insurance details, etc., during Advanced Shipping Notification (ASN) creation in SUS. In India, suppliers also give excise invoice details in an ASN. You can use customer fields to define these additional fields as required by the customer.

Refer to the following SAP Notes to define customer fields:

▶ **458591**: Through versions SAP SRM 3.0

▶ **672960**: From version SAP SRM 4.0 on

▶ **675800**: For customer fields in the business partner master

▶ **752586**: To transfer customer fields to the backend system

▶ **1103956 & 1115579**: For WebDynpro metadata configuration from SAP SRM 2007 on

▶ **762984**: For customer fields in SUS

Refer to the following additional tips to define and use customer fields:

▶ If you want to enable change history for the customer fields, ensure that you select the "Change document" checkbox in the data element definition.

▶ If you want to include the new customer fields in a version comparison, include them in table BBPD_COMP_FIELDS using Transaction SM31. Note that bid invitations have internal (relevant only for purchasers) and external versions (relevant for bidders). Bid invitation customer fields can be included in either the external or internal version, or in both versions.

17.3.2 Determine Driver Function Modules for Backend Systems Integration

This scenario helps you understand the way integration is handled with back-end systems from SAP SRM and how you can modify this integration. We will discuss this with the help of a customer scenario where the customer wants to modify a budget check.

Customer Requirement

The customer does not want to integrate with budget details in SAP ERP as the standard SAP ERP budgeting process is not implemented at his company. The customer has maintained budget details in customer-specific tables and wants to do a budget check in SAP SRM using these tables. Before we suggest a solution for this situation, you need to understand the way SAP SRM accesses information from backend systems and creates documents in backend systems.

Standard Integration with Backend Systems

The SAP SRM system uses meta-BAPIs, among other things, to access information and to create documents in a backend system that correspond to an SAP SRM document. Let us look at an example of a purchase order creation to illustrate this.

The meta-BAPI META_PO_CREATE first determines the designated driver function module for the required backend system. The meta-BAPI calls up the function module META_BAPI_DISPATCH that identifies the driver function module using the business object, the method and the system type from the table BBP_FUNCTION_MAP. The table BBP_FUNCTION_MAP contains the driver function modules for various activities and backend systems. This driver function module then transfers the SAP SRM document into the backend system. Similarly, the META_BUDGET_READ function module is executed to read budget data. This will execute META_BAPI_DISPATCH, which identifies the driver function module from table BBP_FUNCTION_MAP as B470_BUDGET_READ. Note that these driver function modules are different for different systems and system versions. For example, the driver function module for reading budget data from SAP R/3 version 4.6B is B31I_BUDGET_READ.

We will now examine the solution for the given customer requirement.

Solution for Budget Check from Customer Tables

BAdI BBP_DRIVER_DETERMINE can be used to modify the determination of the driver function module. The solution steps are as follows:

1. Create an RFC function module in the SAP ERP system in the customer namespace (z-function module) that extracts budget data from custom tables.
2. Create a driver function module in the SAP SRM system in the customer namespace. This function module should call the newly created ERP function module to extract budget data in SAP ERP.
3. Ensure that the data structures match the budget data extraction requirements.
4. Implement BAdI BBP_DRIVER_DETERMINE to change the driver function module for reading the budget.
5. While reading budget data, function module META_BUDGET_READ will be executed. This will execute META_BAPI_DISPATCH, which calls the BAdI BBP_DRIVER_DETERMINE. Export parameters Object (BUDGET), Pending Method (Read), and Logical System (logical system name of the backend system) will be passed in this case. The values in the brackets are values for the parameters. Based on these parameters, the BAdI returns the new driver function module for reading the budget, which will be passed back to META_BAPI_DISPATCH. Once the control is transferred to META_BUDGET_READ, the function module calls the newly developed function module.
6. The Budget data can now be extracted from custom tables in SAP ERP.

Tip

You can find all driver function modules for most of the interfaces in the table BBP_FUNCTION_MAP. In this table, you will also find driver function modules for external tax systems integration, and for non-SAP systems integration.

17.3.3 Define Grouping Criteria for Local Purchase Orders

One of the sourcing options is the grouping of requirements while creating a purchase order. In this process, if you assign the same source of supply to many requirements, the system groups all of the requirements and creates a single purchase order. Some customers may want to create multiple purchase orders based on customer-specific criteria. BAdI BBP_GROUP_LOC_PO can be used for this purpose. Let us now take a look at a customer's requirement.

Customer Requirement

The following are included in a sample customer's requirement:

▸ Maintenance engineers responsible for a regular weekly preventive maintenance task create shopping carts for the required items.

▸ Many items from these shopping carts can be sourced with a single preferred vendor. This will create a single purchase order in the standard SAP SRM sourcing process.

▸ However, the customer purchasing organization is organized by separate purchasing departments for Process Consumables, Services, Electrical, Technology and Automation, Mechanical, etc. Each purchasing department handles a set of product categories.

▸ The items required for the preventive maintenance task include items from categories of different purchasing departments.

▸ Each purchasing department has expert knowledge on the specific category procurement. They manage sourcing, spend analysis, supplier evaluation, and vendor management for their categories. Hence, it was decided that separate purchase orders should be issued based on the items belonging to each purchasing department.

Solution

The solution steps for the given customer requirement are as follows:

▸ Define purchasing departments in a custom table. The fields in this table should include product category and purchasing department.

▶ Implement BAdI BBP_GROUP_LOC_PO. In the implementation, check the product category in ITEM_DATA. Compare the product category in ITEM_DATA with entries in the custom table for the purchasing department.

▶ Fill the REFNUMBER field based on the purchasing department. For example, group all mechanical requirements and fill the REFNUMBER with value 1. Similarly, group all services requirements and fill the REFNUMBER field with value 2 and so on.

▶ When the Control is passed on to the main grouping program, the shopping cart items are processed based on the REFNUMBER and grouped based on the REFNUMBER field, thus creating different purchase orders.

17.3.4 Archive SAP SRM Documents

SAP SRM provides the functionality to archive SAP SRM documents using standard SAP archiving. The standard archiving programs execute many checks before archiving a document. These checks ensure that a document is not required in the system anymore for processing of any follow-on documents. Sometimes, customers want to modify these checks by adding more checks or removing some of the checks. BAdI BBP_ARCHIVING_BADI can be used to modify the standard SAP archiving process. This BAdI supports multiple methods, of which some important ones are explained here:

▶ **CHECK_LIST_PREPARE**: Changes the list of documents to be chekked for archiving suitability. This is run before preparing the list.

▶ **CHECK_DOCUMENT_ARCHIVABLE**: Overrides the archiving decision (per document). This is prepared after defining the list.

▶ **WRITE_PREPARE**: Used to register additional customer tables that should be archived before the start of the write phase. The table AOBJ does not require an entry for these tables.

We will now look at a sample customer requirement and solution for the requirement.

Customer Requirement

A customer wants the following requirements for archiving contracts:

▶ Expired contracts should be archived after 366 days of the expiry date.

▶ Due to the legal guidelines, contracts with a value of more than $100,000 should not be archived immediately as they should be in the system for an extended period of five years.

Solution

The solution is as follows:

1. Implement BAdI BBP_ARCHIVING_BADI. In the method CHECK_LIST_PRE-PARE, documents that need to be archived are listed in table CT_PDLIST.

2. Check the OBJECT_TYPE for the contract business object.

3. Get details of the contract and check for the value of the contract.

4. If the value is greater than $100,000 and the current date is less than five years from the expiry date, then remove the contract from the list.

> **Tip**
>
> You can also use the BAdI to provide a customer-defined list of documents to be archived without executing the standard checks. You may want to do this to improve the system performance or reduce the number of checks executed in the standard programs. For example, if you do not use SUS invoices, other SUS documents like ASNs, orders, etc., cannot be archived in the standard. If you still want to archive the SUS ASNs and orders, you can use the BAdI to circumvent the standard archiving checks.

17.3.5   Determine the Target Object in the Backend System

You can configure settings in the system to create purchase requisitions, purchase orders, or reservations as the follow-on documents for shopping carts in SAP SRM. You configure these settings in the IMG setting "Define Objects in Backend System (Purch. Reqs, Reservations, Purch. Orders)." The standard settings can be altered by defining customer-specific criteria in the BAdI BBP_TARGET_OBJTYPE. Let us look at a customer requirement and solution.

Customer Requirement

Some customers want to use more criteria for determining the target object type. The requirements of a sample customer are outlined as follows:

- In the IMG settings, the customer has defined that a reservation will be created for the items when stock exists for them.

- However, the customer does not want all users to create reservations for specific product categories. For example, when professional purchasers create a shopping cart, the system should create a purchase requisition or purchase order instead of a reservation.

Solution

The solution steps for the given customer requirement are as follows:

1. Implement BAdI BBP_TARGET_OBJTYPE.

2. Check the product category from table ITEM_DATA.

3. The field ITEM_DATA-OBJ_TO_GEN controls the creation of the bakkend document (1 for Reservation, 2 for Purchase Requisition and 3 for Purchase Order). Therefore, check the user type and overwrite the field ITEM_DATA-OBJ_TO_GEN to create the required document.

Note

The BAdI BBP_TARGET_OBJECTS is replaced with BBP_TARGET_OBJTYPE from SAP SRM 5.0 on.

Tip

When you create a shopping cart item with multiple account assignments, which creates a reservation in the backend system according to configuration settings, the reservation created will have only one account assignment. This is because the reservation in SAP ERP cannot have multiple account assignments. In such cases, you can implement BAdI BBP_TARGET_OBJTYPE to create a purchase requisition instead. Please refer to SAP Note 700526 for a sample implementation.

17.3.6 Transfer Document Data to the Backend System

In this section, we will discuss mapping data between SAP SRM and ERP while creating documents in the ERP system. Depending on the scenario, follow-on documents for shopping carts can be reservations, purchase orders, or purchase requisitions in the backend ERP system. Similarly, the follow-on document from sourcing or bidding can be a purchase order or contract. While creating the documents in the backend system, there may be some data inconsistency between SAP SRM and ERP systems. For example, the purchasing organization and purchasing group in transferred data may be local to the SAP SRM system and may not be available in the ERP system, and in some cases they may be defined with different names in the ERP system. So it is necessary to map the data between SAP SRM and the ERP system.

To make the data transfer flexible, BAdIs are defined in SAP SRM so that data can be changed before sending it to ERP system. The following BAdIs are available for this purpose:

- **BAdI BBP_ECS_PO_OUT_BADI:** In the extended classic scenario, it is possible to override the standard and determine which data from the SAP SRM purchase order is transferred to the backend system.

- **BAdI BBP_CREATE_BE_PO_NEW:** It is possible to change all of the data that is transferred for creating a purchase order in the backend system in the classic scenario using this BAdI. You can also modify item data, account assignment data, and texts being transferred to create a purchase order in backend system.

- **BAdI BBP_CREATE_BE_RQ_NEW**: It is possible to change all of the data that is transferred for creating a purchase requistion in the backend system in classic scenario using this BAdI.

- **BAdI BBP_CREATE_BE_RS_NEW**: It is possible to change all of the data that is transferred for creating a reservation in the backend system in classic Scenario using this BAdI.

- **BAdI BBP_BS_GROUP_BE**: This BAdI is used to group shopping cart items for creating follow-on documents (PR, purchase order, or reservations) in the backend ERP system. You can also use the BAdI to define your own document type or number range. For example, in the standard, you can use only one PR document type for creating PRs from a shopping cart. Using the BAdI, you may use different documents based on customer specific logic.

- **BAdI BBP_CTR_BE_CREATE**: It is possible to change all of the data that is transferred to the backend system for generation of contract using this BAdI.

17.3.7 Change SAP XML Mapping

SAP SRM provides the flexibility to modify the inbound and outbound XML mappings using BAdIs. These are particularly useful in SUS implementations where all documents are exchanged using XML interfaces. Let us discuss briefly inbound and outbound XML mapping BAdIs.

Change SAP XML Inbound Mapping

BAdI BBP_SAPXML1_IN_BADI can be used to override the result of standard mappings of an SAP XML inbound interface to the internal SAP SRM structures. This can be necessary to fill in customer fields and to record additional information from XML messages that is not supported by SAP SRM. When the customer fields in the SAP SRM structure and the fields in the SAP XML message have the same names, it is not necessary to use this BAdI because mapping occurs automatically. Implementation is object-specific and available for all business objects that support creation of documents through XML interfaces.

Change SAP XML Outbound Mapping

BAdI BBP_SAPXML1_OUT_BADI is used to override the result of standard mappings from the internal SAP SRM structures to the SAP XML outbound interfaces. This can be necessary to fill in customer fields and include additional information not supported by the SAP SRM in XML messages. If the customer fields in the SAP SRM structure and the fields in the SAP XML message have the same name, it is not necessary to use this BAdI because mapping occurs automatically. This BAdI is called after the mapping of the SAP XML outbound interface to the SAP XML messages. Implementation of this BAdI is object specific and available for all business objects that support creation of documents through XML interfaces.

In this section, we have discussed simple customer requirements where specific BAdIs are used. In Section 17.4, we will look at enabling several complex customer business scenarios with various BAdIs and enhancements.

17.4 Complex Customer Scenarios

In this section, we will explain the implementation of the following specific customer processes using the enhancement framework in SAP SRM:

▶ Public sector 2-Envelope bidding process
▶ Enabling different price Units of Measure (UOM) in SUS

17.4.1 Public Sector 2-Envelope Bidding Process

The 2-Envelope bidding process is widely used in public sector companies and government departments. It is also used in many private sector companies for project purchases or complex high-value purchases. The 2-Envelope bidding process is explained as follows:

1. RFPs for high-value purchases are typically prepared by a team. Therefore, the team collaborates and prepares the RFP.
2. Purchasers publish the RFP and invite bidders (usually global tenders) to participate.
3. Purchasers invite bidders to submit their bids in two sealed covers before the submission deadline, one cover for a technical bid and another for a price bid.
4. Purchasers provide two separate opening dates for technical and price bids.
5. When the technical bid opening date is reached, purchasers open the technical bids for evaluation. The price bids are not opened at this stage.
6. The technical bids are circulated to an internal evaluation team. The team evaluates the bids and shortlists a few of the bids.
7. Price bids are opened for shortlisted bids on the price bid opening date. The bidder with the lowest price typically wins the bid.

SAP SRM supports normal bidding in the standard but does not support 2-Envelope bidding. Separating technical bids and price bids is a major challenge. Separating the opening of technical bids and price bids is another major challenge. The process needs collaborative document management facilities to prepare RFPs and to evaluate technical bids. Additional controls are necessary to ensure bid confidentiality. Thanks to the flexibility offered by SAP SRM technology, a project solution is feasible. The project solution is live and widely used by many SAP SRM customers. We provide an outline of this project solution in the next section.

Solution

The solution steps for implementing 2-Envelope bidding are as follows:

1. The bidding with collaboration scenario is used to enable the 2-Envelope bidding process. cFolders is used for collaborative document management. A template collaboration is created to ensure that the structure of bid documents is standardized. Status management in cFolders is used to set different statuses for documents, such as Released for Publishing, etc.

2. Receive technical bids in cFolders collaborations assigned to bids, and enter prices in SAP SRM bid pricing screens.

3. Define customer fields in bid invitation (RFP) and bid (quotation) according to SAP Note 672960. Configure additional fields, such as Technical bid opening date, Time, etc.

4. If you want to restrict the additional fields to only certain transaction types, you should create the required transaction types in the IMG. Implement BAdI BBP_CUF_BADI_2 to restrict the additonal fields. In SAP SRM 2007, configure WebDynpro metadata to control the customer field appearance on screens. Refer to SAP Notes 1103956 and 1115579 for more information on WebDynpro metadata configuration.

5. Implement BBP_DOC_CHECK_BADI in the bid invitation. Some checks you should enable are as follows:

   ▶ Ensure the validity of dates. For example, the technical bid opening date should be later than the submission deadline but before the price bid opening date and time.

   ▶ Ensure that an entry is required in certain fields. For example, the fields bid opening date and technical bid opening date should be configured as required fields.

   ▶ Ensure that cFolders collaboration exists for Two-Envelop bidding transaction types.

   ▶ Ensure that the status in cFolders collaboration is "Released for Publishing" before the bid invitation is published. This ensures that all RFP documents are ready before the publishing bid invitation. RFC function modules are created in cFolders to get status information and are called from this BAdI implementation in SAP SRM.

6. Implement BBP_DOC_CHECK_BADI in the bid (quotation). Ensure that a collaboration is created for the bid using this BAdI. You can also incorporate additional checks, if required. For example, some customers may want the

bidder to pay a certain tender fee amount before he can participate in the bidding. You can configure the necessary checks using this BAdI.

7. Implement BAdI BBP_CFOLDER_BADI in SAP SRM to control the integration with cFolders. Several RFC function modules have been created for different tasks in cFolders using the API function modules provided by cFolders. The following enhancements are achieved with this BAdI:

   ▸ When a buyer creates a collaboration from a bid invitation, the system creates the collaboration using the RFC user. Hence, the buyer needs to be provided with administrator authorization rights to the collaboration using this BAdI. In the method COL_CREATE_POST, the RFC function module is called to set the authorizations for the buyer.

   ▸ When a bidder creates a bid, a bidder area is created in the collaboration by copying the folders from the public area. Call the necessary RFC function modules to ensure that only public data is copied to bidder area and internal documents of the buying company are not copied.

   ▸ Ensure that buyer does not have authorization in the bidder area so that he cannot see the bidder's documents.

8. Create a new transaction to open technical bids and add this transaction in the authorization profiles of buyers. The transaction can be executed after the technical bid opening date and time. The transaction provides authorizations for buyers to the bidder areas in the cFolders collaboration of a specific bid invitation. Buyers will have access to all submitted technical bids on executing this transaction.

9. Buyers can access technical bids in cFolders and use the collaboration features to evaluate technical bids.

10. Create a button called Technically Rejected in cFolders using Transaction CFX_UD_BUTTON.

11. Implement BAdI CFX_BUTTONS in cFolders to control the behavior of the new button. The button should not be visible to bidders, but be visible to buyers only at the root folder of the collaboration. It also will not be visible in all folders. When a button is clicked, an RFC function module in SAP SRM is called to reject the bids in SAP SRM.

12. The evaluators click on this new button to technically reject a bid. An RFC function module in SAP SRM is called to reject bids in SAP SRM.

13. Once the price bid opening date and time reached, buyers can open price bids of shortlisted bidders and determine the winner. A follow-on document is created from the winning bid.

The solution outlined here demonstrates how complex processes also can be enabled by leveraging the integration with SAP Business Suite applications and the enhancement framework. If interested, you can contact the authors for more details about this solution.

17.4.2 Enabling Different Price UOMs in SUS

In the chemical industry, it is a common practice to use multiple UOMs in operations. For example, the chemicals are procured in drums (order unit), price is negotiated in kilograms (order price unit), and stores issue the chemicals in kilograms (issue unit). Currently, SUS supports order units but there is only limited support for order price unit. Price units are supported when conversion between order unit and price unit is defined in unit of measurement configuration. For example, conversions like gram and kilogram are supported. In SAP ERP, alternate units and conversions can also be defined at the material level in the material master or at the order level in purchase order items. SUS does not support such conversions. However, a solution can be provided using customer fields, BAdIs, and ABAP code enhancements without modifying the standard code.

When you use price units different from order units in an SAP ERP purchase order and transmit the purchase order to SUS, the following problems are encountered:

▶ SUS does not support price unit. Therefore, the inbound XML message in SUS results in an error.

▶ The order price unit and conversions are not shown in the SUS documents.

▶ The unit price and order value shown in SUS are not correct. The amounts shown will have fractional errors. This may result in variations between goods receipt and invoice values.

One sample definition of units is given here:

▶ Order unit is "drum" and price unit is "KG." One drum equals 50 KG.

▶ The price in the purchase order is $5,933 per 10,000 KG.

▶ The price per drum will be $29.665 (5,933*50/10,000). But, the price is shown in SUS as $29.67.

Solution

Customers expect SAP SRM to support different order price units as SAP ERP supports this functionality. The solution steps for this requirement are outlined below:

▶ Implement SAP Note 921368.

▶ Define customer fields in the SUS purchase order item according to SAP Notes 672960 and 762984. You need to define addition fields for order unit (drum), price unit (KG), price in price unit (USD 5,933), price unit ratio (50), order unit ratio (1) and per price unit (10,000). The values in brackets represent the values from the sample definition of units described in this section.

- ▶ Define the additional customer fields in the order confirmation (SUS PCO), also.

- ▶ Configure the field control settings for additional fields in IMG setting by following the menu path **SPRO • SRM • Supplier Self-Services • Make Field Control Settings for Tables**. This setting enables the fields to be displayed on SUS screens.

- ▶ Create an RFC function module in SAP ERP to get the details of additional fields from the table EKPO.

- ▶ Implement BAdI BBP_SAPXML1_IN_BADI in SUS. In method PURCHASEORDER_SUS, call the RFC function module in SAP ERP and obtain the additional details required for customer fields and map the values to purchase order customer fields. This will ensure that additional fields required for price unit and conversions are filled in tables.

- ▶ To ensure that values shown in SUS are correct and that the correct values are transferred from ASNs and invoices, enhancements have been created using ABAP code enhancements in programs LBBP_BD_MAPPING_SAPXML1FOR, LBBP_PDIGPF51, and LBBP_PDIGPF86.

This solution ensures that order price units and conversions are enabled in the MM-SUS scenario. If you are interested, you can contact the authors for more details about this solution.

17.5 Summary

With more than 250 BAdIs across all levels of infrastructure, SAP SRM provides a large amount of flexibility for customers to define functionalities and processes to suit their requirements. In this chapter, you have learned that SAP SRM leverages the strengths of SAP Business Suite applications in offering end-to-end processes for customers. You have also seen the power of the enhancement framework enabled by NetWeaver to extend the standard SAP SRM processes to enable complex customer requirements. Consultants should explore the available BAdIs and leverage the ABAP code enhancements to provide customers with industry-specific best-processes.

18 Conclusion

This book was written out of the result of our desire to share our passion and experience to enable SAP SRM consultants deliver fast and successful Supplier Relationship Management (SRM) implementations. To see if we succeeded, we tested the efficacy of the content in this book in an internal project, and observed that a new SAP SRM consultant could implement the MM-SUS and EBP-SUS scenarios, including the SAP NetWeaver XI configuration in three days — a very short time indeed.

Now, we would like to leave you with a few final remarks and recommendations to help you be the best SAP SRM consultant you can be:

▶ A good consultant should play different roles at different stages of an SAP SRM implementation. He should play a business process consultant's role during the design phase (Business Blueprint phase in ASAP implementation methodology), and a product expert role during the realization phase. We have shared our in-depth experience gained in numerous SAP ERP and SAP SRM implementations so that SAP SRM consultants can don these roles effortlessly and enable them to deliver more value to their customers.

▶ Implementing SAP SRM should not be restricted to the configuration of the software product. We have taken the case-study approach in this book to explain SAP SRM processes and implementation factors because we believe that a good consultant should keep certain points in mind to ensure a successful SAP SRM implementation, as follows:

  ▶ Consultants should understand the pain points in the procurement processes in an organization and design new processed to address these points. Consultants should also understand the nuances of industry-specific processes and procedures while designing a process.

  ▶ Consultants should become product experts to leverage the strengths of SAP SRM as a component in the SAP Business Suite and make full use of the integrated processes.

  ▶ Consultants should focus both on technical and functional aspects of the product. We have observed that most successful consultants are not only experts in procurement processes, but are also technology-savvy enough that they can offer solutions leveraging the flexibility of the SAP NetWeaver technology platform.

We wish you success in your SAP SRM implementations! Go ahead and delight your customers!

Appendix

A   Commonly Used Abbreviations

Table A.1 lists commonly used abbreviations and what they stand for.

Abbreviation	Definition
ABAP	Advanced Business Application Programming
ADS	Adobe Document Services
ALE	Application Linking and Enabling
APO	Advanced Planning and Optimization
ASN	Advanced Shipping Notification
B2B	Business-to-Business
BAdI	Business Add-In
BAPI	Business Application Programming Interface
BE	Bidding Engine
BI	Business Intelligence
BIW	Business Information Warehouse
BRF	Business Rule Framework
BSP	Business Server Page
BW	Business Information Warehouse
CCM	Catalog Content Management
CLM	Contract Lifecycle Management
CO	Controlling
CPO	Chief Procurement Officer
CRM	Customer Relationship Management
CUA	Central User Management Administration
DB	Database
DMS	Document Management System
EBP	Enterprise Buyer Professional

Table A.1 Commonly Used Abbreviations

Abbreviation	Definition
ECC	ERP Central Component
ECS	Extended Classic Scenario
EDI	Electronic Data Interchange
EP	Enterprise Portal
ERP	Enterprise Resource Planning
ESA	Enterprise Services Architecture
FAQ	Frequently Asked Questions
FI	Financials
FTP	File Transfer Protocol
GOA	Global Outline Agreement
GR	Goods Receipt
HR	Human Resources
IAC	Internet Application Component
IDoc	Intermediate Document
IMG	Implementation Guide
IMS	Invoice Management System
IPC	Internet Pricing Configurator
IT	Information Technology
ITS	Internet Transaction Server
J2EE	Java 2 Enterprise Edition
JCo	Java Connector
JIT	Just-in-Time
KPI	Key Performance Indicator
LAC	Live Auction Cockpit
LCCS	Low-Cost Country Sourcing
LDAP	Lightweight Directory Access Protocol
LIV	Logistics Invoice Verification
MDM	Master Data Management
MM	Materials Management

Table A.1 Commonly Used Abbreviations (Cont.)

Abbreviation	Definition
MNC	Multinational Company
MRO	Maintenance Repair and Operations
MRP	Material Requirements Planning
MS	Microsoft
NW	NetWeaver
OCI	Open Catalog Interface
ODS	Operation Data Storage
OEM	Original Equipment Manufacturer
OLTP	Online Transaction Processing
OPI	Open Partner Interface
OS	Operating System
P-Card	Procurement Card
PDP	Plan-Driven Procurement
PI	Process Integration
PLM	Product Lifecycle Management
PM	Plant Maintenance
PO	Purchase Order
POWL	Personal Object Worklist
PR	Purchase Requisition
PS	Project Systems
RFC	Remote Function Call
RFI	Request for Information
RFP	Request for Proposal
RFQ	Request for Quotation
ROS	Registration of Suppliers (Supplier Self-Registration)
SAR	Scheduling Agreement Release
SBU	Strategic Business Unit
SCM	Supply Chain Management
SDM	Software Deployment Manager

Table A.1 Commonly Used Abbreviations (Cont.)

Abbreviation	Definition
SDN	SAP Developer Network
SLD	System Landscape Directory
SMI	Supplier Managed Inventory
SMTP	Simple Mail Transfer Protocol
SOAP	Simple Object Access Protocol
SRM	Supplier Relationship Management
SSO	Single Sign On
SUS	Supplier Self-Services
TCP/IP	Transmission Control Protocol/Internet Protocol
TREX	Text Retrieval and Extraction
UM	User Management
UNSPSC	Universal Standard Products and Services Classification
UOM	Unit of Measure
URL	Uniform Resource Locator (Web address)
UWL	Universal Worklist
VMC	Virtual Machine Container
VMI	Vendor Managed Inventory
WAS	Web Application Server
WPS	Web Presentation Server
xCLM	SAP xApp Contract Life Cycle Management
xCQM	SAP xApp Cost and Quotation Management
xSA	SAP xAPP Spend Analytics
XI	Exchange Infrastructure
XML	Extensible Markup Language

Table A.1 Commonly Used Abbreviations (Cont.)

B   References

David Marchand, "Master Data Management with SAP Supplier Relationship Management," SAP Developers Network (May 2007). Access the article at *https://www.sdn.sap.com/irj/sdn/bpx-srm*

SAP AG, "Self-Service Procurement: Slashing Costs and Saving Time," SAP Solution in Detail (January 2006). SAP material number: 50061096

SAP AG, "Supplier Enablement with mySAP Supplier Relationship Management," SAP Solution in Detail (January 2003). SAP material number: 50061061s

SAP AG, "Contract Management with mySAP Supplier Relationship Management," SAP Solution in Detail (November 2005). SAP material number: 50077275

SAP AG, "Analytics with mySAP Supplier Relationship Management," SAP Solution in Detail (November 2005). SAP material number: 50076850

SAP AG, "MDM Generic Extractor for Reference Data," from SAP Note 964991 (October 2006).

SAP AG, "mySAP SRM Statement of Direction 2003," SAP Service Marketplace (September 2003).

SAP AG, "mySAP SRM Statement of Direction 2004," SAP Service Marketplace (August 2004).

SAP AG, "mySAP SRM Statement of Direction 2003," SAP Service Marketplace (August 2005).

SAP AG, SAP SRM online help documentation at *http://help.sap.com*

C   Useful Links

The following list includes useful links, which you can refer to during your SAP SRM implementations:

- SDN Wiki at *https:/wiki.sdn.sap.com/wiki/display/SRM*
- SDN SRM Forum at *https://forums.sdn.sap.com/forum.jspa?forumID=143*
- SDN SRM Business Process Expert Community at *https://www.sdn.sap.com/irj/sdn/bpx-srm*
- SDN SRM Blogs at *https:/wiki.sdn.sap.com/wiki/display/SRM/Blogs*
- SRM Master guides, Installation guides, upgrade guides, security guides, etc., can be accessed at *http://service.sap.com/srm-inst*
- Product Availability Matrix at *http://service.sap.com/pam*
- The latest SAP SRM information can be accessed at *http://service.sap.com/srm*

D   Author Biographies

**Ramakrishna Potluri** (Ramki) has 17 years of industry experience, including 12 years in ERP product management and implementations, and 5 years in all materials management functions in the automotive industry. The latter enabled him to learn about and become an expert in supply chain processes. While consulting at IBM and SAP, he provided his expertise to customers of all sizes across verticals (including the automotive, oil and gas, airlines, utilities, retail, engineering, pharmaceuticals, chemical, and property management industries) in transforming supply chain management processes and implementing IT applications.

Ramki's current area of focus is SAP SRM. As head of the SAP SRM Regional Implementation Group, he helps customers, partners, consultants, and SAP teams deliver successful SAP SRM implementations in the Asia Pacific and Japan region. He strongly believes that the potential of SAP SRM is yet to be fully tapped by customers, and that there is a large latent demand for SAP SRM in the market. Ramki works closely with SAP sales and marketing teams in the region to position SAP SRM strongly in the market. He believes that a consultant should strive to delight the customer by delivering value above and beyond the customer's expectations. Ramki strives to be a 'Trusted Advisor' to his customers, colleagues, and partners. He is a regular speaker in the industry and at SAP events.

Ramki holds a B.Tech in Mechanical Engineering and MBA in Finance from XLRI, India. For more information about Ramki, visit

http://www.potluri.co.in and *https://wiki.sdn.sap.com/wiki/x/ZL4.*

PadmaPrasad Munirathinam (Prasad) has 13 years of industry experience, including 10 years in SAP implementation, expert consulting, product development, solutioning, and business development. He was actively involved in the implementation of various SAP solutions during his consulting career. He has been with SAP for the past 7 years, all of it in SAP SRM. His product experience has been with SAP ERP, SAP SRM, SAP CRM, SAP NetWeaver, integration platforms, and marketplace solutions as both technical and process consultant. During his career he has provided and is still providing numerous consulting solutions to customers for industry-specific processes that have been used globally. His solutions for manufacturing and asset-intensive industries in particular have enabled customers to implement effective supplier collaboration and sourcing processes.

Prasad's current area of focus is product development in SAP SRM and he is based out of SAPLABS India. As senior manager of SRM Development, Prasad is responsible for the delivery of new process developments in SAP SRM and involved in developing and delivering next generation Business Suite purchasing processes in SAP SRM. Before joining development, he managed the regional implementation group for SAP SRM for Asia Pacific and Japan based out of Singapore. Prasad has been recognized widely by his colleagues at SAP and by his customers for his dedication and commitment to get the projects he works on delivered successfully, especially in filling the process gaps using his technology process consulting skills. He strongly believes in the fact that software is defined by people, and not the other way around. This belief and confidence has enabled him to deliver solutions for customer satisfaction. Prasad has also delivered numerous lectures on SAP and SAP SRM in regional forums in Asia Pacific.

Prasad holds a Bachelors degree in Engineering with specialization in electronics and communication engineering.

Index

Learn how to integrate
SAP SRM with other
core SAP components

Uncover key insights on
strategies, functionalities,
and methodologies

695 pp., 2007, 69,95 Euro / US$ 69,95
ISBN 978-1-59229-068-0

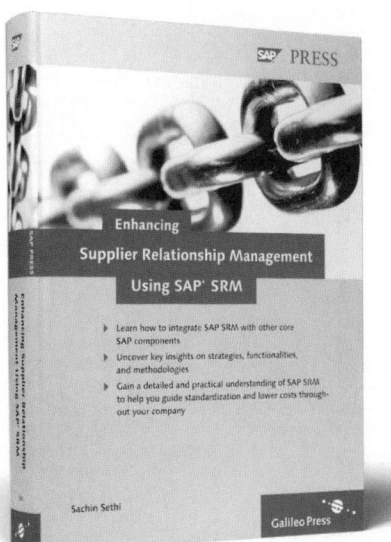

Enhancing Supplier Relationship
Management Using SAP SRM

www.sap-press.com

Sachin Sethi

Enhancing Supplier Relationship Management Using SAP SRM

This book will help readers leverage valuable insights
into strategies and methodologies for implementing
SAP SRM to enhance procurement in their
companies.
Tips and tricks, changes brought about by 5.0 and
customization will be woven in throughout the book.
It will provide detailed information on integration
and dependencies of mySAP SRM with core SAP
components like MM, IM, FI and HR.

Apply SAP SD to your own company's business model and make it work for you

Learn all aspects of SD functionality and essential technical details

365 pp., 69,95 Euro / US$ 69.95
ISBN 978-1-59229-101-4

Effective SAP SD

www.sap-press.com

D. Rajen Iyer

Effective SAP SD

Get the Most Out of Your SAP SD Implementation

From important functionalities to the technical aspects of any SD implementation, this book has the answers. Use it to troubleshoot SD-related problems and learn how BAdIs, BAPIs and IDocs work in the Sales and Distribution area. Understand how SAP SD integrates with modules like MM, FI, CO, and Logistics. Whether you're looking for in-depth SD information or need advice on implementation and upgrades, this practical guide is an invaluable reference.

Customization, functionality, and
complete SAP PS usage details

In-depth coverage of all project
phases from planning to invoicing

Includes exclusive expert insights
on reporting and interfaces

481 pp., 2007, 69,95 Euro / US$ 69,95
ISBN 978-1-59229-125-0

Project Management
with SAP Project System

www.sap-press.com

Mario Franz

Project Management with SAP
Project System

This book provides consultants and project managers
who use SAP PS as well as PS implementation project
team members with a comprehensive overview of the
functions and customization options of SAP Project
System. You learn how to maintain control of the
entire project lifecycle, from design to planning, and
from budgeting to controlling to invoicing and
beyond. This unique reference provides concise and
straightforward information on the many integration
scenarios available for SAP Project System. Focused
chapters provide you with detailed coverage of those
aspects that involve several different project phases,
such as reporting or interfaces to other project
management tools.

Configuration and application of APO-DP and APO-SNP

Business principles made easy

Functions, use, customization, and master data parameters

Fully up-to-date for SAP SCM 5.0

440 pp., 2007, 69,95 Euro / US$ 69,95
ISBN 978-1-59229-123-6

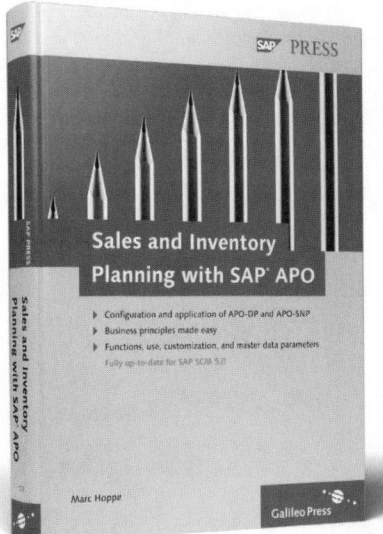

Sales and Inventory Planning with SAP APO

www.sap-press.com

Marc Hoppe

Sales and Inventory Planning with SAP APO

This comprehensive reference shows you how to best use the cross-company modules APO-DP and APO-SNP in your supply chain, for a wide variety of tasks such as carrying out accurate forecasts and optimally utilizing the means of transport.

Learn about the full functionality and technical configuration issues of SAP SD

Get tips, tricks, and references for important OSS Notes

Explore practical examples and real-world scenarios

545 pp., 2008, 69,95 Euro / US$ 69.95
ISBN 978-1-59229-168-7, Feb 2008

SAP SD: Functionality and Technical Configuration

www.sap-press.com

Kapil Sharma

SAP SD: Functionality and Technical Configuration

This detailed and comprehensive SAP SD functionality and configuration guide is a must-have for anyone working on a new or existing SD implementation. You'll learn about core functionality and technical configuration issues, explore real-world tips and scenarios, and find OSS notes that every SAP SD consultant needs. Use this book to configure SAP SD based on the unique requirements of your own company, and deal with your shipping, transportation, mailing, and customer service issues.

2nd edition, completely revised
and up-to-date for SAP ECC 6.0

Gain a comprehensive
understanding of SAP MM and
how it works

Learn the basics and then explore
the full functionality of each part
of SAP MM

588 pp., 2. edition 2008, 69,95 Euro / US$ 69.95
ISBN 978-1-59229-134-2

SAP MM—Functionality and Technical Configuration

www.sap-press.com

Martin Murray

SAP MM—Functionality and Technical Configuration

Fully updated for SAP ERP 6.0, this comprehensive update of the best-selling original is the ultimate MM resource. From dealing with Goods Receipt and Invoice Verification to Balance Sheet Valuation and the Material Ledger, this book is the ultimate reference for anyone looking for MM information.

Processes and customization of SAP PM

Interfaces, controlling, and new technologies in plant maintenance

With examples and workshops on DVD

approx. 555 pp., 69,95 Euro / US$ 69.95
ISBN 978-1-59229-150-2, May 2008

Enterprise Asset Management

www.sap-press.com

Karl Liebstückel

Enterprise Asset Management

This is a must-have guide for anyone interested in learning about the implementation and customization of SAP EAM. Consultants, managers, and administrators will learn about the plant maintenance process, how to evaluate which processes work best for them, and then go on to review the actual configuration steps of these processes. This book includes practical tips and best practices for implementation projects. The companion DVD contains examples, practice tests, presentations, and more. This book is up-to-date for SAP ERP 6.0.

Effectively analyze supply chain processes, inventory and purchasing

Avoid the hassle of custom ABAP reports by using LIS

Up-to-date for ECC 5.0

328 pp., 2007, 69,95 Euro / US$ 69,95
ISBN 978-1-59229-108-3

Understanding the SAP Logistics Information System

www.sap-press.com

Martin Murray

Understanding the SAP Logistics Information System

Gain a holistic understanding of LIS and how you can use it effectively in your own company. From standard to flexible analyses and hierarchies and from the Purchasing Information System to Inventory Controlling, this book is full of crucial information and advice.
Learn how to fully use this flexible SAP tool that allows you to collect, consolidate, and utilize data. Learn how to run reports without any ABAP experience thus saving your clients both time and money.

Interested in reading more?

Please visit our Web site for all
new book releases from SAP PRESS.

www.sap-press.com